T4-AQL-654

ALAN J. HAUSER is professor of biblical studies at
Appalachian State University, Boone, North Carolina.
He is also coeditor of *Art and Meaning: Rhetoric in Biblical
Literature* and coauthor of *From Carmel to Horeb: Elijah in
Crisis* and *Rhetorical Criticism of the Bible: A Comprehensive
Bibliography with Notes on History and Method*.

DUANE F. WATSON is professor of New Testament
studies at Malone College, Canton, Ohio. He is also
the author of *Invention, Arrangement, and Style: Rhetorical
Criticism of Jude and 2 Peter*, editor of *Persuasive Artistry:
Studies in New Testament Rhetoric*, and coauthor of *Rhetorical Criticism of the Bible*.

A HISTORY
of
BIBLICAL INTERPRETATION

VOLUME 1

The Ancient Period

A HISTORY
of
BIBLICAL INTERPRETATION

VOLUME 1

The Ancient Period

Edited by

Alan J. Hauser

&

Duane F. Watson

WILLIAM B. EERDMANS PUBLISHING COMPANY

GRAND RAPIDS, MICHIGAN / CAMBRIDGE, U.K.

© 2003 Wm. B. Eerdmans Publishing Co.
All rights reserved

Wm. B. Eerdmans Publishing Co.
255 Jefferson Ave. S.E., Grand Rapids, Michigan 49503 /
P.O. Box 163, Cambridge CB3 9PU U.K.
www.eerdmans.com

Printed in the United States of America

07 06 05 04 03   5 4 3 2 1

BS
500
.H575
2003
vol. 1

Library of Congress Cataloging-in-Publication Data

A history of biblical interpretation / edited by
Alan J. Hauser & Duane F. Watson
p.   cm.
Includes bibliographical references.
Contents: v. 1. The ancient period.
ISBN 0-8028-4273-9 (hardcover: alk. paper)
1. Bible — Criticism, interpretation, etc. — History.
I. Hauser, Alan J. II. Watson, Duane Frederick.
BS500.H575   2003
220.6′09 — dc21

2002035406

JESUIT - KRAUSS - McCORMICK - LIBRARY
1100 EAST 55th STREET
CHICAGO, ILLINOIS 60615

Contents

Preface

At first glance, it may seem an anomaly that after more than two thousand years of biblical interpretation, there are still major disagreements today among biblical scholars about what the Jewish and Christian Scriptures say, and about how one is to interpret and understand their content. Indeed, the late twentieth century has been witnessing the dissolution of what had been for well over a hundred years at least a substantial consensus among scholars about how to interpret the Bible, and how to understand and explain what it says. To the outsider this may seem amazing, since both the Jewish and Christian Scriptures are a limited corpus of writings, and have been exhaustively studied by Jews and Christians for centuries — indeed, millennia. Why, then, is it necessary for interpretation to continue in the extensive way that is in evidence today, with a rapidly-growing variety of approaches being employed? And, more directly to the point of this multi-volume work on interpretation, why is it necessary to study extensively the many interpreters and methods of interpretation that have been used since the late ancient world? Can we not cut through all this and discern the true message of these Scriptures, discarding all other approaches and teachings as incorrect and therefore unnecessary?

The answer to the last question is clearly "no." The reasons for this negative answer are twofold: the multi-layered richness and open-endedness of the biblical text itself; and the interplay of this diverse richness with the enormous variety in the worldviews of the various communities and individuals, living in many different ages, who have had to interpret the Scriptures in order to provide a direct and vital message for each of these communities and individuals. Thus, one could say that the interpretive possibilities are infinite, a product of the cross-fertilization of the fecundity of the biblical texts themselves with the varying needs and interests of the many interpreters who have wrestled with these texts.

Yet, even though this interpretive process has been multifaceted and infinitely varied throughout the ages, it is clear that many of the same questions have periodically appeared throughout the history of biblical interpretation, nuanced somewhat differently to address the specific concerns of different ages. Along these lines, one thinks of parallels between the more flexible and open-ended forms of the allegorical approach as practiced, for example, by Alexandrine scholars and their heirs, who delved deeply into the diversified intellectual world of their day, and some forms of reader-response criticism and deconstructive criticism as practiced by some scholars today. Likewise, the interests of Origen and Jerome in multi-lingual study of the biblical texts was set aside, ironically enough, by the success which Jerome's *Vulgate* translation encountered. In the Middle Ages, all other texts seemed unnecessary. Due to modern discovery of long-concealed ancient texts, this interest in the utilization of multiple languages in the interpretation of Scripture has reemerged, aided by many newly-developed linguistic tools including, most recently, the computer.

Furthermore, many scholars have sought to find *the* meaning of a particular biblical text, or of the Bible as a whole. Luther was convinced that if the Jews would only see the truth of the Bible as he had uncovered it, they would convert to Christianity, a view the Jews hardly shared with Luther. Many modern higher-critical scholars have seen their scholarly goal to be the recovery of the "true," often defined as the earliest, meaning of particular units of biblical material. Unfortunately, they have long been mired in relentless quibbling among themselves as to how to uncover and identify that "true" meaning, and they have essentially ignored the key issue of whether this is the most useful or meaningful form of the biblical text for contemporary Jewish and Christian communities. Approaches which recognize the considerable variety and open-endedness within the Scriptures themselves, and/or the variety of perspectives brought by different readers to the text, have firmly rejected the notion that it is possible to identify the meaning of Scripture so clearly and unambiguously.

Even in a multi-volume set like this, the attempt to treat the many different methods of interpretation, the many important interpreters who have written in various ages, and the many key issues that have surfaced repeatedly during the course of the history of biblical interpretation, is a daunting task. Not only is there a need to highlight key threads which tie together the complex and diverse materials that are important in understanding this rich history; there also is a need to make difficult decisions as to which individuals, periods, and methods are to receive more extensive treatment, and which less. Inevitably, virtually every decision the editors have made will ruffle someone's feathers, but it is the editors' hope that the readers will agree that, on the whole, the treatment has been comprehensive, fair, and balanced.

Perhaps a few examples of the tough decisions that had to be made will be helpful. Some might argue that Origen should have received a chapter devoted to him alone, and that would indeed seem reasonable. Yet, if there is to be substantial comparison of the Alexandrine and Antiochene schools of interpretation, such comparison must involve extensive discussion of Origen. Thus, if there were a separate treatment of Origen, there would of necessity be much duplication and repetition, a problem in a work such as this, where space is precious. As recent scholarship is beginning to realize, Marcion most likely had a more significant impact on ancient Christian interpretation than the forceful suppression of his works by the church would lead one to think, and he might well have received a separate chapter. Similarly, there is the issue of Gnostic exegesis, however one chooses to define that elusive category of literature and interpretation. Its influence on interpretation was no doubt considerable. It forced the church to respond by countering the various teachings of Gnosticism, and in the process, also led the church to rethink its own teachings and methods of interpretation. A multi-volume history of *ancient* biblical interpretation could allow room for an extensive treatment of Gnostic interpretation, but the current work must cover the entire waterfront of biblical interpretation. One might wish to treat the practices of the Samaritans, who formed one of the passionate, if rather small (in numbers) alternatives to nascent rabbinic Judaism. Yet, while their views form an interesting alternative to other views within Judaism, some of which later became definitive in rabbinic Judaism, their impact on interpretation outside their own group does not appear to have been extensive.

Thus, the selection of articles in this first volume was made only after considerable constraints had been dealt with, and some very tough decisions made. The editors have provided, in the first chapter, a comparative analysis of some of the main points made in each of the articles. The purpose is to give the reader a means of scanning in broad perspective the primary issues and features of ancient biblical interpretation as treated in this volume, and a means of sampling the ways in which these key figures, schools of interpretation, and issues both interweave and contrast with each other.

This volume would not have been possible without the assistance of many persons. We wish first of all to thank the many contributors, without whose special knowledge this volume could not have come into being. Their many years of work in their individual fields of expertise give this volume a rich texture and a depth of treatment which should make it most useful to the reader. We wish especially to thank Schuyler Kaufman, who constructed the subject index, and whose editorial diligence has helped give better shape and form to the volume. We also thank Elizabeth Tester, for her sharp eye and discerning judgment in processing the proofs; Richard Spencer, for his invaluable help in resolving knotty problems; and Thomas P. Benza, Jr. for his help with the subject index. Finally, we wish to thank John Simpson and his colleagues at Eerdmans Press for all the work they have done to bring the book to its polished form.

Future volumes are already well under way, but the editors would welcome comments and suggestions from readers. Subsequent volumes will treat interpretation in: the medieval and Reformation periods; the eighteenth and nineteenth centuries, which saw the rise of modern biblical criticism; and the twentieth century.

ALAN J. HAUSER, *Editor*
DUANE F. WATSON, *Editor*

Abbreviations

AB	Anchor Bible series
ABD	*Anchor Bible Dictionary*
Abr.	Philo, *De Abrahamo (On Abraham)*
AcPil	*Acts of Pilate*
AddEsth	Additions to Esther
Aeter.	Philo, *De aeternitate mundi (On the Eternity of the World)*
Ag.Ap.	Josephus, *Against Apion*
Agr.	Philo, *De agricultura (On Husbandry)*
Ah	Ahiqar
AH	*Aramaic Handbook*
ANF	Ante-Nicene Fathers
ANRW	*Aufstieg und Niedergang der römischen Welt: Geschichte und Kultur Roms im Spiegel der neueren Forschung*
Ant.	Josephus, *Antiquities of the Jews*
ApAb	Apocalypse of Abraham
ApAdam	Apocalypse of Adam
ApDan	Apocalypse of Daniel
ApEl	Apocalypse of Elijah
ApMos	Apocalypse of Moses
Apoc. Ezek	*Apocryphon of Ezekiel*
Apoc. John	*Apocryphon of John,* text from Nag Hammadi
Apol.	*First Apology* of Justin Martyr
ApSedr	Apocalypse of Sedrach
ApZeph	Apocalypse of Zephaniah

ApZeph	Apocalypse of Zephaniah
ArisEx	Aristeas the Exegete
Aristob	Aristobulus
Art	Artapanus
ATR	*Anglican Theological Review*
Aug.	*Augustinianum*
b.	Babylonian Talmud
Bar	Baruch
2 Bar	2 (Syriac Apocalypse of) Baruch
3Bar	3 (Greek Apocalypse of) Baruch
4Bar	4 Baruch
Barn	*Epistle of Barnabas*
BCE	before the common era (= BC)
Bel	Bel and the Dragon
BG	Berlin Gnostic Codex
BHT	Beiträge zur historischen Theologie
Bib	*Biblica*
BIOSCS	*Bulletin of the International Organization for Septuagint and Cognate Studies*
BJRL	*Bulletin of the John Rylands Library*
BTB	*Biblical Theology Bulletin*
BWANT	Beiträge zur Wissenschaft von Alten und Neuen Testament
BZ	*Biblische Zeitschrift*
BZAT	Beiheft der Zeitschrift für die alttestamentliche Wissenschaft
BZAW	Beihefte zur *Zeitschrift für die alttestamentliche Wissenschaft*
c. Faust.	Augustine, *Against Faustus the Manichaean (Contra Faustum Manichaeum):* CSEL, v. 25.
cat. rud.	Augustine, *On Catechizing the Uninstructed (De catechizandis rudibus):* CCSL, v. 46.
CBQ	*Catholic Biblical Quarterly*
CBQMS	Catholic Biblical Quarterly Monograph Series
CD	Q Damascus texts (Cairo Damascus Document)
CE	common era (= AD)
CG	Coptic Gnostic Library
Cher.	Philo, *De cherubim (On the Cherubim)*
civ. dei	Augustine, *De civitate Dei (The City of God):* CCSL, vv. 47-48.
1 Clem	*1 Clement*

2 Clem	*2 Clement*
ClMal	Cleodemus Malchus
CNRS	Centre National de la Recherche Scientifique
Comm. Matt.	Jerome: Commentary on Matthew
con. ev.	Augustine, *Harmony of the Gospels (De consensu evangelistarum):* CSEL, v. 43.
ConBOT	Coniectanea Biblica: Old Testament Series
conf.	Augustine, *Confessions (Confessionum Libri XIII):* CCSL, v. 27.
Conf.	Philo, *De confusione linguarum (On the Confusion of Tongues)*
Congr.	Philo, *De congressu quaerendae eruditionis gratia (On Mating, with the Preliminary Studies)*
Cont.	Philo, *De vita contemplativa* (On the Contemplative Life)
CR:BS	*Currents in Research: Biblical Studies*
CRINT	Compendium rerum ad iudaicarum ad Novum Testamentum
CSCO	Corpus scriptorum christianorum orientalium
CUAPS	Catholic University of America Patristic Series
d.	died
Dec.	Philo, *De decalogo (On the Decalogue)*
Dem.	Demetrius
Det.	Philo, *Quod deterius potior insidiari soleat (The Worse Attacks the Better)*
Dial.	Justin Martyr, *Dialogue with Trypho*
Did.	*Didache*
Diog.	*Epistle to Diognetus*
DJD	Discoveries in the Judaean Desert
doc. chr.	Augustine, *On Christian Doctrine,* or *De doctrina christiana (The Art of Christian Instruction):* R. P. H. Green, ed., *Augustine: De Doctrina Christiana* (Oxford: Clarendon, 1995).
DSS	Dead Sea Scrolls
Ebr.	Philo, *De ebrietate (On Drunkenness)*
EH	Eusebius, *Ecclesiastical History*
ElMod	*Eldad and Modad*
1En	1 (Ethiopic Apocalypse of) Enoch
2En	2 (Slavonic Apocalypse of) Enoch
3En	3 (Hebrew Apocalypse of) Enoch

en. Ps.	Augustine, *Enarrationes in Psalmos (Expositions of the Psalms):* CCSL, vv. 38-40.
ep.	Augustine, *Epistulae (Letters):* CSEL, vv. 34.1-2, 44, 57-58.
EpApost	*Epistula Apostolorum*
ET	English translation
Eup	Eupolemus
EzekTrag	Ezekiel the Tragedian
1 Ezra	1Ezra
4 Ezra	4Ezra
Flacc.	Philo, *In Flaccum (Against Flaccus)*
FoiVie	*Foi et Vie*
Frag. Tg.	*Fragmentary Targum*
frag.	fragment
FrgsPoetWrks	Fragments of Pseudo-Greek Poets
Fug.	Philo, *De fuga et inventione (On Flight and Finding)*
G.Ex.	Greek Exodus
GCS	Griechischen christlichen Schriftsteller
GEbion	*Gospel of the Ebionites*
Gen. Rab.	*Genesis Rabbah*
GHeb	*Gospel of the Hebrews*
Gig.	Philo, *De gigantibus (On the Giants)*
GkApEzra	Greek Apocalypse of Ezra
Gn. adv. man.	Augustine, *De Genesi adversus Manichaeos (On Genesis against the Manichaeans):* PL 34:173-220.
Gn. litt.	Augustine, *De Genesi ad litteram libri XII (The Literal Meaning of Genesis):* CSEL, v. 18.
Gn. litt. imp.	Augustine, *De Genesi ad litteram opus imperfectum (Incomplete Literal Commentary on Genesis):* CSEL, v. 28.
GNaz	*Gospel of the Nazarenes*
GPet	*Gospel of Peter*
GThom	*Gospel of Thomas*
HBT	*Horizons in Biblical Theology*
HelSynPr	Hellenistic Synagogal Prayers
Heres.	Philo, *Quis rerum divinarum heres sit (Who Is the Heir?)*
HistJos	History of Joseph
HistRech	History of the Rechabites
HSS	Harvard Semitic Studies
HTR	*Harvard Theological Review*
HTS	Harvard Theological Studies
HUCA	*Hebrew Union College Annual*

Hypothetica	Philo, *Apologia pro Iudaeis*
Ign. *Eph.*	Ignatius, *Letter to the Ephesians*
Ign. *Magn.*	Ignatius, *Letter to the Magnesians*
Ign. *Phil.*	Ignatius, *Letter to the Philippians*
Ign. *Pol.*	Ignatius, *Letter to Polycarp*
Ign. *Rom.*	Ignatius, *Letter to the Romans*
Ign. *Smyr.*	Ignatius, *Letter to the Smyrnaeans*
Ign. *Trall.*	Ignatius, *Letter to the Trallians*
Immut.	Philo, *Quod deus immutabilis sit (On the Unchangeableness of God)*
Int	*Interpretation*
Iren *Dem.*	Irenaeus, *Demonstration of the Apostolic Preaching*
IRHT	Institut de Recherche et d'Histoire des Textes
ITQ	*Irish Theological Quarterly*
j. (y.)	Jerusalem (Palestinian) Talmud
JanJam	Jannes and Jambres
JBL	*Journal of Biblical Literature*
JBLMS	*Journal of Biblical Literature* Monograph Series
JBR	*Journal of Bible and Religion*
Jdt	Judith
JETS	*Journal of the Evangelical Theological Society*
JJS	*Journal of Jewish Studies*
Jo. ev. tr.	Augustine, *In Johannis evangelium tractatus CXXIV (Tractates on the Gospel according to John):* CCSL, v. 36.
Jos.	Philo, *De Iosepho (On Joseph)*
JosAsen	Joseph and Aseneth
JQR	*Jewish Quarterly Review*
JQRS	*Jewish Quarterly Review* Supplements
JR	*Journal of Religion*
JSHRZ	Jüdische Schriften aus hellenistische-römischer Zeit
JSJ	*Journal for the Study of Judaism in the Persian, Hellenistic, and Roman Periods*
JSNT	*Journal for the Study of the New Testament*
JSNTS	*Journal for the Study of the New Testament* Supplement Series
JSOT	*Journal for the Study of the Old Testament*
JSOTS	*Journal for the Study of the Old Testament* Supplement Series
JSP	*Journal for the Study of the Pseudepigrapha*

JSPS	*Journal for the Study of the Pseudepigrapha* Supplement Series
JSS	*Journal of Semitic Studies*
JTS	*Journal of Theological Studies*
Jub	*Jubilees*
L.	Leipzig Manuscript
LAB	*Liber Antiquitatum Biblicarum*
LadJac	*Ladder of Jacob*
LAE	*Life of Adam and Eve*
Leg.All.	Philo, *Legum allegoriae (Allegorical Interpretation of the Laws)*
Legat.	Philo, *De Legatione ad Gaium (On the Embassy to Gaius)*
LetAris	*Letter of Aristeas*
LetJer	*Letter of Jeremiah*
Lev.Rab	*Leviticus Rabbah*
LivPro	*Lives of the Prophets*
LXX	Septuagint
LXXPs	Septuagint Psalm
m.	*Mishnah*
1 Mac	1 Maccabees
2 Mac	2 Maccabees
3 Mac	3 Maccabees
4 Mac	4 Maccabees
mag.	Augustine, *De magistro (On the Teacher):* CCSL, v. 29.
Magn.	Ignatius, *Letter to the Magnesians*
Mand.	*Shepherd of Hermas, Mandates*
Mart. Pol.	*Martyrdom of Polycarp*
MartIs/AscenIs	*Martyrdom and Ascension of Isaiah*
MC	Mekilta Commentary
Meg.	Megillah/Megilloth
Mek.	Mekilta
Migr.	Philo, *De migratione Abrahami (On the Migration of Abraham)*
mor.	Augustine, *De moribus catholicae ecclesiae et de moribus Manichaeorum (On the Morals of the Catholic Church and of the Manichaeans):* CSEL, v. 90.
Mos.	Philo, *De vita Mosis (On the Life of Moses)*
MT	Masoretic Text
Mut.	Philo, *De mutatione nominum (On the Change of Names)*
MV	Mededelingen en Verhandelingen

NHC	Nag Hammadi Codex
NHS	Nag Hammadi Studies
NovT	*Novum Testamentum*
NovTS	Supplements to *Novum Testamentum*
NRSV	New Revised Standard Version
NT	New Testament
NTOA	Novum Testamentum et Orbis Antiquus
NTS	*New Testament Studies*
NTTS	New Testament Tools and Supplies
NumenS	*Numen: International Review for the History of Religions* Supplement
OdesSol	Odes of Solomon
OG	Old Greek translation
Omn.	Philo, *Quod omnis probus liber sit (Every Good Man Is Free)*
Opif.	Philo, *De opificio mundi (On the Creation of the World)*
Orig. World	*On the Origin of the World* (Nag Hammadi text)
Orph	Orphica
OT	Old Testament
OT	Old Testament
OTA	Old Testament Apocrypha
OTP	Old Testament Pseudepigrapha
OTP	*The Old Testament Pseudepigrapha* (edited by J. H. Charlesworth)
OTS	*Oudtestamentische Studiën*
P.	Paris Manuscript
Pal.	*Palestinian Targum*
Pal.	*Palestinian Targum Pentateuch*
par.	and parallel(s)
PG	J. P. Migne: *Patrologiae cursus completus* Series Graeca, Paris: Migne
PhEPoet	Philo the Epic Poet
PL	J. P. Migne: *Patrologiae cursus Completus* Series Latina, Paris: Migne
Plant.	Philo, *De plantatione (On Noah's Work as a Planter)*
Plea.	Athenagoras, *Plea on Behalf of the Christians*
Pol. *Phil.*	Polycarp, *Letter to the Philippians*
Post.	Philo, *De posteritate Caini (On the Posterity and Exile of Cain)*
POxy	Oxyrhynchus Papyrus

Praem.	Philo, *De praemiis et poenis (On Rewards and Punishments)*
PrAzar	Prayer of Azariah
PrJac	Prayer of Jacob
PrJos	Prayer of Joseph
PrMan	Prayer of Manasseh
ProtJas	*Protevangelium of James*
Prov.	Philo, *De providentia (On Providence)*
Ps-Eud	Pseudo-Eupolemus
Ps-Hec	Pseudo-Hecateus
Ps-Philo	Pseudo-Philo
Ps-Phoc	Pseudo-Phocylides
PssDvd	More Psalms of David
PssSol	Psalms of Solomon
PTMS	Princeton Theological Monograph Series
PVTG	Pseudepigrapha Veteris Testamenti graece
1QapGen	Genesis Apocryphon
1QDM	Words of Moses
1QH	*Hodayot (Hymns of Thanksgiving)*
1QM	*Milhamah (War Scroll)*
1QpHab	Pesher Habakkuk
1QS	*Serekh ha-Yahad (Rule of the Community)*
11QMelch.	Qumran *Melchizedek*
11QPs	Psalms
11QT	Temple Scroll
4QAgesCreat.	*Ages of Creation*
4QD	Deuteronomy
4QFlor	*Florilegium*
4QHab	Habakkuk
4QMMT^c	*Miq'sat Ma'aseh ha-Torah^c*
4QShirShabb	*Songs of the Sabbath Sacrifice*
4QTestim	*Testimonia*
4QTgJob	Targum Job
4QTgLev.	Targum Leviticus
QE	Philo, *Quaestiones et Solutiones in Exodum (Questions and Answers on Exodus)*
QG	Philo, *Quaestiones et Solutiones in Genesin (Questions and Answers on Genesis)*
QuesEzra	Greek Apocalypse of Ezra
RAC	*Reallexikon für Antike und Christentum*

RB	*Revue Biblique*
RevEzra	Revelation of Ezra
RevQ	*Revue de Qumran*
RSR	*Recherche de science religieuse*
RSV	Revised Standard Version
s. dom. mon.	Augustine, *De sermone Domini in monte libri II (On the Lord's Sermon on the Mount)*: CCSL, v. 35.
Sacr.	Philo, *De sacrificiis Abelis et Caini (On the Sacrifices of Abel and Cain)*
Sanh.	Sanhedrin
SBL	Society of Biblical Literature
SBLDS	Society of Biblical Literature Dissertation Series
SBLMS	Society of Biblical Literature Monograph Series
SBLSCS	SBL Septuagint and Cognate Studies
SBLSP	Society of Biblical Literature Seminar Papers
SBLTT	SBL Texts and Translations
SBT	Studies in Biblical Theology
SC	Sources chrétiennes
SCJ	Studies in Christianity and Judaism
SCM	Studies in the Christian Movement
SCS	Septuagint and Cognate Studies
SD	Studies and Documents
SE	*Studia Evangelica*
Sem	*Semitica*
ser.	Augustine, *Sermones (Sermons)*: PL 38 and 39; 46. Cf. CCSL 41 (Sermons 1-50); G. Morin, *Miscellanea Agostiniana* (Rome, 1930), and F. Dolbeau, ed., *Augustin d'Hippone: Vingt-six sermons au peuple d'Afrique* (Paris, 1996).
SibOr	Sibylline Oracles
Sim.	*Shepherd of Hermas, Similitudes*
Simp.	Augustine, *Ad Simplicianum de diversis quaestionibus (To Simplician on Various Questions)*: CCSL, v. 44.
Sir	Sirach
SJLA	Studies in Judaism in Late Antiquity
Sobr.	Philo, *De sobrietate (On Sobriety)*
Somn.	Philo, *De somnis (On Dreams)*
SP	*Studia Philonica*
SPA	*Studia Philonica Annual*
Spec.	Philo, *De specialibus legibus (On the Special Laws)*

spir. et litt.	Augustine, *De spiritu et littera (On the Spirit and the Letter)*: CSEL, v. 60.
SSEJC	Studies in Scripture in Early Judaism and Christianity
STDJ	Studies on the Texts of the Desert of Judah
Strom.	Clement, *Stromateis*
Sus	Susannah
SVTP	Studia in Veteris Testamenti pseudepigrapha
SyrMen	Sentences of Syriac Menander
t.	Tractates of the Tosefta
T.Ps.-J	*Targum Pseudo-Jonathan*
T12P	Testaments of the Twelve Patriarchs
Tab	Testament of Abraham
Tadam	Testament of Adam
Test. Truth	*Testimony of Truth,* text from Nag Hammadi
Tg. Cant.	*Targum Canticles*
Tg. Chron.	*Targum Chronicles*
Tg. Esth.	*Targum Esther*
Tg. Ezek.	*Targum Ezekiel*
Tg. Isa.	*Targum Isaiah*
Tg. Job	*Targum Job*
Tg. Josh.	*Targum Joshua*
Tg. Judg.	*Targum Judges*
Tg. Ket.	*Targum of the Writings*
Tg. Lam.	*Targum Lamentations*
Tg. Lev.	*Targum Leviticus*
Tg. Mal.	*Targum Malachi*
Tg. Neb.	*Targum of the Prophets*
Tg. Neof.	*Targum Neofiti*
Tg. Onq.	*Targum Onqelos*
Tg. Prov.	*Targum Proverbs*
Tg. Pss.	*Targum Psalms*
Tg. Ruth	*Targum Ruth*
Tg. Qoh.	*Targum Qoheleth*
Theod	Theodotus
Tisaac	Testament of Isaac
Tjac	Testament of Jacob
Tjob	Testament of Job
Tjud	Testament of Judah
Tmos	Testament of Moses
Tob	Tobit

TRE	*Theologische Realenzyklopädie*
trin.	Augustine, *On the Trinity (De trinitate):* CCSL, vv. 50-50A.
TrShem	Treatise of Shem
TSAJ	Texte und Studien zum Antiken Judentum
Tsol	Testament of Solomon
TZ	*Theologische Zeitschrift*
util. cred.	Augustine, *De utilitate credendi (On the Usefulness of Believing):* CSEL, v. 25.
V.	Vatican Library Manuscript
VC	*Vigiliae Christianae*
ver. rel.	Augustine, *On True Religion (De vera religione):* CCSL, v. 32
Virt.	Philo, *De virtutibus (On the Virtues)*
Vis.	*Shepherd of Hermas, Visions*
VisEzra	Vision of Ezra
VT	*Vetus Testamentum*
VTS	*Vetus Testamentum* Supplement
WBC	Word Biblical Commentary
WisSol	Wisdom of Solomon
WUNT	Wissenschaftliche Untersuchungen zum Neuen Testament
ZAW	*Zeitschrift für die alttestamentliche Wissenschaft*
ZNW	*Zeitschrift für die neutestamentliche Wissenschaft*
ZRGG	*Zeitschrift für Religions- und Geistesgeschichte*

CHAPTER 1

Introduction and Overview

Alan J. Hauser and Duane F. Watson

This introductory discussion presents an overview and summary of key topics important to the early history of biblical interpretation. The reader is referred to the subsequent chapters in this volume for more extensive discussions.

THE BEGINNINGS OF INTERPRETATION

The history of biblical interpretation begins at that unknown point in time when the first biblical traditions were created ("biblical traditions" is used here to mean any materials, such as laws, stories, sayings, pieces of poetry, hymns, oracles, etc. that subsequently found their way, after incorporation into larger bodies of material, into the biblical text as we now have it). Such creation of necessity involves a deliberate focusing on particular elements chosen from the broader experience of life, such as major events, significant laws, important customs and practices, special clan and tribal affiliations, etc. Furthermore, no tradition can embrace and embody all elements and vantage points of the subject it treats. What is selected in this creative process will be a direct result of the perspectives, social mores, religious beliefs, hopes and fears, and political and economic needs of the person or community that does the creating. Thus, interpretation is already under way.

The next step in the interpretive process comes when these created units are passed on from one generation or group to another. Admittedly, the mere passing on of traditions may not appear to be an act of interpretation, since

1

transmission does not necessarily imply an *intent* to modify or reformulate. Nevertheless, even in clearly neutral contexts for transmission, where there is no conscious desire to alter or emend the tradition(s) received, the transmitters will nevertheless place their own, or their group's, particular perspective onto the material being transmitted, often without being aware that such a shift in perspective is occurring. That *is* interpretation, and it can occur either early in the long process of transmission, when the form is more likely to be oral, or later in the process, when the transmission is more likely to be written. Furthermore, those transmitting the traditions were, in many cases, quite intentionally altering the material they had received to make it suit their own purposes. They would not have seen anything questionable or improper in their doing so.

It is only human nature for any person receiving and conveying important traditions to view them from a perspective that most clearly makes sense in the context of that person's particular religious, cultural, social, economic, and intellectual milieu, which often will not be the same as the milieu presumed earlier by the person or group that created or previously transmitted the tradition(s). The new person or group's own milieu quite understandably becomes, in this context, the only important perspective at that point in time for understanding the materials received. For example, the motif of the exodus experience, including the various traditions and reflections associated with it, would of necessity have been viewed quite differently by a returnee to Palestine after 538 BCE than by a citizen of Solomon's kingdom. Both would have possessed the same essential core to the tradition, namely, the deliverance from Egypt, but each would have seen the shape, significance, and implications of the traditions in quite different ways.

Another example would be the stories in Daniel 1–6. Presuming, as most scholars do, that these stories existed in some earlier form before they were incorporated into the current book of Daniel, it is clear that their emphasis on avoiding idolatry, observing the kosher food laws, and overcoming the evil plotting of dictators and vengeful enemies of the Jews necessarily took on a new and more profound meaning in light of the murderous actions of Antiochus Epiphanes and his cohorts beginning in 168 BCE. So powerful were the reinterpretation and reapplication of those traditions that we today can do little but speculate concerning the focus of these stories in their earlier form(s), and the context(s) that determined their earlier meaning.

Clearly, there normally will have been numerous generations of interpretation/modification of particular biblical traditions before they ever appeared in the form in which we now find them in our biblical text. The earlier, normally oral, stages were followed, as Esther Menn argues in detail in chapter 2, by a long history of conscious utilization and revision of earlier written texts, continuing to the time of the Jewish community's eventual establishment of its canon and standard biblical text. Many examples could be given of the growing importance of written texts within the Israelite/Jewish community, such as the book of the law found in the temple during Josiah's reign (621 BCE, 2 Kgs. 22:8–23:25), Ezra's reading of the book of the law (Neh. 8:1-8), Jeremiah's recording of his prophetic words (Jeremiah 36), and Zechariah's vision of the flying scroll (Zech. 5:1-4). As Menn notes (p. 61), "interpretation of traditional texts was an important component of Israelite culture, before, during, and, most prominently, after the period of exile in Babylon." An especially helpful example of this ongoing expansion on earlier written traditions is the way in which the text of Jeremiah's description of the "70 years" of service to the king of Babylon (Jer. 25:11; 29:10) has been reinterpreted and reapplied repeatedly in later biblical documents (2 Chron. 36:17-21; Zech. 1:12; Dan. 9:24-27). Such interpretation enabled these authoritative texts to maintain their relevance to successive generations of Jews, who continued to need their sacred traditions to address the rapidly changing political, social, economic, religious, and intellectual conditions in which they found themselves.

Hence, at these earlier, precanonical stages, interpretation contributes, often in a major way, to the eventual shaping of the written, canonical text itself. In fact, it would be very difficult to find either oral or written transmissions of traditions that were indeed neutral, that did not grow and adapt, especially before a standard text was generally accepted within the Jewish or Christian communities. If the existence of a set, standard text of both the Tanak (the Hebrew Bible) and the New Testament, with few major deviations or significant disagreements, has not in recent centuries inhibited the creativity of interpreters who are consciously dealing with a specific religious community's clearly defined sacred (and therefore authoritative) texts, it is quite clear that in the earlier, precanonical days, there would have been far fewer inhibitions working against an open-ended reconfiguration of the shape and meaning of a unit of biblical tradition.

Thus, two crucial principles must be kept in mind if one is to have a clear grasp of the early history of biblical interpretation. First, a unit of tradition, whether in the form of an oral unit or a written text, does not convey meaning in a context-neutral manner, without reference to the nature of the audience. Whether it admits it or not, or whether it is aware of it or not, every audience brings a particular perspective through which the text or unit of tradition is screened, and it is by means of this interpretive perspective that the text or unit of material will be (re)focused and understood. The unit itself, as received, will, of course, set some limits on what interpreters may find in it, but as the ancient allegorical approach to interpretation and some contemporary modes of interpretation make clear, these limits can at times be very loose, with the text or unit serving as a Rorschach blot for the interpreter's own sense of what may be legitimately found in the text.

Second, interpretation of the biblical materials as contained in the texts and canons established by the Jewish and Christian communities was often a reflection and expansion of interpretive concerns, issues, and methods that had already appeared long before the consensual establishment of the texts and canons of these communities. Another way to put this is that any community's clearly defined sacred documents, especially ones that have had as long and rich a heritage as the Jewish and Christian Scriptures, constitute in one sense no more than a snapshot in time, a frozen moment in a long journey. Like a photograph taken during a race, they both encapsulate what came before the "Kodak moment" and anticipate what will follow. Canonization and the setting of a standard biblical text thus are carefully preserved moments embedded in the midst of a continually modulating history of interpretation. Consequently, if one is to study the history of biblical interpretation, it would be shortsighted to think of interpretation only in a postcanonical mode, since, as already noted, precanonical and inner-biblical interpretation clearly set the stage for, and in many ways anticipated, major interpretive elements in subsequent ages. This dynamic is further complicated by the fact that both Judaism and Christianity for a long time granted high importance, and indeed for many individuals and subgroups, equal or close to equal authoritative status, to numerous documents that would later be ruled by some or all of these communities to lie outside the domain of accepted Scripture. An excellent example here is *1 Enoch*, which is clearly referred to in the book of Jude (vv. 14-15). Neither the Jewish nor the Christian communities gave canonical status to *Enoch*.

ISSUES OF UNITY AND DIVERSITY

The issue of scriptural unity and authority must also be examined carefully. After the establishment of the canons within Judaism and Christianity, it came to be assumed that the creators and early transmitters of the biblical materials knew that they were creating "Scripture," and therefore were strongly conscious of the need to interweave their teachings carefully with those of other biblical writers in order to provide an integrated whole. However, even though the rabbis and Christian interpreters came fairly early to see the need for an emphasis on the unity of Scripture, especially when confronted by what could at times be a considerable diversity within their own community, there is little to suggest that the biblical writers themselves had a clear concept of the comprehensive authority of Scripture or of the need for careful integration of its components. Indeed, in the earlier, precanonical periods, one does not sense, in the literature as it has come down to us, a concept of long-term, overarching canonical authority intended to stretch far into the future. Rather, such authority as there was appears to have been for and within the context of the immediate time and community, building upon a new understanding of respected traditions from the past. Even when reference was made to a previous authority figure such as Moses and the law he gave to Israel, the "Law of Moses" was the law as perceived at that particular moment for that particular community. Likewise, when Jeremiah had Baruch, at his dictation, write down two successive compendia of Jeremiah's words spoken during the earlier half of his career (Jeremiah 36), he did so in the hopes that the combined strength of his words would alert his contemporaries to the doom he saw to be impending and cause them to change their ways (v. 3), a purpose that appears to have been thwarted, as Jehoiakim's burning of the first copy of the scroll suggests. There is no clear indication that Jeremiah envisioned a purpose for Baruch's two scrolls beyond this. When Paul wrote to his congregations, as in 1 Corinthians, his concern to confront and solve the problems of the specific congregation being addressed was predominant, which is why some details of the discussion elude us. Indeed, one wonders if Paul might not at times have chosen his words more carefully if he had known that for nearly two millennia his epistles would be given microscopic scrutiny by so many generations of Christian interpreters.

If these early individuals addressed their contemporaries rather than unseen future generations, it is also true that they were not focused strongly on carefully coordinating their words with those of others whose works would also eventually find their way into Scripture. Indeed, there is no indication that they would have even understood the concept of Scripture, certainly not in the sense in which the Jewish and Christian communities defined it in the late ancient, medieval, and modern eras. Nor could they have known which books would eventually be placed in the canon. Biblical writers alluded to and quoted other documents (or traditions) as having some sense of authority, which could at times be strong. But that appeal to authority (exemplified where the New Testament quotes or alludes to material from the Tanak) was driven not by an overall, encompassing desire for articulating the comprehensive unity of all Scripture, but rather by the desire to support the point currently being made (for a rather extreme example, see 1 Cor. 9:8-10). It would fall to later teachers within Judaism and Christianity, once the concept of a unified corpus of authoritative religious documents had become an imperative, to try to forge a broad consensus of scriptural teachings that could somehow embrace within it the divergence of perspective that was the inevitable result of hundreds of years of very different religious, cultural, sociological, historical, and economic factors playing on the lives and writings of the many different individuals and communities that produced these numerous documents. No doubt the vehemence with which the church put down Marcion, who argued that the god of the Tanak was not the god of the New Testament, shows how sensitive the church was concerning this matter of the substantial diversity present in Scripture. Marcion was an astute interpreter, and he put his finger on a raw nerve when he pointed to the strong diversity found within and among the numerous documents of Scripture. Even though the church shouted down his voice, the diversity of interpretation in the church for so many centuries certainly arose not only with the diversity of the interpreters but also with the diversity contained in the documents themselves. Marcion saw the diversity of Scripture more accurately than many in the church might like to admit.

The matter of the diversity within Scripture comes to focus especially when one looks at the shape of the canon in the various Jewish Christian communities. For example, the scope of the Tanak in the Jewish and Protestant Christian heritages, when compared to the significantly different Roman Catholic and Orthodox heritages (see pp. 33-36 below), clearly demonstrates this diversity, since the various groups each found it necessary to define and articulate their concept of scriptural unity by including or excluding documents which were seen to aid or inhibit specific ideas defining their own concept of unity. This also constitutes interpretation, at the most foundational level.

Luther is a classic example of one who wished to have a more rigorously defined, tightly-focused concept of scriptural unity. This led him to opt for a shorter canon of Scripture (interestingly enough, the same canon for the Old Testament as that used by the Jewish community, which he later so vehemently vilified). It even led him to call James "an epistle of straw," although there is no indication that he ever sought to remove it from the canon of the New Testament. Luther and his intellectual progeny have consistently pushed for a strongly unified perspective for interpreting Scripture, focused around the distinction of law and gospel.

On the other hand, many Christian interpreters in the ancient period, who often focused on the need for extensive interaction with the rich intellectual environment in which they found themselves, tended to put more emphasis on the ability of Scripture to appeal to a broad spectrum of the population of the ancient Mediterranean world. In this sense they were following the lead of the first-century Jewish interpreter Philo of Alexandria, who was well versed in, and wanted to appeal to, the Hellenistic heritage of the world he knew. It is not surprising that these circles of Christian interpreters preferred the longer canonical list of the Septuagint, since a number of the "additional" documents it contained provided, through their variety, increased opportunity for dialog with the broader world. By the Middle Ages, when the church had come to dominate western civilization in Europe, the church's authority dictated how Scripture was to be interpreted, so the greater diversity in the longer canon of Jerome's *Vulgate* was not seen as a potential threat to the concept of Scriptural unity. The church could simply declare by fiat what the correct interpretation was, thereby preserving the unity of meaning. In any case, at this time the number of those who studied and interpreted the Scriptures of the church was relatively small, and deference to the authority of the church was great. Judaism had, by this time, ceased to debate with any intensity the unity of the Tanak. Jewish scholars focused on details of daily practice in following the laws initially provided in broad scope in the Torah and debated the fine points and seeming contradictions in the Mishnah and the Talmud, far removed from any challenges to the unity of the Tanak text itself.

As indicated above, each new age or generation, due to its own social, political, religious, economic, military, and other contexts, was likely to have its own perspective for assessing and refocusing what earlier generations had enshrined in the traditions passed down. One must be careful, however, not to overemphasize the commonalities and consistency of a particular age, generation, geographical region, or religious community at the expense of the unique perspectives, problems, and geniuses of various individuals living within such a community. Truly gifted interpreters often go beyond and challenge many of the factors which they share with others in their community, and one must therefore be especially sensitive to those points at which such interpreters part company with their contemporaries or intellectual compatriots. The apostle Paul would be an excellent example. While he shared a great deal with the Jewish community in which he was raised, and especially with the Pharisees, whose methods of interpretation he clearly knew and often employed, and while he shared a great deal with other Christian interpreters who understood the Old Testament in light of their belief that Jesus is the Christ, he nevertheless put his own unique stamp on his understanding of the "Scripture" of his day, and in the process dramatically influenced the subsequent history of Christian biblical interpretation. For example, his new understanding of the role and significance of the law in the history of God's people was especially powerful and strongly challenged his Jewish-Christian contemporaries. Jerome also was inclined to give far more credence to the Hebrew text of the books of the Old Testament than were his contemporaries, despite the sharp rebukes he received from some of them, such as Augustine and Theodore of Mopsuestia. Indeed, interpreters separated by considerable periods of time can, on occasion, have more in common with each other than they do with their own contemporaries, despite major differences in the contexts in which they lived. For example, select aspects of interpretation as practiced by Theodore of Mopsuestia in certain ways anticipate some of the perspectives of modern higher criticism. One must, however, be very careful not to make too much of these similarities, as the fundamental interpretive worldviews of the two were quite different.

If the "pre-canonical" Jewish and Christian communities had a tendency to deal with the traditions they had received in a more open, flowing manner and regarded these traditions as fairly malleable, this nevertheless changed considerably as the various Jewish and Christian communities formed a well-developed sense of canon. The Jewish community, especially after the disaster of the Bar Kochba revolt, and Christianity, primarily in the second through fourth centuries CE, both moved toward closed canons. From these periods forward, the text of the canonical books, as best as the text could be established, formed the basis for interpretation, and there was little interest in recovering an earlier form of the text of a particular unit of biblical material under study. Herein lies a major difference between interpretation in the ancient world and modern interpretation of the Bible in the late eighteenth through late twentieth centuries: even though the materials in most biblical books clearly went through numerous stages of transmission, modification, expansion, and integration into larger units, that entire process, important as it was, rarely interested ancient biblical interpreters once the canons were basically set.

Much modern and contemporary interpretation, however, in its attempts to learn about the early church or the early period of Israel's history, has tended to push the canonical text aside in an effort to get behind it, to recover these earlier (and when possible, earliest) forms of the traditions. The expectation is that such recovery provides us with knowledge which is, in the long run, much more useful than the knowledge gained through the study of the canonical texts themselves. To put it simply, recovery of knowledge about "how it really was" in early Israel, during the career of Jesus, or in the earliest church has been seen as the best avenue to useful and satisfying religious knowledge. As later volumes in this history of biblical interpretation will show, canon criticism and numerous forms of interpretation recently practiced by a variety of scholars who have taken a postmodern perspective have seriously challenged a number of the assumptions and methods of "higher-critical" scholarship as practiced for approximately the past 200 years. This does not, of course, imply a return to interpretation as practiced, for example, in the ancient world, but it is likely to have an impact, as yet not clearly in focus, on how we will view and assess biblical interpretation in the ancient world.

Since we have focused in some detail on the way in which the early biblical traditions were reshaped and recontextualized before they reached their stable form in the canonical texts, it would be best to survey briefly those major events in the life of ancient Israel and the early church, as well as the more gradual changes in the religious, economic, social, political, intellectual, and geographical circumstances of those communities, that were most likely to have an impact on the way receptors of the traditions reformulated them in order to make them their own. Clearly, at any point in time, the most recent events and the contemporary life circumstances of the community would have had the most powerful effect on the interpretation and reshaping of the traditions.

MAJOR HISTORICAL EVENTS AND CIRCUMSTANCES INFLUENCING ANCIENT BIBLICAL INTERPRETATION

The following are some of the significant events and circumstances that shaped the interpretation and development of the earlier traditions that eventually found their way into the Tanak/Old Testament, and into the New Testament, and thus would have shaped the form of the different canons:

- the numerous petty conflicts in early Israel's history, which eventually led various clans and tribes to form alliances and share traditions with one another,
- the establishment of the centralized, unified monarchy under David and Solomon,
- the division of the Israelite state into the Northern and Southern Kingdoms (922 BCE),
- the repeated invasion of both kingdoms by major states such as Assyria and Babylonia, which forced both kingdoms to see themselves and their God as actors on a large international stage,
- the destruction of the Northern Kingdom in 721 BCE by Assyria,
- the reform by King Josiah in 621 BCE,

- the destruction of Jerusalem, the temple, and the Southern Kingdom in 587 BCE by Babylonia,
- the exile of many people from the Northern Kingdom (721 BCE) and from Judah (587 BCE), thus beginning the diaspora or spreading of Jews eventually throughout the known world,
- the edict of Cyrus the Persian, allowing various peoples, including Jews, to return to their homeland (538 BCE),
- the rebuilding of the temple in Jerusalem (completed 515 BCE),
- Ezra's proclamation of the Torah and Nehemiah's rebuilding of the walls of Jerusalem (prior to 400 BCE),
- Alexander the Great's conquest of the Near East (336-323 BCE) and the consequent Hellenization of most of the areas where Jews lived,
- the deadly attempt by Antiochus IV Epiphanes to eradicate Judaism (168-165 BCE),
- the takeover of Palestine by Rome (63 BCE), followed by frequent Jewish rebellions,
- the reign of Herod the Great (38-4 BCE) and the rebuilding of the temple in Jerusalem,
- the career and death of Jesus of Nazareth (approximately 30 CE),
- the beginnings of the Jewish Christian community,
- the preaching of Christianity by Paul and others to Gentiles,
- the writing of Paul's epistles,
- the revolt of Jews in Palestine against Rome (beginning in 65 CE),
- Rome's crushing of the Jewish revolt and the destruction of Jerusalem and the temple (70 CE),
- Christianity's gradually becoming a predominantly Gentile religion,
- the beginning of Roman persecution of Christians (60s CE),
- the writing of the Gospels, and
- the Jewish revolt led by Bar Kochba (135 CE).

This is certainly not a complete list of all the significant events that influenced the shaping of the Jewish and Christian canons, but it is enough to give a broad picture.

By the first century CE, Jews had been living in Egypt, Asia Minor, Mesopotamia, Greece, Rome, and numerous other places. Conditions and experiences in each of these places influenced the shaping of traditions which were developed there. Since the interpretation and development of the Tanak and New Testament prior to the canonization of both are on a steadily growing continuum with the interpretation of the Tanak and New Testament *after* the canonization of both, it would be best to continue our list by adding those

events in the late ancient world which influenced Jewish and Christian interpretation during and after the setting of the various canons:

- the codification of the Mishnah by Rabbi Judah (200 CE),
- Christianity being made a legal religion in the Roman Empire by Emperor Constantine (313 CE),
- the Council of Nicea (325 CE),
- the strong steps taken against paganism by Emperor Theodosius I (390s
  CE),
- the growing disfavor toward Jews in the now-Christian Roman Empire,
  and
- the western Roman world's gradual take-over by outsiders.

It would be difficult to list all the significant social, economic, political,
cultural, and religious developments which, interacting with the historical
events mentioned above, would have had an impact on the development and
interpretation of biblical traditions. However, among those to be mentioned
from the period prior to the exile are these (in roughly chronological order):

- the growing sense of community, of what it meant to be a part of Israel,
  among the premonarchic clans and tribes,
- concomitant with this, a growing sense of separation from peoples, regions, and cities not a part of Israel,
- despite this, the unavoidable cross-fertilization with cities, regions,
  countries, and religions with which Israel was in contact,
- the gradual development of wealthy urban classes in the cities of the
  Northern and Southern Kingdoms (10th-6th centuries BCE),
- the persistent influence of Canaanite and other religions on the religion
  of the Israelites,
- the growing importance of the temple in Jerusalem and the priestly
  caste associated with it, in both preexilic Judah and postexilic Palestinian Judaism,
- the growth of the prophetic movement in the two preexilic kingdoms
  and its gradual disappearance during the postexilic period, and
- the growing exposure of preexilic Israelites to international culture and
  wisdom, beginning as early as Solomon, growing especially after approximately 850 BCE, and intensifying dramatically after 587 BCE.

After 587 BCE, two multifaceted factors became primary in shaping and
defining the perspectives through which Jews would interpret the earlier tra-

ditions they had received. The first was the growing interaction of Jews (especially in the diaspora) with the numerous cultural, social, economic, political, religious, and intellectual environments in which they found themselves. The diaspora could be said to have begun with the destruction of the Northern Kingdom in 721 BCE and the deportation of many of its citizens to foreign lands, with additional waves of deportees coming in 597 and 587, when the Southern Kingdom was crippled and then destroyed by the Babylonians. By the first century CE, the diaspora had extended in the Mediterranean world from Spain across to Asia Minor in the north, and across northern Africa to Egypt in the south. East of Palestine, Jews were found in large numbers in Mesopotamia and in areas farther east. While they were also to be found in more peripheral areas, these were the primary areas of Jewish settlement. As these Jews interacted with the various social, economic, cultural, political, religious, and intellectual factors they found in these numerous different environments, the perspectives through which they viewed their own religious traditions were bound to be altered, in some cases quite substantially. Inevitably, the sacred writings of the Jewish community needed to be translated into other languages. Midrash, the interpretive expansion of the sacred writings of the Jewish community, also developed in these contexts. These expansions themselves often came to be written down, even though they did not attain the authority of the sacred writings.

The second and perhaps more influential factor shaping the perspective through which the Jewish community would interpret its sacred traditions in the late ancient world was the rapid dissemination of Hellenistic culture throughout the Mediterranean basin and elsewhere after the conquests of Alexander the Great. The Hellenic culture spread by Alexander blended with the various indigenous cultures to produce the composite Hellenistic culture, which provided the linguistic and cultural glue which held together much of the ancient world during the Roman era. Hellenization first of all provided a language — Greek — through which Jews could be in dialogue with at least the more educated of their Gentile neighbors. This resulted in a growing knowledge of Jewish sacred writings and religious ideas among substantial portions of the Gentile population in areas where there was a significant Jewish community, a factor that also helped lay the groundwork for the rapid growth of Christianity. Judaism, and subsequently also Christianity, were placed side-by-side with the pagan religions of the Greeks and Romans, typically to the detriment of the latter; but the Greek and Roman religions influenced the way in which Jews and Christians came to interpret their own religious heritage.

The spread of Hellenistic culture also led to an extensive impact of Greek methods of interpretation on Jewish interpreters. Greek philosophy, culture, and social mores also impacted those Jewish communities, such as the one in Alexandria, Egypt, that eagerly welcomed dialogue with their Hellenistic neighbors. Even those Jews who were less than interested in dialogue with Hellenistic culture certainly felt a substantial Hellenistic influence, since the world in which they functioned was of necessity pervaded by Hellenism. An example of this is the way in which the Greek emphasis on the individual rather than the community refocused Israel's thinking about the relationship between God and his people, as evidenced especially in the third part of the Jewish canon (the Ketuvim), where emphasis is on the pious individual's relationship to God (see Sanders below, p. 247).

KEY TOPICS AND PERSONALITIES
IN ANCIENT BIBLICAL INTERPRETATION

The Septuagint

The Septuagint (LXX), the earliest known translation of the Hebrew Bible, is an early example of the influence of the Hellenistic world on biblical interpretation within the Jewish community. By the third century BCE, there was a large Jewish community in Alexandria, Egypt, which by this time had become a major center of Hellenistic civilization. Many Jews participated actively in the life of this larger Hellenistic community, so much so that a large number of them lost their ability to speak and read Hebrew, the language of their Scriptures. More pervasive ways in which Hellenism influenced the thinking of these Alexandrine Jews will be treated in the discussion of Philo below. Since translation is always interpretation, signs of the influence of the Hellenistic environment in which these Jews lived may already be seen in the work of the early scholars who provided them with a Greek rendering of their Hebrew Scriptures.

The Pentateuch was translated first, and therefore most likely served in some sense as a model for translations of other books. However, because these various translations of the Tanak were done by numerous scholars over a substantial period of time, there is no unity of method and style. While translations of the Pentateuch lean more toward the literal side of the interpretive spectrum, other books were translated more freely, as in the case of Job, for example. A translation that stuck closely to the Hebrew text would, of course, not always flow well in Greek, while attention to good Greek style had the potential to lead the translator far from the intent of the Hebrew original.

In either case, however, the surrounding Hellenistic culture still exerted its influence on the translator.

Factors complicating our attempt to understand in detail this process of translation/interpretation as embodied in the LXX include: (a) the fact that we no longer possess any copies that can be linked directly to the original translators, (b) our lack of precise knowledge of what Hebrew text(s) lay before the various translators; (c) the tendency of later scribes to modify the Greek to bring it into closer accord with the developing standard Hebrew text; and (d) the question whether later forms of the Greek text are more appropriately called revisions of the LXX (the "Old Greek text"), or should be deemed new translations in their own right. See Greenspoon's chapter below for detailed discussion of these and other associated issues.

As Greenspoon astutely points out, if we are to understand in the most complete manner possible the conceptual world which focused the thought of these translators, we must study not only those features of the Greek where the translations diverge, as far as we can tell, from their presumed Hebrew source, but also those points where the translator rendered the Hebrew in a fairly direct, straightforward manner. It would appear safe to assume that the translator would have diverged from the Hebrew text, rather than rendering it essentially unchanged, in those instances where basic features of the text clashed substantially with the intellectual environment within which the translator operated. Where the world of the Hebrew text meshed with the intellectual world of the translator, change would have been unnecessary. See Greenspoon's article for specific examples of the types of divergence within the Septuagint from its Hebrew sources.

An interesting approach to analyzing the differences in interpretive style among the various translators is to compare the later forms of the Greek text presented by Aquila, Symmachus, and Theodotion. Aquila's interpretive stance toward the Hebrew text was that the more precisely one could convey the syntax and grammatical form of the Hebrew text to the Greek reader, the better, even if that meant producing a Greek rendering that was deficient in regard to Greek grammar and style. At times it is difficult to read Aquila's text if one does not know some Hebrew. Symmachus, on the other hand, produced a translation in flowing Greek style and, as Greenspoon notes (p. 102), operates conceptually from a perspective of "functional equivalence." Theodotion stands between these two, sticking closer to the Hebrew than does Symmachus, but producing better Greek than Aquila's.

It has often been assumed that the Septuagint was the direct source for the Old Testament as quoted in Greek throughout the New Testament by its writers, and it has also been assumed that the extensive use of the Septuagint by Christians led the Jewish community to abandon it. While admitting that the Septuagint no doubt played a considerable role in the formation of the New Testament books, Greenspoon challenges both assumptions (pp. 102-5). Pointing to the discovery among the Dead Sea Scrolls of numerous biblical texts that to varying degrees approximate sources that also lay behind the Septuagint (where the Septuagint differs from the Masoretic Text), he notes that the New Testament writers could just as well have been quoting from and translating a Palestinian Hebrew text closely related to the Septuagint's source rather than quoting the Septuagint itself. Likewise, since the New Testament writers may not always have had a copy of a Greek (or Hebrew) text of the Tanak before them when they wrote, they often may have been quoting from memory, and their memory may not always have been perfect, no matter which Greek translation or Hebrew text they had in their head. Furthermore, the Septuagint clearly existed in a variety of forms rather than one simple, unified translation. These factors complicate any claim that the New Testament writers were quoting from the Septuagint. Concerning the matter of the Jewish community's abandoning the Septuagint, it should be noted that for centuries Jews continued to live in an environment which dictated that Greek would be their native language. They thus would have continued to need a current Greek translation of the Tanak and, as the efforts of figures such as Aquila and Theodotion make clear, there were scholars who were willing to provide such updated forms for Jews as long as that was necessary.

The history of biblical interpretation is filled with countless instances in which the content of Scripture required significant reinterpretation in order to make it more directly applicable to new contexts in which it needed to be understood. The Septuagint, which in its numerous forms adapted the teachings of the Hebrew Scriptures to the Hellenistic world of Alexandrian Jews, is an early example of the interpretation/understanding of Scripture from a new vantage point, an interpretation focused through translation. We now turn to another example of the adaptation of the Hebrew Scriptures to the Hellenistic environment of ancient Alexandria, focusing on the influential first-century CE Jewish philosopher and exegete Philo.

Philo of Alexandria

Philo was thoroughly steeped in the worlds of both early Judaism and Hellenistic culture. As a Jew who was in continual dialogue with the best learning that the Hellenistic world of his time could offer, Philo strove both to make Judaism credible and worthy in the eyes of his Hellenistic friends and to use

Hellenistic philosophy and interpretation as a means of exploring and reveal-ing the depth and power of the Jewish Scriptures. Among the Greek philoso-phers, Philo was especially fond of Plato, and it was from the Stoics that he learned methods of interpreting revered texts. Indeed, so thoroughly versed was Philo in both Judaism and Hellenistic philosophy that scholars could eas-ily debate whether he was principally driven by the world of Judaism or by the world of Greek philosophy and interpretation.

Philo was convinced that a great deal of continuity existed between the wisdom of the Greek sages and the wisdom of the Jewish Scriptures. Accord-ing to Philo, true philosophy was presented by God to Israel through Moses when the Law was given on Mount Sinai. This true philosophy was also given, through different means, to other peoples. It was given to the Greeks in their ancient philosophical heritage, elements of which Philo argues are derived from the teachings of Moses. In fact, Moses is seen by Philo as a teacher rather similar to the ancient Greek philosophers. Thus, Philo works extensively in his exegetical analysis to develop in detail the commonality between Greek philosophy and the teachings of Moses.

A key concept for Philo is the transcendence of God. Philo assumes that God, as he is, cannot be conceived or described by mere mortals. Conse-quently, Philo wishes to move quickly beyond certain aspects of the presenta-tion of God in the Hebrew Scriptures, such as the extensive use of anthro-pomorphisms, which appear to describe God. Showing his background in Platonic philosophy, Philo argues that God is "beyond motion and emotion, beyond evil, and beyond any contact with matter" (Borgen, p. 119 below, quoting Siegert). Thus, Philo maintains that one cannot understand anthropomorphisms in Scripture literally, but must instead find other means for interpreting these passages.

While Philo typically deals with anthropomorphic statements about God by finding in them a deeper meaning, and thus is prone to push aside the literal meaning of these passages, his normal tendency is not to see the deeper meaning of the Scriptures as invalidating the literal meaning of the text. In fact, it is only when one has studied rigorously the closest details of the text (*Fug.* 54: Moses "never puts in a superfluous word") that one is prepared to search for and find the deeper meaning. Thus, Philo frequently interprets the same text on two or three different levels. Nevertheless, while he does not dis-count the validity of the Law in everyday life, he maintains that the primary purpose of Moses when he wrote down the Law was to present correct religious-philosophical teachings, which interpreters must uncover by means of the allegorical method of interpretation.

As Philo sees it, the many particular ordinances in the Law given by Moses "coincide with the universal cosmic principles" (Borgen, p. 120 below). Thus, the careful study of the particulars of the Jewish Law will reveal to the careful scholar, hidden behind the details of the Law, the fundamental truths on which the cosmos is founded and on the basis of which it operates. While some enemies of the Jews might argue that the truths of Greek philosophy undercut the Jewish Scriptures and show them to be imperfect and unworthy, Philo counters that the careful study of the Jewish Scriptures shows them, when properly understood, to be in accord with the true teachings of philosophy. Such an approach to exegesis, in which the fundamental truths of the cosmos can be found hidden behind the surface form of the text, is hardly surprising in one who was an avid student of Plato. Like his mentor, Philo found truth in the meaning (form) that lay behind the given text (material world).

As Borgen notes, Philo continues the theme found in earlier Jewish Hellenistic writings of the "superiority of the Jewish nation" (pp. 114-15), although the sharpest edge of this is removed by his claim that God revealed himself by other means to other people. This edge is further dulled by Philo's notion that the type of education one would receive in the pagan Hellenistic world could be a helpful tool in uncovering the wisdom in the laws of Moses, just as Chaldean wisdom was of benefit to Abraham. Yet, the bottom line is that true wisdom comes first and foremost through the laws of Moses. Not surprisingly, Philo saw the primary purpose for the translation of the Law of Moses into Greek (the Septuagint) to be so that Gentiles might learn the cosmic and universal laws of the one true God, and not so that Greek-speaking Jews who did not know Hebrew could read their own Scriptures. In this we no doubt see mirrored Philo's view of his own role as an interpreter, namely, to convey to his fellow Jews and to the Hellenistic world the universal truths contained within the Jewish Scriptures.

Thus, several purposes are evident in Philo's writings. One would be to confirm in his own mind and to work out the details of the powerful relationship between Jewish teachings, on the one hand, and the teachings of the classical Greek philosophers on the other. Another would be to make credible to non-Jews living in Alexandria the Jewish Scriptures and their basic teachings. A third would be to defend Jewish teachings against those who would see Judaism as a barbaric and unsophisticated religion, whose Scriptures are filled with crude and unsophisticated notions. All three of these purposes played into Philo's thinking, making him and his interpretive perspective very much a product of the Hellenistic world in which he lived.

The Dead Sea Scrolls

When we turn to Philo's Palestinian contemporaries who wrote the Dead Sea Scrolls (DSS), we enter a very different world of interpretation. Here the sacred writings are not viewed through and interwoven with a revered source of knowledge from outside Judaism, as in Philo's use of Greek philosophy to help unlock the true meaning of the Torah. Rather, the writers of the DSS focused their energies entirely on their own Jewish Scriptures. They infused their Scriptures with their own, unique sectarian twist, which is clearly and extensively infused with biblical language and builds on the apocalyptic eschatology of certain portions of Scripture. But their community would have viewed with skepticism such distinctions between Scripture and their own understanding of it, since in their view the former flowed clearly and unavoidably into the latter. They, as the elect, were uncovering Scripture's true meaning, which was being fulfilled in the life of their community.

Certain factors must be kept in mind as one analyzes interpretation as practiced by this community. First, the boundaries of Israel's sacred writings were quite fluid for the writers of the DSS, with no clear delineation between books regarded as unmistakably scriptural and therefore authoritative and books that lay outside the bounds of Scripture (Davies, pp. 144-46 below). Second, the lines between sacred text and interpretation, between authoritative texts and what can at times be equally authoritative interpretation and elucidation of those texts, are quite blurred. In the mind of those interpreting Scripture, the "correct understanding" (their view) or "sectarian twist" (our view) that they placed on the texts was merely an amplification and clarification of the meaning God had already placed in the text, and the lines between sacred text and interpretation were therefore of necessity quite fluid. For example, in the case of scriptural texts which give signs that predict future events, the writers of these scriptural texts, in the view of the writers of the DSS, did not completely control the meanings of the signs contained in the scriptural texts, and as a result they may not have been fully aware of the implications of those signs (Davies, pp. 157-58). Therefore, the texts and their signs needed subsequent interpretation in order to unscramble the code that had been embedded in the text, and thereby to reveal God's true intentions for the end of the age.

Those composing the literature preserved in the DSS believed that, without question, they had the gift to unscramble and interpret the code. An example appears in 1QpHab 7.1-5: "as for the statement 'He who reads it may run,' its interpretation refers to the Teacher of Righteousness, to whom God reveals all the mysteries of his servants the prophets." The community therefore worked diligently to understand more fully the "mystery" words spoken by the scriptural writers. These mysteries could refer to recent events that had been anticipated in the prophetic writings, as in the case of the interpretations in the *Habakkuk Pesher,* or they could predict events yet to happen, as with the interpretations in the *Melchizedek Midrash,* which describe events to come at the time of the end. This latter text is interesting in that, unlike the *Habakkuk Pesher,* which is an extensive elucidation of one biblical book, it interweaves texts from numerous sacred books to form a coherent picture of the end of the age. In doing so, it clearly presupposes that all of Scripture is a unity, and therefore, as a cohesive unit, is useful throughout for helping one learn about the end of times. The growing need in both Judaism and Christianity for an understanding of revealed Scripture as a unity has been discussed above. Clearly, the development of such a concept had already begun in DSS documents such as the *Melchizedek Midrash,* even if there was at this time no attempt (and apparently, no perceived need) to develop a closed list of books in order to articulate this concept in detail.

If there is no clear line between text and interpretation, there is also no need to feel bound to the precise words of the sacred texts. (In this matter of getting beyond the literal words of the text, there is a substantial parallel between Philo and the writers of the DSS.) As Davies notes, "There was *no fundamental conceptual distinction* in the minds of these writers between a scriptural text and a sectarian interpretation." The interpretation only made clear what was already in the text. Not surprisingly, "There is an almost complete spectrum of genres and techniques for converting the implicitly sectarian Scriptures into explicitly sectarian interpretations" (p. 164).

This spectrum of interpretive approaches to the sacred text is very broad. For example, some documents found among the Dead Sea Scrolls, such as the famous *Isaiah Scroll,* are simply copies of scriptural texts quite similar to those we possess from other sources. These texts may simply have been read by the community in light of an implicit sectarian understanding. Other documents constitute paraphrases or retellings of the biblical texts, usually portions of the Pentateuch. The *Genesis Apocryphon,* for example, does not deal with the text of Genesis in an explicitly exegetical manner, as is done in the pesher format, illustrated above by the *Habakkuk Pesher,* which alternates text and interpretation. Rather, exegesis is carried out in the *Genesis Apocryphon* by expansion and embellishment of the Scripture text.

The *Damascus Document* occupies another point on this spectrum of interpretation. It presents a collection of the laws of the community, which were, as the writer saw it, derived from the Torah of Moses by means of an ongoing revelation to the true remnant. In the view of the writer, Moses received God's revealed law early in Israel's history, but preexilic Israel disobeyed that law. It therefore became necessary that a subsequent, divinely-given interpretation of the sacred text be provided in order to restore the true revelation of the will of God. That revelation was contained in the *Damascus Document* (CD 6:2-11), which the community carefully followed. However, because the current age is seen as a period of wickedness, yet another revealed interpretation will be necessary in the future. Here sacred text and interpretation are strongly interwoven, with interpretation seen as a second (and later, a third) revelation that builds on the first and returns to its true meaning. While we today may view this later rewriting as a going beyond the sacred text, as a commentary on the text, Davies raises an interesting point (p. 155): ". . . in the case of the Scriptures, were the varying laws in Exodus, Leviticus, and Deuteronomy meant to replace or interpret each other? Creatively rewriting, and indeed adding, without abrogating the authority of the source, has precedents." Thus, if rewritings and expansions of earlier laws by later biblical writers were seen to be legitimate within the Pentateuch, with both the early and the later forms preserved in the text, would there be any reason to think that writers of documents such as the *Damascus Document* or the *Temple Scroll* saw themselves to be doing anything different from what they had seen done by some of the biblical writers/interpreters within the Pentateuch? Clearly, in the absence of a concept of a closed canon, the writers saw themselves to be part of a continuing process of revelation/interpretation already well established by and within the very documents they were interpreting.

While we cannot discuss here all the varieties of interpretive formats present in the DSS, several additional examples will be helpful. One format already mentioned is an explicit commentary on a specific scriptural text, such as the *Habakkuk Pesher*. In such cases, more than in many other DSS documents, we see a formal distinction between sacred text and the interpreter's explanation of the true meaning of the text. Yet even here it is doubtful that the demarcation between text and interpretation of the text is as clear as it would be in the mind of a twentieth-century interpreter, since the DSS interpreter saw himself to be presenting aspects of God's revelation that were not known to the original writer of the text. Another interpretive category includes documents that collect and interpret texts around a common theme. The *Testimonia*, made up of messianic texts, is such a type of anthology. To a substantial extent, its interpretation is expressed through its choice of specific texts. In their mix, these texts give a particular twist to the notion of the Messiah, one no doubt closely tied to the views of the writer and his associates. A comment Davies makes in another context is also appropriate here (p. 161): "Whether or not explicit comments were written, there was often an implicit reading below the surface of the text pointing to an underlying esoteric narrative."

The last category to be mentioned in this spectrum of interpretation is liturgical documents, which typically are saturated with scriptural language. As Davies notes (p. 161), ". . . in analyzing any hymnody that follows a scriptural idiom, it is often impossible to decide when shared vocabulary is simply generic, when there are conscious or unconscious allusions, and when there is a deliberate quotation of as small a unit as a single word. Taken as a whole, Qumran hymns and psalms have to be seen as scriptural interpretation of a sort, for the allusions and quotations are intended in some way to apply the scriptural language to the experiences and feelings evoked in the later composition." It is not always possible to tell whether or not these liturgies reflect a specifically sectarian origin, as some may have been composed in a different context but nevertheless came to be used by the community because they fit the community's ideology. The *Hymns* (1QH) do, however, contain an ideology typical of the sectarians. They give thanks for deliverance from the lot of the wicked and for revealed knowledge of the divine mysteries. Another example that likely contains sectarian ideology is the *Songs of the Sabbath Sacrifice* (4QShirShabb). Thus, in these various liturgies found among the DSS, scriptural usage and interpretation can range from the employment of words or phrases that are common in the sacred texts and therefore are part of the common religious language of the time, with no passage in particular being alluded to, all the way to substantial utilization of specific texts, as in the case of the dependence of the *Songs of the Sabbath Sacrifice* on Ezekiel 1 and 10. In whatever way the sacred language and text(s) are brought to bear, however, they are typically seen through the prism of sectarian ideology.

Thus, within the DSS documents there was not a clear boundary between sacred texts and subsequent interpretation. Rather, the revelation from God was seen as partially given in the older revered texts, expanded through subsequent revelation to and interpretation by the groups writing the scrolls, and yet to be completed as the time of the end approached. This ongoing revelation, while based on the scriptural documents available to the community, reshaped and expanded those documents as necessary in order to present the new message which God had given to his chosen community.

This view of ongoing revelation certainly was not limited to the writers of the DSS. In fact, many within the broader Jewish community saw themselves as recipients of a subsequent revelation which enabled them to interpret more clearly the content and meaning of Judaism's sacred texts. Perhaps the best-known examples are found in the New Testament, whose writers interpreted the Jewish Scriptures as documents that, properly understood (from their perspective), anticipated the new revelation in Jesus Christ. While the writers of the twenty-seven New Testament documents apparently did not view themselves as writers of "Scripture," they certainly believed that they had participated in a subsequent revelation from God. Before the passage of many years, most of these documents had come to be regarded by the church as revelation on a par with the earlier Jewish sacred texts. While the writings of Josephus, unlike the New Testament documents, did not come to be regarded as revelatory by any particular community, his method of expanding on the Jewish sacred writings certainly parallels interpretive techniques in evidence among the DSS (e.g., the *Genesis Apocryphon*), and there is no reason to suppose that Josephus sharply distinguished the message contained in the sacred texts from his own elucidation of that message. That is, revelation and interpretation were on a continuum.

Targumim

We now turn to another category of literature, the targums, which also blur the line between the sacred text and interpretation of that text. The targums are translations of the Jewish community's Scripture from Hebrew into Aramaic that also interweave substantial interpretation of and expansion on those texts. They are translations, but they carried the full impact of the sacred texts, since they became for Aramaic-speaking Jews their primary avenue of access to God's revelation to his people. These targums were used extensively, over a considerable number of centuries, in the synagogue and in other contexts within the Jewish community, as an understandable form of the scriptural texts for Jews living throughout the Diaspora. The primary areas of usage were Palestine, Syria, Babylon, and northern Mesopotamia.

The earliest translations may have been used for private or scholastic purposes. McNamara suggests (p. 170 below) that this may well have been the case with the Targum of Job from Qumran (4QTgJob, which may date to the second century BCE) and the fragments of a Targum on Leviticus (4QTgLev, from the first century BCE). In these two cases, we are fortunate to have copies of very early texts, which can provide valuable information about the early process of the formation of the targums. However, with other copies of the targums, dating can be an elusive process, primarily due to the nature of these translations as living documents that were modified in successive generations as the needs of each period changed. It has been suggested that targums can be compared to a tell with various strata. A sensitivity to this tell-like character of targums is required since the extant text probably includes stratified elements representing as much as several centuries of targumic development. Midrash, expansive interpretation of the narrative portions of the biblical texts, often developed alongside the targumic texts (see Porton's article below on rabbinic midrash), and elements of this midrashic heritage also worked their way into the targums. The same is true of the developing halachic (legal) traditions of Judaism, which also bled over into the targumic texts. (See the examples below.)

Thus, the nature of the targums as living, evolving translations of the Hebrew text that adapted themselves to subsequent generations points strongly to the interconnectedness of translation and interpretation in the targums. Translation always involves interpretation, as anyone who has ever done a significant amount of translation can affirm. Indeed, the root *trgm* which lies behind the word "targum," as used in Rabbinic Hebrew and the targums themselves, carries the double meaning of "to translate" and "to interpret." In the targums, however, the interpretive element plays a stronger, more obvious, and at times much more expansive role than we would expect to see in any modern translation of the Tanak.

The text of Nehemiah 8, though it does not mention *translation* of the Hebrew Scriptures into another language, presents, with this one needed modification, a clear example of what the targums do. Ezra and his numerous assistants "helped the people to understand the law, while the people remained in their places. And they read from the book, from the law of God, with interpretation, and they gave the sense, so that the people understood the reading" (Neh. 8:7-8). Add the element of translation from Hebrew to Aramaic, and we can see the process wherein the targums present, explain, and expand upon the scriptural text. One can envision a synagogue context in which a portion of the Hebrew Scriptures is read, and then an Aramaic translation is provided. The translation would be provided for those no longer fluent in Hebrew. It is likely that even for those who knew Hebrew well, elements in the Scriptures needed to be explained. Other parts of Scripture may have offended both the theological and cultural sensitivities of the readers/hearers. So an "interpretation" of the text was needed to adapt it to the culture, developing religious beliefs, social forms and practices, intellectual environment, and broader external world of each successive generation during which the targums were used. The following examples of how the targums "explained" the sacred texts show how the communities adapted them to fit the later contexts in which they were used.

At a more foundational level there is, as McNamara notes (p. 172 below), "a tendency in the targumim to turn a metaphorical turn of phrase into something more readily understood, and also to use certain stock phrases and a more limited vocabulary than that found in the Hebrew, with the result that often the particularity, and with it the vitality, of the original text is lost in the process." Thus, Hebrew *zera'*, "seed," is often rendered in Aramaic as "sons" or "descendants of sons." "A land flowing with milk and honey" becomes "a land bearing good fruits, pure as milk and sweet as honey." Contemporary place names are sometimes substituted for biblical names, as when Dan becomes Caesarea (Philippi). The lateness of some of these adaptations may be seen in *Pseudo-Jonathan*, which mentions, in Gen. 21:21, Adisha and Fatima, the wife and daughter of Mohammed. (See pp. 172-73 below for additional examples.)

At a more substantive level, the sacred texts were adapted to reflect contemporary halachic practices, which had often gone well beyond the descriptions in the text. McNamara (p. 173) quotes Smolar and Aberbach as follows: "The central purpose of the Aramaic translation of Biblical texts was not to provide an accurate rendering for the benefit of scholars, but to instruct the masses with an up-to-date version of the Scriptures, one which perforce had to agree with current laws and customs. Inevitably, accuracy and historical truth had to be sacrificed on the altar of halachic orthodoxy." For example, Exod. 23:19; 34:26; and Deut. 14:21 read, "You shall not boil a kid in its mother's milk." *Onqelos* and the *Palestinian Targum* read, "Do not consume meat with milk," reflecting the contemporary halachic practice. Similarly, in treating Lev. 23:29, the *Palestinian Targum* expands on "who is able to fast" by specifying that the sick and the infirm are exempted from this stipulation. Nevertheless, the targums do not always adapt to contemporary practice. Exod. 21:29 stipulates that the owner of an ox with a record of goring who does not keep the ox confined is to be put to death. While Jewish halachah had evolved to require monetary compensation, not execution, *Onqelos* and the *Palestinian Targum* render the text literally, ignoring contemporary practice.

McNamara provides numerous additional categories of translation/interpretation of scriptural texts in the targums, including converse readings, euphemisms, avoidance of anthropomorphisms, and the augmentation of eschatological references. In converse renderings, the Aramaic says the opposite of what the scriptural text says. For example, *Onqelos* and the *Palestinian Targum* render Cain's protest in Gen. 4:14, "From your face I will be hidden," as "It is impossible to hide from before you." The (presumably embarrassing) description in Num. 12:1 of Moses' wife as a "Cushite woman" becomes "like a Cushite in complexion" in the *Palestinian Targum* and simply "beautiful" in *Onqelos*. In euphemisms, offensive passages are rendered innocuous, as when "one urinating against a wall," which is used in 1 Sam. 25:22 and 34 to designate a male, becomes "one knowing knowledge," or when Leah's "weak eyes" in Gen. 29:17 become "beautiful" in *Onqelos* and "raised in prayer" in *Neofiti*. Translators often avoid applying anthropomorphisms directly to the deity, as when "Is the Lord's hand shortened?" in Num. 11:23 becomes in *Neofiti* "Is there deficiency before the Lord?" or "the Lord regretted that he had made man" in Gen. 6:6 becomes in the *Palestinian Targum* "There was regret before the Lord (that he created Adam)." In some passages, the eschatological references are heightened, as in Deut. 32:39, where God's "See now . . . I kill and make alive" becomes in the *Palestinian Targum* "I am he who causes the living to die in this world, and who brings the dead to life in the world to come." God's comment to Adam in Gen. 3:19, "You are dust and to dust shall you return," is extended in the *Palestinian Targum* with the addition of "But from the dust you are to rise again to give an account and a reckoning of all that you have done." Interestingly, one method of dealing with difficult texts, such as the account of Reuben lying with Bilhah, the story of the golden calf, David's offense regarding Bathsheba, and Amnon's rape of Tamar, was to specify that these texts could be read aloud in Hebrew but not rendered into Aramaic (see the Mishnah tractate *Megillah* 4:10). Here, apparently, no amount of euphemism, adaptation, and revision could make the text fit for all Jews.

There also are longer interpretations/expansions of the biblical texts in the targums. For instance, the Hebrew text of Gen. 15:1 reads, "After these things the word of the Lord came to Abraham in a vision, 'Fear not, Abraham, I am your shield; your reward will be very great.'" In the *Palestinian Targum* this becomes:

> After these things, after all the kingdoms of the earth had gathered together and had drawn up battle-lines against Abram and had fallen before him, and he had killed four kings from among them and had brought back nine encampments, Abram thought in his heart and said: "Woe, now, is me! Perhaps I have received the reward of the precepts in this world and there is no portion for me in the world to come. Or perhaps the brothers or relatives of those killed, who fell before me, will go and be in their fortresses and in their cities, and many legions will become allied with them and they will come against me and kill me. Or perhaps there were a few meritorious deeds in my hand the first time they fell before me and they stood in my favor, or perhaps no meritorious deed will be found in my hand the second time and the name of the heavens will be profaned in me." For this reason there was a word of prophecy from before the Lord upon Abram the just, saying: "Do not fear, Abram, for although many legions are allied and come against you to kill (you), my Memra will be a shield for you, and it will be a protection for you in this world; and although I delivered up your enemies before you in this world, the reward of your good works is prepared for you before me in the world to come."

Rabbinic Midrash

When we move from the targums, with their clear focus on providing interpretation, expansion, and, at times, revision of the sacred Scriptures, to
midrashic interpretation, we enter a substantially different environment. As
Porton notes (see p. 202 below), midrash is confined to the world of the rabbis and therefore circulated in much smaller circles than the targums, which
served the general Jewish population. Furthermore, while rabbinic Judaism's
understanding of the Torah and its interpretation would eventually come to
dominate Judaism, early in the first millennium CE, when midrash was first
being developed, rabbinic Judaism was still in competition with other forms
of Judaism.

Midrash is rabbinic interpretation that is directly linked to specific biblical texts, but not necessarily in the form of a running commentary on an entire
biblical book, nor in a form designed for general use by all members of the
Jewish community. As Porton defines it (p. 202), midrash is "a distinctive form
of rabbinic literature and a well-defined intellectual enterprise. Whether written or oral, it begins from the fixed canonical text, which it explicitly cites. This
explicit citation text differentiates midrash from the other significant genre of
early rabbinic literature, Mishnah." Porton also notes (p. 204) that there is a
clearly defined distinction between the scriptural text and its midrashic interpretation (as may also be seen, for example, in the Dead Sea *pesharim*). "The
rabbinic documents mark the separation between Scripture and rabbinic
comments with a number of expressions that introduce the biblical citations,
so that they are not conflated with the rabbis' interpretations."

In order to understand the scope and nature of midrash, we must
briefly examine the broader structure of rabbinic teaching within which midrash was practiced. The rabbis argued that what Moses received on Mount Sinai was not simply a written text that needed to be understood in a straightforward manner, but rather the Torah, the complete and forever authoritative
revelation of God's will for his people Israel and for the world. This revelation
was given in both oral and written form, the oral form containing both methods of interpreting the Torah and teachings not found in the written Torah. It
was the responsibility of the rabbis to study the entire revelation continually
in order to comprehend it ever more fully. Since all of God's will was contained there, it was necessary that each generation deepen its understanding
of the wisdom the revelation contained, applying it to its own age.

The Mishnah (oral Torah, codified and written down by Rabbi Judah in
200 CE) contained the sayings and teaching of the rabbis from the preceding
several centuries, thereby presenting a developed and enriched understand-

ing of the revelation from God. The Babylonian Talmud (500 CE) further expanded on this understanding of the revelation from God, adding as commentary on the Mishnah the much longer exposition called gemara ("completion"). Neither the Mishnah nor the Talmud, however, made a consistent attempt to link these teachings directly with the written Torah. As Porton notes, (p. 203, citing Neusner), the rabbis mentioned in the Mishnah, while they were heavily influenced by the teachings and religious perspectives found in their Scriptures, were focused first and foremost on issues crucial to their own times, which were often determined by problems and concerns independent of matters raised in the written Torah. Thus it would have been impossible to anticipate the issues the rabbis would later address simply by reading the Scriptures themselves.

This lack of a direct link between rabbinic teachings, as they came to be codified in the Mishnah, and the form and shape of issues as they were raised in the written Torah, apparently troubled the rabbis. Over a considerable period of time, a large number of the rabbis developed, piece by piece, the many interpretations now brought together in the various midrashim which have come down to us. In these midrashim, the rabbis interpret the scriptural passages they treat in ways that allow them to justify current rabbinic practice and interpretation. By basing the teachings in the midrashim on scriptural texts, these rabbis were asserting that "one could not merely employ human logic to discover the correct action according to God's will" (Porton, p. 203). Thus, these midrashim comment extensively on scriptural texts (in formats described below) in order to link many of the teachings in the Mishnah and the Talmud directly to the written Torah. In fact, many of the sages cited in the midrashic discussions also participated in the discussions presented in the Mishnah and the Talmud. Therefore, all four elements — the Mishnah and the gemara constructed around it, and the written Torah and the midrashim commenting on it — are part of a larger rabbinic mythic structure whose focus is the exposition and explication of the revelation given to Moses on Mount Sinai (Porton, p. 208). Though each has a different role to play in this process, and each pursues that role by different means, all four have the same goal, the thorough understanding of God's will for Israel and for the world.

Some scholars have argued that the various midrashim arose in response to the needs of the broader Jewish community to understand the written text of Scripture. Porton, however, notes that we cannot discern with absolute certainty the setting in which midrash was born and argues that the midrashim were most likely created in the more narrowly controlled context of the rabbinic schoolhouses, where the rabbis disputed with one another and trained the next generation of rabbinic scholars. "[T]here is virtually no evidence that the rabbis played an important role in the ancient synagogues or delivered popular sermons in that context. Midrash most likely arose in the rabbinic schoolhouse and reflects the supreme importance of the Hebrew Bible within the mythology and the self-definition of the rabbinic class" (pp. 202-3). "The basic framework was a master-disciple relationship between the sage and his students" (p. 206 below). In fact, the connections and allusions in a midrash are often too obscure for non-rabbis, even if they heard them, to have understood them.

If the intent of midrash was to link the oral Torah of the rabbis more closely with the written Torah, the specific manner in which the various midrashim carried out this intent could vary substantially. For example, some midrashim comment on the entire text of a book from the written Torah, as in the case of *Sifra* ("the book"), which comments verse-by-verse, and at times word-by-word, on the entire text of Leviticus. *Mekhilta* ("rule" or "norm") comments on roughly one-third of the book of Exodus, and *Sifre Numbers* and *Sifre Deuteronomy* comment on sizeable portions of the books they treat. *Genesis Rabbah* at times directly parallels the approach of *Sifra,* sticking closely to the verses and words of its given text, but at other times presents elaborate expositions only very loosely connected to the text of Genesis. All these midrashim work their way closely through at least portions of a biblical book, following the sequence of the biblical text. *Leviticus Rabbah* is different, being composed, instead, of thirty-seven homilies on particular themes. It therefore does not necessarily follow the order of the biblical text. *Pesiqta de Rab Kahana* is another homiletical midrash, focusing on the biblical readings from the festivals and the special Sabbaths. It has five chapters in common with *Leviticus Rabbah.*

These various midrashim are not the sustained work of one writer, as in the case of Philo's expositions or works such as the DSS *pesharim* or the *Genesis Apocryphon.* Rather, they are collections of numerous independent units brought together by an editor and most likely modified in subsequent generations. While particular rabbis are often credited with specific interpretations, it is also common for interpretations to be given anonymously and for several interpretations of a particular text to be provided one after another, often with no indication of the relative authority accorded to each interpretation (Porton, p. 208).

Midrash often focuses on minute aspects of the biblical text. An individual word or letter can lead to an exegetical conclusion. Repetitions, peculiar spellings, shapes of letters, minor differences between parallel passages, and word order can all lead to rabbinic conclusions about the meaning and implication of a particular text. See, for example, the illustration provided by Porton (pp. 210-12) of the significance of the particle *'k* (Exod. 31:13) for the discussion concerning when one may violate the Sabbath or the interesting discussion (pp. 215-16) of why the first word in the written Torah begins with *bet,* the *second* letter of the Hebrew alphabet, rather than *aleph,* the first. Since the rabbis began with the premise that written and oral Torah contained the entirety of God's revelation, it is not surprising that the rabbis focused so closely on minute aspects of the text.

Thus, if Philo's writings had as a primary goal the integration of philosophy (which in Philo's opinion was another form of God's revelation to humankind) with the wisdom of the Jewish Scriptures, and if the Septuagint and the targums reveal attempts by their translators to make understandable and to interpret the Jewish Scriptures for the general Jewish population, the midrashim had as their primary goal the connection of the sayings and teachings of the rabbinic sages to the written Scriptures. While Philo's writings clearly were not aimed at the masses, they were directed toward all learned individuals, both Jewish and Gentile, who loved the pursuit of wisdom. The Septuagint and targums circulated quite widely. But the midrashim apparently circulated in much smaller groups, centered around the master-student relationship in the rabbinic academies.

Canon of the Tanak (Old Testament)

Understanding how the Jewish community reached a consensus on which books should be regarded as canonical is crucial to understanding the interpretive process. Before looking at the focus and orientation of the three main sections of the Tanak — the Torah (law), Nebi'im (prophets), and Ketuvim (writings) — we need to discuss briefly the authority of traditions from the time of their origin in early Israel down to the time of the setting of the written canon in its current form near the middle of the second century CE. In part, this question of authority is tied closely to the Semitic, pre-Greek notion of traditions as products of the life of the community. As Sanders notes in treating early Israel, "certain common traditions gave the community identity and norms of conduct in light of that identity. They functioned in much the same way as later canonical Scripture, except that they were remembered and transmitted in fluid, oral forms. That they were not set in stabilized forms in no way diminished their authority" (p. 227 below). Sanders cites the various traditions associated with the exodus from Egypt and the traditions focused around the life of David and the establishment of the Davidic dynasty as examples of the power of such traditions to carry authority in early Israel. While not canonical in quite the same sense as the later literature accepted as canonical by the Jewish community in the second century CE, these earlier traditions nevertheless served a "canonical" function by providing an authoritative, definitional focus for the life and beliefs of early Israel. In time, these traditions became embodied in written form, as in the appearance of an early form of the book of Deuteronomy in 621 BCE, which "most likely marked the first time a written document functioned in a canonical way (as *norma normans*) in ancient Israel/Judah" (Sanders, p. 233). In a sense, everything beyond the earliest days of the creation of Israel's foundational oral traditions is an expansion of these "canonical" traditions, the adding of new traditions, the adaptation of all these traditions to new life situations which Israel encountered, the critique of Israel's subsequent life and conduct in light of these traditions, and the exclusion of certain developing traditions as "dead-ends" in Israel's journey as a people.

Eventually, of course, circumstances led to the "closing" of the canon, that is, to the decision that certain written traditions, and they alone, would henceforth be considered the complete and authoritative statement of God's will for his people. It is crucial here to note the distinction between canon as a cluster of authoritative traditions, which can move into the future in an open-ended, malleable manner, and canon as a closed group of authoritative writings that are no longer open to modification except through interpretation. Another way to say this is that one does not have to have a closed written canon to have authoritative literature. In fact many, such as the community at Qumran, appear to have had both a highly developed concept of scriptural authority and a strong sense of the open-endedness of that authority.

Certainly, the discovery of the Dead Sea Scrolls has dramatically altered our view of the movement within Judaism toward the setting of a closed written canon. As Sanders notes (p. 244), we can now see that Judaism in the centuries leading up to the rise of Christianity was considerably more diverse than just the four parties (Pharisees, Sadducees, Essenes, and Zealots) long thought to be the main forms of pre-Christian Judaism. Certain Jewish groups, such as the Qumran community and the earliest Jewish Christians, did not regard prophecy as having ceased after the time of Ezra and Nehemiah. In this sense, Christianity did not see a rebirth of prophecy after the death and resurrection of Jesus, but rather a continuation of prophecy and revelation in a rejuvenated sense as a result of the appearance of Jesus and the full realization of the significance of his appearance. This is why for Christians the canon could not be closed but had to remain open for the embodiment of a "new covenant" in the New Testament. For them, the new covenant completed what was lacking in the old covenant. Similarly, the Qumran community could hardly develop the notion of a closed canon as long as it saw itself as closely involved in the expansion, deciphering, and realization of the revelation that had been begun in the documents they prized so highly and scrutinized so meticulously.

To say that elements within Judaism, such as the Qumran community and the earliest Christian community, did not have a concept of a closed or completed canon in no way negates the strong concept of canonical scriptural authority within Judaism. In fact, as Sanders argues (p. 241), one can well make the case that both the Torah (Pentateuch) and the Prophets had basically achieved canonical status by 400 BCE (the Pentateuch perhaps in the middle of the fifth century, the prophetic corpus shortly thereafter, toward the end of the fifth century). Here Sanders disagrees with the commonly advanced claim that the Pentateuch achieved canonical status by about 400 BCE, the Prophets by about 200 BCE. He argues, instead, that the two go hand-in-hand: "the Torah and the Prophets hang together as a basic statement of God's dealings with the world and with Israel in fairly clear theological tones. . . . Taken in tandem, [they] present the panorama of the rise and fall of the preexilic adventure called Israel" (p. 241). When one takes into consideration the exilic and postexilic prophets, which are a vital portion of this second section of the canon, "The prophetic corpus provides several metaphors enabling the reader to understand all the adversity that had befallen Israel and Judah, not only as punishment for Israel's corporate sins, but also in the more positive sense of transforming Israel from common nationhood (like all the nations round about) into a people with a God-given mission to the rest of the world" (p. 242). The third section, the Ketuvim (writings), did not reach stabilization, Sanders argues, until the middle of the second century CE, after the Bar Kochba revolt of 135 CE. This is because apocalyptic thinking, which assumes a substantial open-endedness of the canon, lasted well beyond the destruction of Jerusalem in 70 CE. The destruction of Jerusalem has previously been seen as the catalyst for the closing of the canon. As an example of this late survival of apocalyptic thinking, Sanders cites Rabbi Akiba's strong support of Bar Kochba as the Messiah (p. 245). Thus, Sanders sees an early, pre–400 BCE timeframe for the solidification of the basic written canon of the Torah and Prophets, followed by a period of over half a millennium during which the eventual third section, the Writings, was in a state of substantial flux, followed by the eventual closing of the Writings and thus of the entire canon, after the disasters of the Bar Kochba revolt caused the Jewish community to rethink in major ways its understanding of the nature of Scripture.

Since the Christian community also sees the Tanak or Old Testament as foundational, it is interesting to see the varying ways in which Christians and Jews have grouped the books of the Tanak. Although, due to the efforts of Jerome, the *texts* of both canons are the same, since Jerome's translation into Latin is based on the Hebrew text rather than on the Septuagint text, the arrangement of the books in the Jewish canon differs considerably from the arrangement in the Christian canons. For the purposes of this discussion, the differences between the several forms of the Christian canon are not nearly as significant as are the similarities between them (see the chart on pp. 34-35 below).

Concerning the relationship between the three sections of the Jewish canon, Sanders notes: "Whereas the Torah and the Prophets deal in some depth with God's involvement and revelations in world affairs, the Ketuvim at best offer reflections on that involvement as a thing of Israel's past. Outside the book of Daniel, there is no speculation on how God might intervene in history to sort things out, and how one reads Daniel is open to debate" (p. 246). Keeping in mind the large gap in time between the canonization of the Torah and the Prophets, on the one hand, and the Ketuvim on the other, Sanders goes on to note, "The Ketuvim clearly reflect the view of Pharasaic/rabbinic Judaism as it survived and emerged out of the failure of the Bar Kochba Revolt in the mid-second century of the common era: prophecy or revelation had ceased at the time of Ezra and Nehemiah" (p. 246). Chronicles, which comes first in the Ketuvim in the ancient Tiberian manuscripts (unlike contemporary Jewish forms of the Tanak), sets the tone for the Ketuvim. It emphasizes that Judaism, as it took shape in the postexilic restoration, was focused on the temple and the authority vested in the temple's priests and functionaries. This coincided nicely with the idea that prophecy had ceased by the time of Ezra and Nehemiah, and this in turn assisted in the necessary shift, after the Bar Kochba debacle, away from open-ended revelation and an open canon. In addition, Chronicles sets the stage for the remainder of the Ketuvim by emphasizing how all Jews could, as individuals, lead good lives as responsible Jews who pleased God by their obedience. Here one sees within Judaism the growing influence of the Greek emphasis on the individual, which is quite different from the sense of Israel as a community that permeates the first two sections of the canon.

In this context, the book of Psalms can be seen as encouraging individual obedience and responsibility, as in Psalm 1, which opens the book: "Blessed is the person who walks not in the way of the wicked . . . but delights in the Torah of Yahweh, and on that Torah meditates day and night" (Sanders, p. 247 below). The Wisdom literature in the Ketuvim also encourages individuals to lead lives of obedience to God's will. In this context even Daniel, which is typically seen as eschatological literature by Christians, can be understood instead "as a book of encouragement to Jewish individuals to lead lives obedient to the one God" (Sanders, p. 248). Thus, the message of the third section of the Jewish canon provides what post–Bar Kochba rabbinic leaders felt was imperative for the survival of the Jewish community: an emphasis on the pious life of the individual Jew, based on study of and close obedience to the tripartite closed canon.

A close look at the Christian quadripartite canons presents quite a different perspective, as revealed in its sequencing of the Pentateuch, the Historical Books, the Poetic and Wisdom Books, and the Prophets. Books such as Ezra, Nehemiah, and Esther are placed in the second section among the historical books, and in the Catholic and Orthodox canons First, Second, and even Third Maccabees are also added, thereby "stretching the history of God's dealings with Israel and the world as far down to the beginnings of Christianity as possible. The message was clear: revelation had not ceased but God, on the contrary, continued to work in history and did so climactically in Christ and the early church" (Sanders, p. 248). Unlike the Jewish canon, where the prophets were used to explain the righteous judgment of God on his people, in the Christian canon the prophets "are understood as foretelling the coming of Christ" (Sanders, p. 248), as is indicated by their being placed last in the canon and by the inclusion among them of the book of Daniel, which is understood eschatologically. Even though there are some differences among the Christian canons of the Old Testament, they nevertheless, as a group, contrast sharply with the shape of the Jewish canon. "The Tanak provides a way to move on to Mishnah and Talmud, while the First or Christian Old Testament provides a way to move on to the New Testament" (Sanders, p. 249).

Non-Canonical Jewish Literature

What about the Jewish literature that did not become part of the Tanak or the Protestant Old Testament canon? This apocryphal and pseudepigraphical literature was written primarily between 200 BCE and 200 CE and often claims to have been written by Old Testament heroes like Jeremiah, Baruch, and Solomon. The Old Testament Apocrypha is composed of thirteen works found in the Greek manuscripts of the Old Testament. The Pseudepigrapha is a collection of sixty-five writings that claim to be inspired, are related in form and content to the Old Testament, and are falsely attributed to Old Testament fig-

THE HEBREW BIBLE	THE SEPTUAGINT
Torah	Pentateuch
Genesis	Genesis
Exodus	Exodus
Leviticus	Leviticus
Numbers	Numbers
Deuteronomy	Deuteronomy
Former Prophets	History
Joshua	Joshua
Judges	Judges
Samuel	Ruth
Kings	1 Kingdoms (1 Samuel)
Latter Prophets	2 Kingdoms (2 Samuel)
Isaiah	3 Kingdoms (1 Kings)
Jeremiah	4 Kingdoms (2 Kings)
Ezekiel	1 Chronicles
The Twelve:	2 Chronicles
Hosea	*1 Esdras
Joel	2 Esdras (= Ezra-Nehemiah)
Amos	Esther
Obadiah	*Judith
Jonah	*Tobit
Micah	*1 Maccabees
Nahum	*2 Maccabees
Habakkuk	†3 Maccabees
Zephaniah	†4 Maccabees
Haggai	Poetry
Zechariah	Psalms
Malachi	*Odes
Writings (Ketuvim)	Proverbs
Psalms	Ecclesiastes
Job	Song of Solomon
Proverbs	Job
Ruth	*Wisdom (of Solomon)
Song of Solomon	*(Wisdom of) Sirach
Ecclesiastes	(Ecclesiasticus)
Lamentations	Prophets
Esther	†Psalms of Solomon
Daniel	Hosea
Ezra-Nehemiah	Amos
Chronicles	Micah

Joel
Obadiah
Jonah
Nahum
Habakkuk
Zephaniah
Haggai
Zechariah
Malachi
Isaiah
Jeremiah
*Baruch
Lamentations
*Epistle of Jeremiah
Ezekiel
*Susannah
Daniel
*Bel and the Dragon

The Septuagint's order is followed in all Christian canons, except that the Tanak's order is observed in the (Latter) Prophets, with Lamentations and Daniel moved from the Writings to the Prophets.

APOCRYPHA/DEUTEROCANONICAL BOOKS
NOT IN THE SEPTUAGINT
Books in the Greek and Slavonic Bibles; not in the Roman Catholic Canon:
    1 Esdras (= 2 Esdras in Slavonic = 3 Esdras in Appendix to Vulgate)
    Prayer of Manasseh (in Appendix to Vulgate)
    Psalm 151, following Psalm 150 in the Greek Bible
    3 Maccabees
Books in the Slavonic Bible and in the Appendix to the Vulgate:
    2 Esdras (= 3 Esdras in Slavonic = 4 Esdras in Vulgate Appendix)
    (Note: in the Latin Vulgate, Ezra-Nehemiah = 1 and 2 Esdras)
In the Appendix to the Greek Bible:
    4 Maccabees

*Books excluded from the canon or included in the Apocrypha by Protestants. Roman Catholics and Orthodox churches include these books in the Old Testament.
†Books excluded from all Christian canons but often included in modern editions of the Apocrypha/Deuterocanonical books.

ures. Many of these works circulated for a time, often with equal authority, alongside those that would eventually be deemed canonical books.

The Old Testament Apocrypha and Pseudepigrapha emerged out of interpretation of the books that constitute the Old Testament canon. As Charlesworth argues, "The main reason these writings were composed was the appearance of biblical exegesis" (p. 253 below). Their interpretation consisted of a creative dialogue with the books of the Old Testament. Their authors met the new challenges of their communities by modifying and expanding the contents of the books of the Old Testament. They reappropriated Israel's past traditions as a way to develop new theological ideas in concert with their developing understanding of God in relation to Israel and the nations.

The intertextual connections between the Old Testament and the Jewish apocryphal and pseudepigraphical literature are innumerable and of a great variety. These connections may, for a specific book, be limited to a circumscribed portion of the Old Testament, or they may draw on traditions found throughout the Old Testament. For example, the *Testaments of the Twelve Patriarchs* relies on the Genesis narratives of Jacob and his sons, whereas *1 Enoch* 1–36 draws on traditions found throughout the Old Testament. From the Torah or Pentateuch emerged books like *Jubilees* (2nd century BCE), which is a sermonic expansion of Gen. 1:1 to Exod. 12:50. Difficult passages are rewritten so that the biblical narrative is less problematic. For example, Rebecca loves Jacob rather than Esau, not because she mistreated Esau but because Abraham, her father-in-law, foresaw that Esau would not be a worthy heir (*Jub.* 19:16-31). From among the Prophets emerged books often based on Isaiah, Jeremiah, and Ezekiel. *Baruch* (ca. 200-63 BCE) is an exegetical commentary on several books of the Old Testament, especially Jeremiah, Deuteronomy, and Daniel, as well as wisdom traditions. From the Writings emerged additional Psalms of David, many hymns and prayers found scattered throughout Jewish apocryphal and pseudepigraphical literature, and wisdom books. Early Christians utilized many of the books of the Apocrypha and Pseudepigrapha as part of their use of the manuscripts of the Greek Old Testament, often with considerable Christian editing (e.g., *Ascension of Isaiah*).

Christian Interpretation in the Apostolic Period (30-100 CE)

The earliest churches were composed of Jewish Christians living within the Jewish environment of Palestine. In continuity with the Judaism from which they emerged, these earliest Jewish Christians did not use the Old Testament as a canonical collection in the form in which we have it today. Rather they turned to an assortment of authoritative texts that was larger than what eventually became known as the Old Testament. We can refer to these works as "Israel's Scriptures." As explained by Donald Juel, in the earliest years of the church the basic text of Israel's Scriptures may have been Aramaic Targums used in Jewish Christian circles in Palestine and the synagogues in which they initially continued to worship. However, the early Christian movement quickly spread to include Greek-speaking Jews and Gentiles in Syrian Antioch, the northern Mediterranean basin as far as Rome, and Alexandria in Egypt. The basic text of Jewish Scriptures in the churches became the Septuagint written in the Greek language, the language of the new converts and of the writers of the New Testament books.

As we have already seen, Israel's Scriptures testify to the Jewish practice of interpreting and incorporating new community circumstances within an existing understanding of God. These circumstances often presented theological challenges to previous thinking about God and God's relationship with the community of faith. For example, the Babylonian conquest of Jerusalem in 587 BCE and the exile in Babylon destroyed the popular theological concept that Jerusalem was inviolable because it was the seat of the dynasty of David, with whom God had made a covenant. Within the confines of Babylon a new theological emphasis on the conditional nature of covenant emerged, both as a way to explain the enslaved status of a once proud people, and to provide theological and ethical underpinnings for the continuation of the Jews as a people.

For those Jews who accepted it, the proclamation and claims of Jesus and his followers presented a critical theological challenge that required a new understanding and utilization of Israel's Scriptures. Faith that Jesus was the Christ, the fulfillment of the Scriptures' messianic prophecies, required a new reading of those Scriptures. "The confession of Jesus as Christ . . . is not the result of scriptural interpretation but its presupposition" (Juel, p. 296 below). This presupposition to interpretation played a major role in the formation of the church and its self-understanding in relation to Judaism and the world.

The interpretation of Israel's Scriptures was motivated and guided by the needs of worship, proclamation of the gospel, and instruction of new converts. Worship, preaching, and teaching were thus the catalysts of interpretation. The early Christians were predominantly Jews or Gentile proselytes to Judaism who had come to the conviction that Jesus fulfilled the prophecies of Israel's Scriptures. Therefore, the established texts of those Scriptures and the established traditions and methods of their interpretation were predominant in the early church. The use of Israel's Scriptures by the early church and the writers of the New Testament is both a continuation of the reinterpretation and adaptation of the Jewish Scriptures within the Jewish community and a significant departure that sends interpretation in new directions. The continuity is grounded in the fact that the early Christians of Jewish heritage interpreted their Scriptures using traditional methods. They did not understand themselves to be forming a new religion — that self-understanding took time to develop.

However, a significant departure in the interpretation of Israel's Scriptures in the early church could be expected because the church was guided by a new set of convictions. The church confessed that Jesus is the Messiah; that his life, death, and resurrection fulfill messianic prophecy; that the church is the New Israel with which God has established a new covenant; and that the kingdom of God is inaugurated as a spiritual rather than political kingdom. Old Testament passages took on christological meaning, often through the use of typology. The Old Testament was interpreted in light of the understanding that Jesus was the Messiah who had inaugurated the kingdom of God. In fact, the literal fulfillment of Old Testament prophecy was a fundamental hermeneutical principle of early Christianity.

The early Christian use of the Scriptures of Israel is extensive. The New Testament cites or alludes to virtually every book sacred to Judaism in the first century CE, including those of the Hebrew and Greek canons and some pseudepigrapha. Israel's Scriptures are not utilized to create systematic commentary as in Jewish writings (e.g., 1QpHab). Rather they are utilized for quotations, allusions, and echoes of themes and patterns. Quotations are taken from the Hebrew text and from several versions of the Septuagint. These are often modified in light of confession of Christ. For example, "the day of the Lord," referring to God's day of judgment on the enemies of Israel, is given the new referent of the second coming of Jesus as Lord in judgment. Allusions to Israel's Scriptures are common in the New Testament and are of a maddeningly disparate nature. Sometimes they are very close to the written texts and sometimes very loose paraphrases. Allusions are expected in a predominantly oral culture in which written texts and the ability to read are not prevalent.

Several interpretive methods are borrowed from Judaism. The Old Testament is interpreted according to its plain or literal meaning, especially on ethical issues. In Rom. 12:17-21, Paul teaches the Romans not to seek revenge on those who hurt them. He cites Deut. 32:35 ("Vengeance is mine and recompense . . .") and Prov. 25:21-22 ("If your enemies are hungry, give them bread to eat; and if they are thirsty, give them water to drink, for you will heap coals of fire on their heads . . .").

As Juel points out, common in the New Testament is the use of Israel's Scriptures in midrash. This method of interpretation is very alien to the modern reader. Midrash assumes that all words and passages of Scripture are of equal weight and can be used to interpret one another because they all derive from the mind of God. Any word or passage of Scripture can be used to interpret any other word or passage. Historical and literary contexts are not of primary significance. For example, in Gen. 12:7 and 22:17-18 God makes his promises to Abraham and his "seed" or offspring, a collective singular for all offspring. In Gal. 3:15-18 Paul ignores the historical and literary contexts of these passages and restricts the word "seed" to Jesus alone. The early Christian conviction that Jesus was the Messiah ushering in the last days guided the use of midrash to bring passages together into new constellations of texts. The Jewish Scriptures were scoured for passages that now saw fulfillment in him. Many passages that did not have messianic significance in Judaism now did in Christianity. For example, the passage describing the servant of Isaiah who suffered for his people is now seen as a prophecy of the suffering Messiah Jesus (e.g., Isa. 52:13–53:12).

Typology is an interpretive method that combs the Jewish Scriptures to find foreshadowings or prototypes of the work of Christ and the church in persons, events, things, and ideas mentioned in the text. Typological interpretation sees the revelatory connection between two historically distinct but religiously significant persons or events. Matthew and Hebrews best illustrate the typological approach. Matt. 2:17 claims that Herod's killing of the male infants in Bethlehem fulfills Jer. 31:15: "A voice is heard in Ramah, lamentation and bitter weeping. Rachel is weeping for her children; she refuses to be comforted for her children, because they are no more." In Jeremiah this refers to the exile of Israel to Babylon in the sixth century BCE. Matthew sees the earlier event repeated in a new way in his time. Hebrews 7 patterns the priestly office of Jesus after the Old Testament priest Melchizedek (Gen. 14:17-20).

The New Testament writers also utilize Israel's Scriptures for principles inherent in their pages that can be applied in new situations. For example, in 1 Cor. 9:9 Paul defends his right to receive a living while ministering to the gospel. In Judaism, the rabbis were prohibited from taking payment for their services. Paul quotes Deut. 25:4: "You shall not muzzle an ox while it is treading out the grain." The principle is that those working for the benefit of others should partake in the benefit themselves.

The New Testament borrows the allegorical method of interpretation from Hellenistic Judaism, but does not use it often. This method assumes that texts have meaning lying behind the literal meaning. Elements within a narrative are given significance and referents from outside the narrative. In Gal. 4:21–5:1 Paul equates the slave Hagar, the mother of Ishmael, with Mount Sinai, Jerusalem, and Christians who want to observe Jewish law; and he equates Sarah, mother of Isaac, with the heavenly Jerusalem and Christians who want to be free from the Jewish law.

What is crucial to note is that the use of Israel's Scriptures in all modes of Christian interpretation is often guided by intertextual connections inherited from the interpretive traditions of Israel. Particular quotations are used and allusions and midrashim are made because they were standard in Israel's interpretive traditions, which had already made the intertextual connections. The major added feature in early Christian interpretation was the presupposition that Jesus was the Christ, and this reconfigured the intertextual connections of Jewish tradition and created new ones, often through typological interpretation.

The Apostolic Fathers and the Apologists (100-200 CE)

As Trigg points out, the principal Christian literature of the second century was produced by two groups, who have come to be called the Apostolic Fathers and the Apologists. The Apostolic Fathers wrote the earliest Christian literature outside the New Testament, which is typically dated to the first half of the second century. The Apologists wrote defenses of Christianity against charges from their pagan neighbors, typically dating from the second half of the second century. Neither group extensively cited the Jewish Scriptures, wrote commentaries on entire books of Scripture, or presented a developed theory of interpretation as did Origen, Jerome, and Augustine, who followed them. Rather they used the language of Scripture to describe their experiences and provide ethical and theological instruction to meet pastoral needs. To speak in generalities, the Apostolic Fathers understood the books of the New Testament as part of the kerygma or proclamation, and not as Scripture with definitive authority, while the Apologists were beginning to understand the books of the New Testament as Scripture. Both groups understood the Jewish Scriptures as authoritative, as indicated in part by their use of quotation formulas before citations of the Old Testament.

Ignatius of Antioch rarely utilized the Old Testament in his letters (written ca. 110 CE). He does refer to the authority of the law of Moses and the prophets (*Magn.* 8-9; *Philad.* 5; *Smyrn.* 5.1). He understands the gospel to be grounded not in the Old Testament but in the church's experience of Jesus

Christ. He knows the New Testament documents but does not appeal to them as authoritative Scripture. He does not distinguish between the books that eventually became the New Testament and the larger Christian tradition. He uses the New Testament, especially the Pauline epistles, as a resource for ministry rather than as a definitive authority.

Unlike Ignatius, *1 Clement,* a Roman work of Clement, secretary of the Roman church, who wrote about 95 CE, understands the Old Testament as authoritative Scripture in which the founding Christian events are prefigured. Like the Essenes of the Qumran community, Clement sees the Old Testament directly fulfilled in the Corinthian congregation to which he writes. For example, the Christians' prosperity was a fulfillment of Deut. 32:15: "My Beloved ate and drank, and he was enlarged and waxed fat and kicked" (*1 Clem.* 3.1, Loeb translation). He quotes sayings of Jesus, not as Scripture, but as authoritative portions of the kerygma. And he uses the Pauline epistles, not as authoritative Scripture, but as an additional witness to what he is arguing (47.1-2).

In *2 Clement,* a homily possibly coming from Rome, there is evidence that the New Testament writings, especially the epistles of Paul, are coming to be held as Scripture on par with the Old Testament. The *Didache* relies upon the Gospel of Matthew. The *Epistle of Polycarp* shows virtually no use of the Old Testament because Polycarp did not know the Old Testament (12.1), but is dense with allusions to books of the New Testament. However, it cannot be ascertained whether Polycarp or the author of the *Didache* understood these books as Scripture on par with the Old Testament. The *Epistle of Barnabas,* possibly written from Alexandria about 130 CE, moves interpretation in the direction of what will be known as Alexandrian exegesis: describing a deeper insight into Scripture. The author draws on traditional prooftexts or *testimonia,* assuming that the Old Testament is a prophecy of Christ. He understands the legal and ritual provisions of the Old Testament allegorically as moral provisions for the Christian life. The Old Testament is interpreted by means of christocentric allegory and typology. The author does cite Matt. 20:16 and 22:14 with a quotation formula, which may indicate a very early recognition of the Gospel as Scripture on par with the Old Testament (cf. Polycarp, *Phil.* 12.1).

By contrast with the Apostolic Fathers, the Apologists use a body of literature which they regarded as sacred texts, that is, as Scripture. This includes not only the Greek Septuagint but also the four Gospels, Acts, and the Pauline Epistles. Justin Martyr understood the Old Testament as a prophecy of Christ and the church, and thus proof-texts play a large role in his interpretation. His written works are intended to defend this understanding of the Old Testament. In his *Apologies* he tries to prove to pagans that the prophets of the

Old Testament present a philosophy that is superior to Greek philosophy, providing a more reliable and a finer presentation of Greek philosophical ideals. Christianity refines, completes, and corrects Greek philosophy. In his *Dialogue with Trypho* he argues with a Jew that the Old Testament is a prophecy of Jesus as Christ and the church as the New Israel. The Old Testament prophesies Christ in types *(typoi)*, persons or actions that have a function in and beyond the narrative level, and discourses *(logoi)*, that is, prophecies of Christ. Melito of Sardis in his newly discovered homily *On the Passover* uses typology to show that Christ is the Passover lamb and finds types throughout the Old Testament.

Irenaeus is the first interpreter to speak of a Christian Scripture composed of Old and New Testaments. His *Demonstration of the Apostolic Preaching* uses proof-texts to show that the prophets predicted Christ, much in the fashion of Justin Martyr's *Dialogue,* on which it depends. Borrowing from grammatical terminology, Irenaeus's *Against Heresies* presents the important teaching that the Rule of Faith handed down by the apostles to their disciples is the hypothesis *(hypothesis)* or argument of Scripture, a divinely given guideline that provides understanding to the diversity of materials in the two testaments of Scripture. The hypothesis of the Old Testament was not clear until the coming of Christ and the giving of the Rule of Faith. The New Testament makes explicit what is implicit in the Old Testament. This became a key principle of interpretation in Origen's *On First Principles.* Irenaeus also taught that the deeper teachings of Scripture must complement and supplement the plain meaning of the text, but not contradict it. Clear passages of Scripture must govern the interpretation of unclear and ambiguous passages of Scripture. This is found as an important principle in Augustine's *On Christian Teaching.*

The literature of the Apostolic Fathers and the Apologists primarily instructs Christians in doctrine and defends the new faith against Jewish arguments. Its texts use several interpretive approaches. Literal-historical interpretation continued alongside more innovative methods of interpretation. Midrash also continued as a popular method. For example, *Barnabas* 9.8 uses midrash to interpret christologically the number of the 318 men mentioned in Gen. 14:14 and presumably circumcised in Gen. 17:23:

> For it says, "And Abraham circumcised from his household eighteen men and three hundred." What then was the knowledge that was given to him? Notice that he first mentions the eighteen, and after a pause the three hundred. The eighteen is I [= 10] and H [= 8] — you have Jesus — and because the cross was destined to have grace in the T he says "and three

hundred." So he indicates Jesus in the two letters and the cross in the other. (Loeb translation)

Typology was popular, especially types referring to Jesus. For Clement of Rome (*1 Clem.* 12.7) the scarlet cloth that Rahab hung up to signal Joshua's spies foreshadows redemption through the blood of Jesus. For the author of the *Epistle of Barnabas* (12.1-7) two Old Testament passages are types of the cross of Christ: the outstretched arms of Moses that gave Israel victory over Amalek (Exodus 17) and the bronze serpent that Moses lifted up in the wilderness (Numbers 21). Allegory, while not prevalent in the New Testament, was clearly favored by the Apostolic Fathers and in second-century culture in general. For example, *Barnabas* 8 interprets the Old Testament ritual of the red heifer (Numbers 19) allegorically. He draws significance from the details of the story. The red heifer is Jesus and the children who sprinkle its ashes are the apostles who preach the forgiveness of sins.

At the close of the second century, what is becoming more pronounced in interpretation is an appeal to church tradition that had a growing authority all its own. The Rule of Faith was the teachings of the church received by the apostles, transmitted by the episcopate, and formulated in creeds. This tradition would not only guide interpretation along set paths, but also be used to judge the content and theology of Christian books for their suitability for the canon.

Alexandria versus Antioch (150-400 CE)

The heritage of the Christians in the first two centuries of the church was a body of tradition that saw the Old Testament as a source of prophecy fulfilled in Jesus. It had also interpreted the Old Testament and early Christian texts for practical ethical instruction for the guidance of the new community. By the third century Christians were becoming self-conscious about developing their interpretive methods and full-fledged commentaries. Major intellectual centers in Alexandria, Egypt, and Antioch, Syria, had developed their own traditions and methods of interpretation, or "schools." Until recently the differences in the interpretation had been characterized as spiritual or allegorical interpretation in Alexandria and literal and historical interpretation in Antioch. However, the dichotomy of spiritual and literal does not accurately describe the interpretation seen at work in the commentaries and homilies from these schools. Both schools understood that the literal wording of the text of the Bible points to a deeper meaning.

In her article in this volume as in her other work, Frances Young shows that the differences in interpretation between Alexandria and Antioch can be traced to different methods for examining texts, methods borrowed from the schools of grammar, rhetoric, and philosophy. This education included *to methodikon* and *to historikon*. *To methodikon* dealt with linguistic issues of the text: etymologies of words, figures of speech and thought, tropes, and style. *To historikon* dealt with background of the text to explain its content and references. It involved the hypothesis or underlying theme, the flow of argument developing the hypothesis, and the obvious meaning of the narrative. It was concerned with the biblical writers' aims and motivations. Philosophical education stressed that a text had a *hyponoia,* the "undersense" or deeper sense. The Alexandrians emphasized the *to methodikon* and philosophical aspects of their education and the Antiochenes emphasized *to historikon* and the grammatical and rhetorical aspects. Different hermeneutical principles were developed in each center as a result, but these principles had much in common. Use of the simple dichotomy of allegorical versus literal is no longer adequate to describe exegesis in these schools. The rivalry between the Alexandrian and the Antiochene schools can be understood in part in light of the rivalry between the philosophical and rhetorical schools.

The influence of Greek culture on the world began with the conquest of the known world by Alexander the Great beginning in 334 BCE. This Hellenization strongly influenced the large Jewish community in the Egyptian city of Alexandria. Here the Jews translated their Scriptures into Greek and gave us the Septuagint. Here they tried to integrate Greek philosophy, especially that of Plato, with Jewish religious beliefs, especially those attributed to Moses. The main mode of interpretation in Hellenistic Judaism was allegory. The allegorical method was rooted in Platonic philosophy. Plato argued that the material world was only a dull reflection of the perfect spiritual world. Everything on earth had a perfect type in the spiritual world. The allegorical method assumes that the text intends to say something other than its literal wording suggests. In other words, the text's true meaning is assumed to be hidden behind the written words. The details of the text have other significance. The text is really an extended metaphor pointing to meaning lying behind it. The master practitioner of allegory was the Alexandrian Jew Philo (20 BCE–54 CE), who tried to reconcile the Old Testament with the philosophy of Plato and interpreted the Jewish Scriptures allegorically.

In part, early exegesis at Alexandria appears to have been Gnostic in character. The Gnostics Valentinus and Basilides both hailed from Alexandria. The exegesis of the Gnostics treated the Jewish Scriptures as allegories of their cosmology, which rejected the material world and the creator God of

Genesis. The Christian philosopher Clement of Alexandria (150-215) taught in the catechetical school in Alexandria during 190-203 and rejected much of Gnostic interpretation. He did share the Gnostic love of allegory and was a chief proponent of the method. Clement tried to interpret the Bible literally whenever possible. However, like Philo, Clement taught that Scripture had a twofold meaning: the literal and the spiritual. He considered the spiritual meaning to be the more important meaning. He usually understood the spiritual meaning of the text to be what it said about the relationship of Christ and the Church.

Origen (c. 185-254) was educated in Alexandria in Greek literature, philology, and philosophy and brought this education to the task of interpretation. He was perhaps the first in the church to consider interpretation systematically as a subject in itself and to write a formal commentary. He studied the Hebrew of the Old Testament and considered the history of interpretation of the Old Testament within Judaism as valuable. Using the approaches of *to methodikon* Origen produced the *Hexapla*, a critical edition of the Old Testament in six parallel columns containing the Old Testament texts in Hebrew, a Greek transliteration of the Hebrew, the Septuagint, and the Greek versions of Aquila, Symmachus, and Theodotion.

Origen's theory of exegesis is developed in Book IV of his *On First Principles*. He was influenced by Platonic philosophy and the work of Philo and Clement of Alexandria, both of whom established the allegorical method of interpretation as a viable method for interpreting Scripture. He desired to go beyond the literal to the spiritual meaning of a text. Philosophical education stressed that a text had a *hyponoia* or deeper sense. Origen thought that this sense could be discovered by allegorical interpretation. For Platonists like Origen, the material creation and its texts are symbolic of the eternal world of spiritual realities and point beyond the material to those spiritual realities. On the basis of Prov. 22:20-21, Origen argued that biblical texts had three senses — literal or physical, moral, and spiritual — that are analogous to the philosophical division of the human person into body, soul, and spirit. The moral sense would seem to deal with the attainment of virtues and the spiritual sense with messianic realities. However, in Origen's exegesis the distinction between moral and spiritual dissolves, and he often does not set out all three senses for a text. The rhetorical schools distinguished between the content of the text and its wording; the mind or intent *(skopos)* of the text was clothed in the wording. From *to methodikon*, figures like metaphor and allegory naturally led to avenues of interpretation of a text other than the literal and historical. These and other concerns of the schools diverted Origen from the plain meaning of the text as he utilized allegory to uncover the hidden meaning. He had a profound influence in making allegory the dominant method of biblical interpretation into the Middle Ages, especially through the commentaries of Jerome, which relied heavily on Origen's commentaries.

However, as Young points out, Origen's interpretation was not completely nonliteral or ahistorical. He has been accused of being a Platonist who read the Bible allegorically to uncover the hidden meaning of the text while ignoring its historical nature. However, his works give evidence of a concern for the literal as well as for the hidden meaning. His commentaries were some of the first to attempt a verse-by-verse interpretation that placed the biblical books in their historical background, analyzed their themes, and tried to grapple with problems of their interpretation. He applied Greek critical methods to the analysis of the text and did not hesitate to draw on Jewish interpretation of the Old Testament, though he often found it too literal. Neither was Origen's allegorical approach purely arbitrary. He often connected passages of the Old and New Testament together on the basis of christological and typological connections already established in the New Testament or already familiar from Christian tradition and early Christian writings like the *Epistle of Barnabas*. Origen's use of symbols tends to be consistent throughout his interpretation and assumes a unity of Scripture. For example, "temple" refers to the church as the body of Christ. This more structured approach to allegorical interpretation is evident in the newly discovered work of Didymus the blind of Alexandria (c. 313-398), who inherited Origen's methods.

In the Antiochene catechetical school the emphases of rhetorical schooling dominated. The rhetoricians sought morals from classical stories and myth for the purpose of education. Antiochian interpretation emphasized the moral and dogmatic meaning of biblical texts that were thought to be mirrored in the narrative, rather than needing to be discovered by allegory as the philosophers taught. These and other concerns of the rhetorical schools steered the Antiochenes to the plain meaning of the text, but did not make them either completely historical in interpretation or the precursors of modern historical exegesis. They explained the meaning of the text, not necessarily what actually happened. They often interpreted one passage of the Bible on analogy or correspondence with another, rather than using allegory to get a deeper meaning. *Historia,* or the narrative logic of the text, formed the basis of the higher spiritual sense, the *theōria,* often found by analogy with other texts. Allegory was rejected because it ignored the *historia.* As part of *to methodikon,* allegory was treated primarily as figures of speech, not as an interpretive method per se. Literal interpretation was preferred and allegorical interpretation used only when the literal sense was impossible. The Antiochene school reacted negatively to the more pervasive allegorical interpretation of the Alexandrians.

The Antiochene school peaked in its influence in the late fourth and early fifth centuries. Its chief instructors were Eustathius of Antioch (c. 300-377), Theodoret of Cyrrhus (393-460), and Diodore of Tarsus (d. ca. 390) and his two pupils John Chrysostom (c. 347-407) and Theodore of Mopsuestia (c. 350-428). The work of Theodore of Mopsuestia is often considered to epitomize the school. He interpreted the psalms and prophets in light of their original historical contexts and historical references. He saw this literature as addressing the original audience as well as the future, not just the future. He rejected interpretations of the psalms and the prophets that understood them to be christological. He interpreted an Old Testament passage messianically only if the New Testament did so. He rejected the allegorical interpretation of the Song of Songs, which understood it as describing the relationship of Christ to individual souls or to the church. Theodoret of Cyrrhus was more moderate in his views, allowing messianic interpretation of the psalms and prophets and a more mystical interpretation of the Song of Songs. The sermons of John Chrysostom together cover nearly entire books of the Bible and show the application of this literal-historical method of interpretation to preaching.

The school at Antioch had a primary concern with salvation history, that is, those events in which the hand of God for the salvation of the world is most evident. These events included creation, the fall, the incarnation, and the restoration of paradise. Thus special focus was on Genesis 1–3 and the book of Revelation. There was concern that these key events in the foundation of faith should not be allegorized or spiritualized away. The Genesis accounts had been a concern of Irenaeus, the Apologists, and Origen as they grappled with the nature of the human condition. The Antiochian School saw the allegorization of these key texts of salvation history as a threat to the foundation of the faith. Eustathius wrote a work entitled *On the Witch of Endor and against Allegory* that argues against Origen's allegorical interpretation of the creation and paradise accounts.

Jerome and Augustine and the Legacy of the Schools

A chief heir of the Antiochian and Alexandrian schools was Jerome (early 340s-420), who is well known both for his commentaries and for his translation work. He translated several theological works from Greek into Latin, especially the homilies of Origen. However, he is best known for his work of biblical translation. Jerome was competent in Greek, Latin, and Hebrew (which he learned from a Jewish convert to Christianity). His knowledge of Hebrew, rare among early church fathers, placed him in a superior position to guide the translation of the Bible into an official Latin version from the plethora of divergent manuscripts available in his day. The result was the Latin Vulgate, the standard literary form of the Bible of the Western Church, completed in 406 CE. Previously, Jerome had used Origen's Hexaplaric Septuagint and other Greek versions as the textual basis for his earlier translation of the Psalms and several other Old Testament books; however, for the Vulgate, he translated the Old Testament directly from the Hebrew. Of the New Testament books, only the Gospels are certain to be his translation.

As Dennis Brown indicates, Jerome not only utilized traditions and methods of Christian biblical interpretation, but also Jewish interpretation, to which he had access through his rabbinic study. In his commentaries, Jerome demonstrates the influence of Jewish interpretation as well as the hermeneutics of both the Alexandrian and Antiochene schools. Jerome used many Jewish interpretive traditions of the Old Testament that can be broadly categorized as haggadah and halakha. Haggadah is the creative elaboration of the biblical narrative that often uses midrash. Halakha emphasizes implementing sacred texts in practical matters of daily life. From the Alexandrian school Jerome was profoundly influenced by Philo and Clement of Alexandria, but especially by Origen. This is seen most clearly in his use of allegorical interpretation to interpret more difficult passages of Scripture. With the Antiochenes he begins with the literal and historical sense of the passages, but with the Alexandrians he uses allegorical interpretation to find the deeper, spiritual meaning. The content and themes of his commentaries are heavily dependent on those of Origen but also on Jerome's own unique contributions. He left commentaries on the Major and Minor Prophets with the exception of Jeremiah. The format of the commentaries is to provide a translation from the Hebrew and the Septuagint, a literal commentary with notes on the text and Jewish interpretation, and a spiritual, allegorical commentary that often followed the works of Origen quite closely (at points word-for-word). He also left commentaries on Matthew, Galatians, Ephesians, Titus, and Philemon.

Meanwhile, in the West, Augustine (354-430 CE) was developing his own hermeneutics. Trained in classical grammar and rhetoric, Augustine became Professor of Rhetoric at Milan, Italy, and eventually Bishop of Hippo Regius in northern Africa. His understanding of Scripture was molded by his early involvement in Manicheanism, and eventually by the preaching of Ambrose, bishop of Milan. Ambrose utilized the techniques and interpretive traditions of Philo, Origen, and the Alexandrian school. A further connection with the Alexandrian school was made by Augustine's correspondence with Jerome, whose commentaries he read and who supplied him with Latin translations of Origen's commentaries. Augustine stood within the Alexandrian school of interpretation, but not slavishly, for he used its methods and traditions to help him wrestle with his own investigations. Augustine left *Expositions on the Psalms,* allegorical and literal commentaries on Genesis, and several other works. His interpretation of the Old Testament is often shaped by his need to defend it from Manichean attacks.

Augustine equated the wisdom of God with the Neoplatonist "mind" *(nous),* the mind of God expressed in the Word, the Son of God, a wisdom that enlightens every human being. The search for wisdom and truth brings the believer and God into direct communication. God provides the Scriptures to show the way to God. The Scriptures are the external verbal communication of the divine Rhetorician. As Norris explains, this understanding provided the basis for the following presuppositions of Augustine's interpretation: (1) The Scriptures are inspired, for God guided the minds of human authors as they wrote. The intent of the authors agrees with the intent of the mind of God *(sensus),* but may express that mind in diverse ways. Even various versions of the Bible express the same intent in different ways. Augustine was careful here to refute the Manichean assertion that the text of Scripture was inconsistent and corrupted by the orthodox church. (2) Coming from the divine Rhetorician, Scripture has one main theme: Christ is the head of his body, the church, and is bound together with its members. This is the idea of the Old Testament as a foreshadowing of the New Testament: what is hidden in the Old Testament is revealed in the New Testament. For example, Christ is prefigured in Adam. Augustine is careful to refute the Manichean list of antitheses between the testaments and the stress on their incompatibility. (3) Since Scripture has only one ultimate theme, any word, phrase, or image can be understood in the light of its occurrence elsewhere in Scripture, regardless of literary or historical context. (4) God put obscure and difficult passages in Scripture to force believers to delve deeper in their search for God. Such passages require figural or allegorical interpretation.

Augustine's hermeneutics are outlined in his *De doctrina christiana.* He was greatly influenced by Tyconius, a Donatist who wrote *The Book of Rules* (c. 370), which Augustine incorporates into his *De doctrina christiana.* In conjunction with his understanding of signs as representing something deeper than the sign itself can convey, Augustine distinguishes between the letter and spirit of Scripture, between the literal text and the figurative meaning. The literal forms the basis of the figurative by way of analogy between similar passages. Believers need to move beyond the literal to the figurative, the spirit within the letter, for the Scriptures are an expression of the divine mind and that mind needs to be found through the words of Scripture. Words of Scripture are provided by God only to establish communion between God's thoughts and purposes and the minds of humanity. Spiritual or figurative exegesis is warranted when the literal does not directly address morals or the truth of the Church. Scriptures point to the ultimate thing (the *res*), which is one's relationship to God and others through love.

This understanding makes for a problem: what to do with the multiple readings that Christians devise from the same passages. Augustine argues that there is no single true reading of a passage. Truth from the mind of God can have more than one human interpretation. God intended this multiplicity, and all readings are valid that are consistent with the law of love of God and neighbor and the creedal beliefs of the church, the Rule of Faith.

The Emergence of the Canon of the New Testament

The church has always had Scripture, that is, authoritative religious literature. At the beginning it had the Scriptures of Israel as understood through the Greek Septuagint translation. Gradually writings of the early Christian movement itself became Scripture for the church as well. It has been thought that the New Testament canon was formed toward the end of the second century in response to heterodox movements like Gnosticism, Montanism, and Marcionism. In other words, in light of heretical documents, the orthodox church needed to define what documents were authoritative. However, as Harry Gamble argues, the evidence of current study points in another direction. The New Testament canon, a fixed list of authoritative religious literature, was gradually formed up to the fourth and fifth centuries in a long process in which biblical interpretation treated early Christian literature as Scripture. "The emergence of the New Testament canon was itself a result of interpretation of those documents that were ultimately included in it" (p. 408 below). The history of the development of the New Testament canon is the history of interpretation of the early Christian writings that came to be contained in the canon. The interpretation of early Christian writings deemed as Scripture was the prerequisite of the creation of the canon.

Paul's letters were originally addressed to individual churches, but wider dissemination and interpretation facilitated the formation of a Pauline corpus. The use of these letters gradually gave them the status of Scripture. Gamble argues that the "Pauline school" perpetuated the mission and theology of Paul. Its members reappropriated the content of his letters by applying it to new situations in the church; they did so by writing pseudonymous letters, namely 2 Thessalonians, Ephesians, Colossians, 1 and 2 Timothy, and Titus, in the late first and early second centuries. This appropriation of Paul's letters created a collection of letters that was generally known in the early second century among both the orthodox and heterodox. Paul's letters were considered authoritative sources for Christian teaching and preaching.

In the earliest church, Gospels were written by those creatively appropriating the oral tradition about Jesus to provide interpretations of his mission and significance for specific segments of the church. These Gospels circulated regionally until the second century, when they became more widely disseminated. To solve the interpretive problem created by the multiplicity of Gospels and their divergence from one another, scribes conflated readings and harmonized the texts. Tatian even went so far as to homogenize the Gospels of Matthew, Mark, Luke, and John into a continuous narrative, the *Diatessaron.* But the solution that prevailed at the end of the second century was the fourfold Gospel as found in the canon today. It was understood that there were not so much four Gospels as four witnesses to the one gospel. The four Gospels were to be understood as testimonies to the one gospel. They were Gospels "according to" an apostolic writer.

By the beginning of the third century, the collection of the four Gospels and the Pauline Epistles were used widely in the church as Scripture. The seven Catholic Epistles were not brought together as a group until the fourth century. 1 Peter and 1 John were in use, but there is little evidence that James, Jude, 2 Peter, and 2 and 3 John were known and used. Their use in the church was greatly disputed.

Acts did not share the quick and wide acceptance of its sister volume, the Gospel of Luke, and was not in wide use until the end of the second century. Hebrews was disputed in the western church because it is anonymous, but once it was ascribed to Paul the opposition decreased. Revelation was used widely in the second century by the western church. In the eastern church it was used to support chiliasm. In response, Dionysius argued against its apostolic authorship and for the need to interpret it allegorically rather than literally. This argument greatly diminished the authority of Revelation in the eastern church.

Other gospels, acts, epistles, and apocalypses produced by early Christianity were in use throughout the churches. "The availability of these other documents and the popularity of some of them are useful reminders that the canon which eventually emerged was the result not merely of collection, but also of selection" (Gamble, p. 416 below). The canon is the result of a centuries-long sifting and selection process. In the early fourth century this process included the creation of lists of heretical or spurious books, and by the end of the fourth century canon lists were being devised. By the fifth century a genuine canon of Christian Scripture was finalized for both the Latin and Greek churches. This canonization process was not the result of decree by formal councils but the end result of centuries of liturgical and theological use. It was the usefulness of these books for worship, preaching, and teaching that was the decisive factor for their inclusion in a canon. "It was due to their regular and repeated public reading that Christian writings became familiar to the largely illiterate body of Christians, were given close interpretation, gained authority, and thus became normative resources for Christian thought and life" (Gamble, p. 418).

Other factors involved in canonization included apostolicity, which is not so much authorship by an apostle or apostolic aide as origin in the earliest period of the church and apostolic teaching. Yet other factors were catholicity, that is, use by the church as a whole, and orthodoxy. In other words, these books shaped the teaching and theology of the church, and that teaching was in turn a major factor in the inclusion of these books in the canon.

Biblical interpretation in the first five centuries was not hindered by the lack of a clearly defined canon. Early exegetes worked with documents that they considered to share the basic *hypothesis* or *skopos* of Scripture, which they equated with the Rule of Faith received by the apostles, transmitted by the bishops, and encapsulated in creeds. With this understanding, the Septuagint, the four Gospels, and the Pauline Epistles were understood by nearly all as Scripture. It was the perceived central message of Scripture transmitted through the episcopate that guided exegesis. Interpretation was geared for practical application, as is often seen in early patristic commentaries that are basically an assemblage of homilies on biblical books. Among these, the commentaries of Origen are prime examples.

Early Noncanonical Christian Writings

What about early Christian books not included in the canon? How do they do interpretation? As Evans explains, the apocryphal Gospels interpret and appropriate the Old Testament in much the same way as the canonical Gospels do. They, too, quote (with or without quotation formulas), paraphrase, and echo the Old Testament. They utilize the Old Testament for proof-texts to demonstrate the fulfillment of prophecy and to support and provide examples in argumentation, polemics, doctrine, and instruction. They interpret its texts in spiritualizing and moralizing ways and often according to long-established Jewish methods and traditions of interpretation, many of which are exhibited in the Talmuds and Midrashim. The early Gnostic and Christian apocryphal works interpret not only the Jewish Scriptures, but the books of the emerging New Testament canon and independent tradition as well. For example, the *Gospel of Thomas* utilizes the canonical Gospels and allegorizes and alters the sayings of Jesus in order to invest them with new meaning and further Gnostic theology.

The communities within the early church that became known as orthodox and heterodox cannot be distinguished by their use of the Old and New Testaments, for both used these Scriptures. Neither can they be distinguished by the interpretive methods they employed. "The methods of scriptural exegesis do not, therefore, in themselves demarcate boundaries between the bifurcating communities of faith, some moving toward what would eventually be recognized as 'orthodoxy' and others toward what would eventually be condemned as 'heresy'" (C. A. Evans, p. 451 below). Rather, the distinction comes in the use to which Jewish tradition and the earliest Christian tradition were put.

Orthodoxy closely adapts Jewish interpretive traditions and a historical and literal understanding of the life and teachings of Jesus. Gnostic interpretation of the Jewish Scriptures is very diverse, but as a group, Gnostics took a natural and special interest in Genesis. The origin of humanity and the world (cosmogony) and the nature and purpose of the universe (cosmology) were major concerns, for which Genesis provided much from which to speculate, particularly in chs. 1-9 (see Evans for numerous examples). Gnostic interpretation of both Jewish Scripture and Christian writings and traditions employed the interpretative techniques prevalent at the time.

What makes Gnostic interpretation different from that of other branches of emerging Christianity is the rejection of typical Jewish and Christian traditions and interpretation. For example, the Supreme Being is not the God of Judaism or Christianity, who is identified as a demiurge whose inferiority is demonstrated by his portrayal in the Old Testament as a jealous God. And Jesus is portrayed as a heavenly visitor rather than as the Son of God. Along with the God of creation, God's created world is rejected for a transcendent world revealed through the symbols of the Scriptures.

Gnostic literature is a mixture of speculation and exegesis, with interpretation directed to mixtures of texts from many Jewish and Christian Scriptures. In the *Apocryphon of John* allegory is not prominent, but rather the text of Jewish Scripture is often interpreted very literally. For example, if God is said to be a jealous God, then he is not worthy of worship (Isa. 45:5). The narratives of the Jewish Scriptures are often expanded to provide the main characters with motivations for their actions in accordance with the Gnostic myth. In the *Exegesis of the Soul*, allegory plays a prominent role. Texts of the Jewish Scriptures, the New Testament, and classical literature (Homer) are cited to support the elaboration of the cosmology and anthropology of the Gnostic myth.

Gnostics also left behind reasoned hermeneutical speculation, as attested in a letter by the Valentinian Ptolemy, which is preserved in Epiphanius (*Panarion* 33.3.1–33.7.20). It is an attempt to explain the difficulties observed between the Jewish Scriptures and the New Testament. Heracleon, another Valentinian, was the first to leave a commentary on a New Testament book (the Gospel of John).

THE END OF THE ANCIENT PERIOD
OF BIBLICAL INTERPRETATION

As the ancient period of biblical interpretation drew to a close, Judaism and the various forms of Christianity had each gone their separate ways. Yet, what divided them was not so much their methods of interpretation, where there was, in fact, often a remarkable degree of commonality. Rather, what distinguished them from one another was their fundamental presuppositions and beliefs about God, the world, human nature, and Jesus. These, in turn, determined the ends toward which their exegetical methods were directed. Clearly, the same interpretive methods could be employed in pursuit of a wide variety of exegetical goals.

Counting the very earliest instances of biblical interpretation, which were already taking place when the first biblical traditions were being formulated, there had been well over a thousand years of biblical interpretation as the ancient period reached its end. Medieval biblical interpretation would build on this extensive base, but would also need to address new problems that had arisen. The second volume of *A History of Biblical Interpretation* will treat biblical interpretation as it developed within both Judaism and Christianity during the medieval period.

CHAPTER 2

Inner-Biblical Exegesis in the Tanak

Esther Menn

INTRODUCTION

Interpretation of Scripture, which marks the history of Judaism and Christianity as a central religious activity, originated as an ancient and native Israelite phenomenon. Intentional study, exegesis, and revision of authoritative texts emerged as common practices long before the completion of the written works ultimately included in the Jewish biblical canon, commonly known as the Tanak (an acronym based on its three divisions: Torah, Nebi'im or Prophets, and Ketubim or Writings). Certainly there was a remarkable proliferation of extrabiblical exegetical literature in the centuries following the completion of the last books included in the Tanak, which are examined in the other chapters of this volume. To discover the deepest roots of scriptural interpretation, however, one must look even earlier, to the centuries that witnessed the composition of the biblical books themselves.

The narrative depiction of the priestly scribe Ezra and his levitical assistants reading and explaining a certain "book of the law of Moses" before the assembled community in a restored Jerusalem (Neh. 8:1-8) attests to the ascendancy of study and interpretation of key religious texts in postexilic Israel. But this explicit biblical portrayal of scriptural exegesis only confirms what is internally evident throughout the Tanak, in preexilic strata and, even more pervasively, in material from the exilic and postexilic periods. Signs of labor by anonymous scribes and passages that appear to be the work of authors very conscious of their belated position in a literary tradition point to the emergence of a religious imagination characterized by dependence on and

55

preoccupation with traditional texts. The glosses and explications, expansions and revisions, allusive responses and creative constructions of new works in relation to more ancient ones found throughout the Tanak indicate that a text-oriented religion predates the closure of the biblical canon. Although this basic truth often goes unrecognized, the Bible may be understood as an exegetical work in its own right, in addition to serving as the base text for the monumental exegetical cultures of Judaism and Christianity.

Viewed as the product of a long process of transmission, adaptation, and reuse of traditional writings, the Tanak models in itself various approaches to Scripture that attempt to extend historically the divine voice discerned through received texts and to preserve these texts as the preeminent focus of religious intellectual endeavors, while at the same time ensuring their relevance for contemporary communities (Fishbane 1986: 25). In this broad project of addressing present generations through the medium of texts from the past, and thereby honoring these texts even while transforming them, inner-biblical exegesis shares much with scriptural exegesis throughout the ages.

INNER-BIBLICAL EXEGESIS: DELINEATION OF TOPIC

This discussion of inner-biblical exegesis in the Tanak will concentrate narrowly on the phenomenon of biblical texts that seem to clarify, rework, or allude to identifiable precursor texts, many of which are also preserved in the canonical corpus. It will therefore not attempt to survey the broader range of hermeneutical activities undertaken in ancient Israel, many of which have been an object of study for historical-critical scholars since the Enlightenment. For example, there will be no discussion of the biblical appropriation and reinterpretation of mythic patterns from the greater ancient Near East (such as the reemployment in Exod. 15:1-18; Ps. 89:5-18; and Isa. 51:9-11 of cosmic battle imagery found in the Babylonian creation epic *Enuma Elish* and in the Ugaritic myths about Baal), nor of the oral retellings of traditional Israelite narratives and other materials later fixed in writing (for example, the narratives containing the sister-wife motif in Gen. 12:10-20; 20; and 26:6-11), which are commonly studied under the rubrics of tradition criticism and source criticism. Similarly, the interpretive impact of editorial activities generally treated by redaction criticism, such as the addition of introductions and conclusions to older works (Proverbs 1–9; Psalms 1 and 2; and Eccl. 12:9-14), will not receive attention here. While analysis of the wide range of interpretative activities evident in the Tanak suggested by these examples would contribute to a full understanding of the hermeneutical aspects of the canon, limiting the focus to specific instances of textual explication or allusion facilitates exploration of issues raised by the emergence of a religious culture of scriptural interpretation. These issues include the relative authority of traditional texts considered revelatory over against subsequent human interpretation, the purposes and results of inner-biblical exegesis, the contribution of scriptural allusion to the formation of the canon, and the relation between the types of scriptural interpretation found in the Bible and those found in postbiblical interpretive genres.

At the same time, the present discussion of inner-biblical exegesis in the Tanak is broader than it might have been construed. Although in some cases glosses and clarifying comments do seem to have as their goal the explication of an older text (which might be described as "exegesis" in the modern understanding of the word), other treatments of earlier texts appear to have very different aims. Citation and mimicry of traditional writings may serve a variety of purposes that can be determined only through analysis of individual cases (Sommer 1998: ch. 1). Sometimes reference to an earlier text may simply indicate the influence of a literary tradition on a later author, sometimes it may be intended to create a pleasing style by echoing familiar language, and sometimes it may serve to connect the past to the present through a creative appeal to tradition. At other times, the purpose may be to qualify, revise, or polemically refute outdated teachings, or even to replace an earlier version of a written text. So while later usage of traditional writings may affect how one understands the original text, this is not necessarily the result. The terms "exegesis" and "interpretation" are therefore used in this article in an inclusive, and at times imprecise, sense, to designate a whole range of practices indicating a preoccupation with traditional written texts within a literate and literary culture. Indeed, most of the examples analyzed below are, more strictly speaking, allusions to, rather than interpretations of, precursor texts, undertaken for a variety of purposes and with a wide range of results. This expansive understanding of the topic of inner-biblical exegesis is intended to facilitate exploration of the text-based religious culture evident in the Tanak itself in instances of intentional reflection on, citation of, and allusion to precursor texts, rather than to predetermine the scope of that culture by examining only material that might be considered exegetical by modern standards.

ORIGINS OF SCRIPTURAL EXEGESIS

The phenomenon of textual exegesis is of course not unique to Israel, but may be set in the larger context of the ancient Near East, where already by the second millennium scribes and other literate classes had produced written works exemplifying a wide variety of genres, including legal codes, myths, historical chronicles, wisdom literature, and prophecies. The cultural significance of certain of these works may be deduced from the archaeological discovery of multiple copies of the same work and from the presence in many of them of features indicating technical study and reuse of traditional material, including glosses, annotations, corrections, and the like. For example, whereas the Babylonian version of *Enuma Elish* features the divine protagonist Marduk, who establishes Esagila as his temple in Babylon, the Assyrian version of the same myth substitutes the god Ashur, who founds his temple in the metropolis bearing his name. Hittite law codes from the second millennium discovered at Boghazköy clearly describe former legal practices (for example the payment of certain fines for given offenses) and then explicitly stipulate their amendment. From a later period, demotic papyri from the third century BCE offer commentary on earlier, obscure prophecies concerning Egypt's fate.

In a similar way, certain writings attained prestigious status within Israelite culture and came to be perceived as appropriate objects for learned study, and eventually as sources of divine revelation. The preoccupation with written texts that came to characterize many sectors of Israelite society is projected far back into Israel's early history, for example, in the depiction of Moses placing stone tablets inscribed with the commandments in the ark to symbolize the covenant at Sinai (Exod. 25:16; Deut. 10:1-5; 1 Kgs. 8:21). Writing, collecting, and revising texts may have become especially prominent activities during periods of national expansion and revival, for example, during the reigns of David and Solomon in the tenth century and of Hezekiah in the eighth century. According to the biblical record (2 Sam. 8:15-18; 20:23-26; 1 Kgs. 4:1-6; 2 Kgs. 18:18, 37; Prov. 25:1), these kings employed scribal officials, as was the practice in royal courts throughout the wider ancient Near East. These literate members of the court most likely kept state archives (for example, the "Chronicles of the Kings of Israel" and the "Chronicles of the Kings of Judah," mentioned in 1 Kgs. 14:19, 29, and elsewhere), edited traditional materials (as indicated by the superscriptions, annotations, and colophons interspersed unsystematically throughout the books of the Tanak, for example, in Lev. 6:2 [9], 7 [14], 18 [25]; 7:1, 11, 37-38; Num. 5:29-31; Josh. 20:9; Isa. 1:1; Jer. 1:1-3; Pss. 3:1 [superscription]; 51:1 [superscription]; 41:14 [13]; 72:18-20; 89:53 [52]; 106:48; Job 31:40; Prov. 10:1; 30:1; Eccl. 12:9-14), and copied and revised older texts (as Jer. 8:8 notes with dismay). It should be noted, however, that in addition to the royal court several other contexts within Israelite society most likely fostered the intense interest in written texts evident within the Tanak, including circles of priests and temple personnel, judges and legal experts, prophetic figures and their disciples, and sages involved with the education of youth (Fishbane 1985; Kugel 1987: 274-77).

There are many indications in the book of Deuteronomy and in the Deuteronomic History (Joshua through 2 Kings) that dependence on written texts for religious guidance increased substantially beginning in the seventh century. According to the narrative in 2 Kings 22–23, Josiah initiated his religious reform (around 622 BCE) following the discovery of a scroll in the temple. Although this scroll was subjected to interpretation by Huldah the prophetess, the story illustrates a move away from the spoken oracle of the prophet as a medium of divine communication toward reliance on revelatory written texts. Also indicating the ascendancy of written texts, the seventh-century Deuteronomic Code presents Israel's ideal king writing out and studying a copy of "this Torah" (Deut. 17:18-20) as his most important duty. In a similar vein, the Deuteronomic historian tellingly alters a traditional military exhortation when he presents YHWH commanding Joshua to be strong and to meditate constantly on the book of the Torah to ensure success (Josh. 1:2-9; cf. Deut. 31:7-8) and when he presents David commanding his son Solomon to be strong and to keep the commandments as they are written in the Torah of Moses to ensure the continuation of the Davidic dynasty (1 Kgs. 2:1-4). The book of Deuteronomy expresses a consciousness of the importance of stable and authoritative writings that should not be altered and repeatedly portrays Moses urging all Israelites to study the Torah of Moses (for example, Deut. 6:6-9). From a slightly later period, wisdom psalms most likely stemming from the exilic or postexilic periods describe the virtues and benefits associated with meditation on the Torah (Pss. 1:2; 119:12-16, 97-104). Whatever the precise identity of the written "Torah" mentioned in the passages described above, these examples indicate the emergence of a text-centered religious culture that stressed the study of traditional, authoritative writings as a vehicle for understanding the divine intentions for human life. (For additional examples of passages depicting the consultation of written texts, see Dan. 9:2, discussed below, and Neh. 13:1-3.)

Further illustrations of the growing role of texts in Israel's religious life appear in connection with developments within Israelite prophecy. The prophetic call narrative, for example, increasingly portrays the divine word as embodied in written form. Whereas in Jeremiah's call narrative, YHWH places words directly in the prophet's mouth (Jer. 1:9), in Ezekiel's call narrative, YHWH gives the prophet an actual scroll to eat on which are written words of lamentation and woe that he finds surprisingly sweet (Ezek. 2:8–3:3). Another clear illustration of the rise of written texts may be discovered in Jeremiah 36, which depicts Jeremiah's secretary Baruch writing oracles dictated by the prophet on a scroll (Jer. 36:4), only to have to rewrite these oracles along with further additions on another scroll after King Jehoiakim burns the original in his brazier (36:27-32). The literalization of the prophetic word of God formerly associated with the prophet's verbal oracle is even further dramatized in writings attributed to the postexilic prophet Zechariah, who depicts a gigantic scroll flying through the air, inflicting punishment on the wicked (Zech. 5:1-4). This graphic vision of God's word active in history in written form symbolizes the growing power and independence of written texts in the culture's imagination and correlates with a shift in perception of revelatory media from direct theophanies, orally delivered prophetic oracles, technical divination, and dreams, to Scripture and its interpretation.

Once certain traditional writings were perceived as holding an honored and even, in some cases, revelatory status, various types of hermeneutical activities emerged in different sectors of Israelite society to keep these texts comprehensible, applicable, and relevant to audiences of successive generations. At times these activities were stimulated by perceived problems in the text itself (including difficulties in wording and grammar or insufficiencies of detail), but at other times they were motivated by broader changes in the historical or cultural situation (such as the crisis of the exile, the emergence of rival political parties, or innovations in theology) that required adaptation or reauthorization for the present. The exegesis and reuse of texts evident in the Tanak exemplify diverse origins, forms, and purposes, some of which will be illustrated in the selected examples analyzed below.

IDENTIFYING INNER-BIBLICAL EXEGESIS

The examples of inner-biblical exegesis explored below do not appear in distinct exegetical genres that clearly distinguish between scriptural text and interpretive comments, such as those that developed in postbiblical times (including, for example, the pesher at Qumran or the midrashic commentary of rabbinic Judaism). Rather, inner-biblical exegesis in the Tanak is incorporated within the many genres of literature that comprise the canon, including legal codes, historical narratives, liturgical poetry, wisdom literature, and prophetic oracles.

The project of identifying instances of this phenomenon therefore requires various tactics. At times, consciousness of dependence on earlier texts is explicitly indicated through the usage of a citation formula, for example, "as written in the book of the Torah of Moses" (2 Kgs. 14:6) or "as written in the Torah of Moses" (Ezra 3:2; 2 Chron. 23:18), even though the cited passage may not always be found in extant writings (Neh. 10:35 [34]; Num. 21:14). Alternately, this consciousness may be suggested by the use of deictic terms that sometimes introduce gloss-like interpolations into older writings (Josh. 18:13; Esth. 3:7; Exod. 32:1; Ezra 3:12; Isa. 29:9-12, discussed below). In the frequent absence of such clear indicators, however, such as in cases involving implicit reference to a particular text (for example, the allusions in Mal. 1:6–2:9 and Psalms 4 and 67 to the ancient priestly benediction in Num. 6:23-27), or the inclusion of unmarked glosses and explanatory comments (Deut. 22:11; Gen. 30:38; Jer. 25:8-14, discussed below), detecting the phenomenon of inner-biblical exegesis in the Tanak becomes more difficult. In general, the broaching of a common topic through the vehicle of identical terminology in more than one passage suggests a relationship between precursor and later texts, especially when clusters of the same words and phrases are shared. Even in these cases, however, it is not always clear that dependence on an earlier written text best explains the similarities between biblical passages. Other factors such as common religious practice, shared linguistic milieu, or underlying oral tradition may explain these similarities. The problem of identification is further exacerbated because interpreters and alluding authors sometimes obscure the novel aspects of their treatment of traditional material through a variety of techniques, for example, by pseudepigraphy or by reissuing oracles and laws, which formally minimize the gap between divine revelation and human exegesis (Fishbane 1985: 527-42; Levinson 1992).

In the face of these difficulties, identification of instances of inner-biblical exegesis may sometimes be facilitated by comparison between different manuscripts and versions, including the Masoretic Text, the Samaritan Pentateuch, the Septuagint, the targums, and the textual evidence from Qumran. At other times, examination of internal evidence, including the appearance of grammatical irregularities, redundancies, and resumptive repetitions, suggests either the work of later editorial hands or a compositional technique that includes unmarked citation of earlier writings. Despite the difficulties involved in isolating particular instances of dependence on and allusion to earlier writings, the evidence in the Tanak is strong enough to indicate that interpretation of traditional texts was an important component of Israelite culture, before, during, and, most prominently, after the period of exile in Babylon.

EXAMPLES OF INNER-BIBLICAL EXEGESIS

The following sections present illustrative examples of inner-biblical exegesis in the Tanak, including simple glosses and explanatory interpolations found in a number of biblical genres, and more substantial interpretations and reworkings of two selected types of materials, namely laws and oracles. These examples, while far from comprehensive, suggest the wide variety of types of inner-biblical exegesis (see Fishbane 1985 and Zakovitch 1992 for more comprehensive overviews of the phenomenon) and raise a number of critical issues, including the stability and adaptability of written texts in ancient Israel, the authoritative status of received writings and of subsequent reworkings of them, the purposes served by appeal to earlier texts, and the ingenuity of alluding authors who create new works that stand in relation to traditional materials. Following the discussion of the examples and the issues that they raise, two remaining topics will receive attention: the emerging consciousness of a nascent canon or collection of authoritative texts as indicated through certain instances of inner-biblical exegesis, and the continuities between inner-biblical exegesis and the types of exegesis that appear after the composition of the latest biblical books.

Scribal Glosses and Explanatory Interpolations

The simplest examples of inner-biblical exegesis consist of short glosses and explanatory interpolations that one might reasonably attribute to anonymous scribes responsible for copying, correcting, and transmitting written texts. One type of gloss that appears in the Tanak consists of an equivalent word or phrase inserted immediately after a more obscure one. For example, in Josh. 18:13 a gloss clarifies the older geographical name "Luz" by indicating that this place is also known, perhaps more familiarly, as "Bethel" ("Luz, which is Bethel"). Foreign words also receive glosses, as in Esth. 3:7, which identifies the meaning of the loanword *pûr* for an audience without the linguistic background to understand it ("*pûr*, which is the lot"). In both of these cases, a deictic particle (*hî'* or *hû'*, "which is") introduces the interpretive gloss and highlights the explanatory, secondary nature of the insertion (Fishbane 1985: 44-55).

Even in the absence of deictic elements, redundancies consisting of a word or phrase immediately following a difficult reference suggest scribal efforts to clarify unfamiliar terms. For example, in the prohibitions of various types of mixtures in Lev. 19:19, the nature of the "mixed garment" that one should not put on is clarified by a single word, apparently designating a certain kind of cloth ("and a mixed garment, *ša'aṭnēz*, should not be put upon you"). In time, the word *ša'aṭnēz* itself became problematic, so that in Deut. 22:11, this term is defined (or at least paradigmatically illustrated) by the subsequent phrase "wool and linen together" ("You shall not wear *ša'aṭnēz*, wool and linen together"). Similarly, in the description of Jacob's ruse to make Laban's flocks produce speckled and spotted offspring in Gen. 30:38, the obscure phrase "in the runnels" is glossed by the longer explanatory phrase "in the watering troughs" ("He set the rods which he had peeled in front of the flocks in the runnels, in the watering troughs, where the flocks came to drink").

In other instances, inserted words or phrases do not explain specific lexical items but clarify ambiguities due to awkward syntax. For example, Ezra 3:12 contains a description of the people's mixed reactions to the foundation of the second temple that, read one way, seems historically ludicrous: "But many of the priests and levites and heads of fathers' houses, elders who had seen with their eyes the first house *when it was founded* . . . wept with a loud voice, and many with a shout of happiness raised up a loud voice." In this sentence, it is not entirely obvious what the phrase "when it was founded" modifies. If this phrase modifies the preceding phrase, "the first house," then the sentence incredibly asserts that the old men present had actually witnessed the construction of the first temple during Solomon's reign, over 400 years previously! To prevent this infelicity, someone interpolated the disruptive but explanatory phrase "this is the house" (namely the second, rebuilt temple standing during the lifetime of the person responsible for the phrase) to specify the antecedent of the pronoun "it" in the preceding phrase "when it was founded." With this addition, the sentence more credibly states that those who had seen the first temple before it was destroyed in 587 BCE and lived to see the founding of the second temple some seventy years later were overcome with emotion.

At times, however, explanatory interpolations do not simply define obscure lexical items or clarify ambiguous grammar, but more substantially affect the sense of a passage as a whole. An especially striking example occurs in the prophetic denunciation in Isa. 29:9-12, which employs metaphors of drunkenness and sleep to describe loss of spiritual discernment. Since the subject of the passage is not clearly defined in 29:9, one might suppose it to be the population of Jerusalem or the people as a whole, as in the surrounding oracles, especially since the people's dullness is a theme elsewhere in Isaiah (6:9-10). In 29:10, however, a scribe has introduced two glosses, effectively circumscribing the castigation to a single class within Israelite society: "For

YHWH has poured out upon you a spirit of slumber, and he has shut your eyes — namely the prophets — and your heads — the seers — he has covered." The secondary nature of the references to the prophets and seers may be seen in their disruption of the chiastic structure of 29:10b, which originally followed the pattern of verb followed by direct object and direct object followed by verb typical of biblical poetry ("and he has shut your eyes, and your heads he has covered"). These glosses appear to accomplish a revision of the original significance of the text and may be considered a tendentious correction (Luzzatto 1855: 337-38).

Taken together, these examples indicate that the activity of copying and transmitting written works in Israel was not a mechanical occupation, but involved close attention to textual details and ad hoc efforts to render difficult and obscure aspects comprehensible. The presence of brief glosses and interpolations such as those described above also suggests that although the texts in which they are found were at one point in their literary history still fluid enough to allow the incorporation of additional, clarifying words and phrases, they were fixed enough to warrant the preservation of obscure terms and awkward grammar (cf. Deut. 4:2). The conservative retention of original wording alongside later glosses, while certainly intended to serve the dignity of traditional writings, actually highlights the presence of later, interpreting handlers of these texts. Somewhat paradoxically, explanatory glosses and interpolations sometimes significantly transform those very texts whose sense they aim to preserve. This situation is especially evident in the case of Isa. 29:9-12, where later, human exegesis becomes merged with divine oracle, radically altering its sense and redefining Isaiah's prophetic revelation for subsequent generations.

Exegesis of Legal Materials

Exegesis of legal materials in the Tanak presents a special case, since the Pentateuch narratively presents Israel's law, whether civil, criminal, or religious in nature, as divinely revealed to Moses at Sinai. Despite this depiction of commandments and laws as the eternally valid stipulations of the covenant with YHWH, there is clear evidence in the Bible that legal traditions did indeed develop and change, as cases were tried, judicial precedents were set, and social conventions evolved. The legal codes in the Pentateuch (the Covenant Code in Exodus 20:22–23:33, the Holiness Code in Leviticus 17–26, and the Deuteronomic Code in Deuteronomy 12–26) themselves stem from different historical periods, and many of the laws they contain bear signs of application, adaptation, and substantive revision. Outside the Pentateuch as well, in prophetic and historiographic writings, evidence points to the intentional study and reworking of laws in legal and judicial circles, as well as possibly in more scholarly and speculative contexts.

The interpolation of glosses, illustrated above in the discussion of laws concerning garments made of mixed materials (Lev. 19:19; Deut. 22:11), represents a very simple method of clarifying the application of a given law. Reflection on and evolution of legal tradition are also indicated through more extensive clarifications and alterations attached to earlier laws. A telling example appears in the law concerning the sabbatical year in Exod. 23:10-11. This law deals primarily with the management of agricultural fields, which are to be sown and harvested for six years but left fallow for the seventh to benefit poor people and wild animals. At its conclusion, however, an appendage enlarges the law's application: "You shall do likewise with your vineyard and with your olive orchard." Since vineyards and olive orchards are not sown annually, this expansion of the law leaves some questions about acceptable practice unanswered. The revision of the old law from the Covenant Code concerning the sabbatical year in Lev. 25:2-7 subsequently integrates provisions for the pruning and harvesting of vineyards into the main body of the law, parallel to the instructions concerning agricultural fields (Lev. 25:3-5). The secondary nature of this material is confirmed by the awkward retention of the singular possessive suffix in a phrase quoted from the older law, "and you shall gather its produce" (Lev. 25:3), even though one might expect "their produce" since the revised law deals explicitly with both field and vineyard. The levitical law also more broadly defines those who should benefit from the produce of the fallow fields and unpruned vineyards, including the owner himself and his household and domestic animals as well as wild beasts (Lev. 25:6-7).

Similarly, the seventh-century deuteronomic law concerning the release of Hebrew slaves after six years of service (Deut. 15:12-18) restates many elements of an earlier law found in the Covenant Code (Exod. 21:2-6) but also incorporates a number of substantial additions and alterations. For example, the Deuteronomic Code extends the scope of the law to include female slaves as well as male slaves (Deut. 15:12, 17; cf. Exod. 21:2, 7), provides for slaves to receive payment on release (Deut. 15:13-14, 18), changes the location of the ceremony in which a slave announces his intention to stay with his master (Deut. 15:12, 17; cf. Exod. 21:2, 6), and advocates a gracious attitude toward the released slave through appeals to the memory of the exodus from Egypt and the economic benefits of the slave's indenture (Deut. 15:15, 18).

In both cases, the sabbatical year and the law regarding Hebrew slaves, the older law is not entirely rejected but significantly altered, clarified, and extended to additional areas of application, and these adaptations appear to reflect the gradual development of a trajectory of legal tradition.

The situation is radically different in other cases, which do not maintain continuities with older legal traditions, but instead represent decisive ruptures with the past. The legal material in Deuteronomy 12, restricting sacrificial offerings to the single, central site of the Jerusalem temple, presents a good example of such a departure from precedent. To express this innovation, the authors of the deuteronomic passage employ specific terminology and phrases from the older Covenant Code, which presents sacrifice at local sanctuaries as normative in ancient Israel (Exod. 20:24-26). Whereas the older law clearly states that various types of sacrifices are acceptable at altars "in any place" where the divinity causes his "name" to be remembered (Exod. 20:24), the deuteronomic law restricts sacrifices to the single place that the divinity has chosen for his "name" (Deut. 12:5), and cautions against offering sacrifices "at any place" other than that particular one (Deut. 12:13). Fragmented allusions such as these to the earlier law, placed within the new literary context of the Deuteronomic Code, press familiar and venerated language into the service of unprecedented reform. Clearly the Covenant Code was not canonical for the authors of the Deuteronomic Code in the same way that the Torah later became canonical for the rabbis, even though the biblical authors found it imperative to address the old traditions in some fashion. Indeed, one suspects that the new law concerning sacrificial practice in Deuteronomy 12 was intended to replace the old one entirely. In this and similar cases (such as the reformulation of Passover as a pilgrimage festival in Deut. 16:1-8), the reuse of older legal materials in Deuteronomy appears to be programmatic and intended to garner the authority of tradition for innovative measures (Levinson 1991, 1997).

In addition to this type of selective citation of earlier legal material, the authors of the law of centralization in Deuteronomy 12 use another technique to authorize their innovations. They conceal their own authorship by employing the technique of pseudepigraphy, presenting their argument for the transformation of traditional practice in the voice of Moses himself, who claims only to reiterate what YHWH earlier commanded at Sinai (Deut. 12:21). Other interpreters of ancient laws present their legal innovations in markedly different ways, however, as the examples of the treatments of the Sabbath law in Jer. 17:21-22 and of the law against intermarriage in Ezra 9:1-2 illustrate.

Unlike the examples of legal exegesis discussed to this point, the interpretation of one of the ten commandments in Jer. 17:21-22 appears not in any corpus associated with the Sinaitic revelation, but in an oracle attributed to the prophet Jeremiah, who lived centuries after Moses. The divine voice itself alludes to the Sabbath law ascribed to that earlier period and, in language specifically recalling the version of that law found in Deut. 5:12-15 (cf. Exod. 20:8-11), commands those who enter the gates of Jerusalem not to do any work but to keep the Sabbath day holy (Jer. 17:22). The prophetic reissuing of the Sabbath law does more than repeat the original commandment, however, since it prefaces its citation of the deuteronomic version with additional material most likely reflecting this law's long history of interpretation. (For other indications of ongoing reflection on aspects of this law and its application, see Exod. 31:12-17; 34:21; 35:2-3; 16:4-30; Num. 15:32-36; Isa. 58:13-14; Neh. 10:32 [31].) In the Jeremian oracle, keeping the Sabbath day becomes a matter of life or death (Jer. 17:21; cf. Exod. 31:14-15), and the nature of the proscribed work is further defined by two additional clauses: the first prohibits carrying burdens in through the city gates (Jer. 17:21); the second (perhaps a later addition, in light of its more general nature and its absence from the continuation of the oracle in 17:24) prohibits the transfer of any burden from the private to the public domain (17:22). At the conclusion of this expanded rendition of the law, the divine voice, once again alluding to material from the version in Deuteronomy ("as YHWH your God commanded you," Deut. 5:12), presents additions, all as part of the original divine revelation to Israel's ancestors ("as I commanded your fathers," Jer. 17:22). Material arising from the human history of interpretation is thereby presented alongside the commandment itself as stemming from Sinai; and, as in the case of the law of centralization in Deuteronomy 12, novel aspects are not explicitly acknowledged. The goal seems to be to prolong the Sinaitic revelation into later times by obscuring the gap between original and later material through the divine voice's paraphrase of its own words from that foundational period.

In striking contrast to the revealed nature of interpreted law in Jer. 17:21-22, Ezra 9:1-2 presents exegesis of the law forbidding intermarriage with non-Israelite women from Deut. 7:1-6 in entirely human terms. Officials in postexilic Jerusalem report to Ezra that the people, including priests and levites, have married Canaanites, Hittites, Perizzites, Jebusites, Ammonites, Moabites, Egyptians, and Amorites, thus mixing Israel's holy seed. This list recalls Deut. 7:1. There the Israelites entering the land are commanded to refrain from marrying the native inhabitants of Canaan because Israel is a holy people to YHWH. But the postexilic restating of the law contains substantial revisions. In place of two of the original ethnic groups from the period of conquest listed in the deuteronomic law, the officials substitute three foreign peoples encountered by those returning from exile, namely Ammonites, Moabites, and Egyptians. This alteration not only renders the older law relevant to the contemporary situation but also indicates learned reflection on another traditional writing, since these three nations are the subject of laws dealing with exclusions from the assembly of YHWH in Deut. 23:4-9 (3-8). In Ezra's confessional prayer following the officials' report, the scribe associates the deuteronomic law against intermarriage with yet another earlier source, when he identifies the basis for this prohibition as the prophetic warning concerning the defiling abominations of the autochthonous populations (cf. Lev. 18:24-30). This conflation of sources suggests careful scrutiny of the legal corpus and synthesis of material perceived as topically related. Similarly, the solution to the crisis forwarded by the layman Shecaniah, that the men expel the foreign wives and their children "according to the law" (Ezra 10:1-5), represents an innovative addendum to Deut. 7:1-6, most likely informed by the stipulations in Deut. 23:4-9 (3-8) that the descendants of Ammonites and Moabites should be excluded from the assembly of YHWH even to the tenth generation and that the descendants of Egyptians should be admitted only after three generations.

Crediting a specific layman for the interpretation of the practical demands of the law prohibiting intermarriage contrasts remarkably with the techniques of pseudepigraphy and oracular reissue of law illustrated in the previous examples. This contrast suggests a movement from the practice of obscuring the signs of legal development to open validation of human exegesis of laws in the postexilic period. Despite this significant difference, all three cases share the common goal of maintaining the preeminence of revealed law by oscillating between traditional and interpretive material, modifying received texts while seeming to uphold their authority. These examples thus illustrate the central and abiding tension associated with the interpretation of authoritative texts, which must be transformed through exegesis in order to retain their privileged position within a religious system.

Exegesis of Prophetic Oracles

Prophetic oracles constitute another genre that engaged the exegetical energies of interpreters, who sought to clarify the sense of the oracles' often obscure poetic expression to indicate their fulfillment in historical events and to specify their continuing relevance. Although generally delivered orally by the prophets, oracles subsequently came to be preserved in writing (Isa. 8:16), making them available for study by later interpreters.

At times, the evocative mode of poetic expression characteristic of prophetic oracles proved too elusive for later commentators to let stand unaltered. The explanation of vague oracular imagery interpolated into the oracle in Isa. 9:12-16 (13-17) illustrates this point. This passage warns that YHWH will cut off Israel's head and tail, palm branch and reed, all in one day (Isa. 9:13 [14]). The gloss placed immediately after these figurative entities explains that "elders and dignitaries are the head and prophets who teach lies are the tail" (9:14 [15]; cf. 29:10, discussed above). A further example illustrating the practice of inserting phrases to clarify obscure references is Jer. 25:8-14, which describes the invasion of Jerusalem and its environs by "all the peoples of the north" (cf. 1:14-15; 6:1) and then specifies a particular historical figure, "Nebuchadnezzar the king of Babylon, my servant." This identifying phrase, as well as other references to the Babylonian conqueror in the oracle (25:11, 12), appear to be later glosses, judging from their striking absence in the Septuagint version of the oracle. Not only do these glosses clarify the identity of the invading forces, making them in that regard *vaticinium ex eventu* (prophecy from the event), but they also provide closure for at least the first part of the oracle, which in its revised form finds fulfillment in the historical events of the sixth century.

Such concern for the fulfillment of prophetic oracles motivated many exegetical revisions, extensions, and re-predictions intended to provide closure. Biblical prophecies did not always find immediate fulfillment in historical events. For example, two centuries after Micah predicted the destruction of Jerusalem (Mic. 3:9-12), the citizens of that city understood that his prophecy had remained unfulfilled because of the people's repentance (Jer. 26:18-19). This lack of correlation between oracle and historical reality was frequently perceived as problematic, however, as the criterion of true prophecy came to include accuracy of prediction (Deut. 18:22). For example, the prophecy against Moab in Isa. 15:1–16:12 apparently remained unfulfilled longer than expected, since it is reissued in Isa. 16:13-14, which acknowledges that the preceding oracle was formerly the word of YHWH but goes on to allow an extension of an additional three years until Moab's destruction. The oracle concerning the destruction of Tyre and Sidon in Isa. 23:1-12 experienced a much longer period of postponement, so an addition appended to this eighth-century oracle almost two centuries later insists that the destroying forces destined to fulfill the prophet's words are not the Assyrians but the Chaldeans (23:13). The closure provided by this additional remark simultaneously imbues an old oracle with contemporary relevance for the sixth century, since the events it describes are now located not in the distant past but in the present.

This type of adaptation of an older oracle to address changing times may be illustrated through the remarkably fertile history of interpretation of Jeremiah's prediction of a seventy-year period of Babylonian domination over the

Southern Kingdom and the surrounding lands (Jer. 25:8-14). As noted above in the discussion of clarifying glosses in prophetic oracles, the first instance of interpretation occurs within the oracle of doom itself, which specifies "Nebuchadnezzar the king of Babylon, my servant," as the leader of the invading forces from the north (Jer. 25:9). Another early interpretative treatment of this oracle appears later within the book of Jeremiah, in the letter that the prophet sends to the citizens of Jerusalem exiled in Babylon (Jeremiah 29), in which Jeremiah counsels the people to settle in the foreign country until the seventy years of Babylonian hegemony are completed. At that time, YHWH intends to bring them back to Jerusalem and restore their fortunes (29:10). This allusion to the oracle actually transforms its impact, for whereas the original prediction in 25:8-14 stresses the lengthy period of Babylonian rule over Jerusalem and its environs, the letter articulates divine intentions for the exiles' return and the city's restoration following the completion of this period. The letter recalling the earlier oracle of doom therefore addresses later, exilic concerns and alludes to the prediction in order to deliver a message of encouragement and hope for those already experiencing Babylonian domination.

The first allusion to Jeremiah's oracle outside the book itself appears in 2 Chron. 36:17-21. The destruction of the temple in Jerusalem and the exile of the people to Babylon are included as part of the fulfillment of Jeremiah's prophecy, although his original oracle specified only military conquest and a preordained period of foreign domination. Just as striking is the Chronicler's additional explanation that the land was left desolate for the seventy years of Babylonian rule in order to make up for sabbatical years that had been desecrated. This understanding of the period of desolation reveals an interpolation of Jeremiah's oracle in light of Lev. 26:34-35, which presents military defeat, exile, and the fallow wastage of the land as consequences of disobedience to the commandments — particularly those concerning the sabbatical year. Since the larger context in Leviticus 26 consists of an oracle concerning exile and restoration, the conflation of this material occurs rather naturally and reflects a harmonizing and anthologizing consciousness in relation to earlier texts. Following the depiction of the seventy-year period, the Chronicler portrays a time of restoration, consisting of a return from exile for the purpose of rebuilding the temple (2 Chron. 36:22-23; cf. Ezra 1:1-4). Thus the temple, which Jeremiah never mentions in his oracle or in his reference to the oracle in his letter to the exilic community, becomes a central focus of the Chronicler's understanding of the prophecy, in keeping with the concerns of the postexilic community.

This preoccupation with the temple characterizes the postexilic prophet Zechariah's references to the Jeremian oracle as well. When Zechariah asks

YHWH when he will show mercy to Jerusalem and the cities of Judah, with which he has been angry for seventy years (Zech. 1:12; cf. 7:4-7), the oracle that follows emphasizes divine compassion for the city, to be expressed in the near future not only generally through a return of prosperity but specifically through the rebuilding of the temple (1:13-17). It may well be that calculations of the seventy-year period beginning with the destruction of the temple in 587 BCE galvanized the drive to rebuild that structure advocated by Zechariah and his contemporary Haggai and thereby influenced the course of history.

The most elaborate interpretation of Jeremiah's oracle appears in the second-century BCE pseudepigraphic book of Daniel. Narratively set during Babylon's decline in the middle of the sixth century, Daniel 9 depicts a Judean official at the foreign court poring over books containing Jeremiah's prophecy of Jerusalem's seventy years of desolation (Dan. 9:1-2). After confessing Israel's sins that brought on the calamitous events foretold also "in the law of Moses" (9:11, 13, possibly alluding to passages such as Deut. 28:15-45 and Lev. 26:14-39), Daniel prays for forgiveness and requests the speedy restoration of Jerusalem. In response to his prayer, the angel Gabriel appears, and explains that the prophecy's seventy years actually means seventy weeks of years, or a total of 490 years (Dan. 9:24-27), which are further divisible into significant periods. The angelic interpretation of the seventy years in terms of weeks of years may not be an innovation by the author of Daniel, however, but rather a further development of an established trajectory of exegesis, already evident in 2 Chron. 36:17-21, that views Jer. 25:8-14 in light of the land's Sabbaths (the seventh years of fallow rest) described in Lev. 26:34-35. Whatever the case, the interpretation in Daniel extends the time-frame of the Jeremian prophecy by bringing the period of Seleucid rule in the second century BCE (the actual time of Daniel's composition) within its purview. In so doing, it presents a coherent vision of reality and time and holds out hope for future restoration to those suffering under the persecutions of Antiochus IV Epiphanes. This example also illustrates the transition from oral oracles of living prophets to the interpretation of written texts, in this case specifically a prophetic text, as a central means of revelation concerning a contemporary situation. The message of hope to the contemporary community comes through the medium of textual interpretation, albeit in this case angelic interpretation given to a prayerful student of books containing Jeremiah's old prophecy. The angel's interpretation of this scriptural passage, as well as other visions and explications, are in turn bound and sealed in a book (Dan. 12:4, 9), so that Daniel's story attests in more than one way the emergence of a religious culture centered on written texts.

The interpretations of Jeremiah's prophecy described above illustrate how through the medium of exegesis an oracle can be made to address a succession of generations from preexilic, exilic, postexilic, and Hasmonean times. The presence of multiple interpretive layers of a single scriptural passage in the Tanak points to the adaptability of traditional texts to the ongoing life of religious communities.

INNER-BIBLICAL EXEGESIS AND THE EMERGING CANON

Traces of exegetical activity in the Tanak indicate a developing appreciation of and homage to a limited collection of central and authoritative writings — in other words, to a canon, albeit in nascent form. As certain texts achieved prominent and revered status, they came to be studied and interpreted in light of each other as parts of a selected library of texts. The emerging concept of the unity of a limited number of writings may be seen in certain examples of inner-biblical exegesis, found in various genres and parts of Scripture.

The synthetic combination of legal traditions preserved in different parts of the Pentateuch has already been observed in Ezra 9:1-2, which develops the law prohibiting intermarriage in Deut. 7:1-6 by incorporating elements from Deut. 23:3-8 and Lev. 18:24-30. There are also harmonizations of conflicting legal traditions, each of which came to be included in the Pentateuch. One example of this phenomenon occurs in the narration in 2 Chron. 35:13 of the Passover celebrated after Josiah's temple reform, which attempts to take seriously discordant laws concerning the preparation of the Passover sacrifice. Exod. 12:8-9 specifically declares that the sacrifice should be roasted, not boiled, but Deut. 16:7 claims that it should indeed be boiled. To resolve this discrepancy, the Chronicler explains somewhat incongruously that the men of Josiah's time "boiled the Passover lamb in fire according to the ordinance," conflating the two conflicting laws to depict an innovative practice conforming to neither. This example indicates comparative study of the texts now preserved in Exodus and Deuteronomy, most likely within a living legal and judicial context, although scholarly and speculative study of the laws cannot be ruled out. But whatever the social context, both conflicting traditions were esteemed as authoritative and therefore taken seriously in the Chronicler's account of the reformer king's practices.

Another feature pointing to the emergence of intentional study of certain texts in light of each other appears in the superscriptions prefixed to some of the Psalms. Of particular interest are the historical designations of the periods in David's life when he composed certain Psalms, connecting narrative and poetry that are now preserved in two different parts of the Tanak, the

Prophets and the Writings. For example, anonymous editors attribute Psalm 51 to the time that David asked forgiveness for his sin "when the prophet Nathan came to him, after he had gone in to Bathsheba" (Ps. 51:2 [superscription]; cf. 2 Samuel 11–12). The many thematic and verbal links between these two writings attest to the editors' careful scrutiny of the texts and make their association plausible (Childs 1971), but this interpretive movement was by no means inevitable. In making this connection, the editors chose to read Psalm 51 in light of a specific character and event in Israelite history recorded in another text, rather than stressing the universality of important themes in the psalm, such as contrition and petition for forgiveness. The superscription thus reveals the editors' presupposition that the David narratives and the Psalms should be considered a unity and exemplifies the practice of cross-referencing within a corpus of writings and the interpretive process of transforming the lives of national characters into exempla. It also reveals a historicizing tendency in the interpretive activities of the early biblical exegetes, according to which the Psalms are understood as the prayers of specific characters, rather than as set liturgical pieces for performance in the Temple.

The postexilic prophets similarly demonstrate a broad and studied knowledge of their predecessors. Just as Daniel labored over books containing Jeremiah's oracle, prophets living during and after the Babylonian exile also familiarized themselves with earlier prophetic utterances and other writings, as is clear from their frequent references to these works. For example, the material found in Isaiah 40–66, attributed to an anonymous sixth-century prophet (or prophets) sometimes designated in scholarly circles as deutero-Isaiah, cites Jeremiah, Isaiah ben Amoz, the Psalms, and pentateuchal narratives, suggesting that these writings held a certain claim on his imagination (Sommer 1998). For example, Isa. 62:4 recalls the old threat from the Assyrian period in Isa. 1:7 that *"your land* will be *desolate"* and reverses its force by promising that *"your land* will no longer be called *desolate,* but . . . *your land* [will be called] owned." Similarly, the ancient prophecy of hope beginning in 9:1 (2) with the assertion that "the people who walk in *darkness* shall see a great *light"* receives exuberant confirmation in 60:1, which urges a later generation to return from Babylon to Jerusalem: "Arise, shine, for your *light* has come, and the glory of the LORD shines upon you; for now *darkness* covers the earth . . . but the LORD shines upon you!" Indeed, allusions such as these to the oracles of the eighth-century Isaiah ben Amoz in deutero-Isaiah may have been one of the factors impelling the decision to join the two works into one corpus. If this is indeed the case, then inner-biblical exegesis influenced the structure of a biblical book in its final edited form.

Other postexilic prophets, including Haggai, Zechariah, and Malachi, also quote extensively from earlier prophetic material, effectively crafting their oracles from the language of former mantic figures in whose shadow they found themselves. The book of Zechariah, for example, explicitly indicates an awareness of "the former prophets" (Zech. 1:4; cf. 7:7, 12) and incorporates interpretations of their sayings into the series of night visions found in the first part of the work. Specific examples of this practice appear in the third and fourth night visions and their explanations in Zech. 2:5–3:10 (2:1–3:10), which creatively allude to Ezekiel's image of the man with a measuring line (2:5-9 [1-5]; cf. Ezek. 40:3–42:20), to Jeremiah's concept of an influx into Jerusalem from the north (Zech. 2:10 [6]; cf. Jer. 1:13-16), to Isaiah's and Jeremiah's appellation "Branch" for the ideal Davidic king (Zech. 3:8; cf. Isa. 4:2; Jer. 23:5; 33:15), and to Micah's depiction of peaceful security under vine and fig tree (Zech. 3:10; cf. Mic. 4:4). The anthological style that characterizes this passage illustrates the postexilic prophets' employment of ancient oracles to address the changed situation and the unique concerns of the restoration period. The multiple allusions to different prophetic precursors furthermore suggest that the postexilic prophets may have been conscious of a collection of writings forming an early core of the second division of the Tanak, eventually known as the Prophets. In any case, the postexilic prophets' treatment of earlier texts attests to the developing concept of a canon, defined as a collection of a limited number of writings worthy of study and commentary (Smith 1982).

Not only do the examples discussed above reflect an emerging recognition of a limited number of written texts as having a certain status, but, viewed from another angle, this type of reuse of and allusion to traditional textual materials also helps solidify the authority of the books that eventually become part of the canon. The citation and exegesis of traditional materials signal their authority and keep them the focus of attention for the next generation, thus contributing to their inclusion in the Tanak. Inner-biblical exegesis in the Tanak therefore performs vital functions in addition to interpreting specific passages within earlier writings, including contributing to the contents and sometimes even to the structure of biblical books, as well as furthering the formation of the canon by giving prominence to some of the written material eventually included.

CONTINUITY BETWEEN INNER-BIBLICAL EXEGESIS AND LATER INTERPRETIVE ACTIVITIES

One remaining issue concerns the connections between inner-biblical interpretation and the later forms of scriptural interpretation that flourished following the completion of the writings eventually included in the canon. These include the Apocrypha and Pseudepigrapha, the examples of pesher interpretation discovered at Qumran, the works of Philo and Josephus, rabbinic midrash, and Christian exegesis found in the New Testament and the writings of the Church Fathers, which all exploded following the completion of the writings that became included in the canon. A central question expresses this issue succinctly: is there a clear break between the exegesis found in the Tanak and the exegesis of the Tanak found in later works, or do continuities predominate?

Scholars used to stress continuity with later forms of interpretation, including but not limited to rabbinic midrash (Bloch 1957; Vermes 1961), citing such characteristics as close attention to the details of the text, filling of gaps, solving of ambiguities, explicit citation of texts, harmonization of discordant passages, and use of specific exegetical techniques such as the *qal wāḥomer,* a form of argumentation that draws conclusions concerning weighty issues from lesser cases. While there may be a nuanced continuum between specific types of inner-biblical exegesis in the Tanak and postbiblical exegetical activity, including rabbinic commentary, there are significant differences as well. For example, in rabbinic exegesis, a clear demarcation is made between Scripture and later commentary on it, due to the fundamentally different situation arising from the completion of the biblical books and the establishment of a canon, the subsequent demise of rewriting traditional texts as a form of interpretation, and the emergence of clearly exegetical genres, such as the homily and commentary. In addition, interpretation of Scripture in rabbinic Judaism is more systematic and comprehensive in comparison with the ad hoc and occasional quality of the exegesis evident within the Bible itself. Calling the exegetical material in the Bible "midrash," as used to be common, obscures, therefore, real differences between the interpretation preserved in the Bible and the specific forms that emerged much later in rabbinic Judaism. "Inner-biblical" exegesis is a more cautious and accurate term (introduced by Sarna 1963), in that it allows the phenomenon to be described on its own terms.

Despite the validity of these qualifications, it must be acknowledged that the Bible models a great diversity of exegetical procedures and techniques that may be viewed as the antecedents of postbiblical interpretation, although other influences such as Greco-Roman hermeneutics should not be discounted. For example, the pseudepigraphic style of Deuteronomy and Daniel presents biblical precedents for a number of Second Temple works, including *Jubilees,* the *Testaments of the Twelve Patriarchs,* and the *Temple Scroll.* The retelling of biblical narratives, such as the version of Israel's history in Chronicles, which revises the version presented in Samuel-Kings, parallels the retelling of Genesis in *Jubilees* and in the *Genesis Apocryphon*. Allegorical and typological methods, which predominate in the exegetical writings of Philo and the Church Fathers, are anticipated in the allegorical interpretations of laws in the prophets (Jer. 2:3; cf. Lev. 22:14-16), in the typological interpretation of the exodus as a pattern for later episodes of national redemption (Jer. 16:14-15; Isa. 43:16-21; cf. Exodus 14–15), and in the typological interpretation of Abraham as a figure foreshadowing postexilic restoration in the land (Isa. 51:1-3; cf. Gen. 12:1-3). Explicit citation of Scripture and glossing techniques noted in earlier examples bear affinities with the pesher type of interpretation found at Qumran. The anthological style characteristic of the post-exilic prophets is replicated in the Hôdayôt (Thanksgiving Hymns) found at Qumran and in florilegia circulated in Jewish and Christian circles.

Some particular exegetical techniques typical of rabbinic midrash are also found in the Bible itself, including the *qal wāḥomer* type of argument (Ezek. 33:24), although this specific technique may be a universal type of argument, not limited to a single hermeneutical tradition. The precedents for the earliest postbiblical interpretations of Scripture are therefore apparent within Scripture itself, which provides models for later exegetes, or at the very least validates their exegetical intents and energies.

The presence in the Tanak of multiple strata — of texts and interpretive materials that revise, actualize, and reauthorize the traditional literature of the past — establishes through example the fundamental importance of scriptural interpretation as a religious activity. The sacred corpus of Israel represents revelation and interpretation as part of a continuous dialectic process in which successive generations contribute to the received tradition through exegesis, thereby creating a layered textual mode that emerges as a resource for later, postbiblical interpreters. This understanding of the Tanak echoes aspects of the traditional dual Torah doctrine of rabbinic Judaism, which maintains that from the moment of Sinaitic revelation itself there existed a parallel oral transmission and interpretation of the written Torah (Mishnah *'Avot* 1.1; see Danby 1933: 446). This theological statement concerning the value of rabbinic interpretation articulates something akin to the import of the examples of inner-biblical exegesis presented above, namely that Scripture is never transmitted free of an interpretive tradition. The evidence of scriptural exegesis in the Tanak shows that an interpretive tradition, arising from various social origins and exemplifying diverse techniques and purposes, flourished during the period that witnessed the composition of the biblical books and the formation of the canon. The composite, interwoven final form of the Tanak, containing multiple traditions and layers of interpretations, itself makes a theological statement about the value of the interpretation and reinterpretation of Scripture. Religious truth is articulated with a voice that is both old, because it is inspired by and draws on inherited texts, and new, because it reverbalizes, alters, and transforms ancient language to reappropriate tradition for the present generation. The Bible therefore presents Judaism and Christianity not only with a sacred text, but also with illustrative ways of relating to Scripture. Viewed as an interpreting work, the Tanak serves as prelude and invitation to further exegesis.

BIBLIOGRAPHY

Barr, J.

1983   *Holy Scripture: Canon, Authority, Criticism.* Philadelphia: Westminster.

Beentjes, P. C.

1993   "Tradition and Transformation: Aspects of Innerbiblical Interpretation in 2 Chronicles 20." *Bib* 74:258-68.

Blenkinsopp, J.

1977   *Prophecy and Canon: A Contribution to the Study of Jewish Origins.* University of Notre Dame Center for the Study of Judaism and Christianity in Antiquity 3. Notre Dame: University of Notre Dame Press.

Bloch, R.

1957   "Midrash," in *Supplément au Dictionnaire de la Bible* (Paris) vol. 5, cols. 1263-81. ET 1978 by M. H. Calloway: "Midrash," in W. S. Green, ed., *Approaches to Ancient Judaism: Theory and Practice,* 29-50. Brown Judaic Studies 1. Missoula: Scholars.

Childs, B.

1971   "Psalm Titles and Midrashic Exegesis." *JSS* 16:137-50.

1979   *Introduction to the Old Testament as Scripture.* Philadelphia: Fortress.

Danby, H., tr.

1933   *The Mishnah: Translated from the Hebrew with Introduction and Brief Explanatory Notes.* Oxford: Oxford University Press.

Dozeman, T. B.

1989   "Inner-Biblical Interpretation of Yahweh's Gracious and Compassionate Character." *JBL* 108:207-23.

Eyslinger, L.

1992   "Inner-Biblical Exegesis and Inner-Biblical Allusion: The Question of Category." *VT* 42:47-58.

Fishbane, M.

1980   "Revelation and Tradition: Aspects of Inner-Biblical Exegesis." *JBL* 99:343-61.

1985   *Biblical Interpretation in Ancient Israel.* Oxford: Clarendon.

1986 "Inner Biblical Exegesis: Types and Strategies of Interpretation in Ancient Israel." In G. H. Hartman and S. Budick, eds., *Midrash and Literature*, 19-37. New Haven: Yale University Press.

Kugel, J. L.
1987 "The Bible's Earliest Interpreters." *Prooftexts* 7:269-83.

Kugel, J. L., and R. A. Greer
1986 *Early Biblical Interpretation: Two Studies of Exegetical Origins.* Library of Early Christianity 3. Philadelphia: Westminster.

Levinson, B. M.
1991 "The Right Chorale: From the Poetics to the Hermeneutics of the Hebrew Bible." In J. P. Rosenblatt and J. C. Sitterson, Jr., eds., *"Not in Heaven": Coherence and Complexity in Biblical Narrative.* Bloomington: Indiana University Press.
1992 "The Human Voice in Divine Revelation: The Problem of Authority in Biblical Law." In M. A. Williams, C. Cox, and M. S. Jaffee, eds., *Innovation in Religious Traditions: Essays in the Interpretation of Religious Change,* 35-71. Religion and Society 31. New York: de Gruyter.
1997 *Deuteronomy and the Hermeneutics of Legal Innovation.* Oxford: Oxford University Press.

Loewenstamm, S. E.
1992 *The Evolution of the Exodus Tradition.* Translated by B. Schwartz. Jerusalem: Magnes.

Luzzatto, S. D.
1855 *Il Profet Isaia, volgarizzato e commentato.* Padua: Bianchi.

Mason, R.
1990 *Preaching the Tradition: Homily and Hermeneutics after the Exile.* Cambridge: Cambridge University Press.

Sanders, J. A.
1972 *Torah and Canon.* Philadelphia: Fortress.
1976 "Adaptable for Life: The Nature and Function of Canon." In F. Cross, et al., eds., *Magnalia Dei,* 531-60. Garden City: Doubleday.

Sandmel, S.
1961 "The Haggadah within Scripture." *JBL* 80:105-22.

Sarna, N. M.
1963 "Psalm 89: A Study in Inner Biblical Exegesis." In A. Altmann, ed., *Biblical and Other Studies,* 29-46. Brandeis University Studies and Texts 1. Cambridge: Harvard University Press.

Schniedewind, W.
1995 "Are We His People or Not? Biblical Interpretation during Crisis." *Bib* 76:540-50.

Scholem, G.

1971 "Revelation and Tradition as Religious Categories in Judaism." In *The Messianic Idea in Judaism and Other Essays on Jewish Spirituality*, 282-302. New York: Schocken.

Seeligmann, I. L.

1953 "Voraussetzungen der Midraschexegese." In G. W. Anderson, ed., *Congress Volume: Copenhagen*, 150-81. VTS 1. Leiden: Brill.

Smith, J. Z.

1982 "Sacred Persistence: Toward a Redescription of Canon." In *Imagining Religion: From Babylon to Jonestown*, 36-52. Chicago: University of Chicago Press.

Sommer, B. D.

1998 *A Prophet Reads Scripture: Allusion in Isaiah 40–66*. Stanford: Stanford University Press.

Toeg, A.

1973 "Numbers 15:22-31: Midrash Halakha." *Tarbiz* 43:1-20 (in Hebrew).

Vermès, G.

1961 "The Story of Balaam: The Scriptural Origin of Haggadah." In *Scripture and Tradition in Judaism: Haggadic Studies*, 125-77. Studia Post-Biblica 4. Leiden: Brill.

1970 "Bible and Midrash: Early Old Testament Exegesis." In P. R. Ackroyd and C. F. Evans, eds., *The Cambridge History of the Bible* I: *From the Beginnings to Jerome*, 199-231. Cambridge: Cambridge University Press.

Weingreen, J.

1957 "Rabbinic-Type Glosses in the Old Testament." *JSS* 2:149-62.

Zakovitch, Y.

1991 *"And You Shall Tell Your Son . . .": The Concept of the Exodus in the Bible*. Jerusalem: Magnes.

1992 *An Introduction to Inner-Biblical Interpretation*. Even-Yehuda: Reches (in Hebrew).

Zeidl, M.

1955-56 "Parallels between Isaiah and Psalms." *Sinai* 38:149-72, 229-40, 272-80, 333-55 (in Hebrew).

CHAPTER 3

Hebrew into Greek:
Interpretation In, By, and Of the Septuagint

Leonard Greenspoon

All translation involves interpretation, but not all interpretation is the same. This two-part truism, when applied to the Septuagint (LXX) or Old Greek (OG) translation of the Old Testament (a process begun around the third century BCE), yields results that are exciting, yet tantalizingly incomplete.

Before viewing specific illustrations of these observations, readers should consider a number of more general points. Although some of these points are widely applicable to translations of almost any literature at almost any time, others are unique to the context, or rather contexts, in which the Septuagint was produced.

THE SEPTUAGINT: NOT A UNIFIED DOCUMENT

It is commonplace today to view a given Bible translation as the result of a unified effort by a committee, or individual, who applies as consistently as possible predetermined stylistic, lexical, and theological principles. In this regard we would be surprised to find a literal approach taken in Genesis, for example, and a paraphrastic rendering in the book of Job. A formal structure for Exodus, reminiscent of the King James Version, should not be followed by a more colloquial one in Leviticus. A Torah rendered in conformity with conservative Protestant exegesis would be a strange introduction to a version that elsewhere reflects Orthodox Jewish understanding. In general, then, statements made about an individual book in a modern-language version of the Bible can be applied to most, if not all, other books in that translation.

80

None of this holds true for the Greek version we call the Septuagint. The origins of this ancient version are, to a greater or lesser degree, unknown. There is wide agreement that the Five Books of Moses, or the Pentateuch, was the first block of material translated and that this took place sometime in the third century BCE in Alexandria, Egypt (see, e.g., Jellicoe 1968: 52-58; Tov 1988). The primary motivation for this translation was the change within the Alexandrian Jewish community, which had for the most part ceased to speak or even understand the Hebrew language in which most of its sacred text had originally been written (brief portions of the Old Testament were originally written in Aramaic). An ancient document, the *Letter of Aristeas,* dates this activity to the reign of Ptolemy II Philadelphus in the first third of the third century BCE (for a recent translation of this *Letter,* see Shutt 1985). Even though that may be a bit early, most scholars agree that this translation of the Torah into Greek, to which some today would limit the term Septuagint (on this and related terminological issues, see Tov 1987c: 229-31; Greenspoon 1987), was the earliest written foreign-language version of any part of the Old Testament or Hebrew Bible.

In spite of the insistence by *Aristeas,* amplified in later retellings, that the entire Pentateuch was translated into Greek at one time by one group (consisting of 70 or 72 individuals, hence the designation "Septuagint"), there is wide consensus today that even this material is the result of more than one independent translator — probably a different translator for each of these first five books (see especially the authoritative conclusions in Wevers 1996: 95; 1997 *passim*). Lacking any precedent for the translation into Greek of "barbarian" (that is, foreign) sacred texts, these earliest translators wisely opted for a fairly literal approach. What they "saw" in their Hebrew, they "represented" to the best of their ability in their Greek. Even so, they did not seek to produce a concordant or interlinear Hebrew-Greek text. They had a healthy respect for both the sacred Hebrew text they were translating and the resultant Greek version they offered to their coreligionists.

One major strand of both Jewish and Christian tradition viewed these translators as inspired and the Greek they produced as equal in authority to the Hebrew. (The Alexandrian philosopher Philo was a prominent proponent of this view from the Jewish side; among early Christians, the stance of Augustine is representative.) We are without any sure knowledge of how the translators themselves viewed their enterprise.

It is abundantly clear that the Old Greek (OG) or Septuagint (LXX) versions of other biblical books are chronologically later than the Pentateuch. When others prepared Greek renderings of the remaining books of their "Bible" (this happened over a period of a century or so), they were significantly influenced by what these first translators had done (Tov 1981). Some have sought to arrive at relative dates for many of these other books (see especially the discussion in Harl, Dorivan, and Munnich 1994: 86-101); in a few cases, absolute dates have been determined on the basis of what are interpreted as allusions to events contemporaneous with the translators themselves.

Even a cursory examination of the completed "Septuagint" reveals several different styles, the result of different approaches to both the Hebrew text being translated and the Greek text that was produced. Apparently there was no supervisory board that sought to bring unity or consistency to this diverse material. This diversity extended to matters of interpretation as well. In short, we may be able to say something about interpretative elements in one book of the LXX, but we should not assume that these observations apply elsewhere in the Greek text.

WHAT DID THE TRANSLATORS TRANSLATE — AND HOW?

The remarks above describe a set of circumstances that should make any potential investigator of the LXX cautious. Two further observations serve to expand this cautionary note. The first relates to our inability to answer with certainty the question posed at the beginning of this section: What did the translators translate? We would like to know details about the Hebrew text available to the various Greek translators (the *Vorlage*). At times, the Hebrew from which they translated was quite similar to the traditional Masoretic Text (MT) of the sixth to tenth centuries CE which has come down to us today (at least in regard to its consonants, since the ancient text was not provided with vowel points to help in pronunciation and comprehension, as was later the case). Elsewhere, the Greek translators worked with a Hebrew text that varied considerably in regard to its contents, order of material, and length from the MT (e.g., Samuel-Kings and Jeremiah). That, at least, is what we think, because in plain fact we do not know for sure exactly what Hebrew text lay before any particular Greek translator.

Because of this lack of certitude, every statement that we make about the translators' approach, including statements about the nature and extent of their interpretive activity, must remain in the realm of speculation. Nonetheless, careful scholars have been able to demonstrate to the satisfaction of most of their colleagues that Jeremiah, for example, was translated quite literally, while the book of Job falls on the freer end of the spectrum. Orlinsky, Seeligmann, and Tov are among the scholars who have led the way in such methodological considerations; naturally, they have not always agreed among themselves on their substantive results. Only careful, almost microscopic attention to details of translation technique allows us to make convincing arguments about how a given translator handled his Hebrew.

It is important to emphasize what is at stake here. When we find that a segment of LXX text reflects quite closely the Hebrew preserved in the MT, it is methodologically appropriate to argue that the translator was rendering an MT or MT-like text. When, however, the text of the OG clearly differs from the MT, we must decide whether this Greek text results from the OG translator's rendering of a different Hebrew *Vorlage* or from his interpretative handling of a Hebrew identical with (or very close to) the MT. Only the latter cases qualify as examples of interpretative renderings by the Greek translator himself. As we can easily imagine, it is rarely an easy matter to determine in specific cases where the "non-MT" element entered.

TRANSMISSION OF THE SEPTUAGINT

We encounter a further difficulty when we ask, as we must, not only how the original Greek text was produced, but also how this original text was subsequently passed down or transmitted to us in manuscripts — both in Greek and in other languages into which the Greek itself was translated — far removed in time from the third or second century BCE. In one sense, this is a problem common to all ancient literature. With good reason we hypothesize that there was an original or autograph for each book that is found in the LXX. However, we do not have any of these autographs. What we do have are copies of copies of copies . . . in the Greek language and in translations from the Greek into Latin, Syriac, and many other languages.

On the basis of dozens if not hundreds of extant manuscripts, researchers must decide what the wording for each passage was in the original LXX translation. This is the job of textual critics, for whom this quest is both a science and an art. In controversial cases unanimity is rare in the search for original readings, but the general contours are nonetheless agreed upon for most books of the LXX through the application of text-critical insights that are widely applied to ancient literature in general.

There are several other factors unique to the transmission of the text of the LXX in Greek and in its daughter versions (i.e., translations from the Greek). As narrated above, the Greek translation we call the LXX was initially produced by Jews, for Jews, a century or more before the birth of Jesus. When, however, the early church adopted the Greek text as its own "Old Testament," this material was by and large abandoned by Jewish communities (although this may not have been the case; see "The Jews and the Septuagint," below). As a result, almost all sources for the LXX available to us today were transmitted within the context of Christianity.

This observation leads to the following question: Did Christian scribes regularly introduce readings into the text they were copying to bring it into closer conformity with their own theological presuppositions, especially as regards the Old Testament as the predictor of the coming of Jesus Christ? Although such an impulse might seem almost natural, careful study reveals very few sure examples of intentional Christian "tampering" with the original "Jewishness" of the LXX (Kraft 1978). Two factors may be adduced to explain this phenomenon. One is that scribes were probably aware that they were working with Sacred Writ that needed to be handed down as accurately as possible; where Christians saw references to Jesus but Jews did not, these passages could be handled by commentaries rather than by reworking the biblical text itself. Moreover, Christian apologists such as Justin and Origen early on recognized the need to have a biblical text in common with their Jewish contemporaries, with whom they were often engaged in controversy, so as to defuse the claim that Christians had changed the text. Whatever the reasons, we are immeasurably helped in our quest for interpretive elements in the LXX by the fact that the process of transmission was relatively straightforward in this regard.

REVISIONS OF THE SEPTUAGINT

There is, nonetheless, one other complicating factor. In antiquity, as in the modern world, anyone with even a superficial knowledge of both Hebrew and Greek would recognize that the two traditions often diverge (as is especially notable in books like Jeremiah and Proverbs). To those for whom the Hebrew text was uniquely true, this circumstance stimulated a desire to "correct" the LXX on the basis of the truth contained in the Hebrew. The *Letter of Aristeas,* with its insistence that the Septuagint of the Pentateuch was accepted at Alexandria in exactly the same way the Law had been received at Mount Sinai, demonstrates an early recognition of, and hostility to, such revisions.

We know the names and some of the circumstances regarding several individuals responsible for revisions of the Septuagint: Theodotion, Aquila, and Symmachus. These three individuals, all Jews, will be discussed in detail later in this article (see "Revisors and Translators . . . ," below). Here we simply observe that in several instances, most notably in parts of the books of Reigns (Samuel and Kings), Ecclesiastes, and Daniel — these later revisions or reworkings supplanted the older and original Greek text in virtually all manuscripts available to us today. This not only contributes to the "unevenness" of the LXX we spoke of earlier, but also further complicates any effort to formulate statements that would apply across the board to all books of the Septuagint.

ALL IS NOT LOST

With such an array of caveats, uncertainties, and methodological difficulties, some might think it most prudent simply to throw up our hands and admit that we really cannot say anything about interpretative elements in the LXX. As sympathetic as they might be to such extreme action (or, in reality, inaction), most scholars have come to realize that it is not, after all, impossible to make some responsible judgments in this area, so long as we recognize the limitations we must necessarily impose on both our quest and its results. Failure at least to try would rob us of invaluable information about the beliefs and lifestyles of important Hellenistic Jewish communities. These communities are worthy of study in and of themselves and as links between biblical Israel and the Judaism and early Christianity that emerged in the first few centuries CE.

One other observation of the general sort is necessary before we turn to specific examples. As noted several times above, researchers seeking interpretative elements in the LXX are naturally drawn to places where the Greek translators introduced such material either through the insertion of additional words or by the reinterpretation of material contained in their Hebrew *Vorlage*. If, however, we seek to understand fully the conceptual world of these translators, these divergences are only part, albeit an important part, of the study. Where translators were content to render their Hebrew in a straightforward manner, such passages were presumably consistent with their beliefs or presuppositions or thought patterns. Not surprisingly, Jewish translators of the third or second centuries BCE held many beliefs in common with the earlier Hebrew text they were rendering. These instances also need to be taken into account by anyone endeavoring to provide a complete picture of Hellenistic Judaism. Our goal, alas, is considerably less ambitious!

INTERPRETATIVE ELEMENTS IN LXX ISAIAH

We begin with the study of interpretative elements located in several of the individual books found in the LXX. Our starting point is the book of Isaiah. In this connection, Seeligmann (1948: 3-4) points both to the book's unique features and to aspects shared with other translated material in the LXX:

> Every translation is governed by two factors. The original text sets the translator certain limits. . . . But apart from this, the translator's historical background never fails to exert its influence on him subjectively, and thereby on his work. The range and strength of each of these two influences vary from one case to another, and the same is true of the collection of translations preserved in the Septuagint; the translation of Isaiah is characterized in numerous places not only by a fairly considerable independence of the Hebrew text, but also by the fact that it evinces an equally marked influence from the surrounding cultural atmosphere, as well as expressing the author's personal views. This translation, in fact, is almost the only one among the various parts of the Septuagint, which repeatedly reflects contemporaneous history. . . . This realization enables us to take the difference between the original and translation as a basis for an attempt to reconstruct the complex of theological ideas behind the translation, its conception of God, its historical consciousness, and its expectations in regard to the future.

Seeligmann enumerates an impressive number of renderings through which the Greek translator of Isaiah reveals his acquaintance with what had become traditional language and practice of the Alexandrian Jewish community. As his programmatic statement indicates, Seeligmann seeks further specificity through purported references to specific historical events or conditions. Although most translators do betray (if that is the appropriate term) aspects of their cultural and theological setting, it is less common for the specifics of history and government to make their way into such versions.

For LXX Isaiah, these latter factors are in evidence in many ways. As Seeligmann notes (pp. 77-81), the translator of Isaiah had scant knowledge of the details of ancient Israelite geography. Nor did he presuppose such knowledge on the part of his readers. So, the "tendency to contemporization" and "the bringing up to date of geographical facts and names" (pp. 79, 81) was natural. Seeligmann uses his observation of the translator's practice with geographical terms (which admittedly is not all that unexpected) to move to the question of specific historical references in the Septuagint of Isaiah. His findings in this regard are quite remarkable: in the LXX the great satire of ch. 14 contains unmistakable allusions to Antiochus Epiphanes, and ch. 8 to the high priest Onias III (Seeligmann 1948: 83-94). In Seeligmann's elaborated analysis, there are numerous references to historical personalities of the translator's period, and to the Jewish reaction to them. We are, as it were, moved from the eighth and seventh centuries of Isaiah or the sixth century of deutero-Isaiah to the era of the Maccabees, the Seleucids, and especially, given the reputed origins of LXX Isaiah in Alexandria, to Ptolemaic Egypt. It is particularly exciting to follow Seeligmann as he establishes specific historical links with the Oniad-founded temple in Heliopolis, Egypt.

This last reference leads to a consideration of the translator's theological views. In this regard, as in others, "the Isaiah translator . . . cannot be said to have been merely a translator and nothing more" (Seeligmann 1948: 95). Seeligmann carefully analyzes the subtle but cumulatively convincing evidence that this translator made a "conscious attempt to transpose from the Biblical to the Hellenistic sphere of thought [the] nuclear idea of every Jewish theological concept: God, Torah and Israel" (p. 96). Although it is natural to expect any translator, especially a Jewish one, to hold basic theological tenets in common with biblical writers, the Isaiah translator also exhibits a considerable degree of independence from biblical thought, especially in his conception of Torah (pp. 104-108). Seeligmann (pp. 105-107) links Septuagint Isaiah's theological pattern with Alexandrian Jewish theology in general and then takes this idea one bold step further by hypothesizing that some of the language in Greek Isaiah is specifically aimed at a "heretical" group that failed to live up to the standards Isaiah (in Hebrew and in Greek) was thought to have erected.

This was heady material when it was first promulgated by Seeligmann in 1948, and it continues to be so today (see "'Messianizing' in the LXX?" below). Equally apt and fruitful is Seeligmann's characterization of the Isaiah translation as giving "striking insight into the Galuth [Diaspora] psychology of Alexandrian Jewry" (p. 111). As seen through his extensive reworking of, for example, Isaiah 25, this translator observes in such passages "the conditions of his own time and of the state of exile"; the Diaspora "is symbolic of misery and humiliation" (p. 112). Life in Egypt may have offered much even to its Jewish residents, but it could never take the place of Zion for the loyal among them.

However, Seeligmann continues, Septuagint Isaiah was more than a road map of loss and destruction; it was also a blueprint for future redemption and salvation. National deliverance would come. It had been foreseen by Isaiah and other biblical prophets, whose words (at least as recorded in the

Greek of Isaiah) pointed to the very Diaspora community of Alexandria itself as the means of effecting this salvation. As viewed finally through the interpretative prism constructed by Seeligmann, such salvation moved onto a universal stage as Diaspora Jews taught their religion among the Gentile majorities in whose midst they passed their exile. Viewed in this light, the Greek reworking of Isa. 66:5 may be understood as a "fragment of Alexandrian preaching and exhortation to the making of religious propaganda in the hostile Gentile milieu" (p. 118), especially in regard to the teachings of the Torah.

Although Greek Isaiah, along with the remainder of the books of the Septuagint, has been most often read by Christians, this historical phenomenon

> ought not to make us shut our eyes to the fact that the lexicological, historical and religious interpretations presented . . . are Jewish both as to form and content. It is, therefore, as ancient testimonies of the Jewish exegesis, that the Books of the Septuagint must be investigated and understood. (p. 121)

As should be abundantly clear even in this necessarily brief discussion of Seeligmann's monograph, he set the standards, lofty standards at that, for much of the scholarly work that followed in his wake. He has especially set the standard for subsequent studies that continue to focus attention on the book of Isaiah.

Dutch scholar Van der Kooij is among the most productive researchers today on the Greek text of Isaiah. His critique of Koenig (Koenig 1982), and to an extent of Seeligmann, is methodological (although data or results can never be completely severed from the methodology through which they were obtained). Van der Kooij claims that their approach to analysis "is too fragmentary to be conclusive" (1987: 128). In part to overcome such limitations, Van der Kooij subjected an entire pericope, Isa. 19:16-25, to an intense and multi-leveled analysis in order to refine our understanding of just how this translator introduced interpretative elements through the intentional adoption of a free approach.

Among his conclusions is one that may strike readers as too obvious to require (re)statement:

> "Free" renderings in LXX Isa. 19:16-25 do cohere with each other . . . within a verse and between verses. . . . It means that this translation is not the result of a mechanical way of translating a Hebrew text, not of some guesswork, but of "interpretation," not only of some words, or phrases,

but of several verses together. . . . The "free" choice of words . . . turns out to be a deliberate choice of Greek words and phrases, forming parts of a particular interpretation. (1987: 157)

Such a conclusion, which flies in the face of assertions or presuppositions on the part of other scholars (according to Van der Kooij, especially 1987: 151-53), serves alike to vindicate both Van der Kooij and the Greek translator of Isaiah.

One other observation by Van der Kooij (p. 159) has general applicability to all of Greek Isaiah and, applied with due caution, to the entire corpus of translated LXX Greek: "It is likely that the Hebrew original of LXX Isa. 19:16-25 is identical with the Hebrew text [of extant witnesses such as the MT and 1QIsa[a], the Great Isaiah Dead Sea Scroll] where LXX Isaiah differs from it." Only where such a statement is made by a seasoned scholar is it possible to speak of interpretative elements, either sporadic or cohesive, that belong to the Septuagint rather than to its *Vorlage*.

In a very recent study, Porter and Pearson (1998: 542) call attention to Greek Isaiah's rendering of 40:3-6 as reflective of "an event in the course of Hellenistic history which may very well have resonated both with the translator of Isaiah and with his audience — namely, the funeral procession of Alexander the Great." Although that event took place perhaps as much as 200 years earlier than the Greek rendering of Isaiah, it is not farfetched to think that it remained etched in popular imagination, especially if it were kept alive through public ritual in Alexandria.

Porter and Pearson characterize Greek Isaiah's rendering of these verses as "strictly literal" and yet capable of conveying "the theology and historical situation of the translator." As the authors point out, this calls to mind Seeligmann's observation that "passages that were translated literally in a given book of the Septuagint are of equal importance as free paraphrases: both represent fragments of the religious notions of the translator concerned" (Porter and Pearson 1998: 545, 542).

INTERPRETATIVE ELEMENTS IN LXX DEUTERONOMY

For over two decades, Wevers has been working on the mammoth task of preparing a Greek text for each of the books of the Pentateuch, accompanied by a book-by-book textual history in German and a verse-by-verse series of notes in English. A recent summary of his work on Greek Deuteronomy concludes with a section introduced in the following manner:

> The book of Deuteronomy purports to be a report of Moses speaking to
> the Israelites from Transjordan (see 1:1) before the actual conquest of Ca-
> naan, i.e. before crossing the Jordan. The translator lived in the city of Al-
> exandria in the first half of the third century BCE. That occasionally his
> own environment and times should betray itself in his translation is
> hardly surprising; more remarkable is how little of such is evident in
> Deut. (Wevers 1997: 83)

The more tentative phrasing by Wevers, in comparison with scholars working
on Isaiah, is due both to Wevers' general understanding of the Septuagint and
to the specific characteristics of the Greek translator of Deuteronomy, who
(along with the other translators responsible for the Pentateuch) occupies
more literal segments on the literal–free continuum than does Greek Isaiah.

In addition to updated geographical references of the sort already seen
from Seeligmann's work, Wevers points to relatively small changes indicative of
life in Alexandria contemporary with Greek Deuteronomy. For example, in
Deut. 5:30 Moses' order to "return to your tents" becomes "return to your
homes" in keeping with the normal living arrangements of urban Jews. Likewise, references to money, weights, and measures are often updated, as is true in
the more weighty area of politics: for Hebrew "elders," the favorite rendering of
Greek Deuteronomy is the equivalent of "council of elders, senate," probably reflecting the realities of the translator's own times (Wevers 1997: 84-85).

There are also changes for which Wevers discerns a theological motivation. Such exegesis manifests itself not only in expected references to God, but
also in relation to humans. Since God is Israel's only true king, Greek Deuteronomy avoids the standard Greek equivalent for "king" with reference to Israelite monarchs, who are consistently styled "rulers" (Wevers 1997: 87-88; for
an extended discussion of this terminology and its significance, see Freund
1990). In summary, although the evidence of interpretation from Deuteronomy is indeed sparse in comparison with the book of Isaiah, its range is remarkably wide: from the mundane to the sacred.

INTERPRETATIVE ELEMENTS IN LXX ZECHARIAH

Another recent study focuses on the book of Zechariah, which has the advantage of being more manageable in length than a book of the Pentateuch or the
Major Prophets. In a wide-ranging article, dealing only partly with topics under discussion here, Italian researcher Cimosa finds "quite a lot of novelty,"
which in his analysis centers on heightened interest in the figure of the Mes-

siah (in 3:8-10; 6:12; 9:9-10; we return to this topic in "'Messianizing' in the LXX?" below) and on "the progressive spiritualization of the concept of prayer" (1997: 108). In these as well as in other areas, Cimosa seeks to forge a tentative link between practice in Greek Zechariah and the midrashic approach characteristic of rabbinic Judaism. It is to this that we now turn.

LXX AND MIDRASH: GREEK JOSHUA

When Jewish scholars returned, after an extended absence of a millennium and a half, to a study and appreciation of the Septuagint as part of the activity associated with *Wissenschaft des Judentums,* among their first substantive accomplishments was the comparative investigation of midrashic material in the LXX and in classical Jewish sources. Seminal in this regard is the still valuable and in some ways unsurpassed work of Frankel (1851; see also Prijs 1948). It is then fitting that the Israeli scholar Tov has been among the leaders in refocusing attention on this topic in recent decades.

Tov introduces his 1978 article with this definition or description of Midrash (p. 50), which may strike some as overly broad, but in fact suits well the nature of the extant LXX evidence:

> Those elements are considered Midrashic which deviate from the plain sense of the MT and either reflect exegesis actually attested in Rabbinic sources or resemble such exegesis but are not found in any Midrashic source.

Even if such a study can cover all relevant examples, regardless of their origin, Tov continues (p. 51) with a reminder that "ideally a distinction should be made between (1) Midrashic elements which were introduced by the Greek translator, and (2) Midrashic elements which belonged to the Hebrew *Vorlage* of the LXX." Tov (1978: 54-56) provides several examples of each from the book of Joshua: the substitution by the Greek translator of *new* corn for *parched* corn at Josh. 5:11, for example, may parallel rabbinic terminology concerned with when produce can be eaten. Among the exegetically significant passages that may have derived either from the translator's Hebrew *Vorlage* or from the translator himself are Josh. 3:15 (the specification of wheat harvest); 4:6 (the change from your *children* to your *son*, in conformity with Pentateuchal passages like Exod. 13:14 and possibly also under the influence of the wording found in the Passover Haggadah); and 5:6 (where the LXX has the unusual *forty-two* years of wandering through the wilderness in place of the normal *forty* years).

LXX AND MIDRASH: GREEK EXODUS

For Greek Joshua, Tov put forth only sporadic, though admittedly quite interesting examples. A young South African scholar, Büchner, has subjected a
major section of the book of Exodus (chs. 12–23) to a sustained analysis of its
exegetical character (1997) in comparison to the rabbinic commentary on Exodus (Mekilta). Although, as he notes, such a comparison is at least as old as
Frankel, Büchner is able to put to good advantage the expansion of our
knowledge for this period since Frankel's day.

Büchner's conclusions are presented in a clearcut, forthright manner
(p. 419):

> It is clear that the majority of agreements between G Ex [Greek Exodus]
> and MC [Mekilta] lie at the level of halakhic exegesis . . . and more specif-
> ically that type of interpretation that can be called *adaptation of the text
> in translation to the reality of the concrete juridical situation.*

While such concerns on the part of the translator may aptly be termed theological, Büchner judges that

> there is no unified approach to theological issues. . . . The translator drew
> from a hodgepodge of available interpretations, with a definite leaning
> toward a type of intellectual activity that sought to adapt the text in
> translation to the concrete legal situation. (p. 420)

Not all exegesis is theological. Furthermore, not all theological activity needs
to be systematic, even within the same book. In fact, the less systematic approach may provide all the more evidence of a given translator's acquaintance
with a wide range of sources and traditions.

GREEK PROVERBS: HELLENISTIC OR JEWISH?

Our last example drawn from an individual book of the Septuagint is Proverbs. Culminating more than a decade of productive research on this book is
Cook's recent monograph (1997). His primary concern is of direct relevance
to our quest:

> I concentrate on a longstanding issue, namely, whether the Septuagint . . .
> is to be seen as a Hellenistic or a Jewish document. . . . In more concrete

terms it pertains to the question of whether the LXX Proverbs should be seen primarily as a Hellenistic document . . . or whether it is rather a Jewish document. (p. 37)

Acknowledging the problematic nature of developing any hypothesis to cover so complex a question, Cook (p. 39) nonetheless formulates the following hypothesis: "Hellenism did not influence the Septuagint version of Proverbs fundamentally."

Knowing that it is impossible and perhaps not even productive to examine all thirty-one chapters of Proverbs, Cook selected chs. 1, 2, 6, 8, 9, and 31 for in-depth analysis. For most of these chapters, he provides acute commentary on translation technique and compares Greek Proverbs with other versions of the same text as well as with passages outside Proverbs. He then looks at the relevance of these data for determining the exegesis or theology of each chapter.

On the basis of the combined evidence, Cook characterizes the translator's approach toward his *Vorlage* as "free." However, simply characterizing a translator's technique in this way is no more valuable than, say, using the term "literal." Recognizing this, Cook speaks of the Greek translator of Proverbs as an "extremely competent" individual, who approached his task with "the drive to make the intention of his parent text, *as he understood it,* evident to his readers." More specifically, "the translator obviously had a 'religious' intention in his rendering" (pp. 316-17). Concern for the overall intention of his *Vorlage* enabled the translator to insert interpolations and rearrange substantial portions of text where he felt it would clarify matters for his intended audience (as, for example, in ch. 8). Clearly, for this individual, intention is something more, or other, than the sum of details (pp. 217-18).

Cook finds uniqueness in Greek Proverbs' intermingling of the translator's "fundamentally *Jewish* approach" with his application of "typically *non-Jewish* traditions." The former dominated the translator's thinking and *modus operandi;* the latter, in Cook's judgment, entered only when such traditions served "to underscore a 'theological/religious' issue that was already explicit in the Hebrew text" (p. 319). Examples adduced range from the higher realms of philosophy to the practical, observable world of bees and ants.

Cook believes that Greek Proverbs stems from Jerusalem rather than Alexandria. This view, he argues (p. 327), should "be taken seriously as a correction of the views formerly held that Alexandria is the sole provenance for *all* Septuagintal books."

Cook also moves beyond the specifics of Greek Proverbs when he speculates on whether an individual who took such liberties with his parent text, even with the best of intentions, can be called a translator at all. Many modern researchers are skeptical that those responsible for the Septuagint version of any book would have been sufficiently bold to effect the sort of deliberate changes that Cook attributes to Greek Proverbs. These scholars prefer to locate such exegetical activity within the transmission history of the Hebrew text that produced the translator's *Vorlage*.

While not necessarily endorsing all aspects of Cook's view, I fully agree with his well-stated caveat that "dogmatic positions as to what the Greek translators could or would have done are out of order" (1997: 325) Restated, following some further observations of Cook's, we might say that at least in some cases those responsible for the Greek version of certain biblical books saw themselves indistinguishably as translators, editors, scribes, and interpreters. As noted above, such questions are not at the forefront for some sorts of analysis. In many other contexts, however, the distinction is crucial between what a translator found in his *Vorlage* and what he introduced on his own.

ANALYSIS OF TRANSLATION EQUIVALENCES:
POSSIBILITIES AND LIMITATIONS

We have referred to, but not yet concentrated on, another approach that moves beyond discrete blocks of material to study the usage of particular terms or phrases throughout the Septuagint. There is much to be gained from such studies, when due regard is paid to the different contexts of each occurrence and to the differing techniques of individual translators. We will sample the results of these studies through a selection of examples from different categories or areas of thought and activity.

Tov has cautioned against expecting too much from such analysis:

> The majority of translation equivalences derive from linguistic identifications of a given Hebrew word or root with a Greek equivalent; as such they are of importance for our understanding of the linguistic knowledge of the translators, but are of limited importance for our understanding of their conceptual world. (1988: 175)

Into this category he places squarely the identification of the Hebrew root *ṣdq* with Greek *dikaio-*. Both mean "righteous," but also have distinctive nuances and significations that tended to be lost once the two roots were identified. More tentative is his placement into this category of the consistent representation of *gêr* ("stranger" in the specific sense of a foreign-born permanent resident) by *prosēlytos* ("proselyte," p. 175). Nor should we be surprised by the translation of "Torah" as *nomos* (usually, but perhaps inadequately, translated "law"). Given the rich field of associations occupied by the latter Greek term in the Hellenistic period, it is a perfectly appropriate, one might even say natural, equivalence for the all-important Hebrew term (Segal 1990).

More promising are examples from the realm of the cult. A clear case is the distinction made, especially in the Greek Pentateuch and Joshua, between a true altar to God, rendered by the term *thysiastērion*, and a pagan or otherwise unworthy altar, represented by the newly-coined word *bōmos*. Since the Hebrew, consistently using the term *mzbḥ*, makes no such distinction, why would Alexandrian translators feel compelled to do so? In the perceptive analysis of Daniel (1966: chapter 1 and "Conclusion"), those responsible for the Pentateuch felt the need to clarify the nature of the altar in a few key passages: especially, the Golden Calf incident (no blame is to be attached to Aaron) and the brief career of Balaam (who is viewed as an enemy of God). Such a distinction was then carried out in other contexts where "true" and "false" altars appeared in proximity to each other. A similar distinction can be located in the varying Greek renderings of "true" vs. "false" prophets (*prophētēs* vs. *pseudoprophētēs*, esp. in Jeremiah).

Parallel developments occur in the Targums, although not every passage is interpreted in the same way in the two traditions (see Churgin 1933). Even if the depth of theological reflection appears somewhat shallow in such examples, they reflect a rather profound concern on the part of the translators for the sensibilities of their intended audience.

ANTI-ANTHROPOMORPHISM AND -PATHISM?

Since at least as early as Frankel (1851), a similar sensitivity to their audiences' sensibilities has been imputed to a number of Septuagint translators with respect to their handling of anthropomorphic and anthropopathic descriptions of God in the Hebrew text: they are said to have avoided literal renderings of these phrases. Such practices, if documented, would indeed exhibit a sharp distinction between *Vorlage* and translation regarding the appropriate language to apply to the divine.

When subjected to the withering criticism of Orlinsky, this seemingly valuable category of evidence melts away (Orlinsky 1944, 1956, 1959, 1961). Orlinsky's points, based on careful methodological considerations, are sound:

researchers expended all of their efforts on places where they located alleged "anti-s," without dealing effectively with the often equal number of passages where similar phenomena passed relatively unchanged into the Greek text. Scholars of this sort

> began with the assumption that the LXX translator had a "scrupulous aversion to describing God in human terms" and when [they were] confronted by the plain facts of the Greek translation, [they] proceeded to create, ad hoc, psychological, literary, and theological concepts and motivations for the translator — when [they] should simply have given up the gratuitous assumption altogether as a working hypothesis that failed to work. (1959: 156-57)

What they should have been concentrating on, in Orlinsky's opinion, represents "nothing more tendentious than mere stylism" (1944: 157). Subsequent specialists have by and large confirmed Orlinsky's point of view, without, alas, being able to match his vigorous presentation (so, e.g., Soffer 1957).

"MESSIANIZING" IN THE LXX?

Similar in many ways to the quest (described just above) for exegetically significant renderings of specific terms or phrases is the broader search for concepts or themes. Whether restricted to a given book, or as far-ranging as the entire corpus of the Septuagint, such an approach opens the possibility of there being overarching concerns that may well be reflected, consciously or otherwise, by one or more Greek translators. Typically, the focus is on concepts such as Messiah(s) and life-after-death, themes that become important in Judaism and in Christianity, but are either absent from or peripheral in the Hebrew Bible.

This sort of analysis is especially tricky, since there is a tendency to read back into the earliest Greek texts understandings that arose only at a later date (see Lust 1985: 179-80). Researchers must, of course, be vigilant against equating the interests of later readers with the intentions of original translators, but it is an easy trap into which to fall. Careful study of literature contemporary with, say, the Greek Psalter or the Greek prophets is essential, although the determination of what is "contemporary with" is notoriously difficult.

Here, as much as in any other area, we must be willing to eschew the label "negative," when we find that a given concept is not in the Septuagint (or a particular section of it). In many ways, such a conclusion, or the more tentative "we just don't know for sure," is just as "positive" as the argument that the concept *is* in the Septuagint.

Perhaps the best way to illustrate the possibilities as well as the limitations of this approach is to summarize the work of the Belgian scholar Lust, who has been working for over two decades on various aspects of "Messianism and Septuagint" (the title of his 1983 Congress article, which appeared in 1985; for a different approach, see Schaper 1995). His 1983 article (1985) is especially valuable for the methodological considerations it contains. It is not by chance that many of his caveats parallel those issued by Orlinsky (as mentioned above):

> When trying to defend the thesis of the "messianizing" character of the LXX, one should avoid arbitrary selections of proof texts. One should not overlook the many passages in the Greek version where a "messianizing" translation might have been expected but where it is not given. Indeed, many Hebrew texts receiving a messianic interpretation in the Targumim are translated literally by the LXX without any added messianic exegesis. Neither should one overlook those texts in which the messianic connotation has been weakened or given a different nuance by the LXX (Lust 1985: 175).

Questionable decisions in the areas of textual and literary criticism, of both the LXX and the MT, also lead scholars astray, especially when these decisions provide such scholars with just the text they need to make their point (Lust 1985: 179-80).

Lust's detailed analysis of Ezek. 21:30-32 is typical of his approach to Septuagint passages that have been adduced to demonstrate an enhanced interest in the Messiah among its translators. Both the MT and the LXX are subjected to exhaustive investigation. In the process, the historical circumstances of both texts are explicated, especially the Septuagint's. So it is that Lust connects the Old Greek rendering of these Ezekelian verses to events and personalities of the Maccabean period:

> According to the LXX version, the oracle reacts against the unification of the royal and the priestly functions. It condemns the high priest who prefers the royal powers over the priestly ones and announces the coming of a new high priest who will be worthy of the priestly turban. One could call this a priestly messianic expectation as opposed to a royal Davidic messianic expectation. (Lust 1985: 190)

In this case, then, the context favors a messianic interpretation, but one which must be carefully explicated against its textual, literary, and historical context.

Lust's general comments prepare us for other instances, when equally careful analysis of another so-called "Messianic" passage in the LXX leads to a rather different conclusion. This is precisely the case with respect to the oracles of Balaam contained in Numbers 24: "There is hardly any reason to state that the LXX version is more messianic than the MT. The term *anthrōpos* ("man") does not have direct messianic connotations" (1995: 251). A similar circumstance occurs in connection with the oracle found in Ezek. 17:22-24. Here, in Lust's judgment (p. 250), "the OG is [even] less open to an individual messianic interpretation than MT." Moreover, the Greek phrase most susceptible to just such an interpretation ("And I shall hang him [on a lofty mountain]"), although found in the majority of LXX manuscripts, is "probably due to a Christian reworking of the text" (1997: 250).

SEXUAL POLITICS AND (IN?) THE SEPTUAGINT

Sexual politics. Is there any other expression that sounds more current or, according to one's predilections, more faddish? Yet, there are two ways in which this very modern-sounding expression may be relevant for the study of the Septuagint. On the one hand, it may provide an ideological prism through which we of today can judge attitudes and practices of antiquity. On the other, it may be viewed as another exegetical category for translators responsible for the LXX text. As in the case of biblical studies in general, these two perspectives may be complementary, but that is not necessarily the case.

A strong ideological bias informs De Young's analysis of the Septuagint's treatment of homosexuality (1991). Condemning the appeal to Scripture "to justify homosexual behavior," he likewise criticizes those who would in any manner use the LXX to further such a position. (p. 157). He deals with a small group of passages and terms from throughout the Old Testament. His conclusions regarding both the Hebrew and the Greek are not surprising, given such an orientation:

> The LXX translators seem to have exercised deliberation and concern to reproduce appropriately the impact of the Hebrew to their contemporaries centuries after the Hebrew was written. While they use terms more explicit and contemporary than the Hebrew, they have not distorted or contradicted the meaning of the Hebrew, for a homosexual idea was there already. (1991: 177)

Without entering into a debate with De Young, it is telling that his foot-
notes reveal no knowledge of, or at least no interaction with, Septuagintal
scholars or scholarship beyond Jellicoe's introduction (1968). Whether or not
this substantial lacuna invalidates his conclusions, it does expose De Young's
work to the valid criticism that he has not dealt individually or in sufficient
depth with the literary, textual, ideological, and historical contexts of each
Septuagint passage he purports to cover.

In "The Denial of Female Sexuality in the LXX of Genesis," Brayford exhibits considerably more sophistication with respect both to the Septuagint
and to its modern study. Her essay, which centers on a single verse (Gen.
18:12), may also substantiate the validity of an approach that focuses maximal
attention on a minimal number of words. The data obtainable through such
multi-leveled analysis often far exceed the seemingly grander results of more
far-ranging, but inevitably more superficial, examinations.

As Brayford correctly observes, the Septuagint translator of Genesis
presents "a reflection of his theological presuppositions as well as his cultural
ideologies and values." His LXX translation "was not a passive, mechanical
process. . . . Rather, it was an active ideological one of articulating the values
that defined the Alexandrian diaspora Jews" (Brayford 1998: 4 [all references
are to the manuscript in typescript]).

With reference to women, she pointedly continues:

> The differences between the Hebrew and the Greek texts of Genesis repre-
> sent a reconstruction of the ethnic identity of Hellenistic Jews, a recon-
> struction that, among other things, defined the gender roles appropriate
> for a new time and a different place. The differences in the Greek version
> of the stories of Sarah's laughter and Eve's sentencing represent a denial
> of these women's sexuality, a denial that both reflected contemporary val-
> ues of honor/shame and continued to shape attitudes about proper fe-
> male roles and behavior. . . . Their sexuality continued to be controlled by
> their male guardians, the chief one being the translator himself." (pp. 4-5,
> 12)

Has Brayford gone too far in her characterization of LXX Eve and Sarah
as "tamed and shamed [and 'defamed'; see p. 13] foremothers" (p. 14), the literary precursors for later, equally unflattering portrayals in Judaism and in
Christianity? Perhaps she has. But her "feminist" perspective has succeeded in
opening up a whole new dimension to our perception both of the Septuagint
and of the translators responsible for it.

REVISERS AND TRANSLATORS:
THEODOTION, AQUILA, AND SYMMACHUS

Throughout most of our discussion thus far we have been interchangeably using the terms Septuagint, or LXX, and Old Greek (OG). Since we have been focusing on the original (OG) translation (as best it can be recovered), such terminological elasticity was appropriate. When, however, we move beyond the autograph or first translation of each Greek book (none of which are extant) to later texts, we need greater specification in order to avoid, or at least alleviate, confusion.

In this connection, it is useful to distinguish between a translation and a revision. A translation, naturally enough, begins with the foreign language text (or *Vorlage*) being rendered; on the other hand, a revision starts with an already completed translation in the same language as the revision itself. Under the assumption that an individual or group competent to prepare a revision could also produce a fresh translation, such reliance on an existing version suggests considerable respect, even reverence, for its wording and its exegetical stance.

The author of the *Letter of Aristeas,* referred to earlier, goes to great pains to persuade his intended audience (which goes well beyond the single individual to whom this "letter" is ostensibly addressed) that the Septuagint, that is, the Old Greek translation of the Pentateuch, is of a validity and authority equal to the Hebrew text of the Torah. His insistent tone suggests a plea in the face of some opposition.

It is tempting to suggest that the author of *Aristeas* was aware of competing Greek texts of the Pentateuch or parts of the Pentateuch. These texts were almost certainly revisions of the Old Greek with an eye toward accommodating that Greek more closely to what was developing into the authoritative form of the Hebrew text. Such revisers may have felt, as suggested above, that they were paying considerable homage to their Old Greek by retaining as much as possible of that text. For others, keeping the Old Greek in its entirety was the only option (see Greenspoon 1989, and, more broadly, Brock 1988).

It is relevant to chart the exegetical or interpretative significance of these revisions, primarily those attributed to Theodotion (mid-second century CE) and to Aquila (early second century CE). The text of Theodotion contains an early, first century BCE stratum, which is of primary concern here. While it is apparent that not all of the material attributed to Theodotion represents revision (rather than fresh translation), it is beyond doubt that much of it does.

The vast majority of the wording and of the ideology or theology of the Old Greek is retained by these early revisers. Nevertheless, there are places where Old Greek distinctions are abandoned in favor of practices found in the Hebrew. An excellent example of this process is the consistent use by Theodotion and Aquila of *thysiastērion* for "altar" in the face of the Old Greek's lexical variation, which depended on whether the structure was seen as valid or not. But the total of such changes from the Old Greek does not add up to a visibly new, or counter, theology on the part of these revisers. Thus, attempts by Barthélemy (1963) to link each of these revisers with a particular "school" of early rabbinic interpretation foundered when confronted with the lack of such linkage (as well as with the difficulty of determining the historical value of later characterizations of first century CE figures).

This is not, however, to say that the revisions of Theodotion and Aquila, along with the fresh translation attributed to Symmachus (mid-third century CE), are solely motivated by stylistic concerns, although these may predominate. We examine this proposition first with respect to a single word, albeit a fairly important word: "slave." The Hebrew term for "slave," *'bd*, in its basic biblical meaning refers to someone "who is in a subservient relationship to another. This relationship is not necessarily one of ownership *per se*, but may be one of social superiority/inferiority, of relationship to a king, or of relationship to a god" (Wright 1997: 264).

This "monolithic language" (Wright 1997: 272) mirrors the comparatively peripheral role any sort of slavery played in ancient Israel in comparison with the Hellenistic period. The Greek language of this latter era was correspondingly far richer in "slave" vocabulary, and it is certain that LXX translators were aware of both the lexically-changed and culturally-transformed society for which and in which they operated. Surveying all the Jewish authors (not just LXX translators) of the period, Wright (p. 276) concludes: "The evidence . . . warrants the general conclusion that Jewish writers in the Second Temple period are using words for slaves as they know them to be used in their contemporary socio-cultural environment."

If this is true, to a greater or lesser extent, for the translators of the Old Greek, it seems foreign to the (lexical? conceptual?) world of the revisers, for whom *doulos* alone sufficed in almost every occurrence. Although it is tempting to say that this is just another example of their obliterating an Old Greek distinction not warranted by the Hebrew, we might still query as to their reason(s) for this consistent lexical equivalence.

On the larger scale, the versions attributed to Theodotion, Aquila, and Symmachus exhibit sufficiently distinctive features that even a cursory reader will not be likely to confuse one for the other over any extended stretch of text. In his characterization of Aquila's text and its relevance to exegesis, Tov writes:

A translation like Aquila's, for example, reflects mainly linguistic exegesis, since Aquila was interested only in the linguistic identification of the Hebrew words, and did not introduce any exegetical elements in his translation. This tendency is visible in his choice of equivalents which was stereotyped throughout the translation, irrespective of the context. (Tov 1988: 173)

I would nuance the "global" nature of several of Tov's statements; for example, that Aquila did not introduce *any* exegetical elements or that his choice of equivalents was stereotyped *throughout*. Aquila was a bit more complex than most scholars have recognized. Is there no "exegetical element" in his typical stance to the Hebrew text? Is his willingness to sacrifice Greek syntax and grammar to the Hebrew not itself an interpretative stance; namely, that the closer one can bring one's readers to the Hebrew language and to its thoughts, the better?

Symmachus's fresh translation, on the other hand, reads remarkably well as an original Greek composition. Although we have no reason to think that Symmachus wanted his audience to forget the fact that his work was a translation, he does little if anything to call attention to it. This stance, which has its parallels in the many modern-speech translations of the 20th century and its linguistic underpinnings in concepts like functional equivalence, is certainly no more bereft of exegetical considerations than is Aquila's.

In my view, Theodotion stands somewhere in the vast middle on a continuum that can be constructed between Aquila and Symmachus. His version reads far better as Greek than does Aquila's and is far more visibly dependent on the Hebrew than is Symmachus's. As he struggled to accommodate *his* Old Greek (which was not, however, equivalent with *the* Old Greek) version to the then-regnant Hebrew text, Theodotion (or better proto-Theodotion) often retained more of the Greek than he needed to. His loyalties, exegetical as well as stylistic, were divided; compromise was necessary. I judge Theodotion to have been remarkably successful in devising a version that was true to the meaning of the Hebrew, the spirit of the older Greek, and the needs of the Hellenistic Jews for whom he wrote. (For further details and bibliography, see Greenspoon 1992c.)

THE SEPTUAGINT AND THE NEW TESTAMENT

There has been, and continues to be, considerable debate about the linguistic make-up of Palestine in the first centuries BCE and CE. The influence of Aramaic as *lingua franca* was still pervasive, although it no longer served as the preferred means of communication between ruler and ruled, as it once had. Greek had supplanted Aramaic in this regard, although it is difficult to determine how widely Greek was spoken among the Jews of Palestine themselves (see Lieberman 1942, and also Mussies 1992). On the evidence of the Septuagint as well as inscriptions and papyri, it is clear that Greek predominated for Diaspora Jews, at least for those resident in Alexandria, in both intra- as well as extra-communal communication. It was once commonly believed that Hebrew had, for all intents and purposes, ceased by this time to serve as a medium for oral communication, although there might well still have been some expectation that Jews, at least the learned among them, could make their way through the Torah in Hebrew. The discovery at Qumran of so-called sectarian documents in Hebrew has reopened the question of Hebrew's longevity as an everyday language, at least among some groups (see the discussion in Sáenz-Badillos 1993: 112-60).

Those Jews who became active in the founding of what became the Christian religion presumably came from all strata of Jewish society and shared with their coreligionists a number of bi-, tri-, or even multi-lingual arrangements. However, no matter what language they had been reared in or spoke, they all tended to write in Greek (Mussies 1992). For that reason, if for no other, it would not be surprising if their verbal references (quotations? citations? some combination? something else?) to what we call the Old Testament or Hebrew Bible often reflect some knowledge of the OG or Septuagint and its revisers. Indeed, that is the case.

The situation is complicated, however, by a number of factors: (1) Are we to suppose that New Testament writers had access to a copy of the Septuagint or to some already-prepared excerpted lists from the Septuagint, either or both of which they copied scrupulously? (2) Can we imagine that New Testament writers felt at liberty to modify an existing Greek text in order to accommodate it to the literary or theological context of a gospel, epistle, etc.? (3) Is it not likely that on occasion New Testament writers cited a biblical passage from memory?

This leads to another series of queries: (1) Were New Testament writers likely to have access to the Old Greek (no longer extant for us), or is it not more likely that they would be dealing with copies or revisions of the Old Greek? (2) Is it necessary to posit that a given writer used the same approach to the Old Testament throughout his work, even if we think he essentially copied an existent text? (3) Does it follow that the existent text must have been in Greek? What about Hebrew or Aramaic?

Finally, at least one question should be raised about the transmission of

New Testament texts: Could (m)any of the Scriptural citations in the New Testament have been revised or "improved" by copyists intent upon smoothing out perceived inconsistencies between the Testaments and/or among the books of what became the New Testament?

All of these questions, with a variety of answers, have been discussed for so long and by so many different scholars that it might be imagined that there is nothing new to be said. Nothing is further from the truth! Productive discussion, such as is going on in some quarters already, must take into account the following:

1. New developments abound in Septuagint studies, especially with respect to revisions like (proto-)Theodotion, that are certainly pre-Christian, and to early strata of even later recensions, such as that associated with the Antiochene martyr Lucian, continue to emerge. Furthermore, the number of known revisers could easily be overwhelmed by others of whom we know little or nothing. Such a line of inquiry might limit the amount of creativity we attribute to New Testament writers, when, for example, we find a version of an "Old Testament" passage that is apparently not attested elsewhere.

2. The discovery and analysis of the Dead Sea Scrolls are in this case, as in so many others, a cause for rejoicing — and for much reconsideration. Since a number of the scrolls exhibit Hebrew texts at varying degrees of proximity to the *Vorlage* of the Septuagint (where it differs with the MT), many reputed NT-LXX links need to be reexamined, for it is no longer necessary to posit such a link where the New Testament writer might just as well have consulted a Hebrew and not a Greek text (see especially Lim 1997). Moreover, a limited number of Greek-language manuscripts from Qumran exhibit some hitherto unknown developments within the transmission history of the Septuagint.

3. The cumulative effect of these perspectives is difficult to gauge, since in reality we are adding whole new sets of unknowns or barely-knowns to a situation already fraught with possibilities. The end result, however, should be greater precision in our ability to chart the influence of the Septuagint and its revisers on the foundational documents of the emerging Christian Church.

4. The success of all such endeavors depends upon the willingness of scholars to cross what have become tight disciplinary boundaries, in a way that used to be quite common. For example, it was once routine for the New Testament to be considered in the context of Septuagint introductions. Although that remains true in Europe, it is less so in North

America and elsewhere. Regarding the Dead Sea Scrolls, their continued timely publication is making the relevant material available to all interested scholars. It is now up to them to make productive use of the Scrolls.

5. Perhaps it is not inappropriate to add the term "and creative" to the expression "productive use" above. Just as we like on occasion to vary our style, our method, our perspective, so it is appropriate to see ancient individuals — scribes, translators, transmitters, authors, et al. — in the same light. We should limit neither Paul nor the Gospel writers in regard to their access to the Old Testament. The Septuagint is bound to figure in whatever reconstruction we come up with; thus, its legacy for Christianity and Christians should never be in doubt (among the resources interested readers should consult on the myriad of issues raised above are Barr 1994, Barrett 1970, Carson and Williamson [eds.] 1988, Ellis 1991, and Hanson 1980).

THE JEWS AND THE SEPTUAGINT

Is it not true, on the other hand, that adoption (cooption) by early Christians of the Septuagint led to its abandonment by Jews? Although this is a prevailing supposition, it does not appear to be the case.

First of all, its continual revision by Jews — Aquila, (historical) Theodotion, and possibly Symmachus — is, as argued above, not equivalent to abandonment. One of the primary loyalties of a reviser is to the existent text in his own language, in this case an older Greek (if not, *the* Old Greek). Second, as unearthed by De Lange (1996), Greek-speaking Jewish communities continued for many centuries to read the "Hebrew" Bible in their native language, Greek (in addition to? instead of? in Hebrew). De Lange has been able to trace continuing developments in that Greek text, which has Aquila as its basis.

It is then certainly fair to characterize Jewish attitudes toward the Septuagint as different from those adopted by Christians, but we should not imagine its total abandonment as a living, evolving representation of sacred writings.

CONCLUDING REMARKS

Having viewed a wide array of evidence, I largely concur with the cautionary remarks of Tov, who has expended much time and effort on serious consideration of the Septuagint:

> The LXX translation reflects merely some *theologoumena* in a few freely
> translated books as well as several theologically motivated individual ren-
> derings, both the ones that occur occasionally and ones that occur often
> in the LXX. Therefore, to speak of a "theology of Septuaginta" . . . may be
> not only an overstatement but also an ideal that can never be reached un-
> less one defines the term "theology" very loosely. (Tov 1990: 251)

Even if the number of such renderings is relatively small, however, their value
for understanding and appreciating the world and worldview of individual
LXX translators should not be diminished.

What is true specifically for theological exegesis is true also for other
sorts of interpretation, for it is even less likely that a translator in antiquity
would have compartmentalized his environment than it is that today's translators would do so. Tov wisely cautions against the tendency to make too
much of such interpretative elements; being a maximalist at heart, I would
urge researchers to make as much of them as they possibly can — responsibly,
but also creatively.

Imagine a translation of the Bible produced by a number of people over
an extended period of time, with apparently no fixed guidelines beyond the
general principle to reproduce in their language what, to the best of their
knowledge, the Hebrew text says. And, since they are in the very first group of
Bible translators, they lack not only guidelines, but precedents.

This, as I see it, was the situation that confronted those responsible for
the Septuagint or ancient Greek translation of the Hebrew Bible. Lacking either declarations by the translators themselves or statements by contemporaries, we are of necessity forced to look at the Greek text itself for most of our
answers.

On the basis of that text, it is clear that these early Greek translators understood their task in rather varied ways (which is in itself eminently understandable). For some translators, a word-for-word version, even bending
Greek grammar to reflect Hebrew word order, was deemed the most appropriate approach to the sacred Hebrew. Interpretive elements on the part of
such translators would have been rare.

At the other end, as we have seen, are translators for whom the meaning
of the Hebrew is expressible only by radical changes in its wording. This characteristically took the form of updating geographical or cultural terms and
the like. But it could also lead to a re-working of older prophecies and predictions so as to show their fulfillment in the very days of the translator and his
audience.

In between, translators adopted and adapted an array of strategies to render the Hebrew text comprehensible and relevant for their communities. All of these translators, we assert, saw themselves as embarking on the same sacred mission: the text they worked with was holy and the text they produced would be their generation's "Bible." Since Hebrew and Greek are very different languages, the translators naturally struggled, whether or not they consciously introduced elements of interpretation.

Septuagint scholars often labor valiantly to distinguish between interpretations introduced by the translators and those differences (vis-à-vis the received Hebrew text) that they would have found in their Hebrew *Vorlage*. When we think of the Septuagint as a process, such distinctions are vital. For our present purposes, we are more inclined to think of the Septuagint as a finished product, such that the "sources" of interpretive elements are less important than their presence.

Among some Jews of the last two pre-Christian centuries, the Septuagint, however diverse its origins, was considered of equal sanctity with the Hebrew "original." Other Jews, however, saw the Septuagint, whether as process or as finished product, as provisional, standing in need of correction on the basis of the Hebrew and perhaps also other factors. This led to a series of revisions of the Septuagint, beginning in pre-Christian times and perhaps continuing until just a few centuries ago. The general direction of such revisions was toward a more literal reflection of the Hebrew. As a result, overtly interpretative elements, in the form of additional deletions, or lexical choices, became less frequent. It would not, however, be correct to see such movement as free from theological or ideological biases. After all, the decision to remain as close as possible to a Hebrew judged original is an ideological move, just as is the retention of distinctive "Old Testament" beliefs and language — something frequently found throughout the Greek translation.

Finally, we can look at the Septuagint as it was used, re-used, interpreted, and re-interpreted in later Jewish, and then in Christian communities, especially the latter. Since the formative document of early Christianity is the Greek New Testament, it is not surprising that many of the numerous citations of the Old Testament contained within it have distinctive agreements with the Septuagint. But this is not a simple matter, inasmuch as the Old Testament is cited and quoted in many different forms by different, and sometimes by the same, New Testament writers. In revised form, the Septuagint played a central role for Greek-speaking Jews, but their impact on Judaism was hardly as crucial as was that of early Greek-speaking Christians on the history of their new religion.

When all is said and done, the Septuagint is important in and of itself — as the earliest translation of the Bible and as the repository of a substantial body of Hellenistic Jewish interpretation — and as the first in a still-growing and still dynamic process of Bible translation and interpretation. We are cautioned against making too much of interpretive elements, theological and otherwise, in the Septuagint. We should likewise be aware of the danger of undervaluing the rich and unique evidence bequeathed to us by the first translators of the Bible.

BIBLIOGRAPHY

Barr, J.
1994   "Paul and the LXX: A Note on Some Recent Work." *JTS* 45:593-601.

Barrett, C. K.
1970   "The Interpretation of the Old Testament in the New." In P. R. Ackroyd, ed., *The Cambridge History of the Bible* I, 377-411. Cambridge: Cambridge University Press.

Barthélemy, D.
1963   *Les devanciers d'Aquila.* VTS 10. Leiden: Brill.
1965   "L'Ancien Testament a mûri à Alexandrie." *TZ* 21:358-70.

Brayford, S.
1998   "The Denial of Female Sexuality in the LXX of Genesis" (unpublished paper).

Brock, S. P.
1988   "Translating the Old Testament." In Carson and Williamson (eds.) 1988: 87-98.

Brooke, G. J., and B. Lindars, eds.
1992   *Septuagint, Scrolls and Cognate Writings: Papers Presented to the International Symposium on the Septuagint and Its Relations to the Dead Sea Scrolls and Other Writings (Manchester 1990).* SCS 33. Atlanta: Scholars.

Bruce, F. F.
1972   "The Earliest Old Testament Interpretation." *OTS* 17:37-52.
1979   "Prophetic Interpretation in the Septuagint." *BIOSCS* 12:17-26.

Büchner, D.
1987   "On the Relationship between Mekhilta de Rabbi Ishmael and Septuagint Exodus 12–23." In Cox (ed.) 1987: 403-20.

Carson, D. A., and H. G. M. Williamson, eds.
1988   *It Is Written: Scripture Citing Scripture, Essays in Honour of Barnabas Lindars, SSF.* Cambridge: Cambridge University Press.

Churgin, P.
1933   "The Targum and the Septuagint." *JBL* 50:41-65.

Cimosa, M.

1997   "Observations on the Greek Translation of the Book of Zechariah." In Taylor (ed.) 1997: 91-108.

Cook, J. E.

1987   "The Exegesis of the Greek Genesis." In Cox (ed.) 1987: 91-125.

1997   *The Septuagint of Proverbs — Jewish and/or Hellenistic Proverbs? Concerning the Hellenistic Colouring of LXX Proverbs.* VTS 69. Leiden: Brill.

Cox, C. E.

1987   "Methodological Issues in the Exegesis of LXX Job." In Cox (ed.) 1987: 79-89.

Cox, C. E., ed.

1987   *VI Congress of the International Organization for Septuagint and Cognate Studies (Jerusalem 1986).* SCS 23. Atlanta: Scholars.

1991   *VII Congress of the International Organization for Septuagint and Cognate Studies (Leuven 1989).* SCS 31. Atlanta: Scholars.

Daniel, S.

1966   *Recherches sur le vocabulaire du culte dans la Septante.* Études et Commentaires 61. Paris: Librairie C. Klincksieck.

De Lange, N.

1996   *Greek Jewish Texts from the Cairo Genizah.* Tübingen: Mohr (Siebeck).

De Young, J. B.

1991   "The Contributions of the Septuagint to Biblical Sanctions against Homosexuality." *JETS* 34:157-77.

Dines, J. J.

1992   "The Septuagint of Amos: A Study in Interpretation" (Ph.D. dissertation, University of London).

Dodd, C. H.

1935   *The Bible and the Greeks.* London: Hodder and Stoughton.

Dogniez, C.

1995   *Bibliography of the Septuagint/Bibliographie de la Septante (1970-1993).* VTS 60. Leiden: Brill.

Ellis, E. E.

1991   *The Old Testament in Early Christianity: Canon and Interpretation in the Light of Modern Research.* WUNT 54. Tübingen: Mohr (Siebeck).

Fernández Marcos, F.

1979   *Introducción a las versiones griegas de la Biblia.* Textos y estudios "Cardenal Cisneros" 23. Madrid: CSIC.

Frankel, Z.

1851   *Ueber der Einfluss der palästinischen Exegese auf die alexandrinische Hermeneutik.*

Leipzig: Verlag von Joh. Ambr. Barth. Reprint. Farnborough: Gregg International, 1972.

Fraser, P. M.

1984   *Ptolemaic Alexandria*. 2d ed. 3 vols. Oxford: Clarendon Press.

Freund, R. A.

1990   "From Kings to Archons: Jewish Political Ethics and Kingship Passages in the LXX." *JSOT* 2:58-72.

Gard, D. H.

1954   "The Concept of the Future Life according to the Greek Translator of the Book of Job." *JBL* 73:137-43.

Greenspoon, L.

1987   "The Use and Abuse of the Term 'LXX' and Related Terminology in Recent Scholarship." *BIOSCS* 20:21-29.

1989   "Mission to Alexandria: Truth and Legend About the Creation of the First Bible Translation." *BR* 4:34-41.

1992a   "Aquila's Version." In *ABD*, I, 320-21.

1992b   "Symmachus' Version." In *ABD*, VI, 251.

1992c   "Theodotion's Version." In *ABD*, VI, 447-48.

1992d   "Versions, Ancient (Greek)." In *ABD*, VI, 793-94.

Hanson, A. T.

1980   *The New Testament Interpretation of Scripture*. London: SPCK.

1992   "The Treatment in the LXX of the Theme of Seeing God." In Brooke and Lindars (eds.) 1992: 557-68.

Harl, M., G. Dorival, and O. Munnich

1994   *La Bible grecque des Septante. Du Judaïsme hellénistique au Christianisme ancien. Initiations au Christianisme ancien.* 2d ed. Paris: Édition du Cerf.

Hengel, M.

1974   *Judaism and Hellenism.* Translated by John Bowden. 2 vols. Philadelphia: Fortress.

Jellicoe, S.

1968   *The Septuagint and Modern Study.* Oxford: Oxford University Press.

Koenig, J.

1982   *L'herméneutique analogique du judaïsme antique d'après les témoins textuels d'Isaïe.* VTS 33. Leiden: Brill.

Kraft, R. A.

1978   "Christian Transmission of Greek Jewish Scriptures." In *Paganisme, Judaïsme, Christianisme. Mélanges offertes à Marcel Simon*, 207-26. Paris: Éditions E. De Boccard.

Lieberman, S.

1942   *Greek in Jewish Palestine.* Reprint. New York: The Jewish Theological Seminary of America, 1994.

1950   *Hellenism in Jewish Palestine.* Reprint. New York: The Jewish Theological Seminary of America, 1994.

Lim, T. H.

1997   *Holy Scripture in the Qumran Commentaries and Pauline Letters.* Oxford: Oxford University Press.

Lindars, B.

1987   "A Commentary on the Greek Judges?" In C. Cox (ed.) 1987: 167-200.

Lust, J.

1985   "Messianism and Septuagint." In J. A. Emerton, ed., *Congress Volume (Salamanca 1983),* 174-91. VTS 36. Leiden: Brill.

1987   "Exegesis and Theology in the Septuagint of Ezekiel: The Longer 'Pluses' and Ezek 43:1-9." In Cox (ed.) 1987: 201-32.

1991   "Messianism and the Greek Version of Jeremiah." In Cox (ed.) 1991: 87-122.

1995   "The Greek Version of Balaam's Third and Fourth Oracles." In L. Greenspoon and O. Munnich, eds., *VIII Congress of the International Organization for Septuagint and Cognate Studies (Paris 1992),* 233-57. SCS 41. Atlanta: Scholars.

1997   "And I Shall Hang Him on a Lofty Mountain." In Taylor (ed.) 1997: 231-50.

Mussies, G.

1992   "Languages (Greek)." In *ABD,* IV, 195-203.

Oloffson, S.

1990   *The LXX Version: A Guide to the Translation Technique of the Septuagint.* ConBOT 30. Stockholm: Almqvist & Wiksell.

Orlinsky, H. M.

1944   "Review of the Anti-Anthropomorphisms of the Greek Pentateuch." *Crozier Quarterly* 21:156-60.

1956   "The Treatment of Anthropomorphisms and Anthropopathisms in the Septuagint of Isaiah." *HUCA* 27:193-200.

1959   "Studies in the Septuagint of the Book of Job. Chapter III: On the Matter of Anthropomorphisms, Anthropopathisms, and Euphemisms." *HUCA* 30:153-67.

1961   "Studies in the Septuagint of the Book of Job. Chapter III (Continued)." *HUCA* 32:239-68.

1975   "The Septuagint as Holy Writ and the Philosophy of the Translators." *HUCA* 46:89-114.

Pace, S.

1984   "The Stratigraphy of the Text of Daniel and the Question of Theological Tendenz in the Old Greek." *BIOSCS* 17:15-35.

Porter, S. E., and B. W. R. Pearson
1998   "Isaiah through Greek Eyes: The Septuagint of Isaiah." In *Writing and Reading the Scroll of Isaiah* II, 531-46. VTS 70. Leiden: Brill.

Prijs, L.
1948   *Jüdische Tradition in der Septuaginta.* Leiden: Brill.

Sabugal, S.
1979   "La interpretacion septuagintista del Antiguo Testamento." *Aug* 19:341-57.

Sáenz-Badillos, A.
1993   *A History of the Hebrew Language.* Translated by John Elwolde. Cambridge: Cambridge University Press.

Schaper, J.
1995   *Eschatology in the Greek Psalter.* WUNT 2.76. Tübingen: Mohr (Siebeck).

Seeligmann, I. L.
1948   *The Septuagint Version of Isaiah: A Discussion of Its Problems.* MV 9. Leiden: Brill.

Segal, A. F.
1990   "Torah and Nomos in Recent Scholarly Discussion." In *The Other Judaisms of the Late Antiquity,* 131-45. Brown Judaic Studies 127. Atlanta: Scholars.

Shutt, R. J. H.
1985   "Letter of Aristeas, a New Translation and Introduction." In *OTP* II, 7-34.

Smith, D. M.
1988   "The Pauline Literature." In Carson and Williamson (eds.) 1988: 265-91.

Soffer, A.
1957   "The Treatment of Anthropomorphisms and Anthropopathisms in the Septuagint of Psalms." *HUCA* 28:85-107.

Stanton, G.
1988   "Matthew." In Carson and Williamson (eds.) 1988: 205-19.

Taylor, B. A., ed.
1997   *IX Congress of the International Organization for Septuagint and Cognate Studies (Cambridge 1995).* SCS 45. Atlanta: Scholars.

Tov, E.
1978   "Midrash-Type Exegesis in the LXX of Joshua." *RB* 85:50-61.
1981   *Text-Critical Use of the Septuagint in Biblical Research.* Jerusalem: Simor.
1984   "The Rabbinic Tradition concerning the "Alterations" Inserted into the Greek Pentateuch and Their Relation to the Original Text of the LXX." *JSJ* 15:65-89.
1987a   "Die griechischen Bibelübersetzungen." In W. Haase, ed., *ANRW* II.20, 121-89. Berlin: de Gruyter.
1987b   "The Nature and Study of the Translation Technique of the LXX in the Past and Present." In Cox (ed.) 1987: 337-59.

1987c   "Die Septuaginta in ihrem theologischen und traditionsgeschichtlichen Verhältnis zur hebräischen Bibel." In M. Klopfenstein, et al., eds., *Mitte der Schrift?* 237-68. Bern: Lang.

1988   "The Septuagint." In M. J. Mulder, ed., *Mikra*, 161-88. Philadelphia: Fortress.

1990   "Theologically Motivated Exegesis Embedded in the Septuagint." In *Translation of Scripture: Proceedings of a Conference at the Annenberg Research Institute (May 15-16, 1989)*, 215-33. JQRS. Philadelphia: Annenberg Research Institute.

Van der Kooij, A.

1987   "The Old Greek of Isaiah 19:16-25: Translation and Interpretation." In Cox (ed.) 1987: 127-66.

1992   "The Old Greek of Isaiah in Relation to the Qumran Texts of Isaiah: Some General Comments." In Brooke and Lindars (eds.) 1992: 195-213.

Veltri, G.

1994   *Eine Tora für den König Talmai. Untersuchungen zum Übersetzungsverständnis in der jüdisch-hellenistischen und rabbinischen Literatur.* TSAJ 41. Tübingen: Mohr (Siebeck).

Wevers, J. W.

1996   "The Interpretative Character and Significance of the Septuagint Version." In M. Sæbø, ed., *Hebrew Bible/Old Testament: The History of Its Interpretation*, I, 84-107. Göttingen: Vandenhoeck & Ruprecht.

1997   "The LXX Translator of Deuteronomy." In Taylor (ed.) 1997: 57-89.

Wilcox, M.

1988   "Text Form." In Carson and Williamson (eds.) 1988: 193-204.

Wright, B. G.

1997   "Δουλος and Παις as Translations of עבד: Lexical Equivalence and Conceptual Transformations." In Taylor (ed.) 1997: 263-77.

CHAPTER 4

Philo of Alexandria as Exegete

Peder Borgen

Philo as an exegete should be seen against the background of tendencies present in earlier literature preserved from Alexandrian Judaism (Borgen 1992, 1071). Philo continues the approach seen especially in the *Letter of pseudo-Aristeas,* Aristobulus, and the Wisdom of Solomon of interpreting the laws of Moses and Jewish existence by means of Greek ideas and religious traditions. It is particularly important that Aristobulus, in his use of Greek philosophy and quotations and in his method, represents a trend toward Philo's expositions. Like Philo, he stresses the cosmic significance of Judaism, and he shows that Philo's philosophically influenced exegesis was not isolated. According to both, the authentic philosophy was formulated by Moses, and Greek philosophy contained elements of this true philosophy and was in some points derived from the teachings of Moses.

The sharp polemic against polytheistic cults expressed in writings such as *pseudo-Aristeas, Sibylline Oracles* 3, Wisdom, and 3 Maccabees is also found in Philo's interpretations of the laws of Moses. In *pseudo-Aristeas* the one God, the Creator, is contrasted with the idols and idolatry of the Egyptians. *Sibylline Oracles* 3 offers very sharp criticism of Romans and Greeks for their idolatry and adultery. The fragments of Aristobulus also point in the same direction: Orpheus and Aratus had no holy concepts of God since they used polytheistic names of the One God. Harsh criticism is found in Wisdom 13–15, and is a predominant theme of 3 Maccabees. As for Philo, he often levels sharp criticism at polytheistic idolatry, for example, in his exposition of the first of the Ten Commandments (*Dec.* 52-81; *Spec.* 1.12-20). Philo continues the tendency found in the earlier writings to stress the superiority of the Jewish nation, although seen within a cosmic and universal perspective.

Philo also testifies to the continuation of ideological attacks on Jews by non-Jews. Such attacks were already seen in the writings of the Egyptian Manetho. In this connection it should be mentioned that Josephus, *Against Apion,* the anti-Jewish *Acts of the Alexandrian Martyrs,* and Gnostic writings prove that there was a broad stream of anti-Jewish traditions, attitudes, and literature in Egypt. The Jewish polemic against aspects of pagan culture and against some other ethnic groups, such as Egyptians, was at times as pointed. Thus, *Sibylline Oracles* 5, written toward the end of the first century CE, is openly hostile to Gentiles in Egypt and Rome (Collins 1987, 436-38; Hengel 1983; Kasher 1985, 327-45; Kuiper 1986, 595-608; Pearson 1984, 340-41; Tcherikover 1963).

Although Philo has his place in the context of Alexandrian Judaism and its history, it should be remembered that no basic distinction can be drawn between Judaism in the Diaspora and in Palestine. As for Hellenistic influence there is a difference of degree, but not a fundamental gap. The problem of the dating of the rabbinic material makes it difficult to define its relationship to Philo. Nevertheless, points of similarities and differences will be indicated occasionally. In this way the stereotype of an overall contrast between him and the rabbis can be avoided.

PHILO'S EXPOSITORY WRITINGS

Among Philo's writings, his expository treatises are of main interest for a presentation of him as an exegete. They deal primarily with material from the Pentateuch. In addition to Philo's expository works, at times references will be made to the two historical treatises, *Against Flaccus* and *On the Embassy to Gaius* since they give glimpses into problems connected with the interpretation of the laws of Moses in the life of the Alexandrian community.

Philo's expository treatises fall into two main groups: those rewriting the Pentateuch and his exegetical commentaries.

Rewriting the Pentateuch

Philo's works that rewrite the Pentateuch are his expositions of the laws of Moses, *On the Life of Moses,* and *Hypothetica.* The extant writings representing the exegetical works on the laws of Moses are *On the Creation, On Abra-*

ham, On Joseph, On the Decalogue, On the Special Laws, On the Virtues, and *On Rewards and Punishments.* Goodenough named this collection of treatises *The Exposition of the Laws of Moses* (1933, 109-25). *On the Life of Moses* was formerly classed in a group of miscellaneous writings, but Goodenough has shown that these treatises and the *Exposition* were companion works (1933, 109-25; Morris 1987, 854-55). The preserved fragments of the *Hypothetica (Apology for the Jews)* deal with events and laws that cover parts of the Pentateuch from Jacob (Genesis 25) to the conquest of Palestine in the books of Joshua and Judges. In this work the emphasis is placed on a characterization of Judaism in Philo's own time, mainly as a response to criticism leveled against the Jews.

Exegetical Commentaries

Philo's exegetical commentaries include an *Allegorical Commentary on Genesis* and allegorical *Questions and Answers on Genesis and Exodus.* The *Allegorical Commentary on Genesis* consists of the *Allegorical (Interpretation of the) Laws, On the Cherubim, On the Sacrifices of Abel and Cain, The Worse Attacks the Better, On the Posterity and Exile of Cain, On the Giants, On the Unchangeableness of God, On Husbandry, On Noah's Work as a Planter, On Drunkenness, On Sobriety, On the Confusion of Tongues, On the Migration of Abraham, Who is the Heir of Divine Things, On Mating with the Preliminary Studies, On Flight and Finding, On the Change of Names,* and *On Dreams.* This series covers the main parts of Genesis 2–41. In general they have the form of verse-by-verse commentary on the biblical texts.

    Questions and Answers on Genesis and Exodus is a brief commentary in the form of questions and answers on sections of the two first books of the Pentateuch. The extant text of *Questions and Answers on Genesis* begins at Gen. 2:4 and ends at 28:9 (with lacunae), and *Questions and Answers on Exodus* covers parts of Exod. 12:2–28:34 (LXX). All but a small portion of the Greek original has been lost, and for the bulk of the work we must depend on the ancient Armenian version (Hilgert 1991, 1-15).

    In common with the commentaries which have been found among the Dead Sea Scrolls, Philo's *Allegorical Commentary* and *Questions and Answers on Genesis and Exodus* are largely running commentaries that interpret biblical texts largely in sequence, verse-by-verse. Some of the rabbinic *midrashim* also consist of running commentaries on the Pentateuch and other parts of the Hebrew Bible. Dimant's comment on the Dead Sea Scrolls is to the point: ". . . the lemmatic structure and the exegetical techniques used by the

Philo's Writings

The writings of Philo are found in Greek and English in twelve volumes of the Loeb Classical Library series.

I	*De opificio mundi*	On the Creation of the World	Opif.*
	Legum allegoriarum	Allegorical Interpretation of the Laws	Leg. All.†
II	*De cherubim*	On the Cherubim	Cher.†
	De sacrificiis Abelis et Caini	On the Sacrifices of Abel and Cain	Sacr.†
	Quod deterius potiori insidiari soleat	The Worse Attacks the Better	Det.†
	De posteritate Caini	On the Posterity and Exile of Cain	Post.†
	De gigantibus	On the Giants	Gig.†
III	*Quod Deus sit immutabilis*	On the Unchangeableness of God	Immut.†
	De agricultura	On Husbandry	Agr.†
	De plantatione	On Noah's Work as a Planter	Plant.†
	De ebrietate	On Drunkenness	Ebr.†
	De sobrietate	On Sobriety	Sobr.†
IV	*De confusione linguarum*	On the Confusion of Tongues	Conf.†
	De migratione Abrahami	On the Migration of Abraham	Migr.†
	Quis rerum divinarum heres sit	Who Is the Heir?	Heres†
	De congressu quaerendae eruditionis gratia	On Mating, with the Preliminary Studies	Congr.†
V	*De fuga et inventione*	On Flight and Finding	Fug.†
	De mutatione nominum	On the Change of Names	Mut.†
	De somniis	On Dreams	Somn.†
VI	*De Abrahamo*	On Abraham	Abr.*
	De Iosepho	On Joseph	Jos.*
	De vita Mosis	On the Life of Moses	Mos.
VII	*De decalogo*	On the Decalogue	Dec.*
	De specialibus legibus	On the Special Laws	Spec.*
VIII	*De specialibus legibus,* cont.		
	De virtutibus	On the Virtues	Virt.*
	De praemiis et poenis	On Rewards and Punishments	Praem.*
IX	*Quod omnis probus liber sit*	Every Good Man Is Free	Omn.
	De vita contemplativa	On the Contemplative Life	Cont.
	De aeternitate mundi	On the Eternity of the World	Aeter.
	In Flaccum	Against Flaccus	Flacc.
	Apologia pro Iudaeis	Hypothetica	Hypothetica
	De providentia	On Providence	Prov.
X	*De legatione ad Gaium*	On the Embassy to Gaius	Legat.
XI	*Quaestiones et solutiones in Genesin*	Questions and Answers on Genesis	QG
XII	*Quaestiones et solutiones in Exodum*	Questions and Answers on Exodus	QE
	Greek Fragments		

Exposition of the Laws of Moses   †*Allegorical Commentary on Genesis* pesharim link them firmly with other types of lemmatic commentaries, such as the rabbinic midrashim and the commentaries of Philo" (Dimant 1992, 250; cf. Porton 1992, 820).

HERMENEUTICAL PRESUPPOSITIONS
IN PHILO'S EXPOSITORY WRITINGS

Here we will identify some of the hermeneutical presuppositions that guided Philo in his expository enterprise.

God's Laws Proclaimed to the Greek-Speaking World

Some clues to Philo's hermeneutical presuppositions may be found in *Mos.* 2.1-65. Here Philo makes clear that in the Diaspora setting of the Alexandrian Jews the translation of the laws of Moses into Greek was a major revelatory event. The giving of the laws in the Hebrew language at Mount Sinai was for the barbarian half of the human race, while the translation of these laws into Greek on the island Pharos at Alexandria made them known to the Greek half of the world (*Mos.* 2.26-27). This second event took place under Ptolemy Philadelphus, the third in succession to Alexander, the conqueror of Egypt (*Mos.* 2.25-40).

In *Mos.* 2.25-40 Philo gives a summary of the traditional account of the origin of the Greek translation (Swete 1902, 12; cf. Meecham 1932, 121-24): the reason for the translation was not ignorance of Hebrew among Alexandrian Jews but the need for the laws of the Jewish nation, which at the same time were the one God's cosmic and universal laws, to be made known to all nations. In his works, then, Philo continues this *proclamatio Graeca* with the same aim in mind.

The glimpse given by Philo of the Septuagint festival on the island of Pharos shows that there was a large number of non-Jews in Alexandria who were sympathizers with Judaism and took part in at least one Jewish festival, and by implication probably in several of the activities in the Jewish community. These sympathizers, together with the Alexandrian Jews, celebrated the Greek translation of the laws of Moses. Thus, there is reason for believing that Philo had in mind the kind of people present at these Septuagint festivals when he wrote, and that one important setting for his writings is the borderline between the Jews and the surrounding world, especially non-Jewish sympathizers with Judaism.

The Mosaic Law and the Cosmic Law

Is it possible to find a thought-model or some basic presuppositions that might give a hermeneutical clue to Philo's expositions of the Laws of Moses? In a recent article Amir stresses the following points as premises for Philo's exegesis (1988). To Philo the biblical word has authority. This authority is founded on its character as a collection of oracles. "Moses himself learnt it by an oracle and has taught us how it was" (*Det.* 86). Moses is both receiver and transmitter of the divine teaching. Philo uncritically accepted the Septuagint text before him as identical with the Hebrew Bible. Although Philo on the whole recognizes a dual meaning in Scripture, that is, both a literal and an allegorical meaning, his view is that Moses' deepest concern was his religious-philosophical doctrine, which may be arrived at by allegorical interpretation.

According to Siegert the theological basis for Philo's interpretation of Scripture is his strong accent on the transcendence of God (1996, 168-72). Basically God cannot be spoken of. As "the Being One" God is beyond motion and emotion, beyond evil, and beyond any contact with matter. The two powers "God" *(theos)* and "Lord" *(kyrios)* bridge the gap between God's simultaneous transcendence and immanence. Philo's "eclecticism consists in being *a Platonist about transcendence, and a Stoic about immanence*" (Siegert 1996, 170).

Siegert agrees with Amir that to Philo Moses was the author of the laws. Amir stresses here that Philo's view is alien to the rabbis (1988, 434). Siegert also sees the difference between Philo's understanding and the rabbinic view that God speaks immediately in the Torah. Both Amir and Siegert recognize that according to Philo Moses was in a trance when God spoke through him in first person. To Siegert the Philonic concept of inspiration excluded any intellectual activity on the side of humans. On this basis Siegert maintains that in some contexts Philo's supernaturalism is in no way inferior to that of the rabbis (1996, 171).

Amir mentions in passing that according to Philo Moses also receives from within a share of the divine being. He again stresses the contrast between Philo and the rabbis: "Even the fact that in two passages [Exod. 4:16 and 7:1] the Torah conditionally refers to Moses as 'God' — a fact that the rabbis did their best to explain away — is enthusiastically welcomed by Philo" (1988, 436). Amir here overlooks the rabbinic midrash *Tanchuma* (ed. Buber, IV, 51f.): ". . . he [God] called Moses 'God,' as it is said, 'See, I have made you a god to Pharaoh' (Exod. 7:1)" (Meeks 1967, 193).

These analyses by Amir and Siegert give insights into Philo's ideas about the Pentateuch as an inspired and authoritative text. Some further observations need be made on the relationship between the law and the cosmos, which is a central theme in Philo's works (Wolfson 1947: 2, 189-92; Nikiprowetzky 1977, 117-55). He deals with this theme most fully in *Mos.* 2.45-52. In 2.47b Philo considers why Moses began his law-book *(nomothesia)* with history. Part of his answer is:

> in relating the history of early times, and going for its beginning right to the creation of the universe, he [Moses] wished to shew two most essential things: first that the Father and Maker of the cosmos was in the truest sense also Lawgiver, secondly that he who would observe the laws will accept gladly the duty of following nature and live in accordance with the ordering of the universe, so that his deeds are attuned to harmony with his words and his words with his deeds (2.48).

This harmony is also dealt with in *Mos.* 2.52: ". . . the particular enactments . . . seek to attain to the harmony of the universe. . . ." These particular enactments are the specific laws and regulations in the Mosaic laws. This conclusion is supported by *Abr.* 3, where the patriarchs are understood to be archetypes pointing to particular laws in the treatises *On the Decalogue* and *On the Special Laws.*

From this analysis a hermeneutical key can be formulated: *The particular ordinances of the Jewish Law coincide with the universal cosmic principles. Thus to Philo universal and general principles do not undercut or cancel the specific ordinances or events of the Mosaic law.*

Philo furthermore applies the Stoic idea of the cosmos as a city *(Stoicorum veterum fragmenta* 1.262; Cicero, *De natura deorum* 154) to the biblical story of the creation: Moses "considered that to begin his writings with the foundation of a man-made city was below the dignity of the laws . . . , [and] inserted the story of the genesis of the 'Great City,' holding that the laws were the most faithful picture of the world-polity" (*Mos.* 2.51; cf. *Spec.* 1.13-14; *QE* 2.14; *Opif.* 142-44).

By calling the laws of Moses the most faithful picture of the cosmic *politeia,* Philo makes an exclusive claim for these laws. They are both the picture of and the revelatory means by which one can perceive the cosmic commonwealth and its law and live accordingly. The laws of Moses are "stamped with the seals of nature itself" (*Mos.* 2.14; Nikiprowetzky 1977, 117-55).

Israel is a chosen people that has a universal role, just as its law is modeled on the cosmic law. This understanding is formulated in *QE* 2.42 where Exod. 24:12c ("the law and the commandment which I have written . . .") is interpreted: "rightly does He legislate for this race [the contemplative race, i.e., Israel], also prescribing [its law] as a law for the world, for the chosen race is a

likeness of the world, and its Law [is a likeness of the laws] of the world"
(Nikiprowetzky 1977, 118). In this role the people function as the priesthood
of all humankind and their temple and sacrifices have cosmic significance
(*Abr.* 56, 98; *Mos.* 1.149; *Spec.* 1.66-67, 76, 82-97; 2.163-67; *Fug.* 108-9; *Heres* 84;
Somn. 2.188, 231; cf. Josephus, *Antiquities* 3.179-87; see Laporte 1972, 75-190).

The presupposition of these ideas is the biblical tradition that the God
of Israel is also the Creator and that the books of the Mosaic law begin with
the story of creation. There was a broad Jewish tradition built on this biblical
idea. In Sirach the concept of Wisdom was thought to pervade the cosmos
and to have made her home in Israel, in Jerusalem (Sir. 24:3-12). Sirach identified Wisdom with Torah (24:23).

Also in rabbinic writings creation and the revealed Torah are connected
in such a way that the Torah is the cosmic law: heaven and earth cannot exist
without Torah (b. *Nedarim* 32a), and God consulted the Torah when he created the world (*Gen. Rab.* 1:2). Of special interest is Josephus's statement that
everything in the Mosaic law is set forth in keeping with the nature of the universe (*Ant.* 1.24).

The Deeper Meanings

The hermeneutical insights drawn from these observations are that Philo can
in different ways interpret one and the same biblical text basically on two,
sometimes three, levels, for example, on concrete and specific levels, or on the
level of the cosmic and general principles and on the level of the divine realm
of the beyond (cf. Christiansen 1969, 134).

It should be mentioned that a two-level exegesis is present also in other
Jewish writings, for example, in such a way that both levels may be pictured in
concrete and specific terms. Thus, in the *Jubilees* Noah, Abraham, and others
are said to have observed and enjoined the laws *on earth*, but the laws are the
ones inscribed on *heavenly* tablets, which were later given to Moses (*Jub.* 6:17;
15:1; 16:28, *passim*; cf. *Abr.* 276; Bousset 1926, 125, n. 3, and 126 n. 1; Urbach 1975:
1, 335).

In general support of the understanding of Philo's two-level exegesis
outlined above one might refer to the hermeneutical function of Philo's ascents according to *Spec.* 3.1-6. Philo states that his soul ascended to the heavenly sphere. This and successive more moderate ascents enable him to unfold
and reveal in the laws of Moses their deeper meaning, which is not known to
the multitude (*Spec.* 3.6).

This deeper meaning includes allegory, but is not limited to it, as is evident from Philo's *Exposition of the Laws of Moses* of which *On the Special Laws* 3.1-6 is a part. In this comprehensive work of Philo allegorical interpretations as such are not prominent. The general (ethical) meaning behind the specific commandments and regulations are, however, brought out by Philo.

ASPECTS OF PHILO'S EXEGESIS

Philo moves from one level of meaning to another by proceeding from macrocosm to microcosm, from individuals to the virtues and vices they embody, from specific commandments to their ethical meanings, and by anthropomorphic statements and etymologies.

From Macrocosm to Microcosm

In many cases Philo builds his exegesis on the correspondence between macrocosm and microcosm. For example, seen within a macrocosmic context, for Abraham to become a proselyte (*Abr.* 68-84) meant to migrate from the Chaldean search for God within the created order, in astrology, to the recognition that the world is not sovereign but dependent on its Maker. From a microcosmic point of view, Abraham's migration was an ascent via a microcosmic apprehension of a person's invisible mind as the ruler of the senses (Philo connects the name of Haran with the Greek root *charran*, "hole," i.e., sense organ): "It cannot be that while in yourself there is a mind appointed as a ruler which all the community obeys, the cosmos . . . is without a king who holds it together . . ." *(Abr.* 74). Philo's ideas about macrocosm and microcosm should not be seen as alien to rabbinic tradition, since they are also expressed by rabbis (see Meyer 1937, 39-40, 43-44, 126-27, 148-49). More associative analogies can also be seen. For example, Moses compares passion to a tiger, the animal least capable of being tamed (*Leg. All.* 1.69).

In Pythagorean fashion numbers in the biblical text are often interpreted within a cosmic context as well as in the microcosmic context of humanity. Of special importance is the connection between the number seven and the celebration of the completion of the world, the Sabbath, as outlined in *Opif.* 89-128 and *Leg. All.* 1.8-12. The properties of the number seven are seen in things incorporeal, in external creation as heavenly bodies (the seven planets), in the stages of humanity's growth, in all visible existence, and in grammar and music, and as given as a commandment in the decalogue. On a more limited scale Aristobulus developed a similar interpretation already in the second century BCE. Clement of Alexandria also has arithmological sections in which the number seven is seen in the cosmic realm, as in the planets, and in anthropology (*Strom.* 6.16, 139-45; van den Hoek 1988, 201-205; Heinisch 1908, 105).

Etymologies

Philo makes extensive use of etymologies of names using both the Hebrew and Greek languages. For example, on the basis of Hebrew "Israel" is interpreted to mean "the one who sees God," "Abram" as "uplifted father," and "Abraham" as "elect father of sound" (*Abr.* 82). From Greek etymology the river Pheison is interpreted to mean "sparing" (*Leg. All.* 1.66). Etymologies were widely used in Christian exegesis as well, as by Clement. Some of Clement's Hebrew etymologies occur in contexts in which he draws on Philo (van den Hoek 1988, 222), and Clement uses the same etymological explanations of Abram and Abraham (*Strom.* 5.1.8; Heinisch 1908, 109ff.).

Individuals as Embodiments of Virtues and Vices

In ways other than by etymologies specific persons are seen as embodiments of general virtues and vices or of other properties. A central place in Philo's educational philosophy is the view that Abraham, when he failed at first to have a child by Sarah, that is, by wisdom and philosophy, he took the maid Hagar, general education, in her place. Here Philo follows an allegorical interpretation of Homer's Penelope, as is found in pseudo-Plutarch: those who wear themselves out in general studies and fail to master philosophy are like the suitors who could not win Penelope and contented themselves with her maids. By applying this tradition to Abraham's relation to Hagar, Philo brings it into a Jewish context. The relationship between Judaism (Abraham) and non-Jewish culture (Hagar and general education) is a central matter (Borgen 1984a, 255): properly used, pagan education may in a positive way prepare for the revealed wisdom of the laws of Moses and be a useful help for the Jews.

Specific Commandments and Their Ethical Meaning

In his expositions Philo fuses together the specific commandments and observances and their ethical and philosophical meanings. Thus his intention is

not to instruct his readers in the practical specifics of Jewish life. In his interpretation of the dietary laws he does not ignore observance, but he also takes
them as having deeper ethical meanings. In this he is dependent on exegetical
traditions, as can be seen from the agreements with *pseudo-Aristeas*. For example, both say that the laws concerning clean animals, those with parted
hooves, teach humanity that it must distinguish between virtuous and bad
ways of life (*Spec.* 4.106-9; *pseudo-Aristeas* 150). One clue to such ethical interpretations was the idea that observance made it possible to live an orderly,
harmonious, and healthy life free of gluttony and extravagance. Thus Moses
approved neither of rigorous austerity, like the Spartan legislator, nor of luxu-
rious living, as taught to the Ionians and Sybarites (*Spec.* 4.100-102).

Anthropomorphic Statements

One criterion that may show that the literal understanding is to be discarded
and a deeper meaning is meant is formulated by Philo in this way: ". . . to say
that God uses hands or feet or any created part at all is not the true account"
(*Conf.* 98). Thus Philo is a pointed representative of the broad tendency
among Jews, seen also in the Septuagint, Aristobulus, the Targums, and the
Midrashic commentaries, to remove anthropomorphic statements about
God by reading into them deeper meanings (Maybaum 1870; Lauterbach
1910; Heinemann 1936; Fritsch 1943; Wolfson 1947: I, 56-60; II, 127-28; Borgen
1984a, 278).

Other Textual Details

Other details in the text may indicate that a deeper meaning is intended. One
such criterion is formulated by Philo in *On Flight and Finding:* Moses "never
puts in a superfluous word." Thus since the phrase "let him die the death"
(Exod. 21:12) refers redundantly to death, it actually refers to two deaths: bad
people are spiritually dead already while living (*Fug.* 54-55).

The Deeper and Literal Meanings

Although Philo in exceptional cases discards the literal meaning (e.g., *Det.* 95,
167) his basic principle and attitude are that the deeper meaning does not invalidate the literal meaning. Accordingly the deeper meanings of the obser-

vances enjoined in the laws are not to be understood in such a way as to mean the abrogation of the practice of these laws. "Nay we should look on all these outward observances as resembling the body, and their inner meaning as resembling the soul" (*Migr.* 93).

In the employment of these (and other) methods of exegesis Philo follows approaches that existed within Jewish expository traditions in general, including rabbinic exegesis, and that shared features with methods of interpretation in the broader Hellenistic context. In comparison with rabbinic expositions (committed to writing from the late second century on) an important difference is that Philo to a larger extent finds in the texts Greek philosophical ideas, mainly of a Platonic and Stoic bent.

PHILO AS AN EXEGETE IN CONTEXT

Philo was an exegete among other exegetes, and he refers to many others, though not by name (Shroyer 1936, 261-84; Hay 1979-80; 1991a; Borgen 1984a, 259-62; 1984b, 126-28). Here only two examples will be mentioned to indicate different hermeneutical approaches. In *Migr.* 89-93 Philo criticizes some spiritualists who in their interpretation of the Sabbath, feasts, and circumcision were in danger of separating the specific and concrete level from the higher level of general ideas and convictions. Philo keeps both levels together. It is then interesting to note that the specific and concrete levels do not just refer to biblical texts, but to biblical and traditional laws as they were to be practiced in Jewish community life.

Philo also refers to exegetes who do not look for a higher general and cosmic meaning if it is not stated in the text itself. Some examples of this approach are: in Deut. 34:4 God humiliates Moses by not permitting him to enter the promised land (*Migr.* 44-45), in Gen. 11:7-8 the confusion of tongues refers to the origin of the Greek and barbarian languages (*Conf.* 190), Gen. 26:19-32 tells about the actual digging of wells (*Somn.* 1.39), and in Exod. 22:26-27 the material return of the garment is meant (*Somn.* 1.92-102).

Moreover, Philo may deal with concrete and specific human experiences and events, at times seen together with biblical examples. Thus in *Praem.* 11-14 the idea of hope is illustrated by examples from various professions, such as the meaning of hope in the life of a tradesman, a ship captain, a politician, an athlete, and others. Then the biblical figure of Enos expresses every person's need for setting hope in God.

Within Philo's two or three-level hermeneutical perspective there is room for various emphases. Thus the focus may be set on the level of specific

historical events, interpreted by ideas from the higher level of cosmic principles and divine guidance. The treatises *Against Flaccus* and *On the Embassy to
Gaius* belong to this kind of writing. The focus may also primarily be placed
upon the higher level of general cosmic principles and God's realm above the
created world. The *Allegorical Commentary* qualifies for this classification.
Another possibility was to place both the concrete and the deeper levels together in immediate sequence, as especially is the case in several entries in the
Questions and Answers on Genesis and Exodus and parts of *On Abraham* and
On Joseph (Borgen 1987, 22-23, 53-54; Wan 1993, 35, 39). Various aspects of
both levels may be woven together, as is largely the case in Philo's rewriting of
the laws of Moses in *On the Life of Moses, On the Decalogue, On the Special
Laws, On the Virtues,* and *On Rewards and Punishments.*

SOME EXEGETICAL APPROACHES AND FORMS

In this section we will discuss the forms of question and answer, direct exegesis, contrast, paraphrastic rewriting, rewriting of the Bible, and commentary.

Question and Answer

The exegetical form of question and answer is central for a formal analysis of
the works of Philo, since it occurs in the *Exposition of the Laws of Moses, On
the Life of Moses, the Allegorical Commentary,* and the *Questions and Answers
on Genesis and Exodus* (Borgen and Skarsten 1976-77, also printed in Borgen
1983, 191-201; Nikiprowetzky 1977, 170-80; 1983; Hay 1991b; Wan 1993). As seen
by its title, *Questions and Answers on Genesis and Exodus* is a collection of
such questions and answers. Other examples are seen in *Leg. All.* 1.33-41, 48-
52, 70-71, 85-87, 90, 91-92a, 101-104, 105-108; 2.19-21, 42-43, 44-45, 68-70, 80-81;
3.18-19, 49ff., 66-68, 77-78, 184-85, 188; also *Cher.* 21f., 55ff.; *Sacr.* 11ff., 128ff.;
Det. 57ff., 80ff.; *Post.* 33ff., 40ff., 153; *Gig.* 55ff.; *Immut.* 11f., 60ff., 70ff., 86ff., 104,
122; and *Somn.* 1.5ff.; 12f.; 14ff.; 41f.; 2.300ff.

In the *Exposition of the Laws* Philo uses the exegetical form of question
and answer at many points. One is the account of the creation of humankind
(*Opif.* 72-88). Another is in connection with the central event of the giving of
the law at Mount Sinai, where it is asked why, when all the many thousands
were collected in one spot, God thought it good to proclaim the ten commandments to each person, not as to several persons, but with singular "Thou
shalt not . . ." (*Dec.* 36-43). Other questions treat the desert as an unusual place

for setting up a code of laws (*Dec.* 2-17), the lack of penalties for future transgressors of the ten commandments (*Dec.* 176-78), and Moses' unusual use of a story of the creation of the world to begin his legislation (*Mos.* 2.47ff.).

Broadly speaking, Philo's own context is reflected in some passages. The questions asked in *Mos.* 2.47ff. and *Dec.* 176-78 refer to some special features of the Mosaic Law *when compared with other laws* (the creation as introduction to the laws, the lack of specified penalties with the ten commandments). With regard to why the laws were given in the desert, Philo characterizes cities as places of countless evils, such as vanity, pride, and polytheistic worship. This point had special relevance against the background of life in a large city such as that of Alexandria.

In both *Opif.* 72ff. and *Conf.* 168ff. it is asked why the creation of humanity is ascribed not to one Creator but to plural creators. *Leg. All.* 1.101-104 and *QG* 1.15 ask why, when giving the charge to eat of every tree of the garden, God addresses the command to a singular person, but when prohibiting any use of that which causes evil and good, God speaks to plural persons (Gen. 2:16-17; Borgen and Skarsten 1976-77, 2-5). But the answers differ in these two passages. Philo (or a synagogue school tradition behind him) could give different answers to the same question and could express them in the same expository structure of question and answer. Moreover, parallel usage can be found, as in *Opif.* 77 and in *QG* 2.43, where the problem of an unexpected order and rank in two sections of the Pentateuchal story is addressed.

This question and answer form is also seen in rabbinic exegesis, and Philo and the rabbis even sometimes draw on the same traditions. For example, why Adam was created last is asked several times in rabbinic writings (*Gen. Rab.* 8:1ff.; *Lev. Rab.* 14:1; the midrash on Psalm 139; *Tanchuma,* Buber [1885] 32; t. *Sanh.* 8:7; y. *Talmud Sanh.* 4:9). Of special interest is the parallel in form and content between *Opif.* 77

> One should ask the reason why man comes last in the world's creation, for, as the sacred writings show, he was the last whom the Father and Maker fashioned,

and t. *Sanh.* 8:7 and 9 (Zuckermandel 1908):

> Man was created last. And why was he created last?

Furthermore, one answer to this question is shared between the two texts, and it is an answer that goes beyond the text of Genesis (Borgen 1995, 377-79):

Just as givers of a banquet, then, do not send out the summonses to supper till they have put everything in readiness for the feast . . . in the same way the Ruler of all things, like some provider . . . of a banquet, when about to invite man to the enjoyment of a feast . . . made ready beforehand the material . . . in order that on coming into the world man might at once find . . . a banquet . . . full of all things that earth and rivers and sea and air bring forth for use and enjoyment. . . . (*Opif.* 78)

Another matter: So that he might enter the banquet at once. They have made a parable: To what is the matter comparable? To a king who built a palace and dedicated it and prepared a meal and [only] afterwards invited the guests. And so Scripture says, "The wisest of women has built her a house" (Prov. 9:1). This refers to the King of the kings of kings, blessed be He, who built his world in seven days by wisdom. "She has hewn out her seven pillars" (Prov. 9:1) — these are the seven days of creation. "She has killed her beasts and mixed her wine" (Prov. 9:2) — These are the oceans, rivers, wastes, and all the other things which the world needs. . . . (t. *Sanh.* 8:9 according to Neusner 1981, 224)

Moreover, this tradition also occurs elsewhere in the rabbinic writings (y. *Sanh.* 4:9; b. *Sanh.* 38a; *Jalkut, Shemone* 15; cf. *Gen. Rab.* 8:6) and in church writings, such as Gregory of Nyssa, *De hominis opificio* 2, and so was widespread and originated at the time of Philo or before.

Scholars have observed that the question and answer form is found both in the Jewish Alexandrian writer Demetrius (*On the Kings of Judea*, fragment 2) and in Greek commentaries on Plato's *Theaetetus* (*Anonymous Commentary on Theaetetus* 34.9-14; 34.33–35.44) and on the writings of Homer (*Scholia Venetus* A on *Iliad* 1.52, etc.). It was frequently used also in Christian exegesis. Early on, it often reflected controversies between the orthodox and heretic. From the fourth century on, the commentaries treated traditional problems rather than live issues. Thus, the question and answer form represented a very broad and varied exegetical tradition in antiquity (Schaublin 1974, 49-51; Dörrie and Dörries 1966, 347-70).

This analysis has demonstrated the central importance that the exegetical use of the form of question and answer has in Philo's expository writings. The locus of this exegetical method and form seems to be activities in learned settings within Judaism as well as in the wider Hellenistic context. In Jewish communities these learned settings may be located in synagogal or similar contexts, as suggested by Philo's report on the expository activity among the Therapeutae: "the President of the company . . . discusses (*zētei*) some questions arising in the Holy Scriptures or solves *(epilyetai)* one that has been propounded by someone else."

Against this background the term *dialegomai,* "hold converse with," "discuss," when used of expository activity, probably refers to the use of the question and answer method (*Cont.* 31, 79; *Spec.* 2.62; *Mos.* 2.215). Against the background of such expository activity in community meetings, learned persons would themselves employ the same expository method, partly as a rhetorical and literary device. Thus, instead of discussing the possible dependence of the *Allegorical Commentary* on the *Question and Answer Commentary,* as done by scholars (see Borgen 1987, 30; Hay 1991b), one should discuss how far Philo is dependent on traditions and on learned (synagogal) school activity in his extensive use of this form of exegesis (cf. Delling 1974, 141; Nikiprowetzky 1977, 174-77).

Direct Exegesis

Nikiprowetzky suggests that the technique of question and answer was behind Philo's expositions in general (1977, 179-80; 1983, 55-75). This view is too one-sided. There is thus a need for examining other exegetical forms that might be found in Philo's expositions. A large body of such expositions may be classified as direct exegesis, that is, small or large units in which no exegetical question is formulated.

A typical exegetical term used in such direct exegesis is *toutestin,* "this is," "this means," or "that is to say" (cf. Adler 1929, 23). By means of this phrase a word or a phrase is explained by another word, phrase, or sentence. For example, *Leg. All.* 1.24: "'And all the grass of the field,' he says, 'before it sprang up' (Gen. 2:5), that is to say, 'before' the particular objects of sense 'sprang up.'" There are many other examples (*Leg. All.* 1.45, 65, 98; 2.38, 41, 45, 59, 62, 77, 92; 3.11, 16, 20, 28, 46, 52, 95, 142, 143, 145, 153, 154, 176, 230, 232, 242, 244; *Cher.* 17; *Sacr.* 62, 86, 119; *Det.* 10, 59, 119; *Post.* 53, 150, 168, 182; *Gig.* 53, 54; *Plant.* 42, 116; *Ebr.* 40, 53, 70, 95, 125; *Heres* 304; *Congr.* 49; *Fug.* 135, 192, 201; *Somn.* 1.112; 2.76; *Spec.* 1.306).

Other such exegetical terms used by Philo are phrases built on the word *ison,* "equal (to)," as, for example, in *Leg. All.* 1.36: "'Breathed into' (Gen. 2:7), we note, is equivalent to inspired." There are many other examples (*Leg. All.* 1.65, 76; 2.16, 21; 3.51, 119, 189, 219, 246, 247, 253; *Cher.* 7.119; *Sacr.* 12.112; *Det.* 38, 70, 96, 169; *Agr.* 166; *Plant.* 90.114; *Sobr.* 15; *Conf.* 72, 84, 111, 150, 160, 189; *Migr.* 5, 7, 27, 42, 80, 101, 160; *Congr.* 158, 172; *Spec.* 3.133; *Aeter.* 46).

Contrast

Besides question and answer and direct exegesis, many other exegetical terms and methods are used. One meaning may be discarded in contrast to the proper meaning by the contrast "not — but." This is exemplified in *Leg. All.* 1.1, where Gen. 2:1 is cited: "And the heaven and the earth and all their world were completed." Philo's exposition rejects one interpretation over against another: "He [Moses] does not say that either the individual mind or the particular sense perceptions have reached completion, but that the originals have done so."

A contrast may be used to confirm a certain reading of the text against an alternative one (Borgen 1965, 62-65). In *Migr.* 1 and 43 the contrast offers a confirmation of the reading of the text of Gen. 12:1, "into the land that I will show you.": "He says not 'which I am shewing,' but 'which I will shew *(deichō)* thee.'" Such philological confirmation of the reading of a text is used in rabbinic exegesis, as in *Mek. on Exod.* 15:11: "'Doing wonders.' It is not written here 'Who did *('s)* wonders,' but 'who does *('sh)* wonders,' that is, in the future." A NT example is found in Gal. 3:16: "'and to his offspring.' It does not say 'and to offsprings,' as referring to many, but, referring to one, 'and to your offspring,' which is Christ."

The contrast may correct a certain reading, as is the case in *Det.* 47-48: "'Cain rose up against Abel his brother and slew him *(auton)*' (Gen. 4:8). . . . It must be read in this way, 'Cain rose up and slew himself *(heauton)*,' not someone else." *Mek. on Exod.* 16:15 has a rabbinic parallel: "'Man did eat the bread of strong horses (Ps. 78:25).' Do not read 'of strong horses' *('byrym)*, but 'of the limbs' *('ybrym)*, that is, 'bread' that is absorbed by the 'limbs.'" When the Greek verb is translated back into Hebrew, John 6:31-32 is seen to be a parallel: "'Bread from heaven he gave *(edōken / ntn)* them to eat.' Truly, truly I say to you, 'not Moses gave *([d]edōken / ntn)* you the bread from heaven, but my Father gives *(didōsin / nwt)* you the true bread from heaven'" (cf. Exod. 16:4, 15; Ps. 78:24; Borgen 1965, 40-41; Menken 1996, 47-65).

In his expositions Philo often moves from one level of meaning to another one. He may do so by using a modified form of contrast to indicate that he accepts both levels of meaning: "not only — but also." For example *Spec.* 4.149-50: "'Thou shalt not remove thy neighbour's landmarks which thy forerunners have set up.' Now this law, we may consider, applies not merely to allotments and boundaries of land . . . but also to the safeguarding of ancient customs."

Paraphrastic Rewriting

In some forms of exegesis the biblical material has been interpreted by means of rewriting as a paraphrase. One such form draws on the formulation of blessings and curses from the Bible. Philo builds on this form in his rewriting of biblical material in *Praem.* 79-162, drawing mainly on parts of Leviticus 26 and Deuteronomy 28. The future blessings are surveyed in *Praem.* 85-125 and the description of the curses follows in 127-62. Philo ties the two sections together in 126: "These are the blessings invoked upon good men, men who fulfil the laws by their deeds, which blessings will be accomplished by the gift of the bounteous God, who glorifies and rewards moral excellence because of its likeness to Himself. We must now investigate the curses delivered against the law-breakers and transgressors."

Another form of paraphrase is a list of biblical persons or events. Philo lists a series of biblical persons in *Virt.* 198-210. Here Adam, Noah, Abraham, and Isaac are surveyed and characterized (cf. Schmitt 1977). This series of cases from the laws of Moses serves as an argument against the view that nobility of ancestry as such is a criterion of nobility and for the view that the criterion is rather the virtuous life of the person himself. It is worth noticing that, although Philo here illustrates a general principle, he at the same time keeps the idea of Jewish superiority, since he maintains that non-Jews obtain nobility by following Abraham's example and becoming proselytes.

The theme of predestination is illustrated by a chain of biblical examples in *Leg. All.* 3.69-106: Noah, Melchizedek, Abraham, Isaac, Jacob and Esau, Manasseh and Ephraim, those who sacrifice the Passover (Num. 9:1-8), Bezalel, and Moses. Outside Philo's works, one might mention as a parallel Paul's discussion of predestination in Romans 9, in which he gives a brief list in vv. 7-18: Abraham, Isaac, Jacob and Esau, and Pharaoh (Dunn 1988, ad loc.; Fitzmyer 1993, ad loc.). In both *Leg. All.* 3.88 and Rom. 9:10-12, 20-23 the idea illustrated is God's foreknowledge and election of two contrasting persons, Jacob and Esau, even before their birth. Moreover, in both cases God is pictured as a maker of clay pots. These agreements make it probable that Philo and Paul draw here on a common tradition of exposition of Gen. 25:23.

Jewish and early Christian literature contains numerous reviews of biblical history varying in content and length and each adapted to its own context and interpretative function. Lists of biblical persons are found in many places (Sir. 44:1–49:16; Wis. 10:1-21; 1 Macc. 2:49-64; 3 Macc. 2:1-20; 6:1-15; 4 Macc. 16:16-23; 18:11-13; *Apoc. Zeph.* 9:4; *4 Ezra* 7:106-10; Heb. 11:1-39; *1 Clem.* 4.7–6.4; 9.2–12.8; see Attridge 1989, 305-307; Schmitt 1977). In Hebrews 11 Abel, Enoch, Noah, Sarah, Abraham, Isaac and Jacob, Moses, and heroes and events from the time of the judges, the monarchy, and other times are listed to illustrate faith. In *1 Clem.* 4.7–6.4 Christian persons are added to Old Testament figures to illustrate the struggle against envy.

Rewritten Bible

Reviews of material from the Old Testament may also have the form of continuous rewriting in chronologically ordered narratives. A body of laws may be included in the historical scheme. An example is *Virt.* 51-174, which deals with the virtue *philanthropia,* "love of people," "philanthropy." Philo exalts Moses' *philanthropia* by recording some events in his life and by presenting a selection from the Mosaic laws. There seems to be a corresponding structure in parts of the preserved fragments of Philo's *Hypothetica.* Fragment 8.6.1-9 reviews biblical history from Abraham to the exodus and the Hebrews' settlement in Palestine. Then Philo describes the Mosaic constitution and presents the admonitions, prohibitions, and injunctions (6.10–7.20). Josephus gives a corresponding account of the Jewish laws in *Ag. Ap.* 145-56. His stated purpose is to refute criticism of Judaism from Apollonius Molon, Lysimachus, and others. Like Philo in *Virt.* 51-174 and *Hypothetica* 8.6.1–7.19, Josephus also begins with a characterization of Moses and events connected with the exodus (*Ag. Ap.* 2.157-63). Josephus gives a direct polemical response to his critics (2.164-89), and then a selection of the laws follows.

The basic structure of this form is already found in Deuteronomy, which contains a revised repetition of a large part of the history and laws of the first four books of the laws of Moses (Weinfeld 1992). This model can also be traced in Josephus, *Ant.* 4.176-331, where Josephus gives a summary of the laws and events from biblical history, drawing largely on Deuteronomy (4.199-301).

Philo also rewrites biblical events and laws in *On the Decalogue* (cf. *Heres* 167-73) and *Spec.* 1-4. As the title indicates, *On the Decalogue* is a paraphrase of the event at Sinai and a paraphrasing elaboration of the decalogue, which understands the ten commandments as headings for the grouping of laws. In *Spec.* 1-4 Philo generally begins with an elaboration on a given commandment, similar though fuller than in *On the Decalogue,* and then discusses particular requirements that Philo thinks may be set under the particular commandment. He seems to develop in a more systematic fashion a notion also found in Palestinian tradition, that the decalogue contained *in nuce* all the commandments of the Mosaic laws (see Borgen 1984b, 126; 1984a, 239-40, and n. 30; 1987, 26-27). In general, Philo follows in these two treatises the biblical chronology.

Philo's entire exposition of the law of Moses, his *Exposition of the Laws of Moses*, is divided into treatises tied together by transitional statements in which he gives his own perspective and understanding (cf. Borgen 1996). Thus we find in them systematic motifs that demonstrate that Philo is not just an eclectic editor, but is largely an author. The introductory and transitional statements indicate that he has organized and interpreted traditional material with five systematic aspects in view:

> He describes the creation of cosmos and humans (*Opif.*; cf. *Praem.* 1).
> He gives a record of good and bad lives and sentences passed in each generation on both (*Abr.* [*On Isaac; On Jacob*]; *On Joseph*; cf. *Praem.* 2a).
> Having related the lives of the good men, the patriarchs (and their contrasting counterparts), who are portrayed in Scripture as archetypes and founders of "our nation," Philo presents the written laws of Moses, starting in *Dec.* with the ten commandments, understood as the main headings delivered by the voice of God. The particular laws, which are derived from the decalogue and have Moses as the spokesman, are written down in *Spec.* 1.1–4.132 (cf. *Praem.* 2b).
> The virtues that Moses assigned to peace and war are common to all commandments (*Spec.* 4.133-238; *Virt.*; cf. *Praem.* 3).
> After having related the particular laws and the virtues they have in common, Philo proceeds to the rewards and punishments that the good and the bad respectively can expect. *Praem.* covers both aspects (see 3b).

This outline shows that Philo followed some overriding concepts when he interpreted various traditional material in his *Exposition*. Although he is not a systematic philosopher, he has some overarching perspectives when he fuses Jewish and Greek traditions, ideas, and notions together.

In his *Exposition of the Laws of Moses* Philo basically follows the form found in other Jewish books that rewrite (parts of) the Pentateuch. Philo covers the biblical story from creation to Joshua's succession. *Jubilees* narrates the story from creation to the giving of the laws on Mount Sinai. The Qumran *Genesis Apocryphon*, preserved only in parts, covers Genesis from the birth of Noah to Gen. 15:4. The *Biblical Antiquities* of pseudo-Philo contain an abstract of the biblical story from Genesis 5 to the death of Saul. In his *Jewish Antiquities* Josephus begins with creation and relates the whole span of biblical history and goes beyond even to the beginning of the Jewish war in his own time (Borgen 1984a, 233-34; 1987, 18 and 20; Nickelsburg 1984, 97-110; Alexander 1988).

Commentaries

In the rewritten Bible, the *Exposition of the Laws of Moses*, Philo ties the different parts together with interpretative transitional statements and outlines the content of larger units of the work in summary statements. There is a kinship between the *Exposition* and the *Allegorical Commentary* in that both have been subject to extensive editorial activity. In both, references and transitions bind various parts together. But the *Allegorical Commentary* and the *Questions and Answers* differ from the *Exposition* in their general structure since they appear in the form of running commentaries on parts of the Pentateuchal text and not as rewritten Scripture. In the *Questions and Answers* transitional statements are used only in a limited degree.

In the *Allegorical Commentary* Philo has built up the treatises as a running commentary. Their structures and outline vary, however. For example, the complexity of the expositions in the first three treatises, *Leg. All.* 1-3, increases from the first to the second and from the second to the third. The exposition of seventeen verses (Gen. 2:1-17) in the first treatise fills twenty-eight pages in one edition, the exposition of nine verses (2:18–3:1) in the second treatise covers twenty-two pages, and the exposition of eleven verses (3:8b-19) in the third treatise fills fifty-six pages (Adler 1929, 8-24).

In *Leg. All.* 3, and to a lesser degree also in *Leg. All.* 1 and 2, Philo has used the running commentary on the verses from Genesis as headings for related expositions on other parts of the Pentateuch. Thus, the commentary on Gen. 3:8 in *Leg. All.* 3.1-48 (Adam hiding himself) leads into a lengthy exposition of other Pentateuchal verses dealing with the theme of hiding and flight. Similarly, God's cursing of the serpent, Gen. 3:14, is quoted in *Leg. All.* 3.65 and 107, and this leads into a broad exposition of the contrast between lives of pleasure and of virtue based on a list of examples from various parts of the Pentateuch. Such extensive expositions of interrelated passages are quite common in the other treatises of the *Allegorical Commentary* as well. Among the specific problems of Philo's own time that he deals with are temptations at banquets (*Leg. All.* 2.29; 3.155-56, 220-21), temptations of wealth, honors, and offices (2.107), and the temptation to use education only for building one's political career regardless of Jewish values and commitments (3.167).

In *Leg. All.* 1-3 and *Cher.* the exegesis deals with the stories of Adam and Eve and Paradise. *On the Cherubim* is a commentary on two verses, Gen. 3:24 and 4:1. The biblical story of Cain and Abel is dealt with in *On the Sacrifices of Abel and Cain* (on Gen. 4:2-4), *The Worse Attacks the Better* (on Gen. 4:8-15), and *On the Posterity and Exile of Cain* (on Gen. 4:16-22, 25). The story of the appearance of giants on earth, Gen. 6:1-4a, 4b-9, 11-12, is interpreted in the twin treatises *On the Giants* and *On the Unchangeableness of God.*

On Husbandry, On Noah's Work as a Planter, and *On Drunkenness* all deal with the same text, Gen. 9:21-22, and consist of well-organized sections on themes suggested by words in the text. *On Sobriety* interprets Gen. 9:24-27, on Noah's return to sobriety and the curses he then uttered, and follows the structure of a running commentary. Transitional statements tie these treatises together.

The various parts of *On the Confusion of Tongues* are brought together at the beginning by the umbrella quotation of Gen. 11:1-9, the story of the tower of Babel. A running commentary follows. The treatise serves as a defense of the laws of Moses against scoffers who state that the laws contain myths, such as the story of the tower of Babel. *On the Migration of Abraham* covers Gen. 12:1-4, 6 with a topical and running commentary. The long treatise *Who Is the Heir?* (of Abraham) is a running commentary on Gen. 15:2-18.

On Mating, with Preliminary Studies is a running commentary of Gen. 16:1-6a, on Abraham's mating with his handmaid Hagar. The text is applied to Philo's contemporary setting in which the question of Greek general education was an issue. *On Flight and Finding* follows then and interprets Gen. 16:6b-9, 11-12. Philo ties the two treatises together with a transitional statement: "Having in the preceding treatise said what was fitting about the courses of preliminary training and about evil entreatment, we will next proceed to set forth the subject of fugitives" (*Fug.* 2). The text is cited in an umbrella quotation in *Fug.* 1.

On the Change of Names gives a running exposition of Gen. 17:1-5, 15-21, on the names of Abram and Sarai and the promise of a son to Abraham and Sarah. Sections 60–129 are a thematic excursus on the change of names. It serves as a defense against scoffers who ridicule the idea that a change of a letter in a name should have any importance. Finally, the fragment of *On God* is extant only in Armenian. It concerns the revelation to Abraham at the oak of Mamre.

In the two treatises *On Dreams* the form of running commentary serves only as a subordinate element in expositions of dreams in Genesis. The form thus approaches that of *On the Virtues* and *On Rewards and Punishments.* Philo classifies the dreams in three groups: those in which God on his own initiative sends visions to a sleeping person, those in which a person's mind is God-inspired and foretells future events, and those in which the soul, setting itself in motion, foretells the future. This classification seems to follow one such as the one Cicero, *De Divinatione* 1.30, 64 ascribes to Poseidonius. The treatise for Philo's first group of dreams is lost. The first extant treatise deals with the two dreams of Jacob, the ladder (Gen. 28:10-22) and the flock with varied markings (31:10-13). The second treatise deals with the dreams of Joseph (37:8-11), of Pharaoh's baker and butler (40:9-11, 16-17), and of Pharaoh (41:17-24). Allusions and references to Philo's own time are sometimes built into the exposition, as for example in *Somn.* 2.123, where he reports on a dream of his own that a governor of Egypt had attempted to interfere with the Jewish observance of the Sabbath and other laws.

THE LAWS OF MOSES IN THE ALEXANDRIAN CONFLICT

The conflict in Alexandria and Jerusalem during the reign of the Emperor Gaius Caligula and the governor Flaccus was a struggle about the way in which the laws of Moses should be interpreted and practiced in society as civil rights, as a way of life, and as institutional life centered around the synagogues and the Temple. Philo's *Against Flaccus* and *On the Embassy to Gaius* give ample support for this understanding: the Alexandrian Jews experienced an attack on their laws, synagogues, Temple and ancestral customs (see *Flacc.* 41, 47, 50, 53 and *Legat.* 6-7, 115, 117, 152-57, 161, 170, 200, 232, 236, 240, 249, 256). Thus these two treatises should be understood as a report on a struggle for the interpretation and application of the laws of Moses in the context of the Jewish community and its status in Alexandria as well as in Palestine. Thus, to Philo the relationship between the Jewish community and its non-Jewish surroundings was a central factor in his interpretation of the laws of Moses and their role in the life of the Jewish community.

EPILOGUE

Runia sums up the main points about Philo's place in early Christian literature: it has not proven possible to demonstrate beyond doubt that Philo was known to apologists such as Justin, Athenagoras, and Theophilus of Antioch (1993, 335-42). The teachers of the catechetical school in Alexandria — Pantaenus, especially Clement (Runia 1993, 335), and Origen — made use of Philo's writings in making the connection between the biblical sources and philosophical ideas and categories. They also followed Philonic methods of exegesis. A main difference was, of course, that their expositions were written in a setting basically located outside the Jewish community. Moreover, their presupposition was that Christ, not the laws of Moses, was the center of revelation (cf. Paget 1996, 482).

Clement's worldview was akin to that of Philo, and he worked similarly with exegesis on two or more levels. For example, that which belonged to the temple signifies cosmic entities: "Now, connected with the concealment is the special meaning of what is told among the Hebrews about the seven circuits around the old temple, and also the equipment on the robe, whose multicolored symbols allude to celestial phenomena, which indicate the agreement from heaven down to earth" (*Strom.* 5.32.2; van den Hoek 1988, 118; see further *Strom.* 5:32-40). This section on the temple is parallel to parts of Philo's interpretation in *Mos.* 2:87-130 (cf. Josephus, *Ant.* 102-23). Clement seems to draw on Philo only at some points, but the general cosmic perspective follows the model of Philo, Josephus, and the author of the letter to the Hebrews. To Clement the christological application is central: "the robe prophesied the ministry in the flesh by which he [the Logos] was made visible to the world directly" (*Strom.* 5.39.2; van den Hoek 1988, 140; see further pp. 116-47).

Like Philo, Clement uses the image of body and soul. According to Clement, the interpreter's aim is to advance from the body of Scripture to the soul (*Strom.* 5.90.3; Paget 1996, 492). Accordingly he distinguishes between historical-literal exegesis and the deeper meaning of the text. In eliciting the deeper meaning Clement, like Philo, makes use of etymologies and numerological speculations. But Clement is less interested in lexical and stylistic details in his exegesis (Paget 1996, 498).

As seen above, to Philo the Egyptian servant Hagar represents non-Jewish general education and Sarah represents wisdom. Clement develops a related interpretation in *Strom.* 1.28-32. For Philo, non-Jewish education and philosophy should serve the wisdom revealed in the laws of Moses. For Clement, they represent, together with the Jewish law, the preparatory phase which serves the wisdom that is Christ (van den Hoek 1988, 23-47).

The later Alexandrian and Egyptian fathers such as Didymus and Isidore also had a favorable attitude to Philo's exegesis. Eusebius continued the Alexandrian tradition, but in Palestine. He incorporated a lengthy notice regarding Philo in his *Ecclesiastical History* and gave extensive citations from Philo in his apologetic writings. Among the Cappadocian fathers, Gregory of Nyssa especially drew positively on Philo. In the West, Ambrose and Jerome used Philo's exegesis extensively, and from them Augustine gained knowledge of Philo's exegesis and ideas.

In general, early church writers were interested in Philo's paraphrasing rewritten Bible, his *On the Life of Moses* in particular. This material was used in their historical apologetics on the earlier history of Israel. Josephus's writings were utilized by them in the same way. They were also interested in

Philo's expository commentaries. They drew on his rules and procedures of exegesis. His literal exegesis was not overlooked, but the main interest was in his allegorical elaborations and its Platonic bent. Runia emphasizes three areas of influence (1993, 338-39):

> (a) the doctrine of God, with the strong emphasis on unchangeability and essential unknowability; (b) the doctrine of man, created "according to the image" (i.e. the logos), endowed with reason and the capacity to reach out to God and become like unto Him; (c) the doctrine of the virtues or excellences *(aretai)*, taken over from Greek philosophy and adapted to the requirements of allegorical expositions and the differing emphases of biblical thought.

In this way the church's writers learned from Philo how to mediate between the biblical and philosophical traditions.

The Antiochene school of exegesis was critical of Philo. An outstanding representative was Theodore of Mopsuestia, who attacked Philo for his allegorical exegesis. A reaction against Philo grew in the fourth century. He was associated with heretical forms of Christianity, mainly Origenism and Arianism, and direct use of his works diminished, but many Philonic themes were adopted by later authors at second-hand through the writings of the early church fathers.

BIBLIOGRAPHY

Adler, M.
1929   *Studien zu Philon von Alexandreia.* Breslau: Marcus.

Alexander, P. S.
1988   "Retelling the Old Testament." In D. A. Carson and H. G. M. Williamson, eds., *It Is Written: Scripture Citing Scripture,* 99-121. New York: Cambridge University Press.

Amir, Y.
1988   "Authority and Interpretation of Scripture in the Writings of Philo." In M. J. Mulder and H. Sysling, eds., *Mikra: Text, Translation, Reading and Interpretation of the Hebrew Bible in Ancient Judaism and Early Christianity,* 421-53. CRINT 2.1. Assen: Van Gorcum; Philadelphia: Fortress.

Attridge, H.
1989   *Hebrews: A Commentary on the Epistle to the Hebrews.* Hermeneia. Philadelphia: Fortress.

Borgen, P.

1965   *Bread from Heaven.* Reprint. Leiden: Brill, 1981.

1983   *"Paul Preaches Circumcision and Pleases Men" and Other Essays on Christian Origins.* Relieff 8. Trondheim: Tapir.

1984a "Philo of Alexandria." In Stone (ed.) 1984: 233-82.

1984b "Philo of Alexandria. A Critical and Synthetical Survey of Research Since World War II," *ANRW* II.21.1:98-154.

1987   *Philo, John and Paul.* Atlanta: Scholars.

1992   "Judaism in Egypt." In *ABD,* III, 1061-72.

1995   "Man's Sovereignty over Animals and Nature according to Philo of Alexandria." In T. Fornberg and D. Hellholm, eds., *Texts and Contexts,* 369-89. Oslo: Scandinavian University Press.

1996   *Early Christianity and Hellenistic Judaism.* Edinburgh: Clark.

Borgen, P., and R. Skarstene

1976-77 "Quaestiones et Solutiones: Some Observations on the Form of Philo's Exegesis." *SP* 4:1-15.

Bousset, W.

1926   *Die Religion des Judentums im späthellenistischen Zeitalter,* revised by H. Gressmann. 3d ed. Tübingen: Mohr.

Buber, S. (ed.)

1885   *Midrash Tanchuma.* 3 vols. Vilna: Romm.

Christiansen, I.

1969   *Die Technik der allegorischen Auslegungswissenschaft bei Philon von Alexandrien.* Beiträge zur Geschichte der biblische Hermeneutik 7. Tübingen: Mohr.

Collins, J. J.

1987   "The Development of the Sibylline Tradition." *ANRW* II.20.1:421-59.

Delling, G.

1974   "Perspektiven der Erforschungen des hellenistischen Judentums." *HUCA* 45:133-76.

Dimant, D.

1992   "Pesharim, Qumran." In *ABD,* V, 244-51.

Dörrie, H., and H. Dörries

1966   "Erotapokriseis." In *RAC* 6, cols. 342-70.

Dunn, J. D. G.

1988   *Romans.* 2 vols. WBC 38a, 38b. Waco: Word.

Fitzmyer, J. A.

1993   *Romans: A New Translation with Introduction and Commentary.* AB 33. New York: Doubleday.

Fritsch, C.

1943   *The Anti-Anthropomorphisms of the Greek Pentateuch.* Princeton: Princeton University Press.

Goodenough, E. R.

1933   "Philo's Exposition of the Law and His De Vita Mosis." *HTR* 26:109-25.

Hay, D. M.

1979-80 "Philo's References to Other Allegorists." *SPA* 6:41-75.
1991a   "References to Other Exegetes." In Hay (ed.) 1991b: 81-97.

Hay D. M. (ed.)

1991b   *Both Literal and Allegorical: Studies in Philo of Alexandria's Questions and Answers on Genesis and Exodus.* Atlanta: Scholars.

Heinemann, I.

1936   *Altjüdische Allegoristik.* Breslau: Marcus.

Heinisch, P.

1908   *Der Einfluss Philos auf die älteste christliche Exegese.* Alttestamentliche Abhandlungen 1.2. Münster: Aschendorff.

Hengel, M.

1983   "Messianische Hoffnung und politischer 'Radikalismus' in der 'Jüdisch-hellenistischen Diaspora.'" In D. Hellholm (ed.) *Apocalypticism in the Mediterranean World and the Near East,* 655-86. Tübingen: Mohr.

Hilgert, E.

1991   "The *Quaestiones:* Texts and Translations." In Hay (ed.) 1991b, 1-15.

Kasher, A.

1985   *The Jews in Hellenistic and Roman Egypt.* Tübingen: Mohr.

Kuiper, G. J.

1986   "Jewish Literature Composed in Greek." In Schürer, Vermes, and Miller (eds.) 1986-87, 3.1:470-704.

Laporte, J.

1972   *La doctrine eucharistique chez Philon d'Alexandrie.* Theologie historique 16. Paris: Beauchesne.

Lauterbach, J. Z.

1910   "Ancient Jewish Allegorists." *JQ* n.s. 1:291-333, 503-31.

Maybaum, S.

1870   *Die Anthropomorphien und Anthropathien bei Onkelos und den spätern Targumim.* Breslau: Schletter.

Meecham, H. G.

1932   *The Oldest Version of the Bible: "Aristeas" on Its Traditional Origin.* London: Holborn.

Meeks, W. A.

1967   *The Prophet-King.* Leiden: Brill.

Menken, M. J. J.

1996   *Old Testament Quotations in the Fourth Gospel: Studies in Textual Form.* Kampen: Kok Pharos.

Meyer, R.

1937   *Hellenistisches in der rabbinischen Anthropologie.* BWANT 4.22. Stuttgart: W. Kohlhammer.

Morris, J.

1987   "The Jewish Philosopher Philo." In Schürer, Vermes, and Miller (eds.) 1986-87, 3.2:809-89.

Mulder, M. J., and H. Sysling (eds.)

1988   *Mikra: Text, Translation, Reading and Interpretation of the Hebrew Bible in Ancient Judaism and Early Christianity.* CRINT 2.1. Assen: Van Gorcum; Philadelphia: Fortress.

Neusner, J. (trans.)

1981   *The Tosefta. Fourth Division: Neziqin.* New York: Ktav.

Nickelsburg, G. W. E.

1984   "The Bible Rewritten and Expanded." In Stone (ed.) 1984: 89-156.

Nikiprowetzky, V.

1977   *Le commentaire de l'Écriture chez Philon d'Alexandrie.* Leiden: Brill.

1983   "L'exégèse de Philon d'Alexandrie dans le De Gigantibus et le Quod Deus." In D. Winston and J. Dillon (eds.) 1983, 5-75.

Paget, J. N. B.

1996   "The Christian Exegesis of the Old Testament in the Alexandrian Tradition." In M. Sæbø (ed.) 1996, 478-542.

Pearson, B. A.

1984   "Philo and Gnosticism." *ANRW* 2.21.1: 295-342.

Porton, G. G.

1992   "Midrash." In *ABD*, IV, 818-22.

Runia, D.

1993   *Philo in Early Christian Literature.* Assen: Van Gorcum; Philadelphia: Fortress.

Sæbø, M. (ed.)

1996   *Hebrew Bible: The History of Its Interpretation.* 1.1, *Antiquity.* Berlin, Göttingen: Vandenhoeck & Ruprecht.

Schaublin, C.

1974   *Untersuchungen zu Methode und Herkunft der antiochenischen Exegese.* Köln: Hanstein.

Schmitt, A.
1977   "Struktur, Herkunft und Bedeutung der Beispielreihe in Weish 10." *BZ* n.s. 21:1-22.

Schroyer, M. J.
1936   "Alexandrian Jewish Literalists." *JBL* 55:261-84.

Schulz-Flügel, E.
1996   "The Latin Old Testament Tradition." In Sæbø (ed.) 1996: 642-62.

Schürer, E., G. Vermes, and F. Miller (eds.)
1986-87 *The History of the Jewish People in the Age of Jesus Christ (175 B.C.-A.D. 135).* 3 vols. Edinburgh: Clark.

Siegert, F.
1996   "Early Jewish Interpretation in a Hellenistic Style." In Saebø (ed.) 1996, 130-98.

Skarsaune, O.
1996   "The Development of Scriptural Interpretation in the Second and Third Centuries — except Clement and Origen." In Sæbø (ed.) 1996: 373-442.

Stein, S.
1957   "The Dietary Laws in Rabbinic and Patristic Literature." In K. Aland and F. L. Cross, eds., *Studia Patristica,* 64:141-54. Berlin: Akademie.

Stone, M. E. (ed.)
1984   *Jewish Writings of the Second Temple Period.* CRINT 2.2. Assen: Van Gorcum; Philadelphia: Fortress.

Swete, H. B.
1902   *An Introduction to the Old Testament in Greek.* Cambridge: Cambridge University Press.

Tcherikover, V.
1963   "The Decline of the Jewish Diaspora in Egypt in the Roman Period." *JJS* 14:1-32.

Urbach, E. E.
1975   *The Sages: Their Concepts and Beliefs.* 2 vols. Jerusalem: Magnes, Hebrew University.

Van den Hoek, A.
1988   *Clement of Alexandria and His Use of Philo in the* Stromateis. Leiden: Brill.

Wan, S.
1993   "Philo's *Quaestiones et solutiones in Genesim:* A Synoptic Approach." In E. H. Lovering, ed., *Society of Biblical Literature 1993 Seminar Papers,* 22-53. Atlanta: Scholars.

Weinfeld, M.
1992   "Deuteronomy, Book of." In *ABD,* II, 168-83.

Winston, D., and J. Dillon (eds.)

1983   *Two Treatises of Philo of Alexandria: A Commentary on De Gigantibus and Quod Deus sit immutabilis.* Chico: Scholars.

Wolfson, H. A.

1947   *Philo.* 2 vols. Cambridge: Harvard University Press.

Zuckemandel, M. S. (ed.)

1908   *Tosefta, Mishna und Boraitha in ihrem Verhältnis zueinander, oder pälastinische und babylonische Halacha.* Frankfurt: Band.

CHAPTER 5

Biblical Interpretation in the Dead Sea Scrolls

Philip R. Davies

SCRIPTURE AT QUMRAN?

The adjective "biblical" with reference to Qumran is not strictly correct. Not only were there no Bibles during the period of Qumran literary activity (ca. third century BCE–first century CE), but there also was no single canon of Scripture that such a Bible might have included. That authoritative writings were recognized and interpreted by the authors of these scrolls cannot, however, be disputed. We can therefore conveniently speak of "Scriptures," that is, scrolls and scroll collections that had achieved a canonized status; however, we cannot be certain in every respect how precisely the boundaries were determined among the authors of the Qumran scrolls, nor can we infer a generalized way of treating such writings. Indeed, the way in which the scrolls were transmitted, revised, glossed, and commented on suggests that our modern reverence for a canonical text as verbally sacrosanct does not apply to the writers of the Qumran scrolls.

These authors do, however, refer to "law" and "prophets" as canonical collections, both separately and together. In 1QS 1.3, for example, we find "as he [God] commanded by the hand of Moses and all his servants the prophets," while a similar conjunction of "Moses" and "the prophets" occurs in 1QS 8.15-16 and CD 5.21–6.1. Separately, "law of Moses" occurs in 1QS 1.2-3; 5.8; 8.22; 4QDibHam^a 3.12-13; CD 15.2; 9.12, etc., while in CD 7.17 the "books of the prophets" are mentioned on their own. The "law of Moses" comprises the five books of the Masoretic canon, and, even though none actually contains the end of one book *and* the beginning of another, there are three fragments that appear to have contained at least two consecutive Torah books. These fragments perhaps once belonged to a single Torah scroll of the kind used in synagogues since the rabbinic period at least. A few of the scrolls of Mosaic books are written in the old Hebrew script. While this might attest either a greater veneration for the Mosaic writings, or a belief that they were much older than other texts, there is no other significant difference between these and other scriptural scrolls.

The Scriptures referred to in the Qumran scrolls as "prophets" may, of course, have extended to books later classified in the "Writings," or even to books not represented in the Masoretic canon at all. Quite possibly, Daniel and Psalms were treated in this way. However, in 4QMMT C11 we encounter the expression ". . . the book of Moses and the books of the prophets and of David and [the deeds of] each succeeding generation (*[bema'asey] dōr wadōr*)*," which may suggest that the (historical) books of the "Former Prophets" are regarded as a separate category (as Psalms apparently were); but equally, Chronicles, Ezra, Nehemiah and possibly other books could be meant.

How might we tell further whether or not a particular text was counted as scriptural? A number of factors have been suggested that might indicate this: multiple copies, fixity of text, and use of citation formulas.

1. The number of "biblical" scrolls found at Qumran is as follows:

Psalms	36	1-2 Samuel	4
Deuteronomy	29	Song of Songs	4
Isaiah	21	Ruth	4
Exodus	17	Lamentations	4
Genesis	15	Judges	3
Leviticus	13	Ecclesiastes	3
Numbers	8	Joshua	2
Twelve Prophets	8	Proverbs	2
Daniel	8	Ezra	?
Jeremiah	6	1-2 Chronicles	1
Ezekiel	6		

But we ought to put alongside these figures the numbers of some "non-biblical" texts, namely *Jubilees* (15) and *1 Enoch* (11), and of works that appear to have been authoritative within a certain community, such as CD or 1QS — although being authoritative does not necessarily make a scroll scriptural. The list of Qumran Scriptures could nevertheless have included works not so viewed in other Judaisms (for example, the Samaritans did regard, and Sadducees may have regarded, only Torah as canon). Thus, when arguing with opponents, some authors of Qumran texts used works that both sides accepted as scriptural. In matters of internal discipline or esoteric lore, however, when there was no need to dialogue with outsiders, other texts (*Jubilees* or *Enoch,* for example) may also have enjoyed scriptural status.

2. The extent to which the text of a scroll has been fixed might also point towards a canonical status. Genesis and Leviticus for the most part display a high degree of uniformity. Exodus and Numbers, on the other hand, are represented in two versions, while Deuteronomy has the most fluid text of all the Mosaic books. The "prophetic" texts show rather less stability than the Torah, and there is generally no evidence of a concern to fix texts of works regarded as scriptural. The scroll of Psalms from Cave 11 has excited particular interest because, although it parallels the order of the biblical book of Psalms up to a point, beyond that point the order diverges, and additional psalms are appended at the end. Is this a "biblical scroll" from Qumran? It is hard to deny that the writers would have regarded it as their Davidic psalm book (see Sanders 1967) — or could it have been *one* of their Davidic psalm books?

3. Citing a text with the formula "as it is written" has been taken by some scholars as an indication of scriptural status. This formula occurs in references to all five books of the Mosaic canon and is applied, as well, to select books within the "former prophets" (Joshua, Samuel) and the "latter prophets" (Isaiah, Ezekiel, Hosea, Amos, Micah, Zechariah and Malachi) and to Psalms and Proverbs (see Fishbane 1988: 347-56). It is doubtful, however, how useful this information is. The texts that contain the total of seventy or so such citations are actually rather few (CD, 1QS, 4QFlor, 4QTestim, 11QMelch and 1QM) and hardly give us a comprehensive view. There is also at least one such citation of a book that is *not* in the Masoretic canon (CD 4.15 of a statement of Levi son of Jacob). It is not certain, in any case, that a specific formula is invariably applied for citing scriptural books only. The number of allusions to supposedly scriptural books *without* the use of a citation formula is also very large, while, without the formula, CD 16.3-4 refers the reader to the book of *Jubilees* in a way that suggests it may have had scriptural authority (and in fact fragments of at least fifteen copies have been found at Qumran). Given the status accorded to *1 Enoch* by the conservative ben Sira at the beginning of the second century BCE (Sir. 44:16; 49:14), it may well be that an Enochic collection was given such authority even by him, and also by the Qumran writers (not to mention the author of the New Testament letter of Jude: see v. 14). Perhaps Tobit and Sirach also need to be added.

FROM "TEXT" TO "INTERPRETATION"

It is fashionable nowadays to assert that there are no texts, only interpretations, in the light of the claim that readers rather than authors make meanings, and that texts have no intrinsically objective meanings of their own. It is quite clear that in antiquity reading and interpretation were equally hard to disentangle, as is shown particularly by the genre now referred to as "rewritten Bible," in which the scriptural texts are not explicitly *interpreted*, but retold (e.g., 1QapGen, 4Q123, 4Q364-67) and, outside Qumran, by the earliest Greek translations of the Hebrew text, by Josephus and the Targums. Readers of the Jewish Scriptures differed considerably over what they took to be the "objective" meaning of the text. There is, however, a more material problem. Given the variation of textual forms and the fragmentary nature of most of the materials, it is sometimes difficult to distinguish clearly when a fragment represents a scriptural text and when, given a certain level of deviation from the mean, it constitutes instead an adaptation, expansion, or abridgment of a scriptural text. Indeed, the transmission of the Qumran scriptural texts itself offers some examples of interpretation on the part of the copyist as he adds, omits, or changes. We have, in fact, a spectrum of texts. At one end are clearly scriptural scrolls and translations (three Aramaic targums: two of Job, one of Leviticus). There are phylacteries *(tefillin)* and *mezuzoth* that contain excerpts of scriptural texts but are not scriptural scrolls; and there are other texts that appear to display excerpted scriptural passages, both with and without additions (4Q252). Some of these are sequences of texts joined so as to form a kind of theme or plot, and supplied with a linking commentary (4Q364-367). We also encounter paraphrases, commentaries, halakhic rules based on scriptural laws, and, at the other end of the spectrum, texts or passages permeated with scriptural language and allusions which make no explicit citations. The entire range, which will presently be rather sketchily surveyed, shows that these authors undoubtedly were not only familiar with the scriptural texts, but also had inherited and developed a variety of ways in which these texts were presented, represented, interpreted, and applied.

How do we best analyze and interpret this enormous variety, of which, until the fairly recent definitive publication of Cave 4 texts, we had little expectation? There is continuing uncertainty about how "sectarian" the Qumran scrolls are, but the ways in which Scriptures were used here clearly represent a wider pattern of Jewish hermeneutics. Can we therefore speak of any *distinctive* Qumranic interpretation? To an extent, we can, though the peculiarities lie as much in the *content* of the interpretation as in the techniques and genres employed. The material for direct comparison is unfortunately not extensive, since very few exegetical documents have survived from the same time and place as the scrolls. The closest documents — the writings of Philo (who did not live in Judah), Josephus, the New Testament, the early rabbinic texts — are all different in significant ways. Among the closest comparisons, in fact, is a scriptural text itself: the book of Daniel.

EXPLICIT AND IMPLICIT ALLUSION TO SCRIPTURE

As Brooke points out (1985: 36-37), virtually *all* the Qumran texts are to some extent derived from or inspired by Scripture. However, having indicated some of the problems involved with the category of "scriptural" scrolls at Qumran, we may set these (some 25 percent of the total) aside. A useful next step is to survey the substantially preserved interpretive works:

1. **Works of explicit scriptural interpretation (midrashic works):**
   Genesis commentaries (4Q252-254)
   Isaiah *Pesher* (4Q161-165; 3Q4)
   Hosea *Pesher* (4Q166-167)
   Micah *Pesher* (1Q14; 4Q168)
   Nahum *Pesher* (4Q169)
   Habakkuk *Pesher* (1QpHab)
   Zephaniah *Pesher* (1Q15, 4Q170)
   Psalms *Pesher* (1Q16; 4Q171, 173)
   Florilegium (4Q174)
   Catena A (4Q177) (4Q174 + 4Q177 = Eschatological Midrash)
   Testimonia (4Q175)
   Melchizedek Midrash (11Q13)
   Tanhumim (4Q176)

2. **Works that substantially recapitulate or implicitly invoke Scripture:**
   Damascus Document (CD, 4QD266-273; 5QD; 6QD)
   4QMMT (4Q394-399)
   Temple Scroll (11Q19)
   Ordinances (4Q159)
   Tohorot (4Q274, 276-277)
   Jubilees
   Words of Moses (1Q22, 1QDM)
   Genesis Apocryphon
   Genesis-Exodus Paraphrase (4Q422)

"Reworked Pentateuch" (4Q158, 4Q364-367)
"Ages of Creation" (4Q181)
Hodayoth (1QH)

This classification is convenient rather than definitive, since several works contain passages that fall into both categories. Nevertheless, it will serve to distinguish what might be called "interpretation" in the narrow sense ("commentary") from the wider definition. In the case of the Qumran scrolls it is vitally necessary to recognize how prevalent is scriptural interpretation *in the wider sense*.

The distinction between explicit/formal and implicit interpretation generates a spectrum. At one end stands an explicit citation of a scriptural passage, including a citation formula; at the other end, we find the slightest of allusions to a scriptural phrase without any formal indication. We have, then, a series of phrase-by-phrase commentaries on consecutive scriptural text *(pesharim)*, where text and commentary are set side by side, in the manner (though not with the hermeneutics!) of a modern scholarly commentary. Since the writers of these texts were thoroughly familiar with the scriptural literature (see Fishbane 1988: 356-59) and indeed may have spent much of their time copying it, their own compositions not surprisingly make extensive use of scriptural language and vocabulary. At this end of the spectrum it can be difficult to decide whether a scriptural phrase carries enough weight that its use may be called "exegetical." Thus, for example, when the writer of CD 4.19 first alludes to a group he calls the "builders of the wall" *(bwny hhyṣ)*, is he consciously alluding to Ezek. 13:10: ". . . because they have misled my people, saying 'Peace' when there is no peace; and because, when the people build a wall, these prophets daub it with whitewash . . ."? Is it his intention to direct the reader's mind to what he sees as either a similar situation in the past, or even a prophetic prediction of present-day conditions? Or does the phrase simply betray a biblically-steeped author who recalls an apt epithet? In the case of CD, a very good case can in fact be made that the writer has composed a text almost entirely on a structure of scriptural passages and phrases (Campbell 1995).

HALAKHIC AND HAGGADIC INTERPRETATION

The most useful way of reviewing this very wide range of interpretative modes is one that is readily drawn from rabbinic literature: the distinction between *halakhic* and *haggadic* interpretation. Halakhic interpretation (see

Fishbane 1988: 368-70) defines the rules by which a Jew (the texts themselves would say: a "child of Israel" or "member of the covenant") should live according to the revealed divine will. The end is in principle practical, even if (as is sometimes the case) the practice itself cannot be carried out because of barriers imposed by humans or by God. Two alternative goals in such exegesis can then be further distinguished: to develop a set of regulations either for the life of the whole people of Israel or for a sectarian lifestyle seen as a temporary dispensation. Broadly speaking, the former is ideal, in that the conditions for their fulfillment are not met at the time of composition, while the latter is real, in that it is for a group or community defined by its adherence to certain practices understood as being in accordance with the "Torah of Moses."

Haggadic exegesis (see Fishbane 1988: 371-73) for the most part aims to discover from the text some truth from the past or about the future, and thus contributes to the development of a worldview: it is directed toward understanding rather than behavior and seeks to impart a lesson. The Qumran haggadic texts can also be broadly divided into two kinds: those reflecting on the past and those deducing the future (Fishbane [1988: 373-75] describes "prophetic exegesis" as a distinct type). Broadly, then, these two foci can be related to the topic of "history" if we conceive history to cover the course of human life on earth, not only the past but also the present and future.

The above distinctions are no more watertight than any of the others so far introduced: a text like *Jubilees* (of which there are several copies at Qumran) is not generally regarded as a sectarian text, and, though narrative in form, it also serves some halakhic purposes, at least in part. The distinction between an idealized law for a "congregation of Israel" and a real law for a particular Jewish community may also be blurred, because the principles behind both laws must be the same: divine revelation in Scripture. Also, from the laws for all Israel, certain actual practices for particular groups may be implicit. In the case of haggadah, too, reflection on the past may often have as a subtext a belief about the future, as, for example, when the Flood is interpreted as a prototype of an eschatological disaster to fall upon the wicked. For the most part, however, it seems helpful to follow the classification proposed.

Not every Qumran text will be covered by the categories of "halakhic" and "haggadic." Three other sets of broadly interpretative texts also need to be mentioned. A particularly difficult case is presented by liturgical texts, which do not fall clearly into either of the above categories. Although they often use scriptural language very widely, one may debate whether or not they fall into the category of "interpretive," if that is narrowly defined. Their function is performative rather than explanatory, and the role of Scripture in such texts may be largely traditional. Nevertheless, liturgical *forms* and traditional vocabulary do function as vehicles of exegesis, and some account ought to be taken of this aspect of scriptural interpretation at Qumran.

Another category to be mentioned is the wisdom texts, of which a relatively large number have been published recently. As with the liturgical works, it is doubtful that they may be called exegetical in the narrow sense; they are didactic, but their language and imagery are drawn from the scriptural wisdom books. Their educational value derives, in part, from their scriptural antecedents, as does the liturgical power of the hymns and prayers. Apart from explicitly wisdom texts, there are substantial portions of other texts that would have to be classified as "wisdom" and an even larger range of broadly exegetical texts in which "knowledge" and "perception" play an important hermeneutical role.

"PARABIBLICAL" TEXTS

The third category of "broadly interpretive" texts to be considered is the one with which we ought to begin. We need to deal first with those texts that blur the distinction between "biblical texts" and "interpretation"; they fall into a category that is hard to define, but may loosely be termed paraphrase or retelling. While some interpretative intent is to be assumed in these texts, there is usually little or no explicit exegesis present. They can be either halakhic or haggadic in character, depending on the nature of the text they are reworking. It is significant, however, that such texts almost always deal with the Pentateuch, and in particular with Genesis.

The *Genesis Apocryphon* (1QGen Ap) covers some of the same material as the scriptural book, but differently. It is an Aramaic retelling of the story of Noah and Abraham. Because it is ascribed to Lamech, Noah's father, and then to Abraham, it is also (perhaps uniquely) a "double" pseudepigraphon, and hence is to be distinguished from a targum, although its retelling of the story is often reminiscent of the expansive Pseudo-Jonathan Targum. It deals extensively with Noah's miraculous birth (also providing his mother's name, Bitenosh) and even more extensively with the life of Abraham. It does not exhibit any halakhic purpose, but embellishes the story-line with the aim of adding colorful detail, such as Abraham's premonition in a dream of the danger to Sarai (col. 19), details of Sarah's beauty and Abraham's healing of Pharaoh (col. 20).

Another important, but more difficult, text is 4Q252 (see Brooke 1994, 1996), which seems to be made up of a series of episodes from Genesis loosely linked. It deals with the flood, Abraham, Sodom and Gomorrah, and the destruction of Amalek and the blessings of Jacob; but whether or not there is a common thread, a single purpose behind the text, is hard to know. Possibly it has to do with the writers' claim to be the legitimate heirs of the promises, while their contemporaries inherit the curses. This would be consistent with part of the argument of the "Admonition" of CD. In the flood account, the writer seems most interested in arranging the chronology to fit the solar calendar. In the case of Abraham, the writer seems concerned with the details of God's promises and their fulfillment; while in the Sodom and Gomorrah episode, the writer perhaps underlines the destruction that attends illicit sexual behavior. As with several other texts from Qumran, this "Genesis Commentary" defies any single generic categorization, and seems to fluctuate between a paraphrased biblical text, a glossed biblical text, and a text with explicit commentary.

Another curious text recently published in full (Tov 1994; 1992) belongs to the same genre and is called *4QReworked Pentateuch*. It is believed to have originally contained the entire Pentateuch. The four copies, now represented only by fragments, offer an extensive text. This work consists of a running text of the Pentateuch, but with omissions and additions, the additions taking the form of comments. Sometimes the scriptural sequence is even altered. A particularly problematic aspect of this text, however, is that it blurs the distinction between a "biblical scroll" and an "exegetical scroll." In content it very largely resembles a biblical scroll, and were it not so extensively preserved, no doubt fragments of it would have been regarded as such. Perhaps "annotated scriptural scroll" is a suitable description.

One of its more notorious additions is a poem appended to the Song of Moses (Exodus 15) and sharing several features with it. It is possible (see White in Trebolle Barrera 1992: 217-28) that this is supposed to be the Song of Miriam (mentioned in Exod. 15:20-21). In another instance, the two passages in Numbers dealing with the daughters of Zelophehad (chs. 27 and 36) are juxtaposed. One of the fragments, in fact (4Q365, fragment 28), overlaps with cols. 41-42 of the Temple Scroll (non-scriptural material), and indeed it is the (halakhic) Temple Scroll that this text closely resembles in many ways when it reorganizes the sequence of scriptural texts according to subject matter. The Genesis-Exodus Paraphrase (4Q422) belongs to the same genre as this text, if indeed we can speak here of a single genre at all.

HALAKHAH: SCRIPTURE AS LAW

We can now consider more explicitly interpretative texts. Under this rubric we should regard as relating primarily to *community* practice the collections of sectarian rules in the *Damascus Document* (and other fragmentary texts); and as relating to *Israelite* practice the systematic reorganization of Mosaic torah in the *Temple Scroll* and the purity rules as advocated in the letter 4QMMT.

The hermeneutical theory of the QDamascus (CD) texts is fairly simple, stated several times in the *Admonition* (CD A). The law that was revealed by Moses was disobeyed by preexilic Israel, which was punished; a preserved remnant was given a true revelation of God's desires, to which it has subsequently adhered (CD 6.2-11). The rest of Israel, however, has continued to be led astray by Belial, so that it does not obey the true law of Moses and God. Examples of this are marriage between uncle and niece and permitting of divorce (CD 4.13–5.11). Both of these criticisms, however, are supported and defended not by newly-revealed *texts,* but by an interpretation of the scriptural Mosaic Torah. Thus, on the first count, the argument is made that Scripture forbids a woman to marry her nephew and "the regulation regarding incest is written for the male, but women likewise" (5.9-10), while on divorce the writer appeals not only to Gen. 1:27 (see also Matt. 19:4; Mark 10:6) but also to the "two and two" that Noah took into the ark (examples of non-legal scriptural texts used to support a halakhic argument can also be found in rabbinic texts).

The difference lies, then, in the *interpretation,* which the writers claim to be divinely given, and given to their group alone. A distinction is thus made between "revealed" *(nigleh)* and "hidden" *(nistar)* revelation, the latter giving the true meaning of the former (see Schiffman 1975). The name given to the correct interpretation is *perush* (or *perush ha-torah,* CD 6.14). Appropriately, the title given to the person credited with having founded the Damascus sect is *doresh ha-torah,* "interpreter of the law" (6.7).

Much of the Damascus Document is taken up by collections of community laws derived from Scripture. In some cases (9.2, 8; 16.6, 10) the law is preceded by an explicit citation formula, "as it says" *(asher 'amar),* but elsewhere it is stated without such backing, although the laws are always traceable to a scriptural origin, and indeed the formulas often used to introduce the laws follow scriptural precedents ("let no one . . ."). However, the "Damascus" group(s) have also decided "not to come into the sanctuary so as to kindle His altar in vain," a statement backed up by an explicit citation from Mal. 1:10 (CD 6.12), thereby, apparently, withdrawing to some degree from direct participation in the cult. Hence, the laws under which they are living, though derived from Scripture, are "for the period of wickedness" (6.14). Thus, the body of interpreted law is provisional, and will apply only until "one who will teach righteousness at the end of days" arrives (6.11). Thus, just as the "interpreter of the law" brought a revealed interpretation in the past, so another revealed interpretation will be brought in the future. The laws of CD are in reality derived from the application of practical rules (and inherited customs, no doubt), in large measure developed from, or in relation to, the scriptural Torah of Moses, but also guaranteed by a separate revelation. Such a twofold source of authority will be found elsewhere in Qumran exegesis, though not without exception.

One of the exceptions, indeed, is found in 4QMMT (see Qimron and Strugnell 1994). In this text, which apparently represents a letter from one group to another (or to an individual, a ruler of the nation), a number of differences in cultic practice are listed. But the writers refer to "our rulings" (B1), writing "but *we* reckon" (*'nḥnw*). There is no clear appeal to revealed knowledge. Rather, the writers urge, (C10) "we have [written] to you so that you may perceive (*tbyn*) in the Torah of Moses and the books of the prophets. . . ." It is unlikely, though not impossible, that the root *byn* refers to revealed or privileged knowledge rather than to intelligence. The writers in fact go on to appeal to the Scriptures as predicting what was happening in their own time, apparently expecting their addressee(s) to be convinced.

This text reveals to us only that at least two different sets of traditional interpretations of purity laws were in effect. Scripture is always implied, and the topics of impurity are undoubtedly those dictated by the scriptural legislation (e.g., the "red heifer," B13, or firstfruits, B63). But Scripture is rarely cited, and no exegetical *arguments* are deployed. There are grounds for connecting this text historically in some way with the Damascus texts, but the hermeneutics are rather different. For the most part, the Damascus texts relate not to disputes with others but to intra-community regulations, in which, for whatever reason, the scriptural text, as we have seen, lies closer to the surface (which it sometimes breaks).

A third important case of halakhic exegesis is the Temple Scroll (11QT), which is a compilation of scriptural texts (mostly from Deuteronomy) into systematic form; but it also introduces several non-scriptural items. Notably, as with all Qumran texts that deal with calendrical matters, it adopts a 364-day calendar. In re-presenting scriptural laws, it transforms the (Mosaic) third-person speech of Deuteronomy into first-person, so making more explicit their divine authorship (as elsewhere in the Pentateuch) — but it does the same for laws not found in the Scriptures! It also harmonizes the wording of similar scriptural passages, sometimes to clarify variant formulations, but sometimes to extend or create new laws (e.g., Lev. 23:15-21 and Num. 28:26-31 at 11QT 18ff.; Lev. 16; 23:27-32; and Num. 29:7-11 at 11QT 25.10ff.). Is the Temple Scroll, then, intended to be an authoritative torah, replacing the scriptural form of the Mosaic Pentateuch, or is it a commentary?

A similar question may be asked of *Jubilees,* and it is hard to answer. Perhaps that is because the question may be invalid. After all, in the case of the Scriptures, were the varying laws in Exodus, Leviticus, and Deuteronomy meant to replace or interpret each other? Creatively rewriting, and indeed adding, without abrogating the authority of the source has precedents. Somewhat later, we encounter the *Diatessaron* of Tatian, a harmonization of the four New Testament Gospels, which in some churches had a canonical status alongside those Gospels (see conveniently Petersen 1992). In the present case, it is clear that no authoritative Jewish law could afford to dispense with the agency of Moses. On the other hand, we obviously are not dealing with a "fundamentalist" attitude to the scriptural form of that law. While its substance is certainly authoritative, interpretation may need to go to extreme lengths to bring the text of that Mosaic law into line with its "correct" meaning.

Other text, such as the *tohorot* or ordinances also comprise legal rulings clearly based on scriptural categories but without explicit citations, and indeed without presenting their laws as exegetically derived. This is also the case with 4QMMT, though, as we have seen, that text clearly claims to champion the "law of Moses." There is no doubt that these rules were also understood to be Mosaic, even though they were not scripturally explicit. This phenomenon is interesting, but by no means unexpected. Neusner's analysis of the development of the Mishnah (1981) concluded that its laws were not, in fact, presented from the outset as exegetically derived, even though the general structure of the legal categories was unmistakably scriptural. The rabbinic notion of the Oral Law, whereby rulings not in the scriptural text of the Torah are regarded as nonetheless part of the divine revelation to Moses on Sinai, is a device to accommodate just this kind of eventuality, though this observation does *not* mean that we have an "oral law" in the Qumran texts. Rather, in these writings the scriptural laws could be appealed to verbatim in disputes and would be held to be authoritative; but in the development of codes of behavior, whether social or cultic, exegetical expansion of scriptural texts did not *necessarily* play a fundamental role (though we have seen that the laws in CD do contain some citations of Scripture). Scriptural *categories* were observed, though not necessarily because they were scriptural — they may have been a common cultural/cultic denominator — but in matters such as the

calendar or the insertion of certain festivals (as in the Temple Scroll), where
there was no scriptural basis, Scripture was ignored, or, as in a case we shall
consider presently, Scripture could be rewritten! The "law of Moses" was not
coextensive with the written text of the five scrolls of the Pentateuch, but designated the authoritative (and necessarily Mosaic) code by which a "Judaism"
(an "Israel") lived, expressed in its actual practices and rules.

SCRIPTURE AS HISTORY LESSON

The insight that Scripture did not always (or usually) function *verbatim* as a
legal authority applies particularly well to the non-legal material also. It is
clear (cf. Sir. 44–49; Josephus, *Ag. Ap.* 1.37-43) that in addition to being the
written basis of Torah, the Scriptures functioned as a *story* of Israel's past, one
that taught lessons for the present and the future. It was the story itself, rather
than a "canonical" account of it, that mattered. Now, in a society where oral
culture thrives alongside a smaller, elite literary culture, stories do not persist
in fixed, canonical forms: stories exist to be told, and in the recreating of the
story clearer, better, or just different meanings can be taught through it. This
understanding of the ongoing vitality of the retold story explains, perhaps,
why so many of the texts from Qumran, in narrating Israel's past, do not always adhere to the scriptural details. Indeed, there is sometimes quite a variation. The simplest and most effective way to exegete a story, in other words, is
to retell it; and scriptural stories were evidently not exempted from this procedure.

A simple example is contained in CD 2.14–3.20, where the writer is urging the readers to follow the path of God's will and not their own inclinations.
For "many have gone astray on these issues. Heroes have been brought down
because of them" (2.16-17). The first example given of this recurrent pattern is
of the "Heavenly Watchers"; then Noah and his sons, the Israelites in Egypt,
and then the kings of Israel. The picture painted is of virtually continuous
disobedience, and the scriptural story is summed up in a certain way so as to
support the claim. As for detail, the story of the "Watchers" is preserved in *Jubilees* and *1 Enoch*, telling of a revolt of some of these heavenly beings who fell
to earth and corrupted it. The story, truncated and revised in Gen. 6:1-4 (including in the Qumran Genesis scrolls) does not say this much; the writer of
CD nevertheless takes it for granted that everyone knows what the scriptural
story was *really* about.

We can now turn to some more elaborate cases of retold scriptural stories. The book of *Jubilees*, previously known in full in Ethiopic translation,

should be mentioned first, because several fragments in its original language (Hebrew) have been found at Qumran. *Jubilees* is almost certainly the text cited in CD 16.2-4 as a source for "the specifications of the periods of Israel's blindness," and it claims to be an account revealed to Moses on Sinai of history up to that point (as covered in Genesis and Exodus). Its main features are the role of Mastema (Satan, Belial) as the instigator of evil (including the testing of Abraham with the sacrifice of Isaac), and the obedience of the patriarchs to the law of Moses, though this law prescribes a solar calendar (364 days a year), especially regarding the scrupulous observation of sabbath rest. It also follows ("imposes" would be better) a chronology of "weeks" (composed of seven years) and "jubilees" (seven "weeks" of years). This system is also found in several other writings of the period, including Daniel 9, *1 Enoch* and the *Melchizedek Midrash*, though these others have a more evidently eschatological focus to their calendar. As with many of the Qumran interpretative texts, *Jubilees* is virtually impossible to classify generically: it has features of both halakhic and haggadic midrash, paraphrase, apocalypse, testament, and historiography. As midrash, it interprets both the scriptural story and certain scriptural laws, providing a very useful and important reminder that the uses of Scripture in the Qumran scrolls cannot always be neatly compartmentalized.

A large number of texts present figures from the past who issue warnings about the behavior of Israel, exhorting Israel to observe the will of God and avoid catastrophe. Sometimes these addresses are embedded in narrative. They include (the list cannot be exhaustive) the *Words of Moses* (1Q22, 1QDM), to which can be added several other Moses pseudepigrapha from Cave 4, apocrypha of Samuel, Jeremiah, Ezekiel, and Daniel, all too fragmentary to deal with here. There are also various testaments of patriarchs: Jacob, Judah, Levi, as well as the lesser-known figures Qahat and Amram, grandfather and father of Moses respectively. While such compositions at times contain predictive elements, anticipating future events, their main function is usually exhortation. In other words, eschatological judgment and salvation are not the subjects of detailed prediction, but rather are prompts to ethical behavior.

While there is a sense (as we have seen) in which Scripture as history is used to disclose and warn about the future, most of the Qumran texts that explicitly treat Scripture as predicting the future (and that means the "last days") adopt a different hermeneutic, which we may call "mantic." Manticism is the culture of divination, a major science in the ancient world, especially in Babylonia. It took the form of examining natural or unnatural phenomena that it interpreted as heavenly "clues" to what would happen. Such phenomena could take the form of dreams, animal entrails, meteorological events, or anomalous animal births, to name the most common. Sometimes these phenomena were artificially induced, and sometimes not.

In the case of the Qumran texts, the "signs" are scriptural texts, which are, accordingly, understood as conveying their meaning by means of a code, rather than through the obvious surface sense. The writers of these scriptural texts, then, did not control the meaning, and were not necessarily fully aware of it. This code, embedded by God in his revealed words, needed to be interpreted in order for the prediction to be discovered. It is worth observing that this approach to prophetic texts fully adopted the view that they were inspired verbatim by God and intended for the attention of future generations, not the prophets' own generations.

The technique is evident in Daniel 9, where a text from Jeremiah is interpreted to Daniel by a heavenly being. It also constitutes the interpretive method of the group of commentaries from Qumran called *pesharim*. These commentaries are confined to prophetic books, plus Psalms. The book of Psalms was often used at Qumran, as well as in the New Testament, as a source of predictions, since David, the presumed writer of the Psalms, was considered a prophet. The name of these commentaries, *pesharim,* derives from the format of citing a phrase or sentence from the chosen scroll, then appending its "interpretation" (Hebrew *pesher*). Such a device is also found in other texts, such as the Florilegium (4QFlor) and the Melchizedek midrash (11QMelch), which do not exhibit this form overall. There is, however, an important difference between the *pesharim* proper and these other texts. The purpose of the *pesharim* is not to reveal the future, but to show *that what was predicted long ago in Scripture has already taken place.* The point of this claim is not just to demonstrate that the end times have already begun but also to emphasize the central role in these events played by the group authoring the *pesher.* The interpretation of the prophetic book turns out to be an account of the origins and history of a figure called the "teacher of righteousness," his opponents, and the groups which he founded (these details are confirmed in CD 1 and 19–20). The teacher's gift of interpretation was apparently bequeathed to his followers, from whom the composers of the *pesharim* are evidently drawn.

The hermeneutic just described is in fact very neatly summarized in the Habakkuk commentary:

> And God told Habakkuk to write that which was to happen to the final generation, but he did not reveal to him when time would come to an end. And as for the statement "He who reads it may run," its interpreta-

tion refers to the teacher of righteousness, to whom God revealed all the mysteries of his servants the prophets. (1QpHab 7.1-5)

If the *pesharim* are primarily concerned with identifying recent events as being those foretold in Scripture, another group of midrashim deal with events still ahead of the writer. They include the Melchizedek midrash and the Eschatological Midrash (Florilegium + Catena A: see Steudel 1994).

In the Melchizedek midrash (11QMelch) we find phrases from various scriptural scrolls, including some from all three sections of the Masoretic canon, combined into a literary form different from the *pesharim* in that it does not deal with a single scriptural book. There are, in fact, some sections in which the *pesher* technique (including the technical terminology) is applied over a single verse. More commonly, however, this midrash weaves texts from different Scriptures into a coherent argument about the end of world history. The importance of this technique is that it already implies at this early date what the rabbis were later to accept, namely, that *all* scriptural texts form a unity and that the meaning of a passage in one scroll may be elucidated by a passage in another. Rather than one scroll containing a series of disconnected and coded oracles about future events, the source of this midrash is an entire set of scriptural writings, all of which, when put together in the right way, contain a message about the end. Whether this message is, as with the *pesharim,* understood as encoded and claimed to be reached by some kind of divinely-given revelation or insight, or, as with the rabbis, is recognized as the outcome of putting different texts together in a rational sequence, is hard to say. The distinction may be ours alone. We have already seen that exegetically-derived laws can be presented as a new revelation. To the minds of the authors of these texts the two perspectives are not incompatible: any process of human thought can be claimed as a divine prompting. This may explain the embedding of *pesher* segments within this midrash.

The preserved text, of which the beginning is lost, opens in the middle of an explanation of the jubilee year, citing Lev. 25:13 and Deut. 15:2, focusing on the release of slaves and debts. This law is then expanded by means of Isa. 61:1, which also speaks of the release of prisoners. Therefore, the text refers to a jubilee. Since debts to God take the form of sins (note the different wording of the "Lord's prayer" in Matt. 6:12 [*opheilēmata*] and Luke 11:4 [*hamartia*]) and are atoned for on behalf of all Israel every year by the High Priest at the Day of Atonement, the agent of this final release of debts to God will be the heavenly High Priest on the final day of atonement in history. This heavenly figure is identified as Melchizedek, and the date is "the end of the tenth jubilee," that is, after 490 or 500 years from the start of the calendar (which is the destruction of the temple and the beginning of the Babylonian exile), depending on whether one counts a jubilee as 49 or 50 years.

A similar though not quite identical mixture of devices is found in the "Eschatological Midrash" reconstructed by Steudel (1994) from the Florilegium and Catena A (that they form a single text is very likely, though not conclusively shown). This, like the *pesharim*, is apparently based on a sequence of quotations from a single scroll, the Psalms, and follows their canonical order. Unlike the *pesharim*, it does not address every single verse in a single psalm, but individual verses from a whole sequence of psalms. Each interpretation is buttressed in turn by other quotations from the Prophets. The *pesher* formula is used for the Psalms quotations, but different formulas (e.g., "as it is written") are employed for the non-Psalms texts. The explication of texts from one scroll by texts from others follows the principle of the Melchizedek midrash, but the execution is carried out differently, and the plot of the midrash is more difficult to discern. Its subject matter is the experiences of the men of the same community (the *yahad*) as those in the *pesharim*, though it does not mention their teacher. From the texts dealt with it emerges that these people (who now call themselves "children of light") will be assailed by their enemies ("children of Belial") but may expect vindication and return to Jerusalem, while their enemies and persecutors, the "children of Belial," are to be destroyed.

In addition to explicit commentaries, we also find at Qumran collections of texts on a common theme, or anthologies. One of these, called *Testimonia*, has as its theme messianic predictions. After an introduction from Deuteronomy 5 about keeping the commandments, it starts with the promise in Deuteronomy 18 of a future prophet. It continues with the "star" prophecy of Balaam (Num. 24:15-17) and the blessing on Levi from Deut. 33:8-11, which is probably to be understood as referring to the Messiah of Levi. It ends, strangely, with Josh. 6:26, which curses the one who will rebuild Jericho. This is followed by a comment that someone, a "son of Belial," has rebuilt it and has also made Jerusalem a "fortress of impiety."

The similar collection of texts called *Tanhumim* ("Consolations") opens with a selection of passages from Isaiah on the theme of God's comforting Israel during or after her sufferings. Like the *Testimonia*, it closes with an apparent attempt to explain why God permits suffering (it is a "mystery"), and alludes to the rewards of the righteous.

Finally, there is a text called *Ages of Creation*, which opens with the phrase "Interpretation *(pesher)* concerning the ages that God has created." It initiates a series of such "interpretations" concerning Azazel (the leader of the fallen "Watchers" — see above), and Sodom and Gomorrah. The use of the word *pesher* here suggests perhaps a conscious esoteric understanding of the history as narrated in the scriptural books. This would mean, for instance, that what may appear as the history of Israel is really the history of a struggle between forces of light and darkness (or angelic and human forces). This history is perhaps being continued in the history of the authoring sect rather than in the fortunes of the Jewish people as a whole. Unfortunately, the text, like so many, is too fragmentary to confirm fully whether or not this understanding is correct. It can be said with some probability, however, that the whole of Scripture could be, and was, read as a sectarian history by those who regarded themselves as the true Israel. Whether or not explicit comments were written, there was often an implicit reading below the surface of the text pointing to an underlying esoteric narrative.

LITURGY AS SCRIPTURAL INTERPRETATION

It hardly needs remarking that the liturgy of the Qumran scrolls is permeated with scriptural language and that this language both reinforces the ancient and divine background of the liturgy and, at times, pushes it in the direction of a new worldview. This statement is, however, true of nearly all psalmody of the late Second Temple period (Holm-Nielsen 1960: 19; Schuller 1986: 10-12). When surveying the Qumran liturgies, we cannot in every case decide whether we are dealing with a specifically sectarian liturgy, that is, one that was composed *for* the sect rather than just being used *by* the sect. Two texts do, however, fairly clearly suggest some kind of sectarian ideology: the Hymns (1QH), and the Songs of the Sabbath Sacrifice (4QShirShabb). A sectarian origin for the non-apocryphal Psalms (4Q380-81) is not so obvious.

Of course, in analyzing any hymnody that follows a scriptural idiom, it is often impossible to decide when shared vocabulary is simply generic, when there are conscious or unconscious allusions, and when there is a deliberate quotation of as small a unit as a single word. Taken as a whole, Qumran hymns and psalms have to be seen as scriptural interpretation of a sort, for the allusions and quotations are intended in some way to apply the scriptural language to the experiences and feelings evoked in the later composition. The Hymns (1QH) are a clear example of the way in which scriptural language is used pervasively to exploit a rather non-scriptural theology (see Holm-Neilsen's extensive discussion [1960]). The main themes of the *Hodayoth* are thanksgiving for having been rescued from the "lot" of the wicked (a dualistic concept) and having been given knowledge of the divine mysteries. The biographical references contained in the scriptural psalms of lament in particular, which are underlined by the use of superscriptions assigning them to episodes in David's life (both the LXX and the Q11 Psalms scroll have more of these than does the MT), are here interwoven into these themes. Consequently, some scholars have tended to assign them to the founder of the *yahad*, the "Teacher of Righteousness." Thus, the "wicked" and "treacherous" of the scriptural psalms become the author's own enemies. Whereas the Psalms *pesher* makes the scriptural text formally predictive, these hymns make it typological: the scriptural language applies with particular appropriateness to the figure writing at the "end of days." This hermeneutic makes it difficult to decide whether, or to what extent, we can reconstruct a reliable biography of the author from these poems, or whether we should instead consider these descriptions to be inspired by the stereotyped language of scriptural psalms. New Testament scholars have a similar difficulty with parts of the Passion narratives.

The Songs of the Sabbath Sacrifice is a cycle describing the liturgy of the angels (called variously *'elohim, mal'akim,* and *qedoshim*), covering thirteen sabbaths, a quarter of a 364-day year. (In another Qumran text, the 11Q Psalms Scroll, however, David is credited with 52 "songs for the sacrifice of the sabbaths.") This cycle displays a particular dependence on Ezekiel 1 and 10, in which the chariot-throne is described (Newsom 1985: 55-56). From our point of view, the interesting question is whether this text reflects a practice or literary tradition (including the names of angels) that is largely excluded from the scriptural texts: a practice that acknowledged, perhaps, the Jerusalem temple as being a material copy of a heavenly one. Alternatively, and more probably in the view of most scholars, this cycle may be a development peculiar to a group excluded from the Jerusalem temple and thus obliged to focus its liturgy on the heavenly cult. In the former case, it could be argued that Ezekiel is already reflecting beliefs (and practices?) of an earlier time; while in the latter case, the relationship between the Qumran text and Ezekiel will have been a creatively exegetical one. It is conceivable that *no* practice actually underlies the Qumran text at all, or that it is an aid to a mystical experience, in which case it might be classified as an expanded midrash on Ezekiel.

As for the apocryphal psalms, Schuller (1986: 34-38) has noted that they rely very largely on the scriptural psalms (unsurprisingly) and has classified the use of Scripture in the non-canonical psalms as follows: quotation of more than a bicolon of a scriptural text, linkage to a specific text, and use of only sporadic quotations. Among the first are cases of as much as five consecutive lines. The second group shares a good deal of vocabulary with a particular scriptural psalm, though in these cases extensive verbatim quotation is rare. Rather, these psalms rework the language of the scriptural text. In the case of the last group, where biblical citation amounts to the occasional word or short phrase, it may even be questioned whether such vocabulary is direct quotation or simply common liturgical stock.

WISDOM AS SCRIPTURAL INTERPRETATION

In common with late Second Temple psalmody, the Qumran psalms reflect an increased employment of wisdom terminology, especially in the roots *byn* ("perceive," "understand") and *śkl* ("be wise, discerning"). The general prevalence both of wisdom texts and of wisdom vocabulary and ideology in the scrolls makes it important to consider wisdom as an aspect of scriptural interpretation in the Qumran literature.

In the books of Proverbs and ben Sira, the ancient Near Eastern genre of instructional wisdom is represented: here learning the conventional and empirically derived rules of social conduct offers the reward of a good life and a good reputation. Another strand of "wisdom," using overlapping vocabulary, regards wisdom more and more in terms of esoteric knowledge, and the "wise" person as one who has received, by virtue of allegiance to a certain group, discernment into things not generally knowable. Knowledge, in short, becomes the means of salvation: God is sometimes even called the "God of knowledge" (e.g., 1QS 3.15), and terms like *maśkil* ("sage") and *mebin* ("perceptive"), both key wisdom terms, are used to denote respectively the master and the pupil within the sectarian community.

The term "wisdom" text might be applied to a great deal of the Qumran literature, and both 1QS and CD have sections of wisdom teaching. However, here we should concentrate on texts that interpret scriptural wisdom. The most famous, entitled "Wiles of the Wicked Woman" (4Q184; see Allegro 1968: 82-85), illustrates a typical dilemma facing Qumran scholars. It describes a woman who is generally understood to be the evil woman of Proverbs 7 (from which a good deal of the language and imagery is clearly borrowed). Is this merely a reprise of the scriptural warning against folly, or is it a sectarian warning against defection? Or is it directed against women in general, in a possibly celibate community, since, among other things, this woman "makes the simple rebel against God" (line 15). Another wisdom hymn (4Q185) describes something or someone (the pronoun is feminine) that will bless the righteous as he seeks her out. Other wisdom texts such as 4Q413, 416-18 appear to offer a wider range of advice on various life situations where the right conduct is needed. Now and then in these texts one encounters passages that speak of "mysteries" (in particular, the curious expression "mystery of what is," or "is to be," *rz nhyh*), and allude to final distress and judgment, and to a person's "spirit." These references show that despite stretches of "non-sectarian" traditional wisdom language, there is a very different world-view lying behind these compositions. As has been said earlier, the importance of this insight is not only that these texts are, after all, possibly "sectarian," but also that they show how the scriptural texts were being *understood* as they were read. For if it is true, as it undoubtedly is, that the writers of the Qumran literature, and the readers as well, were students of the Scriptures, it follows that they found in these Scriptures the confirmation of their own way of life, of their history, beliefs, and of their expectations for the future.

CONCLUSION: SCRIPTURE AS SECTARIAN

We can say with some justification that among those addressed by the Qumran scrolls, including one or more sects, the Scriptures themselves were "sectarianized" in the very act of reading. There was *no fundamental conceptual distinction* in the minds of these writers between a scriptural text and a sectarian interpretation. The interpretation, after all, only seeks to make clear what the text itself means. If this is fully appreciated, then it becomes easier to understand why, among the Qumran writings, there is an almost complete spectrum of genres and techniques for converting the implicitly sectarian Scriptures into explicitly sectarian interpretations: from scriptural scroll to rewritten scriptural scroll to explicit commentary to wisdom or liturgical texts in scriptural language. The Scriptures provided, to the writers and readers of these scrolls, the worldview of Qumran Judaism(s), and for the most part, that worldview was sectarian — even if only from our point of view. From their perspective, then, everything they wrote did no more than make clear Scripture's true meaning, and in it they saw their own selves.

BIBLIOGRAPHY

Allegro, J. M. [with A. A. Anderson]
1968   *Qumran Cave 4:I*. DJD 5. Oxford: Clarendon.

Attridge, H., et al. (eds.)
1994   *Qumran Cave 4, VIII. Parabiblical Texts*. DJD 13. Oxford: Clarendon.

Brooke, G. J.
1985   *Exegesis at Qumran: 4QFlorilegium in Its Jewish Context*. JSOTS 29. Sheffield: JSOT.
1994   "The Thematic Content of 4Q252." *JQR* 85:33-59.
1996   "4Q252 as Early Jewish Commentary." *RevQ* 17:385-401.

Campbell, J. G.

1995   *The Use of Scripture in the Damascus Document 1-8, 19-20.* BZAW 228. Berlin: de Gruyter.

Davies, P. R.

1990   "Halakhah at Qumran." In P. R. Davies and R. T. White (eds.) *A Tribute to Geza Vermes: Essays on Jewish and Christian Literature and History,* 37-50. JSOTS 100. Sheffield: JSOT.

Fishbane, M.

1988   "Use, Authority and Interpretation of Mikra at Qumran." In M. J. Mulder (ed.) *Mikra: Text, Translation, Reading and Interpretation of the Hebrew Bible in Ancient Judaism and Early Christianity,* 339-77. CRINT 1. Assen: Van Gorcum.

Holm-Nielsen, S.

1960   *Hodayot: Psalms from Qumran.* Aarhus: Universitetsvorlaget.

Neusner, J.

1981   *Judaism: The Evidence of the Mishnah.* Chicago: Chicago University Press.

Newsom, C. A.

1985   *Songs of the Sabbath Sacrifice: A Critical Edition.* HSS 27. Atlanta: Scholars.

Petersen, W. L.

1992   "Diatesseron." In *ABD,* II, 189-90.

Qimron, E. and J. Strugnell

1994   *Qumran Cave 4,V Miqṣat Maʿaśe Ha-Torah.* DJD 10. Oxford: Clarendon.

Sanders, J. A.

1967   *The Dead Sea Psalms Scroll.* Ithaca: Cornell University Press.

Schiffman, L. H.

1975   *The Halakhah at Qumran.* Leiden: Brill.

Schuller, E. M.

1986   *Non-Canonical Psalms from Qumran: A Pseudepigraphic Collection.* HSS 28. Atlanta: Scholars.

Steudel, A.

1994   *Der Midrasche zur Eschatologie aus der Qumrangemeinde (4QMidrEsch[a.b]).* Leiden: Brill.

Tov, E.

1992   "The Textual Status of 4Q364-367 (4QPP)," in Trebolle Berrara and Montaner (eds.) 1992: 43-82.

1994   "364-367: 4Q Reworked Pentateuch[b-e] and 365a.4QTemple?" in Attridge, et al. (eds.) 1994: 187-97.

Trebolle Barrera, J., and L. Vegas Montaner (eds.)
1992   *The Madrid Qumran Congress: Proceedings of the International Congress on the Dead Sea Scrolls, Madrid 18-21 March 1991.* Leiden: Brill.

White, S. C.
1992   "4Q364 & 365: A Preliminary Report." In Trebolle Barrera and Montaner (eds.) 1992: 217-28.

CHAPTER 6

Interpretation of Scripture in the Targumim

Martin McNamara

The targumim are early Jewish translations of books of the Hebrew Bible into Aramaic. They are, by definition and in practice, interpretations at two levels: through translation of the Hebrew texts and through their efforts to bring out what was perceived to be the meaning of these same texts for later generations.

ORIGIN AND DEVELOPMENT OF TARGUMIC TRADITION

Rabbinic tradition (y. *Meg.* 74d; b. *Meg.* 3a) traces the origin of targumic translation back to the solemn reading of the law of Moses by Ezra in the seventh year of the Persian king Artaxerxes (458 or 398 BCE), as recounted in Neh. 8:1-3, 8, interpreting v. 8 as referring to translation. It is very doubtful, however, that this text refers to translation into Aramaic. Hebrew was still probably the language of the Jewish people in Judah and Jerusalem, making an Aramaic translation or interpretation unnecessary.

But by the turn of the era, and well before 70 CE, Aramaic was the vernacular of Jewish communities in Palestine, Syria, Mesopotamia, and elsewhere. Ezra's task, that of reading and explaining the Scriptures, particularly the Pentateuch, was a central part of Jewish life in these areas. With the aim of bringing out the meaning, or rather multiple meanings, of the text, the Scriptures were the object of philological examination and religious, devotional reflection. Rabbinic Midrash (see chapter 7 below) records some of this reflection on the text. The reflection took place in a bilingual setting, where the

The Targums

We possess three targumim of the Pentateuch: *Targum Onqelos*, the *Palestinian Targum,* represented by Codex *Neofiti* 1 and the fragmentary targumim, and the *Targum of Pseudo-Jonathan.*

 Targum Onqelos (Tg. Onq.) contains all five books of the Pentateuch. It was composed before 135 CE and revised later. It is preserved in more than sixty manuscripts. For the most part it aims at translating the sense of the Hebrew text both idiomatically and as closely as possible to literal meaning. In debated issues of *halakah* it favors the school of Rabbi Aqiba against that of Rabbi Ishmael (see Grossfeld 1988b: 33). It also contains non-halakic midrash (see Vermes 1963) and in a number of instances agrees with the midrashic paraphrase of the Palestinian targumim (e.g., Gen. 49:10; Num. 20:18-20; 24:17-19). Behind our present text of *Targum Onqelos* there seems to stand an old form of a Palestinian targum represented also by *Targum Neofiti* and the fragmentary targumim. Since *Onqelos* became the official targum of Babylonian Judaism in the second century and later of Western Judaism, its text is cited in rabbinic writings as an authoritative understanding of the Torah.

 The different forms of the *Palestinian Targum of the Pentateuch (Pal.)* are all possibly based on a first-century CE prototype, though the wording we have in the extant manuscripts comes from no earlier than the third century CE. *Codex Neofiti 1* was copied out in 1504 (or 1499) and contains many glosses and evidence of considerable reworking of the text prior to the manuscript, though much of the text seems to be from the first century CE. It includes the entire Pentateuch except for sixteen or so omitted verses. Apart from the beginning (Gen. 1:1–3:4) and the ending (Deut. 29:17[18]–34:12), which are probably from another Palestinian targum manuscript, *Neofiti* represents a unitary translation. It is a literary work, not a pastiche of traditions or compilation of different pieces of translation. Words and phrases of the Hebrew Text tend to be translated in the same manner throughout the entire work. The fragmentary targums preserve portions of the *Palestinian Targum* in manuscripts in Paris (P, fifteenth century), the Vatican Library (V, thirteenth century), Nuremberg (N, thirteenth century), and Leipzig (L, thirteenth-fourteenth centuries). Fragmentary texts from the eighth to thirteenth centuries were also found in the Cairo synagogue genizah.

 Pseudo Jonathan (Tg. Ps.-J.) was composed in the seventh to ninth centuries and printed in 1591 from a manuscript now lost. It is also preserved in a British Library manuscript of the fifteenth or sixteenth century. It is now generally recognized that *Pseudo-Jonathan* should not properly be classified as representing the *Palestinian targum*. It uses sections of the *Palestinian targumim* and of *Targum Onqelos,* but also apocryphal and other writings. It is the work of a scholar and was not intended for synagogue use.

The *Targum of the Prophets* (*Tg. Neb.,* from Hebrew *Nebi'im*) contains both the "Former Prophets" (Joshua, Judges, 1-2 Samuel, and 1-2 Kings = *Tg. Josh.,* etc.) and the "Latter Prophets" (Isaiah, Jeremiah, Ezekiel, and the Twelve Minor Prophets = *Tg. Isa.,* etc.) of the Hebrew canon. It was originally composed before 135 CE, though whether before or after 70 CE is disputed, and revised later. It is now preserved in more than twenty manuscripts.

The T*argum of the Writings* (*Tg. Ket.,* from Hebrew *Ketubim*) contains the third part of the Hebrew canon except for Daniel, Ezra, and Nehemiah, of which no targum is known. The text of *Targum Psalms (Tg. Pss.)* goes back to the seventh to ninth centuries and is preserved in fourteen manuscripts. The text of *Targum Job (Tg. Job)* goes back to the seventh to ninth centuries and is also preserved in fourteen manuscripts. The date of origin of *Targum Proverbs (Tg. Prov.)* is uncertain (second to seventh centuries). It is preserved in at least eight manuscripts from the thirteenth to sixteenth centuries. The date of *Targum Ruth (Tg. Ruth)* is also uncertain (third to seventh centuries); it is preserved in many manuscripts from Europe and Yemen. *Targum Canticles (Tg. Cant.)* is preserved in two distinct forms, Yemenite and Western, and is very similar in language to *Targum Lamentations (Tg. Lam).* It was composed possibly in the seventh century and is preserved in over sixty manuscripts of varying provenance and date. *Targum Qoheleth (Tg. Qoh.)* was probably composed in Palestine in the seventh century and is preserved in over seven manuscripts. *Targum Lamentations,* is preserved in two recensions, Western and Yemenite, like *Tg. Cant.* probably of the same date (possibly seventh century). The two related *Targums of Esther (Tg. Esth.),* distinguished as *1 Tg. Esth.* and *2 Tg. Esth.* (= *Targum Sheni),* are of uncertain date (fifth to tenth centuries?) and are preserved in many manuscripts of the twelfth to sixteenth centuries. *Targum Chronicles (Tg. Chron.),* probably originally composed in the fourth century but receiving its final redaction in the seventh or eighth century, is preserved in three German manuscripts of the thirteenth and fourteenth centuries.

vernacular was Aramaic and the teachers bilingual. The results of this study of the Scriptures was conveyed to the people in Aramaic.

The evidence does not present clear indications as to when Aramaic translations were first introduced into the use and explanation of the scriptures in the synagogues. The first Aramaic translations may have been for private or scholastic, rather than liturgical, use. The Qumran scrolls include a "Reworked Pentateuch" (4Q364-67, 4Q158) in a late Hasmonean or early Herodian hand, which carries a running text of the Pentateuch interspersed with exegetical additions and omissions, a targum of Job (4QTg. Job and 11QTg. Job), possibly from the second century BCE, and fragments of a targum of Leviticus (4QTg. Lev.), from the first century BCE. Rabbinic literature (t. *Shabb.* 13:2-3; cf. y. *Shabb.* 15c; b. *Shabb.* 115a) associates copies of Job targumim with Rabban Gamaliel and his grandson Gamaliel II (both first century CE; McNamara 1972: 64-65).

It is reasonable to assume that an Aramaic targum of the Pentateuch, and probably also of the Prophets, came into existence at a relatively early date, possibly in the closing century of the Second Temple. Some scholars hold that a Palestinian targum, on which both *Targum Onqelos* and our present Palestinian targumim depend, was composed in the first century of our era (see Kaufman 1994: 130; Kutscher 1965: 10), and a targum of the Prophets (from which our present text descends) about the same time (Tal 1975; English summary p. x). In that age, an Aramaic targum could have served the needs of all parts of Aramaic-speaking Jewry. Even if we grant that targumim such as these were basically literal in character (not including, that is, expansive midrash), it still seems likely that portions of the "translation" were highly influenced by a midrashic understanding of the text, for instance in Num. 21:16-20. Even if we restrict the presence of midrashic development in these "original" targumim, we should not forget that the interpretative tradition in which they originated continued to exist and expand alongside the Aramaic translation and might indeed invade the targum at any later stage of its transmission with either haggadic or halakic interpretation.

The existence of such an early targum or targumim would be in keeping with early rabbinic tradition. They are legislated for in the Mishnah (*Yadayim* 4:5; *Meg.* 4:10). Certain Aramaic translations of Pentateuch passages were cited, sometimes for censure, in the second to fourth centuries. Rabbis of about 250-300 CE recommended reading at home the Aramaic translation of the section of Scripture currently being read in the synagogue (b. *Ber.* 8; see McNamara 1978: 45-60; 1972: 82-85). This evidence would seem to indicate the existence of written targum texts in Palestine at that time.

Such early targum texts could undergo change from a rich variety of sources and motives. One (as also in the case of Greek translation of the Scriptures) would be revision to conform them with the normative Hebrew text. Another would be revision to conform the translation to a given halakic tradition (as may have happened with *Targum Onqelos* in relation to the *halakah* of the school of Rabbi Aqiba). Midrashic expansions of the biblical text, arising from the text and still current in the community, could be inserted into the targum text itself. The form of the language into which the targum was originally rendered could easily be changed without affecting the underlying translation itself. At some given time these various forms of the text attained a certain fixed status and were transmitted as such and conveyed to Jewish communities outside their Babylonian or Palestinian place of origin. Other and later translations of biblical books could also be made, some not quite in the literary genre of the earlier targumim (for instance, *Targum Canticles* and *Targum Pseudo-Jonathan*).

While all this possible development over the centuries has to be borne in mind, we should not look on the targum corpus we possess as a haphazard assembly of diverse elements put together over the centuries. For the most part we find in them a common approach to the Scriptures and common terms, phrases, and theological concepts. We may legitimately presume that many of these common elements were present from an early age, possibly even from the very origins of the proto-rabbinic or rabbinic targum tradition. Close examination of these features, in fact, helps us to understand the targumic interpretation of the Scriptures.

CHARACTERISTICS OF TARGUMIC TRANSLATIONS

Translations of the Hebrew Text

With few exceptions (such as *Targum Canticles, Targum Qoheleth*), the primary aim of the targumim known to us seems to have been, in the words of Neh. 8:8, to "give the sense so that the people understood the reading." This is true in a particular way of the *Palestinian Targumim of the Pentateuch*, of *Targum Onqelos,* and of the *Targum of the Prophets*. The more or less uniform translation technique in *Targum Neofiti* seems to indicate that the rendering was well planned and in no way haphazard. The import of certain words of the Hebrew text must at times have appeared unclear or uncertain to the Aramaic translator. In some such cases the targumim translate the Hebrew by two or more terms. Thus *swp,* occurring twice in Gen. 3:15 (RSV "bruise"), is rendered as "aim at and smite" and "aim at and bite." Likewise *b-ʿqb* in the same verse is translated both as "in the heel" and "in the future" ("in the days of King Messiah"). Sometimes the targumist uses two words ("targumic doublets") to bring out the sense of a single word of the Hebrew text, for example, *nś* (*ś't*, RSV, "it will be accepted") is rendered as *sry wsbq*, "loose and forgive" (a pair of words, we may note, occurring rather regularly in *Pal.*; for additional examples, see *Tg. Neof.* Gen. 4:13; 18:26; 50:17; Exod. 23:21; 32:32; Num. 14:18).

Stylized Translation

In the targumim we find certain fixed translation terms and formulas, sometimes differing from one targum to another. Thus, *zera'* ("seed") in the Hebrew Text, when human progeny is intended, is rendered by "sons" (*Tg. Neof.*), or "descendants of sons" (*Tg. Neof.* margin and other texts). When respect for persons rather than adoration of the God of Israel is intended, Hebrew *hsthwh* is rendered as "inquire about the welfare (of)," to which "according to the custom of the land" is added if the Hebrew adds *'arsah* ("to the ground"). "A land flowing with milk and honey" becomes "a land bearing good fruits, pure as milk and sweet as honey" (see McNamara 1992: 31, 103; Beattie and McNamara 1994: 3-6). There is a tendency in the targumim to turn a metaphorical turn of phrase into something more readily understood, and also to use certain stock phrases and a more limited vocabulary than that found in the Hebrew, with the result that often the particularity, and with it the vitality, of the original text is lost in the process (with regard to this tendency in *Tg. Neb.*, see Cathcart and Gordon 1989: 2; for *Tg. Chron.* see McIvor 1994: 22).

Contemporizing of Names

In the targumim many names in the biblical text tend to be identified with what were probably regarded by the targumists as their contemporary equivalent. Together with this we find later place names that are not in the biblical text. Sometimes such identifications can help us regarding the presumed location of biblical events. Bashan becomes Batanea in the *Palestinian Targum* and Matnan in *Targum Onqelos* and the *Targum of the Prophets;* Dan becomes Caesarea (Philippi); Hamath becomes Antioch (on the Orontes); Erech becomes Edessa; Kalneh becomes Ctesiphon; Lesha (Gen. 10:19) becomes Callirrhoe; Kadesh becomes Reqem (i.e., Petra); Kadesh Barnea becomes the nearby Reqem de-Gaya;

Shur near the Egyptian border and Bered become Halusa in the *Palestinian Targum* and Hagra in *Targum Onqelos* and the *Targum of the Prophets*. All the identifications in the *Palestinian Targum* and the *Targum of the Prophets* are attested from the first centuries of our era. *Targum Pseudo-Jonathan* (Num. 24:24) mentions Constantinople and also Adisha and Fatima (Gen. 21:21), the wife and daughter of Mohammed. It is recognized that at least in its present form *Pseudo-Jonathan* is a late composition (for the place names in the *Pal.* see McNamara 1972: 190-205; McNamara and Maher 1995: 8-21; for *Tg. Neb.* see Smolar and Aberbach 1983: 63-128; for *Tg. Chron.* see McIvor 1994: 19-20).

Contemporizing of *Halakah*

Jewish *halakah* regulated the main thrust and the details of Jewish life, as it was believed this should be lived in keeping with the biblical tradition and current Jewish understanding of itself. The main basis for *halakah* was the Law of Moses as set out in the Pentateuch, although the Prophets and other biblical books also had to be reckoned with. The Aramaic translations, intended to interpret the biblical message for the common people, had perforce to take account of the contemporary understanding of the *halakah*. At the end of their discussion of the *halakah* in *Targum Jonathan of the Prophets,* Smolar and Aberbach (1983: 61) write:

> Summing up, it may be confidently stated that the evidence leaves no doubt that the laws and customs depicted in *[Targum Jonathan]* are not necessarily what they were in biblical times, but a retrojection of halachic practice in the Talmudic age. It cannot be sufficiently emphasized that the central purpose of the Aramaic translation of Biblical texts was not to provide an accurate rendering for the benefit of scholars, but to instruct the masses with an up-to-date version of the Scriptures, one which perforce had to agree with current laws and customs. Inevitably, accuracy and historical truth had to be sacrificed on the altar of halachic orthodoxy.

The principal targum presenting halakic interpretation of the Pentateuch was and is *Targum Onqelos*. Whether with regard to *Onqelos* or the *Palestinian Targumim,* it should be borne in mind that the entire Aramaic translation need not conform verbally with the official *halakah*. Alongside the Bible and its translation, Judaism had its legal institutions, which interpreted the authoritative texts. Implementation of some texts depended on the courts or judges, even though many of the biblical prescriptions were intended directly for the entire community. Exod. 21:29 stipulates that in the case of an ox that has already gored twice, killing someone, the ox was to be stoned and its owner also put to death. Contrary to the wording of the text, according to Jewish *halakah*, the owner was not to be executed but was to make monetary compensation. Despite this, *Targum Onqelos* renders literally (as does *Pal.*), *not* according to the *halakah*. The same seems true with regard to "an eye for an eye . . ." of Exod. 21:24, which *Onqelos* again (as apparently also *Pal.*) renders literally, although the *halakah* stipulates monetary compensation (on both texts see Grossfeld 1994: 229).

Matters are different with regard to some other *halakoth*. Exodus 12:46 stipulates that the Paschal lamb be "eaten in one house," which *Targum Onqelos,* in accordance with the *halakah,* renders: "it should be consumed by one *group*." The *Palestinian Targum (Tg. Neof.)* likewise replaces "house" with "groups." Exodus 23:19; 34:26; and Deut. 14:21 command: "Do not boil a kid in its mother's milk." In keeping with the official *halakah, Onqelos* translates: "Do not consume meat with milk," as does *Pal.* Other examples in which the targum interprets in accordance with the *halakah* are Lev. 23:11, 15, where "the day after the Sabbath" is rendered "after the first day of the Passover" (*Tg. Neof.; Tg. Onq.:* "after the festival"), in keeping with the well-known Pharisaic interpretation of this verse, against the Sadducees (see Grossfeld 1988c: 51). The *Palestinian Targum* in Lev. 23:29 (not, however, *Tg. Onq.* or *Tg. Neof.* margin) adds "who is able to fast" to the biblical text to make allowance for the sick and the infirm who are unable to fast on the Day of Atonement. In Pal. Exod. 22:17 (not, however, in *Tg. Onq.*), in keeping with rabbinic halakic texts, the death penalty prescribed for the "sorceress" in the biblical text is expanded to include the male sorcerer as well. While noting such agreements of targumim with *halakoth*, one should remember that there was a certain diversity in Jewish tradition with regard to some *halakoth*, and the extent of inclusion of halakic material in the Aramaic translation probably varied from age to age (see Grossfeld 1994: 238-39).

Converse Translations

Sometimes the Aramaic translation says the opposite of what is in the biblical text. There can be a variety of reasons, whether theological or midrashic, for instance, belief that the biblical text took from the honor of God or the honor due to Israel. In Gen. 4:14, Cain says to God "from your face I will be hidden," but all the targumim (*Tg. Onq.* and *Pal.*) have "it is impossible to hide from before you." In Deut. 2:6 God tells Israel to purchase food and water from the sons of Esau. Not so in *Pal. (Tg. Neof.)* which renders: "You have no need to buy food from them for money because manna descends for you from heaven, and you have no need to buy water from them for money, because the well of water comes up with you." A text might also be altered slightly to avoid the plain meaning, as in Num. 12:1, which says that Moses married a Cushite; it is made to say Moses' wife was "like a Cushite in complexion" *(Pal.)*, or "Cushite" is simply rendered as "beautiful" *(Tg. Onq.)*. We have a straightforward case of converse translation in *Tg. Mal.* 2:16a, where the Hebrew text "For I hate [or 'he hates'] divorce, says the Lord" is rendered as "but if you hate her, divorce her, says the Lord." This converse translation may have been influenced by Rabbi Aqiba's interpretation and his liberal views on divorce (see the discussion in Smolar and Aberbach 1983: 3, and the note to this verse in Cathcart and Gordon 1989: 235). We may note that Jerome's Vulgate rendering is in the tradition of the targum: *cum odio habueris, dimitte,* "when you hate her, put her away."

Euphemistic Translations and Respect for the Elders

The rabbis and the targumists were profoundly committed to clean language. The principle possibly led to "a maiden or two for every man" (as war spoil) of the biblical text being translated in *Tg. Judg.* 5:30 as "a man and his house to everyone," without any philological basis. "One urinating against a wall" in 1 Sam. 25:22, 34; 1 Kgs. 14:10; 21:21 and elsewhere is rendered as "one knowing knowledge" — itself a euphemism for "male," the rendering adopted by most modern English translations. The vivid sexual metaphors occurring in Ezekiel 16 and 23 presented special problems for synagogue audiences (see further below).

Related to the above is the delicacy required in treating the respect due to Israel's elders and the rendering (or non-rendering) of phrases or passages in the Bible detrimental to this respect. Such phrases and passages tended to be toned down or changed in translation. This sort of change is present already in the Septuagint and possibly already in the Elohist's presentation of Abraham's untruths (compare Gen. 20:12-13 with Gen. 12:19). Genesis 29:17 says that Leah's eyes were weak, a description translated literally in some early *Pal.* texts, it would appear. This rendering was objected to by the rabbis about 250 CE. *Targum Onqelos* renders it as "beautiful"; *Targum Neofiti* as "raised in prayer." Gen. 29:31, 33 says that Leah was "hated" by Jacob. While *Neofiti* and *Onqelos* render this literally, a Cairo Genizah text (manuscript E) and a marginal gloss in *Neofiti* make it "she was not loved in the face of her husband."

Forbidden Targumim

The end of the Mishnah treatise *Megillah* (4:10) lists certain texts to be read out in Hebrew rather than rendered into Aramaic. The texts in question (with the exception of the blessing of the priests, Num. 6:24-26) were detrimental to the honor of Israel: the story of Reuben lying with Bilhah, his father's concubine (Gen. 35:22), the second story of the golden calf (Exodus 32), the story of David and Bathsheba (2 Sam. 11:2-17), and the story of Amnon and Tamar (2 Samuel 13). Since some of these passages are actually translated in our targum manuscripts, there was evidently a certain fluidity in the application of the principle "to be read but not translated."

Converse Translation in Targum Ezekiel 16

Ezekiel 16 and 23 presented a special problem for the Aramaic translator because of their explicit sexual language. An added difficulty in ch. 16 was its ruthless condemnation of the people of Jerusalem and Judah: "Your origin and your birth are in the land of the Canaanites; your father was an Amorite and your mother a Hittite" (v. 3). One early rabbi (Eliezer) held that this was sufficient reason for omitting the entire chapter from synagogue readings, but his opinion was not universally accepted. *Targum Ezekiel* 16 allegorizes the sexual references. For example, "Your breasts were formed, and your hair had grown; yet you were naked and bare" (v. 7b) becomes "and because of the good deeds of your forefathers, the time had come for the redemption of your congregation, because you were enslaved and oppressed." The targum does not translate the biblical text but instead transforms the entire chapter. In Levey's words (1987: 51):

> The targumic exegesis . . . is . . . designed to counteract the prophetic denunciation of Israel as a worthless piece of brush by its very nature (Ezek. 15:5), and Jerusalem as an offshoot of the Amorites and Hittites in v. 3. Instead, it harks back to the biblical story of Abraham, and the promise of redemption from Egyptian slavery, the invocation of the Merit of the Fathers to drive out the Amorites and the Hittites to make way for Israel.

Throughout the chapter a word or two from the Hebrew text is used as a springboard for the midrashic interpretation. This is an instance in which, contrary to Neh. 8:8, the targumist saw to it that the people did *not* get the message of the Hebrew text.

Derogatory Translations

The targumim generally use translation to speak in a derogatory fashion of the gods and worship practices of pagan nations. "Gods" (*'lhym*), when referring to pagan gods, is rendered as "idols" (literally "errors"). Pagan priests and pagan altars are designated by terms different from those employed for Jewish priests and altars. Any incautious statement on this matter in the biblical books is carefully recast. Thus, as one among many, Mic. 4:5, "all the peoples walk each in the name of its god," becomes "all the peoples shall be guilty because they worshipped idols" (see further Smolar and Aberbach 1983: 150-56).

Avoidance of Anthropomorphisms and of God as Subject or Object

The Bible, particularly in the earlier writings, has certain anthropomorphic ways of speaking of God (hands, eyes, or face of God, divine anger, etc.). Later biblical writings tend toward greater abstraction. This tendency becomes much more general in the targumim, especially in the stronger cases of anthropomorphisms. Such phrases as "hands of God" or "face of God" are rephrased in different ways. For example, "Is the Lord's hand shortened?" in Num. 11:23 becomes in *Targum Neofiti* "Is there deficiency before the Lord?"; in *Targum Onqelos* it becomes "Can the *Memra* of the Lord be restrained?" The rephrasing of anthropomorphic statements is not, however, consistent. Some have been allowed to remain. "If I have found favor in your sight" in Gen. 18:3 is given in *Neofiti* and *Onqelos* as "If I have found favor in your face." "The sanctuary which your hands have established" in Exod. 15:17 is translated almost intact in *Onqelos* and *Pal.*: ". . . your sanctuary, O Lord, your two hands have perfected it."

In keeping with this anti-anthropomorphic tendency, the targumim avoid having God as the direct subject or object of an action. Rather than God doing things, these are done "before the Lord," or God's *Memra*, Glory (*yeqara*, *'yqar*), Presence, or Shekinah does them. "The Lord regretted that he had made man" in Gen. 6:6 becomes in *Pal.* "There was regret before the Lord . . ."; more clumsily *Onqelos*: "The Lord regretted through his *Memra*. . . ." The targumim tend to replace such phrases as "the Lord was angry" with "there was anger before the Lord." For example, Jer. 7:19a, "Is it I whom they provoke to anger?" becomes "Do they imagine that it is before me that they are provoking anger?" "The Lord saw" tends to become "it was revealed (or 'manifest') before the Lord" (*Pal.* Gen 1:4, etc.).

God or the Lord as the direct object of such verbs as seek, find, and cling to presented special difficulty for targumists. *Targum Onqelos* renders these as seek, find, cling to "the fear (or 'reverence,' *dhlyt'*) of God," the point apparently being that the believer seeks and finds not God but only evidences and manifestations of God's presence (see further Grossfeld 1988b: 32). The *Targum of the Prophets* is in the same tradition as *Onqelos* (see Smolar and Aberbach 1983: 139-41). *Targum Neofiti* has the same concern with regard to these verbs and also fear, forget, and return to, so the object becomes "the instruction of the law of the Lord." *Neofiti* includes "love" in this category. Thus, "love the Lord your God" in *Neofiti* becomes "love the instruction of the law of the Lord your God" (*Tg. Neof.* Deut. 6:5; 10:12; 11:1, etc.), where *Onqelos* retains "God" as the direct object.

The biblical text often speaks of God or the Lord being with a person, or a prayer might say that God may "be with" the one praying. This expression, too, is perceived in the targumim as too anthropomorphic; God is, rather, "at the aid or help" of a person. Thus, for example, "God was with the boy" in Gen. 21:20 becomes in *Targum Onqelos* "the Memra of the Lord was at the aid/assistance of the boy." In *Targum Neofiti*, however, this is not universal. There Gen. 21:20 and other texts are rendered literally. The paraphrase "at the assistance of" may have been a later, internal targumic development, absent from the earlier stages of the tradition.

"Before" is a very common word in the targumim in such contexts. Thus Ps. 51:6, "To you [*l*^e*ka*] alone have I sinned, and what is evil in your sight I have done," becomes in the targum: "Before you alone have I sinned and what is evil before you have I done." It must be noted, however, that such use of "before" is not restricted to the targumim. It occurs also in secular and in other religious Aramaic texts as a polite form of expression.

Divine Immanence and Transcendence, *Memra* of the Lord, Glory, Shekinah

"*Memra* (of the Lord)" is one of the most characteristic terms of the targumim, one not attested in other Jewish sources. The word (from the root *'mr*, "say") generally means "word." On occasion, but rarely, it means "command." Sometimes in the targumim it can be used of persons other than the God of Israel, in which cases it probably means "self," as, for instance, *Tg. 2 Chron.* 16:3, where Asa says to Benhadad: "There is a covenant between my Memra and your Memra," that is, "between me and you," and *Tg. 2 Chron.* 32:1: "the Lord decided in his Memra to . . ." followed by "Sennacherib . . . said in his Memra to . . . ." Generally, however, "*Memra*" is used to avoid making God the subject or object of an action and may have no greater theological significance than this. For example, "And the *Memra* of the Lord said 'Let there be light.' . . . And the *Memra* of the Lord separated the light from the darkness. . . . And the *Memra* of the Lord called the light daytime . . ." (*Tg. Neof.* Gen. 1:3-5).

The problem of maintaining a balance in the expression of divine immanence and transcendence was felt early in the Bible. We have it in the "name" theology of the deuteronomic writings. God is in heaven, but present on earth through his name. No one can see God and live (Exod. 33:20). The rabbis early noted that Exod. 24:10, "they saw the God of Israel," cannot be translated literally. It must be rendered "they saw the glory of the God of Israel." "The glory *(kabod)* of the Lord" is a good biblical expression, and the equivalent Aramaic term for "glory," *y^eqar* or *'yqar,* is very common in the targumim, where the frequency of its use probably represents a religious attitude that used such language in speaking of God.

"*Shekinah*," meaning divine presence (from the root *šakan,* "dwell"), is used frequently in all the traditional targumim of God's presence with his people and especially the manifestation of that presence in particular circumstances. A peculiarity of *Targum Neofiti* is that it speaks of "the glory of the *Shekinah*" rather than of the *Shekinah* alone. In this targum it is used in particular in association with certain verbs such as dwell, be revealed, lead, go up, rebel against, tempt, meet, see, accompany, and be in the midst of.

Another term found in such contexts in the targumim, though rarely, is *dibbera,* in the sense of divine discourse or revelation. As a designation for God, its use in the targumim is unstable in its attestation and at times is found in one text where a parallel targum passage might have *Memra* (see *Tg. Neof.* Exod. 33:22-23).

While each of these terms probably originally had a particular theology and range of usages attached to it, in some texts one wonders whether through the passage of time some of these terms came simply to be regarded as synonyms, as buffer words to protect the divine transcendence. This is true in particular of "*Memra*" and "glory" in *Targum Neofiti,* as in Gen. 1:26-28: "And the Lord said 'Let us create man . . .'; and the *Memra* of the Lord created the man . . . and the Glory of the Lord blessed them, and the *Memra* of the Lord said to them. . . ." The combination of these terms in some paraphrases can become cumbersome. Thus, for instance, *Tg. Neof.* Exod. 33:22-23: "And it shall come to pass that when the glory of my *Shekinah* passes by, I will place you in a cleft of the rock. And I will spread my palm over you until the troops of angels which you will see pass by. And I will make the troops of angels pass by and they will stand and minister before me, and you will see the *Dibbera* of the Glory of Shekinah, but it is not possible that you see the face of the Glory of my Shekinah" (the biblical text: "I will cover you with my hand until I pass by; then I will take away my hand, and you will see my back; but my face shall not be seen").

The Holy Spirit and the Father in Heaven

Occasionally the Bible speaks of certain persons being endowed with the spirit of God, the sense being that they have received special gifts. In *Targum Neofiti* in general, "spirit" in these texts is paraphrased as "a spirit of holiness from before the Lord." For instance, in Gen. 41:38 Pharaoh seeks "a man . . . in whom is the spirit of God," and in *Neofiti* this becomes ". . . upon whom there dwells a holy spirit from before the Lord." The usage is extended to include texts without explicit mention of the spirit in the Bible. Outside *Neofiti* the usual expression is "the spirit of prophecy."

"Father in Heaven" as a designation for God occurs in the Palestinian targumim, but rarely, and what attestation there is is unevenly distributed. In all we find thirteen occurrences, and only in one single instance do all the *Pal.* texts have it, that being Exod. 1:19, in the words of the Hebrew midwives to Pharaoh: "Because the Hebrew women are not like the Egyptian women, for they are vigorous. Before the midwife comes to them, *they pray before their Father in heaven, and he answers them and* they give birth." "Father in Heaven" is found in three contexts in the targumim: prayer before the Father, reward before the Father, and mercy like that of the Father in heaven (texts in McNamara 1992: 35-36). The designation itself would seem to be a very early one, even though it has not strongly affected the targumic tradition.

The Law, Good Deeds, and Reward in Heaven

Reference to the Torah is ubiquitous in the targumim, and somewhat less frequently there is reference to good deeds, to action in keeping with the law. The Palestinian targumim, and *Targum Neofiti* in particular, are replete with references to "the instruction of the Law," so much so that on occasion the expression seems to function somewhat as "*Memra* of the Lord," as a sort of buffer word for God, as in such stock phrases as "love (or seek, return to, adhere to) the instruction of the law of the Lord."

The targumim have a theology of the law based on the identification of the law with wisdom (Prov. 8:22-31), that which was created before the world and is with God daily (Hebrew *yôm yôm*, literally "day day" = two days; midrashically = 2000 years; see Ps. 90:4; 2 Pet. 3:8). For example, *Pal.* Gen. 3:24:

> And he banished *Adam;* and he had made *the Glory of his Shekinah* dwell *from the beginning* to the east of the Garden of Eden, *between the two* cherubim. *Two thousand years before he created the world he had created the Law; he had prepared the Garden of Eden for the just and Gehenna for the wicked. He had prepared the Garden of Eden for the just that they might eat and delight themselves from the fruits of the tree because they had kept precepts of the Law in this world and fulfilled the commandments. For the wicked he prepared Gehenna, which is comparable to a sharp sword devouring with both edges. He prepared within it darts of fire and burning coals for the wicked to be avenged of them in the world to come because they did not observe the precepts of the Law in this world. For the Law is a tree of* life *for everyone who toils in it and keeps the commandments: he lives and endures like* the tree of life *in the world to come. The Law is good for all who labor in it in this world like the fruit of the tree of life.*

The *Palestinian Targum* has also some touching excurses on reward in heaven, as in the expansive introduction to Gen. 15:1:

> After these things, *after all the kingdoms of the earth had gathered together and had drawn up battle-lines against Abram and had fallen before him, and he had killed four kings from among them and had brought back nine encampments, Abram thought in his heart and said: "Woe, now, is me! Perhaps I have received the reward of the precepts in this world and there is no portion for me in the world to come. Or perhaps the brothers or relatives of those killed, who fell before me, will go and will be in their fortresses and in their cities, and many legions will become allied with them and they will come against me and kill me. Or perhaps there were a few meritorious deeds in my hand the first time they fell before me and they stood in my favor, or perhaps no meritorious deed will be found in my hand the second time and the name of the heavens will be profaned in me." For this reason there was a word of prophecy from before* the Lord upon Abram *the just,* saying: "Do not fear, Abram, *for although many legions are allied and come against you to kill (you), my Memra will* be a shield for you, *and it will be a protection for you in this world; and although I delivered up your enemies before you in this world, the reward of your good works is prepared for you before me in the world to come."*

Eschatology, Resurrection of the Dead,
the World to Come, the Messiah

The targumim evidence in paraphrases and occasional excursuses an overall view of the next life and of the place of this life as a preparation for it (on *Pal.* see McNamara 1972: 133-41; on *Tg. Neb.* see Smolar and Aberbach 1983: 179-87). This eschatology appears to have originated in an apocalyptic matrix and to represent central Pharisaic and rabbinic Judaism, though its origins were probably multiple. Jews would naturally have attempted to associate their beliefs with, if not base them on, biblical texts, particularly the Pentateuch.

In 4 Maccabees, a work originating in a Stoic Hellenistic context with belief in immortality rather than in resurrection of the body, the mother exhorts her children to face death, reminding them of the Scripture texts by which their father used to confirm their faith (4 Macc. 18:6-19). It is interesting that three of these texts (Prov. 3:18; Ezek. 37:2-3; Deut. 32:39 with 30:20) were understood in rabbinic Judaism as implying the doctrine of bodily resurrection. The Pharisaic tradition was particularly interested in founding belief in the resurrection on texts of the Pentateuch. We have such belief expressed in two texts of the *Palestinian Targum,* Gen. 3:19 and Deut. 32:39. To God's words to Adam (Gen. 3:19) "You are dust and to dust you shall return," the *Palestinian Targum* adds "But from the dust you are to arise again to give an account and a reckoning of all that you have done." In Deut. 32:39 God says, "I kill and make live." In the *Palestinian Targum* (not in *Targum Onqelos*) this becomes: "I am he who causes the living to die in this world and who brings the dead to life in the world to come."

In similar manner, as the texts present themselves, the targumist slips into the translation mention of "this world, the world to come," "the day of great judgment," the sufferings in Gehenna, and the rewards in Paradise. Sometimes we get a lengthy paraphrase, giving an insight into the larger picture of the beliefs which the targumists carried within them. An example of this is seen in *Pal.* Gen 3:24, cited above.

There are relatively few references in the targumim to a Messiah (or King Messiah as he is called in the *Palestinian targumim*). In *Targum Onqelos* and the *Palestinian targumim,* Gen. 49:10-12 is interpreted messianically, as is Num. 24:7, 17. King Messiah is mentioned in a prophecy ascribed to Eldad and Medad in *Pal.* Num. 11:26 and in a beautiful composition on the "Four Nights" in *Pal.* Exod. 12:42, which we shall consider below. It is interesting to see a messianic reference included in the midrashic interpretation of the Protevangelium (Gen. 3:15) preserved in the Palestinian targumim. The text reads:

And I will put enmity between you and the woman and between *your sons and her sons. And it will come about that when her sons observe the Law and do the commandments they will aim at you and smite you* on your head and *kill you. But when they forsake the commandments of the Law* you will aim and *bite him* on his heel *and make him ill. For her sons, however, there will be a remedy, but for you, O serpent, there will not be a remedy, since they are to make appeasement in the end, in the day of King Messiah.*

LECTIO DIVINA AND THE ORIGIN
OF TARGUMIC TRADITIONS

By *lectio divina* I here mean devotional, reflective reading of the Scriptures. Such reflection can be seen as enjoined on Israel by the context of the Shema itself (Deut. 6:4-7). The ideal Israelite is described in Ps. 1:2 as one who delights in the law and meditates on it day and night. An examination of the evidence would seem to indicate that one of the factors operative in the formation of the targumic tradition was precisely this attitude toward the Scriptures, toward God's law and revelation. Furthermore, some of the midrashic compositions of this sort in our targumim are demonstrably very early. We shall consider some of these targumic interpretations here.

Prayer

One of the prominent features in the targumim is prayer (for the targumim in general see Maher 1990 and 1993; for *Tg. Neb.* see Smolar and Aberbach 1983: 164-69). Rabbinic tradition lists thirteen words in the Hebrew Bible which were regarded as synonyms for prayer. The targumim in general agree here with rabbinic tradition, rendering these words and some others as referring to prayer. Some of the words in question are: bless, inquire, seek, cry out, entreat, make supplication, groan, draw near, prostrate oneself, raise (one's hands), serve, worship, pass by, stand, answer, entreat, intercede, pray, stretch forth one's hand, cry (*ṣʿq*), call on (*qr'*), cry out in entreaty (*rnn*), meditate (*śwḥ, śyḥ*), bow down, and hear. It is, then, not surprising to find in the Palestinian targumim of the Pentateuch, and in the other targumim as well, frequent mention of prayer. As an example we may give Gen. 12:8, where Abraham calls on the name of the Lord. This becomes in *Targum Neofiti:* "he worshiped and prayed in the name of the *Memra* of the Lord." The "still small voice" that Elijah hears in Horeb (1 Kgs. 19:12b) becomes in the *Targum of the Prophets* "the voice of them that praise [God] softly (or 'silently, in a whisper')."

The Four Gifts

We have in the targumim what appears to be a very informative midrash on the gifts that God gave to Israel in the wilderness wanderings — the manna, the well, and the pillar of cloud. In the midrash these three (or four, if the quails are included) gifts are brought together as a reminder of God's loving providence toward his people.

The section of the midrash on the well that followed Israel itself origi-nated in various references to water and a rock in the biblical account (Marah, Exod. 15:23; Meribah, Num. 20:1-11). The midrash is summarized most succinctly in the *Biblical Antiquities* of pseudo-Philo (20.8), a work originating most probably in the first century CE:

> And after Moses died, the *manna stopped* descending on *the sons of Israel* [see Josh. 5:12], and then they began to *eat from the fruits of the land*. And these are the three things that God gave to his people on account of the three persons: the well of water of Marah for Miriam, the pillar of cloud for Aaron, and the manna for Moses. And when these came to their end, these three things were taken away from them.

The four gifts, including Miriam's well, are mentioned in *Biblical Antiquities* 10.7:

> Now he led his people into the wilderness; for forty years *he rained down for them bread from heaven* and brought *quail* to them *from the sea* and brought forth a well of water to follow them. *Now with a pillar of cloud he led them by day, and with a pillar of fire he gave them light by night.*

We have a further and informative mention of the well in *Biblical Antiquities* 11.25 in a section dealing with the giving of the Law:

> And there he commanded him [Moses] many things and *showed him the tree* of life, from which he cut off and took and threw into *Marah,* and the water *of Marah became sweet.* And it followed them in the wilderness forty years and went up into the mountain with them and went down with them into the plains.

This first-century text is almost targum-like in its composition, passing from biblical narrative into midrash and back again to biblical text.

We have a similar treatment of the biblical text in the *Palestinian*

Targum immediately after the account of the death of Aaron and before a major text on the well that followed Israel (*Tg. Neof.* Num. 20:28–21:1):

> And [Moses] stripped Aaron of his garments and put them on Eleazar his son; and Aaron died there on the top of the mountain, and Moses and Eleazar came down from the mountain. And all *the people of* the congregation saw that Aaron had died, and the whole house of Israel wept for Aaron thirty days. And the Canaanite, the king of Arad, who was dwelling in the south heard *that Aaron, the pious man for whose merits the clouds of the glory used to lead Israel forth, had been removed; and that Miriam the prophetess, for whose merits the well used to come up for them, had been removed;* that Israel had reached the route *through which the spies had come up.* And they waged war on Israel and took captives from among them.

The well is spoken of in Num. 21:16-20. As currently understood this biblical text mentions the place name Beer (in Hebrew meaning "well") and then a well said to be connected with Moses, and goes on to give further place names in Israel's itinerary. The targumim of this passage are interesting in that, instead of translation, midrash has taken over completely and given us an extended account of the well. The place names are interpreted as common nouns. The paraphrase is practically the same as the description of the well in *Biblical Antiquities* (*Tg. Neof.* Num. 21:16-20):

> And from there the well *was given to them.* This is the well of which the Lord said to Moses: "Gather the people together and I will give them water." Then Israel sung this song *of praise;* "Spring up, O well"; they sang to it; *and it sprang up.* It is the well which the princes *of the world, Abraham, Isaac and Jacob, dug from the beginning; the intelligent ones of the people perfected it, the seventy sages who were distinguished; the scribes of Israel, Moses and Aaron measured it* with their rods; and from the wilderness *it was given to them* (as) a gift. *And after the well had been given to them as a gift, it went on to become for them swelling torrents; and after it had become swelling torrents, it went on to go up with them to the tops of the mountains and to go down with them to the deep valleys; and after it had gone up with them to the tops of the high mountains* and had gone down with them to the deep glens, it was hidden from them in the valley which is at the *boundaries* of *the Moab*ites, the top *of the height which* looks out opposite *Beth Jeshimon.*

Further evidence of the early date of this entire text is its almost identical appearance in *Targum Onqelos*, a text rarely identical with the *Palestinian Targum* for any length:

> *At that time the well was given to them,* that is the well about which the Lord spoke to Moses, "Gather the people together, and I will give them water." So Israel offered their praise, "Rise, O well; sing to it." The well which the princes dug, the leaders of the people dug, *the scribes,* with their *staffs,* and it was given to them, since wilderness [times]. *Now since it was given to them, it went down with them to the valleys, and from the valleys it went up with them to the high country. From the high country* to the descents of the Moabite *fields,* as the summit of *the height,* which looks out towards *Beth Yeshimon.*

A further instance of the influence of the midrash concerning Miriam and her merits can be seen in the *Palestinian Targum* paraphrase of Num. 12:15-16:

> And Miriam was shut up outside the camp for seven days; and the people did not journey until such time as Miriam was *healed. Although Miriam the prophetess was sentenced to become leprous, there is much teaching (in this) for the sages and for those who keep the law, that for a small precept which a man does, he receives for it* a great reward. *Because Miriam stood on the bank of the river to know what would be the end of Moses, Israel became sixty myriads — which is a total of eighty legions. And the clouds of the glory and the well did not move nor journey from their places until such time as the prophetess Miriam was healed of her leprosy. (And after the prophetess Miriam was healed of her leprosy,)* after this the people moved from Hazeroth and camped in the wilderness of Paran.

The Four Nights

A long history of prayerful reflection on the biblical narrative very likely stands behind the following beautiful text on the high points of sacred history summed up in four nights. The text is found only in the Palestinian targumim of the Pentateuch, and its point of insertion is the biblical text on the night of Passover: "So this same night is a night of watching kept to the Lord by all the people of Israel throughout their generations" (Exod. 12:42). Here *Targum Neofiti's* text is translated; the text in angle brackets, on the Messiah, is absent from *Neofiti* and reproduced from the other *Palestinian Targum* texts (the *Palestinian Targum* text and context have been examined in detail by Le Déaut [1963]):

> It is a night reserved *and set aside* for *redemption to the name of the Lord at the time the children of Israel* were brought out *redeemed from the land of Egypt.*
>
> *Truly, four nights are those that are written in the Book of Memorials.*
>
> *The first night: when the Lord was revealed over the world to create it. The world was without form and void and darkness was spread over the face of the abyss and the Memra of the Lord was the Light, and it shone; and he called it the First Night.*
>
> *The second night: when the Lord was revealed to Abram, a man of a hundred years, and Sarah his wife, who was a woman of ninety years to fulfill what the Scripture says: Will Abram, a man of a hundred years beget, and will his wife Sarah, a woman of ninety years, bear? And Isaac was thirty-seven years when he was offered upon the altar. The heavens were bowed down and descended and Isaac saw their perfection, and his eyes were dimmed because of their perfection, and he called it the Second Night.*
>
> *The third night: when the Lord was revealed against the Egyptians at midnight; his hand slew the firstborn of the Egyptians and his right hand protected the firstborn of Israel to fulfill what the Scripture says: Israel is my firstborn son. And he called it the Third Night.*
>
> *The fourth night: When the world reaches its appointed time to be redeemed: the iron yokes shall be broken and the generations of wickedness shall be blotted out and Moses will go up from the midst of the desert <and the king Messiah from the midst of Rome>. One will lead at the head of the flock and the other will lead at the head of the flock and his Memra will lead between the two of them, and I and they will proceed together.*
>
> This is the night *of the Passover to the name of* the Lord: it is a night reserved and set aside for the *redemption of* all Israel, throughout their generations.

Imitation of God's Humility and Kindness

Targum Pseudo-Jonathan paraphrases Lev. 22:28 as follows: "My people, children of Israel, just as I am [a variant has "just as your Father is"] merciful in heaven, so shall you be merciful on earth." Although this paraphrase is not found in the *Palestinian Targum*, its sentiments are well expressed in this midrash in *Pal.* Gen. 35:8-9, which is also further evidence of deep reflection on God's nature as revealed in the sacred text:

> And Deborah, Rebekah's nurse, died and she was buried under the oak and he called the name of the oak "Weeping." *O God of eternity — may his name be blessed for ever and for ever and ever — your humility and your rectitude and your justice and your strength and your glory and your splendor will not pass for ever and ever. You have taught us to bless the bridegroom and the bride from Adam and his consort* [see Gen. 1:28]. *And again you have taught us to visit those who are ill from our father Abraham, the righteous one, when you were revealed to him in the Valley of the Vision while he was still suffering from circumcision* [cf. Gen. 17:1, 9-14; 18:1]. *And you taught us to console the mourners from our father Jacob the righteous one. The way of the world overtook Deborah, the foster mother of Rebekah his mother. And Rachel died beside him on his journey and he sat down crying aloud and he wept and lamented and wailed and was dejected. But you in your good mercies were revealed to him and blessed him; (with) the blessing of the mourners you blessed him and consoled him. For thus the Scripture explains and says: And the Lord was revealed to Jacob a second time* when he came from Paddan-aram and blessed him.

Moses, the Model Dispenser of Justice

The Pentateuch has four texts in which Moses gives judgment on practical cases of law infringement (Lev. 24:12; Num. 9:8; 15:34; 27:5). In the Palestinian targumim these four cases are worked into a midrash on Moses as a model for judges. This midrash is inserted fully at the translation of each of the four texts. The midrash itself grew out of reflection on the texts, but is inserted rather awkwardly into the translation, as is clear from the *Pal.* Num. 9:8-10, where the Hebrew Text has: "And Moses said to them, 'Arise and I will make (you) hear what the Lord will command concerning you'":

> And he said to them: *This is one of the four legal cases which came up before Moses; in two of them Moses was quick and in two of them Moses was slow. In (the case of) the unclean persons who were not able to keep the Passover at its appointed time and in the judgment of the daughters of Zelophehad Moses was quick because such judgments were judgments concerning wealth. In (the case of) the wood-gatherer who willfully profaned the Sabbath, and in the case of the blasphemer who pronounced the sacred Name with blasphemies*

Moses was slow because such cases were capital cases, to teach the judges to arise after Moses that they be quick in judgments of wealth and slow in capital cases, lest they precipitately put to death someone who should be put to death by law, and lest they be ashamed to say: We have not heard (a similar case), since Moses our master said: I have not heard; and Moses said to them: Arise *now* and I will make *you* hear what *is established before* the Lord *that* you should do. And the Lord spoke with Moses, saying: Speak with the children of Israel, saying: If any one of you or of your (future) generations is unclean through the *defilement* of the corpse of a *man,* or is afar off on a journey, he shall keep the Passover before the Lord.

BIBLIOGRAPHY

The Aramaic Bible (M. J. McNamara, Project Director)

Cathcart, K. J., and R. P. Gordon
1989   *The Targum of the Minor Prophets.* Aramaic Bible 14. Wilmington: Glazier/Edinburgh: Clark.

Chilton, B.
1987   *The Isaiah Targum.* Aramaic Bible 11. Wilmington: Glazier/Edinburgh: Clark.

Clarke, E. G.
1995   *Targum Pseudo-Jonathan: Deuteronomy.* Aramaic Bible 5b. Collegeville: Liturgical/ Edinburgh: Clark.

Grossfeld, B.
1988a   *The Targum Onqelos to the Torah: Deuteronomy.* Aramaic Bible 9. Wilmington: Glazier/Edinburgh: Clark.
1988b   *The Targum Onqelos to the Torah: Genesis.* Aramaic Bible 6. Wilmington: Glazier/ Edinburgh: Clark.
1988c   *The Targum Onqelos to the Torah: Leviticus and Numbers.* Aramaic Bible 8. Wilmington: Glazier/Edinburgh: Clark.
1988d   *The Targum Onqelos to the Torah: Exodus.* Aramaic Bible 7. Wilmington: Glazier/ Edinburgh: Clark.
1991   *The Two Targums of Esther.* Aramaic Bible 18. Collegeville: Liturgical/Edinburgh: Clark.

Harrington, D. J., and A. J. Saldarini
1987   *The Targum Jonathan of the Former Prophets.* Aramaic Bible 10. Wilmington: Glazier/Edinburgh: Clark.

Hayward, R.

1987　　*The Targum of Jeremiah.* Aramaic Bible 12. Wilmington: Glazier/Edinburgh: Clark.

Levey, S. H.

1987　　*The Targum of Ezekiel.* Aramaic Bible 13. Wilmington: Glazier/Edinburgh: Clark.

Maher, M.

1992　　*Targum Pseudo-Jonathan: Genesis.* Aramaic Bible 1B. Collegeville: Liturgical/Edinburgh: Clark.

Mangan, C., J. F. Healey, and P. S. Knobel

1991　　*The Targums of Job, Proverbs, and Qohelet.* Aramaic Bible 15. Collegeville: Liturgical/Edinburgh: Clark.

McIvor, J. S., and D. R. G. Beattie

1994　　*The Targums of Ruth and Chronicles.* Aramaic Bible 19. Collegeville: Liturgical/Edinburgh: Clark.

McNamara, M. J.

1992　　*Targum Neofiti 1: Genesis.* Aramaic Bible 1a. Collegeville: Liturgical/Edinburgh: Clark.

1997　　*Targum Neofiti 1: Deuteronomy.* Aramaic Bible 5A. Collegeville: Liturgical/Edinburgh: Clark.

McNamara, M. J., and E. G. Clarke

1995　　*Targums Neofiti 1 and Pseudo-Jonathan: Numbers.* Aramaic Bible 4. Collegeville: Liturgical/Edinburgh: Clark.

McNamara, M. J., M. Maher, and R. Hayward.

1994a　　*Targums Neofiti 1 and Pseudo-Jonathan: Leviticus.* Aramaic Bible 3. Collegeville: Liturgical/Edinburgh: Clark.

1994b　　*Targum Neofiti 1 and Pseudo-Jonathan: Exodus.* Aramaic Bible 2. Collegeville: Liturgical/Edinburgh: Clark.

Other Works

Aberbach, M., and B. Grossfeld

1982　　*Targum Onkelos to Genesis.* University of Denver Center for Judaic Studies; New York: Ktav.

Alexander, P. S.

1985　　"The Targumim and the Rabbinic Rules for the Delivery of the Targum." In J. A. Emerton, ed., *Congress Volume. Salamanca 1983,* 14-28. VTS 36; Leiden: Brill.

1988　　"Jewish Aramaic Translations of Hebrew Scriptures." In M. J. Mulder, ed., *Mikra: Text, Translation, Reading and Interpretation of the Hebrew Bible in Ancient Judaism and Early Christianity,* 217-54. CRINT 5. Assen/Maastricht: Van Gorcum / Philadelphia: Fortress.

1989 "The Aramaic Version of the Song of Songs." In G. Contamine, ed., *Traduction et traducteurs au Moyen Age. Proceedings of the Colloque international du CNRS, 26-28 mai 1986*, 119-31. Paris: Éditions de CNRS.

1992 "Targum, Targumim." In *ABD*, VI, 320-31.

1994 "Tradition and Originality in the Targum of the Song of Songs," in D. R. G. Beattie and M. J. McNamara, eds., 1994: 319-39.

Bacher, W.

1899, *Die exegetische Terminologie der jüdischen Traditionsliteratur* I, II. Reprint (two vol-
1905 umes in one), Darmstadt: Wissenschaftliche Buchgesellschaft, 1965.

Beattie, D. R. G., and M. J. McNamara (eds.)

1994 *The Aramaic Bible: Targums in Their Historical Context.* JSOTS 166; Sheffield: JSOT.

Black, M.

1967 *An Aramaic Approach to the Gospels and Acts.* Oxford: Blackwell.

Bloch, R.

1957 "Midrash." In *Dictionnaire de la Bible. Supplement* V, cols. 1263-81. Paris: Letouzey. ET by M. H. Callaway in W. S. Green, ed., 1978: 29-49.

Boccaccini, G.

1994 "Targumic Neofiti as a Proto-Rabbinic Document: A Systemic Analysis." In Beattie and McNamara, eds., 1994: 254-63.

Bomberg, D. (ed.)

1591 *The Hebrew Bible: Pentateuch.* Venice: Asher Forins.

Bowker, J.

1969 *The Targums and Rabbinic Literature: An Introduction to Jewish Interpretations of Scripture.* Cambridge: Cambridge University Press.

Cathcart, K. J., and M. Maher (eds.)

1996 *Targumic and Cognate Studies: Essays in Honor of Martin McNamara.* JSOTS 230. Sheffield: Sheffield Academic.

Chilton, B.

1983 *The Glory of Israel: The Theology and Provenience of the Isaiah Targum.* JSOTS 2. Sheffield: JSOT.

1984 *A Galilean Rabbi and His Bible: Jesus' Use of the Interpreted Scripture of His Time.* Wilmington: Glazier.

1986 *Targumic Approaches to the Gospels: Essays in the Mutual Definition of Judaism and Christianity.* Studies in Judaism. Lanham: University Press of America.

Churgin, P.

1927 *Targum Jonathan to the Prophets.* Yale Oriental Series. Researches, vol. 14. New Haven: Yale University Press. See Smolar and Aberbach 1983 for revised edition.

Cisneros, Cardinal F. J. de (ed.)
1522   *Biblia Sacra Polyglotta* (The Complutensian Polyglot). 6 vols. Guillen de Brocar: Alcala de Henerares.

Clarke, E. G., with W. E. Aufrecht, J. C. Hurd, and F. Spitzer
1984   *Targum Pseudo-Jonathan of the Pentateuch: Text and Concordance.* Hoboken: Ktav.

Cook, E. M.
1986   "Rewriting the Bible: The Text and Language of the Pseudo-Jonathan Targum." Ph.D. dissertation, University of California at Los Angeles.
1994   "A New Perspective on the Language of Onqelos and Jonathan." In Beattie and McNamara, eds., 1994: 142-56.

Díez Macho, A.
1960   "The Recently Discovered Palestinian Targum: Its Antiquity and Relationship with the Other Targums." In G. W. Anderson, et al., eds., *Congress Volume Oxford 1957,* 222-45. VTS 7. Leiden: Brill.

Díez Macho, A. (ed.)
1968   *Neofyti 1: 1. Genesis* Targum Palestinense. MS de la Biblioteca Vaticana. Madrid/Barcelona: Consejo Superior de Investigaciones Científicas.
1970   *Neofyti 1: 2. Exodo* Targum Palestinense. MS de la Biblioteca Vaticana. Madrid/Barcelona: Consejo Superior de Investigaciones Científicas.
1971   *Neofyti 1: 3. Levitico* Targum Palestinense. MS de la Biblioteca Vaticana. Madrid/Barcelona: Consejo Superior de Investigaciones Científicas.
1974   *Neofyti 1: 4. Numeros* Targum Palestinense. MS de la Biblioteca Vaticana. Madrid/Barcelona: Consejo Superior de Investigaciones Científicas.
1977   *4. Numeri; Biblia Polyglotta Matriensia.* Series IV. *Targum Palaestinense in Pentateuchum.* Additus Targum pseudohonathan ejiusque hispanica versio. Madrid: Consejo Superior de Investigaciones Científicas.
1978   *Neofyti 1: 5. Deuteronomio* Targum Palestinense. MS de la Biblioteca Vaticana. Madrid/Barcelona: Consejo Superior de Investigaciones Científicas.
1980a   *2. Exodo; Biblia Polyglotta Matriensia.* Series IV. *Targum Palaestinense in Pentateuchum.* Additus Targum pseudohonathan ejiusque hispanica versio. Madrid: Consejo Superior de Investigaciones Científicas.
1980b   *3. Levitico; Biblia Polyglotta Matriensia.* Series IV. *Targum Palaestinense in Pentateuchum.* Additus Targum pseudohonathan ejiusque hispanica versio. Madrid: Consejo Superior de Investigaciones Científicas.
1980c   *5. Deuteronomium; Biblia Polyglotta Matriensia.* Series IV. *Targum Palaestinense in Pentateuchum.* Additus Targum pseudohonathan ejiusque hispanica versio. Madrid: Consejo Superior de Investigaciones Científicas.
1989   *1. Genesis; Biblia Polyglotta Matriensia.* Series IV. *Targum Palaestinense in Pentateuchum.* Additus Targum pseudohonathan ejiusque hispanica versio. Madrid: Consejo Superior de Investigaciones Científicas.

Díez Merino, L.

1982   *Targum de Salmos. Edición principe del Ms. Villa-Amil n. 5 de Alfonso de Zamora.*
        Madrid: Consejo Superior de Investigaciones Científicas.

Drazin, I.

1982   *Targum Onkelos to Deuteronomy.* New York: Ktav.

Fitzmyer, J.

1968a   Review of McNamara 1966, *Theological Studies* 29:321-26.
1968b   Review of Black 1967, *CBQ* 30:417-28.

Flesher, P. V. M. (ed.)

1992   *Targum Studies. Vol. 1. Textual and Contextual Studies in the Pentateuchal Targums.*
        USF Studies in the History of Judaism. Atlanta: Scholars.

Forestell, J. T.

1979   *Targumic Traditions and the New Testament.* SBL Aramaic Studies. Chico: Scholars.

Geiger, A.

1857   *Urschrift und Übersetzungen der Bibel.* 1st edition. Breslau (2nd edition ed. P. Kahle
        and N. Czorthoski. Frankfurt am Main: Madda, 1928).

Ginsburger, M.

1903   *Pseudo-Jonathan (Thargum-Jonathan ben Usiël zum Pentateuch) nach der Londoner
        Handschrift (Brit. Mus. 27031).* Berlin: Calvary.

Gordon, R. P.

1988   "Targum as Midrash: Contemporizing in the Targum to the Prophets." In
        M. Goshen-Gottstein, ed., *Proceedings of the Ninth World Congress of Jewish
        Studies. Jerusalem. August 4-12, 1985. Panel Sessions. Bible Studies and the Ancient
        Near East,* 61-73. Jerusalem: World Union of Jewish Studies.
1994a   "Dialogue and Disputation in the Targum to the Prophets." *JSS* 39:7-17.
1994b   *Studies in the Targum to the Twelve Prophets: From Nahum to Malachi.* VTS 51.
        Leiden: Brill.

Goshen-Gottstein, M. H.

1988   "Aspects of Targum Studies." In M. H. Goshen-Gottstein, ed., 1988: 35-44.

Goshen-Gottstein, M. H. (ed.)

1988   *Proceedings of the Ninth World Congress of Jewish Studies. Panel Sessions. Bible
        Studies and Ancient Near East.* Jerusalem: World Union of Jewish Studies.

Grabbe, L. L.

1979   "The Jannes/Jambres Tradition in Targum Pseudo-Jonathan and Its Date." *JBL* 98:
        393-401.

Green, W. S. (ed.)

1978   *Approaches to Ancient Judaism: Theory and Practice.* Missoula: Scholars.

Grossfeld, B.
1979 "The Relationship between Biblical Hebrew *brh* and *nws* and Their Corresponding Aramaic Equivalents in the Targum — ʿrq, ʾpk, ʾzl: A Preliminary Study in Aramaic-Hebrew Lexicography." *ZAW* 91:107-23.
1982 See under Aberbach, M.
1994 "Targum Onqelos, Halakha and the Halakhic Midrashim." In D. R. G. Beattie and M. J. McNamara, eds., 1994: 228-46.

Harrington, D. J.
1985 "The Biblical Antiquities of Pseudo-Philo." In J. H. Charlesworth, ed., *The Old Testament Pseudepigrapha*, vol. 2, 297-377. London: Darton, Longman and Todd.

Kahle, P.
1930 *Masoreten des Westens*. II: *Das palästinische-Pentateuch Targum, die palästinische Punktuation, der Bibeltext des Ben Neftali*. Stuttgart: Kohlhammer. Reprint Hildesheim: Olms, 1967.
1947 *The Cairo Geniza*. Schweich Lectures. London: British Museum (2nd ed. Oxford: Blackwell, 1959).

Kaufman, S. A.
1994 "Dating the Language of the Palestinian Targums and Their Use in the Study of First Century CE Texts." In Beattie and McNamara, eds., 1994: 118-41.

Kaufman, S. A., and Y. Maori
1991 "The Targumim to Exodus 20: Reconstructing the Palestinian Targum." In M. Goshen-Gottstein, ed., *Textus: Studies of the Hebrew University Bible Project* 16, 13-78. Jerusalem: Magnes.

Kaufman, S. A., and M. Sokoloff
1993 *A Key-in-Context Concordance to Targum Neofiti*. Baltimore: Johns Hopkins University Press.

Kutscher, E. Y.
1965 "The Language of the 'Genesis Apocryphon.'" In C. Rabin and Y. Yadin, eds., *Scripta Hierosolymitana*. IV: *Aspects of the Dead Sea Scrolls*, 1-35. Reprint. Jerusalem: Magnes (1958).

Le Déaut, R.
1963 *La nuit pascale. Essai sur la signification de la Pâque juive à partir du Targum d'Exode XII 42*. Rome: Biblical Institute Press.
1974a "The Current State of Targumic Studies." *BTB* 4:3-32.
1974b "Targumic Literature and New Testament Interpretation." *BTB* 4:243-89.

LeJay, G. M. (ed.)
1629-45 *Biblia* (The Paris Polyglot). 10 vols. Paris.

Levine, E.
1973 *The Aramaic Version of Ruth*. Analecta Biblica 56. Rome: Biblical Institute Press.

Levy, B. B.
1986   *Targum Neophyti 1. A Textual Study*. Vol. 1. *Introduction, Genesis, Exodus*. Studies in Judaism. Lanham: University Press of America.
1987   *Targum Neophyti 1. A Textual Study*. Vol. 2. *Leviticus, Numbers, Deuteronomy*. Studies in Judaism. Lanham: University Press of America.

Lewy, J.
1954   "Section 70 of the Bisutum Inscription." *HUCA* 25:169-208.

McNamara, M.
1966   "Targumic Studies." *CBQ* 28:1-19.
1972   *Targum and Testament. Aramaic Paraphrases of the Hebrew Bible: A Light on the New Testament*. Shannon: Irish University Press/Grand Rapids: Eerdmans.
1978   *The New Testament and the Palestinian Targum to the Pentateuch*. Reprint with supplement. Analecta Biblica 27A. Rome: Biblical Institute Press (Analecta Biblica 27, 1966).
1983   *Palestinian Judaism and the New Testament*. Wilmington: Glazier/Edinburgh: Clark.
1996   "The Song of Songs as Historical Allegory: Notes on the Development of an Exegetical Tradition." In K. Cathcart and M. Maher, eds., 1996: 14-29.

Maher, M.
1990   "The Meturgemanim and Prayer." *JJS* 41:226-46.
1993   "The Meturgemanim and Prayer (2)." *JJS* 44:220-34.

Montana, B. A. (ed.)
1569-71 *Biblia Sacra Polyglotta* (The Antwerp Polyglot/Biblia Regia/Royal Polyglot). 5 vols. Antwerp: Platinus.

Moor, J. C. de
1996   "Research Programme on the Targum of the Prophets at Kampen, The Netherlands." *Newsletter for Targumic and Cognate Studies* 23, 2: 111-12. Reproduced in *Proceedings of the Irish Biblical Association* 19 (1996).

Moor, J. C. de (ed.)
1995-97 *A Bilingual Concordance to the Targum of the Prophets*. Vols. 1-8: Joshua to Kings. Leiden: Brill.

Moore, G. F.
1927-30 *Judaism in the First Centuries of the Christian Era: The Age of the Tannaim*. 3 vols. Cambridge: Cambridge University Press.

Munk, L.
1876   *Targum Sheni zum Buiche Esther: Nebst Variae Lectiones*. Berlin.

Pratensis, F. (ed.)
1517-18 *The First Rabbinic Bible*. 2nd edition 1528. Venice: Bomburg.
1524-25 *The Second Rabbinic Bible*. Edited by Jacob ben Hayyim ben Adonijah. Venice: Bomburg.

Rabin, C.

1963   "Hittite Words in Hebrew." *Orientalia* 32:134-36.

Rieder, D.

1984-85 *Pseudo-Jonathan: Targum Jonathan ben Uziel on the Pentateuch Copied from the London MS.* Brit. Mus. Add. 27031. With Hebrew translations and notes. 2 vols. Reprint Jerusalem: Solomon (1974).

Rodriguez Carmona, A.

1978   *Targum y resurrección. Estudio de los textos del Targum Palestinense sobre la resurrección.* Granada: Facultad de teologia.

Rosenthal, A.: see Tal (Rosenthal), A.

Shinan, A.

1992   *The Embroidered Targum — The Aggadah in Targum Pseudo-Jonathan to the Pentateuch* (in Hebrew). Jerusalem.

1994   "The Aggadah of the Palestinian Targum of the Pentateuch and Rabbinic Aggadah: Some Methodological Considerations." In Beattie and McNamara, eds., 1994: 203-17.

Smolar, L., and M. Aberbach (eds.)

1983   *Studies in Targum Jonathan to the Prophets* and *Targum Jonathan to the Prophets* by P. Churgin (1927; see under Churgin). New York: Ktav.

Sperber, A.

1959   *The Bible in Aramaic.* II: *The Former Prophets according to Targum Jonathan.* Leiden: Brill. Reprint 1992.

1963   *The Bible in Aramaic.* III: *The Latter Prophets according to Targum Jonathan.* Leiden: Brill. Reprint 1992.

Stec, D. M.

1989   *The Text of the Targum of Job.* Ph.D. dissertation, University of Manchester. Sheffield: Sheffield Academic.

Tal (Rosenthal), A.

1975   *The Language of the Targum of the Former Prophets and Its Position within the Aramaic Dialects* (in Hebrew). Tel Aviv: Tel Aviv University Press.

Vermes, G.

1963   "Haggadah in the Onkelos Targum." *JJS* 8: 159-69. Reprint in Vermes, *Post-Biblical Jewish Studies,* 127-38. Studies in Judaism and Late Antiquity 8. Leiden: Brill, 1975.

Walton, B. (ed.)

1653-57 *Biblia Sacra Polyglotta* (London Polyglot/Walton Polyglot). London: Roycroft. Reprint Graz: Akademische, 1965.

York, A. D.

1979   "The Targum in the Synagogue and in the School." *JSJ* 10:74-86.

Zijl, J. B. van

1979   *A Concordance to the Targum of Isaiah.* SBL Aramaic Studies 3. Missoula: Scholars.

Zunz, L.

1892   *Die gottesdienstlichen Vorträge der Juden historisch entwickelt.* 1st edition 1832. Reprint Hildesheim, 1966. 2nd edition, Frankfurt am Main: Kaufmann.

CHAPTER 7

Rabbinic Midrash

Gary G. Porton

The rabbis were an elite intellectual class of the Jewish communities of Palestine and Babylonia during late antiquity, roughly the first nine centuries CE. They transformed the Israelite religion into Judaism, a system centered on the written and the oral Torahs as the accurate record of the Lord's revelation and on the human body as the medium through which Jews could put the Lord's commands recorded in the dual Torah into practice.

Each Jewish community of antiquity looked back to the biblical text in light of the group's distinctive theology and view of the world. Each group portrayed the biblical myths of exile, redemption, election, and covenant in its own way. At least in part on the basis of these interpretations, each group developed its own rituals, its own ethical and legal agenda, and its own set of priorities to allow its members to participate "correctly" and "authentically" in the Hebrew Bible's mythic structures. Although all these interpretations focused on the same document, each group had its own styles and methods of explaining Holy Scripture, as we see elsewhere in this volume: the writers at Qumran, Philo, Paul, the other writers in the New Testament, and the rabbis all used the ancient texts for their own purposes, and each differed from the others in the particular manner of biblical interpretation employed. For example, Josephus (*Ant.* 13.297-98) claims that a major difference between the Sadducees and Pharisees was that the former rejected the latter's "laws which were not recorded in the Law of Moses"; that is, the two differed over what one could and could not connect to a biblical text. In other ways the other Jewish (and Christian-Jewish) writers and groups defined themselves over against each other by reference to differing interpretations of Scripture.

Collections and Translations of Rabbinic Midrash

This list includes only the most frequently cited midrashic collections.

Sifra is an early collection of exegetical statements on Leviticus. Sifra means "the book," an early designation for the book of Leviticus. The Sifra we now have comments on the entire book of Leviticus, verse-by-verse, often word-by-word. It is either contemporaneous with the Mishnah or slightly post-dates it (Strack and Stemberger 1991: 283-89). Neusner 1988c is the only English translation of the collection.

Mekhilta is an exegesis of parts of the book of Exodus, specifically 12:1–23:19; 31:12-17; and 35:1-3. "Mekhilta" is the Aramaic word for "rule" or "norm." The earliest clear reference to our present Mekhilta is from the eleventh century. The work is called the Mekhilta of Rabbi Ishmael because the body of the collection was considered to have begun with Pisha 2, Pisha 1 being considered the introduction, which opens with a reference to Ishmael. Mekhilta does not cover all the legal portions of Exodus, especially omitting the building of the tabernacle, and it treats some of the narrative portions of the biblical book, especially the Song of the Sea, Exodus 15. It has undergone numerous redactions, making it difficult to date its origin as an exegetical collection (Strack and Stemberger 1991: 274-80). Although most scholars would place its origin somewhere in the second to the third centuries of the common era, Wacholder (1968) claims that Mekhilta is a unified work, composed by one author shortly before the ninth century. Lauterbach published a critical edition with an English translation (1933). His translation is often paraphrastic, but his idioms accurately reflect the Hebrew text. Neusner (1988b) also gives an English translation of the text. Goldin produced a translation with a superb commentary to Mekhilta on the Song of the Sea (1971).

Sifré means "books," and in the Babylonian Talmud it refers to a commentary on Exodus, Numbers, and Deuteronomy. By the Middle Ages, however, the term was limited to commentaries on only the last two books of the Torah. Sifré Numbers begins with the first legal material in the book and covers chs. 5–12; 15; 18–19; 25:1-13; 26:52–31:24; and 35:9-34. The consensus of scholarly opinion dates this midrash after the middle of the third century (Strack and Stemberger 1991: 290-93). Levertoff's paraphrastic English translation (1926) covers about twenty percent of the text, while Neusner (1986a) has translated one hundred fifteen of the one hundred sixty-one *parashot* into English.

Sifré Deuteronomy is a midrash on Deuteronomy 1:1-30; 3:23-29; 6:4-

9; 11:10–26:15; and 31:14–32:34; therefore, it covers both legal and narrative portions of the biblical book. Most scholars believe that the exegetical portions at the beginning and end of the collection are of a different origin from the midrash's central legal core. The collection is usually dated to the late third century (Strack and Stemberger 1991: 294-99). Hammer (1986) offers a complete translation of the work with notes citing important parallel passages, indicating the issues involved in the midrashic passages, and offering literal or alternate translations of particular passages. Neusner (1987b) translated the text, and Basser has translated the material on the Song of Moses (1984). Fraade (1991) contains a translation and interpretation of large portions of Sifré Deuteronomy.

The meaning of "Rabbah" in the titles of midrashic collections is a matter of dispute. Some have argued that Genesis Rabbah is the "great" midrash on Genesis, while others have suggested that the name comes from Rabbi Oshayah Rabbah, a sage cited early in the collection (for detailed discussions of both positions, see Strack-Stemberger 1991). The midrash includes everything from close readings of verses, sometimes word-by-word, to elaborate expositions with little connection to the text. The redactor of this collection seems to have drawn material from a wide range of rabbinic texts. Although direct quotations are difficult to demonstrate, especially given the state of the manuscripts we now have, it seems that those behind Genesis Rabbah knew the contents of Mishnah, Tosefta, Sifra, Sifré, Mekhilta, and the targums. The midrash was most likely edited in the first half of the fifth century (Strack and Stemberger 1991: 300-16). Freedman rendered the text into English (1939), as did Neusner (1985).

Leviticus Rabbah and Pesiqta deRab Kahana are constructed around themes rather than the order of the biblical text. They are therefore usually described as homiletical midrashim, while those described above are often called expositional midrashim. Leviticus Rabbah consists of thirty-seven homilies. Most scholars agree that it was redacted sometime in the fifth

The rabbis' relative lack of an apocalyptic perspective (Saldarini 1979) caused them to read the Bible very differently from those at Qumran who composed the *pesharim*. The members of the Dead Sea sect saw in Nathan's and Habakkuk's prophecies references to their community's history, which they believed was marking the end of the era and signaling the coming of the messianic age. Rabbinic midrash, in contrast, does not apply the prophetic century (Strack and Stemberger 1991: 316-17). Israelstam and Slotki produced the first English translation (1939), and Neusner (1986b) also renders the text into English.

Pesiqta de Rab Kahana is constructed around the biblical readings for the festivals and the special Sabbaths, that is, the four Sabbaths after Hanukkah, the three Sabbaths before the ninth of Av, the fast-day on which Jews recall the destructions of the First and Second Temples, the seven Sabbaths of comfort after the ninth of Av, and the two Sabbaths after the New Year. The Pesiqta has five chapters in common with Leviticus Rabbah. Most contemporary scholars would date the core of this midrash to the fifth century, about the same time as the redaction of Leviticus Rabbah (Strack and Stemberger 1991: 321-22). Braude and Kapstein (1975) published a translation of the text with helpful notes. Unfortunately, the translation often tends to paraphrase the Hebrew and Aramaic, and it is frequently difficult to imagine exactly what the original text might say. Neusner (1987a) is much more faithful to the original text.

There are three useful midrash anthologies in English. Neusner (1988a) contains an outline of his important new ideas concerning the place of the midrashic enterprise within the rabbinic system. It also includes selections from Sifra, Sifré Numbers, Genesis Rabbah, Leviticus Rabbah, the Pesiqta deRab Kahana, the Fathers according to Rabbi Nathan, and examples of the use of the biblical text in both talmuds. Each section is introduced by a discussion of the collection. Also included are selected vocalized Hebrew texts. Neusner's other anthology (1990) presents selections from Sifré Numbers, Sifré Deuteronomy, Sifra, Mekhilta, Genesis Rabbah, Leviticus Rabbah, Pesiqta deRab Kahana, and Song of Songs Rabbah. Porton (1985a) offers translations of extended passages from Sifra, Mekhilta, Sifré Numbers, Sifré Deuteronomy, Genesis Rabbah, and Leviticus Rabbah. The translations are followed by notes designed to aid the readers' comprehension of the midrashic text and its structure and themes.

texts to its heroes or to non-Jewish contemporaries in comparable ways. The lack of allegorical interpretations in rabbinic midrash as compared to Philo's expoundings of Scripture also points to the different environments in which these exegeses were undertaken. Philo's work reflects Alexandria's Hellenistic environment, which was different from the rabbis' Palestinian Hellenistic world (Borgen 1984: 259-79; Arnaldez 1984; Cazeaux 1984).

THE BIBLE AND MIDRASH

The rabbis believed that their authority derived directly from Moses' conversations with the Lord on Mount Sinai and that what occurred in their own schools paralleled the encounters between the Lord and Moses at the time of revelation. But they still consciously separated their interpretations of the holy writings from the scriptural text itself. Juxtaposing the rabbinic mythology concerning Scripture and some aspects of recent literary theory has led some scholars (such as Boyarin, Bruns, and Handelman) to conclude that the rabbis did not clearly distinguish between their interpretations and the biblical text itself. There are a number of reasons for rejecting this view and maintaining that the rabbis did understand that their interpretations stood apart from the written Torah. While their intellectual endeavors were part of the oral Torah, that Torah was always recognized as being distinct from the written Torah, the Pentateuch.

The written Torah was available to all and was contained in the biblical books of Genesis, Exodus, Leviticus, Numbers, and Deuteronomy. The oral Torah was in the possession of the rabbis alone. Each rabbi learned the oral Torah from his rabbi, who had learned it from his rabbi, in a continuous chain of tradition that originated on Mount Sinai with Moses, "our" (in the sense of the preeminent) rabbi (Neusner 1971: I:11-23; 1972: 73-74), when he heard the oral Torah from the Lord face to face (Deut. 34:10) and then transmitted it to Joshua (m. 'Avot 1.1). The rabbis, therefore, were the only members of the Jewish community who could legitimately claim to know the entirety of God's revelation to Moses and to live a life totally in accord with the Lord's will. With this in mind, they set out to delineate, analyze, and organize what they knew about the Lord's expectations of humankind. These deliberations made up the content of the oral Torah. It was the rabbis' task to elucidate the details of those commandments so that Jews could do what the Lord expected of them. That is, without the rabbis analyzing and teaching the two Torahs, Jews could not fulfill their part of the plan which the Lord had created for human beings.

Midrash is a distinctive form of rabbinic literature and a well-defined intellectual enterprise. Whether written or oral, it begins from the fixed canonical text, which it explicitly cites. This explicit citation text differentiates midrash from the other significant genre of early rabbinic literature, Mishnah. Many have claimed that midrash arose in the ancient synagogues from the sermonic practices of the rabbis. But there is virtually no evidence that the rabbis played an important role in the ancient synagogues or delivered popular sermons in that context. Midrash most likely arose in the rabbinic schoolhouse and reflects the supreme importance of the Hebrew Bible within the mythology and the self-definition of the rabbinic class.

The Mishnah, the basic document of the talmuds, was compiled about 200 CE. It is "a philosophical law code, covering topics of both a theoretical and practical character" (Neusner 1994: 98). Its authors "failed to signal the relationship between their document and Scripture" (p. 124), so that "the Mishnah contains scarcely a handful of exegesis of Scripture. These, where they occur, play a trivial and tangential role" (p. 126). It is not that the authors of the Mishnah worked with no concern for Scripture. Rather, they were not limited by the biblical text and did not overtly connect their statements with Scripture.

> The framers of ideas ultimately to be located in the Mishnaic system drew heavily and informedly upon what they found in the Scriptures. But they drew upon materials they found relevant to concerns already defined, framed essentially independent of issues and themes paramount in Scripture itself. . . . [W]hat topics the philosophers of the end product will choose for their reflection is not to be foretold on the basis of a mere reading of Scripture. (Neusner 1981: 168-69)

In contrast to the Mishnah, midrash always relies on a direct connection to specific passages in the Hebrew Bible. Two of the earlier midrashic collections, Sifra on Leviticus and Sifré on Numbers, were composed primarily to demonstrate that logic unaided by reference to Scripture would produce the incorrect decision concerning God's will (Neusner 1988c; 1986a; 1994: 272-327). These documents explicitly connected some of Mishnah's statements to the biblical text, even though these overt correlations produced no practical difference in the passages' ultimate teachings or meanings. At issue was neither what was said nor what point was made but rather disparate opinions on the ability of the human mind to comprehend the Lord's plan. One could not merely employ human logic to discover the correct action according to God's will. One could discover the Truth only by direct recourse to God's revelation to Moses. For instance m. *Hullin* 9.4 states:

> "[If] there was [flesh] on [a piece of animal skin] equal to two [separate] half-olive's bulk, it conveys uncleanness by carrying, but not by touching" — the words of R. Ishmael.

> R. Aqiba says: "It does not convey uncleanness either by carrying or by touching."

Sifra *Shemini Parashah* 10:6 reads:

> [*And if any animal of which you may eat dies, he who touches*] *its carcass*
> [*shall be unclean until the evening*] (Lev. 11:39).

> *Its carcass* [but] not two half olives' bulk [of meat] which is on the skin.
> "One might think that [one who] carries [the skin which contains the
> two half olives' bulk of meat] does not become unclean; however, Scrip-
> ture says, *shall be unclean*" — the words of R. Ishmael. R. Aqiba says: "One
> who carries and one who touches [such a skin does not become un-
> clean]."

A non-midrashic dispute from the Mishnah is formulated as a midrashic dispute in Sifra. There is no practical or legal difference between the two passages; however, one is explicitly connected to the Hebrew Bible, while the
other is not.

The rabbinic documents mark the separation between Scripture and
rabbinic comments with a number of expressions that introduce the biblical
citations, so that they are not conflated with the rabbis' interpretations
(Green 1987: 160). The Torah was more than mere text, while the rabbinic interpretations were simply text, for they did not achieve the same status as sacred objects. Furthermore, the rabbis were well aware of their stretching the
Torah. M. *Hagigah* 1:8 states:

> [The rules concerning] releases from vows hover in the air, and they do
> not have anything to support them. The laws of the Sabbath, the festival-
> offerings, and sacrilege are like mountains hanging by a hair, for [their
> supports in] Scripture are few, but [their] laws are many. The [rules
> about] court cases [involving property], the [Temple] services, what is
> clean, what is unclean, and the forbidden sexual degrees, have [verses in
> the Bible] to support them, and they are the essence of the Torah.

There is also the famous story in the Babylonian Talmud, *Menahot* 29b, in
which Aqiba, through midrashic interpretation, deduced massive amounts of
law from the crowns on the Hebrew letters written in the Torah. Moses, who
was able to attend one of Aqiba's teaching sessions, did not recognize his own
Torah until Aqiba stated that the laws were given to Moses at Sinai.
Handelman (1982: 38) uses this story to demonstrate the Torah's multiplicity
of meanings and its containing "all the secrets of creation." On the other
hand, one could argue that the passage demonstrates that the rabbis were

aware of the fact that they had moved a good distance from the Torah Moses had received from God on Sinai, for Moses did not recognize it until Aqiba identified it as part of God's revelation to Moses. The story makes it absolutely clear that the meaning of the biblical text, as Moses is forced to concede, is what Aqiba says it is and not the text as Moses heard, copied, or transmitted it. While this gives the rabbis an enormous amount of authority and power, it also demonstrates that the rabbis understood that what they were doing was different from what occurred on Sinai when God spoke to Moses.

Several writers (e.g., Bloch 1957; Vermes 1970; Heinemann 1970) have suggested that midrash developed out of the need for the Hebrew Bible to be updated to fit an age different from the ones which provided the backgrounds for the biblical authors. While there is probably truth to this claim, it presents a one-dimensional picture of the role of the Bible in Jewish society and of the midrashic enterprise. Many have described the Bible as the "constitution" of Judaism (as described in Porton 1979: 112-18), which, like the American constitution, is in need of constant reinterpretation, so that it may continually serve as the sole foundational document of the culture. This argument holds that as the Jews of the last few centuries of the previous era and the first few centuries of the common era developed new rituals, practices, and beliefs, midrash provided the means for relating them to Scripture and for making the Bible relevant to their evolving way of life (Brownlee 1951: 60-62; Zunz 1832: 42-43; Weingreen 1951-52: 190; Bloch 1957: 1265-72). The canon is characterized by "the openness of what is written; that is, its applicability to the time of its interpretation, its need for actualization" (Bruns 1990: 201). Midrash allows the ancient biblical text to maintain its central place within Judaism and supplies the substance of Jewish practice. It "embodies the principles of interpretative elasticity that are the basic invigorating forces of that traditionality" (Gruenwald 1993: 6).

Despite these claims, there is no evidence that the Bible functioned as the "constitution" of the post-biblical Jewish community. The role of the Hebrew Bible in Jewish culture of late antiquity is complex. 1 Macc. 1:56 mentions that the Syrians tore asunder all of the Torahs they found, presumably in private hands. Only in the first century, however, do we find evidence that the Bible played a liturgical function in Judaism beyond the priests' recitation of portions in the context of the Temple rituals. Nor is it clear that it served as the major source of information about God's will or plan (Porton 1979: 116-17). Until the Maccabean priesthood appropriated for themselves the priestly prerogatives, the high priest and his staff seem to have been the major resource for gaining knowledge about God's desires for humankind (pp. 113-14).

The Bible certainly was important for a wide variety of Jewish communities of the first centuries CE. But they also had other sources of wisdom and guides for activity. Would they have felt the need to "actualize" or "contemporize" the Hebrew Bible? Clearly some did, as witnessed by the New Testament and the *pesharim*. However, much of the legislation in the Qumran documents is not connected to Scripture, and there is much in the New Testament which does not relate to the Old. Similarly, while the rabbis after the Bar Kokhba War sought to ground the rabbinate and its traditions in the Sinai event, they created a phenomenon which was parallel to Scripture, not one which merely actualized it, as Neusner has shown (1981). As we noted above, only later did some of the rabbis recognize and become troubled by the Mishnah's independence from the Bible. They created some of the early midrashim to remedy this bothersome situation. But the overall point is that, in its origin, the oral Torah holds a place *alongside* the written Torah, a distinct element of the revelation at Sinai. The oral Torah stands as an independent entity and not merely as a commentary on, completion of, or actualization of the written Torah.

THE SETTING OF MIDRASH

For the most part, those who stress that midrash results from a need to make the Torah relevant also subscribe to the scholarly tradition that holds that rabbinic midrash originated in sermons rabbis delivered in the Palestinian synagogues of late antiquity, in which they would use Scripture as the foundation of their remarks, whether we have actual sermons in the midrash collections or mere outlines (Zunz 1832; Geiger 1857; Heinemann 1970). But the midrashim as we now have them are literary creations, and no one has conclusively demonstrated that they are derived from oral originals (Sarason 1982). While at the turn of the eras we do begin to find evidence that the reading of the Torah was a major feature of synagogue worship (Porton 1979: 112-18; Levine 1987: 15-19), the extent of the rabbis' participation in synagogue worship is unclear (Neusner 1968: 234-38; 1969: 149-51).

The arena of rabbinic life was the rabbinic academy in which rabbis trained other rabbis. These schools were not formal, permanent institutions in Palestine until at least the third century and perhaps even later. The basic framework was a master-disciple relationship between the sage and his students, which came to an end with the master's death (Goodblatt 1975; Levine 1989: 28-29). The rabbis' influence on and concern for the general population are matters of debate, but probably were not extensive (Levine 1989: 98-133;

Neusner 1968: 95-194, 272-338; 1969). Their main goal was to study Torah and to train other rabbis, which meant introducing their students to the oral Torah, as well as to their interpretations of the written Torah (Neusner 1972: 44-97).

Handelman, Boyarin, and Bruns, among others, have underscored the fact that we often find several rabbinic interpretations attached to a single verse. For these literary scholars this points to the open nature of the biblical text, which does not have one fixed meaning. The multifarious interpretations of a text are an important feature of some modern theories of literature. Green has noted, however (1987: 160-61), that in most cases the various rabbinic interpretations are not as different as they may appear. In fact, the range of meanings given to one biblical verse is usually quite limited (pp. 161-65; Gruenwald 1993: 12-13). The various rabbinic comments are generally variations on a single theme, not a collection of dissimilar interpretations. Idel (especially 1993: 46-47) also stresses the limited possibilities of midrashic interpretation, especially when one compares midrash to the mystical forms of biblical interpretation. In reality, the variety of midrashic interpretations occurs within a border which is carefully circumscribed by rabbinic culture and theology. The rabbis did not believe that the Torah was an open-ended document which could be manipulated in an unlimited number of ways. The Torah could not be interpreted freely; its meanings had to fall into a rather narrow range of culturally approved possibilities.

Neusner (1983) argues that the crisis produced by Mishnah's unique style engendered not only the *gemarot,* those parts of the Babylonian and Palestinian Talmuds which comment upon the Mishnah, but also midrash. The *gemarot* relate to the Mishnah in the same way that the midrashim relate to the Bible. Because Mishnah's infrequent biblical citations leave the impression that it is independent of the Bible, one could view the Mishnah, the recognized authoritative law produced in the Patriarch's court, as an independent document which stood alongside the Bible as the legitimate source of God's will, instead of a text dependent upon the Holy Scripture. Neusner shows that the early midrashim, such as Sifra, set out to demonstrate that Mishnah's laws were in fact derived from the Bible. He argues that the Palestinian Talmud also devotes much of its time to proving that the Mishnah is secondary to the biblical text and not independent of it. Neusner even demonstrates that the midrashim and the *gemarot* employ the same units of discourse (1994: 9-13).

The rabbinic myth claims that virtually everything is "Torah given to Moses at Sinai." But in reality, the documents clearly recognize distinct levels of the texts, different exegetical methods, and different relationships among the various documents and the rabbinic arguments and interpretations. The written Torah was clearly perceived as different from the oral Torah, and the various subsets of the oral Torah were different from one another. Their crucial underlying similarity was that they were all part of God's revelation to Moses at Sinai. But the rabbis clearly marked distinctive moments of that revelation. They knew, and they wanted us to know, what were parts of the written Torah and what were segments of the oral Torah. They may all have originated at Sinai, but they were not all the same or all of equal stature and standing.

THE FORM OF MIDRASHIC INTERPRETATION

Unlike many of the other forms of Jewish biblical exegesis in late antiquity, rabbinic midrashim are collections of independent units. Unlike the Qumran *pesharim* or the *Genesis Apocryphon,* the rabbinic midrashic collections are not the sustained work or interpretations of one author. Their sequential arrangement is the work of each document's editor(s). Rabbinic midrash is also the only form of Jewish exegetical text that more often than not contains several interpretations of the biblical text joined together, and often it is impossible to distinguish among interpretations in terms of their importance or validity. Even in the legal passages, we often find a ruling based on several biblical texts, with no indication that the editors or the tradents prefer one exegetical strategy over another. Many of the non-rabbinic exegetical texts are anonymous, and even a large number of the exegetical remarks in the rabbinic collections are also transmitted anonymously. But much of the exegetical material in the rabbinic corpus is attributed to named sages. Still, even here, the arrangement of the attributed interpretations need not reflect the actual chronology of the sages' lives and is manifestly the work of the collections' editors. Like all rabbinic texts, the midrashim include the names of authorities who, with very few exceptions, are known only from the rabbinic documents.

Some midrashic interpretations are simple explanations of the biblical text; others may be part of a dialogue, a story, or an extended soliloquy. The comment may answer a question that refers to the text but need not be connected with the text to be comprehensible. Some comments reflect actual problems in the biblical text, while others create anomalies in the text in order to deal with them. Some interpretations are "obvious"; others are not. This variety of forms and techniques does not appear in any other single Jewish community which interpreted the Bible.

Rabbinic midrash often atomizes the biblical text. Each word or letter may serve as the basis for an exegetical remark. Repetitions, unusual spellings, minor differences among passages, shapes of letters, sequences of words, and many other phenomena led to rabbinic comments. The targumim and the Septuagint are the only other Jewish exegetical endeavors which pay such close attention to the details of the Hebrew text. Finally, uniquely among the Jewish exegetical texts, the midrashic passages often enumerate the specific methods on which the interpretation is based.

EXAMPLES OF RABBINIC MIDRASH

The following passage (adapted from Porton 1985a: 20-22) from the opening of Sifra illustrates Neusner's point that there were those who argued that logic alone could not lead one to the proper understanding of the Lord's actions. Here, the midrash asks why in Lev. 1:1 the Lord both *called* and *spoke to* Moses when he could have just called him or spoken to him. That is, why are there two verbs when one would have been sufficient? This reflects the midrash's concern with the exact wording of Scripture. The passage offers an explanation and then demonstrates that using logical methods, such as allegory or a prototype, one could not reach the correct conclusion that the Lord's calling always preceded his speaking to Moses from the Tent of Meeting.

> *And [the Lord] called [to Moses] and spoke [to him]* (Lev. 1:1). [This teaches us] that "calling" precedes "speaking." But cannot [this be established by means of] an argument by analogy, [so that we do not need to learn it from this verse? Here is the argument: The holy] speech is mentioned here, and [the holy] speech is mentioned in connection with the [burning] bush, [for Ex. 3:4 states: *When the Lord saw that he turned aside to see, God called to him out of the bush.... Then He said: ...]*. Just as with regard to the [holy] speech which was mentioned at the [burning] bush, "calling" preceded "speaking," so also with regard to the [holy] speech which was mentioned here, "calling" preceded "speaking." No, [these two instances are not analogous]. If you say concerning the [holy] speech at the [burning] bush, which was the first time [that God] spoke [to Moses and that God's calling preceded His speaking], need you reason that, with regard to the speech at the Tent of Meeting, which was not the first time [that God] spoke [to Moses], He likewise began by calling [to Moses? Rather], the [holy] speech at Mount Sinai supports [your claim that you can use an argument by analogy], for [Mount Sinai] was not the first oc-

casion on which God spoke to Moses, yet, even so, [God] began there by
"calling" and followed by "speaking." No, [these two instances are not
analogous]. If you say concerning the [holy] speech at Mount Sinai,
which [was addressed] to all of Israel, [that "calling" preceded "speaking"], need you reason [that "calling" preceded "speaking"] in the case of
the [holy] speech at the Tent of Meeting, which was [addressed to Moses
alone and] not to all of Israel? [You need not.] Behold, you can argue
[that "calling" always should precede "speaking"] by means of a prototype. [You can] not [claim that] the [holy] speech at the [burning] bush
where He first spoke [to Moses] is like the [holy] speech at Mount Sinai,
which was not the first occasion on which God spoke [to Moses], and
[you can] not [claim that] the [holy] speech at Mount Sinai, where He
spoke to all of Israel, is like the [holy] speech at the [burning] bush, where
He did not speak to all of Israel. The common element between [the
speech at Mount Sinai and the speech at the burning bush] is that they
are [both holy] speech[es] and [that they] were from the mouth of the
Holy One to Moses and that "calling" preceded "speaking" [in both
places]; therefore, in every [place] where there is a [holy] speech which is
from the mouth of the Holy One to Moses [one might reason that] "calling" preceded "speaking." Not [necessarily. You could argue] that just as
the common element between [the speech at Mount Sinai and the speech
at the burning bush] is that they are [holy] speech[es spoken] through
fire from the mouth of the Holy One to Moses and [in both places] "calling" preceded "speaking," so also only [in]a [place where] there is a [holy]
speech [spoken] through fire from the mouth of the Holy One to Moses
will "calling" precede "speaking." [This would] exclude the [holy] speech
at the Tent of Meeting, for it was not [spoken] through fire. [Therefore],
Scripture [must] say: *[and the Lord] called [to Moses] and spoke [to him]*
(Lev. 1:1) [to teach us that also here, where the holy speech was not spoken
through fire,] "calling" preceded "speaking." You might think that "calling" [occurred] only with reference to this [act] of speaking alone. And
on what basis [do we learn that "calling" preceded] all [acts of "speaking"
which are in the Torah]? Scripture says: *[the Lord called to Moses and spoke
to him] from the Tent of Meeting* (Lev. 1:1). On the basis of this passage let
us hold that "calling" preceded "speaking" in the case of all [the words of
God] which [came] from the Tent of Meeting.

The following passage from Mekhilta de Rabbi Ishmael (adapted from
Porton 1985a: 55-56) begins and ends by focusing on the particle *'k,* "indeed,"
with which Exod. 31:13 opens. This serves to illustrate again the midrash's fre-

quent concern with every word in the Bible. What is of interest to us is the narrative about the five sages. There is a well-known principle that one may save a life in violation of the biblical injunction against work on the Sabbath. In response to the question concerning how one learns this principle, Ishmael offers an interpretation of Exod. 22:1-2, while the other sages use logic to support the principle. One can see that here, unlike in the previous passage, there is no devaluation of logic. Furthermore, the narrative does not deal with the verse upon which this section of Mekhilta focuses. It is here because the subject is relevant, as the context makes clear.

> *Indeed (ʾk) you shall keep My Sabbaths* (Exod. 31:13). Why was this said? [It was said] because it says [in Exod 20:10:] *You shall not do any type of work.* [From Ex. 20:10] I [can learn] only [about] acts which are [considered] a type of work. On what basis [can I learn about] acts which [merely detract from one's] resting [on the Sabbath]? Scripture says: *Indeed you shall keep My Sabbaths* to include actions which [merely detract from one's] resting [on the Sabbath]. One time Rabbi Ishmael, Rabbi Eleazar the son of Azariah, and Rabbi Aqiba were walking on the road, and Levi the netmaker and Rabbi Ishmael the son of Rabbi Eleazar the son of Azariah were walking on the road after them, and this question was asked before [the former by the latter]: "On what basis [do we learn that] saving a life supersedes [the commandment of not working on] the Sabbath?" Rabbi Ishmael answered and said: "Behold it says, *If a thief is found breaking in [and is struck so that he dies, there shall be no bloodguilt on account of him; but if the sun has risen upon him, there shall be bloodguilt on account of him]* (Exod. 22:1-2). And what [type of case] is this? [The verse refers to a case in which] there is uncertainty about whether [the intruder] came to steal or to murder. Now, behold [this] case [forms the basis of] an *a fortiori* argument: Now, if the spilling of blood, which renders the Land [of Israel] unclean, and which causes the Holy Presence to remove Herself [from the Land], supersedes [the commandment not to work on the Sabbath], how much the more the saving of a life, [which does not render the Land unclean and which does not cause the Holy Presence to remove Herself from the Land], should supersede [the commandment not to work on the] Sabbath." Rabbi Eleazar the son of Azariah answered and said: "Just as circumcision, [which affects positively] only one limb of a man's body, supersedes [the commandment not to work on the] Sabbath, [for one may be circumcised on the Sabbath], how much the more [may one engage in an act which affects positively] the rest of a man's body [on the Sabbath]." They said to him: "From the case which you bring [us we

can learn only that one may violate the commandment not to work on the Sabbath when there is certainty.] Just as there [in your example] it is certain [that the Sabbath is the eighth day after the male's birth, so he must be circumcised on that day or be subject to the penalty of being 'cut off' from among his people], so also here [in the case of a life on the Sabbath there must be] certainty [that if we do not violate the Sabbath the person will die]." Rabbi Aqiba says: "If the [execution of] a murderer supersedes the performance of the worship service, [for we read in Exod 21:14 that *if a man willfully attacks another to kill him treacherously, you shall take him from My altar, that he may die,]* and [the worship service] supersedes the commandment not to work on the] Sabbath, [for the regular sacrifice is offered before the special Sabbath sacrifice,] how much the more does the saving of a life supersede [the commandment not to work on the] Sabbath." Rabbi Yosi the Galilean says: "When it says, *Indeed you shall keep My Sabbaths,* [the particle] *indeed, 'k,* [indicates that there are] distinctions [among the Sabbaths; for instance], there are Sabbaths which you may supersede, and there are Sabbaths [which you may not] supersede.

The following example from Sifré Numbers (adapted from Porton 1985a: 84-85) offers several interpretations of Num. 18:7, demonstrating that without the verse, one could not logically discover what the Lord demanded of the priesthood. Note that one verse teaches two things: the non-priest, *the stranger,* is put to death (1) only when he approaches the altar to perform the sacrificial service, and (2) even if he is ritually pure. Ishmael and Yohanan the son of Nuri disagree about the method of punishment, and the passage indicates which is correct.

For the stranger who draws near shall be put to death (Num. 18:7). [This verse refers to a stranger who comes near to perform] the Temple service. You say [this verse refers to a stranger who comes near to] perform the Temple service. Or [perhaps] you say [it refers both to one who comes near to perform] the Temple service and [to one who comes near but] not [to perform] the Temple service. Now, just as [a priest] who has a defect, and who, [should he offer a sacrifice,] is not punished by death [because of his defect], is not punished by death [at all] until [he comes near to perform] the Temple service, so also a stranger, [that is, a nonpriest,] who, [should he offer a sacrifice,] is punished by death, how much the more should he not be punished [under the rule of Num. 18:7] unless [he comes near to perform] the Temple service. Behold, what does Scripture say? *For a stranger who draws near shall be put to death.* [This applies only if he comes near to perform] the Temple service. *For the stranger who draws near shall be put to death* even if he performs the Temple service while he is pure. Or perhaps it refers only to a case in which he performed the Temple service while he is impure. You may reason: If the one who enters [the Temple precincts] while impure is [still] culpable even though [he did not perform] the Temple service, how much the more [should he be culpable if he drew near] to perform the Temple service [while he was impure]. Behold, why did Scripture say, *For the stranger who draws near shall be put to death?* [This was said to teach us that contrary to reason the stranger who comes near is put to death] even if he performs the Temple service while he is pure. *Shall be put to death* (Num. 18:7). Rabbi Ishmael says: "*Shall put to death* is said here and *shall be put to death* is said elsewhere [in Deut. 13:6, *And that prophet or that dreamer of dreams shall be put to death*]. Just as *shall be put to death* which is said elsewhere [refers to death by] stoning, so also *shall be put to death* which is said here [refers to death by] stoning." Rabbi Yohanan the son of Nuri says: "*Shall be put to death* is said here, and *shall be put to death* is said elsewhere. Just as *shall be put to death* which is said elsewhere [refers to death by] strangulation, so also *shall be put to death* which is said here [refers to death] by strangulation." *For the stranger who draws near shall be put to death.* [In this verse,] we learn [about] the punishment. But the warning we have not [yet] learned; [therefore, we need Num. 18:4, for] Scripture says: *A stranger shall not draw near to you.*

The following midrash (adapted from Porton 1985a: 130-31) is from Sifré Deuteronomy. Scripture states that a person should "bind these words upon your hand," and this is the passage from which the practice of binding the *tefilin,* phylactaries, comes. The problem is that the phylactery is tied to the inner side of the upper left arm, not on the hand as the literal interpretation of the biblical verse requires. In this passage, several sages interpret the biblical injunction in ways that justify the actual rabbinic practice and show that it is faithful to the scriptural commandment. Note how many different things we learn from the phrase "on your hand."

And you shall bind them for a sign on your hand (Deut. 6:8). [There should be] one roll with four inscriptions, for it is an argument by analogy: Because [the] Torah said [to] put [the] *tefilin* on your hand and [to] place the *tefilin* on your head, [I might think that] just as on the head there are four [rolls with] inscriptions, so also on the hand there should be four [rolls with] inscriptions; [however,] Scripture says, *And you shall bind them for a sign on your hand* [the singular form of the word *sign* means that there should be] one roll with four inscriptions. Or, [perhaps, you can reason as follows:] Just as on the hand there is one roll, so also [the *tefilin*] of the head [should contain] one roll [with four inscriptions; however,] Scripture says: *And they shall be ttpt* (Deut. 6:8), *ttpt* (Exod. 13:16), *twtpt* (Deut. 11:18); [the repetition of the word in addition to the extra letter added in Deut. 11:18 means that] four inscriptions are mentioned. Or, [perhaps] one should make four receptacles for four inscriptions; [however,] Scripture says: *As a memorial between your eyes* (Exod. 13:9); [the singular *memorial* means that there should be] one receptacle [which contains] four inscriptions. *On your hand* [means] the thick part of the upper arm. You say [it refers to] the thick part of the upper arm or *on your hand* in its literal sense. One can make an argument by analogy: Because Scripture said [to] put [the] *tefilin* on your head [and to] put [the] *tefilin* on your hand, [you might conclude that] just as [with regard to your head you put it on] the thick part of [your] upper head, so also *on your hand* [means you should put it] on the thick part of your upper arm, [and this line of reasoning is correct]. Rabbi Eliezer says: "*On your hand* [means] on the thick part of your upper arm. You say [it means] on the thick part of your upper arm or [it means] *on your hand* in its literal sense; [however,] Scripture says: *And it shall be a sign for you on your hand* (Exod. 13:9). *It shall be a sign for you,* but it shall not be a sign for others; [therefore, you should put it on the inside of your upper arm]." Rabbi Isaac says: "[You should put the *tefilin* on] the thick part of your upper arm. You say [it means] on the thick part of your upper arm or [it means] *on your hand* in its literal sense; [however,] Scripture says: *And these words . . . shall be upon your heart* (Deut. 6:8) [which means] opposite your heart. And which [place] is this [that is opposite your heart? It is] the thick part of your upper [left] arm. *On your hand.* This [refers to your] left hand. You say this is [your] left hand or, perhaps, it [refers to] only [your] right hand? Even though there is no clear proof for the matter, there is a hint [supporting] this position, [for it is said:] *My hand laid the foundations of the earth, and My right hand spread out the heavens* (Isa. 48:13); and it says, *She put her hand to the tent peg and her right hand to the workman's mallet; she struck Sisera a blow, she crushed his head, she shattered and pierced his temple* (Jdgs. 5:26). Behold, in every place [where] *your hand is* said, [it refers to] only the left hand." Rabbi Nathan says: "*And you shall bind them* (Deut. 6:8), *And you shall write them* (Deut. 6:9). Just as writing [is done] with the right hand, so also [the] binding [should be done] with the right hand [which means that it must be placed on the left arm]." Rabbi Yosi the net-maker says: "[Contrary to the claim you have just made,] we find that also the right hand is called [merely] 'hand,' for it is said: *When Joseph saw that his father laid his right hand upon the head of Ephraim, it displeased him; so he took his father's hand, to remove it from Ephraim's head to Manasseh's head* (Gen. 48:17). If this is so, why does Scripture say *on your hand*? [It said this] to include the one [who merely] has a stump [for his left arm] so that he might place [the *tefilin*] on [his] right arm."

The following example from Genesis Rabbah focuses on the first letter of the written Torah, *bet.* If *aleph* is the first letter of the alphabet, why did the Lord begin the Torah, or the creation of the world, with *bet,* the second letter of the alphabet? The passage contains several different answers to this question. Again, we see that the midrash can be concerned with the smallest detail of the biblical text. Notice, however, the small range of possible interpretations given.

Yonah in the name of R. Levi [said]: "Why was the world created with [the second letter of the alphabet], a *bet* [for the Torah begins with *br'št*]? Just as a *bet* is closed on its side and open from its front, so also you are not permitted to inquire about what is above [the heavens] and what is below [the earth] and what [God did before creating our world] and what [is after our world]." Bar Qappara said: "*But, do not inquire about the ages that have come before you, from the day* (Deut. 4:32). *From the day* that the waters were created you may inquire, but you may not inquire about the days before that. *From one end of the heavens until the other* (Deut. 4:32) you may examine, but you may not examine what is before that." R. Judah b. Pazzi expounded on the Deeds of Creation according to the words of Bar Qappara. Why [was the world created] with a *bet*? To make known to you that there are two worlds [this world and the world to come which correspond to the numerical value of the letter *bet,* two]. Another matter: Why [was the world created] with a *bet*? Because [the *bet*] is an expression of blessing [for the *bet* is the first letter of the Hebrew word *brkh,* blessing]. And why [was the world] not [created] with an *aleph* [the first letter of the alphabet]? Because it is an expression of a curse [for it is the first letter of the Hebrew word for curse, *arwrh*]. Rather, the Holy One, blessed be He, said, "Behold, I will create it with a blessing and with luck, it will stand [forever]." Another matter: Why [was it created] with a *bet*? It has two stems, one [points] upward and one [points] after it. They said to it [the *bet*], "who created you?" Then it shows them [who created it by pointing upward with its stem]. It says, "This [one] who is above created me." "And what is his name?" they ask. Then it shows them with its stem which [points] afterward, "the Lord is his name." R. Leazar the son of Abinah in the name of R. Aha [said]: "[For] twenty-six generations the *aleph* would complain before the Holy One, blessed be He. It would say before Him, 'Lord of the Universe, I am the first of the letters and you did not create your world with me!?' The Holy One, blessed be He, said to it, 'The world and its fullness was created only for the sake of the Torah. Tomorrow I will come and give my Torah on Sinai, and I will begin [that Revelation] with you [for it begins with] *I (`anky) am the Lord your God* (Exod. 20:2).'"

Our last example (adapted from Porton 1985a: 200-202), from Leviticus Rabbah, opens by explaining the importance of the Tent of Meeting, for it was where the people learned the commandments from God. Because of this interaction with God, Israel has the best prophets, if not the only prophets, in the world, and Moses is the best among the Israelite prophets.

From the Tent of Meeting (Lev. 1:1). Said Rabbi Eleazar: "Even though the Torah was given as a fence to Israel [to protect her and to prevent her from violating the Lord's commandments] at Sinai, they were not punished [for violating its precepts] until it was repeated for them at the Tent of Meeting. It is a parable. [It can be compared] to an ordinance written and sealed and brought into a country. The people of the country were not punished [for violating the ordinance] until it was explained to them in the public baths of the country. Thus, even though the Torah was given to Israel at Sinai, they were not punished [for violating it] until it was repeated in the Tent of Meeting. Thus it is written: *Until I had brought it into my mother's house, and into the chamber of her that conceived me* (Cant. 3:4). *Into my mother's house,* this is Sinai. *And into the chamber of her that conceived me (hwrty),* this is the Tent of Meeting, for from there Israel was commanded [to follow] the teaching[s *(hwr'h)* of the Torah]." Said Rabbi Joshua the son of Levi: "If [the rest of] the nations of the world would have known how wonderful the Tent of Meeting was for them [Israel], they would have surrounded it with camps and fortifications [to prevent Israel from entering it.] You find that before the Tabernacle was set up, [the rest of] the nations of the world would hear the voice of [God's] speech, and they would be frightened in their camps; thus it is written: *For who is there among all flesh who heard the voice of*

God and lived (Deut. 5:23)." Said Rabbi Simon: "The speech [of God]
went forth [from the Tent of Meeting] with a double nature: life for Israel
and the poison of death for [the rest of] the nations of the world. Thus it
is said: *When you heard it and lived* (Deut. 4:33) [which means] you [Is-
rael] heard and lived, but [the rest of] the nations of the world heard [it]
and died. For Rabbi Hiyya taught: '*From the Tent of Meeting* teaches [us]
that the voice [of God] would stop and would not go outside of the Tent
of Meeting.'" Said Rabbi Isaac: "Before the Tent of Meeting was set up,
prophecy was found throughout the nations of the world. After the Tent
of Meeting was set up, [prophecy] was removed from among [the rest of
the nations of the world]; thus it is written: *I held it and would not let it go*
(Cant. 3:4)." They said to him [Isaac]: "Behold, Balaam prophesied, [and
he was not an Israelite." Isaac] said to them: "He prophesied only for the
good of Israel, [for it is said:] *Who can count the dust of Jacob* (Num.
23:10), *He has not beheld misfortune in Jacob* (Num. 23:23), *How fair are
your tents, O Jacob* (Num. 24:5), *A star shall come forth from Jacob* (Num.
24:17), *By Jacob shall dominion be exercised* (Num. 24:19)." What [differ-
ence] is there between the prophets of Israel and the prophets of [the rest
of] the nations of the world? Rabbi Hama the son of Rabbi Hanina and
Rabbi Issacar of the village of Mandi [discussed this question]. Rabbi
Hama the son of Rabbi Hanina said: "The Holy One, blessed be He, revealed [Himself] to the prophets of [the rest of] the nations of the world
only through partial speech; thus, what do you say? *And God called (wyqr)*
[without the last letter of the Hebrew root] *to Balaam* (Num. 23:4). But
[He revealed Himself to] the prophets of Israel through a complete
speech, for it is written: *And [the Lord] called (wyqr') to Moses* (Lev. 1:1)."
Said Rabbi Issacar of the village of Mandi: "Should this [reception of
prophecy] be their reward? This expression, *And He called (wyqr),* is only
an expression of uncleanness [for *wyqr* is spelled similarly to *mqrh*]; thus
you say, *But if there shall be a man among you who is not clean because of
what happened (mqrh) at night* (Deut. 23:11). But [He revealed Himself to]
the prophets of Israel through an expression of holiness, with an expression of cleanness, in a clear expression, in the [Hebrew] language with
which the angels of service praise Him. Thus you say: *And they called
(qr'), this one to that one, and said* (Isa. 6:3)." Said Rabbi Eleazar the son of
Menahem: "It is written: *the Lord is far from the evil ones but He hears the
prayers of the righteous* (Prov. 15:29). *Far from the evil ones,* these are the
prophets of [the rest of] the nations of the world. *But he hears the prayers
of the righteous,* these are the prophets of Israel. You find that the Holy
One, blessed be He, revealed [Himself] to the prophets of [the rest of] the

nations of the world only like a man who comes from a faraway land; thus you say: *They have come to Me from a faraway land, from Babylon* (Isa. 39:3). But [He revealed Himself to] the prophets of Israel immediately [without coming from a faraway place, thus it is written: *And the Lord] appeared [to him] and He called* (Gen. 18:1)." Said Rabbi Yosi the son of Biba: "The Holy One, blessed be He, revealed Himself to the prophets of [the rest of] the nations of the world only at night, when normally human beings are separated from one another, [for it is said:] *Amid thoughts from visions of the night, when deep sleep falls upon men* (Job 4:13), and *Now a word was brought to me stealthily, my ear received a whisper of it* (Job 4:12)." Rabbi Hanana the son of Pappa and the rabbis [discussed this matter]. Rabbi Hanana the son of Pappa said: "It is a parable. [It can be compared] to a king when he and his lover were placed in a hall and a curtain was between them. When he spoke with his lover, he doubled up the curtain and spoke to his lover." The rabbis said: "[It is comparable] to a king who had a wife and a concubine. When he walks with his wife, he walks freely and openly. When he walks with his concubine, he walks in secrecy. Thus, the Holy One, blessed be He, reveals Himself to the prophets of [the rest of] the nations of the world only at night, for it is written: *And the Lord came to Abimelech in a dream of the night* (Gen. 20:3). And it is written: *And God came to Laban the Arami in a dream of the night* (Gen. 31:24). *And God came to Balaam at night* (Num. 22:20). But [He revealed Himself to] the prophets of Israel during the day: *And he sat near the door of the tent in the heat of the day* (Gen. 18:1). *On the day when the Lord spoke to Moses in the Land of Egypt* (Exod. 6:28). *On the day that He commanded the Children of Israel* (Lev. 7:38). *These are the generations of Aaron and Moses on the day that the Lord spoke to Moses on Mount Sinai* (Num. 3:1)." What is [the difference] between Moses and the rest of the prophets? Rabbi Judah the son of Ilai and the rabbis [discussed this matter]. Rabbi Judah said: "All [the other] prophets saw [their visions] through nine window panes. Thus it is written: *And the vision which I saw was like the vision which I had seen when He came to destroy the city and like the vision which I had seen by the river of Chebar, and I fell on my face* (Ezek. 43:3) [for the Hebrew root *r'h* appears eight times plus one plural form for nine occurrences]. But Moses saw [his visions] through one window pane, *[With him I speak mouth to mouth] clearly and not in dark speech* (Num. 12:8)." But the rabbis said: "All [the other] prophets saw [their visions] through a dim glass, for it is written: *I spoke to the prophets, and I increased visions* (Hos. 12:11). But Moses saw [his visions] through a polished glass; thus it is written: *He beholds the form of the Lord* (Num. 12:8)."

Rabbi Phinehas in the name of Rabbi Hoshiya [said: "It is comparable] to a king who revealed himself to his household only through his image, for in this world the Holy Presence reveals Herself to the special ones. But [with reference] to the world-to-come, what is written? *And the glory of the Lord will be revealed, and they shall see [it]* (Isa. 40:5)."

BIBLIOGRAPHY

Arnaldez, R.

1984   "L'influence de la Traduction des Septante sur le Commentaire de Philon." In R. Kuntzmann and J. Schlosser, eds., 1984: 251-66.

Basser, H. W.

1984   *Sifre Haazinu: Midrashic Interpretations of the Song of Moses.* New York: Lang.

Bickerman, E.

1962   *From Ezra to the Last of the Maccabees: Foundations of Post-Biblical Judaism.* 1st ed. New York: Schocken.

Bietenhard, H.

1984   *Der tannaitische Midrasch "Sifre Deuteronomium."* Bern: Lang.

Bloch, R.

1957   "Midrash." In *Dictionnaire de la Bible, Supplement,* 1263-81. Paris: Letouzey et Ané.

Borgen, P.

1984   "Philo of Alexandria." In M. E. Stone, ed., *Jewish Writings of the Second Temple Period: Apocrypha, Pseudepigrapha, Qumran Sectarian Writings, Philo, Josephus,* 233-82. CRINT II. Assen: van Gorcum/Philadelphia: Fortress.

Boyarin, D.

1990   *Intertextuality and the Reading of Midrash.* Bloomington: Indiana University Press.

Braude, W. G., and I. J. Kapstein

1975   *Pesikta de-Rab Kahana: R. Kahana's Compilation of Discourses for Sabbaths and Festal Days.* Philadelphia: Jewish Publication Society.

Brownlee, W. H.

1951   "Biblical Interpretation among the Sectaries of the Dead Sea Scrolls." *Biblical Archaeologist* 14 (3): 54-76.

Bruns, G. L.

1990   "The Hermeneutics of Midrash." In R. Schwartz, ed., *The Book and the Text: The Bible and Literary Theory,* 189-213. Oxford: Blackwell.

Cazeaux, J.

1984   "Philon, L'allégorie et l'obsession de la Totalité." In R. Kuntzmann and J. Schlosser, eds., 1984.

Daube, D.

1949   "Rabbinic Methods of Interpretation and Hellenistic Rhetoric." *Hebrew Union College Annual* 22:234-64.

Finkelstein, L.

1969   *Sifre on Deuteronomy.* New York: Jewish Theological Seminary of America.

1989   *Sifra on Leviticus.* New York: Jewish Theological Seminary of America.

Fishbane, M.

1985   *Biblical Interpretation in Ancient Israel.* Oxford: Clarendon.

Fishbane, M. (ed.)

1993   *The Midrashic Imagination: Jewish Exegesis, Thought, and History.* Albany: State University of New York Press.

Fraade, S. D.

1991   *From Tradition to Commentary: Torah and Its Interpretation in the Midrash Sifre to Deuteronomy.* Albany: State University of New York Press.

Freedman, H.

1939   *Midrash Rabbah: Genesis.* London: Soncino.

Geiger, A.

1857   *Urschrift und Uebersetzungen der Bibel in Ihrer Abhängigkeit von innern Entwicklung des Judenthums.* Breslau: Heinauer.

Goldin, J.

1971   *The Song at the Sea.* New Haven: Yale University Press.

Goodblatt, D.

1975   *Rabbinic Instruction in Sassanian Babylonia.* Leiden: Brill.

Green, W. S.

1987   "Romancing the Tome: Rabbinic Hermeneutics and the Theory of Literature." *Semeia* 40:147-68.

Gruenwald, I.

1993   "Midrash and the 'Midrashic Condition': Preliminary Considerations." In M. Fishbane, ed., 1993: 6-22.

Halivni, D. W.

1986   *Midrash, Mishnah, and Gemara: The Jewish Predilection for Justified Law.* Cambridge: Harvard University Press.

Hammer, R.

1986   *Sifre: A Tannaitic Commentary on the Book of Deuteronomy.* New Haven: Yale University Press.

Handelman, S. A.

1982 *The Slayers of Moses: The Emergence of Rabbinic Interpretation in Modern Literary Theory.* Albany: State University of New York Press.

Hartman, G. H., and S. Budick (eds.)

1986 *Midrash and Literature.* New Haven: Yale University Press.

Heinemann, I.

1954 *The Paths of the Aggadah.* 2nd ed. Jerusalem: Magnes.

Heinemann, J.

1970 *Sermons in the Community in the Period of the Talmud.* Hebrew ed. Jerusalem: Mosad Bialik.

1986 "The Nature of the Aggadah." In G. H. Hartman and S. Budick, eds., 1986: 41-47.

Hengel, M.

1974 *Judaism and Hellenism: Studies in Their Encounter in Palestine during the Early Hellenistic Period.* ET J. Bowden. Philadelphia: Fortress.

Horovitz, H. S.

1966 *Siphre D'be Rab Fasciculus primus: Siphre ad Numeros adjecto Siphre zutta.* Reprint. Jerusalem: Wahrmann (1917).

Horovitz, H. S., and I. A. Rabin

1960 *Mechilta D'Rabbi Ismael.* Reprint. Jerusalem: Bamberger & Wahrman (1931).

Idel, M.

1993 "Midrashic Versus Other Forms of Jewish Hermeneutics: Some Comparative Reflections." In M. Fishbane, ed., 1993: 45-58.

Israelstam, J., and J. J. Slotki

1939 *Midrash Rabbah: Leviticus.* London: Soncino.

Jacobson, H.

1983 *The Exagoge of Ezekiel.* Cambridge: Cambridge University Press.

Kugel, J. L.

1986 "Two Introductions to Midrash." In G. Hartman and S. Budick, eds., 1986: 77-104.

Kuhn, K. G.

1959 *Der tannaitische Midrasch Sifre zu Numeri übersetzt und erklärt.* Stuttgart: Kohlhammer.

Kuntzmann, R., and J. Schlosser (eds.)

1984 *Études sur le Judaïsme hellénistique.* Paris: Cerf.

Lauterbach, J. Z.

1933 *Mekhilta de-Rabbi Ishmael.* Philadelphia: Jewish Publication Society of America.

Levertoff, P. P.

1926 *Midrash Sifre on Numbers.* London: Golub.

Levine, L. I.

1987   "The Second Temple Synagogue: The Formative Years." In L. I. Levine, ed., *The Synagogue in Late Antiquity*, 7-32. Philadelphia: American Schools of Oriental Research.

1989   *The Rabbinic Class of Roman Palestine in Late Antiquity.* New York: Jewish Theological Seminary of America.

Lieberman, S.

1950   *Hellenism in Jewish Palestine.* New York: Jewish Theological Seminary of America.

Mandelbaum, B.

1962   *Pesikta de Rab Kahana.* New York: Jewish Theological Seminary of America.

Margulies, M.

1953   *Midrash Wayyikra Rabbah: A Critical Edition Based on Manuscripts and Genizah Fragments with Variants and Notes.* Jerusalem: Ministry of Education and Culture of Israel.

Neusner, J.

1968   *A History of the Jews in Babylonia III: From Shapur I to Shapur II.* Leiden: Brill.

1969   *A History of the Jews in Babylonia IV: The Age of Shapur II.* Leiden: Brill.

1970   *The Modern Study of the Mishnah.* Leiden: Brill.

1971   *The Rabbinic Traditions About the Pharisees Before 70.* 3 vols. Leiden: Brill.

1972   *There We Sat Down: The Story of Classical Judaism in the Period in Which It Was Taking Shape.* Nashville: Abingdon Press.

1981   *Judaism: The Evidence of Mishnah.* Chicago: University of Chicago Press.

1983   *Midrash in Context: Exegesis in Formative Judaism.* Philadelphia: Fortress.

1985   *Genesis Rabbah: The Judaic Commentary to the Book of Genesis. A New American Translation.* Atlanta: Scholars.

1986a   *Sifre to Numbers: An American Translation and Explanation.* Atlanta: Scholars.

1986b   *Judaism and Scripture: The Evidence of Leviticus Rabbah.* Chicago: University of Chicago Press.

1987a   *Pesiqta de Rab Kahana: An Analytical Translation and Explanation.* Atlanta: Scholars.

1987b   *Sifre to Deuteronomy: An Analytical Translation.* Atlanta: Scholars.

1988a   *Invitation to Midrash: The Working of Rabbinic Bible Interpretation. A Teaching Book.* San Francisco: Harper and Row.

1988b   *Mekhilta Attributed to R. Ishmael: An Analytical Translation.* Atlanta: Scholars.

1988c   *Sifra: An Analytical Translation.* Atlanta: Scholars.

1990   *A Midrash Reader.* Minneapolis: Fortress.

1994   *Introduction to Rabbinic Literature.* The Anchor Bible Reference Library. New York: Doubleday.

Novak, D.

1983   *The Image of the Non-Jew in Judaism: An Historical and Constructive Study of the Noahide Laws.* New York: Mellen.

Pfeiffer, R.

1971   *History of Classical Scholarship.* Oxford: Oxford University Press.

Porton, G. G.

1977   *The Traditions of Rabbi Ishmael.* II: *Exegetical Comments in Tannaitic Collections.* Leiden: Brill.

1979   "Midrash: Palestinian Jews and the Hebrew Bible in the Greco-Roman Period." In H. Temporini and H. Haase, eds., *Aufstieg und Niedergang der Römischen Welt,* II.19.2, 103-38. Berlin: de Gruyter.

1982   *The Traditions of Rabbi Ishmael.* IV: *The Materials as a Whole.* Leiden: Brill.

1985a *Understanding Rabbinic Midrash: Text and Commentary.* Hoboken: Ktav.

1985b "Sects and Sectarianism during the Period of the Second Temple: The Case of the Sadducees." In N. Stampfer, ed., *The Solomon Goldman Lectures: Perspectives in Jewish Learning.* IV, 135-48. Chicago: Spertus College of Judaica Press.

1987   "Rabbi Ishmael and His Thirteen Middot." In J. Neusner, et al., eds., *New Perspectives on Ancient Judaism.* I: *Religion, Literature, and Society in Ancient Israel, Formative Christianity and Judaism,* 1-18. Lanham: University Press of America.

Ruether, R. R.

1974   *Faith and Fratricide: The Theological Roots of Anti-Semitism.* New York: Seabury.

Saldarini, A. J.

1979   "Apocalypses and 'Apocalyptic' in Rabbinic Literature and Mysticism." *Semeia* 14:187-205.

1988   *Pharisees, Scribes, and Sadducees: A Sociological Approach.* Wilmington: Glazier.

Sanders, J. A.

1972   *Torah and Canon.* Philadelphia: Fortress.

Sarason, R.

1981   "Road to a New Agendum for the Study of Rabbinic Midrashic Literature." In J. J. Petuchowski and E. Fleischer, eds., *Studies in Aggadah, Targum and Jewish Liturgy in Memory of Joseph Heinemann,* 55-73. Jerusalem: Magnes.

1982   "The Petihot in Leviticus Rabba: Oral Homilies or Redactional Constructions?" *Journal of Jewish Studies* 33:557-67.

Smith, M.

1968   *Tannaitic Parallels to the Gospels.* JBLMS 6. Corrected reprint. Philadelphia: Society of Biblical Literature.

1971   *Palestinian Parties and Politics That Shaped the Old Testament.* New York: Columbia University Press.

Spiro, M. E.

1987   "Religion: Problems of Definition and Explanation." In B. Kilborne and L. Langness, eds., *Cultural and Human Nature: Theoretical Papers of Melford E. Spiro,* 187-222. Chicago: University of Chicago Press.

Strack, H. L., and G. Stemberger

1991   *Introduction to the Talmud and Midrash.* 1st ed. Trans. Markus Bockmuehl. Edinburgh: Clark.

Theodor, J., and C. Albeck

1965   *Midrash Bereshit Rabba. Critical Edition with Notes and Commentary,* with additional corrections by C. Albeck. Jerusalem: Wahrmann.

Towner, W. S.

1973   *The Rabbinic "Enumeration of Scriptural Examples."* Leiden: Brill.

Vermes, G.

1961   *Scripture and Tradition in Judaism.* Leiden: Brill.

1970   "Bible and Midrash: Early Old Testament Exegesis." In P. R. Ackroyd and C. F. Evans, eds., *The Cambridge History of the Bible.* I: *From the Beginnings to Jerome,* 199-231. Cambridge: Cambridge University Press.

Wacholder, B. Z.

1968   "The Date of the Mekilta de-Rabbi Ishmael." *Hebrew Union College Annual* 39:117-144.

Weingreen, J.

1951-52 "The Rabbinic Approach to the Study of the Old Testament." *Bulletin of the John Rylands Library* 34:166-90.

Weiss, I. H.

1947   *Sifra deBe Rab: Torah Kohanim.* Reprint. New York: Om (1862).

Winter, J., and A. Wünsche

1990   *Mechiltha, ein tannaitischer Midrasch zu Exodus.* Reprint. Hildesheim: Olms (1909).

Wright, A

1967   *The Literary Genre Midrash.* New York: Alba.

Wünsche, A.

1967   *Bibliotheca Rabbinica: Eine Sammlung alter Midraschim: Zur ersten Male ins Deutsche übertragen.* Reprint. Hildesheim: Olms (1881).

Zunz, L.

1832   *Die gottesdienstlichen Vorträge der Juden.* Berlin: Asher.

CHAPTER 8

The Stabilization of the Tanak

James A. Sanders

THE MEANING OF "CANON"
AND THE NOTION OF AUTHORSHIP

The word "canon" can be used in either of two ways. Most commonly it is used to mean a closed list of writings in a certain order (Latin *norma normata*, "norm normed"). The second usage indicates how such writings function in a believing community (in Latin, *norma normans*, "norm norming"). It is important to distinguish between the two meanings and to be aware of how the word is used in a given instance. The first indicates shape, the second function.

The first meaning connotes a five-foot shelf of literature that is considered some kind of standard by the community that holds that literature in high regard (Gorak 1991; Bloom 1994). The word itself derives from Semitic and Greek roots which designated a rod or reed that was firm and straight (see also Latin *canna*, English "cannon"). In Greek the word might indicate a stave, a weaver's rod, a curtain rod, a bedpost, a stick kept for drawing a straight line, or a reference for measuring, such as a level, a plumb line, or a ruler. Thereafter it took on metaphoric meanings such as model, standard, paradigm, boundary, chronological list, or tax and tariff schedule. In the New Testament it means "rule, standard" (Phil. 3:16 in some manuscripts; Gal. 6:16) or "limit" (2 Cor. 10:13, 15-16). In early church literature it came to refer to biblical law, an ideal person, an article of faith, doctrine, catalog, table of contents, or a list of persons ordained or sainted (Metzger 1987: 289-93; McDonald 1995: 1-5). Athanasius (d. 373) is the first known to have used the word for a list of inspired books, though Origen (d. 254) may have done so earlier *(Letter to Africanus)*. In his Easter letter of 367 Athanasius listed the twenty-seven books of the New Testament. It is clear from these early, varied uses of the term that it could indicate either an instrument used for measuring or the act of measuring itself — shape or function. Both senses have continued ever since as denotations of the word "canon" (Sanders 1992: 839).

Some religions are scriptured (Judaism, Samaritanism, Christianity, Islam, Confucianism, Taoism, Buddhism, Hinduism, and Zoroastrianism); others are not (W. Smith 1993). Whereas the Scripture of Islam, the Quran, designates the record of divine revelation to one individual, in Judaism and Christianity Scripture designates an anthology of human responses to divine revelations, in dialogue with each other. Most documents in the Jewish and Christian canons are anonymous. Because of the growing influence of Greek culture on Judaism in the pre-Christian period, pressure grew to assign "canonical" literature to great names in the particular community's past. Greek culture, considerably more than Semitic cultures, stressed the worth and responsibility of individuals. Everyone knew who wrote the *Iliad* and the *Odyssey*, and other great Greek literature. By the same token, Jews and early Christians felt they had to come up with names of individuals as authors of their well-known literature, whether "canonical" yet or not. Thus ensued the attribution of anonymous literature to great names of Israel's past.

As strange as it may seem to the Western (Greek-influenced) mind, the four canonical Gospels are basically anonymous. For example, not only do we not know who Luke was, the Gospel that bears his name did not even have an attribution (*kata Loukan*, "according to Luke") until well into the second century CE, when Christianity was beginning to leave its Jewish matrix to become a separate religion. It is a very western notion, due to the Renaissance of Greek culture in the fourteenth to sixteenth centuries, to think that we would know more about the third Gospel if we knew who its author was. It is only an assumption that the Luke whose name was affixed to the Gospel was the "beloved physician" to whom the writer of Colossians refers (4:14). It is the same with the other Gospels and some of the letters attributed to Paul.

Greek cultural pressure was so great that Jews felt they had to answer the question of individual authorship in order to gain respect for their community literature and for Jewish culture in general. The kinds of apologetic arguments that Philo and Josephus engaged in were directed toward seeking acceptance of Judaism in the Greek cultural world. It was not until some time in the third to second centuries BCE that Jews began to attribute the whole Pentateuch to Moses, all the Psalms to David, the whole of the anthology of wisdom in the Book of Proverbs to Solomon, etc. The western, Greek-shaped mind fears that if Paul did not write Ephesians or Colossians, for example, those books would have less authority. Even the superscriptions to the books in the prophetic corpus of the Hebrew Bible did not indicate authorship so much as what God was doing for Israel and the world through certain charismatic persons in their particular time-space frames. The focus was not on the worth and authority of those individuals but on the work of God through them and their contemporaries.

THE REPETITION OF TRADITIONS IN EARLY ISRAEL

Long before there was anything close to an agreed-upon table of contents specifying the literature which the Jewish community held to be "canonical," certain common traditions gave the community identity and norms of conduct in the light of that identity. They functioned in much the same way as later canonical Scripture, except that they were remembered and transmitted in fluid, oral forms. That they were not set in stabilized forms in no way diminished their authority. Consider, for instance, the innumerable times the exodus event is referred to in preexilic literature. Such references were not casual but intentional, undergirding the points otherwise made by prophets, psalmists, or historians possessing community authority. That the stories of those community-defining events were recited in different ways for different purposes did not diminish that authority (compare Taussig 1980).

Reference to two great events in Israel's past powerfully conveyed such authority. One, the exodus, created the people called Israel: "the people come out of Egypt." The other was the call of David and the establishment of his dynasty. In addition, the patriarchal traditions, and eventually the belief in creation as God's initial great act of grace, also functioned canonically as references of authority (Sanders 1972: 13-28). The great preexilic prophets (with the possible exception of the eighth-century Isaiah) referred to God's freeing of the slaves from Egypt to substantiate their claims that the God of the exodus could and would free the people from their slavery to and idolatry of God's gifts of land, city, and temple. In doing so, these prophets brought a different hermeneutic to bear in understanding the authority of the Mosaic and Davidic traditions, since the common people chose instead to understand these same community traditions as guaranteeing those gifts. Largely because of their quite unpopular application of those sacred traditions, "no prophet was acceptable in his own country" (Luke 4:24).

It is often assumed that most prophetic books record some kind of "call of the prophet" so that subsequent disciples or "schools" could thereby establish the prophet's authority, and the authority of his later followers, to say the kinds of things they claimed he said and did. While this is basically correct, the prophets also referred to Israel's corporate "call" to claim authority for what they said and did. That is, in order to lend authority to their ministry and message, they referred "canonically," as it were, to the common traditions that gave the people their essential identity. That same kind of appeal to authority later would be made to those traditions, and many others, when they had become stabilized in a written canon.

One example of prophetic reference to the exodus events may suffice to illustrate the point. The book of Amos records a sermon that extends from 1:3 to 3:2 (probably the sermon referred to in 7:10-11, when Amos was in the royal sanctuary at Bethel). It is a remarkably powerful sermon in a number of ways, not the least being its rhetorical style, which was drawn to some degree from international wisdom thought. The sermon starts out with numerous oracles against Israel's surrounding neighbors. Each indictment and sentence against those peoples begins with an *incipit* common to them all. The same *incipit* then intones indictments and sentences not only against Judah, but even against northern Israel, where the sermon was delivered. The indictments against the neighbors (with the exception of Judah) are all directed against some act of inhumanity committed toward a neighbor. The sentences all include fire as part of the punishment. In the case of neighboring Judah, however, the indictment is simply that Judah had rejected the Torah of Yahweh and believed in the lies by which they lived (2:4-5). In the case of Israel itself, the indictment is about acts of inhumanity, but not acts directed against neighbors but against the poor and dispossessed in Israel's own land, as well as acts of idolatry against God (2:6-8). The sentences declaimed against Israel do not follow the indictments directly, as in all the other cases, but come after a reference to what God did for Israel in the exodus, wanderings, and entrance events of Israel's sacred story (2:9-11).

The power in the utilization of the "canonical" reference to the exodus events lies in the contrast between what Israel was doing to the poor in its own land and what Yahweh had done for the Israelites when their heads were in the dust of the land of Egypt (2:7). When Israel was powerless in Egypt, Yahweh stooped in grace to release them from the suffering and shame to create a people out of slaves. Israel, on the other hand, when it gained some power and a place to call its own, failed to follow the way of Yahweh, following instead the way of Pharaoh (Muilenburg 1961). Israel was selling the righteous for silver and the needy for sandals, trampling into the dust of the earth the heads of the poor in their own land (Amos 8:4-6). The power Israel attained corrupted Israel.

Hosea and Jeremiah, alone among the prophets, expressed the view that Israel had been devoted and dedicated in the wilderness period after the exodus, up to the point of entering the promise and settling the land (Hos. 2:14-15; 9:10; Jer. 2:2-3). Amos does not say it quite that way, but he clearly implies that when Israel came into the heritage of the land and hence into power of their own, they became corrupt. The reference to the "gospel" (God's story) of the exodus, wanderings, and entrance provides a marked contrast between what God has done for Israel and what Israel is doing to her own powerless and poor people, her own in-land neighbors. To reinforce the point at issue, the entrance into the land is mentioned first, and then the exodus and the forty years in the desert (Amos 2:9-11).

Recitals of Israel's identifying past can be found throughout the Bible. The shortest such recital is in 1 Sam. 12:8, part of a speech that Samuel addressed to the assembly gathered at Gilgal to anoint Saul. That one verse covers Israel's story from Jacob to the entrance into the land. In the immediately preceding verse Samuel titles the little recital "the saving deeds of the Lord" (RSV/NRSV), literally "the righteousnesses of Yahweh." The same title is also used in Judg. 5:11 and Mic. 6:5. The implication is clearly that each act of God was a righteousness. In Hebrew the word translated "righteousness" can indeed have the very concrete meaning of an act of God as it appears in these little "canonical" recitals. One knew what a righteousness was because Israel's identifying stories, which came to be repeated regularly, told one so. It was an act of God for Israel and the world.

The recitals could also be very long, with more details of the story included. For example, at the climax of Deuteronomy, Moses gives instructions to each Israelite who has entered the promised land, and these include reciting Israel's story (26:5-9). The recitals clearly became confessions of Israel's identity. Regular recital of this story meant that Israel's people would always know their essential identity no matter what happened to them or where they were. At the summit conference at Shechem after settlement in the land, Joshua recites a fuller account (Josh. 24:2-13). Even longer ones appear in Psalms 105–106 and 135–136, Sirach 44–50, Acts 7, Hebrews 11, and other passages.

Recitals of the Davidic traditions of the election of David as king based on 1 Samuel 16–17 and 2 Samuel 7 are found principally in the Psalter and in the book of Isaiah. Psalm 78 and Exodus 15 combine the two traditions, as does the fuller story contained in the Torah and the Former Prophets (Genesis to 2 Kings). In fact, the fullest recital of the Mosaic traditions is actually the whole of Exodus through Joshua, with Genesis as a kind of global introduction.

In preexilic times there was no stabilized and uniform way of referring to Israel's common identifying past. Nevertheless, the function of the traditions worked in the same authoritative way that later Scripture would work when the Torah and the Prophets became Israel's Scripture.

In the exilic and postexilic period we find the beginnings of more stabilized references to Israel's past and to the growing body of Israel's traditions. Fishbane (1985) has brilliantly described the development of the process in the earliest Jewish (or postexilic) portions of Scripture. Most likely, the literature that ended up in the Jewish canon was only about ten percent of the literature Israel had created over the centuries. The Hebrew Bible itself refers to twenty-four noncanonical works (Leiman 1976: 19-20). In an extended history of repetition and recitation of the sort described above in the book of Amos, some of Israel's traditions landed on a kind of tenure track toward what would eventually be Israel's canon as *norma normata*. There was no council of authoritative persons who made the decisions about what was to be in or not in the canon (Lewis 1964). Rather, it was the common and frequent repetition of certain traditions in community that determined the content of the eventual canon.

CHARACTERISTICS OF THE BIBLE AS CANON,
THE HERMENEUTICAL TRIANGLE

Such repetition and recitation are together only one of the major characteristics of canonical traditions or literature. Another is the resignification that took place whenever Israel's identifying stories were repeated in ever-changing circumstances and socio-political situations. This is true also for Scripture whenever it is recited. Resignification is a constant and steady characteristic of Scripture as canon. While there are as many canons as there are distinct communities of faith, and their stability is therefore to that limited extent uncertain, all canons are viewed by their adherents as constantly relevant to their lives. This characteristic may be called its adaptability-stability quotient. Literature that is canonical for a community of faith is by its very nature adaptable (Sanders 1976). The properties of resignification and adaptability have their limits, however. If the tradition or Scripture is resignified or adapted beyond recognition by the community, it loses its power in that use. It cannot be so bent to purpose that it gets out of recognizable shape. Canonical shape and function work together and neither can overwhelm the other.

Canonical traditions and literature are also both multivalent and pluralistic. These are the main properties that render them relevant. They are multivalent in the sense that all really good poetry and most prose have the ability to speak to widely different situations. This is the principal literary reason canonical literature has lasted so long and continues to draw people to its messages. Literature as canon is also pluralistic — in the case of the Jewish and Christian canons, if perhaps not the Muslim. The Bible was formed over a period of time lasting at least twelve hundred years. As noted earlier, the Jewish and Christian Bibles are dialogical anthologies which may be viewed as collections of numerous human responses to divine revelations.

The Hebrew Bible has two distinct histories, the one that goes from Genesis through Kings and the other in the books of Chronicles. Both tell the same basic story, but in quite different ways with distinctly different emphases and theological points of view. Similarly, since Tatian's *Diatessaron* did not gain wide acceptance within Christianity, the Christian canon has four distinct Gospels, four different points of view on what God was doing in Christ. The churches in the late second and early third centuries said, in effect, that one should not harmonize God's truth so that it can be called coherent by human standards. God cannot be fully comprehended by the limited human intellect. God, the churches said, is as much *absconditus* (hidden from human reason) as *revelatus* (understood by human reason), and that has been the classical theological position of Christianity through the ages. Human limitations are thus taken into account in the shape and function of the canon, Jewish and Christian. The juxtaposition of Genesis 1 and Genesis 2 is a felicitous hermeneutical statement by which to read the rest of the text: God is both transcendent and immanent, awesome and pastoral. The two divine traits cannot and should not be collapsed into a proposition humans can reasonably comprehend; each is fully and completely true. God is both a high god who inhabits only the heavens and a local deity who condescends to grant his presence among the people; God is both transcendent and itinerant, both ineffable and personal.

The Bible as canon includes constraints that prevent readers from making it say whatever they want it to say (Sanders 1995: 4), and it bears within it, between its lines from beginning to end, the hermeneutic by which it should be read and applied to ever-changing situations. The thrust of the whole, both Jewish and Christian, is in its monotheizing hermeneutic. The canonical process, through which its various parts passed, filtered out any serious or meaningful polytheistic reading of its texts. Truth is presented as having its own integrity, the oneness of God.

This is the hermeneutical message not only of the first three of the Ten Commandments but also of the whole, including the Christian New Testament. The trinitarian effort to understand the oneness of God must never be confused with polytheism; it was simply an effort to meet humans where they were in their Greco-Roman limitations to comprehend truth. Like the heavenly council in the Hebrew Bible, the trinitarian formula was a clear way of denying power and authority to the many who were thought to serve the heavenly courts.

The natural human bent is toward polytheism because it seems to grant humans more control of the world in which they think they live. Idolatry, prohibited in the Second Commandment, is the self-serving tendency of humans to worship what God has given them instead of worshiping God the giver. Co-opting God's name for one human point of view, whether in courts of law or courts of theology, violates the Third Commandment. The Bible's pervasive monotheizing hermeneutic is not to be thought of only as a major theme or message of the Bible; it is the mode by which all its parts should be read and reread in order to hear clearly what the Bible continues to say to a world constantly threatened by chaos.

At the close of Amos's sermon at Bethel (3:1-2), the prophet apparently (by inferential exegesis) was interrupted by a hearer, perhaps Amaziah, the priest of Bethel (7:10). This person protested vigorously against Amos's message of God's judgments against the people of Israel: "Sir, we are the only family of the earth with whom God has a covenant relationship; therefore God will prosper us!" Amos's recorded response is sharp and clear: Quite correct! says God. The tradition is right, but the conclusion is wrong. "You only have I known of all the families of the earth; therefore I will punish you for all your iniquities" (3:2).

Three factors must always be kept in mind in reading any passage of Scripture: the tradition being recited, the socio-political situation to which it was (and is) being applied, and the hermeneutic by which it was (and should be) applied to that situation. These three factors form the hermeneutical triangle of any truly critical reading of the Bible. The hermeneutic Amaziah used was that of God as Israel's redeemer God. Amos used the hermeneutic that God was also creator of all peoples (9:1-8), on the basis of which he declaimed God's judgments against Israel's neighbors in the Bethel sermon (1:3–2:5) before he indicted and sentenced Israel (2:6-16; Sanders 1987a: 87-103).

These basic characteristics of the Bible as canon — repetition, recitation, resignification, adaptability, stability, multivalence, pluralism, constraints on its readers, and the monotheizing hermeneutic — and the hermeneutical triangle should be kept in mind in order not to violate the Bible's true integrity, the oneness of God, which is discernible in and through its pluriformity (Sanders 1991b). In our day of the apparent triumph of criticism and reason, it is only in the combination of a critical and faithful reading of the Bible that the mystery of its staying power through the centuries can be discerned. A critical reading alone may reveal only the differentness and irretrievability of its past (Johnson 1996). A faithful reading alone may only confirm the hermeneutic (like Amaziah's) that the community brought to it.

THE COALESCING OF THE TRADITIONS FROM GENESIS TO 2 KINGS

The discovery and promulgation of an early form of the scroll of Deuteronomy, found in the Temple in 621 BCE during King Josiah's reformation, most likely marked the first time a written document functioned in a canonical way (as *norma normans*) in ancient Israel/Judah. Josiah is reported to have accepted the scroll as authentic and to have made it the basis of his Mosaic/Yahwistic reformation (2 Kings 22–23). In the story line that runs from Genesis through Kings in the Jewish canon, Deuteronomy purports to be the last will and testament of Moses before his death on Mount Pisgah, near where Israel made its last camp site on the east bank of the Jordan River. In the old pre-Deuteronomic story-line the narrative clearly had gone from traditions now contained in Numbers directly to the story of the entrance into the land, as described in Joshua. The acceptance of Deuteronomy, most importantly by the exilic communities that received the old traditions, caused it to disrupt the old sequence by its insinuation between Numbers and Joshua (Sanders 1972).

Exilic adherents to the deuteronomic point of view (sometimes called the deuteronomistic historians) probably edited the older versions to bring them into line with the exilic-deuteronomic point of view. That point of view was not greatly modified when the later priestly editors put their stamp on the whole before it was finally edited in Babylonia and brought back to Jerusalem by Ezra in 445 BCE (cf. Nehemiah 8). In fact, as one reads the whole story that runs now from Genesis through Kings one can discern, among other points made, a clear four-point message that is affirmed vigorously in Deuteronomy 29–31. Those four points strongly reflect the experience of destitution and exile: (A) it is not God who let us down; (B) it is we who let God down by polytheism, idolatry, and foolishly co-opting Yahweh's name for a self-serving theology; (C) if we take the whole experience to heart, as the prophets and Deuteronomy interpreted it, it will be God's great joy to restore us not only to our former estate but to even better and more prosperous conditions; and (D) God sent prophets early and often precisely to tell us how this truly is in the divine economy and what our theology ought to have been (Sanders 1989, 1992).

This four-fold message came to reside at the heart and at the climax of the Torah as it was edited and stabilized in the Babylonian exile at the height of the Persian hegemony of the Ancient Near East. The traditional date assigned to Ezra's return to Jerusalem, with the edited Torah in hand, is 445 BCE (for recent discussion concerning the date, see Eskenazi 1993). It is recorded that Ezra read the Torah from morning until noon on a dais built for the occasion in the Water Gate of Jerusalem (Nehemiah 8). The people had lost the ability to understand Hebrew, so it was translated passage by passage into Aramaic by Levites standing on either side of Ezra as he read. The Deuteronomy scroll had the function of canon for Josiah's Judah, but now Ezra's Torah had both the function and the shape of a community's canon. This was truly the beginning of the Bible as *norma normata,* as well as *norma normans* (Gorak 1991: 9-43).

The Torah that Ezra brought to Jerusalem, edited in exile, was clearly the Torah as we know it in both the Masoretic Text and the Septuagint, with the possibility of a bit of editing yet to be done. The Torah that Ezra read in community that day was basically stable for all time to come. Its message included not only the already-mentioned four Deuteronomic points but other points as well. Yahweh, the God of Israel, was actually the creator God of all heaven and earth, indeed of everything in creation. Yahweh established creation as a divine order that would keep the forces of chaos and outer darkness at bay. Righteousness and justice were the marks of God's creation, that is, of the order God had wrought out of the morass of chaos (Clifford 1994). God was the sole god of all creation. What others thought of as the many gods of polytheism were really only ministering servants of God in the heavenly order or chthonian (underworld) deities who represented chaos but who had no ultimate power of their own. Genesis 1–11 set the stage of creation's order of justice and righteousness. Because of the human tendency to violate the order of God's creation, God engaged in a pact with a couple who lived in Haran in Mesopotamia. Abram and Sarai were invited to accompany God on a journey, going where they knew not. They were given therewith two promises: progeny and a place for them and their progeny to live (Gen. 12:1-3).

Though the promises often seemed to fail, or seemed continually not to come true, eventually they were indeed fulfilled. In fact, if one is looking for a biblical theme of promise and fulfillment, it is found within the broader Torah story that finds completion, not in the Moses/Ezra Pentateuch but in the Former Prophets, which soon were added to the Torah Ezra read in the Water Gate. The promises of both progeny and land were fulfilled by the end of the book of Joshua, though they were not yet secure. The security of fulfillment, of the sort humans seek, is clearly assured by 1 Kings 10. The Queen of Sheba visited Jerusalem to witness for herself the great wisdom for which Solomon had become internationally famous, according to the immediate text. In the larger context of the broader Torah story the Queen of Sheba plays the role of the international witness to God's fulfillment of the two promises to Abraham and Sarah, progeny and land. The borders of the united kingdom under Solomon were as extended as ever they would be, and the land was teeming with heirs of the Abraham/Sarah promises. "All the king's vessels were of gold; none was of silver . . ." (10:21).

But alas, God appointed three *satans* (testers) to Solomon, and he failed all three tests. By the end of the next chapter (1 Kgs. 11:14, 23, 26) the kingdom had split and there was dissension on every side. Solomon succumbed to polytheism and idolatry, apparently due in part to the flattery of foreign adulation. In the story line that runs from Genesis through 2 Kings, the movement after 1 Kings 11 is downhill all the way to the dissolution of the whole experiment — the defeat of the northern kingdom in 722 BCE and of the southern kingdom in 587 BCE (1 Kings 11–2 Kings 25). In the Jewish canon, this is where the story line ends. King Jehoiachin, who is taken hostage in 597 BCE at the end of 2 Kings, is invited by the new Babylonian monarch to dine at the king's table. He would at that time have been fifty-five years of age. The move from prison to more comfortable quarters, with board at the king's table, was surely welcome; nevertheless, the surviving king of Judah still lived only by the graces of Evil-merodach (2 Kgs. 25:27-30). The story that began in Genesis thus ends in total defeat and subjugation.

At this point one poignantly remembers that the whole Torah story insists that God is the God of fallings as well as risings, of defeat as well as of victory, of both honor and shame, of what humans call evil or bad, as well as of what they call good (Deut. 32:39; 1 Sam. 2:6-7; 2 Sam. 22:27; Isa. 45:7; Luke 1:52-53; see Sanders 1988, 1992). In fact, much of the Bible is devoted to explaining defeat under the sovereignty of God — the defeat of the northern kingdom by Assyria and of the southern kingdom by Babylonia, tight hegemony by the Persians, conquest by Greece and subjugation by the Ptolemies and the Seleucids, conquest and oppression by Rome, the fall of Jerusalem in 70 CE, the crucifixion of a teacher from Galilee, persecution of Christians on all sides, and the apparent failure of the parousia in the first century CE.

In Christian canons one can go on to read the books of Chronicles immediately after Kings and sense some relief from the disaster, but not so in the Tanak, or Jewish canon. In the Tanak this strange story of beginnings and endings, fulfillment and subsequent disappointment, is immediately followed by fifteen prophetic books, the books of the Three, Isaiah, Jeremiah, and

Ezekiel (in that order in most manuscripts), and of the Twelve, the so-called minor prophets. In other words, the fuller Torah story, in its full canonical extent, including the so-called Former Prophets (ending in 2 Kings), is followed by the so-called Latter Prophets, fifteen case histories that substantiate the fourfold message noted above in the deuteronomic history. God had indeed sent prophets early and often to tell the people and their leaders how it was in the divine economy. Those prophets, in one way or another, made the same points: it was indeed the people who had broken the covenant, not God; but there was a second chance, in destitution, to learn what God had by the prophets tried to teach them, that if they repented and came to their senses God would restore them more handsomely than before. There would be resurrection on the corporate level, as Ezekiel affirmed (ch. 37).

THE PROPHETIC PERSPECTIVE ON ISRAEL'S FUTURE

Of these fifteen case histories that substantiate the fourfold message of Deuteronomy and the deuteronomi(sti)c history, a few arose in the exilic period, reflecting on the catastrophes and their aftermath, but most of them present the words and actions of prophets who date from before the final fall of Jerusalem and the defeat of Judah in 587 BCE. The preexilic prophets consistently convey the message that God was God in the defeats of Israel as well as in Israel's earlier fulfillment. They fairly consistently indict the people as a whole, beginning with their leaders, for polytheism and idolatry, especially the idolatry of loving God's gifts more than God the giver, or, just as bad, adhering to their view of God as one obligated by the covenant to prosper them. But the prophets also consistently offer hope beyond the disaster, if the people, in destitution, take the prophetic message to heart. In one way or another they interpret the coming disasters as having not only punitive effect because of the people's sins, but also transformative effect that would prepare them for the subsequent restoration — if they would take it all to heart (Deuteronomy 29–31). Even the book of Amos (if not the historical person Amos) offers hope beyond disaster (Amos 9). Hosea very clearly says that the defeat of Samaria may be looked at as a Valley of Achor that God will turn into a Door of Hope — if the people return to the devotion of their youth (Hos. 2:14-15; 5:15–6:3). Jeremiah has much the same message, suggesting that in adversity God is in effect a surgeon suturing God's Torah onto the heart of the people corporately (Jer. 31:31-34). The book of Isaiah is a virtual paradigm in how God's judgments may be understood as preparing Israel to be God's teacher of Torah to the world (especially Isa. 1:21-27; 28:14-22; see Sweeney 1988).

Ezekiel presses the surgical metaphor used by Hosea and Jeremiah further, affirming that in adversity God is conducting a heart transplant, taking out the old heart of stone and putting in a heart of flesh, giving the people a new heart and a new spirit so that they can be obedient and faithful when restored to the land God gave them in the first place (Ezek. 36:25-28). Ezekiel goes on to affirm that God is resurrecting the bones of old Israel and Judah and making them into a new united people under God's pastoral oversight (Ezekiel 37).

Each of the preexilic prophets in one way or another affirmed that defeat and even death would not stump God; God was indeed the God of fallings and risings, as well as of risings and fallings. A remarkable thing to note about historical biblical criticism is that it has not been able to date these prophets, as individuals, after the catastrophic event. When New Testament scholarship sees Jesus, in the Gospels, speaking prophetically of the coming fall of Jerusalem, it usually claims that this is a *vaticinium post eventum* placed in the mouth of Jesus by the Gospel-writers. Not so with the prophets. They state clearly that God is the God of both victory and defeat. This is a (theo)logical consequence of belief in one God only. Adversity in the monotheizing thrust of the Bible cannot be ascribed to a bad God, and prosperity to "our good God." Nothing in the Bible, in either testament, would affirm such a position. In fact, it is reasonable to speculate that Jesus may have believed that the first-century Jewish world in Palestine would eventually fall to the Romans. Given that Jesus was apparently born just before the turmoil of the War of Varus, which followed the death of Herod, and witnessed personally the cruel oppression of Roman occupation thereafter, the fall of Jerusalem might have been for him, just as for the preexilic prophets, a (theo)logical consequence of belief in one God. The key to understanding it all was the Torah story and its belief that death does not stump God, that God can indeed reach in and through defeat and death to new life, for both belong to God.

THE TENSION BETWEEN CORPORATE AND INDIVIDUAL FOCUS

It is helpful to understand that the Bible resides in a kind of tension between focus on corporate worth and responsibility, on the one hand, and focus on individual worth and responsibility, on the other, and that this tension pervades both testaments. Most of the literature in the Bible, as noted above, is anonymous and was viewed as corporately owned. To call passages in biblical

literature "secondary" because they were "added by a later hand" is to deny
the community dimension of the Bible. The names of the patriarchs in Genesis are largely eponymous. Scholarship has long since accepted the corporate
dimension of names like Abraham, Isaac, and Jacob. The current conservative
(actually Greek-shaped) mind feels that authority is somehow denied to the
Bible by recognition of this Semitic dimension of it. Skilled historians know
that when we deal with history, we deal with a very different and irretrievable
past (Johnson 1996). The Bible is indeed a book very strange to the western
mind, whether it recognizes this or not (Sanders 1988). Its strangeness provides a dimension of authenticity that familiarity denies: we can never claim
to comprehend it fully or dismiss it. Like Jacob with the "man" at Peniel, one
wrestles with the text as with a human, later to find that one had somehow
been wrestling with God (Gen. 32:22-32). The concept of its being, or conveying, the word of God means that, like God, it cannot be fully comprehended.
The history of modern historical criticism of the Bible has indeed shown that
the "assured results" of one generation of biblical criticism are often challenged by the next. Modern thinking perceives the challenges as improve-
ments on the way to claiming the truth of the text. Postmodern thinking, on
the contrary, understands that the process of challenge and response, even
within the most rigorous pursuit of critical method, is the nature of critical
inquiry. The very strangeness of Scripture challenges the assumption that
"the best" in modern, western cultural awareness is what God wants. The best
thinking, conservative or liberal, of any generation will always fall short of
truth in ultimate terms.

As noted, much of the Bible is engaged in explaining adversity and defeat. The deuteronomic historians portray all preexilic Israel and Judah as sinful, for that alone would explain such a catastrophe. Yet, they were not saying
that each individual was sinful so much as saying, with Paul citing Scripture,
"none was righteous, no, not one" (Rom. 3:10). It was necessary to explain the
disaster. In fact, it has been noted that the Bible presents many mirrors for
identity, but hardly any models for morality (Sanders 1987a: 69-73). The popular tendency would have been to blame God for letting the people down, but
the prophets, historians, and psalmists who end up in the Bible clearly state
that it was the fault of Israel, not God. The deuteronomic historians laid special blame on the leaders, notably the kings of Israel and Judah, eponymically
representing the people as a whole. King Manasseh, who reigned through
most of the seventh century BCE in Judah (2 Kgs. 21:1-18), was a primary example. For the deuteronomists, Manasseh was a kind of scapegoat explaining
the destitution. The focus was corporate, however, for the king represented
the whole people. The indictments of the preexilic prophets were directed at

Israel as a whole, the entire nation. None would escape the righteous judgments of God. The concept of a remnant was not that some would escape the judgment but that some would be reshaped by it while retaining their Yahwistic identity in and beyond the disaster.

Not long before the fall of Jerusalem to Babylonia in 587 BCE, both Jeremiah and Ezekiel told the people that they should no longer quote the old proverb that the children's teeth were set on edge because their ancestors had eaten sour grapes (Jer. 31:29-30; Ezekiel 18). Ezekiel developed the idea of individual responsibility in ch. 18 in a way that contradicted the clear statement in the Torah of corporate responsibility (Exod. 34:7). This caused questions to be raised in early rabbinic literature as to whether the book of Ezekiel "soiled the hands," that is, was inspired. The book of Job stands as a monument to the tension between understandings of corporate and individual responsibility. Job's friends laid the full blame for his low estate on Job himself, in effect, laying on him, as an individual, what the prophets and the deuteronomists had called the corporate sins of Israel as a whole. Job, throughout the poem (chs. 3–31), resists the implication with all his being. He tends to blame God for his disasters, sure that he will again experience the intimate relation with God in destitution that he has experienced in comfort, just as Jeremiah experienced it in both comfort and apparent abandonment (Jer. 15:15-21; Job 13:20-28; 19:23-29; 29:1-4) The whirlwind speeches, on the contrary, call Job to humility and recognition of his limited human understanding of God's work in nature, and hence in history (Job 38–42; Lundberg 1995). They thus herald belief in God's increasing remoteness, transcendence, and inaccessibility, both in Semitic and in Greek religious thought of the time.

THE GROWING DOMINANCE OF FOCUS ON THE INDIVIDUAL

As Greek culture became more and more influential in Semitic, and especially Jewish thinking, increasing attention was given to the moral struggles of the individual, as in Ecclesiastes and the Psalter. This became so much the case that the Chronicler told of King Manasseh's repentance and of God's acceptance of his repentance to the point of restoring him to the throne (2 Chron. 33:10-17). The Chronicler, however, failed to record a prayer of repentance for Manasseh. Eventually such a prayer was attributed to Manasseh, and today is present in Greek and Slavonic Orthodox canons, but not in Protestant or Catholic canons (Sanders 1993). God's acceptance of the repentance of individuals, no matter how heinous their sins or character, became a cornerstone of Judaism, which focuses on the belief that God can be obeyed and pleased by human effort.

The expansion and rapid growth of Christianity in the Greek world was due in large part to its core message contradicting the generally accepted view that God was remote, transcendent, and ineffable. Christians went about the Mediterranean world claiming that, on the contrary, God had just been sighted on the hills of the Galilee and had succumbed in crucifixion to the numbing cruelty of Roman repression for the sake of all humanity. Christianity's dramatic spread was also based on the Greek idea that an individual could choose his or her basic identity and convert from whatever had been his religious identity at birth to take on a different identity. Indeed, Judaism had become so influenced by Greek thought that in the centuries immediately before the birth of Christianity, it was said that Pharisees would go to great lengths to seek converts to Judaism (Lieberman 1942).

The New Testament, like other early Jewish literature, is a splendid mix of Semitic and Greek cultures. The concept in Paul and John of the church being "in Christ" is basically Semitic. Paul arrived at his ecclesiology through midrash on Gen. 21:12 (Rom. 9:7), which states that all Israel was "called in Isaac." The Christian idea that the church is the body of Christ resurrected is basically Semitic in concept. Nevertheless, Christians, even today, need to acknowledge that the idea of God's being incarnate in one person appeared, and appears, to less Hellenized or Greek-influenced Jews, to be too Greek or pagan a notion to accept seriously. Some Jewish philosophers, like Rosenzweig, Buber, and Fishbane, have advanced the idea of God being incarnate in Scripture (Fishbane 1989). Others, like Maimonides and Heschel, sponsored the belief that God is incarnate in Israel as a people (ha'am, Heschel 1982). Those ideas are compatible with Semitic cultural thinking. The notion that God was incarnate in one individual needed a sufficiently cross-culturally Hellenized Jewish mind to find acceptance.

THE TRANSFORMATION OF ISRAEL'S IDENTITY

It is quite probable that something like the present prophetic corpus of the second part of the tripartite Jewish canon functioned canonically for many Jews not long after Ezra brought the Torah back with him from Babylon in about 445 BCE. These texts go together as a statement of what early Judaism understood itself to be. Together they would have provided the identity Judaism needed to survive as a discrete religion in the period of Persian dominance and hegemony in the Ancient Near East. As Yeivin has noted, the most stable part of the Jewish canon, from the earliest manuscript evidence through to the very stabilized printed editions of the Tanak, was and is the Genesis to Kings sequence (1980: 38). This story line guaranteed the community's stability — even when scrolls were used, before common use of the codex in Jewish communities some time in the third or fourth century CE. The fifteen-book section that follows, called the Latter Prophets, was not so stable in order, but it nonetheless was probably fairly well set in the Persian period in terms of what was included.

Before the discovery of the Dead Sea Scrolls it was commonly believed that the Pentateuch was canonized by about 400 BCE, the Prophets around 200 BCE, and the Writings, or Ketuvim, at the council of Jewish leaders held at Yavneh/Jamnia around 90 CE (Leiman 1976, Beckwith 1985, contrast Carr 1996). The date for the Pentateuch or Torah is about right, or could be advanced to the middle of the fifth century. The date for stabilization of the prophetic corpus should probably be set back to the late fifth century, soon after the Torah. But the date for the stabilization of the Ketuvim should be advanced to some time after the Bar Kochba revolt, more toward the middle of the second century CE (Lewis 1964, McDonald 1995, Carr 1996). As argued above, the Torah and the Prophets hang together as a basic statement of God's dealings with the world and with Israel in fairly clear theological tones. Yahweh, the God of ancient Israel, turns out to be the one God of all the world who is the God of all and of everything, the God of risings and fallings, what humans call good and what they call evil (according to the limited time and circumstances in which they live). The Pentateuch, indeed the Hexateuch, can be called an apologia for the *Landnahme*, or Israel's taking over the Land of Canaan (Knierim 1995). The Law and the Prophets as a two-part unit, on the other hand, when taken in tandem, present the panorama of the rise and fall of the preexilic adventure called Israel, God's apparent plan for bringing salvation to a fallen world.

One of the functions of the anthology called Isaiah was to resignify that divine plan in the light of Israel's Assyrian, Babylonian, and Persian experiences. Looking back from the vantage point of Persian hegemony, and all that meant, the school of Isaiah perceived the loss of self-government as divine discipline and instruction transforming Israel into God's teacher of Torah to all the world (Sanders 1955, Sweeney 1988). By that time Israel had settled into accepting and understanding her survival not as an autochthonous nation but as an international religion, in part shaped by Persian policy and expectations. Its mission had become rather clear to those whose literature would itself survive the canonical process of repetition/recitation, as well as adaptation/stabilizaton. Israel, apparently in contrast to all her neighbors, survived with an identity based on the enduring preexilic traditions, but transformed into God's new Israel with a mission to the rest of the world.

The prophetic corpus provides several metaphors enabling the reader to understand the adversity that had befallen Israel and Judah, not only as punishment for Israel's corporate sins, but also in the more positive sense of transforming Israel from common nationhood (like all the nations round about) into a people with a God-given mission to the rest of the world. The people of Israel could not simply accept their survival in their transformed state as the will of God, but had to understand why they survived in and through all the adversity. This survival, in contrast to the assimilation of her neighbors into Assyrian or Babylonian dominant cultures, had to be explained, but the adversity had to be explained as well. Various metaphors were used, and the basic one depicted God disciplining his people for a purpose. Other metaphors were purgational and surgical. The book of Isaiah stresses the purgational metaphor, that the adversities suffered under Assyria and Babylonia were to be understood as God's purging of his people, either cleansing by flood or smelting by fire (Isa. 1:21-26; 8:5-8; 28:17-19). Jeremiah and Ezekiel suggest surgical metaphors, God suturing Torah onto the collective heart of Israel corporately (Jer. 30:12-17; 31:31-34) or replacing Israel's heart of stone with a heart of flesh, and indeed implanting the divine spirit into Israel so that in the transformed state Israel would be obedient (Ezek. 36:16-37:14). Whether the metaphor for understanding the survival through suffering was disciplinary, purgational, or surgical, the statement was the same: Israel survived disaster, whereas other peoples had not, and survived for a purpose (Sanders 1972: 74-90).

As long as Israel subsisted under the foreign domination of Egypt, Assyria, Babylonia, or Persia, there was no drastic *cultural* challenge to its people's thinking, for all four powers were also Near Eastern in culture, two of them also Semitic. It was in and through those experiences of rising, falling, and rising again in a transformed state that the Torah and the Prophets were forged and shaped in the canonical process. This was the literature that survived with Israel. With the stabilization of Judaism in the postexilic period as essentially a priestly religion came the stabilization of a bipartite Scripture which, if recited regularly no matter where they lived, reminded Jews of who they were, how they got that way, what they essentially stood for, and what they should do with their lives.

The lives of the Jews were to change rather dramatically, however, with the rise of Greek political and cultural influence on most aspects of Jewish life. For the first time a dominant European culture provided challenges to Jewish self-understanding. The most salient contributions of Greek culture to Semitic culture were the Greek focus on the *polis,* or city, and on individual worth and responsibility, with the attendant humanism that was sponsored by both foci. As noted above, Greek philosophy raised the worth of the individual, and of individual thinking, to a degree unheard of in Semitic culture.

The book of Sirach, or Ecclesiasticus as it has been called in its Latin translation and hence in most English translations, brought a new dimension to Jewish thinking about individuals. In contrast to Semitic practice, the Jewish writer signed his name to his work — Jesus ben Sira — hence, the Greek-derived title of the book, Sirach. More than that, the writer, although he wrote in Hebrew, borrowed Greek literary devices, one of which was the encomium, a form of writing in which individual humans were praised. Chapter 44 begins with the startling clause "Let us now sing the praises of famous men. . . ." It was the first time such a phrase was used in known Jewish literature, and it would have been shocking to the traditional Jewish ear, which would have expected instead "Let us now sing the praises of God. . . ." The poem then goes on for seven chapters reciting the expanded Torah story (noted above as occurring frequently in biblical literature), but does so focusing on the great deeds of the individuals in the story. There had been no such form in the famous old recitals.

Ben Sira praises God and frequently mentions God as approving or disapproving of this or that act of the humans involved, but God is not the focus of praise in the encomium. The author weaves together, in magnificent cadences, the old Torah story recital and the newer Greek emphasis on the worth of individual humans (Mack 1985). Such weaving together of the Semitic Jewish and the Greek was part of the Hellenization process, and from that time forward for several centuries it would be a major trait of Jewish literature, to a greater or lesser degree (M. Smith 1967, chapter 3). Nearly all Jewish literature from the early Jewish period, including the New Testament, exhibits, to one degree or another, a weaving together of the Semitic and Hellenistic traits in Judaism. In fact, the New Testament is a prime example of Hellenistic Jewish literature.

LATE MOVEMENT TOWARD THE
CANONIZATION OF THE TORAH

One of the major results of extensive study of the Dead Sea Scrolls has been the realization that while rabbinic Jewish literature may not be a major help in understanding the birth of Christianity, the Qumran literature on the other hand is very helpful (Talmon 1991, 1993). The discovery and study of the Scrolls have induced a dramatic modification of our understanding of the history of early Judaism. Two major revisions are: (a) Judaism in the pre-Christian period was very diverse, and not limited to the "parties" listed in the classical sources, and (b) for some Jewish groups of the time, prophecy had not ceased at the time of Ezra and Nehemiah in the fifth century BCE.

Here at Qumran there existed an eschatologically oriented Jewish community which, like the Christian community, was looking for divine intervention to deal with all the forces of evil in a world dominated and repressed by Rome and did not believe that prophecy or revelation ceased at the time of Ezra and Nehemiah. Prior to the finding of the scrolls, it had been commonplace for scholars to assert that almost everyone within Judaism had come to believe that divine revelation ceased at the time of Ezra. Now, however, we see that such was not the case for all forms of early Judaism. The Qumran and Christian communities are two forms of early Judaism that contradict this idea. In fact, much of the so-called intertestamental literature from early Judaism, later set aside by rabbinic Judaism, came from Jewish communities that believed that God was still very active in history and could indeed bring it to a satisfactory close in the face of all the evil abroad at the time.

The literature discovered in Palestine since 1947 has caused a number of revisions in the history of early Judaism, the rise of Christianity, and the birth of rabbinic Judaism. In addition to highlighting the pluralism of early Judaism, the finds have caused a major revision of the history of transmission of the texts of the Bible, as well as a major revision of the history of the stabilization of the Jewish and Christian canons. It is now clear that the history of the transmission of the text and the history of the canonical process go hand in hand (Sanders 1976, 1979). It is also clear that the third section of the tripartite Jewish canon, the Ketuvim, was not stabilized until after the failure of the Bar Kochba revolt in the second century CE.

If one compares the Jewish and Christian canons of the Tanak (see the parallel lists on pp. 34-35 above), one sees major differences in the structures. Whenever one speaks of canon, one must state clearly which community's canon is being discussed, Jewish or Christian, and, within that community, which subgroup's canon one has in mind. The Qumran literature has shown that the Qumran community's canon contained two major sections, the Torah and the Prophets, but beyond that was amorphous or not yet stable. Thirty years of study of the Psalms Scrolls from Qumran has shown that the Psalter itself was not yet stable at Qumran, whether or not it was in other forms of Judaism (Sanders 1967, Wilson 1985, Flint 1996 and 1997). The situation with the Septuagint (LXX) is similar. In 1964, a year before publication of the large Psalms Scroll and the Temple Scroll, both from Qumran Cave 11, Sundberg demonstrated that there was no stabilized canon reflected in the

LXX manuscripts of the Tanak (Sundberg 1964). What he found can now be rephrased to indicate that there was not yet a clear stabilization of anything beyond the Pentateuch and the Prophets. At about the same time, Barthélemy's magisterial study of the Greek Minor Prophets scroll from Wadi Habra showed that the text of the LXX was, in the first century of the common era, in the process of being stabilized from its rather fluid, early translations of the Prophets, to conform more closely to the stabilization process going on at about the same time with Hebrew texts of the Tanak (Barthélemy 1963). By the end of the first century CE, certainly the beginning of the second century, translations of Jewish Scripture into Greek would be very literal and rigid, parallel to the rise of belief in verbal, and even literal, inspiration of Scripture (Sanders 1979).

A clear pattern has emerged from review of the situation of Scripture in the first century. The third section of the Jewish canon was not stabilized into its rabbinic, proto-Masoretic form until after the failure of the Bar Kochba revolt. Apocalyptic thinking remained vital in the forms of Judaism that survived the fall of Jerusalem and the destruction of the temple by Rome in 70 CE (Silberman 1989). Of this there can be little doubt when one remembers that Rabbi Akiba supported Bar Kochba as the messiah. Bar Kochba's revolt failed miserably. Jerusalem was sown by Rome with salt, and what was left received a Roman name, Aelia Capitolina. A growing consensus sees Rome's forceful suppression of the Bar Kochba revolt as the principal event that caused closure of the rabbinic Jewish canon (McDonald 1995, Carr 1996).

THE KETUVIM; THE TANAK AND THE CHRISTIAN OLD TESTAMENT

A careful look at the Tanak as we have inherited it from the Masoretes shows that its tripartite structure makes a very different statement from that of the Christian quadripartite First (Old) Testament. In the case of comparison of the Jewish and the Christian Protestant canons (see again pp. 34-35 above), the two structures *(norma normata)* are quite different, although the texts of the two are essentially the same. This was not always the case. The texts are the same because Jerome, in the fourth century CE, was convinced that the Latin translation of the Christian First Testament should be based on the Hebrew text (his principle of *Hebraica Veritas*) and not on the Greek translation. Since the early churches were so influenced by Greco-Roman culture, the first Scriptures of the early Christian movement were Greek translations of Jewish Scriptures. Paul knew the Jewish Scriptures in both forms, as did probably the con-

tributors to Mark, Matthew, and John. But Luke and others in the New
Testament used only the Greek translations. As the churches moved further
out into the Greco-Roman world, Greek came to be used almost exclusively.
Even Bibles in Syriac (a Semitic language) in eastern churches were considerably influenced by the Greek translations of Jewish Scripture.

The Torah had been translated into Greek by the end of the third century BCE, and the Prophets soon thereafter, with portions of the rather amorphous third section of the Jewish canon being translated as Greek-speaking
Jewish communities needed them in the pre-Christian period (Bickerman
1976). It is crucial to remember that we have the text of these Greek translations only because the churches copied, preserved, and used them. We are really not sure what the structure *(norma normata)* of a Greek translation of
the Hebrew Bible would have looked like in the world of the Hellenistic Jewish synagogue. What we know is that the structure of the Greek First Testament is very different from the structure of the Hebrew Bible, once one goes
outside the Pentateuch. Comparison of them is very instructive.

The considerable difference between the message of the Torah and the
Prophets, the first two parts of the Jewish canon, and the Ketuvim, the third
part, is striking. As argued above, the Torah and the Prophets make a fairly
clear statement about how to understand the world under one God, the God
of both risings and fallings. But the third section of the Jewish canon is quite
different. Whereas the Torah and the Prophets deal in some depth with God's
involvement and revelations in world affairs, the Ketuvim at best offer reflections on that involvement as a thing of Israel's past. Outside the book of Daniel, there is no speculation on how God might intervene in history to sort
things out, and how one reads Daniel is open to debate. Whereas Daniel is always counted among the Prophets in Christian canons, it is but one of the
Ketuvim in the Jewish canon. In other words, the Ketuvim clearly reflect the
view of Pharisaic/rabbinic Judaism as it survived and emerged out of the failure of the Bar Kochba Revolt in the mid-second century of the common era:
prophecy or revelation had ceased at the time of Ezra and Nehemiah.

Extant classical, Tiberian, Masoretic manuscripts of the Hebrew Bible
all place the book of Chronicles at the beginning of the Ketuvim, although
the Babylonian Talmud at *Baba Bathra* 14b puts it last in the Ketuvim. Placed
at the beginning, Chronicles sets the tone for the Ketuvim in a way that the
Psalter does not. Chronicles makes the reader reconsider the deuteronomic
view of what happened in the experiment called Israel. Chronicles treats the
beginnings of the world, not as in the Torah, but rather by a genealogy from
Adam through nine chapters straight to the situation in the restored temple
in postexilic Jerusalem. All the families of the various priests, Levites, and

other temple functionaries are described and set in place by the authority of genealogy. The postexilic authority of the priesthood of the restored temple is thus validated. Then Chronicles moves to the political arena and offers a revised history of what happened from the united kingdom of Israel to the fall of Jerusalem and the beginning of the exile (1 Chronicles 10–2 Chronicles 36), with a paragraph added about the restoration of the temple authorized politically by King Cyrus of Persia (2 Chron. 36:22-23).

Several revisions of the perspective of the old deuteronomic history are noteworthy. Whereas the deuteronomic history was designed in large part to affirm that God was the God of risings and fallings and could reach through defeat and death to create new life, the Chronicler's interest built on that, delineating more specifically where God was going with the new rising of Israel: Judaism as it took shape in the postexilic restoration of the Temple with authority vested in the Temple's priests and functionaries. Another major revision was the emphasis on individual worth and responsibility, thus establishing Judaism's firm belief that individual Jews, though scattered around the Persian (and later Greco-Roman) Empire, could obey God and could repent of their sins and be restored as individual Jews.

Chronicles thus sets the tone for the remainder of the Ketuvim with its emphasis on how Jews, though clearly having a corporate identity within the covenant of God with Israel, could manage, as individuals, to obey and please God wherever they were. That was precisely the ancient authority needed, after the traumatic Bar Kochba Revolt of the second century CE, for Jews to live lives pleasing to God wherever they found themselves. One can move directly from Chronicles to the Mishnah to see how Jews could live their lives wherever they were, no matter the repression and outside rejection, in stasis in Jewish communities anywhere. In the Mishnah, time is measured in terms of the activities that would have gone on in the Temple, were it still standing. The Jewish liturgical calendar is based on living lives as though the Temple were still functioning in Jerusalem.

The Psalter follows Chronicles in the great Tiberian manuscripts. In the great codices one moves from 2 Chronicles 36 to Ps. 1:1-2: "Blessed is the person who walks not in the way of the wicked . . . but delights in the Torah of Yahweh, and on that Torah meditates day and night." In other words, one moves from a revisionist history that emphasizes individual worth and responsibility, directly to a psalm that encourages individual obedience and responsibility. Even though much of the Psalter dates back to preexilic times, recounting God's mighty deeds in the covenant relationship with Israel, some of the early royal psalms which sang of God's relationship with Israel through their king proved to be directly adaptable, in the postexilic period, to recitation by individual Jews wherever they were scattered. In fact, there was a strong taboo against reciting the royal psalms in their preexilic manner until the Messiah came (Sanders 1987b).

The Wisdom literature that makes up a good bit of the Ketuvim targets individuals who sought to live lives of obedience and probity. As noted above, the book of Job stands as a monument to the struggle in early Judaism to adapt preexilic prophetic theology to the postexilic Jewish situation. The Ketuvim include the "Five Scrolls" (Ruth, The Song, Qoheleth, Lamentations, and Esther), which were recited at feasts and a fast in the early Jewish calendars. Daniel would have been read, not as eschatological literature as Christians do, but as a book of encouragement to Jewish individuals to live lives obedient to the one God. In the Ketuvim, Esther and Daniel usually appear one after the other as stories about brave young Jews, like Joseph in Genesis, who remained faithful to Yahweh even though they functioned in foreign courts, where polytheism was viewed as normal. Ezra-Nehemiah conclude the books of the Jewish canon with a message of strict resistance to assimilation and foreign influence.

There can be little doubt that the message of the third section of the Jewish tripartite canon was one that the surviving Pharisaic/rabbinic Jewish leaders felt was needed after the disastrous failures of the three Jewish revolts against Rome: the War of Varus after the death of Herod, the major revolt in 66-73 CE, and the Bar Kochba Revolt of 132-35 CE. Belief that revelation or prophecy had ceased at the time of Ezra and Nehemiah was the keystone of the new Rabbinic Judaism born out of those disasters, and the Ketuvim sponsor that view.

By contrast, Christian quadripartite canons make a totally different statement. The four sections are the Pentateuch, the Historical Books, the Poetic Wisdom Books, and the Prophets. Ruth, Esther, Daniel and Chronicles/Ezra-Nehemiah in most manuscripts of the Septuagint were put together following the Former Prophets or books about the history of pre-exilic Israel and Judah (with Ruth after Judges because of its first sentence). A glance at the Catholic and Orthodox canons show that other books deemed historical also appear in the second section, in effect stretching the history of God's dealings with Israel and the world as far down to the beginnings of Christianity as possible. The message was clear: revelation had not ceased but God, on the contrary, continued to work in history and did so climactically in Christ and the early church. The third section contained the poetic-wisdom literature and the fourth the Prophets. The Prophets are no longer placed to explain the uses of adversity and the righteousness judgments of God, but rather are understood as foretelling the coming of Christ (Sanders 1995).

Even though the texts of the Jewish Bible and the Protestant First Testament are essentially the same, the structures of the two canons (in the sense of *norma normata*) convey very different messages. The text of the First Testament in Roman Catholic canons is also essentially the same as the text of the Jewish canon, with the addition of a few books, whereas the texts of the Orthodox canons still reflect the old Greek and other church translations and compositions. But no matter how the content differs among the several Christian canons, the structure and message of the Christian canons, as a group, contrast significantly with those of the Jewish canon. The Tanak provides a way to move on to Mishnah and Talmud, while the First or Christian Old Testament provides a way to move on to the New Testament. Modern historical biblical criticism frequently reads particular parts of the canon in ways which create tension with the overall structure of both the Jewish and the Christian canons. Taken positively, this can be seen as a gift from biblical criticism whereby the Bible, in either canonical form, may be enhanced as a dialogical literature open to the future (Weis and Carr 1996).

BIBLIOGRAPHY

Barthélemy, D.

1963   *Les Devanciers d'Aquila.* VTS 10. Leiden: Brill.

Beckwith, R. T.

1985   *The Old Testament Canon of the New Testament Church and Its Background in Early Judaism.* Grand Rapids: Eerdmans.

Bickerman, E.

1976   *Studies in Jewish and Christian History.* Leiden: Brill.

Bloom, H.

1994   *The Western Canon: The Books and Schools of the Ages.* New York: Harcourt Brace.

Carr, D.

1996   "Canonization in the Context of Community: An Outline of the Formation of the Tanakh and the Christian Bible." In Weis and Carr, eds., 1996: 22-64.

Clifford, R. J.

1994   *Creation Accounts in the Ancient Near East and in the Bible.* CBQMS 26. Washington: Catholic Biblical Association of America.

Eskenazi, T. C.

1993   "Current Perspectives on Ezra-Nehemiah and the Persian Period." *CR:BS* 1:59-86.

Fishbane, M.

1985   *Biblical Interpretation in Ancient Israel.* Oxford: Clarendon.

1989   *The Garments of Torah: Essays in Biblical Hermeneutics.* Bloomington: Indiana University Press.

Flint, P.

1996   "Of Psalms and Psalters: James Sanders's Investigation of the Psalms Scrolls." In Weis and Carr, eds., 1996: 65-83.

1997   *The Dead Sea Psalms Scroll and the Book of Psalms.* STDJ 17. Leiden: Brill.

Gorak, J.

1991   *The Making of the Modern Canon: Genesis and Crisis of a Literary Idea.* Atlantic Highlands: Athlone.

Heschel, A. J.

1982   *Maimonides: A Biography.* New York: Farrar, Straus, and Giroux.

Johnson, G.

1996   *Fire in the Mind.* New York: Knopf.

Knierim, R.

1995   *The Task of Old Testament Theology: Substance, Method, and Cases.* Grand Rapids: Eerdmans.

Leiman, S. Z.

1976   *The Canonization of Hebrew Scripture: The Talmudic and Midrashic Evidence.* Hamden: Archon.

Lewis, J. P.

1964   "What Do We Mean by Jabneh?" *JBR* 32:125-32.

Lieberman, S.

1942   *Greek in Jewish Palestine: Studies in the Life and Manners of Jewish Palestine in the II-IV Centuries.* New York: Jewish Theological Seminary of America.

Lundberg, M.

1995   "So That Hidden Things May Be Brought to Light: A Concept Analysis of the Yahweh Speeches in the Book of Job" (Ph.D. dissertation, Claremont Graduate School).

Mack, B.

1985   *Wisdom and the Hebrew Epic: Ben Sira's Hymn in Praise of the Fathers.* Chicago: University of Chicago Press.

McDonald, L. M.

1995   *The Formation of the Christian Biblical Canon.* Revised and expanded edition. Peabody: Hendrickson.

Metzger, B. M.
1987   *The Canon of the New Testament: Its Origin, Development, and Significance.* Oxford: Clarendon.

Muilenburg, J.
1961   *The Way of Israel.* New York: Harper and Row.

Sanders, J. A.
1955   *Suffering as Divine Discipline in the Old Testament and Post-Biblical Judaism.* Special Issue of *Colgate Rochester Divinity School Bulletin* 28.
1967   *The Dead Sea Psalms Scroll.* Ithaca: Cornell University Press.
1972   *Torah and Canon.* Minneapolis: Fortress.
1976   "Adaptable for Life: The Nature and Function of Canon." In F. M. Cross, et al., eds., *Magnalia Dei, The Mighty Acts of God: Essays on the Bible and Archaeology in Memory of G. Ernest Wright,* 531-60. Garden City: Doubleday.
1979   "Text and Canon: Concepts and Method." *JBL* 98:5-29.
1987a   *From Sacred Story to Sacred Text: Canon as Paradigm.* Minneapolis: Fortress.
1987b   "A New Testament Hermeneutic Fabric: Ps 118 in the Entrance Narrative." In C. A. Evans and W. F. Stinespring, eds., *Early Jewish and Christian Exegesis: Studies in Memory of William Hugh Brownlee,* 177-90. Atlanta: Scholars.
1988   "The Strangeness of the Bible." *Union Seminary Quarterly Review* 42:33-37.
1989   "Deuteronomy." In Bernhard W. Anderson, ed., *The Books of the Bible.* I: *The Old Testament/The Hebrew Bible,* 89-102. New York: Scribner.
1991a   "The Integrity of Biblical Pluralism." In J. P. Rosenblatt and J. C. Sitterson, Jr., eds., *"Not in Heaven": Coherence and Complexity in Biblical Narrative,* 154-69. Bloomington: Indiana University Press.
1991b   "Stability and Fluidity in Text and Canon." In G. Norton and S. Pisano, eds., *Tradition of the Text: Studies Offered to Dominique Barthélemy in Celebration of His 70th Birthday,* 203-17. Göttingen: Vandenhoeck & Ruprecht.
1992   "Canon: Hebrew Bible." In *ABD,* I, 837-52.
1993   "Prayer of Manasseh." In W. A. Meeks, et al., eds., *The HarperCollins Study Bible,* 1746-48. San Francisco: HarperCollins.
1995   "Hermeneutics of Text Criticism." In A. Rofé, ed., *Textus: Studies of the Hebrew University Bible Project* 18, 1-16. Jerusalem: Magnes.
1997   "The Impact of the Dead Sea Scrolls on Biblical Studies." In D. W. Parry and E. Ulrich, eds., *1996 International Conference on the Dead Sea Scrolls,* 47-57. Provo: Brigham Young University Press.
1998   "Intertextuality and Canon." In S. Winter and S. Cook, eds., *On the Way to Nineveh: Studies in Honor of George M. Landes,* 316-33. Baltimore: American Schools of Oriental Research.

Silberman, L.
1989   "From Apocalyptic Proclamation to Moral Prescript: *Abot* 2,15-16." *JJS* 40:55-60.

Smith, M.
1967   *Palestinian Parties and Politics That Shaped the Old Testament.* New York: Columbia University Press.

Smith, W. C.

1993   *What Is Scripture? A Comparative Approach.* Minneapolis: Fortress.

Sundberg, A. C.

1964   *The Old Testament of the Early Church.* HTS 20. Cambridge: Harvard University Press.

Sweeney, M.

1988   *Isaiah 1–4 and the Post-Exilic Understanding of the Isaianic Tradition.* BZAW 171. Berlin: de Gruyter.

Talmon, S.

1991   "Oral Tradition and Written Transmission, or the Heard and the Seen Word in Judaism of the Second Temple Period." In H. Wansbrough, ed., *Jesus and the Oral Gospel Tradition,* 21-58. JSNTS 64. Sheffield: Sheffield Academic.

1993   "Die Gemeinde des Erneuerten Bundes von Qumran zwischen rabbinischem Judentum und Christentum." In F. Hahn et al., eds., *Zion — Ort der Begegnung: Festschrift für Laurentius Klein zur Vollendung des 65. Lebensjahres,* 295-312. Bodenheim: Athenaum Hain Hanstein.

Taussig, M. T.

1980   *The Devil and Commodity Fetishism in South America.* Chapel Hill: University of North Carolina Press.

Weis, R. D., and D. M. Carr (eds.)

1996   *A Gift of God in Due Season: Essays on Scripture and Community in Honor of James A. Sanders.* JSOTS 225. Sheffield: Sheffield Academic.

Wilson, G. H.

1985   *The Editing of the Hebrew Psalter.* Atlanta: Scholars.

Yeivin, I.

1980   *Introduction to the Tiberian Masorah.* Translated and edited by E. J. Revell. Atlanta: Scholars.

CHAPTER 9

The Interpretation of the Tanak
in the Jewish Apocrypha and Pseudepigrapha

James H. Charlesworth

The Jewish writings found in the Apocrypha and Pseudepigrapha of the Old Testament, which are referred to together as apocryphal writings, were composed from about 300 BCE (before the last book of the Hebrew Bible, Daniel) to 200 CE. The main reason these writings were composed was the appearance of biblical exegesis, that is, interpretation of the writings that would come to compose the Tanak. If the crucible of the extracanonical writings was biblical exegesis, then perhaps the encounter and conflict of the Greek and Hebrew cultures provided the fire for the crucible.

While the Torah was set before the second century BCE, the Prophets and the Writings were not defined canonically until the second century CE. Jeremiah and 1 and 2 Samuel had two quite different forms prior to 70 CE. Moreover, before 70 CE, some of the books in the Torah have readings, according to the Hebrew manuscripts found in the eleven Qumran caves, that are markedly different from those in the received Hebrew text (the so-called Masoretic Text [MT]). So most of the writings of the Apocrypha and Pseudepigrapha were written as the Tanak's movement toward canonization was still in progress.

Furthermore, many of the apocryphal Jewish writings rivaled the authority of those that would later be canonized. For example, the Qumran *Temple Scroll* preserves a version of Deuteronomy in which God speaks in the first person (in Deuteronomy he speaks in the third person). Thus, for some Jews at Qumran and elsewhere the *Temple Scroll* may well have been considered more authoritative than Deuteronomy. Other writings, roughly contemporaneous with the *Temple Scroll*, were deemed full of direct or indirect revelation; such writings include the *Books of Enoch* (often called

The Apocrypha/Deuterocanonical Books

1 Ezra   Letter of Jeremiah
Tobit   Prayer of Azariah
Judith   Susanna
Additions to Esther   Bel and the Dragon
Wisdom of Solomon   1 Maccabees
Sirach   2 Maccabees
Baruch

The Pseudepigrapha

Apocalypse of Abraham   Testament of Isaac
Testament of Abraham   Martyrdom and Ascension of Isaiah
Apocalypse of Adam   Ladder of Jacob
Testament of Adam   Prayer of Jacob
Life of Adam and Eve   Testament of Jacob
Ahiqar   Jannes and Jambres
Aristeas the Exegete   Testament of Job
Letter of Aristeas   Joseph and Aseneth
Aristobulus   History of Joseph
Atrapanus   Prayer of Joseph

1 *Enoch*), *Jubilees*, Sirach, the Wisdom of Solomon, and the *Testaments of the Twelve Patriarchs*.

For both these reasons, it can be misleading and anachronistic to state that "the Bible" gave birth to the apocryphal writings.

The Apocrypha and Pseudepigrapha are distinguished by the inclusion of the Apocrypha in the Septuagint. According to the minimum (and most useful) number, the Old Testament Apocrypha (OTA) include thirteen works, but some Septuagint manuscripts contain documents that are more conveniently placed among the Old Testament Pseudepigrapha (OTP), the fullest collection of which contains sixty-five documents. (In this chapter, works in the Apocrypha are cited according to the *HarperCollins Study Bible: New Revised Standard Version* (New York: HarperCollins, 1993), and works of the Pseudepigrapha are cited according to *OTP*.) The Dead Sea Scrolls are not reckoned among the apocryphal writings, though fragments of some works

2 (Syriac Apocalypse of) Baruch	Jubilees
3 (Greek Apocalypse of) Baruch	3 Maccabees
4 Baruch	4 Maccabees
Cleodemus Malchus	Prayer of Manasseh
Apocalypse of Daniel	Sentences of Syriac Menander
More Psalms of David	Testament of Moses
Demetrius	Orphica
Eldad and Modad	Philo the Epic Poet
Apocalypse of Elijah	Pseudo-Philo
1 (Ethiopic Apocalypse of) Enoch	Pseudo-Phocylides
2 (Slavonic Apocalypse of) Enoch	Fragments of Pseudo-Greek Poets
3 (Hebrew Apocalypse of) Enoch	Lives of the Prophets
Eupolemus	History of the Rechabites
Pseudo-Eupolemus	Apocalypse of Sedrach
Apocryphon of Ezekiel	Treatise of Shem
Ezekiel the Tragedian	Sibylline Oracles
4 Ezra	Odes of Solomon
Greek Apocalypse of Ezra	Psalms of Solomon
Questions of Ezra	Testament of Solomon
Revelation of Ezra	Theodotus
Vision of Ezra	Testaments of the Twelve Patriarchs
Pseudo-Hecateus	Apocalypse of Zephaniah
Hellenistic Synagogal Prayers	

that are — notably *Jubilees,* the *Books of Enoch,* and the basis for the *Testaments of the Twelve Patriarchs* — were found among the scrolls.

INTERPRETATION OF THE TORAH

The Torah, especially Genesis, Exodus, and Deuteronomy, spawned numerous Jewish apocryphal writings.

The *Books of Enoch* and *Jubilees*

The authors of the *Books of Enoch* and *Jubilees* claimed that their writings were divinely inspired and contained God's word for his people. These books

were thus revelations and sacred Scripture, at least to some Jews during the
Second Temple period.

The *Books of Enoch,* written in Hebrew or Aramaic from probably the
third century BCE to the close of the first century BCE, are essentially built on
Genesis. Aramaic manuscripts found in Qumran Cave 4 date from the early
second century BCE, thus antedating the biblical apocalypse called Daniel,
which was composed in about 164 BCE.

This makes parts of *Enoch* the earliest apocalypse composed by Jews.

There are at least five sections to this library of Enochic books: the Book
of the Watchers (chs. 1–36), the Parables of Enoch (chs. 37–71), the Astronomical Book (chs. 72–82), the Dream Visions (chs. 83–90), and the Admonitions
of Enoch (chs. 91–105). Chs. 106–108 seem to be excerpted from a *Book of
Noah* (see *Jub.* 10:13; 21:10). The *Books of Enoch* thus reflect the Torah: five
books were attributed to Enoch as five were attributed to Moses. The five
books of the Psalter — attributed to David — are also indicative of early Jewish traditions that books should have five sections or that five is the right
number for a library of books.

First and foremost, this pseudepigraphon is dependent on Genesis because the biblical hero chosen is Enoch. According to Gen. 5:23, Enoch lived
365 years and then walked with God. The author of Genesis adds that "he was
not, for God took him." The authors of the *Books of Enoch* interpret this verse
to mean that the 365-day calendar alone is endorsed by Scripture and God,
that Enoch was perfect morally and spiritually, and that he did not die. He remained alive to communicate with the chosen Jews who were faithful on
earth. The books stress the heavenly origin of the solar calendar, but they are
much more liberal than *Jubilees.*

The Dream Visions (chs. 83–90) contain the "Animal Apocalypse,"
which is an example of early apocalyptic reviews of sacred history, in this case
from the time of the Great Flood to the victories of Judas Maccabeus. It depicts the people of Israel as sheep and their enemies as dogs and foxes. Noah
is the "bovid" (or "snow-white cow") who "became a person" and who built a
large boat and lived in it (89:1). Judas Maccabeus seems to have been still alive
when the author composed this section of *1 Enoch,* because "that ram" (= Judas) is engaged in fighting (90:13-16). The Tanak is interpreted so that God remains faithful and hope can be seen in contemporary crises.

An anti-Moses polemic from the Enoch group may be found in the review of the exodus from Egypt, since the master is not one of the sheep. He is,
rather, "their Lord, their leader" (89:24), "the Holy and Great One" (84:1); that
is, he is God, not Moses. But one must be reserved in deriving that conclusion, because Moses is clearly "that sheep" who ascended "that lofty rock"

(i.e., Sinai or Horeb), led the others out of the wilderness, and "fell asleep," that is, died (89:28-37). Also, though there is an entrance into the land, "a land beautiful and glorious" (89:40), there is no conquest, and Joshua is only obliquely depicted (89:39).

Jubilees, written in Hebrew in the second century BCE, is a sermonic expansion of Gen. 1:1 to Exod. 12:50. Its fifty chapters claim to be a revelation by the Angel of the Presence to Moses (1:29–2:1). *Jubilees* emphasizes the Sabbath law more than any other early Jewish composition does, including the Qumran *Angelic Liturgy* and *Songs of the Sabbath Sacrifice*. According to the author of *Jubilees*, the Sabbath is celebrated by angels, and its observance is written in the heavenly tablets (compare the strict rules for the Sabbath found in the Qumran *Damascus Document* [CD]).

The Jew who composed *Jubilees* rewrote the biblical accounts found in Genesis and Exodus and was by no means constrained by the Hebrew text. The author adds names and places to the biblical account and generally explains problems in the text. In a striking way he removes embarrassing episodes by rewriting history in a creative fashion. For example, according to Genesis, Rebecca does not love her son Esau and shows affection only for his brother Jacob. Is that not immoral? According to *Jubilees*, Rebecca did so because her father-in-law Abraham commanded her to love only Jacob, having foreseen Esau's deeds and comprehended that only Jacob was worthy to be the true heir (*Jub.* 19:16-31). In fact, Abraham calls Jacob "my beloved son" (19:27) and blesses him: "may the Lord God be for you and for the people a father always and may you be a firstborn son" (19:29). In contrast, Isaac, the husband of Rebecca and the father of Jacob and Esau, loved Esau more than Jacob (19:15, 31).

The author of *Jubilees* is proud to be a Jew. He reports that Enoch created the art of writing, Noah invented medicine, and Abraham discovered the skill of plowing. While other nations may be guarded by an angel, Israel is protected by God. This is the most conservative writing among the Pseudepigrapha: Jews are to remain exclusive and separate: they must not marry non-Jews, they alone follow the heavenly solar calendar, and they alone are blessed by the joys of Torah.

The *Ladder of Jacob* and Other Works

Genesis also gave rise to many other apocryphal stories and books. One example is especially interesting. Genesis 28 reports the well-known story of Jacob's dream at Bethel: "And he dreamed that there was a ladder set up on the earth, the top of it reaching to heaven; and the angels of God were ascending and descending on it" (Gen. 28:12). This story was so famous that the author of the Gospel of John could simply allude to it when he talked about the cosmic importance of the one he revered as the Son of God ("Jesus said to Nathaniel, 'Very truly, I tell you, you will see heaven opened and the angels of God ascending and descending upon the Son of Man'" [John 1:51]).

Perhaps some time not too far from the date of the Gospel, a Jew composed a work titled the *Ladder of Jacob* based on Genesis 28. According to this pseudepigraphon, Sariel, the angel in charge of dreams, tells Jacob:

> You have seen a ladder with twelve steps, each step having two human faces which kept changing their appearance. The ladder is this age, and the twelve steps are the periods of this age. (*LadJac* 5:11-3)

The meaning obtained from Genesis 28 is quite different than its author had intended. While the author of Genesis 28 stressed the trustworthiness of God's promise of "the land on which you lie" (v. 13) and offspring as numerous as the "dust of the earth" (v. 14), the author of the *Ladder of Jacob* shifts the meaning to the concept of time. The ladder that Jacob saw had twelve steps, and for the author of this pseudepigraphon the meaning is clear: the ladder and its steps represent time. This document indicates a preoccupation, even obsession, with time and the new age because of, mainly, the occupation by pagans — the Romans — of the land given to Abraham and his descendants and the delay in the fulfillment of God's promises found in the Tanak. This explanation of the meaning of time in Genesis stresses that God is reliable and just and that his word can be trusted: "the expected one will come, whose path will not be noticed by anyone" (*LadJac* 7:9).

Of Jewish documents other than the *Books of Enoch, Jubilees,* and the *Ladder of Jacob* composed as expansions of the Torah prior to 136 CE, the most important are the *Apocalypse of Abraham,* the *Testament of Abraham,* the *Apocalypse of Adam,* the *Testament of Adam,* the *Life of Adam and Eve, Eldad and Modad,* the *Apocalypse of Elijah,* 2 (Slavonic) *Enoch,* the *Testaments of Isaac, Jacob,* and *Joseph, Jannes and Jambres, Joseph and Aseneth,* the *Prayer of Joseph,* the *Lost Tribes,* the *Apocalypse of Moses,* the *Assumption of Moses* (= the *Testament of Moses*), the *Book of Noah,* the *Liber Antiquitatum Biblicarum* (an expansion of Genesis–2 Samuel), the *Treatise of Shem,* and the *Testaments of the Twelve Patriarchs.*

During the Second Temple period, it was not so much a concern for history as an interest in Jewish lore and a focus on written Scripture that motivated the composition of sacred books. And these so-called apocryphal works are not to be understood as sitting on the fringes of the Tanak, which would be to anachronistically assume the later closing of the biblical canon. Reading of Scripture raised questions, for example, who were the men who opposed Moses during the exodus? As early as 100 BCE it is clear that Jews called them "Jannes and Jambres" (CD 5.18-19; cf. b. Menahot 85a). These men defied the truth and Moses (2 Tim. 3:8-9). Eventually a Jew composed a pseude-pigraphon, *Jannes and Jambres,* about these two wicked opponents. Jannes tells his brother Jambres (or Mambres) that

> I your brother did not die unjustly, but indeed justly, and the judgment will go against me, since I was more clever than all clever magicians, and opposed the two brothers, Moses and Aaron, who performed great signs and wonders. As a result I died and was brought from among (the living) to the netherworld where there is great burning and the pit of perdition, whence no ascent is possible. (*JanJam* 24)

If the most gifted magician is sent to "Hades" and suffers in "great burning," then — and even more so — one faithless to the Lord of the earth and Over-seer of the universe will not be able to escape eternal damnation, since judg-ment is unquestionably facing all who live. The story of *Jannes and Jambres,* thus, was composed to clarify and expand the Tanak in light of Greek culture and to exhort Jews to live upright lives.

Searches continue for writings that may also be Jewish and antedate the rabbinic period. One of these lost pseudepigrapha is *Eldad and Modad.* It supplies the prophecies of two men, prophets, mentioned in Num. 11:26-29, who "prophesied in the camp" (v. 26) and upset Joshua, who asked Moses to "stop them" (v. 28). Only a small fragment of *Eldad and Modad* is preserved. It is found in the *Shepherd of Hermas:* " 'The Lord is near to those who turn (to him),' as it is written in the (book of) Eldad and Modad, who prophesied in the desert to the people" (*Vis.* 2.3.4). Other lost writings from the first mil-lennium CE include the *Apocalypse of Lamech,* mentioned in the *List of Sixty Books* (see Denis 1970) and in the Slavic list of pseudepigraphical books, but now lost.

Tobit, in the Apocrypha, is a didactic fiction based on numerous books in the Tanak. It recalls and builds on the patriarchal narratives found in Gen-esis. The spirituality of the main Jewish characters reflects the command-ments and laws in the Torah and elsewhere. The teachings in deutero- and trito-Isaiah most likely helped shape the narrative. Wisdom and apocalyptic traditions in many writings, especially *Ahiqar,* Daniel, the *Books of Enoch,* and Sirach, most likely inspired the author of Tobit.

INTERPRETATION OF THE PROPHETS

The canon of the prophets, that is, Joshua–Kings and the books of Isaiah, Jeremiah, Ezekiel, and the Twelve ("minor prophets"), was considered closed by the early second century BCE, at least by those Jews who evolved and later produced and codified the Mishnah and other rabbinic writings. For other groups of Jews, including the Qumranites, the Samaritans, and the Palestinian Jesus Movement, prophecy had not ceased.

The Influence of Isaiah, Jeremiah, and Ezekiel on Interpretation

Among the Prophets, the ideas and dreams of the last three major prophets, Isaiah, Jeremiah (along with his assistant Baruch), and Ezekiel attracted Jewish authors. Before the defeat of Bar Kokhba in 136 CE, the following works circulated under the names of these prophets (and their scribes) and were often considered authentic (that is, derived from them or from reliable records of their teachings): the *Martyrdom of Isaiah,* the *Vision of Isaiah,* the *Letter of Jeremiah,* Baruch, 2 (Syriac) *Baruch,* 3 (Greek) *Baruch, 4 Baruch,* and the *Apocryphon of Ezekiel* (which is extant in Jewish and Christian sources).

A few examples will indicate how the prophetic books left their impression on and shaped the Pseudepigrapha. Expanding on the record in the Tanak, a Jewish scholar described the execution of Isaiah:

> Because of these visions, therefore, Beliar was angry with Isaiah, and he dwelt in the heart of Manasseh, and he sawed Isaiah in half with a wooden saw. . . . And while Isaiah was being sawed in half, he did not cry out, or weep, but his mouth spoke with the Holy Spirit until he was sawed in two. (*MartIsa* 5:1-14)

The tomb in which Isaiah was subsequently buried is mentioned in the *Lives of the Prophets:*

> Isaiah, from Jerusalem, died under Manasseh by being sawn in two, and was buried underneath the Oak of Rogel, near the place where the path crosses the aqueduct whose water Hezekiah shut off by blocking its source. And God worked the miracle of Siloam for the prophet's sake, for being faint before he died, he prayed for water to drink, and immediately it was sent to him from it; therefore it is called Siloam, which means "sent." (*LivPro* 1:1-2)

Of course, archaeologists have found no evidence of the tomb of Isaiah or of any of the prophets in or near Jerusalem — or anywhere else.

The death and burial of Jeremiah is also amplified from the Tanak:

Jeremiah was from Anathoth, and he died in Taphnai of Egypt, having been stoned by his people. He was buried in the environs of Pharaoh's palace, because the Egyptians held him in high esteem, having been bene-fited through him. (*LivPro* 2:12)

Jeremiah's martyrdom is again amplified and explained in a Christian work:

[Jeremiah took a stone] and said, "Light of the aeons, make this stone look just like me until I have described everything I saw to Baruch and Abimelech." Then the stone, by the command of God, took on the like-ness of Jeremiah. And they were stoning the stone, thinking it was Jere-miah. But Jeremiah delivered all the mysteries that he had seen to Baruch and Abimelech, and then he simply stood in the midst of the people, de-siring to bring his stewardship to an end. Then the stone cried out, saying, "O stupid children of Israel, why do you stone me, thinking that I am Jer-emiah? Behold, Jeremiah stands in your midst!" And when they saw him, they immediately ran at him with many stones, and his stewardship was fulfilled. And Baruch and Abimelech came and buried him, and they took the stone and put (it) on his tomb after inscribing (it) thus: "This is the stone (that was) the ally of Jeremiah." (*4 Bar.* 9:26-32)

Ezekiel was killed by the Israelites because he castigated them for wor-shiping idols. He was buried in a tomb that had a double cave:

for Abraham also made Sarah's tomb in Hebron like it. It is called "dou-ble" because there is a twisting passage and an upper room which is hid-den from the ground floor, and it is hung over the ground level in the cliff. (*LivPro* 3:3-4)

The hope of Jews in the Second Temple period seems reflected in Ezekiel's teachings, especially what is found in Ezekiel 37:

When the people was being destroyed by its enemies, he went to the (en-emy) leaders and, terrified by the prodigies, they ceased. He used to say this to them: "Are we lost? Has our hope perished?" and in the wonder of the dead bones he persuaded them that there is hope for Israel both here and in the coming [age]. (*LivPro* 3:11-12)

Ezekiel 37 was not taken to refer to the resurrection of the dead, as Christians have often claimed; it is rightly taken to refer to the resurrection of the nation Israel. The concept is thoroughly Jewish. The hope of the Jew is not lost or "perished."

Judith and the *Words of Gad the Seer*

Judith, in the Old Testament Apocrypha/Deuterocanonical Books, is a didactic fiction or creative history set in the time of Nebuchadnezzar (1:1). The message of Judith — who is exceedingly attractive — is that the people of Israel have nothing to fear if they worship only the God of Israel faithfully and passionately and uphold their covenant with God. Before preparing her body to excite and confuse Holofernes so that she can slay this commander of the Assyrian army, she prays to God to help her lie:

> Make my deceitful words bring wound and bruise on those who have planned cruel things against your covenant, and against your sacred house, and against Mount Zion, and against the house your children possess. Let your whole nation and every tribe know and understand that you are God, the God of all power and might, and that there is no other who protects the people of Israel but you alone! (9:13-14)

After decapitating Holofernes with his own sword, Judith offers a hymn of praise that rings with ideas and themes so typical of the theologies in the Tanak:

> I will sing to my God a new song: . . .
> Let all your creatures serve you,
>   for you spoke, and they were made. . . .
> For every sacrifice as a fragrant
>   offering is a small thing,
> and the fat of all whole burnt offerings to
>   you is a very little thing;
> but whoever fears the Lord is great forever.   (16:13-16)

This hymn is most likely modeled on the song of Moses preserved in Exodus 15. The account of creation according to Genesis 1 is also evident.

It is possible that the *Words of Gad the Seer* is an ancient Jewish text pseudepigraphically attributed to Gad, David's prophet (1 Sam. 22:5; cf.

1 Chron. 29:29). It is mentioned in the *Chronicles of the Jews of Cochin,* an eighteenth-century compilation that took shape in Cochin, India. The text was published by J. G. Eichorn over two hundred years ago (1787-89), but virtually no one today seems to know about it. M. Bar-Ilan is working on the text and is publishing it. According to the chronicle, Shalmaneser, King of Assyria, exiled 460 Jews to Yemen. These exiled Jews took with them the following books:

> a book of Moses' Torah, book of Joshua, book of Ruth, book of Judges, first and second books of Samuel, books of: 1 Kings, Song of Songs of Solomon, Songs of Hallel — David, Assaf, Heiman and the sons of Korah, Proverbs, Ecclesiastes of Solomon, as well as his Riddles, *prophecies of Gad,* Nathan, Shemaiah and Ahijah, age-old Job, Jonah, and a book of Isaiah. . . . (Bar-Ilan 1993: 96)

The chronicle indicates that the Jews who had been expelled from Assyria also left Yemen for India. The above excerpt obviously knows and expands on 2 Kings 17. The chronicle also mentions a work that seems to have been called the *Riddles of Solomon,* which is unknown.

The Jeremiah Cycle

Most important in this group is the Jeremiah cycle with writings pseudonymously attributed to Jeremiah and his scribe, Baruch. The earliest writing in the Jeremiah Cycle is the Letter of Jeremiah in the Apocrypha. It is quoted in 2 Maccabees (2:1-3) and so must date before the end of the second century BCE when 2 Maccabees was composed. A Greek fragment of the letter was found in Qumran Cave VII, and it dates from about 100 BCE. The letter may have been written anytime in the preceding two centuries. It develops Jeremiah's ideas (especially Jer. 10:2-16, 29) and stresses the evil and absurdity of idolatry: "Their tongues are smoothed by the carpenter . . . , but they are false and cannot speak" (6:8).

The book of Baruch, also in the Apocrypha, consists of three compositions. Each is an exegetical commentary on works in the Tanak, especially Jeremiah, but also Deuteronomy, Daniel, and the Jewish Wisdom traditions (especially Job). The book is impossible to date, and may have been composed anytime between about 200 BCE and 63 BCE. In contrast to *1 Enoch,* according to which Wisdom could not find a home on earth and so returned to heaven, the author of Baruch identifies Wisdom with Torah: God gave Wisdom "to his servant Jacob and to Israel, whom he loved. Afterward she appeared on earth and lived with humankind" (3:36-37). Israel is in exile because its people have forsaken Wisdom (3:12).

There are four works in the Jeremiah cycle in the Pseudepigrapha: 2 (Syriac) *Baruch*, 3 (Greek) *Baruch*, 4 *Baruch*, and the *History of the Rechabites*. The earliest and most important of these is 2 *Baruch*, which was composed around 100 CE. The author has answers for the horrifying destruction of Jerusalem in 70 CE. Because of the unfaithfulness of his people, God sent his angels to destroy the Holy City and the Temple. Afterward, the heathen armies were allowed to enter, since God had left the city. The author predicates that the Messiah will be a militant warrior: "my Anointed One (= the Messiah) will convict him (= the last ruler) . . . he will kill him and protect the rest of my people who will be found in that place that I have chosen" (40:1-2). The document is close to the tradition associated with the rabbinic school of Akiba, who probably declared Bar Kokhba the Messiah of Israel. The problem of evil is solved by affirming free will: "Adam is, therefore, not the cause, except only for himself, but each of us has become our own Adam" (54:19). The author may be answering the utter pessimism of 4 *Ezra* and those whom he represents (his community). For the author of 2 *Baruch* the Torah is the answer. The Torah is "the lamp of the eternal law which exists forever and ever illuminated all those who sat in darkness" (59:2).

The Jewish core of the *History of the Rechabites* was probably originally composed in Hebrew sometime between the first and fourth centuries CE (see the rubric in Syriac MS D folios 209r-210v). The work seems to be originally Jewish with massive Christian editing. It is something like a midrashic expansion of Jeremiah 35. Other parts of the Tanak have provided the narrative for some chapters; for example, chs. 7-10 and 12:3a are exegetical reflections on Genesis 1–3. If the work is Jewish and early, then it shows that all the contiguous cultures have influenced Jewish theology prior to 136 CE, since it contains ideas found in Persian, Egyptian, Roman, Greek, and Syrian compositions. The speakers are often "the sons of Rechab" (8:1a) who "departed from the world to this place . . . in that time when Jeremiah, the prophet, announced and prophesied the ravaging and devastation (of) Jerusalem because of the sins of the sons of Israel . . ." (8:2).

The interpenetration of Greek culture into Palestinian Judaism is proved by the recovery of Samaritan papyri with seals bearing images from the Homeric legends. It is conceivable, perhaps probable, that Stoicism shaped the apocryphal works through the argument that the Torah is an immanent law, that is, a divine force working within the created order, and that Platonism helped give rise to the apocalyptic emphasis on the hiddenness of the creating God. Platonism may be seen in the *Letter of Aristeas,* since the banquet scene there seems to reflect the Platonic symposium. Perhaps apocalypticism and its emphasis that the good world is above the earth have also been shaped by Platonic thought. These are possibilities, but it is certain that the Tanak was the crucible in which the apocryphal compositions were shaped.

INTERPRETATION OF THE WRITINGS

The "Writings" section of the Tanak includes Psalms, Proverbs, Job, Song of Songs, Ruth, Lamentations, Ecclesiastes, Esther, Daniel, Ezra, Nehemiah, and Chronicles. Many documents in the Apocrypha and Pseudepigrapha were modeled after or inspired by the ideas and narratives found in the Writings.

The Additional *Psalms of David* and the *Psalms of Solomon*

Most important in the literature inspired by the Writings are five additional *Psalms of David,* composed in the last three centuries BCE under the influence of the biblical psalter. Psalm 151A — as well as Psalms 151B, 152, and 153 — was composed to represent biographical reflections by David:

> I was the smallest among my brothers,
> and the youngest among the sons of my father;
> and he made me shepherd of his flocks,
> and the ruler of his kids.
>
> My hands made a flute,
> and my fingers a lyre;
> and I shall render glory to the Lord,
> I thought within myself. . . .
>
> He sent his prophet to anoint me,
> Samuel to make me great;
> my brothers went out to meet him,
> handsome of figure and handsome of appearance.
>
> (Although) their stature was tall,
> (and) their hair handsome,

the Lord God
did not choose them.

But he sent and took me from behind the flock,
and he anointed me with holy oil,
and he made me leader for his people,
and ruler over the sons of his covenant.   (151A:1-7 Hebrew)

This psalm dates perhaps from the third century BCE. The Syriac version is later since it adds to the story of David in the Tanak a reference to the Lord's angel: "He sent his angel; and removed me from the sheep of my father" (151A:4). An early date within Second Temple Judaism may be evident in the reference to the anointing of David, but without messianic overtones. Psalms 154 and 155 are pseudepigraphically attributed to Hezekiah in the Syriac tradition. While the opening of 154 is lost in Hebrew, the Hebrew of 155 has no caption or rubric.

Not only did Jews attribute more psalms to David, they also composed an entire psalter attributed to Solomon. Like the additional *Psalms of David*, the *Psalms of Solomon* were modeled after the biblical psalter, employing the *parallelismus membrorum* so typical there but so different from the poetic form of the near contemporary *Hodayot*. The psalms were composed by Pharisaic-like Jews in Jerusalem after the entrance of the Romans under Pompey into Jerusalem. They purport to be an eyewitness account of what Pompey did in Jerusalem:

Arrogantly the sinner broke down the strong walls
    with a battering ram . . .
Gentile foreigners went up to your place of sacrifice;
    they arrogantly trampled (it) with their sandals.   (*PssSol* 2:1-2)

One of the clearest descriptions of the tasks of the Messiah is found in *Psalms of Solomon*. In light of the desecration of Jerusalem mentioned in Psalm 2, it is understandable why Jerusalemites would want the Temple and the Holy City purified. Note the following excerpt:

And he will purge Jerusalem
    (and make it) holy as it was even from the beginning,
    (for) nations to come from the ends of the earth to see his glory,
        to bring as gifts her children who had been driven out,
    and to see the glory of the Lord

with which God has glorified her.
And he will be a righteous king over them, taught by God.
There will be no unrighteousness among them in his days,
    for all shall be holy, and their king shall be the Lord Messiah.

(PssSol 17:30-32)

This expression of messianic hope is a pastiche of passages from the Tanak, the portion quoted here beginning with an allusion to Isa. 55:5 and ending with a reworking of Jer. 23:5.

How shall the Messiah achieve these victories? The date of the *Psalms of Solomon* (the second half of the first century BCE) is reflected in the apocalyptic — that is, otherworldly — power of the Messiah. Psalm 17 continues:

(For) he will not rely on horse and rider and bow,
    nor will he collect gold and silver for war.
Nor will he build up hope in a multitude for a day of war.
The Lord himself is his king,
    the hope of the one who has a strong hope in God.
He shall be compassionate to all nations
    (who) reverently (stand) before him.
He will strike the earth with the word of his mouth forever;
    he will bless the Lord's people with wisdom and happiness.
And he himself (will be) free from sin, (in order) to rule
    a great people.   (*PssSol* 17:33-36)

This celebration of the tasks of the Messiah seems to serve as a warning that those who gather "a multitude for a day of war" are not to be saluted as messiahs. The subservience of the Messiah to "the Lord" is exceptional. It may reflect a tendency of some Jews to speak against those who believed the Messiah will come and function on his own. What seems most important for a perception of how the Tanak became the basis for biblical exegesis and was the crucible in which the Pseudepigrapha was shaped is the observation that the last quoted line represents Jewish reflections on Isa. 11:3-4 ("He shall not judge by what his eyes see, . . . but with righteousness he shall judge the poor, and decide with equity for the meek of the earth; he shall strike the earth with the rod of his mouth, and with the breath of his lips he shall kill the wicked"). What Isaiah predicted about the shoot that "shall come from the stump of Jesse" (Isa 11:1) has been transferred to the Messiah. It becomes clear that *Psalms of Solomon* 17:35-36 is a messianic exegesis of Isa. 11:4.

Hymns, Prayers, and Wisdom Tradition

Many of the apocryphal works have hymns and prayers in them and these move the narrative forward, show the link with ancient traditions, especially the Tanak, and punctuate the narrative. For example, this is evident in the additions to Daniel in "the Prayer of Azariah and the Song of the Three Jews" and in the additions to Esther in "the Prayer of Mordecai" and "the Prayer of Esther." Probably later than the time of Bar Kokhba are the *Hellenistic Synagogal Prayers;* this work, however, is modeled more on a Jewish hymnbook than on the Psalter.

There were not two canons in Jewish antiquity. The Septuagint, the Greek translation of the Tanak and the books known as the Apocrypha, was not a different canon used by Egyptian Jews. Obviously, in many circles the books in the Septuagint were considered a depository of God's inspired word. One of the most distinguished compositions in some copies of the Septuagint, but a work now placed among the Pseudepigrapha, is the *Prayer of Manasseh,* which was written to supply a prayer mentioned by the author of Chronicles (2 Chron. 33:12-13) but not found in the Tanak. This prayer elevates to the sublime the recognition and confession of sin:

> And now behold I am bending the knees of my heart before you;
> and I am beseeching your kindness.
> I have sinned, O Lord, I have sinned;
> and certainly I know my sins.   (*PrMan* 11-12)

The influence of this refrain remains unnoticed by specialists. As Chronicles has directly influenced the author of the *Prayer of Manasseh,* so he has influenced at least two subsequent Jewish authors. The author of *ApMos* (but not the author of the almost identical work called *Vita Adae et Evae*) portrays Eve praying as her husband Adam is dying. This scene takes on poignancy when one reflects that Adam was the first to die from old age. Eve's observing his death caused some intense reflection among early Jews. Some of Eve's words are derived from the *Prayer of Manasseh:*

> I have sinned, O God; I have sinned,
> O Father of all; I have sinned against you. . . .   (*ApMos* 32:1-2)

Eve seems to be taking on herself the blame for Adam's aging and eventual death. The same refrain from the *Prayer of Manasseh* reappears in *Joseph and*

Aseneth, which is a midrashic and legendary expansion of material in the Tanak. Aseneth's prayer contains this confession and prayer for acceptance:

> I have sinned, Lord,
> before you, I have sinned. . . .
>
> *(JosAsen* 12:5)

So the author of Chronicles has influenced directly the *Prayer of Manasseh,* and indirectly the authors of the *Apocalypse of Moses* and *Joseph and Aseneth.* Since both of the later works highlight women and are from about the first century CE, perhaps they can help us understand such works as the paintings in the House of Mysteries at Pompeii. As in the *Apocalypse of Moses* and *Joseph and Aseneth,* a woman is in central focus, and as in *Joseph and Aseneth,* her elevation is achieved through confession and revelation. Mystery and wonder and the yearning for personal salvation help us understand the spiritual search of Jews in Egypt and Romans in Italy. Such reflections may have little to inform us about how powerful the Tanak has been in shaping the so-called parabiblical works — that is already evident; but these thoughts help us to grasp that there are no boundaries to the human quest for the creator.

The Wisdom traditions, found primarily in Proverbs, stimulated the writing of numerous Jewish compositions. In the Apocrypha the Wisdom tradition produced the Wisdom of Solomon and Ecclesiasticus (Sirach), and in the Pseudepigrapha especially *3* and *4 Maccabees,* as well as *Pseudo-Phocylides* and the *Sentences of the Syriac Menander.* The Wisdom traditions also helped shape and provided the hero for the *Testament of Solomon,* since Solomon, it was said, knew all wisdom, including the control of demons.

The Historical Writings, Especially the Ezra Cycle

The histories of the lives of Abraham, Joseph, Moses, David, Solomon, and others that are preserved in the Tanak helped shape later historical writings, including what Mendels has rightly called "creative history" (1988). Most important among these historical books would be our only real reliable histories, which, of course, need to be studied in light of their *Tendenzen,* namely 1 Maccabees and Josephus' compositions, the *War of the Jews* and *Jewish Antiquities.* More creative historical works are 2 Maccabees and the more romantic and fictional works such as Tobit, Judith, Susanna, Bel and the Dragon, the *Martyrdom of Isaiah,* the *Life of Adam and Eve,* the *Ladder of Jacob, 4 Baruch, Jannes and Jambres,* the *History of the Rechabites, Eldad and Modad,* and *Joseph and Aseneth.* The *Ethiopic History of Joseph* seems to be

Jewish and may derive from Judaea, written in some yet unspecified time, but it is shaped by later, even Arabic, cultures. It is an elaboration with dramatic flair of the story of Joseph in Genesis 37 and 39–48.

The biblical hero Job is the basis for the interesting *Testament of Job,* which adds to the story the name of Job's wife: Sitis. The "Lament for Sitis" is a stunning example of expansion of the biblical text: "Who is not amazed that this is Sitis, the wife of Job? Who used to have fourteen draperies. . . . Now she exchanges her hair for loaves!" (25:1-3).

The Apocrypha significantly expands on Esther and Daniel. *The Apocalypse of Sedrach* — the name of one of Daniel's associates — is too late for our survey; it was composed long after the fourth century CE and the establishment of Christianity as the official religion of Rome (see S. Agourides in *OTP*).

Ezra may be the most important biblical hero for the composition of pseudepigrapha. An Ezra cycle developed from the second century BCE to well into the Christian era. Most important are the *Fourth Book of Ezra* (which contains a Jewish work entitled *4 Ezra*), the *Apocalypse of Ezra,* the *Questions of Ezra,* the *Revelation of Ezra,* and the *Vision of Ezra.* Among these the most brilliant and earliest, and the stimulus for most of the others, is *4 Ezra.* It is easy to imagine why Jews composed documents and attributed them to Ezra. He was the quintessential scribe for most Jews, as was Enoch for the Enoch groups. To write was to take up the occupation of a scribe. *4 Ezra* is a pseudepigraphon that takes off from the Tanak, especially Ezra. Ezra's pseudonym is Salathiel, who, in this famous pseudepigraphon, is in captivity with Israel in Babylon. It was composed probably in Hebrew in the decades that followed the burning of Jerusalem and the Temple by the Roman army in 70 CE. It consists of seven visions. Uriel must confess before Ezra and his piercing questions that he does not know everything, an unprecedented confession for an archangel. The theodicy in this pseudepigraphon has no easy solution. The concept of the Messiah is developed; but even he is not the answer to the profound and honest questions raised by the author of this masterpiece. The Messiah will simply come and die (7:29). He will neither drive the Gentiles out of Jerusalem nor inaugurate the eschaton (contrast *PssSol* 17–18).

Ezra's lament is penetrating and realistic. It seems as if the author has been choked by the smoke of a holocaust: "O Adam, what have you done? For though it was you who sinned, the fall was not yours alone, but ours also who are your descendants" (7:48 [118]). The refrain characterizes this pessimistic apocalypse: ". . . we have miserably failed . . . we have lived wickedly . . . we have walked in the most wicked ways . . . we have lived in unseemly places . . . our faces shall be blacker than darkness . . . we have lived and committed iniquity . . ." (7:51-56 [121-26]). Not only was the Jewish author devastated by the events of 70 CE, but also a Christian editor felt obliged to add a preface and an ending and so provide his own answers in light of Christian theology.

Reading the laments in *4 Ezra* should never lead one to think that Jews were more wicked in the first century than in any other; that would smack of Christian polemics and false historical reconstructions of the crucifixion of Jesus. The Jewish author — perhaps the author of the best work on theodicy ever written — attributed his work to the famous scribe of the Tanak, the optimistic Ezra, but he did not have an answer for a world that had gone up in smoke. The author feels no obligation to make his explanation coherent with the one given in the Tanak.

APOCALYPTIC LITERATURE

We have repeatedly used the word "apocalyptic" in the preceding pages. The adjective apocalyptic denotes concepts, beliefs, and ideas that are shaped by the contention that meaning does not come from present historical situations, but understanding must be aided by revelation by God, through an intermediary, who explains present, and especially future, history and time in terms of another world, either above or in the future. Apocalyptic thought appears full-blown in an apocalypse. The only apocalypse in the Tanak is the latest book in the collection, the book of Daniel. Daniel may have been shaped by traditions preserved in the *Books of Enoch* — which may contain the oldest apocalyptic work — and became the paradigm for such apocalypses or apocalyptic compositions as *2 (Slavonic Apocalypse of) Enoch*, the *Sibylline Oracles*, the *Apocryphon of Ezekiel*, the *Apocalypse of Zephaniah*, the *Fourth Book of Ezra*, *2 (Syriac Apocalypse of) Baruch*, *3 (Greek Apocalypse of) Baruch*, the *Apocalypse of Abraham*, the *Apocalypse of Adam* (in its putative original form), and the *Apocalypse of Elijah*.

An apocalypse is a revelatory narrative, often with bizarre images and symbols, that usually describes an ascent into heaven by a person mentioned in the Tanak. An angel reveals to the seer what is happening in heaven and what is about to happen in the future in the cosmos, especially on earth. The apocalypse redefines concepts, so that those being conquered on earth are actually conquerors in view of heaven and eternity. It often has a moral message that a seer such as Enoch brings back to God's faithful on earth. The function of an apocalypse is to give encouragement to the righteous who are suffering on earth and to promise them a better future, usually in light of dreams and promises envisioned by the prophets and preserved in the Tanak. History is sometimes presented with people portrayed as animals. The readers can see how time and history began and will end. The dualism of Satan and God is usually extreme, but such dualism is always modified. God alone is powerful and will win in the end. Thus eschatology, reflection on the end of time, is typical of a full-blown apocalypse. The apocalyptic writer knew the mystery of life and the universe, wanted his theology to represent the human and the cosmic, and in the midst of a pessimistic culture dared to dream about a future and better world. The source of his optimism, and some of his inspiration, derived from the promises that characterize the Tanak.

For example, from *4 Ezra:*

two ages:
He (Uriel) answered me and said, "The Most High made this world for the sake of many, but the world to come for the sake of few." (8:1)

vision:
And I looked, and behold, the woman was no longer visible to me, but there was an established city (= Jerusalem), and a place of huge foundations showed itself. Then I was afraid, and cried with a loud voice and said, "Where is Uriel, who came to me at first? For it was he who brought me into this overpowering bewilderment; my end has become corruption, and my prayer a reproach." (10:17-28)

And as for the lion that you saw rousing up out of the forest and roaring and speaking to the eagle and reproving him for his unrighteousness, and as for all his words that you have heard, this is the Messiah whom the Most High has kept until the end of days. . . ." (12:31-32)

review of history:
On the second night I had a dream, and behold, there came up from the sea an eagle that had twelve feathered wings and three heads. . . . He said to me, "This is the interpretation of this vision which you have seen: The eagle which you saw coming up from the sea is the fourth kingdom which appeared in a vision to your brother Daniel. But it was not explained to him as I now explain or have explained it to you." (11:1; 12:10-12)

REWRITTEN BIBLE

Problems in the Tanak or issues left frustratingly open to Jewish readers were solved or handled by Jewish writers. In his book *Revealed Histories,* Hall described these writings as "Inspired Historical Sermons" (1991). As Aune has noted, these writings usually contain the claim "that the Torah can only be properly understood if God himself grants divine insight to his people" (1993: 149).

Here I will draw attention to "the Story of Jael and the Hymn of Deborah," the "Lament of Seila," and the "Hymn of Hannah," which are all preserved in the *Liber Antiquitatum Biblicarum (= LAB)*, which is also called pseudo-Philo's *Biblical Antiquities*. This work seems to have been composed in Hebrew sometime in the first century CE, probably in Palestine. The author quotes the Tanak but also expands on and explains problems there, beginning with Adam and ending with the death of Saul. The excerpts below bring out the emerging sensitivity to women represented by this pseudepigraphon (cf. also *OdesSol* 19). Examples include terms like "woman of God" (*mulier Dei*, 33:1) and "the bosom of her mothers" (*in sinum matrum suarum*, 40:4) and especially the Lord's word concerning Seila "I have seen that the virgin is wise in contrast to her father and perceptive in contrast to all the wise men who are here" (40:4). Another example is the explanation of Tamar's intercourse with Judah: she needed to avoid intercourse with Gentiles (9:5).

The Story of Jael and the Hymn of Deborah

In Judges 4–5, Deborah, a prophetess (4:4), and the Israelites under the command of Barak battle against Sisera, the commander of the army of King Jabin of Canaan, whose capital was Hazor (4:1-2). Jabin has treated the Israelites cruelly for twenty years (4:3). Deborah summons Barak and informs him that he and the Israelites will defeat Sisera near Mount Tabor. Sisera's troops are all killed in battle, but he escapes on foot and flees to the tent of Jael, the wife of Heber the Kenite. While he is sleeping Jael drives a tent peg through his temple and into the ground (4:21). After Sisera's death the Israelites destroy King Jabin.

This story raises a question: How could Jael's act be moral since the Kenites were at peace with King Jabin (4:17) and since Sisera, having sought water to drink and rest in the tent of one whom he could trust, was murdered in his sleep? The "Song of Deborah" in Judges 5 is sprinkled with gruesome details, for example, that Jael "struck Sisera a blow, she crushed his head, she shattered and pierced his temple" (5:26). Even in surrounding cultures, the simple-minded knew that one must treat an enemy honorably in one's own tent; that is, as if he were from one's own tribe, for maybe three days. Jael's violation of this primitive custom must have bothered Jews who read Judges.

The author of LAB knew the account had to be "cleaned up" — it had to be rewritten.

In this rewritten form, Jael repeatedly asks for assurance that this apparently dastardly deed is in accordance with God's will. She is very beautiful and adorns herself to meet Sisera (31:3). He asks for water to drink, as in the Tanak. She tells him to rest first (which seems odd; 31:4). While he is sleeping, she goes out to milk the sheep. She speaks with the Lord, appealing to "the Most Powerful One," who likens Israel to a ram that leads the flock, that she is taking milk from sheep for Sisera to drink (the paronomasia is intentional). In contrast to the story in the Tanak, she asks the Lord for "the sign" (*hoc autem signum*) that the Lord is acting with her: "when I enter while Sisera is asleep, he will rise up and ask me again and again, saying, *'Give me water to drink,'* then I know that my prayer has been heard" (31:5, italicized words are from Tanak). The sign is given, but Jael asks for another "sign" (*hoc signum*): "I will throw him down on the ground from the bed on which he sleeps; and if he does not feel it, I know that he has been handed over" (31:7). She pushes him off the bed, and he does not feel it. She asks God for strength and then drives the peg through Sisera's temple. He tells her "I die like a woman" (31:7).

Sisera's mother, given the name Themech in this pseudepigraphon, boasts to "her ladies" that her son will come home to her with the spoils of war (31:8). Barak appears, sees the corpse, and states: "Blessed be the Lord, who sent his spirit and said, 'Into the hand of a woman (*in manum mulieris*) Sisera will be handed over'" (31:9).

The author of LAB rewrote Tanak so that it becomes a story about women, in the process stressing that Jael clearly followed God's will. The author not only expanded the story in the Tanak but also corrected some moral and theological difficulties in the story, according to later refined sensitivities.

The "Hymn of Deborah" (*LAB* 32) is also quite different from the "Song of Deborah" in the Tanak (Judges 5). In fact, almost the full hymn is found only in *LAB*. Here is a major part of it:

> And now in these days Sisera arose to enslave us.
> And we cried out to our Lord,
> and he commanded the stars and said,
> "Depart from your positions
> and burn up my enemies
> so that they may know my power."
> And the stars came down
> and attacked their camp
> and guarded us without any strain.

So we will not cease singing praise,
nor will our mouth be silent in telling his wonders,
because he has remembered both his recent and ancient promises
and shown his saving power to us.
And so Jael is glorified among women,
because she alone has made straight the way to success
by killing Sisera with her own hands.

(32:11-12, versification original here)

This rewriting of Tanak not only raises Jael prominently as a heroine; it also brings into the present the conviction that God remembers his recent and past promises. In *Pseudo-Philo: Rewriting the Bible,* Murphy rightly states that *LAB* is "a creative work that meant to reflect and influence its own day. It is the product of an author with strong faith in God's faithfulness to Israel, even though he sees Israel oppressed by foreigners without and doubt and misunderstanding within" (1993: 269).

The Lament of Seila

Names are not given for many women mentioned in the Tanak; they are identified only in relation to a male figure. For example, Pharaoh's daughter, Potiphar's wife, Samson's mother, and Jephthah's daughter. The authors of many early Jewish apocryphal writings supply names for them (see Ilan 1993), such as Jephthah's daughter, called Seila in *LAB.*

Seila is a nonbiblical name, but perhaps it was chosen because in Hebrew *seila* is a feminine noun meaning "request," as in a prayer for that which is essential for crops and sustenance, namely rain. This origin would fit nicely with the prayer for rain found in the ninth petition of the Eighteen Benedictions (the *Shemoneh 'Esreh* or *Amidah*). If the author of LAB called her Seila because she fulfilled her father's vow, then the author of *LAB* supplied a name that brought before the reader the reason for her death at the hands of her father. He added to his request to God for victory that he would sacrifice whatever would come to him out of his village, perhaps a dog. But it was his daughter. Seila could conceivably derive from "lamb," *śh,* in Hebrew, as Ilan contends (1993: 30). But "lamb" does not fit the narrative in *LAB* as well as "request" or "petition." For example, note *LAB* 40:8: "they named her tomb in keeping with her name: 'Seila.'"

The author of *LAB* also answers questions regarding Seila's obedient response to her father's vow, which was unthinkable for Jews of the first cen-

tury CE. She salutes her father's commitment: "And now do not annul everything you have vowed, but carry it out" (40:3). She asks only that she and her
virgin companions may go into the mountains so that "I will pour out my
tears there and tell of the sadness of my youth." Her explanation cuts to the
heart: "For I am not sad because I am to die . . . but because my father was
caught up in the snare of his vow . . ." (40:3). Then the author adds a lament
of Seila:

> Hear, you mountains, my lamentation; . . .
> O Mother, in vain have you borne your only daughter,
> because Sheol has become my bridal chamber,
> and on earth there is only my woman's chamber. . . .
> You trees, bow down your branches and weep over my youth. . . .
>
> (LAB 40:5-7)

After her lament, she returns to her father, and he sacrifices her. If *LAB* dates
from before 70 CE, then how did the Jews relate to Seila and her lament? Did
some of them think of Israel as God's "only daughter *(unigenitam)*," about to
be annihilated?

The Hymn of Hannah

Hannah, the barren and therefore scorned wife of Elkanah, rejoices with the
"Song of Hannah" after she has dedicated her son to the tabernacle service
(1 Samuel 2). *LAB* gives here a different poetic piece, the Hymn of Hannah,
which differs in form, teaching, and the role given to Hannah (Cook 1991:
103). It is a pastiche of phrases from 1 Samuel, Isaiah, Jeremiah, Job, and
Psalms.

Eli tells her that her request was "promised previously to the tribes. And
through this boy your womb has been justified so that you might provide advantage for the peoples and set up the milk of your breasts as a fountain for
the twelve tribes" (*LAB* 51:2). On hearing Eli's words Hannah offers her hymn,
which draws particular attention to her:

> Come to my voice, all you nations . . .
> and my lips have been commanded to sing a hymn to the Lord.
> Drip, my breasts, and tell your testimonies,
> because you have been commanded to give milk.
> For he who is milked from you will be raised up. . . .   (51:3)

These thoughts would have given encouragement to the Jews living during the Roman occupation of Palestine, whether before or after the destruction of Jerusalem.

There is a significant parallel, but no evidence of influence, between this hymn and the *Odes of Solomon* in the concept of "he who is milked":

> The Son is the cup,
> And the Father is He who was milked;
> And the Holy Spirit is She who milked Him. . . .   (*OdesSol.* 19:2)

This parallel is significant because of the roughly contemporaneous date of the two compositions and the unusual concept of "he who was milked" for Samuel and God the Father.

Again, note how central Hannah is in her own hymn:

> Speak, speak, Hannah, and do not be silent.
> Sing a hymn, daughter of Batuel,
> about the miracles that God has performed with you.   (*LAB* 51:6)

The author of *LAB* has been thinking of others beside Hannah; that seems obvious since he refers to "the miracles" *(mirabilibus)* that God has shown to his people Israel. After the hymn, Samuel is anointed and the people chant, "Let the prophet live among the people, and may he be a light to this nation for a long time!" (51:7). Clearly, the author is thinking about both Samuel's time and his own time.

CONCLUSION

We have seen that the Jewish apocryphal works took form out of a crucible that may be described as hermeneutical exegesis of Scripture. The authors of the apocryphal works revered the books in the Tanak; they considered them sacred and authoritative. Moreover, the books in the Tanak were in process of obtaining canonical shape and status. The authors of numerous apocryphal works often claimed that Torah was fully comprehensible only to those who were divinely guided in their interpretation. That is to say, the authors of many apocryphal works wrote under the assumption, and perhaps experience, that they were divinely inspired.

Alongside the Jewish apocryphal works and the Dead Sea Scrolls, though "canonized" only around 200 CE, is the Mishnah. This great and classical work is extant in a Hebrew form related to and evolved out of the Hebrew of the Scriptures. As Neusner states in *The Mishnah: A New Translation,* the Mishnah "is important because it is a principal component of the canon of Judaism" (1988: xiv).

This insight warns against assuming a clear barrier ever separated sacred Scripture from inspired additions to Scripture (or, the apocryphal writings). As the greatest work in the Mishnah, *Pirkei Aboth* (Sayings of the Fathers) begins, "Moses received Torah from Sinai and handed it to Joshua. Joshua (handed it) to the Elders. The Elders (handed it) to the Prophets. The Prophets handed it to the men of the Great Assembly" (1.1, translation mine). Thus Moses received on Sinai a Torah consisting of two forms: the written Torah and the oral Torah. In this study we have seen an added dimension of the Mishnah's claim that "Moses received Torah from Sinai."

My thesis is that *biblical exegesis was the crucible in which the Pseudepigrapha took shape.* This claim is supported by the penetrating observations by Sanders: "One common feature of the pluriformity within Judaism that emerges with clarity is the pervasive and radical influence of Scripture on Judaism." Sanders continues, "All of the literature of the period was written Scripturally in one sense or another, and to one degree or another. The depth and extent of Scriptural intertextuality in this literature is perhaps its most marked common feature" (1993: 15). It would be wrong to assume that such later compositions were deemed inferior to the earlier ones in the Tanak, since the so-called apocryphal works usually claimed or were assumed to be inspired by God — perhaps directly but usually indirectly through an angel or archangel.

As we contemplate the composing of the "parabiblical" masterpieces, we should not picture the Tanak as a closed set of books. Not only were there no books or codices, but works circulated independently as individual scrolls that often could contain only one or two books. Moreover, the shape of the books in the Tanak was surprisingly fluid. There were circulating in Jerusalem, before 70 CE, sometimes over twelve different versions of a particular book in the Tanak, and sometimes the versions were markedly different. Hence, when we think about how Jews were composing parabiblical works, we need to keep in mind how the same or related Jews, at the same time, were shaping the documents in *the* Book.

BIBLIOGRAPHY

Agourides, S.

1983   "Apocalypse of Sedrach." In Charlesworth, ed., 1983: 605-13.

Aune, D. E.

1993   "Charismatic Exegesis in Early Judaism and Early Christianity." In Charlesworth and Evans, eds., 1993: 126-50.

Bar-Ilan, M.

1993   "The Discovery of The Words of Gad the Seer." *JSP* 11:95-107.

Barton, J.

1986   *Oracles of God: Perceptions of Ancient Prophecy in Israel After the Exile.* London: Darton, Longman and Todd.

Beckwith, R. T.

1985   *The Old Testament Canon of the New Testament Church and Its Background in Early Judaism.* Grand Rapids: Eerdmans.

1988   "Formation of the Hebrew Bible." In Mulder and Sysling, eds., 1988: 39-86.

Black, M. (ed.)

1970   *Apocalypsis Henochi Graece.* PVTG 3. Leiden: Brill.

Böttrich, G.

1996   *Das slavische Henochbuch.* JSHRZ 5.7. Gütersloh: Gütersloher Verlagshaus.

Brox, N. (ed.)

1977   *Pseudepigraphie in der Heidnischen und Jüdisch-christlichen Antike.* Wege der Forschung 484. Darmstadt: Wissenschaftliche Buchgesellschaft.

Charlesworth, J. H.

1977   *The Odes of Solomon.* Oxford: Clarendon.

1981   "A Definition of the Pseudepigrapha." In Charlesworth, Dykers and Charlesworth, eds., 1981: 17-25.

1983   "Introduction for the General Reader." In *OTP* I, xxi-xxxiv.

1986   "Greek, Persian, Roman, Syrian, and Egyptian Influences in Early Jewish Theology." In A. Caquot, et al., eds., *Hellenica et Judaica: Hommage à Valentin Nikiprowetzky,* 219-43. Leuven: Peeters.

1993   "In the Crucible: The Pseudepigrapha as Biblical Interpretation." In Charlesworth and Evans, eds., 1993: 20-43.

1997   "Pseudepigraphen des Alten Testaments" *TRE* 27.4/5:639-45.

1998a   *Critical Reflections on the Odes of Solomon.* JSPS 22. Sheffield: Sheffield Academic.

1998b   *The Old Testament Pseudepigrapha and the New Testament: Prolegomena for the Study of Christian Origins.* Harrisburg: Trinity Press International.

Charlesworth, J. H. (ed.)

1982   *The History of the Rechabites: I: The Greek Recension.* SBLTT 17. Pseudepigrapha Series 10. Chico: Scholars.

1983   *Old Testament Pseudepigrapha*, vol. I. Garden City: Doubleday.
1985   *Old Testament Pseudepigrapha*, vol. II. Garden City: Doubleday.

Charlesworth, J. H., with P. Dykers and M. J. H. Charlesworth (eds.)
1981   *The Pseudepigrapha and Modern Research with a Supplement.* SBLSCS 7. Chico: Scholars.

Charlesworth, J. H., and C. A. Evans (eds.)
1993   *The Pseudepigrapha and Early Biblical Interpretation.* JSPS 14. Sheffield: Sheffield Academic.

Charlesworth, J. H., H. Lichtenberger, and G. S. Oegema (eds.)
1994-   *The Dead Sea Scrolls: Hebrew, Aramaic, and Greek Texts with English Translation.* The Princeton Theological Seminary Dead Sea Scrolls Project. Tübingen: Mohr Siebeck/Louisville: Westminster/John Knox.
1998   *Qumran-Messianism.* Tübingen: Mohr.

Chesnutt, R. D.
1995   *From Death to Life: Conversion in Joseph and Aseneth.* JSPS 16. Sheffield: Sheffield Academic.

Cook, J .E.
1991   "Pseudo-Philo's Song of Hannah: Testament of a Mother of Israel." *JSP* 9:103-14.

Denis, A.-M.
1970   *Introduction aux pseudépigraphes grecs d'Ancien Testament.* SVTP 1. Leiden: Brill.

Dimant, D.
1988   "Use and Interpretation of Mikra in the Apocrypha and Pseudepigrapha." In Mulder and Sysling, eds., 1988: 379-419.

Eichorn, J. G.
1787-89 *Allgemeine Bibliothek der biblischen Literatur.* 2 vols. Leipzig: Weidmann.

Eron, L. J.
1991   "'That Women Have Mastery Over Both King and Beggar' (TJud. 15.5)." *JSP* 9:43-66.

Evans, C. A.
1992   *Noncanonical Writings and New Testament Introduction.* Peabody: Hendrickson.

Frankfurter, D.
1993   *Elijah in Upper Egypt: The Apocalypse of Elijah and Early Christian Christianity.* Studies in Antiquity and Christianity. Minneapolis: Fortress.

Fröhlich, I.
1996   "The Beginnings of the Tradition of the 'Rewritten Bibles': Historiography in the Book of Jubilees." In *"Time and Times and Half a Time": Historical Consciousness in the Jewish Literature of the Persian and Hellenistic Eras,* 91-104. JSPS 19. Sheffield: Sheffield Academic.

Gafni, I. M.

1987   "'Pre-Histories' of Jerusalem in Hellenistic, Jewish and Christian Literature." *JSP* 1:5-22.

Hall, R. G.

1991   *Revealed Histories: Techniques for Ancient Jewish and Christian Historiography.* JSPS 6. Sheffield: Sheffield Academic.

Harrington, D. J., et al. (eds.)

1976   *Pseudo-Philon: Les Antiquités Bibliques.* SC 229. Paris: Cerf.

Hirsch, S. R.

1989   *Chapters of the Fathers.* ET G. Hirschler. Revised ed. Jerusalem: Feldheim.

Ilan, T.

1993   "Biblical Women's Names in the Apocryphal Traditions." *JSP* 11:3-67.

Isaac, E.

1990   "The Ethiopic History of Joseph: Translation with Introduction and Notes." *JSP* 6:3-125.

Jacobson, H.

1989   "Biblical Quotation and Editorial Function in Pseudo-Philo's *Liber Antiquitatum Biblicarum.*" *JSP* 5:47-64.

Klijn, A. F. J. (ed.)

1992   *Die Esra-Apokalypse (IV. Esra): Nach dem lateinischen Text unter Benutzung der anderen Versionen übersetzt und herausgegeben.* GCS. Berlin: Akademie.

Knibb, M. A. (ed.)

1978   *The Ethiopic Book of Enoch: A New Edition in the Light of the Aramaic Dead Sea Fragments.* 2 vols. Oxford: Clarendon.

Knights, C. H.

1997   "A Century of Research into the Story/Apocalypse of Zosmius and/or the History of the Rechabites." *JSP* 15:53-66.

Lehnardt, A.

1999   *Bibliographie zu den Jüdische Schriften aus hellenistisch-römischer Zeit.* JSHRZ 6 Supplementa. Gütersloh: Gütersloher Verlagshaus.

Levison, J. R.

1988   *Portraits of Adam in Early Judaism: From Sirach to 2 Baruch.* JSPS 1. Sheffield: Sheffield Academic.

Meeks, W. A., and M. Bassler (eds.)

1993   *HarperCollins Study Bible: New Revised Standard Version.* New York: HarperCollins.

Mendels, D.

1988   "'Creative History' in the Hellenistic Near East in the Third and Second Centuries BCE." *JSP* 2:13-20.

Mueller, J. R.
1994   *The Five Fragments of the Apocryphon of Ezekiel: A Critical Study*. JSPS 5. Sheffield: Sheffield Academic.

Mulder, M. J., and Sysling, H. (eds.)
1988   *Mikra*. CRINT II.1. Assen-Mastricht: Gorcum/Philadelphia: Fortress.

Murphy, F. J.
1993   *Pseudo-Philo: Rewriting the Bible*. New York: Oxford University Press.

Neusner, J.
1988   *The Mishnah: A New Translation*. New Haven: Yale University Press.

Nickelsburg, G. W.
1984   "The Bible Rewritten and Expanded." In M. E. Stone, ed., CRINT II.2, 89-156. Assen-Maastricht: Gorcum/Philadelphia: Fortress.

Russell, D. S.
1987   *The Old Testament Pseudepigrapha*. Philadelphia: Fortress.

Sanders, J. A.
1993   "Introduction: Why the Pseudepigrapha?" In Charlesworth and Evans, eds., 1993: 13-19.

Satran, D.
1995   *Biblical Prophets in Byzantine Palestine: Reassessing the Lives of the Prophets*. SVTP 11. Leiden: Brill.

Schwemer, A. M.
1997   *Vitae Prophetarum*. JSHRZ 1.7. Gütersloh: Gütersloher Verlagshaus.

Stone, M. E.
1989   "New Discoveries Relating to the Armenian Adam Books." *JSP* 5:101-109.

Uhlig, S.
1984   *Das Äthiopische Henochbuch*. JSHRZ 5.6. Gütersloh: Gütersloher Verlagshaus.

Van der Horst, P. W.
1989   "Portraits of Women in Pseudo-Philo's *Liber Antiquitatum Biblicarum*." *JSP* 5:29-46.

VanderKam, J. C.
1984   *Enoch and the Growth of an Apocalyptic Tradition*. CBQMS 16. Washington: Catholic Biblical Association of America.
1989   *The Book of Jubilees: A Critical Text*. 2 vols. CSCO 510-11, Scriptores Aethiopici 87-88. Louvain: Peeters.

Willett, T. W.
1989   *Eschatology in the Theodicies of 2 Baruch and 4 Ezra*. JSPS 4. Sheffield: Sheffield Academic.

CHAPTER 10

Interpreting Israel's Scriptures
in the New Testament

Donald H. Juel

PRELIMINARY CONSIDERATIONS

Interpreting the Bible was a major form of theological conversation and formation in early Christian circles. Appreciating the role of interpretation in the development of tradition and its place in the narrative and epistolary literature of the New Testament is an important task of modern biblical scholarship. The enterprise requires discipline, especially because the early Christians among whom the Bible was interpreted were different from most of us who read their work today. The "Bible" for the New Testament community was obviously not the collection of books we regard as the "Old" and "New" Testaments. Followers of Jesus read and interpreted the "Bible" before the New Testament was written; most New Testament authors did not know the works of other New Testament writers and did not regard their own productions as being on the same level as "the Bible."

Less clear to many modern interpreters is that terms like "Hebrew Bible" and "Tanak" are inappropriate in studies of the New Testament, because the New Testament community to which we have access read their Bibles in Greek. "The Bible" means something more like "Israel's Scriptures," read in Greek. While there was surely a period of interpretation during which the text read and heard was in Aramaic and Hebrew, that period lies in the past for the communities out of which and for which the Greek New Testament was written. Even though reconstructing a history of Christian exegetical tradition must attend to such an early stage, the interpretation of Israel's Bible in Greek is more crucial for understanding the Greek New Testament. Greek-speaking

Judaism did not descend directly from Aramaic and Hebrew-speaking circles, nor did its interpretive traditions. The same, we may assume, is true of New Testament communities.

It seems appropriate, therefore, to use the term "Scriptures" and "Israel's Scriptures" to designate those books regarded by New Testament authors as the Bible. Although there are many questions about the particular text forms available to New Testament communities, for convenience we will use the term "the Bible," meaning something approximating what we know as "the Septuagint."

Such a statement immediately raises important questions about the scope of "the Bible." Israel's Scriptures in Greek contain a number of books not included in the Hebrew Bible. Whether to include these "apocryphal" books or not has been a vexing problem, posed most poignantly in the debate between Augustine and Jerome. For his Latin version, Jerome proposed translating the Hebrew Bible as the Christian Old Testament; Augustine favored translating the Septuagint, including the extra books, since this had been the Bible of the early church. Jerome prevailed in his translation, but in the western tradition the Roman Catholic Bible has included the so-called "apocryphal" books as well. Even when the list of Old Testament books in Christian Bibles corresponds to the Hebrew rather than the Greek canon, the order is closer to that of the Greek than the Hebrew. It is important to note which works New Testament authors cite and draw on as "the Scriptures." As we shall see, there is no agreement about this among biblical scholars.

Finally, we should be clear about our topic. "Interpreting the Scriptures" has popular as well as academic dimensions. From the intense interest in training public readers of the Scripture for worship in the early church (Gamble 1995: 203-41 and literature cited), it is clear that interpretation involves "making sense" at the level of public engagement. Biblical works were written to be read aloud, and there is no reading that does not involve interpretation. Knowing where to make breaks and pauses and when to take breaths may make all the difference in making sense of a passage to an audience. Modern scholarship has not taken with sufficient seriousness the oral character of engagement with the Scriptures, both in the past and present. Although the focus of this essay is the more academic question of scriptural interpretation in the New Testament, modern proposals about scriptural "echoes" will require that we pay some attention to the biblical text as experienced in both written and oral form.

The Data

Terminology in the New Testament identifying "the Scriptures" (Matt. 21:42; Luke 4:21; John 5:39; Rom. 1:2, etc.), particular divisions of the Bible (e.g., "the Law and the Prophets" [Matt. 5:17; Luke 16:16; John 1:45; Rom. 3:21], "the law of Moses, the Prophets, and the Psalms" [Luke 24:44]), or individual biblical works, varies little from contemporary Jewish usage. This is significant because all the New Testament writers presume a relationship to Israel (including their contemporaries in various Jewish groups) very different from the relationship that developed in subsequent centuries. "Christian" is not a term used to distinguish a believer from a "Jew." The term, used only three times in the New Testament, at best identifies a particular group within the Jewish family. For that reason, it would be best to avoid terms like "Christian" and "Old Testament" in our descriptions of first-century works. Understanding "early Christianity" involves knowing as much as possible about the Hellenistic world and Hellenistic culture, but the particular investment in Israel's heritage and Israel's Scriptures suggests that the most helpful analogies for our study will be other Jewish scriptural interpretation, as practiced, of course, in the Hellenized world.

The index at the back of the Nestle-Aland editions of the Greek New Testament (1979) identifies quotations and allusions to virtually every book in the Hebrew canon, to several works in the Greek (3 and 4 Esdras, 1-4 Maccabees, Tobit, Sirach, etc.), and even works included in neither canon but belonging to the so-called "Pseudepigrapha" (*Enoch, Jubilees,* etc.). The Nestle-Aland editors themselves provide an important qualification: "Opinions differ greatly in identifying quotations and allusions . . ." (p. 72). Those who check the suggested intertextual connections will discover considerable variance in the certainty of the reference. Quotations are least problematic, though false ascriptions raise interesting questions (Mark 1:2), as do references to versions of a text at variance with known Hebrew or Greek text forms. Allusions containing a string of identical words are likewise not problematic. More difficult are connections that may seem possible, but in which there is little evidence of shared wording, or where the words in common are quite ordinary.

Given qualifications, there is evidence that New Testament authors regarded as "scriptural" those books so viewed by the Pharisaic community. We do not need to make a decision about the precise boundaries of such "scriptural" works — a topic that has generated some insightful scholarship but hardly a consensus. Still problematic are the so-called "apocryphal" and "pseudepigraphical" works. Because New Testament authors do not actually quote such material, even evidence of an allusion does not prove that the works were regarded by writer and audience as having the same authority as books of the Bible (Childs 1992:65).

Formal Matters

Significantly, the New Testament is quite different in genre from the literary remains of other Jewish communities. The New Testament contains no commentaries, no retelling of the biblical story as in the *Genesis Apocryphon* or the *Biblical Antiquities* of pseudo-Philo. It is set off from rabbinic midrashic collections or the Qumran *pesharim,* and all such literature of schools. The New Testament contains letters and narratives and an apocalypse. There are passages that explicitly interpret scriptural texts (e.g., Galatians 3, Romans 9–11, Hebrews 1, and the speeches in Acts). Other material presumes interpretation but does not do it overtly. The Apocalypse of John, for example, contains more allusions to scriptural passages than does any other book in the New Testament, but it does not quote a single passage. It uses images and phrases from the Scriptures like stones in a mosaic. It is reasonable to presume a logic to their selection and use, but the "interpretation" must be reconstructed.

That the New Testament is not a collection of school literature does not mean there were not such "schools" or learned interpretation within the circles of Jesus' followers. On the contrary, the New Testament presumes a period of extensive interpretation of Israel's Scriptures. A series of quotations in Matthew, introduced with formulas like "These were done to fulfill what was written in the prophet Isaiah," betray a kind of learned sophistication that has led scholars to speak of a "Matthean School" (Stendahl 1954). The Gospel itself is not a product of such a school, but it presupposes and draws on a kind of scriptural interpretation similar to that of the later rabbis or the Essene circles at Qumran. The speeches in Acts likewise give evidence of learned interpretation.

THE USE OF THE SCRIPTURES

Because the New Testament does not contain commentaries or hermeneutical essays, we must begin by observing the use of Scripture in the New Testament writings. The simple phrase "use of Scripture" does not reveal the complexity of the phenomena.

For instance, biblical passages appear in explicit arguments. Paul marshals an impressive constellation of passages to convince the Galatians that faith in Christ, not circumcision, makes one a child of Abraham (Galatians 3). Jesus cites Hosea in a dispute with the Pharisees about the company he keeps at meals (Matt. 9:13). Peter forges a tight scriptural argument from Psalms 16 and 110 to demonstrate that by raising Jesus from the dead, God "has made him both Lord and Christ, this Jesus whom you crucified" (Acts 2:36). Describing the use of Israel's Scriptures in the New Testament includes attention to such explicit argument.

The "use of Scripture" also includes allusions. In Mark's Passion narrative, words from Psalm 22 are employed to tell the story of Jesus' death: soldiers cast lots for his garments (Mark 15:24 = Ps. 22:19); those who pass by shake their heads (Mark 15:29 = Ps. 22:8); and Jesus' last words, "My God, my God . . ." echo the opening verse of the psalm (Mark 15:34 = Ps. 22:2). The offer of vinegar may allude to Psalm 69 (Mark 15:36 = Ps. 69:22). No formula makes the point that "all this happened to fulfill what was written." Yet there is a kind of argument implied by the use of the terminology, even though it is not explicitly made, and even if, in this and other instances, the respective New Testament authors did not "intend" the argument consciously. Probably from the outset, the language of the Scriptures was used to tell the story of Jesus' death by people who were convinced it was "in accordance with the Scriptures."

Identifying allusions and understanding the kind of scriptural use and argument they imply is less certain than interpreting explicit argument. Where striking similarities in wording suggest an allusion, we may assume there is some reason for using the very words of Israel's Scriptures in telling the story. Understanding why precisely these words are used, however, may involve reconstructing traditions of interpretation that New Testament writers presupposed. Some of the New Testament authors may not even have been aware of the intertextual connections in traditions they inherited; some early readers may well have missed the allusions. The logic of using language from Psalms 22 and 69 to speak of Jesus' death is not apparent in any of the actual Gospel narratives. That the allusions lend a "scriptural" tone to the account is apparent; the reasons for using words from just these psalms is not. The level at which interpreters among the circles of Jesus' followers actually identified and assembled particular biblical passages — the point at which we may appreciate the logic and character of interpretation — is often available to us only as a construct. Understanding the allusions will require, then, a sense of the history of scriptural interpretation, set within the larger context of scriptural use in the wider culture.

Perhaps most difficult are intertextual connections proposed by modern commentators that have to do with large themes and/or patterns in Israel's Bible as much as with identical wording. These "echoes of the Scriptures" would likewise constitute a usage that implies some interpretive approach and even conclusions about the meaning of passages in the Hebrew Bible. Identifying such intertextual connections and drawing inferences about early Christian scriptural interpretation must be still more tentative than in the preceding instances. They presume knowledge of reading practices and usage that is largely unavailable to us.

The Task

Beginning with observations about the use of the Scriptures of Israel, we may proceed in various directions. A first task might be to distinguish the different ways in which the Scriptures are used, including attention to formal issues. Where is the scriptural argument overt and where is it implied? How might we distinguish among the uses of the Scriptures in prayers, hymns, confessions, or visions — formal units that are now included in letters and narratives? What is the difference between actual citation and allusion, or between allusion and an "echo"? (Hays 1989; Brawley 1995).

A second task will involve some reconstruction of interpretive traditions that must underlie the usage we encounter in the New Testament. How is it, for example, that certain passages, like Isaiah 53, came to be used to speak of Jesus? Does the usage reveal a logic, or is the process random and haphazard? In unpacking Paul's argument in Galatians 3 or Peter's speech in Acts 2, how are we to account for the particular selection and combination of texts? Much is presumed and left unsaid. What light can be shed on such matters? It remains to be seen if we can observe a logic in such usage, even to the point of offering a reconstruction of early Christian interpretive tradition (Dodd 1952; Lindars 1961; Juel 1988).

A third task will be to understand the mechanics and logic of all the "premodern" exegesis within the New Testament in light of what we know of the use of texts elsewhere in the ancient world. Although such a general assessment of "New Testament interpretation of Israel's Scriptures" is only an aspect of understanding the various letters and narratives, it is nevertheless useful for readers of letters and Gospels. We need to learn the rules taken for granted in another culture, as it read texts and constructed arguments. These rules in many cases are different from our own.

We will touch lightly on the first, and focus on the second and third tasks in the rest of this essay.

Reading the Scriptures: Rules of the Game

Writing and reading are social enterprises. They depend on shared systems of signs and proceed by largely unspecified "rules" that can be taken for granted. Because social systems differ, interpreting written material from another culture requires knowledge of that culture and its conventions. Basic assumptions about the nature of written texts underlie the whole enterprise of reading and interpretation. That is certainly true for the New Testament and its use of Israel's Scriptures.

Allegory. Allegorical interpretation, while not a respected mode of interpretation among contemporary scholars, was an accepted strategy for dealing with texts up to the time of the Enlightenment. While this strategy is not common in the New Testament, there are some examples. When Paul reads the story of Sarah and Hagar in Genesis 21, he sees in the story something beyond the literal meaning:

> Now this is an allegory: these women are two covenants. Now Hagar is Mount Sinai in Arabia and corresponds to the present Jerusalem, for she is in slavery with her children. But the other woman corresponds to the Jerusalem above; she is free, and she is our mother. (Gal. 4:24-26)

The words of the text mean something other than what they appear to mean. Philo of Alexandria, a Jewish contemporary of Paul whose volumes comprise a precious deposit of first-century Greek-speaking Judaism in Egypt, shared such assumptions. His interpretation of the migration of Abraham as the story of reason's journey from the realm of the senses to the realm of pure Mind operates with similar assumptions. While refusing to abandon the literal meaning of the law and adherence to it, Philo believed the most important meaning of words is other than the literal (*Migr.* 89-93, 183-84). God's command that Abraham "Leave your land, your kindred, and your father's house" is actually a command to leave the realm of ordinary sensual life:

> God begins the carrying out of His will to cleanse man's soul by giving it a starting point for full salvation in its removal out of three localities, namely, body, sense-perception, and speech. "Land" or "country" is a

symbol of body, "kindred" of sense-perception, "father's house" of speech. (par. 2; Colson and Whitaker 1932: 133)

Such reading operates with a particular logic. Philo, for example, frequently engages in word-play and etymology to make a point. "Land" can be a symbolic term for "body"

> because the body took its substance of our earth (or land) and is again resolved into earth. Moses is a witness to this, when he said, "Earth thou art and into earth shalt thou return" (Gen. 3:19); indeed he also says that the body was clay formed into human shape by God's moulding hand, and what suffers solution must needs be resolved into the elements which were united to form it. (par. 3; Colson and Whitaker 1932: 133)

Philo's allegorical reading is more elaborate than Paul's, operates from a different philosophical orientation, and comes to different conclusions. Nevertheless, both share common assumptions about reading texts. For allegorists, texts are cryptograms to be deciphered; meaning is located at a level "beneath" the literal. Interpretation of texts is related to the interpretation of dreams, a vocation in which at least two of Israel's heroes, Joseph and Daniel, excelled. To appreciate allegorical interpretation fully, it would be helpful to know as much as possible about the store of symbols on which interpreters drew, some of which appear in actual lists (Froehlich 1984:19).

If for Philo and later Christian interpreters allegorical method is fundamental, the approach is rarely used in the New Testament.

Midrash. It has become a commonplace among New Testament scholars to refer to early Christian interpretation as "midrash." The term is Hebrew, from the verb "to interpret." While specialists rightly object to the broad and imprecise meaning the term has acquired in recent usage, the designation is helpful as a cross-cultural reminder of the potential distance between our modes of interpretation and those of others.

The identification needs qualification. "Midrash" has a history of usage within Jewish circles of Hebrew Bible interpreters. For the New Testament, a corresponding Greek term like "exegesis" would be more apt, since the authors read and spoke and wrote in Greek. Unfortunately, there is no corresponding Greek term with the same connotations.

"Midrash" can be used to refer to a body of literature ("the midrashim"), the product of rabbinic schools beginning in the second century, though collections were not edited until the fifth century c.e. and later (see chapter 7 above). The New Testament does not contain this type of "midrash," that is, it includes no commentary on a biblical work.

"Midrash" is also used to speak of a specific methodology, identified with lists of rules by Hillel, Ishmael, and Eliezer ben Jose ha-Gelili. The lists of principles *(middoth)* were formulated well after the actual interpreting had taken shape. Although they are interesting, they do not provide the most useful access to the spirit and mechanisms of midrash. Of the various principles, only two are widely practiced within New Testament writings: the principle of analogy *(gezera shawa)* and inference from the light to the weighty *(qal wahomer)* — both strategies of argument that Jewish interpreters shared with other readers of texts in the Greco-Roman world (Froehlich 1984: 4-7).

The term is employed here in a highly generalized sense to identify an approach to the task of interpretation that was widely used not only by Jews, but also by other heirs of Hellenistic culture. This approach (or these approaches) to reading and interpreting texts are typical of cultures almost until the Enlightenment and the dawning of historical consciousness.

For modern interpreters, the most significant feature of midrash (or exegesis) that sets it apart from contemporary modes of interpretation is perhaps the construal of context. Today, students are taught that the meaning of words and sentences is tied to context, both literary and historical. Commentators writing on the book of Isaiah distinguish between "first" and "second" Isaiah (sometimes even a "third"), arguing that the collections of oracles do not derive from the same period of time and must first of all be located in their respective historical setting to be understood properly. The rabbis make no such distinctions. Their interpretation is ahistorical from the perspective of most contemporary readers. Although they are quite capable of making historical observations about passages, the meaning in which they are usually interested is not bound in any way to the setting in which the words were first spoken or written. It may be, in fact, that the real meaning of a prophetic oracle was not available to the prophet and his contemporaries, as the commentary on Habakkuk from the Dead Sea Scrolls states. Concerning the famous watchtower passage from Hab. 2:1-2, the commentator writes,

> and God told Habakkuk to write down that which would happen to the final generation, but He did not make known to him when time would come to an end. And as for that which He said, "That he who reads may read it speedily," interpreted this concerns the Teacher of Righteousness, to whom God made known all the mysteries of the words of His servants the Prophets. (1QpHab VII, Vermes 1995: 343)

The words from Paul's letter to the Corinthians make the same point. After a running commentary on Israel's experience in the wilderness, Paul says,

> These things happened to them to serve as an example, and they were written down to instruct us, on whom the ends of the ages have come. (1 Cor. 10:11)

The Scriptures are about and for later times. Only later generations — and perhaps only particular inspired individuals — can know the real meaning of the biblical passages.

If historical context is not decisive in determining meaning, neither is the immediate literary context. For those who accepted the Torah, the prophets, and the writings as Scriptures, all were part of the same "mind of God" to which the Scriptures provided access. They were on the same level, even if some passages were more important (and more interesting) than others. Thus the meaning of a word in Deuteronomy could appropriately be determined by the use of the same word in Isaiah, and light could be shed on both from a verse in the Psalms. This is precisely what we find to be the case in the New Testament. Here are two examples of such reading of the Scriptures:

(1) Paul's letter to the Galatians includes an extended scriptural argument about the heritage of Abraham. In 3:16 Paul makes what seems an extraordinary claim. In paraphrasing one of the versions of God's promise to Abraham in Genesis (Gen. 13:15; 17:8; 24:7), Paul says, "to Abraham were the promises made, and to his offspring." He continues, focusing on the singular form of the noun: "It does not say, 'and to his offsprings,' as of many; but it says, 'and to your offspring,' that is, to one person, who is Christ" (Gal. 3:16).

Modern commentators are quick to point out that the singular noun, "offspring" (literally "seed"), is collective. One of the passages to which Paul is referring reads as follows:

> for all the land that you see I will give to you and to your offspring forever. I will make your offspring like the dust of the earth; so that if one can count the dust of the earth, your offspring can also be counted. (Gen. 13:15-16)

The context suggests that God is speaking about Abraham's "seed" as a group, a whole people, and the promise is explicitly about possessing the land. Paul speaks of "inheritance" without mentioning the land, however, and he obviously does not read "offspring" (seed) as a collective noun. From the perspective of modern common sense, Paul does violence to the plain meaning of the text.

His interpretation makes good sense, however, if all of Scripture provides the context for understanding the unidentified "seed" in Genesis who will be Abraham's heir. There are other candidates for understanding the specific occurrence of "offspring." One might point to 2 Sam. 7:10-14, God's promise of an eternal dynasty to David through the prophet Nathan:

> "I will raise up your *offspring* [singular] after you, who will come forth from your body, and I will establish his kingdom. He will build a house for my name, and I will establish the throne of his kingdom forever. I will be a father to him, and he will be a son to me." (vv. 12-14)

One might argue that in the literary and historical context of this promise, it refers to Solomon. God did not "establish the throne of his [Solomon's] kingdom forever," however. Later generations came to read this passage as a prophecy of *the* king to come, the "Messiah." Such is the case among the Essenes at Qumran. Of this passage, the Qumran commentator says,

> He is the Branch of David who shall arise with the Interpreter of the Law [to rule] in Zion [at the end] of time. (4QFlor 11-12; Vermes 1995: 354)

"Branch of David" is an expression borrowed from Jer. 23:5; 33:15 and Zech. 6:12, where it also refers to a future king from the line of David. The Qumran commentary presumes that all these passages refer to the same figure, the Messiah-King who will arise at the end of days.

Paul's interpretation presumes the same reading of 2 Sam. 7:12, now with an additional step: he argues that this royal "seed" promised to David is the specific "seed" to whom God promises Abraham's heritage. Abraham's inheritance, in other words, now flows through the promised Christ. That others held such a view prior to Paul is apparent perhaps even within the Scriptures. In Psalm 2, the Lord's "anointed" (Christ) — whom God calls "my son" (v. 7) — is told, "I will make the nations your heritage, and the ends of the earth your possession" (v. 8). According to the psalmist, it is this one whom God calls "my son" who will inherit not only the land promised to Abraham and his "seed" but also "the ends of the earth." Through this offspring Abraham will become "the father of a multitude of nations."

To understand Paul's argument, one needs to know that "seed" in the singular is used both in Gen. 13:16 and in 2 Sam. 7:12 in promises God makes about Israel's future. The unspecified usage in Genesis is interpreted via

2 Samuel. "Seed" is singular, according to this argument, not because it is a collective noun but because God had in mind the "seed" promised to David that would be Abraham's single heir, through whom all — Jews and Gentiles — would be blessed. The analogy (a form of argument identified as *gezera shawa*) is an accepted form of scriptural interpretation and provides here a way of discovering how God's promise to Abraham could be interpreted "messianically."

The analogies explain other features of Paul's argument here as well. Paul's way of proceeding is completely within the bounds of established Jewish interpretive practice, though he argues for a conclusion with which no rabbi would agree. In making a case that Jesus' coming means the end of the law for all those who have faith, Paul employs the Scriptures once again to make his point:

> Why then the law? It was added because of transgressions, until the offspring would come to whom the promise had been made. (Gal. 3:19)

"Until the offspring would come to whom the promise had been made" paraphrases Gen. 49:10:

> The scepter shall not depart from Judah
> nor the ruler's staff from between his feet
> *until tribute comes to him.*

The oracle is about Judah, from whom David was descended and the Messiah was to arise. The phrase translated in the NRSV as "until tribute comes to him" is translated in the Septuagint as "until the one comes to whom the promises belong." It is this reading Paul presumes. That this figure is called the "offspring" in Gal. 3:19 means that Gen. 49:10 is being read in light of 2 Sam. 7:12. The "seed" promised to Abraham is the same as the "seed" promised to David — the king — who is the "one" to whom promises belong according to Genesis 49. The formation of such constellations of passages through verbal analogies is one of the principal mechanisms by which the Scriptures are interpreted.

Such interpretation violates modern conventions about what makes for a convincing argument. It disregards the specific literary and historical settings of Genesis 13 and 49 and 2 Samuel 7. Within its own setting, however, the New Testament follows procedures for "scientific" interpretation. The constellation of "messianic" texts is not haphazardly formed. Beginning with royal oracles whose future verbs came to be read as pertaining to the distant (i.e., messianic) future, connections with other scriptural passages were established through verbal analogy.

Such observations do not constitute adequate interpretations of the verses from Galatians. Paul takes most of the christological reading of the Scriptures for granted. He was certainly not the first to associate 2 Samuel 7 and Genesis 49. Beginning with the "assured results" of the developing exegetical tradition within the circles of Jesus' followers, Paul argues for the social implications of his christological reading of the Scriptures. Appreciating the nature of the scriptural argument, however, is essential to a full understanding of Paul's letter and of the tradition to which he belongs. Interpreters will need to know what suggested the links in the first place, how these constellations of biblical interpretations differ from alternatives, and how Paul could use the same methods as those employed by other readers of Israel's Scriptures while arriving at diametrically opposed conclusions.

(2) The process of "messianic exegesis" can also help explain New Testament use of other scriptural passages that no one had previously connected with the Messiah. Isaiah 42 and 53, familiar passages in Christian tradition, are used in the New Testament to speak of Jesus. Isaiah 42:1 is quoted in Matt. 12:18-21. The voice from heaven at Jesus' baptism and transfiguration shows traces of the passage ("with you I am well-pleased," Mark 1:11 par.; "the chosen one," Luke 3:22; 9:35; 23:35). Even more prominent is Isa. 52:13–53:12, with quotations in John 12:38; Matt. 8:17; Acts 8:32-33, an extended comment in 1 Pet. 2:22-25, and numerous allusions throughout the New Testament. The unprecedented use of these passages to speak of Jesus the Christ depends on the establishment of intertextual connections. Both Isaiah 42 and 53 speak of an unidentified "servant of God" (42:1; 52:13) and may be read as "messianic" because the Messiah-King is called God's "servant" elsewhere in the Scriptures (Ps. 89:50-51; Zech. 3:8).

Other connections might have been made. "Servant" in Isa. 52:13–53:12 might be used of Moses, who is called "servant" elsewhere in the Scriptures. Precisely such a move is made in the Babylonian Talmud (b. *Sotah* 14a; Juel 1988:123). References to Isaiah's "servant" could be used of Elijah, since he is spoken of as a servant of God (Sir. 48:9-10, alluding to Isa. 49:6). Isa. 42:1, speaking of "my servant," could, in light of analogies, be taken as referring to Israel — as in the Septuagint ("Behold my servant Jacob . . .") — or to any "servant" of God — in light of usage in the psalms and the prophetic writings — as it is when Paul applies the words to himself (Rom. 10:16, quoting Isa. 53:1).

Appreciating the mechanisms by which intertextual links are established is not the end of interpretation. To understand Paul (and other New Testament writers), we need to know why one association is preferred over

another. Where is the catalyst for formation of these constellations of passages? The particular christological readings of the Scriptures make most
sense in light of the story of Jesus the crucified Christ — the descendant of
David who ended his career on a Roman cross as "The King of the Jews." That
this most unlikely messianic candidate was vindicated by God "on the third
day" required of his followers a rereading of the Scriptures to understand how
the God of Israel could confirm ancient promises in such an unconventional
manner. The confession of Jesus as Christ, in other words, is not the result of
scriptural interpretation but its presupposition (Dahl 1991).

Common Convictions

To understand scriptural interpretation among the various New Testament
authors, we need to know as much as possible about the interpreters and their
argument. We need to study their works within the larger context of ancient
Jewish scriptural interpretation, which will involve asking why disagreements
arose that were strong enough to divide communities. Regardless of conclusions drawn, however, all of the interpreters of the famous passages in Isaiah,
Jeremiah, Zechariah, Genesis, 2 Samuel, and the Psalms, share certain common notions about the Bible and the task of interpretation:
      1. The words' meaning is not limited to (or even necessarily connected
with) their immediate literary or historical setting. When the passages are
prophetic oracles, interpreters have argued that the prophet did not know
what the passage "really" meant. Similar statements can be made about passages from the Torah. The later rabbis had confidence in reasonable conversation as the way to get at the deeper meanings. Jesus' followers, like the Essenes
at Qumran, believed that the meaning is clear only to those "on whom the
end of the ages has come" or who have the Spirit of God.
      2. The meaning of the Bible is not separated from words and sentences.
It is not the disembodied or abstracted ideas that are the locus of meaning,
but the words and sentences themselves. For the more schoolish rabbis, the
precise order of words and the numerical meaning of letters invited curiosity.
Several pages in the midrashic commentary on Exodus are devoted to the
phrase, "And the Lord spoke to Moses and Aaron in the land of Egypt saying . . . ," asking if the order of the names "Moses and Aaron" implies a corresponding hierarchy in authority (Lauterbach 1949: 1-3; tractate *Pisga*). Is Moses more important than Aaron? Does the opening verse in Genesis 1, "In the
beginning God created the heavens and the earth," suggest that the heavens
are more important than the earth? The New Testament, like the Qumran

scrolls, is less playful — but attention to the particulars of the text is no less apparent (cf. Paul's appeal to the singular form of the noun "seed").

3. The whole scriptural testimony is part of a single fabric. All the biblical books are on the same plane. Any verse can be used to interpret any other. They all disclose the "mind of God." The hymnic passage from the Wisdom of Sirach puts the matter nicely: Wisdom, who proceeded from the mouth of God "in the beginning," has now become embodied in the words of the Scriptures: "All this is the book of the covenant of the Most High God, the law that Moses commanded us as an inheritance for the congregations of Jacob" (Sir. 24:23).

4. While it may seem that preconceptions determine what one sees and that exegetical method is simply a way of making the Scriptures say what is already known, that is far too simple an explanation of the data. Some preconception has always been necessary to open the Scriptures, and it still is. Followers of Jesus, like others within the Jewish community, came to the Bible with experiences and questions that determined the shape and direction of interpretation. The Bible likewise exercised an influence on the outcome and on the shape of the developing tradition.

Several striking examples come to mind. That what happened to Jesus after his death should be discussed, using the language of exaltation and return, has everything to do with the use of passages like Ps. 110:1 and Dan. 7:13. Such biblical passages were not simply proof-texts; they provided the means by which Jesus' followers could understand and speak about his — and their — future. Paul's "doctrine" of justification by faith has a great deal to do with the language of the Scriptures, in particular Hab. 2:4 and Gen. 15:6. References to "the name" of Jesus in Luke-Acts and Romans are tied to the use of Joel 2:32. What is distinctive is the interplay between events and the Scriptures.

5. While interpretation could be motivated by simple curiosity and a desire to make the unclear clear (Vermes 1975: 63-80), most "midrash" was done with the intent of making sense of the Scriptures for the present life of the faithful. Interpretation was a way of making the Bible present and active.

Echoes

It is far more difficult to assess the mode of interpretation behind what Hays (1989) and others have called "echoes of Scripture." Clearly, the followers of Jesus read the Bible, as did others in the ancient world, with particular attention to the words and sentences. But was this the only form in which the Scriptures exercised influence? Is the more "midrashic," word-and-sentence oriented, interpretation even the most common form of scriptural argument? While it is not difficult to detect citations and allusions — the precise wording is the clue — it is far more difficult to detect play on biblical texts in which shared wording is limited or where the alleged associations have to do with larger themes or constructs.

In our own time, for most people, "echoes" of biblical passages appear to be the most common form of interaction with the Scriptures. The Bible exercises most influence in hymns, liturgies, confessions, prayers, and oratorios like Handel's "Messiah." The kind of intertextual play common to a group that shares a canon of stories and images is the most obvious form of scriptural use and interpretation. The question is the degree to which that was also the case in New Testament times, or, more importantly, the degree to which we have sufficient access to the life of those communities to offer an evaluation.

There are numerous proposals. Students of Luke's Gospel, for example, argue that the narrative is a play on major themes in Deuteronomy (Moessner 1989; Sanders and Evans 1994). Hays (1989) proposes that a single allusion to Job in the opening chapter of Philippians suggests that the apostle is drawing a parallel between Job and himself: "Paul the prisoner tacitly assumes the role of the righteous sufferer, as paradigmatically figured by Job" (1989: 22). Mark is a variation on major themes from second Isaiah (Marcus 1992: 26-47).

What makes the arguments worth consideration is that many of the proposed echoes are plausible. What makes them plausible, however, may have little to do with ancient modes of scriptural interpretation. Present readers are quite capable of "detecting" intertextual relationships between Old and New Testament passages that no one has seen before — perhaps not even the author of the passage. Learned interpretation, however, has found controls for this in arguments for precedents: Matthew or Paul or John "intended" such an association; their readers would have detected such echoes. Demonstrating this proves difficult, however. In a sophisticated discussion of "tests" for determining the degree of certainty of a proposed intertextual link, Hays proposes seven criteria for "hearing echoes" (1989: 29-32), including historical criteria (material, historical plausibility and history of interpretation) and literary criteria ("volume," recurrence, thematic coherence, and "satisfaction"). Literary criteria have to do with the present experience of reading a text; historical criteria have to do with precedent. The argument for precedent requires knowledge of historical context, in particular, familiarity with ancient reading practices.

We know about ancient reading practices in the synagogue, though things become clearer after the second century and beyond. It seems certain that at the major Sabbath service there was a reading from the Torah and from the Prophets. Festival days included reading from the *Megilloth* (Song of Songs, Ruth, Lamentations, Ecclesiastes, and Esther) (Gamble 1995: 208-10, with literature cited). Important work has been done on the use of the Scriptures in the life of the synagogue, including attempts to reconstruct a three-year cycle of liturgical readings, correlating readings from the Torah with readings from the Prophets. Scholars have explored the relationship between major festivals and the interpretation of particular Bible stories. One of the most interesting is the work of Le Deaut and others on the place of the "Binding of Isaac" in Passover tradition (see Le Déaut 1963). Such work has been challenged, however, by other scholars who do not see the proposed links and are unconvinced by the evidence (Chilton 1978; Davies 1979).

The New Testament — Luke-Acts in particular — presumes public reading of the Scriptures in the synagogue (Luke 4:16-20; Acts 17:2, 11). 1 Timothy speaks of "the public reading of Scripture" among believers in Jesus (4:13). Paul assumes that Gentile Christians in the Galatian churches know the Bible and can follow careful scriptural argument. Beyond this, however, we do not know precisely what portions of Israel's Scriptures were read, how they were read, or even in what form they were available. That all churches owned copies of the Scriptures is highly unlikely. Contact with written texts mediated by "testimony books" remains a possibility (Gamble 1995: 24-28).

The difficulty in arguing for more broadly and loosely defined intertextual echoes is apparent in Marcus's work on Mark (1992). He interprets the "Old Testament" in terms of "patterns and themes" in the context of which, he argues, Mark and his readers would have heard the story of Jesus.

> A major thesis of our study . . . has been that Mark takes up patterns and themes from the Old Testament and uses them to make clear to his biblically literate readers various aspects of Jesus' identity and his relationship to the community whose existence was inaugurated by his life, death, and resurrection. It makes sense to conclude that these Old Testament motifs have also played a considerable role in shaping Mark's own conception of Jesus. (p. 202)

The problem is anachronism. Marcus employs constructs such as "the Righteous Sufferer" and "the Suffering Servant" that appear to be modern, not ancient, images. To make sense of Mark's use of the phrase "the way" in 1:2 and 10:30-34, he appeals to "the Deutero-Isaian picture of Yahweh's triumphant processional march" (p. 35), a theme that "in Deutero-Isaiah, however . . . has been fused with that of the holy war of conquest" (p. 36). While references to deutero-Isaiah may make sense to modern students of the Hebrew

Bible, they do not reflect the perspective of first-century readers, and there is little evidence that anyone prior to the modern era has detected such "patterns and themes."

Marcus's work may be an extreme example, but it illustrates the difficulty of knowing how to reconstruct a "biblically literate readership." We require knowledge of reading practices and liturgical traditions in the first century, which is largely unavailable. In the case of our closest analogies, rabbinic interpretation, there is little obvious relationship between interpretation of texts and their usage. Knowledge that the psalms are songs has apparently little to do with their use as Scripture. The Midrash on Psalms is a (late) collection of commentary in which the form of the psalms as songs to be performed has no appreciable impact on the comments. The psalms are read as texts. They disclose meaning as do other texts. Interpreters make sense of them by using techniques appropriate to texts, that is, dealing with words and sentences. Almost half the comments in the interpretation of Psalm 22 are devoted to deciphering the cryptic words in the title of the psalm (Braude 1959: 297-326). The case seems much the same in the New Testament. To make sense of the use of Psalms 2, 8, 16, 22, 45, 69, 89, 110, 118, and 132, it is unnecessary to know how they were employed in worship or even that they were performed. They function as scriptural texts whose words and sentences are the focus of attention.

If the proposals of Hays on Philippians and Romans (1989), Moessner (1989) and Brawley (1995) on Luke, or Marcus on Mark (1992), were not plausible, there would be no interest in "echoes of Scripture" and in these more general forms of intertextuality. Their least convincing arguments, however, are generally those that must claim historical precedent. Passages like Galatians 3, Romans 9–11, the opening chapters of Hebrews and 1 Peter, and the speeches in Acts provide clear evidence of forms of interpretation familiar from sources contemporary with the New Testament authors. Paul's allegorical reading of the Sarah-Hagar story in Genesis is likewise at home in his first-century environment. It is appropriate, perhaps, that an essay about biblical interpretation — in contrast to a topic like "the influence of the Old Testament on the New Testament" — should focus on those phenomena that reveal a form of argumentation that can be documented. That Paul could draw on large blocks of material with which he could assume familiarity and that Luke's anachronistic "biblical" language is a subtle form of argument for people in whose consciousness the Scriptures were deeply embedded remain possibilities. Yet what makes the particular intertextual proposals appealing — and convincing — may have more to do with contemporary reading patterns and less with our ability to demonstrate historical precedent.

CONCLUSIONS

In considering interpretation of Israel's Scriptures in the New Testament, it is unnecessary to resolve such matters even if it were possible to do so. Discussions about appropriate forms of scriptural interpretation — including contemporary appreciation and use of intertextual echoes of all sorts in interpretations of the New Testament — can benefit from cross-cultural conversation. Obviously, readers at other times and places have construed texts and engagement with texts differently. Discovering a logic in scriptural interpretation within Jewish circles in the first century of our present era may help to illumine aspects of the New Testament that seem foreign and nonsensical. To what extent these alternative modes of appreciating written texts should shape our own practice is another matter and cannot be answered in advance.

BIBLIOGRAPHY

Braude, W. G. (trans.)

1959   *The Midrash on Psalms.* New Haven: Yale University Press.

Brawley, R.

1995   *Text to Text Pours Forth Speech: Voices of Scripture in Luke-Acts.* Bloomington: Indiana University Press.

Childs, B.

1993   *Biblical Theology of the Old and New Testaments.* Minneapolis: Fortress.

Chilton, B.

1978   "The Aqedah: A Revised Tradition History." *CBQ* 40:514-46.

Colson, F. H., and G. H. Whitaker (trans.)

1932   *Philo.* Loeb Classical Library 4. Cambridge: Harvard University Press.

Dahl, N. A.

1991   *Jesus the Christ: The Historical Origins of Christological Doctrine.* Minneapolis: Fortress.

Davies, P. R.

1979   "Passover and the Dating of the Akedah." *JJS* 30:59-67.

Dodd, C. H.

1952   *According to the Scriptures: The Sub-Structure of New Testament Theology.* London: Nisbit.

Evans, C. A.

1993   *Luke and the Scriptures: The Function of Sacred Tradition in Luke-Acts.* Minneapolis: Fortress.

Froehlich, K.

1984   *Biblical Interpretation in the Early Church.* Minneapolis: Fortress.

Gamble, H.

1995   *Books and Readers in the Early Church: A History of Early Christian Texts.* New Haven: Yale University Press.

Greer, R., and J. Kugel

1986   *Early Biblical Interpretation.* Philadelphia: Westminster.

Hays, R.

1989   *Echoes of Scriptures in the Letters of Paul.* New Haven: Yale University Press.

Juel, D.

1981   "Social Dimensions of Exegesis: The Use of Psalm 16 in Acts 2." *CBQ* 43:543-56.

1988   *Messianic Exegesis: Christological Interpretation of the Old Testament in Early Christianity.* Minneapolis: Fortress.

Lauterbach, J. Z. (ed.)

1949   *Mekilta de Rabbi Ishmael.* Philadelphia: Jewish Publication Society of America.

Le Déaut, R.

1963   "La présentation targumique du sacrifice d'Isaac et la sotériologie paulinienne." *Studiorum Paulinorum Congressus Catholicus 1961.* Analecta Biblica 17-18. Rome: Pontifical Biblical Institute.

1971   "Apropos a Definition of Midrash." *Interpretation* 25:259-82.

Lindars, B.

1961   *New Testament Apologetic.* London: SCM.

1963   *La nuit paschale.* Analecta Biblica 22. Rome: Pontifical Biblical Institute.

Marcus, J.

1992   *The Way of the Lord: Christological Exegesis of the Old Testament in the Gospel of Mark.* Louisville: Westminster/John Knox.

Moessner, D.

1989   *Lord of the Banquet: The Literary and Theological Significance of the Lukan Travel Narrative.* Minneapolis: Fortress.

Nestle, E., and K. Aland

1979   *Novum Testamentum Graece.* 26th ed. Stuttgart: Deutsche Bibelstiftung.

Neusner, J.

1983   *Midrash in Context: Exegesis in Formative Judaism.* Philadelphia: Fortress.

Porton, G. G.

1985   *Understanding Rabbinic Midrash.* Hoboken: Ktav.

Sanders, J. A., and C. Evans

1994   *The Gospels and the Scriptures of Israel.* Sheffield: Sheffield Academic.

Schürer, E.

1971-87 *The History of the Jewish People in the Age of Jesus Christ.* 3 vols. G. Vermes, F. Millar, and M. Black, eds. Edinburgh: Clark.

Spiegel, S.

1969 *Last Trial: On the Legends and Lore of the Aqedah.* Trans. J. Goldin. New York: Shocken.

Stendahl, K.

1954 *The School of St. Matthew.* Philadelphia: Fortress.

Vermes, G.

1975 *Post-Biblical Jewish Studies.* Leiden: Brill.

1995 *The Dead Sea Scrolls in English.* 4th ed. Sheffield: Sheffield Academic.

CHAPTER 11

The Apostolic Fathers and Apologists

Joseph Trigg

Just two generations separate Ignatius of Antioch (d. ca. 101) from Irenaeus of Lyons (d. ca. 177). Irenaeus knew and respected Ignatius's writings, and they shared a human connection: on his way to Rome and martyrdom, Ignatius wrote his one surviving personal letter to Polycarp, whom Irenaeus knew during his youth in Asia Minor. There is, moreover, considerable continuity in their teaching, particularly in their understanding of the nature and work of Christ. Nonetheless, the differences between the ways Ignatius and Irenaeus approach Scripture make plain how vital these two generations were in the history of Christian biblical interpretation. It is a period that saw the development of what were to become classic approaches to Scripture, even as the Scriptural canon itself was in process of formation. It is impossible to speak of Ignatius as oriented toward anything like our Christian Bible. By the time of Irenaeus, we see a broad consensus on the shape of the Christian Bible — the Hebrew Bible in the Septuagint version maintaining its scriptural status as a Christian Old Testament; and the four Gospels, Acts, and the Pauline Epistles forming the core of a Christian New Testament.

Apart from some Gnostic literature and the New Testament Apocrypha (dealt with elsewhere in this volume), the principal Christian literature of the second century consists of the writers known collectively as Apostolic Fathers and the Apologists, to which we can add the works of the second century's most eminent theologian, Irenaeus. The term "Apostolic Fathers" has served since the seventeenth century as a classification of convenience for some of the most ancient Christian literature outside the New Testament canon. It includes works, such as the Ignatian letters, about which we can be fairly confident in ascribing authorship; works, such as the *Didache* (see Draper 1996), that are anonymous; and others, such as the *Letter of Barnabas* (see Hvalvik 1996), which are pseudonymous. In genre, most of these works are letters, but they also include a work that appears to be a homily (the so-called *Second Letter of Clement;* see Knopf 1920), an apology by an unknown author (the *Letter to Diognetus;* see Grant 1989), and an apocalypse (the *Shepherd* of Hermas; see Dibelius 1923). The Apologists wrote, for the most part, a generation later. They are known as such because their principal surviving works seek to clear Christianity of charges thought to justify persecution of Christians. The Apologists include Justin Martyr, his pupil Tatian, Athenagoras, and Theophilus of Antioch. They also include Melito of Sardis, whose apology has been lost, but whose homily *On the Passover* has recently been discovered.

None of the Apostolic Fathers or Apologists wrote learned commentaries on whole books of Scripture with close examination of each verse and its relationship to the book as a whole (Theophilus's discussion of the opening chapters of Genesis is as close as we come to such an approach; see Simonetti 1972). Neither do they present any developed theory of interpretation. Some, like Ignatius, seem to have little use for the concept of an authoritative Scripture. To appreciate their role in the history of biblical interpretation, we must understand biblical interpretation in a large sense. It is not simply what we might call "explicit interpretation" — citing a Scriptural text and saying what it means. Although some of the figures we shall be examining do engage in this sort of interpretation, a much more characteristic way of interpretation is implicit rather than explicit. All of these writers use Scripture extensively, often without explicit citation, to make sense of their experience, to provide moral guidance, to establish doctrine, or simply as a language for devotion. In this way, Scripture provides a specifically Christian language. While later Christians — notably Origen, Theodore of Mopsuestia, and Augustine — would write detailed commentaries and expound hermeneutical theories, implicit interpretation, using Scripture as a Christian language, would remain a salient characteristic of Christian literature for many centuries to come.

THE APOSTOLIC FATHERS

Ignatius of Antioch

Ignatius wrote some time between 100 and 118 CE. His audience was a Christian community still in the process of deciding what writings it will consider authoritative and how it will relate to them. Thus, although he anticipates Irenaeus and later orthodoxy in his teaching on christology and church order, his orientation toward Scripture has something in common with the Gnostics (see Simonetti 1985: 27; Young 1997: 59). This is not to say that he shared the Gnostic view that the Old Testament could be ascribed to a god other than the God and Father of Jesus Christ. In *Smyrn.* 4.2–5.1 Ignatius writes that "the Prophets and the Law of Moses" along with "the gospel" — presumably, as in the New Testament, the proclamation of the good news of Jesus' resurrection rather than a written document (see Schoedel 1985: 207-11) — and "our own individual sufferings" testify that Jesus did not accomplish what he did only in appearance. Likewise, in *Philad.* 5.2 he writes that "we love the Prophets because they made their proclamation looking toward the gospel and hoped in [Jesus] and awaited him, believing in whom they have also been saved." Nonetheless, one sees little indication in Ignatius's letters that the Old Testament had any important continuing role in the life of the Christian community.

His letters evidence little interest in or familiarity with the Old Testament. Only two of them explicitly cite the Old Testament as Scripture, each citing a brief saying from Proverbs with the formula "it is written" *(gegraptai)*. In *Eph.* 5.3, *gegraptai* introduces Prov. 3:34, "God resists the proud" (which is also quoted in Jas. 4:6 and 1 Pet. 5:5, but without *gegraptai*). Likewise, in *Magn.* 12 *gegraptai* introduces Prov. 18:17, "the righteous man is his own accuser." In *Trall.* 8.2 another saying, "For woe to the one through whom my name is blasphemed by some in vain" appears to be a garbled version of Isa. 52:5. It is not introduced as Scripture but, since God speaks in the first person, Ignatius must have intended it to be understood as a prophetic oracle. In another handful of passages, he seamlessly incorporates phrases from the Old Testament into his own argument. Thus, "who spoke and it came to pass" in *Eph.* 15:1 echoes Ps. 33:9 or 148:5; "he will raise a standard" in *Smyrn.* 1.2 alludes to Isa. 5:26; and "all things that he does" in *Magn.* 13.1 may allude to Ps. 1:3. Other allusions to Old Testament texts come, most likely, by way of New Testament documents.

In *Philad.* 8.2, Ignatius seems to indicate that he had on some occasion found himself at a loss in dealing with opponents who asked him to provide scriptural backing for a claim:

> I beseech you not to act out of partisanship, but out of what you have learned in Christ. Because I have heard some saying "If I do not find it in the archives, I do not believe that it is in the gospel." And when I said "It has been written," they answered me, "That is the question." But for me

the archives are Jesus Christ, and the inviolable archives are his cross, death, and resurrection and faith through him, in which I want, with your prayer, to be justified.

Here, Ignatius is recording an unpleasant experience when he was challenged to validate a claim from the "archives" *(ta archeia),* which must be the Old Testament. His vague "it is written" (meaning "it's in there somewhere") elicited the sensible rejoinder "That is the question." On reflection, Ignatius tells the Philadelphians he has decided that the real criterion for the validity of the gospel is not the Old Testament, but the Christian community's contemporary experience of Jesus Christ. From this passage, Young argues that "as already for Paul and the Epistle to the Hebrews, Christ has become the hermeneutical key which relativizes the texts, even as they confirm the Christian testimony" (1997: 16).

Ignatius seems to have been more familiar with what we would consider the New Testament (or much of it), even though he does not appeal to it and probably did not think of it as authoritative Scripture. He does not introduce passages taken or adapted from the New Testament with *gegraptai* but, as with some of his references to the Old Testament, simply incorporates its phraseology into his style. He probably knew the Gospels of John and Matthew, although, conceivably, he was actually familiar with oral traditions incorporated into those Gospels. At any rate, as Grant has pointed out, he does not seem to have distinguished between New Testament scripture and tradition (1967: 52). Thus, for example, he writes in Ign. *Eph.* 17: "For this reason the Lord received myrrh on his head, in order to breathe imperishability upon the church." Not only does Ignatius evidently know the story, recounted in Matthew 26 and John 12, of the woman who poured ointment on Jesus' head, but he seems to presuppose that his readers will also be familiar with it.

On the other hand, Ignatius knew Paul's letters, including the Pastorals, well. Furthermore, Paul, the imprisoned apostle whose letters provided authoritative guidance to individual churches and persons, evidently provided the model for Ignatius's personal conduct and his writing style. Turns of phrase from the Pauline corpus occur frequently on every page. Thus, for example, in *Phld.* 3.3, Ignatius takes the language of 1 Cor. 6:9-10 and adapts it for his own purposes: "Do not be in error, my brothers and sisters, if anyone follows someone who is in schism, that person *will not inherit the kingdom of God.*" It would thus appear that Ignatius uses the Pauline epistles, not as a definitive authority, but as a model and resource for an ongoing ministry in continuity with Paul's own.

1 Clement

We see a similar attitude to the Pauline epistles in *1 Clement,* a letter from the Roman church to the Corinthian church from roughly the same period. It is traditionally attributed to Clement, thought to be an early bishop of Rome. It was written to urge the Corinthians to restore their former leaders, and it justifies this advice with a lengthy exhortation against insubordination, jealousy, and pride and in favor of unity and humility. The letters of Paul, specifically the Corinthian correspondence with its warnings against schism, again provide both a model and, to a lesser extent, a means of expression. Clement, indeed, recommends that the Corinthians "take up the letter [*sic*] of blessed Paul the Apostle. What did he first write to you in the beginning of the gospel? Truly he commanded you spiritually concerning himself as well as Cephas and Apollos, because even then you had predilections for one or the other" (*1 Clem.* 47.1-3). Nonetheless, Paul's letter is presented not as authoritative Scripture but as a testimony to the same message Clement presents on his own. Sayings of Jesus, though not cited as Scripture, are quoted as authoritative, evidently because they belong to the apostolic *kērygma* (the apostolic proclamation of the gospel).

By contrast, Clement accepted the authority of the Old Testament and expected the same of his readers. He addresses them at one point saying: "For you know and know well the holy Scriptures, beloved, and you have scrutinized God's oracles. Therefore we write these things to remind you" (53.1). Whether or not they knew and accepted the Old Testament as Scripture, Clement evidently did. He draws easily on a broad range of books, concentrating, in keeping with the purpose of his letter, on passages that provide moral exhortation. His Old Testament included Judith (55.4-5) and Wisdom (27.5), which he is the earliest author to cite. There is every reason to believe that he saw the Old Testament's authority not simply as morally compelling, but as legally binding. Thus, he quotes Isa. 60:17 in the Septuagint version, "I will appoint their bishops in righteousness and their deacons in faith" (42.5), to buttress his contention that the Corinthian church's previously established order was divinely instituted. His frequent quotation of extended passages is an indication that he had manuscripts readily accessible. Interestingly, he introduces one such passage, Ps. 33:12-18, as an exhortation from Christ himself, addressing the Corinthian Christians through the Holy Spirit (ch. 22).

Clement's work provides one of our earliest windows, after the New Testament, on early Christian biblical interpretation. Thus, he provides an example of the early Christian tendency to see events in the New Testament mysteriously prefigured in the Old when he states that the scarlet thread hung from Rahab's house prefigures the blood of Christ (12.7). The citation of Psalm 33 mentioned above is an early example of what Rondeau (1982: 2:22-23) refers to as "prosopological exegesis," interpretation that identifies the "person" (Greek, *prosōpon*) speaking in a given scriptural passage. In another passage, Clement identifies the Holy Spirit as the person speaking the words of Ps. 21:7-9. Such interpretation, which we find already in the New Testament, would become a major preoccupation of later patristic interpreters. As in the genre of interpretation called *pesharim*, found in the Dead Sea Scrolls, which applies the text to contemporary concerns of the community, Clement has no hesitation in applying Scripture directly to the Corinthians' current situation, arguing (3.1) that the saying in Deut. 32:15, "My beloved was eating and drinking, and he grew fat and robust and began to kick," has been fulfilled in them. Daniélou finds other examples of characteristically Jewish exegesis. He points to "the presence of a dossier of texts in which the resurrection is suggested by the introduction of the verb *anistanai* (to rise again)." He ascribes this "dossier" to Clement's reliance on a series of proof-texts (known to biblical scholars as *testimonia*) to the resurrection. These amount to Christian application of the Jewish *targumim*, interpretive paraphrases of the text (see Daniélou 1964: 94-95). Daniélou also finds Clement using what is, in effect, a Jewish-Christian *midrash*, an application of the biblical text to a contemporary situation, on Ezekiel (see 1964: 105 on *1 Clem.* 8.2-3).

2 Clement

The work traditionally known, in spite of its lack of epistolary form, as the *Second Letter of Clement to the Corinthians*, seems to come from a milieu similar to that of *First Clement*. Rather than a letter, Second Clement seems to be a homily urging a proper appreciation of and wholehearted response to the salvation wrought by Christ.

After a brief paragraph setting forth the theme, the author reinforces it with an interpretation of Isa. 54:1:

When it says "Rejoice, you who were sterile and have not borne children" it speaks about us, for our church was sterile before she was given children. When it says "Cry out, you who did not endure birth-pangs," it is saying this, that we should offer up our prayers before God simply and that we should not be remiss like women in the throes of birth-pangs. But when it says, "Because the children of the abandoned woman are more numerous than those of the woman who has a husband," it is because it

seemed that our people was abandoned by God, but now those who believe have become more numerous than those who seemed to possess
God. (2.1-3)

This application of the passage to the church, presumably as opposed to the
synagogue, does not go beyond the use of the same passage in Gal. 4:26-27,
where it is applied to "the Jerusalem above," free from the law, "which is the
mother of us all."

More interesting is the interpretation of Gen. 1:27:

I do not suppose you are ignorant, brothers, that the living church is the
body of Christ, for Scripture says "God made the human being male and
female." The male is Christ, the female is the church, and yet the books *(ta
biblia)* and the apostles say that the church is not just now but from the
beginning, for it was spiritual, as was our Jesus, but he appeared at the
end of days in order to save us. But the church, being spiritual, has appeared in the flesh of Christ, showing us that if any of us keeps it in the
flesh and does not corrupt it, he will receive it back in the Holy Spirit. Because this flesh is the antitype of the Spirit, no one who corrupts the
antitype will receive the original. (2:11-23)

The application of the creation narrative to Christ and the church seems a
logical extension of the similar application of Gen. 2:23-24 in Eph. 5:30-32,
which also suggests the identification of the church with Christ's flesh. Such
an interpretation, as commentators have noted (see, for example, Knopf 1920:
174), also has affinities with Gnostic speculation about preexistent syzygies.
"The books" are, most likely, the Old Testament Scriptures and "the apostles,"
that is, the Pauline epistles. Mentioning them as separate authorities is an indication that New Testament writings are coming to be recognized as having
the same authority as the Old. Another such indication is the reference in
2 Clem. 2.4 to Matt. 9:13, "I have not come to call the righteous, but sinners to
repentance" as a "Scripture" *(graphē).* 2 Clement places these authoritative
writings on much the same level as several sayings of Jesus not otherwise attested and a prophecy of unknown derivation, also cited in *1 Clement.* We
thus see an emerging (but not at all developed) sense of a Christian Bible and
a conviction that its message is directly applicable, through moral exhortation or through recondite symbolism, to the church in the writer's own time.

The *Didache*

Like the epistles of Ignatius and Clement, the *Didache* probably dates from
the decades around 100 CE. A somewhat miscellaneous work evidently drawing on several sources, it is perhaps best described as a manual of church order. Although it may have achieved its present form at a somewhat later date,
most scholars agree that it draws on early sources (see articles in Draper
1996). It begins with a discussion of Christian behavior as defined by "two
ways," the way of life and the way of death, a form that has its roots, as we now
know from the discovery of similar themes in the Dead Sea Scrolls, in Jewish
tradition. This opening section is, in effect, a Christian *halakha*, that is, an interpretation providing instruction on conduct. Its author draws heavily on
the Gospels, particularly Matthew, from which he quotes, among other
things, the Lord's Prayer (with the concluding doxology). Like Clement and
Ignatius, however, he does not cite the Gospels as Scripture. Echoing Deuteronomy, he insists on the continuing validity of the Law: "Do not abandon the
Lord's commandments, but guard what you have received, neither adding nor
taking away" (5.13; see Deut. 4:2; 12:32).

The *Epistle* and *Martyrdom of Polycarp*

Some time before his martyrdom around 156 CE, Polycarp, the bishop of
Smyrna, one of the recipients of Ignatius's letters, wrote a letter to the church
at Philippi. It provides continuing testimony to the Christian community's
understanding of Scripture as directly relevant to the community's ongoing
life of faith. Polycarp exhorts the Philippians to hold to faith in Jesus Christ in
the face of persecution and the spread of false teaching. Like Clement, whom
he echoes, Polycarp asserts that his readers will be well exercised in the holy
Scriptures (*Phil.* 12.1). Whether or not he considered it Scripture, Polycarp
was certainly steeped in the New Testament. Like Ignatius, Polycarp finds not
just models, but almost all of his language, in earlier Christian epistolary literature. He knew the Pauline corpus well — along with 1 and 2 John and
1 Clement — but seems to have had a special affinity for 1 Peter. A brief passage from his work provides an example of his style:

> Therefore, girding your loins, serve God in fear and in truth, abandoning
> empty vain-speaking and the deceit of the many, believing in the one who
> raised Jesus Christ our Lord from the dead and gave him glory and a
> throne at his right hand, to whom he subjected all things heavenly and

earthly, whom every breath worships, who will come as judge of the living and the dead, whose blood God will require of those who disbelieve in him. (*Phil.* 2.1)

This one typical sentence alludes in turn to 1 Pet. 1:13; Ps. 2:11; 1 Pet. 1:21; Phil. 3:21 and 2:10; Ps. 150:6; Isa. 57:16; Acts 10:42; Gen. 42:22; Luke 11:50; and 1 Pet. 4:17 and possibly also to Eph. 1:14; 2 Tim. 4:1; and 1 Pet. 4:5.

The *Martyrdom of Polycarp,* a near-contemporary account of Polycarp's arrest, trial, and execution, uses Scripture similarly, though it is not so dense with allusions. As might be expected from its subject matter, it makes relatively more use of the Gospels, especially the Passion narratives.

The *Shepherd of Hermas*

The *Visions, Mandates,* and *Similitudes* of Hermas constitute by far the longest work conventionally included among the works of the Apostolic Fathers. It is also the one work of early Christian literature, apart from the Revelation to John, to present itself as an original prophecy (Brox 1991: 33-43). As such, it rarely quotes Scripture as authoritative, although it contains many allusions to both Testaments. One work it does quote as Scripture is the lost Jewish apocalyptic book of Eldad and Modad (*Vis.* 3.1.4). Often these allusions are interpretative, as in *Sim.* 9.12.2, "God's Son is a predecessor to all his creation, so that he became to the Father his counselor," a Christianizing allusion to Prov. 8:27-30.

Like other second-century authors, Hermas exhibits an interest in the Genesis creation narrative. His opening vision contains an implicit interpretation of Genesis 1: "God dwelling in the heavens, who created the things that exist from what does not exist and increased and multiplied them for the sake of his holy church, is angry at you, because you have sinned against me." Here two aspects of Hermas's reading reflect earlier Jewish interpretation. One is the affirmation that God created *ex nihilo,* probably taken from 2 Macc. 7:28, which describes God as "creating and articulating all things and making all things to exist out of what does not exist," a passage Hermas actually quotes in *Mand.* 1.1. The other is the tradition that creation is for the sake of Israel, here changed to the church (Dibelius 1923: 433-34).

The *Epistle of Barnabas*

We do not know who wrote *The Epistle of Barnabas* or where it was written. Since it has some affinities to Philo and later Alexandrian exegesis, it is often assumed to have been written in Alexandria. An apparent reference to the Romans' building a temple to Zeus on the site of the destroyed Temple in Jerusalem (16.3-4) is an indication that it was written around 130 CE (Hvalvik 1996: 18-25). Its author states that his purpose is to convey to readers "the perfect knowledge" *(teleia hē gnōsis)* so that it may accompany their faith (1.5), and the context makes evident that such knowledge is a deeper insight into God's will through correct biblical interpretation. Thus, unlike the works discussed so far, in which biblical interpretation is incidental and almost always implicit, *Barnabas* is *about* biblical interpretation. He draws on Hellenistic Jewish and Jewish Christian traditions, including, most notably, traditional proof-texts. Following a practice already attested in the Qumran Jewish community, these were drawn up in lists, known today as *testimonia*. We can infer that *Barnabas* drew on them because many of the same texts he uses occur, often in the same variant form, in later writers such as Justin.

Hvalvik shows that the interpretation of these texts in *Barnabas* is, in its own way, as radical as that of Marcion, a contemporary (1996: 102-36). For Marcion, the Old Testament was valid for Jews, but not for Christians, since it is the product of an inferior god, just but not good, who created the world and gave the Torah. *Barnabas*, on the other hand, argues in effect that it is valid for Christians, but not for Jews. He urges his readers

> not to make yourselves like certain persons, heaping up your sins and saying "The covenant is theirs [the Jews'] and ours [the Christians']." It is ours, but they completely lost it as soon as Moses received it. For Scripture says: "And Moses was on the mountain fasting forty days and forty nights and he received the covenant from the Lord, stone tablets written by the finger of the hand of the Lord" [Exod. 34:28]. But, by turning to idols, they lost it. For the Lord said: "Moses, Moses, go down quickly, for your people, whom you led out of the land of Egypt, has acted lawlessly" [Exod. 32:7]. And Moses understood and threw down the two tablets from his hands, and their covenant was shattered, so that that of Jesus the beloved might be sealed inwardly on our hearts in hope of faith in him. (4.6-8)

It is not as if the Jews have or ever had an old covenant, inferior and superseded; God's only covenant is the covenant of Jesus in the hearts of Christians.

The ritual and ceremonial provisions of the Torah may still be understood as moral directives. *Barnabas* draws on such prophetic passages as Isa.
1:11-13 and 58:5-10 to argue that God never asked for sacrifice or fasting. So, by
implication, to understand the Torah in that sense is mistaken (chs. 2–3).
Thus, for instance, the prohibition against eating pigs is really an exhortation
to avoid people who act like swine, neglecting God when they are doing well
and turning to him only when they are in need. And the other dietary provisions have similar moral interpretations (ch. 10). For the most part, though,
the Torah is to be understood as a prophecy of Christ. Thus, the provisions in
Leviticus 16 or Numbers 19 for the scapegoat and the heifer are prophecies of
Christ (*Barn.* 7), the Temple symbolizes the presence of God in our hearts
(ch. 16), and the Sabbath the second coming of Christ (15). None of the institutions, practices, or hopes of Judaism escape the author's reinterpretation.
The first commandment of the Torah, the commandment to circumcise given
to Abraham (Genesis 17), was actually a prophecy of Christ, because Abraham
circumcised 318 males, a number in which (when written as a numeral in the
Greek manner) we see the name of Jesus and the cross. The Jews resorted to
physical circumcision because an evil angel misled them (ch. 9).

The author's reinterpretation of the "good land" of Exod. 33:1 provides
an example of his argumentation. After quoting proof-texts from Isaiah and
the Psalms, he asks:

> What does the other prophet, Moses, say to them? "See, the Lord God says
> this: 'Enter into the good land, which the Lord of Abraham, Isaac and Ja-
> cob promised and set aside as an inheritance, a land flowing with milk
> and honey'" [Exod. 33:1, 3]. Learn what knowledge (*gnōsis*) says. "Hope,"
> it says, "in Jesus [or Joshua] who is going to appear in the flesh for you."
> For the land, the one suffering, is man, for from the face of the land came
> about the fashioning of Adam. Why, therefore, does he say "a land flow-
> ing with milk and honey"? Blessed be our Lord, brothers, who places in us
> wisdom and an understanding of hidden things. For the prophet speaks a
> similitude (*parabolē*) of the Lord, though who will understand it except a
> wise and perceptive person who loves his Lord? Therefore when he had
> renewed us by the remission of sins, he made us another type (*typos*),
> having our souls in such a childlike way, that it was as if he had refash-
> ioned us. For Scripture speaks about us as he says to his Son, "Let us make
> man in our image and likeness and they shall rule over the beasts of the
> land and over the birds of the heaven and over the fishes of the sea" [Gen.
> 1:26]. And the Lord says, on seeing our beautiful fashioning, "Increase
> and multiply and fill the land" [1:28]. He says these things to the Son. But

I shall show you again how he speaks to us. He has made a second fashioning in the last days. But the Lord says, "See, I am making the last things to be as the first." Therefore this is what the prophet announced, saying "Enter into a land flowing with milk and honey and rule over it" [Exod. 33:3; Gen. 1:28]. See, therefore, we have been refashioned, and again in another prophet he says "See, says the Lord, I shall take from them" — that is, from those whom the Spirit of the Lord had foreseen — "the stony hearts and I shall place in them fleshly ones" [Ezek. 36:26] because he himself was going to appear in the flesh and to dwell in us. For, my brothers, the Lord's dwelling-place in our hearts is a holy temple. (6.8-15)

The loose way *Barnabas* uses the Greek words *parabolē* and *typos* is characteristic of the exegetical terminology in this (and later) periods (see Curti, et al., 1987). Here an occult *gnōsis* accessible to "the wise and perceptive person who loves his Lord" reveals what the Old Testament describes and prescribes for the spiritual life of Christian readers. Such an assertion links *Barnabas* with the Alexandrian tradition as it was to emerge in the writings of Clement of Alexandria and Origen.

The *Epistle to Diognetus*

Another work commonly included among the Apostolic Fathers is the short apologetic work, presumably from the second century, known as the *Epistle to Diognetus*. This work exhibits a hostility to Jewish beliefs and practices similar to that of *Barnabas*. Somewhat like *Barnabas*, its author commends a divinely given *gnōsis* that makes possible an understanding of the mystery of God's plan. It is, in fact, a concern to recommend such *gnōsis* that brings him to his one explicitly exegetical passage. This passage deals, not surprisingly, with Genesis 2–3, which he applies to the spiritual life of Christians much as *Barnabas* does with the "good land." Speaking of those who have understood the Christian message and "who have become a paradise of delight, cultivating in themselves a flourishing tree with all kinds of fruit," the author seeks to allay suspicions that the text disparages knowledge. Conceding that the primordial couple were forbidden to eat from the fruit of the tree of knowledge and punished for doing so, he goes on to argue that "it is not the tree of knowledge (*gnōsis*) that destroys, but disobedience destroys. For what was written is not without significance, namely how God from the beginning planted a tree of knowledge and a tree of life in the midst of paradise, showing that life is through knowledge" (12.1-3).

THE APOLOGISTS

Justin Martyr

Of the Apologists, the one we know best is Justin Martyr, whose surviving works, the *Dialogue with Trypho* and the two *Apologies,* are more extensive than those of any other Christian writer before Irenaeus. Born in the early second century in Samaria of Gentile parents, Justin, by his own account in the *Dialogue,* found Christianity when, after being disappointed with the various Greek philosophical traditions, he sought another source of truth.

> There were certain persons more ancient than all these persons reputed to be philosophers, blessed, just, and God-loving men speaking by a divine spirit and predicting things that were in the future but are now happening; they are called prophets. These men alone have known the truth and proclaimed it to men without being at all timid and shy or susceptible to vainglory, but saying only those things that they had heard and that they had seen while filled with a holy Spirit. Their writings still exist and, provided that he believes them, someone who happens on them can be most benefited concerning original principles, purposes and those things that a philosopher must know. (*Dial. 7*)

These were, of course, the Hebrew prophets, whose ability to predict events in advance convinced Justin that they had access to a truth toward which Greek philosophy was imperfectly striving. Since Justin believed that Moses, if not Adam, was the first of the prophets (see *1 Ap.* 31.9–32.1), "the prophets" are the whole Old Testament interpreted in the Christian church as pointing toward Christ. In becoming a Christian, Justin joined a community that, in continuity with the synagogue, made the reading and exposition of Scripture a central activity in its life (see Gamble 1995, especially pp. 203-18).

Justin himself is a key witness to the development of a Christian Bible. In describing an ordinary Sunday eucharist, he states that:

> On the day called Sunday there is a meeting for all residing either in towns or in the country and the memoirs of the apostles and the writings of the prophets are read as time permits. Then, when the reader has finished, the presiding officer through a discourse makes a rebuke and an exhortation to the imitation of these good things. (*1 Ap.* 67.3-4)

Here, presumably, the "memoirs of the Apostles" are the four Gospels, with which Justin's work shows he was familiar, although he also knew the words of Jesus from harmonies like the one later produced by his pupil Tatian. He relied on Paul's interpretation of Old Testament prophecies but did not cite him as an authority (see Grant 1989: 58-59). In the context of Christian worship and, most likely, study under Christian teachers, Justin became familiar with a number of Christian traditions that isolated particular Old Testament texts and interpreted them as prophecies of Christ and the church.

Skarsaune (1987) has shown how Justin, in his written work, utilized several distinct proof-text traditions. One of these, the Old Testament texts that Paul appealed to in his epistles, we know well. Justin may also have found texts in other early Christian literature such as the now lost *Dialogue of Jason and Papiscus* by Aristo of Pella and in actual *testimonia* lists handed down in Christian school traditions, at least one of which *Barnabas* also drew on. He also shows that Justin knew the Old Testament at first hand, probably in manuscripts obtained from Greek-speaking Jews (Skarsaune 1987). Justin believed that his interpretation of the Old Testament came from Christ himself, "the interpreter of unrecognized prophecies" (*1 Ap.* 32.2), whose grace has revealed to Christians those prophecies that they have understood from the Old Testament (*Dial.* 100.2). Christ himself taught this interpretation to his Apostles, and they in turn have passed it on to the church.

Justin usually stresses the clarity and accessibility of this interpretation. Thus, he states, the existence of "another God," the Logos, alongside God the Father in Genesis 18 "does not have to be interpreted but only heard" (*Dial.* 55-56). This is because the coming of Christ brings into the open an interpretation of the Old Testament that, until then, was hidden and obscure. Nonetheless, he suggests at least once that the prophets actually hide the truth in parables and types so that most people will not understand them easily, and those who are seeking to find them will have to work (*Dial.* 90). Evidently the correct interpretation is not so obvious that a teacher is unnecessary. With this assumption, Justin set himself up as a teacher of "Christian philosophy" in Rome, where he was eventually martyred around 165 CE.

Justin encountered challenges to his understanding of the Old Testament as a prophecy of Christ on three fronts. Heretical Christians such as Marcion denied that the God of the Old Testament, who inspired the prophets, was the same as the God and Father of Jesus Christ; pagans would deny that the prophets offered a philosophy superior to that of the Greeks; and Jews would deny that Jesus Christ genuinely fulfilled Old Testament prophecies. Justin's major writings sought to vindicate his understanding of Old Testament prophecy against each of these groups. His first major work, a *Treatise (Syntagma) Against All the Heresies That Have Arisen,* addressed the heretics. It is now lost, but provided important material to Irenaeus and Tertullian. His second and third major works survive. The second, the *Apologies* (which may be considered a single work, the second being a supplement to the first), addresses pagans. The third, a *Dialogue with Trypho,* addresses Jewish objections. It would seem that in all these works Justin creatively wove together the proof-text traditions he had received, supplementing them with an understanding of the Logos as subject of the Old Testament theophanies that he seems to have developed on his own.

The *Apologies* makes an eloquent plea for toleration of Christians, arguing that Christianity provides a far truer expression of the finest ideals of Greek philosophy than does paganism. Christian doctrine is a more solid basis for belief than the doctrines of any philosophical school because the Bible is divinely inspired. The argument from prophecy proves their reliability:

> But so that no one may contradict us by saying "What rules out that this one whom you call Christ was man entirely human who accomplished by means of magic art the deeds of power we speak of and by such means appeared to be God's son?" we have our demonstration ready. We are not simply believing hearsay, but we are necessarily persuaded by those who prophesied before these things occurred, because with our own eyes we see things that are happening and have happened as they were prophesied. In our opinion this very thing will also seem to you to be the greatest and truest demonstration. (*1 Ap.* 30)

Like Philo before him (see pp. 114-43 above), Justin sought to show that Plato himself, the philosopher he considered closest to Christianity, actually used the Bible, taking from it his teachings on moral responsibility and on creation. He even makes the fanciful claim that Plato's reference to the world soul as "placed like an X" (*Timaeus* 36bc) is taken from Moses' account of the cross-shaped brazen serpent in Numbers 21, itself a prophecy of the cross as a means of salvation. In this case, Plato read the passage without understanding it accurately (*1 Ap.* 60.1-5). The implication is that the Bible does not invalidate Greek philosophy, but completes and corrects it (see Droge 1989).

Justin's interpretation of Jacob's blessing of Judah shows his characteristic way of making the argument from the fulfillment of prophecy in the *First Apology:*

> Moses, who was the first of the prophets, said in these very words: "A ruler shall not be lacking from Judah nor a leader from his loins, until he shall come to whom it is reserved, and he shall be the expectation of nations, tying his foal to the vine and washing his robe in the blood of the

grape" [Gen. 49:10-11]. It is your task to examine carefully and learn until what time there was among the Jews a ruler and king who belonged to them. It was until the appearance of Jesus Christ, our teacher and the interpreter of misunderstood prophecies, as it was announced ahead of time by the divine holy prophetic Spirit through Moses that a ruler would not be lacking from the Jews, until he should come to whom the kingdom was reserved. For Judah was the forefather of the Jews, from whom the Jews take their name. And you [Romans, to whom the *Apology* is addressed], after his appearance had occurred, have had sovereignty over the Jews and have taken control of their entire land. "He shall be the expectation of nations" means that people from all the nations shall expect his reappearance, the very thing that you can see before your eyes so that you may be persuaded by the occurrence. Indeed from all nations men are expecting him who was the one crucified in Judea just before you gained control of the Jews and dominion over the whole land. "Tying his foal to the vine and washing his robe in the blood of the grape" is a symbol indicating what was to happen to Christ and what he was going to do. For a certain foal of an ass was tied to a vine at the entrance to a certain village, which he then ordered his comrades to bring to him, and when it was brought to him he mounted it and, sitting on it, he entered Jerusalem, where the Jews' great temple was, which you later destroyed, and after this he was crucified, so that the rest of the prophecy might be fulfilled. "Washing his robe in the blood of the grape" was an announcement in advance of the passion he would undergo, cleansing by his blood those who believe in him. For what is called a "robe" by the divine Spirit through the prophet is the men who believe in him, in whom there dwells the seed that comes from God, the Logos. The expression "blood of the grape" means that he who was to appear had blood, but not from human seed, but from divine power. But the first power after God the Father and Master of all things is a Son, the Logos. How he was made flesh and became a man we shall say below. For just as it was God and not a human being who made the blood of the vine, so this means that he did not arise from human seed, but from the power of God, as we have just said. (*1 Ap.* 32.1-10)

Here we see how Justin seeks to relate the prophecy to details of the Christian gospel, at the same time excluding other interpretations. Characteristically, Justin applies the prophecy, not just to Christ's passion, but to its effects, cleansing Christian believers from sin.

The *Dialogue with Trypho* argues against a learned and skeptical Jew that the Old Testament does indeed prophesy Jesus as the Messiah and the church as the new Israel. There Justin argues that the Jews have misunderstood the Old Testament because they have understood it "meanly" *(tapeinōs)* or meagerly *(psilōs)* and do not wish to accept that the prophecies have already been accomplished in Christ, whose incarnation provides the necessary key to Scripture (see *Dial.* 100.112). In making this argument, Justin had to deal with the discrepancy between the proof-texts from the Old Testament (often, in effect, interpretive paraphrases that amount to Jewish-Christian targums that he, like the author of *Barnabas,* had received as *testimonia*) and the Old Testament text actually used by Greek-speaking Jews. He argued that Jews had altered their texts to eliminate passages that were clearly prophecies of Christ such as "from the wood" in Ps. 95(96):10, which he knew as "Say among the nations, 'the Lord has reigned from the wood'" (*Dial.* 72-73).

Although, as we have seen, Justin believed that the Jews misunderstood the Old Testament, he avoided the radical position of *Barnabas.* He did this by making a distinction between two ways in which the Old Testament prophesies Christ, in *typoi* (types) and in *logoi* (discourses; see *Dial.* 114.1).

The concept of a *typos,* already attested in such New Testament passages as Rom. 5:14, where Adam is a *typos* of the Christ who is to come, and in 1 Pet. 3:21, where Noah's flood is a *typos* of baptism, allows two levels of meaning. *Typoi* thus are persons or actions that have validity on one level in their own time but also, on a higher level, foreshadow Christ and the church. In Justin, the Passover lamb was a sacrificial offering enjoined on the Hebrew people and is also a *typos* of Christ, by whose blood we are saved from death (*Dial.* 40.1). Likewise, the commandment to circumcise was given to the Hebrews, but it is also a *typos* of the genuine circumcision by which Christians are circumcised from error and wickedness (*Dial.* 41.4). The Jews were mistaken, not in taking the ritual and ceremonial provisions of the Torah as commandments to be followed (because they could not keep a spiritual law), but in failing to recognize the deeper, prophetic significance of the commandments. Human beings can also be *typoi,* so that Joshua, who brought the people of Israel into the promised land, is a type of Christ, who brings all people into eternal salvation (*Dial.* 75, 113). Eve is effectively a *typos* of Mary (*Dial.* 100.5).

Logoi are verbal prophecies of Christ. The Jews misunderstand these as well, but for a different reason. Here they fail to recognize the *prosōpon* (person or character) in which or to whom such prophecies are spoken. Sometimes the Logos who moves them has the prophets speak in their own *prosōpon,* but at other times they assume the *prosōpon* of God the Father or Christ (*1 Ap.* 36; see Rondeau 1982-85: 2.24-29). Examples of prophecies spoken in the *prosōpon* of Christ are Isa. 65:2, "I spread out my hands over unbelieving and contradicting people . . . ," and 50:6-8, "I have offered my back to whippings and my cheeks to blows . . ." (*1 Ap.* 38.1-2). On the other hand, Ps. 109(110):1, "Sit at my right hand . . . ," is spoken in the *prosōpon* of God the Father to another God, his Logos (*Dial.* 56.14). Justin argues that, because they fail to recognize the application of these passages to Christ, the Jews attempt to apply such prophecies to David or to some other Old Testament figure to whom they do not properly apply, as when, in the case of Psalm 109, Trypho considers Hezekiah the addressee.

Tatian

Justin's pupil Tatian took a different tack from his teacher in his one writing that survives, a *Discourse to the Greeks.* In this work, which seldom refers to the Bible, he sought to show that the barbarians, that is, the Jews and Christians, draw on an older and more authoritative tradition than that of the Greeks, which is, in any event, totally vitiated by licentiousness. Tatian's more properly exegetical works have been lost. In the *Discourse* (15), Tatian states that in another work, *On Animals,* he has set forth most accurately what it means for mankind to be created in the image and likeness of God (Gen. 1:26). He also wrote the *Diatessaron,* a harmony of the Gospels that was well received for a time among Syriac-speaking Christians, and a work called *Problems,* in which, according to Eusebius (Tatian, fragment 4 in Eusebius, *EH* 5.13.8), he undertook to set forth "the obscure and hidden parts of the divine Scriptures." Clement of Alexandria criticizes Tatian for eventually becoming an Encratite, if not a Gnostic, giving as evidence his interpretation of Paul in another work, *On Perfection according to the Savior.* Here, Tatian argues that 1 Corinthians 7 effectively condemns marriage and that the Jewish Law, identified as the old husband of Romans 7, was promulgated by another God (Tatian, fragments 5 and 6 in Clement, *Strom.* 3.12).

Athenagoras

In contrast to Tatian, Athenagoras was friendly to Greco-Roman culture. He wrote an apology, the *Plea on Behalf of Christians,* addressed to Marcus Aurelius, between 176 and 180, and may also have written a treatise *On the Resurrection.* Addressing pagans in their own terms, he rarely uses or alludes to the Bible, even though he writes that God used the prophets as a flute-player plays a flute (*Plea* 9). He does commend Jesus' moral teaching in the

Sermon on the Mount and takes arguments against idolatry from the Second
Isaiah.

Melito

The apology addressed to Marcus Aurelius by Melito of Sardis has been lost, as
have other works that made him one of the more prolific Christian writers of
the second century. Even before the discovery of his homily *On the Passover,* he
was a figure of interest in the history of biblical interpretation. We are told that
in his lost work *On Baptism* (fragment 12), he compared the Greek version of
Genesis 22 with Hebrew and Syriac versions, to establish that the ram hung on
the bush just as Christ did on the cross. Finding Old Testament types of Christ
is common in the second century, but this interest in Hebrew is not. *On the
Passover* exhibits no comparable interest in philology, but confirms Melito's importance (Daniélou 1973: 234-36; Young 1997: 231-35). Well into the third century, Christian churches continued the ancient Jewish liturgical custom of
reading about the institution of Passover in Exodus 12 — even churches that did
not, like Melito's church in Asia Minor, still keep the *Pascha* (the Jewish Passover, now celebrated as Easter) on the Fourteenth of Nisan. This custom invited
homilies that sought to relate the original Jewish Passover, which brought about
deliverance from Egypt, to the Christian commemoration of Christ's suffering,
death and resurrection, which brought about deliverance of humanity from sin
and death. Melito, like Origen, whose homily *On the Passover* has also been re-
discovered recently, was evidently glad to take up that invitation.

Melito's work, written in the florid Asiatic style characteristic of
second-century rhetoric, has images from Scripture in practically every line.
He does not simply make a connection between Christ and the Passover
lamb, but finds types throughout the Old Testament. They are there because:

> The Lord had planned in advance his own sufferings in the patriarchs and
> prophets and in the whole people, so that the law and the prophets ratify
> their validity. For the future event that would occur in a new and grand
> way he had planned long in advance, so that when it should occur, it
> would be credible, having been prefigured long before. (fragment 57)

In addition to the Passover lamb, Melito claims to see Christ prefigured in the
murder of Abel, the binding of Isaac, the sale of Joseph, the exposure of Moses, the persecution of David, and the sufferings of the prophets (fragments
59, 69; see Perler 1970).

On the Passover begins with a magnificent passage that has left some scholars with the impression that the work might better be considered a liturgical Easter poem, like the *Exultet,* rather than a homily. Melito concludes this passage with a doxology that identifies the Old Testament "type," "the mystery of the Passover," with the "truth," the whole saving work of Christ, God and man:

> Thus, the slaughter of the sheep,
> > The rite of Passover,
> > And the writing of the Law
> > Have come to Christ
> For whose sake everything in the old Law occurred
> And even more in the new Word.
> > And indeed the Law has become Word,
> > The Old New
> > > — Coming out of Zion and Jerusalem —
> > The commandment grace,
> > The type truth,
> > The sheep a man,
> > And the man God,
> As indeed the Son has been given birth,
> > As the lamb has been led forth,
> > As the sheep has been slaughtered,
> > And as the man has been buried
> God has arisen from the dead
> By nature God and man.
> He who is all things:
> > As the one who judges, law;
> > As the one who teaches, word;
> > As the one who saves, grace;
> > As the one who gives birth, father;
> > As the one who is given birth, Son;
> > As the one who suffers, sheep;
> > As the one who is buried, man;
> > As the one who rises, God.
> This is Jesus the Christ,
> To whom be glory for ever, Amen.
> This is the mystery of the Passover,
> As it is written in the Law,
> As it has just been read.
> (fragments 6-10)

In the course of his homily, Melito goes on to claim that it was, in fact, this mystery that stayed the angel of death on that first Passover night:

> Tell me, angel, what overawed you: the slaughter of the sheep or the life of the Lord? the death of the sheep or the type of the Lord? the blood of the sheep or the spirit of the Lord? It is evident that you were overawed by seeing the mystery of the Lord taking place in the sheep, the life of the Lord in the slaughter of the sheep, and the type of the Lord in the death of the sheep. Therefore you did not strike Israel but deprived the Egyptians alone of their children. (fragments 32-33)

This leads Melito into a more detailed discussion of the relationship between the words and events of the Old Testament and those of the New than we find anywhere else before Irenaeus:

> What is this new mystery, Egypt beaten so as to be destroyed, but Israel protected so as to be saved? Hear the power of the mystery. What is said *(to legomenon)* and what has happened *(to ginomenon)* amount to nothing, beloved, apart from similitude *(parabolē)* and pattern *(prokentēma)*. Everything that happens or is spoken participates in illustrative value — what is spoken in similitude, what has happened in prefiguration *(protupōsis)* — so that, as what happens is manifested by its prototype just as what is spoken is illuminated by its similitude. Unless there is a model *(prokataskeuē)* a work is not raised *(anistatai)*. Or does not one see the future work through the image that prefigures it *(dia tēs eikonos tupikēs)*? This is the purpose of a pattern of the future work out of wax, clay or wood. It exists so that one may see the future object raised loftier in grandeur, mightier in strength, lovelier in form, and richer in preparation through the small and perishable *(phtharton)* pattern. But when that is raised for which exists the type *(typos)*, which once bore the image of the future work, then the type is destroyed as being of no further use, for it has yielded its image to the real thing. But what was once precious becomes worthless, when the precious thing has appeared. For to each is its proper time, to the type its proper time, to the matter *(hylē)* its proper time. You make the type of the truth. You desire it because you see in it the image of the one who is to come. You provide the matter for the type. You desire this because the one who is to come is raised in it. (fragments 34-38)

The implication of the supersession of the type by the truth is the definitive replacement of Judaism by Christianity; the pattern is of no further use once the work itself has appeared. By using the verb *anistēmi* ("raise") for the replacement of the type (characterized as "perishable" and as an "image," words echoing Paul's discussion of the resurrection in 1 Corinthians 15), Melito implicitly suggests that this movement from type to truth is itself of a piece with the resurrection of Christ that Christians celebrate on their Passover. Given the beauty and originality of *On the Passover*, our pleasure at its recovery must be all the more tempered by regret that we have lost the rest of Melito's work.

Theophilus of Antioch

Theophilus of Antioch probably completed his apology, *To Autolycus*, around 180 CE. It marks a stage in the development of the New Testament by treating the Pauline epistles (not just the Gospels, as in Justin) as part of Holy Scripture (see Simonetti 1972). This makes it all the more odd that Theophilus says nothing about the cross or about Christ, even when explaining the word "Christian" (1.12), and he presents a Logos theology that could have come from a Hellenistic Jew like Philo (see Runia 1993: 110-16). As Simonetti puts it, "Theophilus seems to express himself basically in a theological scheme . . . that includes in the activity of one mediator, conceived as God but in subordination to the supreme God, every possibility of contact from God to the world and from the world to God" (1972: 199). This Mediator, responsible for the divine inspiration of the Scriptures, is known with no consistent differentiation as the Logos, Wisdom, or the Holy Spirit. Thus, the Scriptural authors are "Spirit-bearers (*pneumatophoroi*) of the Holy Spirit" who spoke through Wisdom about the creation of the world (2.9), and "the divine Logos" (3.14) exhorts us in the Pauline epistles. He also argues that the three days prior to the creation of the luminous bodies are types (*typoi*) of the triad of God, his Logos, and his Wisdom (2.15).

Simonetti argues that in *To Autolycus* 2-3 Theophilus takes arguments about the harmony of Scripture that he has developed in controversy with the Gnostics and applies them to controversy with pagans (1972: 199-201). This enables him to set the unanimous and accurate testimony of the scriptural authors about creation and primeval history (Genesis 1–3) against the inconsistent and often absurd testimony of Greek poets, philosophers, and historians, providing, in the process, the earliest surviving Christian commentary on the opening chapters of Genesis. His claim that the biblical account is accurate commits Theophilus to present these chapters as a straightforward and convincing account of actual events. In specifics, his interpretation of this account often derives from previous Jewish interpreters (see Grant 1967: 133-42). Theophilus accepts that the three days before the creation of the sun were real days (2.15), their light coming from the Logos, who shone like a lamp in a closed room (2.13), and that God actually rested on the seventh day (2.19). Without inquiring too closely into details, he treats the second creation account, in Genesis 2, as a further explanation of the account already given in Genesis 1.

Although he is willing to speak of the spirit in material terms, the notion that God walked in Paradise (Gen. 3:8) does give him pause, since he has insisted earlier, against the pagans, that God is ineffable, uncontainable, and invisible (1.3-5) and that such a God cannot be in any given place. Nonetheless, he argues that the account can stand as it is, since it is not God himself who walks, but God's "voice," that is, his Logos, who assumes God's character (prosōpon) and speaks with Adam:

> You will ask me: "You say that God must not be contained in a place, and now how is it that you say that he walked in paradise?" Hear what I say. The God and Father of the Universe is uncontained and is not to be found in a place, indeed there is no place of his rest [Isa. 66:1]. But his Logos, through whom he made all things, being his power and wisdom [1 Cor. 1:24]. Taking the prosōpon of the Father and the Lord of the Universe, he is the one who appeared in paradise in God's persona and conversed with Adam. (2.22)

God is absolutely transcendent, but the mediator, Logos/Wisdom/Spirit, can even be physically immanent in the cosmos, not just walking in the garden, but actually mixing with water. Thus, Theophilus asserts that "the spirit borne over the waters was the one that God gave to vivify the creation, just as a soul vivifies a man, by mixing something thin with something thin (for the Spirit is thin and the water is thin), so that the spirit might nourish the water, and the water with the spirit might nourish the creation by penetrating it from all sides" (2.13).

While seeking to present the Genesis account as an accurate and straightforward account, Theophilus's interpretation may lead in unpredictable directions by theological concerns or by his desire to find edifying moral examples. Thus, the quadrupeds and wild beasts are types of men who are ignorant and impious in relation to God, have their minds on earthly things, and do not repent (2.17). More fancifully, in his discussion of the creation of the waters, Theophilus compares the world to a sea that is prevented from becoming too salty by the sweetness of the law of God and the prophets. Warming to his subject, Theophilus states that this sea has fertile islands with safe harbors, and barren and rocky islands. The former are like the churches that provide safe haven from the wrath of God; the latter are the assemblies of heretics where souls are destroyed by error (2.14). Even though he has no problem ascribing wrath to God (1.3), Theophilus's account evidences his care to absolve the God revealed in the Old Testament from the arbitrariness and cruelty ascribed to him by Gnostics. Thus, he states that the expulsion from Paradise was therapeutic, enabling the man to expiate his sin (2.26), and the same is true of Cain's exile (2.29). As Droge points out (1989: 103), Theophilus also implicitly revises the Genesis account by being careful to deny that God intended to withhold knowledge from the first couple, as if he were jealous of Adam. Rather, God told Adam not to eat from the tree of knowledge because, as a newly-created infant, he was not yet ready for it (1.25). Theological considerations also seem to have led Theophilus to pass in silence over the third and fourth commandments in a brief discussion of the Decalogue, probably because Jesus himself was accused of taking God's name in vain and because Christians did not observe the Jewish Sabbath (3.9). For Theophilus, the interpretation of the Bible is thus determined, in large part, by the needs of the Christian community and by a tradition that defines how Old Testament types relate to New Testament fulfillment.

IRENAEUS AND THE LEGACY OF THE APOSTOLIC FATHERS AND APOLOGISTS

With Irenaeus, we reach a turning point in the history of biblical interpretation. He is the first person, so far as we know, to speak explicitly of a Christian Scripture consisting of an Old Testament and a New Testament. His *Demonstration of the Apostolic Preaching* provides the first comprehensive overview of Christian teaching. There, Irenaeus speaks of guarding "the unbending Rule of Faith" received from the Apostles (Iren. *Dem.* 3). He fleshes out this rule in the first part of that book, which relies heavily on the opening chapters of Genesis to explain the human condition, and goes on to explain how the coming and death of Christ address that condition. The second part of the *Demonstration* provides a scriptural proof from prophecy much like that in Justin's *Dialogue*, on which it depends. Here Irenaeus cites divine theophanies in the Old Testament as evidence of the preexistence of the Logos. These include the appearance of the three young men to Abraham at the oaks of Mamre (Genesis 18), which Irenaeus interprets as an appearance of the Son of God accompanied by two angels (Iren. *Dem.* 45), and the theophany at the burning bush (Exodus 3). He uses prosopological interpretation, as Justin did, to argue that God the Father is speaking with his Son in Ps. 109(110):1 and

Isa. 45:1 (Iren. *Dem.* 48-49). Irenaeus also uses proof-texts to demonstrate that the prophets predicted Christ's virgin birth and Davidic ancestry (Iren. *Dem.* 53-67), his miracles, Passion, and glorification (Iren. *Dem.* 68-85), and the calling of the Gentiles to be a new people of God (Iren. *Dem.* 86-97). Irenaeus thus relies on an already well established tradition of interpreting Scripture, one we have already encountered in *Barnabas* and Justin, to give a comprehensive and compelling account of the Christian faith.

Irenaeus's *Detection and Refutation of Gnosis Falsely So Called,* better known as *Against Heresies,* defends the account of the faith set forth in the *Demonstration* against Gnostic accounts that also, in many cases, claim a basis in Scripture. In this defense he relies on concepts taken from Greco-Roman literary studies, the field known in Antiquity as "grammar" and taught as part of rhetorical training (see Grant 1997: 46-51). Ancient grammar spoke of the "plot" or "argument" *(hypothesis)* of a work reflecting the "planning" or "arrangement" *(oikonomia)* of its author. Relying on its usage by the Apologists and in such passages as Eph. 1:10, Irenaeus identified this *oikonomia* with the saving plan of God, beginning in creation, continuing with the call of Israel, and reaching its summation (*anakephalaiōsis,* another grammatical term used in Ephesians) in the death and resurrection of Christ and the calling of the Gentiles. Irenaeus could thus argue that the Rule of Faith handed down by the Apostles through the principal churches they founded was itself the *hypothesis* of Scripture, reflecting the divine *oikonomia.* As the *hypothesis* of Scripture, the Rule of Faith is not some external guideline foreign to Scripture itself. Rather, it is simply the correct way to give meaning and order to the heterogeneous mass of information Scripture contains. Thus, the Rule of Faith clarifies Scripture, giving the reader true, spiritual insight into its meaning and, in the process, guaranteeing the unity of the two Testaments. As Daniélou points out, for Irenaeus, "the novelty of the New Testament lies not in the message, but in the affirmation that these things have come to pass" (1973: 233).

Gnostic heretics, Irenaeus claims, seek to substitute an alternative *hypothesis,* not inherent in Scripture itself but artificially imposed on it and fundamentally distorting its meaning. He compares them to the authors of Homeric centos, who took verses from here and there in the *Iliad* and the *Odyssey* and put them together to tell a new story, and he provides an example of such a work (*AH* 1.9.4). Using an even more powerful image, he compares them to persons who take apart a mosaic, using its individual *tesserae* to make a completely different image:

> Such is their *hypothesis,* which the Prophets did not proclaim, the Lord did not teach, and the Apostles did not hand down, but which they boast

that they understand better than all others, gathering it from sources other than Scripture and, in the words of a proverb, they make a practice of weaving ropes from sand, trying to harmonize plausibly with their own assertions either the dominical parables, the prophetic oracles or the apostolic discourses, so that their fiction may not seem altogether unsupported. They disregard the order and logical connection of the Scriptures and, in so far as they can, they dismember the truth. They transfer passages and recombine them and, by turning one thing into another, they deceive many with their ill-constructed fantasies, made by twisting the Lord's sayings. It is as if someone should take an image of a king, which a wise artist had carefully constructed out of precious stones and, breaking the underlying image of a man, reassemble the stones to make the image of a dog or a fox, and that wretchedly put together, and then claim that this was that fine image of the king, which the wise artist constructed, pointing out that the stones were indeed the very ones well put together by the first artist as an image of the king. (*AH* 1.8.1)

Implicit in Irenaeus's image is the assumption that, while the *hypothesis* of the Old Testament would not have been fully apparent until the coming of Christ, the Rule of Faith now makes it plain. He makes this clear when he interprets the treasure in a field of Matt. 13:44 as Christ, who was hidden in the Old Testament, but for Christians is now brought to light by his advent:

[Christ] is indeed the treasure hidden in a field (for "a field" is the world). Christ is truly the treasure hidden in the Scriptures [cf. *AH* 4.26.1], since he was signified by types *(typoi)* and parables *(parabolai)*. How could his human nature be understood before the consummation arrived of those things prophesied, namely Christ's advent? On this account the prophet Daniel said: "Shut up the discourses, and seal the book until the time of consummation, until many learn and knowledge be completed. For in that time, when the dispersion shall be accomplished, they shall know all these things" [Dan. 12:4, 7]. But Jeremiah also said: "In the last days they shall understand them" [Jer. 23:20]. For every prophecy, before it comes to pass, is, for humanity, full of enigmas and ambiguities. But when the time comes and that which was prophesied happens, then the prophecies have a clear and certain exposition. (*AH* 2.28.3)

We should not, however, assume that, in Irenaeus's view, the meaning of Scripture is altogether plain and transparent even now that Christ has come. He claims, rather, that Scripture is often hard, if not impossible, for us to un-

derstand and holds out the possibility that we may continually learn from
Scripture about God's plan, not just in this life, but in the life to come (*AH*
28.3). He does not in principle deny the possibility of the Gnostic claim that
the Apostles understood some of these difficult passages and transmitted
them in secret to certain select followers. Instead he argues that, had the
Apostles handed down secret mysteries, they would have transmitted them to
the persons they left in charge of the churches after them, and that those persons would in turn have transmitted them to their successors in apostolic succession (*AH* 3.3.1). Nonetheless, he claims that any deeper understanding of
Scripture, whether on the basis of deeper insight or secret tradition, must
supplement rather than contradict its plain meaning. Thus, what is obscure
in Scripture, such as the meaning of the Gospel parables, must be interpreted
on the basis of what is plain, such as the identity of the God and Father of Jesus Christ with the Creator of the Universe. The Gnostics err by bringing
Scripture's plain and unambiguous teaching into question on the basis of
their idiosyncratic interpretation of obscure passages (*AH* 2.27.1).

The Irenaeus's Scriptural interpretation, itself in many ways a recapitulation
of the interpretation of the Apostolic Fathers and Apologists, is one of his
great legacies to the subsequent Christian tradition. He fully articulates the
idea of a Christian Bible, in which both Testaments give the same teaching,
the New simply stating explicitly a doctrine implicit in the Old. He also articulates important principles that would govern future interpretation. One of
these is the principle that the apostolic Rule of Faith — understood not as
something apart from Scripture but as an authoritative interpretation of
Scripture which can be demonstrated out of Scripture itself — is the fundamental "argument" (*hypothesis*) that clarifies the Bible's meaning. Another is
the principle that clear and unambiguous passages govern the interpretation
of those that are obscure and ambiguous.

The two great treatises dealing with biblical interpretation later on in
the patristic era show Irenaeus's legacy. Origen's *On First Principles* sets forth
the apostolic Rule of Faith as the basis of a theological investigation seeking
to understand the fuller implications of Scripture; Augustine's *On Christian
Teaching* insists on the priority of clear passages over ambiguous ones. Both
Origen and Augustine, along with other great patristic interpreters, would
also follow Irenaeus and the Apologists in looking to the early chapters of
Genesis for an understanding of the human condition and in applying the resources of Greco-Roman grammar to biblical interpretation. However, even
as Christian theologians in the patristic era became more sophisticated in
their interpretation of Scripture, they never abandoned the fundamental
scriptural orientation we already find among the Apostolic Fathers, who use

the Bible, not simply to give an account of the Christian faith, but also to guide them in everyday conduct, both individually and as a community, and to provide them an indispensable language of worship.

BIBLIOGRAPHY

Ackroyd, P. R., and C. F. Evans (eds.)
1970   *The Cambridge History of the Bible* I: *From the Beginnings to Jerome.* Cambridge: Cambridge University Press.

Blowers, P. M.
1997   *The Bible in Greek Christian Antiquity.* Notre Dame: University of Notre Dame Press.

Brox, N.
1991   *Der Hirt des Hermas* = *Kommentar zu den Apostolischen Vätern* VII. Göttingen: Vandenhoeck und Ruprecht.

Curti, C., et al.
1987   *La terminologia esegetica nell'antichità: Atti del Primo Seminario di antichità christiane, Bari, 25 ottobre 1984.* Bari: Università di Bari.

Daniélou, J.
1956   *The Bible and the Liturgy.* Notre Dame: Notre Dame University Press.
1962   "Figure et événement chez Méliton de Sardes." In A. N. Wilder, ed., *Neotestamentica et Patristica: Eine Freundesgabe Herrn Professor Dr. Oscar Cullmann zu seinem 60. Geburtstag überreicht,* 282-92. Leiden: Brill.
1964   *The Theology of Jewish Christianity: A History of Early Christian Doctrine before the Council of Nicaea* I. Trans. J. A. Baker. Philadelphia: Westminster.
1967   *Études d'exégèse judéo-chrétienne (Les Testimonia).* Paris: Beauchesne.
1973   *Gospel Message and Hellenistic Culture: A History of Early Christian Doctrine before the Council of Nicaea* II. Trans. J. A. Baker. Philadelphia: Westminster.

Dawson, D.
1992   *Allegorical Readers and Cultural Relativism in Ancient Alexandria.* Berkeley: University of California Press.

Dibelius, M.
1923   *Der Hirt des Hermas.* Handbuch zum Neuen Testament, Ergänzungs-Band, Die Apostolischen Väter IV. Tübingen: Mohr.

Donfried, K. P.
1974   *The Setting of Second Clement in Early Christianity.* Leiden: Brill.

Draper, J. A.
1996   *The* Didache *in Modern Research.* Leiden: Brill.

Droge, A. J.

1989   *Homer or Moses? Early Christian Interpretations of the History of Culture.* Tübingen: Mohr.

Gamble, H. Y.

1995   *Books and Readers in the Early Church: A History of Early Christian Texts.* New Haven: Yale University Press.

Granfield, P., and J. A. Jungmann (eds.)

1970   *KYRIAKON: Festschrift Johannes Quasten.* Münster: Aschendorff.

Grant, R. M.

1957   *The Letter and the Spirit.* London: Macmillan.

1967   *After the New Testament: Studies in Early Christian Literature and Philosophy.* Philadelphia: Fortress.

1984   *Short History of the Interpretation of the Bible.* 2d ed. Philadelphia: Fortress.

1989   *Greek Apologists of the Second Century.* Philadelphia: Westminster.

1993   *Heresy and Criticism: The Search for Authenticity in Early Christian Literature.* Louisville: Westminster/John Knox.

1997   *Irenaeus of Lyons.* London: Routledge.

Hall, S. G.

1970   "Melito PERI PASCHA 1 and 2: Text and Interpretation." In P. Granfield and J. A. Jungmann, eds., 1970: II:236-48.

Hvalvik, R.

1996   *The Struggle for Scripture and Covenant: The Purpose of the Epistle of Barnabas and Jewish-Christian Competition in the Second Century.* Tübingen: Mohr.

Knopf, R.

1920   *Lehre der zwölf Apostel, Zwei Klemensbriefe.* Handbuch zum Neuen Testament, Ergänzungs-Band, Die Apostolischen Väter 1. Tübingen: Mohr.

Kugel, J. L., and R. Greer

1986   *Early Biblical Interpretation.* Philadelphia: Westminster.

Margerie, B. de

1980-83 *Introduction à l'histoire de l'exégèse.* 3 vols. Paris: Cerf.

Pépin, J.

1976   *Mythe et allégorie: Les origines grecques et les contestations judéo-chrétiennes.* Paris: Études Augustiniennes.

Perler, O.

1970   "Typologie der Leiden des Herrn in Melitons PERI PASCHA." In P. Granfield and J. A. Jungmann (eds.) 1970: I, 256-65.

Rondeau, M.-J.

1982   *Les commentaires patristiques du Psautier* I: *IIIe-Ve siècles.* Orientalia Christiana Analecta 219 and 220. Rome: Pont. Institutum Studiorum Orientalium.

Runia, D. T.
1993   *Philo in Early Christian Literature: A Survey.* Assen: van Gorcum/Philadelphia: Fortress.

Schoedel, W. L.
1985   *Ignatius of Antioch.* Philadelphia: Fortress.

Simonetti, M.
1972   "La sacra scrittura in Teofilo d'Antiochia." In J. Fontaine and C. Kannengiesser, eds., *EPEKTASIS: Mélanges patristiques offerts au Cardinal Jean Daniélou,* 197-207. Paris: Beauchesne.
1985   *Lettera e/o allegoria. Un contributo all storia dell'esegesi patristica.* Rome: Augustinianum.

Skarsaune, O.
1987   *The Proof from Prophecy: A Study of Justin Martyr's Proof-Text Tradition: Text-Type, Provenance, Theological Profile.* Leiden: Brill.

Windisch, H.
1920   *Der Barnabasbrief.* Handbuch zum Neuen Testament, Ergänzungs-Band, Die Apostolischen Väter 3. Tübingen: Mohr.

Young, F. M.
1997   *Biblical Exegesis and the Formation of Christian Culture.* Cambridge: Cambridge University Press.

CHAPTER 12

Alexandrian and Antiochene Exegesis

Frances Young

The exegetes of the third and fourth centuries inherited a body of traditional interpretations, notably those that understood Old Testament texts as prophecy of New Testament fulfillments. Their contribution was to introduce more systematic methods, to produce running commentaries, and to engage in discussion of what we would now call hermeneutical principles: thus the Antiochenes in the fourth century challenged the allegorical approach adopted by the Alexandrians in the third. Into this more systematic exegesis the traditional interpretations were incorporated. Thus the important shift revealed in the extant material is from prophetic or parenetic use of particular texts abstracted from their contexts to the development of biblical scholarship and more self-conscious exegetical techniques.

In that regard the work of Origen must take center stage in discussion of Alexandrian methodology — he was the first real scholar. But he had significant precursors. Clement of Alexandria left no systematic commentaries, but the way in which he used scriptural texts and his hermeneutical approach to the Bible were nevertheless formative. Even more important is the work of the first-century Jewish philosopher Philo (see chapter 4 above). Even though Origen acknowledges his debt to neither Philo nor Clement, their influence can hardly be discounted. Until recently scholarly discussion focused on the allegorical methods developed by Origen on the foundations laid by these predecessors, and against which the Antiochenes later reacted.

ALLEGORY

Origen has generally been regarded as a Platonist enabled by allegory to read the Bible in accordance with his philosophical presuppositions, though the primacy of his exegetical activity was emphasized by Crouzel (e.g., 1989). It seemed clear that Origen spelled out his techniques in Book IV of the *De Principiis,* though most investigators were then somewhat exercised to explain exactly how these methods were applied in the commentaries and homilies that have come down to us. As will become apparent, research has more recently given a new slant to this discussion, but it is worth beginning with Origen's own presentation of his hermeneutics as it has been generally read. The following five points are repeated in standard literature:

1. Origen attributed "literal" interpretation to the Jews, and expected Christians to go beyond the mere letter to the spiritual meaning.
2. He believed that there were three levels of meaning in Scripture analogous to the body, soul and spirit; he developed this analogy from Philo's dichotomous analogy of body and soul, and justified it on the basis of Prov. 22:20-21, "Describe these things in a threefold way." These three senses were literal, moral, and spiritual. Simple believers might remain at the level of the letter, but the elite should progress to the higher levels.
3. Origen found "stumbling-blocks," problems, impossibilities *(aporiai)* at the literal level in Scripture — indeed not every passage has a literal sense. These problems he thought were intended by the Holy Spirit in order to alert the reader to the need to look for the spiritual meaning.
4. Adopting the Jewish claim that every jot and tittle is significant, Origen encouraged often far-fetched allegorical explanations of details that have no obvious spiritual import.
5. Origen accepted without question the unity of the Bible and found it in the Holy Spirit's *skopos* (aim) to impart the truth but to conceal it in a narrative dealing with the visible creation so that proper examination of these records would point to spiritual truths.

On this basis, and by comparison with contemporary philosophical allegorization of Homer, Origen was said to have a poor grasp of the historical nature of the biblical material and to be interested principally in the *hyponoia* or "undersense" discovered by reading the text allegorically; therefore he did not really understand the Bible at all (Hanson 1959, especially).

Origen could, of course, justify his search for spiritual meanings on the basis of scriptural texts: Gal. 4:22-26; 1 Cor. 2:7-8; 9:9-10; 10:1-4; Col. 2:17; Eph.

5:32; and Heb. 8:5; 10:1. These texts were his principal warrants, to which some key Old Testament texts were added, such as: "I will open my mouth in parables; I will utter dark sayings *(problēmata)* from the beginning." (LXX Ps. 77:2). Allegory was also encouraged by the "oracular" approach to Scripture, which, from the earliest days of Christianity, had treated texts as riddles pointing to Christ; indeed, Origen took up traditional "types" and Messianic interpretations into his spiritual sense.

But most modern discussions have treated his approach as alien to the Bible and drawn from the Hellenistic environment. For all his scriptural justifications, Origen, it has been said, really worked from Clement's position that, as all religious language was in the form of oracles, enigmas, mysteries, and symbols — this was true of Plato's myths as well as those of the mystery religions — the truth of Scripture also came through a veil, and the key to unlock the hidden mysteries was Christ (Clement, *Strom.* 5.4.20–10.66).

This approach to describing and assessing Origen's exegesis, however, constantly finds itself in difficulties. It has been recognized that the attribution of "literal" interpretation to Jews of the time does less than justice to contemporary Jewish exegesis or to Origen's own debt to Jewish scholars (de Lange 1976). So far from working with three levels, it was often noted that in practice Origen's commentaries and homilies evidenced a twofold interpretation, as indeed he affirmed to Celsus (*C. Cels.* 7.20); and so far from evacuating the literal sense if it was difficult, Origen often took enormous trouble over it:

> He admits that the measurements given for the ark appear at first sight totally inadequate to house fourteen specimens of every clean and four of every unclean animal in the world, but claims on the authority of a learned Jew that the cubits there mentioned are to be understood as geometric cubits and therefore all the measurements need in practice to be squared. (Wiles 1970: 471)

To confuse things further one often finds a whole series of suggested interpretations, most of a "spiritual" kind, maybe psychological, mystical, moral, ecclesiological, christological, or eschatological. Such descriptions refer to content, of course, rather than method, and alert us to the importance of the reference of the text. For the Origen of the commentaries, the "tropological" or metaphorical character of the language usually pointed to a range of potential spiritual and moral references. Torjesen (1985a) relates these multiple readings to the various needs of the hearers: Origen never intended his threefold classification to apply to different "senses" of Scripture or separate classes of Christian; rather they correspond to different stages on a progressive journey to perfection. But meanwhile the perplexing questions concerning Origen's different senses were complicated further by the discussion of typology.

In the 1950s, Daniélou's attempt to distinguish typology and allegory began to have an impact, particularly in English through the publication of *Essays on Typology* by Lampe and Woollcombe (1957). The result was general acceptance of the view that typology presupposed a sense of history where allegory did not, and that whereas modern exegesis had problems with allegory, ". . . we can have no objection to a typology which seeks to discover and make explicit the real correspondences in historical events which have been brought about by the recurring rhythms of the divine activity" (Lampe 1957:29). This meant distinguishing biblical from platonic typology. Thus the Alexandrians were credited with having confused historical with symbolic typology — that is, with allegory. This analysis having gained widespread acceptance, standard accounts of early Christian exegesis described patristic exegetical methods in terms of three senses: literal, typological, and allegorical (e.g., Grant and Tracy 1984; Simonetti 1994). Typology, it was suggested, had biblical roots and was reclaimed (or indeed formally developed, Guinot 1989) by the Antiochenes as an acceptable method that did not evacuate biblical history (cf. Greer 1961; Wiles 1970; Kugel and Greer 1986, etc.). Meanwhile Origen incorporated many traditional types into his fundamentally allegorical reading.

The chief weakness of this definition of typology, however, is inherent in that last point: in practice drawing a line between typology and allegory in early Christian literature is impossible, not just in Origen's work, where prophetic and symbolic types are fully integrated into his unitive understanding of what the Bible is about, but also, for example, in the tradition of Paschal Homilies beginning with the *Peri Pascha* of Melito. As for history, its supposed importance for typology is already threatened by the evident use of typology in Hebrews and *Barnabas,* where repeated rituals rather than past events provide types of Christ's atonement. The word "typology" is in any case not in patristic vocabulary: it is a modern coinage (Charity 1966). Typology may still prove a useful heuristic tool (Young 1994, 1997), but in the attempt to analyze exegetical methods it is a distraction.

More significant for the light thrown on Origen have been studies of commentaries by the fourth-century Alexandrian Didymus the Blind, which were discovered among the Tura Papyri in a munitions dump during the Second World War (Bienert 1972, Tigcheler 1977). Origen's allegory had always had an arbitrary feel about it because of the multiplicity of meanings he was prepared to give a particular passage, but at the same time, as already noted, it seemed to work essentially at two levels. At first Didymus seemed to confirm this: although he used a range of terms *(anagōgē, allēgoria, theōria, tropologia, dianoia)*, they all referred to a "higher meaning" reached by interpreting symbolically, mystically, or spiritually. Bienert (1972), however, argues that *anagōgē* was restricted to christological meanings and that Didymus had a strong sense of the unity of Scripture, with Christ as the key.

Tigcheler (1977) concentrates on the structure of Didymus's hermeneutics. Didymus distinguished sense and reference, first at the level of the wording, that is, the literal sense and the factual reference, and then at the level of figurative discourse. Here a series of traditional "figures" (such as Jerusalem = church) were consistently applied to reach the sense, and then enquiry followed as to whether, understood this way, the text referred to some reality in the spiritual world. *Allēgoria* led to the recognition of a figurative sense in the language, *anagōgē* to the spiritual reality referred to. The importance of this analysis is twofold: (1) it took account of how Didymus collects scriptural texts to establish consistent scriptural senses and metaphors, thus demonstrating that allegory was not simply arbitrary; (2) it drew attention to the distinction between the roles of sense and reference in determining meaning. Both will prove important as we return to a reassessment of the work of Origen.

As noted, most accounts of Origen's exegetical methods take *De Principiis* 4 as their starting point, but there are two reasons for being cautious in this regard. The first is that Origen is clearly in "apologetic" mode there. He is concerned to show why the Scriptures are to be accepted as divinely inspired (4.1) and how to avoid the misunderstandings of Scripture found among Jews and heretics (4.2). He is justifying controversial aspects of Christian interpretation rather than giving an account of exegetical methodology. The second reason is that he devoted a huge span of his life to biblical scholarship, and an examination of what remains soon reveals that *De Principiis* provides no description of what he did as a text critic, commentator, and preacher. He enunciates certain principles but does not describe methods, most of which were learned in school and never articulated.

PHILOLOGY

The exegetical practice of the schools gives us the clue to Origen's methodology (as already indicated by Hatch 1888). Origen was a philologist (Neuschafer 1987) who exploited school methods to interpret and defend the

Bible (Grant 1961; Young 1997). If we are to understand Origen's methodology we need to understand how texts were interpreted in the schools of grammar, rhetoric, and philosophy in the Greco-Roman world, where texts were the basis of education (see, e.g., Marrou 1948). This will also give access to the methodological objections advanced by the Antiochenes against Origen's use of allegory (Young 1989).

The school exegesis presumed by Origen was divided into *methodikon* and *historikon*. 1. *To methodikon* dealt with the practical problems of reading texts. This was a world in which all copies were handwritten without word division or punctuation. Text-critical questions and problems of construal were bound to occupy the class. So were discussions of archaic words and forms (e.g., in Homer), as well as the identification of figures of speech. This was attending to the "letter" of the text, its "physical" form, and is what Origen was engaged in when he compiled the Hexapla, made comments on variant readings in his commentaries, traced the "idioms" of the Bible by compiling catenae of texts (using the Bible to interpret the Bible as Porphyry used Homer to interpret Homer), or engaged in etymological explanations or identified "tropes," that is, figures of speech.

A whole range of terms could be used for this examination of the "wording," and often they are translated as if they referred to the "literal sense"; but this does not correspond exactly with what we might mean by a "literal" reading, still less have they to do with the "historical" reference of the text. Indeed, the identification of figures of speech would lead to the conclusion that a reading "according to the letter" was wrong: metaphor implies another meaning, etymology opened up other possibilities of interpretation, and allegory itself was a recognized figure of speech. Origen exploited all this. His emulator Didymus attended to the "letter" in a similar way: hence some of the features noted by Tigcheler. Of the terms thought to describe the allegorical or "higher" sense, the most common, *tropologia,* is the identification of metaphorical language — nothing more and nothing less!

2. *To historikon* would then engage the school pupil. This was the assemblage of explanatory comments in order to illuminate the content and reference. Depending on the text it could draw on geographical, astronomical, musical, or any other kind of knowledge. It could spell out the full version or variant versions of narratives alluded to in the text, including not just historical facts but mythological events and characters. Origen was a typical scholar following methods well-tried in relation to the Greek classics, but in his case researching the necessary background information for the "barbarian" literature that had become authoritative for the church. Often he fell into the trap of showing off his erudition, a fault against which the Roman educationalist,

Quintilian, issued warnings, but this is why we find discussion of differences between the Gospels as well as questions about where all the refuse went in the Ark.

3. The rhetoricians of antiquity distinguished between the content or matter of the text *(ho pragmatikos topos)* and its wording *(ho lektikos topos)*. The "mind" *(dianoia)* was clothed in the "letter" *(gramma)*. It was evidently possible to say the same thing in many different ways, just as one could express the same idea in different languages. So the budding rhetor would learn to consider the appropriate style for the matter in hand, and since the schools took classical texts as models, the pupil would learn to look for the way the style fitted the material, and the underlying theme or argument *(hypothesis)*.

Origen saw the "wording" of Scripture as the "veil" in which the Spirit clothed the divine intent *(skopos)*. For Origen attention to the words was important precisely because they both revealed and concealed what they signified. The multiplicity of words, the inconsistencies, were to be regarded as different medicines adapted to different needs. Untrained people might think they were discordant, but all were really in harmony, the various notes of Scripture producing a single sound of salvation from the one perfectly attuned instrument of God. Origen was adapting a classic rhetorical distinction to demonstrate the inspired nature of the Scriptures (Young 1997).

4. It was important for the budding lawyer to be able to challenge the plausibility of narratives delivered by the opposition in court. Methods of *anaskeuē* (refutation) and *kataskeuē* (confirmation) were therefore taught in the schools through the medium of literature (Grant 1961). A narrative might be incredible because of the character to whom the action is attributed, the nature of the action, its timing or mode of performance, or the motive or reason adduced. If a literary narrative was shown to be implausible, it was taken to have some other significance.

Origen was adept at these techniques and turned them to good use in his argument with Celsus. They also enabled him to point out impossibilities and inconsistences in Scripture. He substituted the more biblical words "enigma" and "parable" for "myth" and "fiction," but essentially applied the rationalistic criticism of the schools to biblical narratives. He thought God could adopt such genres for the benefit of the audience, just as an orator could.

5. Plato's classic attack on the poets as morally subversive, echoed by Plutarch, who could speak of poetry as a seductive form of deception, stimulated the school tradition that literature should be read as morally edificatory. In reading literature, therefore, moral judgment *(krisis)* was essential. Plutarch himself demonstrates how admonition and instruction were found in tales and myths, how text was critically weighed against text, how the inextri-

cable mixture of good and bad was taken to be true to life and therefore useful for exercising moral discrimination. Another defense of traditional narratives found to be immoral, especially among philosophers such as the Stoics, was their allegorization.

Origen exercised the same *krisis* in relation to biblical material. Its moral teachings were generally to be followed, but not without discrimination. Its characters were often types on which to model one's behavior, but where this was obviously not the case, the import of the text must lie somewhere else.

Origen's commentaries and homilies demonstrate these standard methods at work. As we shall see, the Antiochenes shared these techniques and assumptions with Origen. They had more in common with him than might at first appear. Why then did they react against the Origenist tradition? The presentation just given hints time and again at the way in which the very practice of scholarship allowed Origen to be diverted from the "plain" meaning of the text, the "obvious" narrative sequence, and enabled him to read the text in ways that appear alien to common sense. At the very least the Antiochenes, like more recent critics, instinctively felt that Origen had not got at what the text was about.

HISTORIA

Holy Scripture knows the term "allegory" but not its application. Even the blessed Paul uses the term . . . [in Gal. 4:24]. But his use of the word and his application is different from that of the Greeks. The Greeks speak of allegory when something is understood in one way but said in another. . . . Let me give an example. The Greeks say that Zeus, changing himself into a bull, seized Europa and carried her across the sea to foreign places. This story . . . is taken to mean that Europa was carried across the sea having boarded a ship with a bull as a figurehead. . . . This is allegory. Or another example: Zeus called Hera his sister and his wife. . . . [In other words] Zeus had intercourse with his sister Hera. . . . This is what the letter suggests: but the Greeks allegorize it to mean that, when ether, a fiery element, mingles with air, it produces a certain mixture which influences events on earth. . . . Of such kind are the allegories of the Greeks. . . . Holy Scripture does not speak of allegory in this way.

This statement appears in the preface to a commentary on Psalm 118 now generally attributed to Diodore of Tarsus, a leading figure in the Antiochene school (translation from Froehlich 1984: 87-88). It implies exactly that common sense reaction while at the same time carrying the charge that allegory is an alien import into the biblical texts. The examples show how immoralities and impossibilities (a bull could never swim that far!) led to rationalizing or philosophizing alternative readings. Diodore thinks it inappropriate to apply such methods to Scripture.

In their anti-allegorical statements the Antiochenes stressed the *historia*. In their commentaries they debated such questions as whether Paul had visited Colossae or not (Theodore took one view, Theodoret the opposite). Notoriously, Theodore even challenged many traditional messianic interpretations, setting the message of the prophets in the context of their own time. It is perhaps hardly surprising that there has been a tendency for the classic modern studies almost to imply that the Antiochene reaction against allegory had the same concerns as modern historical critics.

> The school of Antioch insisted on the historical reality of the biblical revelation. They were unwilling to lose it in a world of symbols and shadows. . . . (Grant and Tracy 1984: 66)

> Theodore, largely because of his sense of history, concentrated on giving a fair exposition of what the text really meant when it was first written. (Greer 1961: 105)

Thus, interested in the literal sense because they had a sense of history, they developed historical typology (see above) as the way to *theōria* (contemplative insight):

> Where the Alexandrians used the word *theory* as equivalent to allegorical interpretation, the Antiochene exegetes used it for a sense of scripture higher and deeper than the literal or historical meaning, but firmly based on the letter. This understanding does not deny the literal meaning of scripture but is grounded on it. . . . (Grant and Tracy 1984: 66)

Thus, it is the standard view that, despite their unfortunate tendency to be distracted by dogmatic and anti-heretical concerns — they were after all children of their own time — the Antiochenes' historical grounding meant that they understood the Bible much better than did Origen and the allegorists.

That may indeed be true, but what similarity there is with modern commentators lies much more in the fact that the roots of all commentary ultimately lie in the activities of the schools, outlined above (Hatch 1888). Commentaries follow through the text providing explanatory notes on a variety of different kinds of problems. Some kinds of difficulty are perennial: all commentators of every age face similar philological problems, problems of text, construal, vocabulary, etc. Other issues are generated by the cultural and intellectual context within which the Bible is read. The Antiochenes' concern with *historia* was not the same as the modernist's questions about historicity.

> No contrast was drawn between the historical and theological meaning of Scripture; the *historia* was the obvious narrative meaning of the text and must not be confused with the modern use of "history" as a way of talking about the reconstruction of what really happened by using the texts as historical evidence. (Kugel and Greer 1986: 195)

Miracles and prophecies, Adam and Satan — none of these were then challenged by science or psychology; ironically, the Antiochenes would have dismissed the modern historical critic as they did the allegorist when it comes to rationalizing away stories such as the Fall. Their problems were dogmatic rather than historical. We shall understand their reaction against allegory much better if we set them firmly in their own time.

The key features of the Antiochene commentaries and homilies belong to the school tradition already sketched (Young 1989; 1997). Characteristic of both are opening paragraphs setting out the *hypothesis* of the text — they want to understand the subject matter (*pragma*[*ta*]). Details of the text are then examined point by point. Comments range from discussion of alternative readings to matters like correct punctuation and proper construal of sentences. Questions of translation and etymology, explanations of foreign words, and attention to metaphor and figures of speech all feature, as do mini-concordances arguing the special biblical flavor of particular words and phrases. Here is *to methodikon* of the schools. Then they explore sequence of thought, test text against text, and provide background material, often utilizing other texts in the Bible to set the text in question in its appropriate context. Here they speak of the *historia,* and they were concerned to get it right, to show, for example, how a prophet's word fit its historical context as evidenced in the biblical narrative, to describe Paul's Corinth, and so on. What they are engaged in is *to historikon* of the schools. The concerns shown in the *hypothesis* feed into this verse-by-verse commentary: summary and paraphrase are persistent techniques used by the Antiochenes to bring out the gist of the argument or the sequence of the narrative, together with the relationship of either or both to the circumstantial detail produced by their "historical" investigation. So context and thrust are not lost under the mass of detailed commentary. Like the school exegetes they sought to discern the underlying idea dressed up in the words and style of the text. They often showed concern with the sequence *(akolouthia)* of an argument or story and discussed genre and the particular literary characteristics of, for example, prophecy.

Their methods, then, were philological and literary. It has been suggested (Young 1989; hinted at by Froehlich 1984) that the Antiochene reaction against Origen's allegory can be understood best against the background of the centuries-old struggle between the rhetorical and philosophical schools. Philosophy since Plato had accused rhetoric of teaching people to make lies plausible and encouraged withdrawal from the corruptions of public life to contemplation of truth. Rhetoric had countered by sneering at philosophy as useless speculation and emphasizing that their teachers did teach morality since it was the key to social success. Associated with this was a different approach to texts. Rhetoricians found morals in the stories and myths of the classic texts that were the basis of education through the kind of *krisis* outlined above; philosophers used allegory to uncover the deeper truth enshrined in texts they criticized for immorality. Of course, the contrast cannot be pressed too far: Aristotle and the Stoics had developed much of the linguistic analysis and rhetorical method used in all the schools, and allegory was not confined to philosophers. Key witnesses belonged to both traditions, as indeed did Origen. It is nevertheless useful to note that rhetoricians and philosophers had different approaches to reading texts, and these seem to underlie the different hermeneutical principles espoused by Origen and the Antiochenes.

No modern historical critic would find morals and dogma in the texts in the same way that the Antiochenes did; on the other hand, it was precisely here that the Antiochenes wanted to retain the *historia*. The difference between their moral reading and allegorical interpretation is well illustrated by comparing Origen's treatment of the feeding story with that of John Chrysostom. Origen took the story as symbolic of spiritual feeding. The desert place represented the desert condition of the masses without the law and word of God, and the disciples were given power to nourish the crowds with rational food. The five loaves and two fish symbolized Scripture and the Logos. Chrysostom, however, suggests that Christ looked up to heaven to prove he is of the Father and used the loaves and fish rather than creating food out of nothing to stop the mouths of dualist heretics like Marcion and Manichaeus. He let the crowds become hungry and only gave them loaves and fish, equally distributed, to teach the crowd humility, temperance, and charity and to have all things in common. He wanted to be sure they did not become slaves to the belly. Chrysostom's points were grounded in the *historia*.

What then did the Antiochenes mean by *historia?* Ancient usage is crucial to answering this. On the one hand, *to historikon* embraced all kinds of background information; on the other, narrative criticism assessed the plausibility of stories and classed them as "myth," "fiction," or *historia.* While the last was expected to be a "true story" (Wheeldon 1989), more often than not it went far beyond such expectations because of the rhetorical inventiveness of the authors (Josephus reports a speech delivered just before all the witnesses committed suicide!), their dramatic construction of events around the tragic themes of fate and fortune, the propensity to provide variant versions so that the audience could make up its own mind, and the inclusion of a similar range of subjects as those embraced by *to historikon.* "History" was a rhetorical genre intended to improve as much as inform, and novelistic romances parodied the conventions of history. Against that background, let us look back at Antiochene discussions, beginning with Eustathius of Antioch, who wrote the first anti-allegorical treatise, *On the Witch of Endor and against Origen.*

"Eustathius rejects not only Origen's interpretation of this particular passage but his entire allegorical exegesis because it deprives scripture of its historical character." So Quasten (1962-64: 3:303). But this is simply not borne out by the text (see Greer 1973; Young 1989, 1997). Eustathius begins by attacking Origen for paying attention to *onomata* (names, terms) not *pragmata* (deeds, things), or in other words, the wording, not the subject matter. It appears that Origen had made certain deductions about the resurrection on the basis of the statement that the witch summoned up Samuel from Hades. Eustathius argues that only God can raise the dead, therefore the witch cannot have done it, and Samuel was not raised at all. He goes on to explain that the devil used the witch to play upon the mad mind of Saul and induce him to believe he saw Samuel. True, in a long aside Eustathius objects to the fact that Origen allegorizes Moses' accounts of creation, Paradise and many other things including Gospel narratives; he regards it as scandalous to allegorize those key narratives and then treat this story "according to the letter." Origen is misled by fastening on words and ignoring the thrust of the narrative. After all, as Eustathius points out, the very word *engastrimythos* shows that the storywriter meant to imply the witch was false: she generates myths in her inner parts, her stomach rather than her mind, myths fathered by the devil. Etymology thus favors Eustathius's interest in showing that Origen's lexical approach is wrong because it destroys narrative coherence. That is what he means by taking away the *historia* — not sticking to the story. Ironically, Origen is too "literal."

But Eustathius has provided us with another clue. Time and again we

find that the primary concern of these critics is about the allegorization of the
narratives of creation, Paradise, the Fall, the Gospel stories, the resurrection
of the body and the kingdom of God. This reveals an anxiety for the overarching story of the Rule of Faith — for what we might call "salvation history," and especially for the narratives that provided the beginning and ending of the biblical story. They were not to be treated as dreams or fantasies, as
metaphor or parable. The attack on allegory was an aspect of the wider
Origenist controversy of the fourth century — the material and bodily existence that is human life on earth was not to be spiritualized away. It was the
narrative logic of the entire biblical text that mattered.

> Diodore of Tarsus, denying the presence of allegory in scripture, admits
> that there is metaphor, parable and enigma: When the author writes:
> "The serpent said to the woman"; "the woman said to the serpent"; "God
> said to the serpent," we have enigmas. Not that there was no serpent; in-
> deed there was a serpent, but the devil acted through it. . . . The reality
> was the serpent but, since a serpent is by nature irrational and yet was
> speaking, it is obvious that it spoke empowered by the devil. (ET:
> Froehlich 1984: 90)

Diodore is as anxious as Origen or the modern critic about the talking serpent, but he refuses to evacuate the thrust of the story. Scripture never repu-
diates the *historia*, though one story may be illuminating of another through
insight *(theōria)*. This is what Paul meant when he used the word "allegory"
of Sarah and Hagar.

Theodore of Mopsuestia, too, discussing this same point — that Paul
used the word "allegory"— is soon diverted into a protest against those who

> claim that Adam is not Adam, paradise is not paradise, the serpent not
> the serpent. I should like to tell them this: If they make history serve their
> own ends, they will have no history left.

His rhetoric depends on two senses of "history": the first use refers to the
"story" that they twist or evacuate, the second to "salvation history." Theodore goes on to argue that the evacuation of the Adam story undermines the
gospel:

> The apostle says that Christ canceled Adam's disobedience and annulled
> the death sentence. What were those events in the distant past to which he
> refers, and where did they take place, if the historical account relating

them does not signify real events but something else, as those people
maintain? . . . In many instances the apostle clearly uses the historical account of the ancient writers as the truth and nothing but the truth.
(translation from Froehlich 1984: 97)

Modern reading of these statements is necessarily colored by the use of "fact"
or "event" to translate *pragma[ta]*; for the Antiochenes the terminology first
implied the subject matter of the narratives as distinct from their wording.
Yet it did matter that the Fall had happened. Diodore defined *historia* as a
pure account of a *pragma gegonos* (something that happened). Theodore protested the reduction of "the entire *historia* of divine Scripture" to "dreams in
the night."

THEŌRIA

Historia is the foundation and basis for the higher sense. Diodore indicates
that the Antiochenes had no wish to hinder *anagōgē* or higher *theōria*, but
this was not to be confused with allegory. He suggests that, with the historical
account as his firm foundation, Paul develops his *theōria* on top of it *(epi-
theōrei)*, interpreting the underlying "facts" as "events" on a higher level. Thus
Paul does not do away with the *historia* of Sarah and Hagar; rather he draws
out a correspondence, a similarity (Theodore). This, the Antiochenes claim,
is the kind of thing Paul calls allegory. Neither Diodore nor Theodore resorts
to the word "type" in this discussion, though we can see why typology as defined above has been associated with the Antiochenes (e.g., Greer 1961). Wiles
attributes Theodore's willingness to admit the "parallel between Jonah's three
days in the whale's belly and Christ's three days in the bowels of the earth" to a
recognition of "a parallel of historical events . . . and therefore one falling
within the range of acceptable historical typology" (Wiles 1970). Rather than
"history," I suggest, it was the "correspondence" in the shapes of the stories
that was crucial for Theodore. *Mimēsis* was a key literary category and one
clue to the possibility of "theorizing on top of" the narrative without dismantling it: we may recall Chrysostom's moralizing. Typology may be an appropriate term for some of this, but certainly not for all of it (see further Young
1994, 1997).

The work of these exegetes was rooted in *to methodikon* of the schools.
Allegory was a recognized figure of speech on a spectrum between metaphor
and irony. Other Antiochene material indicates that, as long as allegory was
confined to a *trope* signaled in the text, these exegetes were prepared to admit

its presence in Scripture. "Everywhere in Scripture there is this law, that when it allegorizes, it also gives the explanation of the allegory," says Chrysostom (Grant 1984; Bultmann 1984). In fact, Diodore's context is a discussion of figures of speech, and Theodore resorts to standard figures of speech to handle what Paul means by allegory. What the Antiochenes object to is a hermeneutic that misidentifies and misapplies figures of speech.

It is instructive to look closely at a little treatise on scriptural interpretation by one Adrianos entitled *Isagōgē ad Sacras Scripturas* (*PG* 98.1273-1312), which has been identified as an Antiochene work (Bultmann 1984; Young 1997a). This treatise bears no explicit marks of the controversy. What Adrianos is concerned to do is to analyze the particular literary characteristics and idioms of Hebrew texts. His first section deals with the mind, or intent *(dianoia)*, of Scripture. Here he is working with the standard rhetorical distinction between wording and the sense. He inquires, in particular, how God's activities *(energeiai)* are represented by human attributes — in other words he deals with the anthropomorphic language of the Bible and its underlying sense, which is to be distinguished from the wording *(lexis)* of the text. No more than Origen does he take literally reference to God's eyes, mouth, hands, feet, anger, or passion, nor indeed to God sitting, walking, or being clothed, but he never employs the term "allegory" to describe what he is doing when he suggests that it is God's knowledge that is expressed in the phrase "God's eyes on us" and God's mercy in the suggestion that God has ears to hear.

Adrianos's second section concentrates on *lexis*, wording and style, noting the use of metonymy, epitasis, parable, simile and metaphor, rhetorical questions, and so on. The third section looks at the principles of composition *(synthesis)*, and after providing examples of ellipsis, tautology, antistrophe, hyperbaton, transposition, epitasis, and pleonasm (every point discussed in this treatise is in fact illustrated by quotations from the scriptural text), he turns to figures of speech *(tropoi)*, covering the great list of figures of speech distinguished in ancient theory. The list begins with metaphor, parable, syncrisis, and hypodeigma and goes on through periphrasis, anakephalaiosis, prosopopoia, and hyperbole, then irony, sarcasm, ainigma, and parenesis — the whole list is about two dozen. In the midst of all this appears allegory, given only four lines, whereas hyperbole merits sixteen. In other words, allegory is recognized as a figure of speech but not treated as very important. Hyperbole certainly was important.

The Antiochenes were fascinated by providence and prophecy, and the presence of prophecy was identified by the use of hyperbole in the text. To return to Diodore:

In predicting future events, the prophets adapted their words both to the time in which they were speaking and to later times. Their words sounded hyperbolic in their contemporary setting but were entirely fitting and consistent at the time when the prophecies were fulfilled.

Diodore adds an example. The words of Ps. 29:1-3 (LXX)

did fit Hezekiah when he was delivered from his ills; but they also fit all human beings when they obtain the promised resurrection. . . . Hezekiah seems to have used hyperbole to describe his own situation; he was not actually rescued from Hades but from circumstances comparable to Hades on account of his very serious illness. . . .

As to the following verse,

it is quite clear that by the pit the author means death, but when he first uttered these words they were used hyperbolically. When he actually rises from the dead, the former hyperbole will come true; the events themselves will have moved in the direction of the formerly hyperbolic expression. (translation from Froehlich 1984: 91-92)

In their use of hyperbole, the Antiochenes rooted their higher sense in a different figure of speech from the *allēgoria* chosen by Origen (who understood it as grounded in *tropologia*) and the philosophic tradition.

Adrianos confirms the Antiochene interest in the sequence *(akolouthia)* of the text and identifies two genres in the Bible, *historia* and prophecy. Diodore states that the prophetic genre is divided into future, present, and past. He regards Moses' account of Adam and very early times from the beginning as prophecy — presumably because it had to be disclosed to Moses; for disclosure of hidden things in the present is equally prophetic, as the story of Ananias and Sapphira shows. Prediction of the future is most prominent, however. This analysis is motivated both by literary interests and by the sense of a time-bound narrative concerned with God's providence. Both methodological and dogmatic concerns colored the Antiochenes' approach.

The various features of Antiochene exegesis noted so far may be illustrated with aspects of the Psalms commentaries of Diodore and Theodore. Diodore indicates his aims in his introduction: he wants people to understand the Psalms as they sing them "from the depth of their *dianoia* [mind, meaning]," so he will provide an exposition of the *hypothesis* of each psalm and provide an exegesis according to the plain text. He wants people to grasp the *akolouthia* (sequence). He thinks the *hypothesis* of the whole psalter has two parts, ethical and dogmatic. Some psalms correct the moral behavior of the individual, others the Jewish people, and others human beings in general, and he will specify in each case to which group the psalm belongs. As for their doctrine, the psalms present proofs that

> all being has one and the same God and creator, that his providence ex-
> tends even to the smallest things, and nothing which owes him its exis-
> tence escapes his continuing providence. (translation from Froehlich
> 1984: 83-84)

Other *hypotheses* include the Babylonian captivity and past events like the exodus recalled for the benefit of later generations. Those referring to the Babylonian captivity, however, belong to the "predictive genre," as do those that fit Jeremiah and Ezekiel specifically, and indeed the Maccabean psalms, "spoken in the person of specific individuals such as Onias and leaders like him": the Holy Spirit was providing a remedy in advance for those who suffered. Diodore and Theodore never questioned Davidic authorship, though they recognized that the context of some psalms postdated David.

Theodore's most controversial claims can be understood in the light of these statements by Diodore. Theodore argued that Psalms 22 and 69, though quoted in the Gospels, could not refer to Christ. The argument was that each psalm is spoken by a single persona and has a single aim, or intent *(skopos)*. David prophetically adopted the persona of Solomon, Hezekiah, and even Christ in Psalms 2, 8, and 45, but this could not be so in the case of Psalm 22 since the author refers to his sins. Theodore relates Psalm 22 to the context of Absalom's revolt and Psalm 69 to the time of the Maccabees. Clearly Theodore was applying school methods to the text, and it is the consistency of the text that he was concerned about: he was anxious to ensure that sense and reference were not at odds. This was a philological principle. Prophecy was not being challenged by any kind of historical realism. Indeed, as Wiles notes (1970: 502), Theodore could admit a "secondary" application to Christ. He proved this secondary nature by noting how the New Testament changes the original words of certain psalms to make them fit the time of Jesus better — "ears" is changed to "body" when Psalm 40 is quoted in Hebrews 10.

Similarly, Theodore's criticism of those who found christological references in the prophets rested on the consistency of the prophet's message. To apply successive verses to Christ and Zerubbabel was simply to ignore the text's connectedness. Theodore would admit only one prophecy that referred to Christ, Mal. 4:5-6, though he again allowed secondary references when the

New Testament provided a precedent. In his commentary Theodore ignores even some of these, concentrating on the context of the prophet's time. Only five verses are given a secondary Christian interpretation, and it is easy to see why Theodore was accused of Jewish interpretation. For it is largely true that, as Wiles states (cf. Greer 1961), "the direct prophetic message always stays for Theodore restricted to the period before the coming of Christ" (1970: 503). Why should Theodore not "have allowed also direct prediction of events at the time of Christ"? The answer seems to lie in his remarkably clear appreciation of the eschatological newness of the New Testament and therefore his tendency to see a radical break between the two ages or dispensations, before and after Christ. He opposed the reduction of this novelty that follows on seeing Christ everywhere in the Old Testament. For him as for the other Antiochenes, God's providential activity was seen in the "economy": God's plan was worked out in the whole story from creation to the end. The only history that mattered was salvation history. This was what the Bible was about.

The real difference between the Antiochenes and Alexandrians lay here. For Origen the Platonist, both the created order and the text of Scripture were symbolic of the eternal world of spiritual realities. Symbols and types he understood in terms of something standing for something else, so that the words of Scripture became a kind of code to be cracked by allegorical reading. The *dianoia*, the real meaning, was veiled — that was the intent of the Spirit. The Antiochenes, on the other hand, had the same concern as Irenaeus in his argument with Gnostics: he had accused them of composing a *cento* — a literary game whereby a new poem was created by selecting and stitching together lines and phrases from Homer or some other classic. Those in the know would recognize the words but not the *hypothesis*, he said; the story was dismantled. As for Irenaeus, so for the Antiochenes — the narrative mattered, and any prophetic, moral, or dogmatic meaning was mirrored in the narrative. This is what they meant by *theōria* not taking away *historia*. This might be called "ikonic" exegesis (Young 1997). Anything that turned any part of the story into a docetic charade threatened the reality of salvation. To that extent Greer's emphasis (1973) on the theological and christological differences is an important element in painting the whole complex picture of the Antiochene attack on Alexandrian allegory.

CONCLUSION

Ancient literary criticism understood texts of all kinds in terms of *mimēsis*, that is, as representations of life intended to instruct. There was some anec-

dotal interest in the author and the circumstances of the text's composition, as
well as in any circumstances that might elucidate the content, but there was no
genuinely historical criticism (Russell 1981). Reading was anachronistic, for the
intent of the author was simply to persuade the reader. Both Origen and the
Antiochenes used the analytical methods of the schools, but their conception
of literary *mimēsis* was different. One stemmed from the treatment of texts in
the rhetorical schools, the other from their handling in the philosophical
schools. The differing results were not the outcome of literal reading opposed
to spiritual sense, for both knew, unlike modernists but perhaps not
postmodernists, that the wording of the Bible carried deeper meanings and
that the immediate sense or reference pointed beyond itself. So it was that, particularly in the hands of the less radical Antiochene, Theodoret of Cyrrhus,
traditional "allegories" reappear — both he and Origen treat the Song of
Songs as an allegory of the love between Christ and his church. The difference
lay not so much in exegetical method as in hermeneutical principles.

BIBLIOGRAPHY

Ackroyd, P., and C. F. Evans (eds.)
1970   *The Cambridge History of the Bible.* Cambridge: Cambridge University Press.

Bienert, W. A.
1972   *"Allegoria" und "Anagoge" bei Didymus dem Blinden.* Berlin: de Gruyter.

Bultmann, R.
1984   *Die Exegese des Theodor von Mopsuestia.* Habilitationsschrift, posthumously pub-
        lished. Stuttgart: Kohlhammer.

Charity, A. C.
1966   *Events and Their Afterlife: The Dialectics of Christian Typology in the Bible.* Cam-
        bridge: Cambridge University Press.

Crouzel, H.
1989   *Origen.* ET by A. S. Worrall. Edinburgh: Clark.

Daniélou, J.
1955   *Origène.* Paris: La Table Ronde, 1948. ET by W. Mitchell. New York: Sheed and Ward.
1958   *The Lord of History.* ET by Nigel Abercrombie. London: Longmans.
1960   *From Shadows to Reality: Studies in the Biblical Typology of the Fathers.* London:
        Burns and Oates.

Devreesse, R.
1948   *Essai sur Theodore de Mopsueste.* Studi e Testi. Vatican: Biblioteca Apostolica
        Vaticana.

Froehlich, K.

1984   *Biblical Interpretation in the Early Church*. Sources of Early Christian Thought. Philadelphia: Fortress.

Grant, R. M.

1961   *The Earliest Lives of Jesus*. London: SPCK.

Grant, R. M., with D. Tracy

1984   *A Short History of the Interpretation of the Bible*. 2d ed. revised and enlarged. London: SCM.

Greer, R. A.

1961   *Theodore of Mopsuestia: Exegete and Theologian*. Westminster: Faith.

1973   *The Captain of Our Salvation: A Study in the Patristic Exegesis of Hebrews*. Tübingen: Mohr.

Guillet, J.

1947   "Les Exégèses d'Alexandrie et d'Antioche: Conflit ou malentendu?" *Recherches de Science Religieuse* 34:257-302.

Guinot, J.-N.

1989   "La typologie comme technique herméneutique." In *Figures de L'Ancien Testament chez les Pères*, 1-34. Cahiers de *Biblia Patristica* 2. Strasbourg: Centre d'analyse et de documentation patristiques.

Hanson, R. P. C.

1959   *Allegory and Event*. London: SCM.

Hatch, E.

1888   *The Influence of Greek Ideas on Christianity*. Reprint 1957. New York: Harper. Originally London: Williams and Norgate.

Kugel, J. L., and R. A. Greer

1986   *Early Biblical Interpretation*, Library of Early Christianity. Philadelphia: Westminster.

Lampe, G. W. H., and K. J. Woollcombe

1957   *Essays in Typology*. SBT 22. London: SCM.

Lange, N. de

1976   *Origen and the Jews*. Cambridge: Cambridge University Press.

Marrou, H.-I.

1948   *Histoire de l'Education dans l'Antiquité*. Paris: Editions du Seuil. ET G. Lamb. London: Sheed and Ward, 1956.

Migne, J. P.

1857-66 *Patrologia Graeca*. Patrologiae cursus completus. Paris: Migne.

Neuschafer, B.

1987   *Origenes als Philologe*. Basel: Reinhardt.

Quasten, J.
1962-64 *Patrology.* 3 vols. Utrecht: Spectrum.

Russell, D. A.
1981   *Criticism in Antiquity.* London: Duckworth.

Schaublin, C.
1974   *Untersuchungen zu Methode und Herkunft der antiochenischen Exegese.* Cologne:
        Hanstein.

Simonetti, M.
1994   *Biblical Interpretation in the Early Church: An Historical Introduction to Patristic
        Exegesis.* ET by J. A. Hughes. Edinburgh: Clark.

Tigcheler, J. H.
1977   *Didyme l'Aveugle et l'exégèse allegorique, son commentaire sur Zacharie.* Nijmegen:
        Dekker & van de Vegt.

Torjesen, K. J.
1985a   *Hermeneutical Procedure and Theological Method in Origen's Exegesis.* Berlin: de
        Gruyter.
1985b   "'Body,' 'Soul,' and 'Spirit' in Origen's Theory of Exegesis." *Anglican Theological Re-
        view* 67:17-30.

Trigg, J. W.
1985   *Origen: The Bible and Philosophy in the Third-Century Church.* London: SCM.

Wheeldon, M. J.
1989   "'True Stories': The Reception of Historiography in Antiquity." In A. Cameron, ed.,
        History as Text. London: Duckworth.

Wiles, M. F.
1970a   "Origen as Biblical Scholar." In P. Ackroyd and C. F. Evans, eds., 103-38.
1970b   "Theodore of Mopsuestia as Representative of the Antiochene School." In P.
        Ackroyd and C. F. Evans, eds., 454-510.

Young, F. M.
1989   "The Rhetorical Schools and Their Influence on Patristic Exegesis." In R. A. Wil-
        liams (ed.), *The Making of Orthodoxy: Essays in Honour of Henry Chadwick,* 182-99.
        Cambridge: Cambridge University Press.
1994   "Typology." In S. E. Porter, P. Joyce and D. E. Orton, eds., *Crossing the Boundaries:
        Essays in Biblical Interpretation in Honour of Michael D. Goulder,* 29-48. Leiden:
        Brill.
1997a   "The Fourth Century Reaction against Allegory." *Studia Patristica* 30:120-25.
1997b   *Biblical Exegesis and the Formation of Christian Culture.* Cambridge: Cambridge
        University Press.

CHAPTER 13

Jerome and the Vulgate

Dennis Brown

Eusebius Sophronius Hieronymus, better known as St. Jerome, Doctor of the Church, was one of the most important interpreters of the Bible in the early centuries of Christianity. He was probably born sometime in the early 340s of the Christian era in the town of Stridon in present-day Croatia. He died in 420, having acquired an international reputation for biblical scholarship, for extensive literary activity, and for living a holy and ascetic life.

The curriculum of Jerome's secondary education in Rome would have been principally concerned with the rules of grammar, particularly the correct analysis and use of language, and classical literature. Favorite authors were Virgil (poet and founder of liberal Latin culture), Terence (the comic playwright), the historian Sallust, and the stylist, orator and philosopher, Cicero. Jerome's works are full of quotations and allusions to classical literature. At 15 or 16, Jerome would have graduated to a Roman school of rhetoric, where he would have learned the art of public speaking with a view, perhaps, to entering a legal career or the civil service. His later writings show how well he learned the art of rhetoric, with its stylized procedures, stock emotional phrases, and tendency to exaggeration (see *Commentary on Galatians* 2.1; for fuller information on Jerome's education, see Kelly 1975: 10-17).

JEROME AS A TRANSLATOR

Hebrew

Before it was possible to interpret the text properly, it was necessary to have the best text available. This meant that Jerome had to learn the original languages of the Bible. As far as the New Testament was concerned, Jerome encountered no problems, for he had learned Greek at school and had attended the lectures of Gregory of Nazianzus in Constantinople. But for the text of the Old Testament, Jerome was faced with a considerable hurdle for, apart from Origen, very few other Christian scholars had any knowledge of Hebrew. Jerome took lessons in Hebrew from a Jewish convert to Christianity, and it is clear that he found it difficult to master. No grammars or concordances were available, so he had to learn the language orally, memorizing the sounds of the consonants and vocabulary. Presumably, he practiced writing the Hebrew characters by copying out manuscripts. Of his Hebrew studies, Jerome says: "What labor I spent on this task, what difficulties I went through, how often I despaired and how often I gave up and in my eagerness to learn, started again" (*Epistle* 125.12).

Jerome believed, with the rest of the ancient Jewish and Christian world, that Hebrew was the world's original language. Regardless of its antiquity, however, Jerome found it a barbarous language, which affected his Latin style. In the preface to his *Commentary on Galatians,* Jerome apologizes for his unliterary style, blaming it partly on eye trouble and problems with copyists, but also on his study of Hebrew: "I leave it to others to judge how far my unflagging study of Hebrew has profited me; what I have lost in my own language, I can tell."

It is clear that Jerome had a much more extensive and profound knowledge of Hebrew than did any other Christian scholar, including Origen. Jerome had the same quantitative use of Hebrew as did Origen, but he added to it a qualitative use of Hebrew as a guide to the right *meanings* (cf. Barr 1966: 282). This qualitative use manifests itself in various ways. The very fact, for instance, that Jerome undertook the task of translating the Old Testament from Hebrew points toward his possessing a high degree of ability in Hebrew. Even bearing in mind that he had the previous Greek translations of Theodotion, Symmachus, and especially of Aquila, which must have been of considerable value to him, Jerome's own translation from the Hebrew was a quite remarkable achievement, especially when it is seen to be a generally accurate and faithful translation.

A second way of showing Jerome's extensive understanding of Hebrew is to look at his vocalizations of the language. The Hebrew text with which Jerome worked was unpointed (i.e., without vowels). Distinctions in meaning could be brought about by different vocalizations of the same consonants. The following example comes from Jerome's *Commentary on Jeremiah* (9:22): "The Hebrew word which is written with the three letters 'd-b-r' (it has no vowels in it), according to the natural progression of the passage and the judgment of the reader, if 'dabar' is read it means 'word'; if 'deber,' it means 'death'; and if 'dabber,' it means 'speak.'" The three words were identical in the unvocalized text. It was possible to discern the correct grammatical construction (the first two instances are nouns, the third is a verb) and the meaning of the word only by studying its position in the sentence. In this example, Jerome is combating the incorrect translations of the word in the Greek versions, based on different vocalizations. The Septuagint omitted the word, Origen's *Hexapla* interpreted it as "death," and Aquila understood it as "speak," as had Symmachus.

It has been suggested (Barr 1966: 293) that Jerome may have been influenced here by the Jewish *al-tiqre* interpretation: "do not read [the word in the text] but [a similar one]." This was a midrashic technique used to introduce alternative readings to a text for purely homiletic purposes. It was understood as a legitimate extension of the literal exegesis of a passage. But this seems unlikely here because, if Jerome had been using this technique, he would have used the different possibilities of vocalization in his own interpretation. It is more likely that he is merely reveling in his good knowledge of Hebrew and showing off to his Christian readers by exhibiting his mastery of the language. It was this extensive knowledge of Hebrew that helped Jerome so much in his major task of translating the Bible from its original languages.

The Need for a Translation

Jerome was, as he himself says, a *vir trilinguis,* knowing Hebrew, Greek, and Latin. One of the greatest achievements for which he is remembered is the "Vulgate," his translation of the Bible into Latin. The term "Vulgate" comes from Latin *vulgata* meaning "common." It is used of the Latin version of the Bible followed by the Roman Catholic Church, often attributed to Jerome. Jerome used the term himself to refer to his own translation of the Bible, because he wanted to make the scriptural texts available to everyone, not just to scholars who could understand Greek and Hebrew (see Sutcliffe 1948a: 250).

Jerome, more than any other single person, was responsible for fixing the literary form of the Bible for the entire western church. The complicated history of the Vulgate translation and Jerome's involvement in it began in 383, when Pope Damasus came to the conclusion that, because of the proliferation of variant readings in the Latin Bible of the day, a thorough revision was imperative. For this task, he commissioned Jerome. Although we do not have the actual words of his commission, we get a very clear idea of the pope's wishes from Jerome's preface to the four Gospels:

> You urge me to compose a new work from the old, and, as it were, to sit in judgement on the copies of the Scriptures which are now scattered throughout the world; and, inasmuch as they differ from one another, you would have me decide which of them agrees with the Greek original. The labour is one of love, but at the same time dangerous and presumptuous; for in judging others I must be content to be judged by all; and how can I change the language of the world in its old age, and carry it back to its early childhood? Is there a man, learned or unlearned, who will not, when he takes the volume in his hands, and sees that what he reads does not suit his settled tastes, break out immediately into violent language and call me a forger and a profane person for having had the audacity to add anything to the ancient books, or to make any changes or corrections in them?

The Old Latin Versions

Jerome was, however, prepared to risk this castigation for two reasons. First, he explains, is the pope's command. Second is the terrible diversity of Old Latin manuscripts. He exclaims that there are "almost as many forms of text as there are manuscripts." His younger contemporary Augustine confirms this fact when he laments: "Those who translated the Scriptures from Hebrew into Greek can be counted, but the Latin translators are out of all number. For in the early days of the faith, every man who happened to gain possession of a Greek manuscript [of the New Testament] and who imagined he had any facility in both languages, however slight that might have been, dared to make a translation" (Augustine: *On Christian Doctrine* 2.16).

Jerome's and Augustine's statements were not mere hyperbole, but based on sound factual information. The Old Latin version was begun in the second century, simultaneously in Africa and Western Europe. By the fourth century, it existed in a bewildering number of forms, showing a huge number of variant readings. This was partly because the task of translation had been undertaken by different scholars at different times in different areas, and partly because of errors in translation and careless transcription. The Latin of those early versions was very odd, as the language was adapted to Christian usage, with special vocabulary created for the new translation (see Brown 1993: 98ff.). The idiom of this form of Latin often recalled the Greek on which the Christian vocabulary was based, and, because it was written for an uneducated people, it had a strongly colloquial feel (see Metzger 1977: 285-330).

Jerome's statement concerning the many text-types of the Old Latin version would also seem to be substantiated, for the modern scholarly consensus distinguishes four main text-types among Old Latin manuscripts: African, European, Italian, and Spanish (Hort 1890: 81ff.; Metzger 1963: 121-41; for versions of the Old Latin texts, see Metzger 1977).

The Vulgate Translation

Faced with a great array of variant readings and different text types, Jerome prepared to carry out Pope Damasus's wish to revise the Latin Bible and create (or re-create) a uniform text. Naturally enough, he began his revision with the four Gospels. Pope Damasus did not commission Jerome to make a *fresh translation* of the Bible, but Jerome found himself checking the accuracy of the Latin text by referring constantly to the Greek original. He was conscious, however, of his commission to *revise* the existing Old Latin version and changed this text only when it was necessary. He finished his revision of the four Gospels and presented it to the pope, with prefaces to each of the Gospels, in 384.

That Jerome revised the four Gospels is certain. Less certain, however, is how much of the remainder of the Old Latin New Testament Jerome revised. In *On Famous Men* 135 and elsewhere (*Epistles* 71.5; 112.20), he claims to have "restored the New Testament to its Greek original." Scholars have expressed opposing views on this statement. Some, notably Chapman (1923), believed that Jerome did, in fact, revise the whole of the New Testament. Chapman argued that Jerome's quotations from Paul in *Epistle* 27 show his intention of publishing in the near future a revision of the Pauline epistles. The lack of prefaces to other New Testament books can easily be explained, Chapman claims. The Pope, for whom Jerome was making the revision, died soon after the Gospels and their prefaces were completed, and Jerome did not wish to write prefaces to any of the other books. Chapman also attempts to explain why Jerome's quotations from the Pauline epistles often differ from those in the Vulgate: he often quotes readings with which he disagrees and he may have thought a certain reading to be a fairly good one, his own suggestion being meant only to explain the real force of the Greek, not to serve as a tolerable Latin rendering. Jerome is often inconsistent anyway, and the differences between the Vulgate readings and those found in Jerome's works do not necessarily prove that he was not the author of the Vulgate of the Pauline epistles. Chapman cites examples from the Gospels that vary from the Vulgate. Those who argue that Jerome did not revise the text of the Pauline epistles because his quotations differ from the Vulgate must also conclude that he did not revise the text of the Gospels, which is absurd. Stylistically, he says, the Vulgate New Testament is the work of a single author, and that author must be Jerome. Furthermore, Jerome is always accurate when enumerating his own works, so when he says he has revised the whole New Testament, he must have done so. Chapman dates the revision of the complete New Testament to 391.

This traditional belief that Jerome revised the entire text of the New Testament has been seriously questioned by other scholars. Cavallera (1922) made a detailed study of the Vulgate of Acts, the Pauline epistles, and Revelation and noted especially the discrepancies between the Vulgate and quotations in Jerome's works. Sometimes Jerome employs a text that coincides more or less with the Vulgate, but more often he quotes one that differs. Sometimes he rejects readings found in the Vulgate. It is very important to note in this context that, in his commentaries on Galatians, Ephesians, Philemon, and Titus, written about 387, shortly after his supposed revision of these letters, he never attributes the Latin text he uses to himself. On the contrary, he often uses the phrase *Latinus interpres* ("a translator of Latin") of the translator. He sometimes disagrees with their readings. More recently, Kelly (1975) has stated his opinion that the style of the Vulgate of Acts is against Jerome's authorship. Kelly has also asserted categorically that "the only tenable conclusion is that Jerome, for whatever reason, abandoned the idea of revising the rest of the New Testament (if indeed he ever entertained it at all) once he had completed the Gospels" (p. 88).

Before he left Rome in 385, after having revised the text of the Gospels, Jerome revised the Latin text of the Psalter according to the Septuagint. He says that he revised this book very quickly, but made substantial changes. This revision used to be identified as the "Roman Psalter," but recent work has indicated that, while the Roman Psalter is not the version which Jerome made at Rome in 384, it may well represent the text on which he worked and which he corrected (DeBruyne 1930; Vaccari 1920: 211-21). A few years later (387-88), Jerome made another translation of the Psalms, this time using Origen's Hexaplaric Septuagint text as his basis. This version is known as the "Gallican Psalter," as it was first accepted for use in the churches of Gaul. It also remained in greater use than his later translation of the Psalms from Hebrew, and so became included in the edition of the Vulgate ratified by the Council of Trent in the sixteenth century. In this "Gallican Psalter," Jerome included Origen's diacritical signs, which were intended to show where the Septuagint text differed from the Hebrew original.

In the same period, Jerome also translated Job, 1 and 2 Chronicles, Proverbs, Ecclesiastes, and Song of Songs. The Psalter, Job (in two manuscripts), and Song of Songs (in only one manuscript), are all that remain of this translation of parts of the Old Testament from Origen's critical Hexaplaric Septuagint text. The other books are not now extant. In 416, when Augustine asked to consult Jerome's revised Septuagint, the latter had to inform the African Bishop that, due to someone's deceit, he no longer had a copy of the other books.

By 390, Jerome had become convinced of the necessity to make a fresh translation of the Old Testament from the Hebrew text, and, encouraged by friends and his desire to demolish the arguments of the Jews, he began to translate each of the books of the Hebrew canon, a task that was not completed until 406. It is probable that Jerome began this new translation with the books of Samuel and Kings. After explaining that the Hebrew canon has three divisions — Law, Prophets and "Hagiographa" — Jerome goes on to say:

> This preface to the Scriptures may serve as a "helmeted" introduction to all the books which I translate from Hebrew into Latin. . . . Read first, then, my Samuel and Kings; mine, I say, mine. For whatever by careful translation and cautious correction I have learnt and comprehended, is my very own. And when you understand anything of which you were ignorant before, either (if you are grateful) consider me a translator, or (if ungrateful) a paraphraser, although I am not at all conscious of having deviated from the Hebrew original. (*Preface to Samuel and Kings; Epistle 49.4*)

It sounds as if Jerome is writing this preface as a general introduction to his whole translation of the Old Testament, discussing the contents and limits of the Old Testament canon. He refers to the preface as "helmeted" *(galeatus)* because he arms himself in advance to defend himself from the critics he knows will rise up against him.

Soon after he had finished the translation of Samuel and Kings, Jerome started on Job, the Psalter, and the Prophets. His friend Sophronius made an "elegant Greek translation" of Jerome's rendering of Job and the Psalter, and in *Epistle 49*, composed in 393-94, Jerome informs Pammachius that he has translated the sixteen prophets (thus including Daniel) and Job, of which Pammachius will be able to borrow a copy from his cousin Marcella. Of this book, Jerome says: "Read it in both Greek and Latin, and compare the old version with my rendering. You will then see clearly that the difference between them is that between truth and falsehood." He also tells Pammachius that he has translated Samuel and Kings. He does not mention Psalms, but this must have been an oversight on Jerome's part. Ezra, Nahum, and Chronicles were translated in 394-95.

It was not until late 404 and early 405 that Jerome translated more of the Hebrew Old Testament. He gave no reason for the long delay, but it was very probably due to his involvement in the Origenist controversy from 393 to 402-403, and also to the fact that he wrote several commentaries in this period. He first translated the Pentateuch, having been asked to do so by his friend Desiderius. His preface makes it clear that he thinks there is still a good deal to be done before his translation of the Old Testament would be complete.

Next, he translated Joshua, Judges, and Ruth in early 405. In the preface, he expresses his relief at having finished the Pentateuch: "Having at last finished Moses' Pentateuch, I feel like a man released from a crippling load of debt." The rest of the Old Testament books were completed by early 406, thus bringing a labor of some fourteen years to an end.

Other Translation Work

Jerome did not restrict his translation activities solely to Scripture. He is also responsible for translating into Latin a considerable number of Greek theological works (see Brown 1993: 91-96; Kelly 1975: 73-77). The first of these translations was made in 380, when he rendered Eusebius of Caesarea's *Chronicle* into Latin (Helm 1956). Presumably, having spent several years studying the works of Greek theologians, Jerome was anxious that the Latin-speaking world should have the opportunity of benefiting from the scholarship of Greek Christians. Interestingly enough, Jerome was not content in this work simply to translate; he omitted sections he thought unnecessary and added a new section, bringing the *Chronicle* up to date and thereby providing the western world with a history of the world from Abraham to 379. He then turned to translating into Latin the works of Origen, from whose exegetical writings he had learned so much. Jerome was interested in translating most, if not all, of Origen's works, but was prevented from doing so by a painful eye irritation caused by constant reading, and by a lack of copyists, owing to a shortage of money. Jerome did succeed, however, in translating quite a number of Origen's homilies. He also translated a work of Didymus the Blind, *On the Holy Spirit,* from Greek into Latin. This work, along with some of Origen's homilies, are now lost in Greek, and Jerome's translation is the only way we can know these important works today.

Implications for the Canon

One of the major results of Jerome's translations of biblical books was the resolution (to his satisfaction) of the question of the extent of the canon. In Jerome's early works, he often quotes from "apocryphal" books, that is, books that were not in the Hebrew Bible but were accepted by Christians because they were included in the Septuagint version. The Septuagint had been the accepted Christian version of the Old Testament since the second century and had taken on the mantle of divine inspiration. Several different versions of the Greek Old Testament existed in Jerome's day, and this diversity was one of the main reasons that he undertook the long task of translating the biblical books from the original languages. His most balanced statement on the relation between his translations from the Hebrew and earlier translations is seen in the *Preface to Samuel and Kings:*

> I beg you, brother, not to think that my work is in any way meant to debase the old translators. Each one offers the service of the tabernacle of God what he can; some gold and silver and precious stones, others linen and blue and purple and scarlet; we shall do well if we offer skins and goats' hair.

There were several lists of canonical books in Jerome's writings. One such is found in *Epistle* 53.8, where Jerome includes all the books in the Hebrew Bible, but the order in which they are recorded is influenced by the Septuagint in that the Minor Prophets are placed before the other prophetic books and Daniel is placed at the end of the Prophets, ostensibly as one of them (see the chart on pp. 34-35 above). This is a good example of the ambivalent attitude Jerome showed toward the canon. The serious scholar is influenced by the Hebrew canon, while the churchman cannot stray too far from the revered tradition of the Septuagint canon (for further on this, see Brown 1993: 62-71).

As regards the New Testament canon, Jerome's views are relatively straightforward. He confirms the books that are now in the New Testament canon, with the possible exception of 2 and 3 John, concerning which he expresses some doubt about whether they were composed by John the Apostle or John the Presbyter. However, he includes both in the canon (*On Famous Men* 9). He did much to stabilize the opinion of the western church concerning the positions of Hebrews and Revelation. He recognized that various sections of the church rejected those books because of doubt concerning their apostolic authorship, but he says:

> The epistle which is inscribed to the Hebrews is received not only by the churches in the east, but also by all church writers of the Greek language before our days, as of Paul the apostle, though many think that it is from Barnabas or Clement. And it makes no difference whose it is, since it is from a churchman, and is celebrated in the daily readings of the churches. And if the usage of the Latin does not receive it among the canonical Scriptures, neither indeed by the same liberty do the churches of the Greeks receive the Revelation of John. And yet we receive both, in that we follow by no means the habit of today, but the authority of ancient writers, who for the most part quote each of them . . . as canonical and churchly. (*Epistle* 129.3)

BIBLICAL INTERPRETATION

Jerome inherited a long tradition of biblical interpretation, both Jewish and Christian. In Judaism, rabbinic scholars had developed a system of interpretative rules and techniques for studying biblical texts. These may be broadly classified under two headings: haggadah and halakhah. Haggadah ("information" or "anecdote") is seen largely in collections of midrash (see chapter 7 above) and often takes the form of moralizing exegesis. Various techniques were used to achieve this, including juxtaposing originally discrete biblical texts, creative elaboration of the biblical narrative, and the use of parable. This midrashic method could provide profound theological insights. Jerome used a great deal of haggadic material in his works and was the main source through which echoes of the haggadah reached some of the western church Fathers. Halakhah ("procedure") was concerned with the implementation of the Torah into practical matters and with ensuring that the Torah could be successfully adapted to the changing conditions in the life of Jews. Jerome also used this halakhic principle in his own exegesis of Scripture.

One Jewish scholar who found favor with Jerome was Philo of Alexandria. Jerome calls Philo an "ecclesiastical" writer, on the grounds that Philo praises Christians at Alexandria and mentions that Christianity is present in other provinces (Jerome, *On Famous Men* 11). Philo had been aware of the haggadic and halakhic traditions, but found that the "impossibilities" and "absurdities" produced by a literal reading of Scripture could be unraveled by using an allegorical method based on Stoic ethics and Platonic cosmology. By searching carefully in Scripture for clues like contradictions, strange expressions, word derivations, and mysterious numbers, the interpreter could discover the real message that God intended to convey (see chapter 4 above).

This allegorical interpretation of biblical texts spread from Philo to Christianity and became widely used by the catechetical school at Alexandria, particularly by its two greatest scholars, Clement and Origen. For Clement, most of Scripture was expressed in enigmas, and it was the task of the interpreter, who had received the deeper knowledge *(gnōsis)* given by Christ to his apostles after the resurrection, to unlock the spiritual truth of biblical language to those capable of understanding. Following Philo, Clement allegorized the Old Testament freely. His hermeneutical principle for identifying the true meaning was an eclectic mixture of Hellenistic (and Gnostic) cosmology, soteriology, and morality, combined with the conviction that, in the Logos-Christ, all foreshadowing of truth had found its goal.

Although Jerome spoke approvingly of Clement, it is clear that he was much more profoundly influenced by the other great Alexandrian exegete, Origen. Much of Origen's huge literary output was devoted to the interpretation of the Bible. Jerome classified Origen's works into three categories: scholia (short explanatory glosses), commentaries, and homilies. Origen dealt with most of the biblical books in one or more of these forms. In *De Principiis* Origen had set out to show systematically how the diversity of the world came about and will eventually return to a divine unity. Fundamental to this structure is the role of Scripture and its interpretation. The divinely inspired Scriptures have a spiritual purpose; therefore, to give them a simplistic understanding was to insult the divine author of the writings. Origen argued that texts like Prov. 22:20-21 suggest a threefold sense of Scripture analogous to the tripartite anthropology of the philosophers: just as humans consist of body, soul, and spirit, so Scripture has literal, moral, and spiritual senses. All biblical texts have a spiritual sense, though not all have a literal one. If no spiritual sense is apparent on the surface, the interpreter must understand the surface sense symbolically. Allegory is the method that will provide the key to unlock the hidden, symbolic meaning of texts, and it was Origen whose influence made allegory the dominant method of biblical interpretation down to the Middle Ages. Jerome was responsible, to an extent, for ensuring that Origen's writings were transmitted to the western Church, thus disseminating more widely Origen's allegorizing exegesis.

Not all Christian scholars were convinced, however, that allegorical exegesis was the best method of discovering the truth of Scripture. The "school" of Antioch developed in reaction against the allegorizing tendencies of Alexandria. The school's early history is associated with the name of Lucian, the teacher of Arius, but the most influential Antiochenes were Diodore of Tarsus, Theodore of Mopsuestia, and John Chrysostom. The Antiochenes insisted on the historical basis of the text of Scripture and that, wherever possible, it should be interpreted literally. Only where this could not be done was the typological or allegorical sense to be explored. The Antiochene emphasis on the literal or historical sense is seen in Lucian's emphasis on the details of the text of Scripture. He knew Hebrew and corrected the Septuagint from the original Hebrew. Jerome praised this recension and used it widely in his own work on the biblical text (see chapter 12 above for a detailed treatment of Antiochene exegesis).

Jerome's Commentaries

By far the major part of Jerome's literary output is in commentary form. He wrote commentaries on almost all the books of the Old Testament and on some of the New Testament.

One of his earliest works was the *Hebrew Question on Genesis*, which was more a grammatical and etymological study of some passages in Genesis. He paid special attention to the (supposed) meaning and etymology of Hebrew words, and intended this book to be the first of a series of such volumes. But he dropped this project when he began his translation of the Hebrew text of the Old Testament. The work dates from about 390 (Hayward 1995: 23-27). A little earlier, in 386-87, Jerome wrote his *Commentary on Ecclesiastes,* dedicated to the young widow Blesilla, whom he had taught in Rome. He used Origen as his main source, but the short work shows traces of originality. It is based on the Hebrew text.

During the period of 391-406, Jerome wrote commentaries on all the Minor Prophets. Again, he made use of Origen's commentaries and referred to both the Hebrew and Greek texts. In these commentaries, as in his other commentaries, Jerome sought to combine historical and spiritual interpretations. He gave double translations of the text, one from Hebrew and the other from Greek (Latin texts in Adraien 1963a, b; no English translation available). The *Commentary on Jonah* is interesting because it follows earlier Christian exegesis of this story in seeing in Jonah a prefiguration of Christ and his resurrection. Jerome treats the story as genuinely historical, arguing strongly that Jonah really did spend three days in the belly of the whale. On the spiritual level, he argues for Jonah as a "type" of Christ, and interpreted many of the details of the story in this light. Thus, Jonah's flight from the Lord's face points to the Son's descent from the heavenly realm, and his preaching to Nineveh points to Christ's postresurrection command to preach to the nations (text and French translation in Antin 1956; see Duval 1973).

The *Commentary on Daniel*, composed in 407, is a study of selected passages from Daniel, based on Jerome's own translation from the Hebrew. This is one of Jerome's most interesting commentaries, for he spends much of the book criticizing the anti-Christian polemic of the third-century Neoplatonist philosopher Porphyry, who had argued (correctly) that Daniel was not a prophecy dating from the sixth century BCE but rather a tract for the times, written to encourage Jews who were suffering persecution at the hands of Antiochus IV Epiphanes. Jerome, on the other hand, rejected this interpretation and argued that the revelation of Christ was to be found throughout the book. So, for instance, he suggests that "the stone . . . cut from a mountain by no human hand" (Dan. 2:45) was none other than the Savior, who was conceived without human intercourse (Latin text in Glorie 1964; English translation in Archer 1958; study and partial translation in Braverman 1978).

Jerome's most extensive commentary was on Isaiah, finished in 410 and consisting of eighteen books, each with its own preface. Jerome labored under the false impression that Isaiah was the work of one man, but followed his normal practice of alternating literal with spiritual exegesis, although he reproduced the Greek version only where it differed significantly from the Hebrew, in order to avoid excessive length (Latin text in Adraien 1963a-b; no English translation available; French study in Jay 1985).

Jerome's final commentary on the Old Testament was his unfinished work on Jeremiah. This was begun in 414 or 415, and was interrupted by Jerome's involvement in the Pelagian controversy. The commentary covers only thirty-two of Jeremiah's fifty-two chapters, but contains several interesting features. There is an increasing emphasis on the Hebrew text, and Jerome argues that the Septuagint text is unreliable, having been corrupted by copyists (*Commentary on Jeremiah* 17.1-4). Also interesting is the fact that Jerome criticizes his former hero, Origen, very severely. This is probably because of the Pelagians (who considered themselves to be the disciples of Origen), against whose beliefs Jerome wrote a treatise at this time (*Dialogue against the Pelagians*, PL 23; no English translation available). A third point of interest in this commentary is Jerome's concentration on straightforward literal interpretation of the text rather than on allegorical exegesis. This may be partly because he was writing for his friend Eusebius of Cremona, who preferred the literal sense (on these points, see Kelly 1975: 316).

Jerome stated that the purpose of a commentary is "to discuss what is obscure, to touch on the obvious, to dwell at length on what is doubtful" (*Commentary on Galatians* 4.6). Scripture, for Jerome, was full of obscurities and a reliable guide is needed. A commentary ought to "repeat the opinions of the many . . . so that the judicious reader, when he has perused the different explanations . . . may judge which is the best and, like a good banker, reject the money from a spurious mint" (*Apology against Rufinus* 1.16). In most of his commentaries, Jerome acknowledges the previous authors from whom he has borrowed. His citations are valuable because they transmit a great wealth of comments from other scholars, some of which would otherwise have been lost.

Literal and Allegorical Understanding

Jerome gave a great value to the literal sense of Scripture. Even in his very first piece of exegesis on the call of Isaiah, Jerome begins with a strictly literal historical exposition of "who this Uzziah was, how many years he had reigned and who among the other kings were his contemporaries" (*Epistle* 18A.1). Only after this does he move on to the spiritual interpretation of the passage.

Again, in the *Commentary on Ephesians*, composed in 388, Jerome interprets "Therefore it is said, 'Awake, O sleeper, and arise from the dead, and Christ shall give you light'" (5:14) by explaining that the words were spoken to Adam, who was buried at Calvary, where Christ was crucified. The place was called Calvary because the head of some ancient man had been buried there and because, when Christ was crucified, he was hanging directly above the place where it was buried. It is likely, though Jerome does not acknowledge it, that he is mainly dependent here on a work by Apollinarius of Laodicea (cf. Grützmacher 1901-08: II, 40).

While Jerome followed the Antiochene school's emphasis on the priority of the historical sense, he nevertheless believed that Christians must go beyond this to discover the fuller, deeper meaning of a passage. It was possible to understand this deeper meaning only with the aid of the allegorical or spiritual method.

When we study Jerome's allegorical exegesis, we see that he takes many of the specific interpretations directly from Origen, even to the extent of verbal borrowing. This is the case both before the Origenist controversy and later on, when Jerome had renounced Origen's theology as heretical. The influence of Origen, whom Jerome had once proudly called "my master," can be seen on almost every page of Jerome's writings.

One example of this influence is seen in Jerome's *Commentary on Matthew*. This is an interesting example, because Origen's comments on this passage are also extant. Jerome wrote this commentary in fourteen days, in order to provide a friend with some reading matter on a long sea voyage. In his interpretation of the parable of the hidden treasure (Matt. 13:44) Jerome has clearly followed Origen. The main points of their respective interpretations are set out below:

> The treasure is the word of God which appears to be hidden in the body of Christ, or the holy Scriptures in which rests the knowledge of the Savior. When the treasure is discovered, one must give up all the *emolumenta* ["benefits"] in order to possess it. (Jerome, *Comm. Matt. II*, 13:44; see Hurst and Adriaen, 1969)

> This is not a parable but a similitude. The field equals the Scripture. The treasure equals the mysteries lying within the Scripture, and finding the treasure a man hides it, thinking it dangerous to reveal to all and sundry the secrets of Scripture. He goes, sells all his possessions, and works until he can buy the field, in order that he may possess the great treasure. (Origen, *Comm. Matt.* on 13:44, GCS 40, 5)

Jerome's interpretation appears to have links with Origen's beyond the similarities one would expect in interpretation of this parable. Yet Jerome's interpretation is simpler and more direct than Origen's in its application of the meaning of the parable. Jerome is not interested in Origen's distinction between a parable and a similitude, the latter being a generic term, the former representing a particular form of similitude. It should be noted that Jerome sets down two different interpretations of the treasure — it is either the word of God hidden in the body of Christ or the knowledge of the Savior hidden in Scripture. His first interpretation does not stem from Origen, but comes rather from Jerome's characteristic ascetic interests.

It is not only specific passages of spiritual interpretation that Jerome borrows from Origen in the *Commentary on Matthew,* but also certain themes. One of these, very important for Origen, was the goodness of God, which Origen used to combat the Gnosticism of the day. This theme is seen running through Jerome's commentary, even though Gnosticism was not a problem he had to fight in his own situation.

Toward the end of his life, after the trauma of the Origenist controversy, Jerome was more critical of some of Origen's contentious exegetical interpretations, though he continued to use several specific examples of Origen's exegesis.

This trend may be seen most clearly in his *Commentary on Jeremiah*, where he denounces Origen as "that allegorist," fiercely attacks his unorthodox views, and relies less on Origen's allegorical interpretations than in any other commentary.

Jerome, then, used specific interpretations from representatives of both the Alexandrian and Antiochene schools for his own purposes. He was also the only church Father in the fourth century to have learned Hebrew, having taken lessons from leading Jewish scholars.

Use of Jewish Exegesis

One of the reasons for which Jerome is important in the history of biblical interpretation is that he used many Jewish interpretations of scriptural passages. Jerome believed that Jewish traditions of exegesis were of great importance for Christians in their interpretation of the Old Testament, so long as they were consistent with the teaching of the Bible.

In his *Commentary on Daniel* (5:2), Jerome records the following Jewish tradition concerning Belshazzar:

> The Hebrews hand down a story of this sort: Belshazzar, thinking that God's promise had remained without effect until the seventieth year, by which Jeremiah had said that the captivity of the Jewish people would have to be ended [cf. Jer. 25:12; 29:10ff.] — a matter of which Zechariah also speaks in the first part of his book [cf. Zech. 1:12ff.] — and turning the occasion of the failed promise into a celebration, gave a great banquet by way of mocking the expectation of the Jews and the vessels of the Temple of God.

Jeremiah had promised Israel that their exile would be temporary. After seventy years they would return to their own land and glory in the destruction of their oppressors, the Babylonians. The chronological problem is to determine which year begins the seventy-year period. B. *Megillah* 11b explains that Belshazzar began his count with the first year of Nebuchadnezzar's reign (605 BCE) but was mistaken in his calculations, a point which is implicit in Jerome's statement. The seventy-year period should have begun from the second year of Nebuchadnezzar's reign, not the first (cf. 2 Kgs. 24:1).

Scholars studying Jerome's use of rabbinic traditions have usually assumed that he took those traditions direct from Jewish sources (e.g., Braverman 1978; Penna 1950; Rahmer 1861, 1902; Jay 1985). There are, however, a few instances where it is clear that he has copied out the Jewish material from the writings of Origen, who also made some use of Jewish traditions. One example is seen in one of Jerome's early letters (*Epistle* 18A.15) dealing with the topic of the two seraphim in Isa. 6:6-9, where Jerome compares Isaiah and Moses. He says that he has discussed this with some Jews and reassures his reader that this tradition comes from an excellent (Jewish) source and should be accepted. Jerome gives the impression that he has gleaned this tradition from direct conversation and study with Jews. In fact, however, he borrowed it from Origen, who had reported it in his sixth *Homily on Isaiah*, saying that both Isaiah and Moses had refused God's command at first, on the basis of their unworthiness, but had subsequently accepted it.

JEROME'S LEGACY

Jerome was essentially an eclectic scholar. He searched diligently in the works of others and drew the best points from each, while striving to avoid their errors. This holds true also of the different "schools" of interpretation accessible to Jerome — Alexandrian, Antiochene, and Jewish.

From the Antiochene school, Jerome learned that interpreters of the Bible must first study and explain the literal, plain sense, and only after this has been accomplished should they venture beyond this to the deeper, spiritual interpretation. From the Alexandrian school, especially Origen, Jerome borrowed many specific allegorical interpretations. Jerome cites Alexandrian authors much more frequently than he does Antiochenes, not because he was more dependent on the former, but rather because the works of Alexandrian exegetes were more readily accessible. Also, the Antiochene school was still in its youth when Jerome was writing and had produced a relatively small collection of commentaries from which he could borrow. From Jewish exegesis, Jerome learned the primary importance of the Hebrew text of the Old Testament. He was unique among the early Fathers of the church in his use of the Hebrew text as the basis for his exegesis of the Old Testament.

Even during his lifetime, Jerome was held by many to be a great authority on the interpretation of the Bible. Jerome's contemporary, Sulpicius Severus, wrote in 405: "I would be surprised if he [Jerome] were not already known to you through his writings since he is read throughout the world" (*Dialogues* 1.8).

In the centuries following Jerome's death, he was universally acknowledged as the prince of Christian biblical scholars, and his translation of the Bible became accepted everywhere as the standard biblical text in the western church. His works became a fertile ground for the labors of subsequent exegetes who recognized that his immense and intimate knowledge and understanding of the Bible surpassed that of any other Christian scholar for centuries.

Although Jerome wrote commentaries on several of the Pauline letters and on Matthew's Gospel, it is for his Old Testament commentaries that he is chiefly remembered. He is the only ancient author who commented on all the Major and Minor Prophets. Jerome saw it as his special task to explain these Old Testament books because they were more difficult to understand than the books of the New Testament.

Jerome's enormous erudition is exhibited on every page of his writings. He quotes frequently from classical authors as well as from the Bible and other Christian writers. In addition, Jerome, with his highly developed powers of observation, makes many suggestive and original contributions to the understanding of the biblical text.

The writings of Jerome are of lasting value to Christians today because they offer us a splendid example of the state of biblical interpretation in the West in the fourth century, because they give us an interesting insight into relations between Christians and Jews in the generations after Christianity became the religion of the State, and also because they paint for us, in vivid colors, a picture of the "irascible monk" who devoted his life to the study of the sacred Scriptures — in his own words: "What other life can there be without the knowledge of the Scriptures, for through these Christ himself, who is the life of the faithful, becomes known" (*Epistle* 30.7).

BIBLIOGRAPHY

Adraien, M. (ed.)

1963a   *Commentariorum in Essaiam Libri I-XI.* Corpus Christianorum Series Latina 73. Turnhout.

1963b   *Commentariorum in Essaiam Libri XII-XVIII.* Corpus Christianorum Series Latina 73a. Turnhout.

Allgeier, A.

1926   "Ist das Psalterium iuxta Hebraeos die letzte (3) Psalmen — Übersetzung des hl. Hieronymus?" *Theologie und Glaube* 18:671-87.

1930   "Der Brief an Sunnia und Fretela und seine Bedeutung fur die Textherstellung der Vulgata," *Biblica* 11:86-107.

1931   "Die erste Psalmenübersetzung des hl. Hieronymus und das Psalterium Romanum." *Biblica* 12:447-82.

Antin, P.

1956   *St. Jerome, In Ionam.* Sources Chrétiennes 43. Paris: Cerf.

Archer, G. L. (trans.)

1958   *Jerome's Commentary on Daniel.* Grand Rapids: Baker.

Arns, E. P.

1953   *La Technique du Livre d'après S. Jérôme.* Paris: de Boccard.

Bardy, G.

1934   "S. Jérôme et ses maîtres Hébreux." *Revue Bénédictine* 46:145-64.

Barr, J.

1966   "St. Jerome's Appreciation of Hebrew." *Bulletin of the John Rylands Library* 49:280-302.

1967   "St. Jerome and the Sound of Hebrew." *JSS* 12:1-36.

Bartelink, G. J. M.

1980   *Hieronymus: Liber de Optimo Genere Interpretandi (Epistula 57). Ein Kommentar.* Leiden: Brill.

Berger, S.

1893   *Histoire de la Vulgate.* Paris: Hachette.

Bevenot, H.

1924   "Hieronymus und die Vulgata des N.T." *Theologische Revue* 23:241-44.

Bihlmeyer, P.

1920   "Hieronymus und die lateinische Bibel." *Benediktiner Monatsschrift* 2:407-24.

Bonnard, E.

1977   *Saint Jerome: Commentaire sur S. Matthieu I* (Livres I-II). Sources Chrétiennes. Paris: Cerf.

Braverman, J.

1978   *Jerome's Commentary on Daniel: A Study of Comparative Jewish and Christian Interpretations of the Hebrew Bible.* CBQMS 7. Washington: Catholic Biblical Association of America.

Brown, D.

1993   *Vir Trilinguis: A Study in the Biblical Exegesis of Saint Jerome.* Kampen: Kok Pharos.

Bruyne, D. de

1920   *Préfaces de la Bible Latine.* Namur: Godenna.

1929   "La lettre de Jérôme à Sunnia et Fretela sur le Psautier." *ZNW* 28:1-13.

1930   "Le problème du psautier romain." *Revue Biblique* 42: 101-26.

Burkitt, F. C.

1896   *The Old Latin and the Itala.* Cambridge: Cambridge University Press.

Burstein, E.

1975   "La compétence de Jérôme en Hébreu. Explication de certaines erreurs." *Revue des Études Augustiniennes* 21:3-12.

Cannon, W. W.

1927   "Jerome and Symmachus: Some Points in the Vulgate Translation of Koheleth."
        ZAW 45:191-99.

Cavallera, F.

1922   *Saint Jérôme. Sa Vie et son oeuvre.* 2 vols. Paris: Champion.

Chapman, J.

1908   *Notes on the Early History of the Vulgate Gospels.* Oxford: Oxford University Press.

1923   "St. Jerome and the Vulgate New Testament." *JTS* 24:33-51, 113-25, 282-99.

Condamin, A.

1911-12 "Les caractères de la traduction de la bible par S. Jérôme." *RSR* 2:425-40; 3:105-38.

1914   "L'Influence de la tradition juive dans la version de S. Jérôme." *RSR* 5:1-21.

Cooper, C. M.

1950   "Jerome's 'Hebrew Psalter' and the New Latin Version." *JBL* 69:233-44.

Cottineau, L. H.

1920   "Chronologie des versions bibliques de S. Jérôme." In *Miscellanea Geronimiana,*
        43-68. Rome: Vatican Press.

Cummings, J. T.

1975   "St. Jerome as Translator and Exegete." In E. A. Livingstone, ed., *Texte und Unter-
        suchungen,* 279-82. Studia Patristica 12. Berlin: Akademie.

Durand, D.

1916   "S. Jérôme et notre N.T. latin." *RSR* 7:531-49.

Duval, Y. M.

1968   "Saint Jérôme devant le baptême des hérétiques." *Revue des Études Augustiniennes*
        14:145-81.

1973   *Le Livre de Jonas dans la littérature chrétienne grecque et latine. Sources et influence
        du Commentaire sur Jonas de saint Jérôme.* 2 vols. Paris: Institute d'Études
        Augustiniennes.

1985   "Jérôme et les prophètes. Histoire, prophétie, actualité et actualisation dans les
        Commentaires de Nahum, Michée, Abdias et Joel." In VTS 36, 108-31. Leiden: Brill.

Estin, C.

1984   *Les Psautiers de Jérôme à la lumière des traductions juives antérieures.* Collectanea
        Biblica Latina XV. Rome: Biblia Sacra.

Ginzberg, L.

1933   "Die Haggada bei den Kirchenvätern: V. Der Kommentar des Hieronymus zu
        Koheleth." In V. Aptowitzer, A. J. Schwarz, and S. Katz, eds., *Abhandlungen zur
        Erinnerung an Hirsch Perez Chajes,* 22-50. Vienna: Ayer.

1935   "Die Haggada bei den Kirchenvätern VI. Der Kommentar des Hieronymus zu
        Jesaya." In S. W. Baron and A. Marx, eds., *Jewish Studies in Memory of George A.
        Kohut,* 279-314. New York.

Glorie, F. (ed.)

1964   *Commentariorum in Hiezechielem Libri XIV.* Corpus Christianorum, Series Latina 75. Brussels: Turnhout.

Glunz, H. H.

1933   *History of the Vulgate in England.* Cambridge: Cambridge University Press.

Gorce, D.

1974   "St. Jerome et son environnement artistique et liturgique." *Collectanea Cisterciensia* 36:150-78.

Gordon, C. H.

1930   "Rabbinic Exegesis in the Vulgate of Proverbs." *JBL* 49:384-416.

Grützmacher, G.

1901-08 *Hieronymus: Eine biographische Studie zur alten Kirchengeschichte.* 3 vols. Berlin.

Hagendahl, H.

1958   *Latin Fathers and the Classics.* Göteborg: Almqvist and Wiksell.
1974   "Jerome and the Latin Classics." *Vigiliae Christianae* 28:216-27.

Harden, J. M.

1922   *Psalterium iuxta Hebraeos Hieronymi.* London: SPCK.

Hayward, C. T. R.

1985   "Jewish Traditions in Jerome's Commentary on Jeremiah and the Targum of Jeremiah." *Proceedings of the Irish Biblical Association* 9:100-120.
1987   "Saint Jerome and the Aramaic Targumim." *JSS* 32:105-23.
1990   *Jerome's Hebrew Questions on Genesis.* Oxford: Clarendon.

Helm, R. (ed.)

1956   *Die Chronik des Hieronymus.* Die griechischen Christlichen Schriftsteller der ersten Jahrhunderte 47. Berlin.

Hort, F. J. A.

1890   "Introduction." In Westcott and Hort, eds., 1881-96, vol. 2, 1-261.

Howarth, H. H.

1908-12 "The Influence of St. Jerome on the Canon of the Western Church." *JTS* 10:481-96; 11:321-47; 13:1-18.

Hritzu, J. N.

1939   *The Style of the Letters of St. Jerome.* CUAPS 60. Washington: Catholic University of America Press.

Hulley, K. K.

1944   "Principles of Textual Criticism Known to St. Jerome." *Harvard Studies in Classical Philology* 55:87-109.

Hurst, D., and M. Adraien
1969   "Jerome: Commentary on Matthew 13:44." In *Commentariorum in Mattheum Libri IV.* Corpus Christianorum, Series Latina 77. Brussels: Turnhout.

Jay, P.
1973   "Sur la date de naissance de Saint Jérôme." *Revue des Études latines* 51:262-80.
1980   "Saint Jérôme et le triple sens de l'Écriture." *Revue des Études Augustiniennes* 26:214-27.
1982   "La datation des premières traductions de l'Ancien Testament sur l'Hébreu par Saint Jérôme." *Revue des Études Augustiniennes* 28:208-12.
1985   *L'Exégèse de saint Jérôme d'après son Commentaire sur Isaie.* Paris: Institute d'Études Augustiniennes.

Johannesohn, M.
1948   "Hieronymus und die jüngeren griechischen Übersetzungen des A.T." *Theologische Literaturzeitung* 73:145-52.
1952   "Zur Entstehung der Ausdrucksweise der lateinischen Vulgate aus den jüngeren alttestamentlichen Übersetzungen." *ZNW* 44:90-102.

Kamesar, A.
1993   *Jerome, Greek Scholarship and the Hebrew Bible.* Oxford: Oxford University Press.

Kedar-Kopfstein, B.
1968   *The Vulgate as a Translation: Some Semantic and Syntactical Aspects of Jerome's Version of the Hebrew Bible.* Jerusalem: Hebrew University of Jerusalem Press.

Kelly, J. N. D.
1975   *Jerome: His Life, Writings and Controversies.* London: Duckworth.

Lagrange, M. J.
1898   "S. Jérôme et la tradition juive dans la Genèse." *RB* 7:563-66.
1917   "La Vulgate Latine de l'Épitre aux Galates et le Texte Grec." *RB* n.s. 14:424-50.
1918   "La Révision de la Vulgate par S. Jérôme." *RB* n.s. 15:254-57.

Larbaud, V.
1956   *Sankt Hieronymus, Schutzpatron der Übersetzer.* Munich: Kügel.

Lardet, P.
1991   *L'Apologie de Jérôme contre Rufin. Un commentaire.* Leiden: Brill.

Lawlor, T. C.
1963   *The Letters of St. Jerome* I. London: Paulist.

Mangenot, E.
1900   "Les manuscrits grecs des Évangiles employés par S. Jérôme." *Revue des sciences ecclésiastiques* 81:56-73.
1918   "Saint Jérôme réviseur du Nouveau Testament." *RB* n.s. 15:244-53.

Marks, J. H.
1956   *Der textkritische Wert des Psalterium Hieronymi juxta Hebraeos.* Winterthur: Keller.

Meershoek, G. Q. A.

1966　*Le Latin biblique d'après Saint Jérôme.* Latinitas Christianorum Primaeva 20. Utrecht: Ecker en Vande Vegt.

Metlin, M.

1937　"Letter of St. Jerome to the Gothic Clergymen Sunnia and Fritila concerning Places in Their Copy of the Psalter Which Had Been Corrupted from the Septuagint." *Journal of English and Germanic Philology* 86:515-42.

Metzger, B. M.

1977　"St. Jerome's Explicit References to Variant Readings in Manuscripts of the New Testament." In E. Best and R. McL. Wilson (eds.), *Text and Interpretation: Studies in the New Testament Presented to Matthew Black,* 179-210. Cambridge: Cambridge University Press.

Metzger B. M. (ed.)

1963　*The Text of the New Testament.* Oxford: Oxford University Press.

Murphy, F. X. (ed.)

1952　*A Monument to St. Jerome.* New York: Sheed and Ward.

Nautin, P.

1973-74 "Études de chronologie hieronymienne (393-397)." *Revue des Études Augustiniennes* 19:69-86, 213-39; 20:251-84.

Newton, W. L.

1943　"Influences on St. Jerome's Translation of the Old Testament." *CBQ* 5:17-33.

Nowack, W.

1875　*Die Bedeutung des Hieronymus für die Alttestamentliche Textkritik.* Göttingen: Vandenhoeck und Ruprecht.

Penna, A.

1950　*Principe e carattere dell' esegesi di S. Girolamo.* Rome: Pontifical Biblical Institute.

Pope, H.

1914　"St. Jerome's Latin Text of St. Paul's Epistles." *ITQ* 9:413-45.

Rahmer, M.

1861　*Die hebräischen Traditionen in den Werken des Hieronymus. Quaestiones in Genesim.* Breslau: Schletter.

1902　*Die hebräischen Traditionen in den Werken des Hieronymus. Die Kommentarien zu der 12 kleinen Propheten.* 2 vols. Berlin: Poppelauer.

Rehm, M.

1954　"Die Bedeutung hebräischen Worter bei Hieronymus." *Biblica* 29:174-97.

Reuschenbach, F.

1948　*Hieronymus als Übersetzer der Genesis.* Limburg: Lahn.

Ronsch, H.
1875   *Itala und Vulgata*. 2nd edition. Marburg: Elwert.

Rousseau, P.
1978   *Ascetics, Authority and the Church in the Age of Jerome and Cassian*. Oxford: Oxford University Press.

Schatkin, M. A.
1970   "The Influence of Origen upon St. Jerome's Commentary on Galatians." *Vigiliae Christianae* 24:49-58.

Schaublin, C.
1973   "Textkritisches zu den Briefen des Hieronymus." *Museum Helvidium* 30:55-62.

Scourfield, J. H. D.
1993   *Consoling Heliodorus: A Commentary on Jerome Letter 60*. Oxford: Oxford University Press.

Semple, W. H.
1965   "St. Jerome as a Biblical Translator." *Bulletin of the John Rylands Library* 48:227-43.

Siegfried, C.
1884   "Die Aussprache des hebräischen bei Hieronymus." *ZAW* 4:34-83.

Siegfried, O.
1883   "Midraschisches zu Hieronymus und Pseudo-Hieronymus." *Jahrbücher für protestantische Theologie* 9:346-52.

Skehan, P. W.
1952   "St. Jerome and the Canon of the Holy Scriptures." In F. X. Murphy (ed.), *A Monument to St. Jerome*, 259-87. New York: Sheed and Ward.

Smith, H. P.
1891   "The Value of the Vulgate Old Testament for Textual Criticism." *Presbyterian and Reformed Review* 2:216-34.

Spanier, M.
1896   *Exegetische Beiträge zu Hieronymus Onomastikon*. Magdeburg: Heinrichshofen.

Studer, B.
1968   "À propos des traductions d'Origène par Jérôme et Rufin." *Vet. Christ.* 5:137-55.

Stummer, F.
1929   "Einige Beobachtungen über die Arbeitsweise des Hieronymus bei den Übersetzung des Alten Testaments aus der hebraica veritas." *Biblica* 10:1-30.
1937   "Beiträge zu dem Problem 'Hieronymus und die Targumim.'" *Biblica* 18:174-81.

Süss, W.
1933   *Studien zur lateinischen Bibel*. Tartu: Tartu University Press.

Sutcliffe, E. F.

1948a   "The Name 'Vulgate.'" *Biblica* 29:345-52.
1948b   "St. Jerome's Hebrew Manuscripts." *Biblica* 29:195-204.
1948c   "St. Jerome's Pronunciation of Hebrew." *Biblica* 29:112-25.

Vaccari, A.

1920   "I Fattori dell' exegesi geronimiana." *Biblica* 1:458-80.
1952   *Scritti di erudizione e di filologia,* vol. I. Rome.

Vogels, H. J.

1928   *Vulgatastudien: Die Evangelien der Vulgata untersucht auf ihre lateinische und griechische Vorlage.* Münster: Aschendorf.

Ward, A.

1932   "Jerome's Work on the Psalter." *Expository Times* 44:87-92.

Weber, R.

1953   *Le Psautier Romain et les autres anciens Psautiers Latins.* Collectanea Biblica 10. Rome: Abbaye Saint-Jérôme.

Westcott, B. F., and F. J. A. Hort (eds.)

1881-96 *The New Testament in the Original Greek.* 2 vols. New York: Harper and Brothers.

Wutz, F. X.

1933   *Die Transkriptionen von der Septuaginta bis zu Hieronymus.* Berlin.

Ziegler, L.

1879   *Lateinischen Bibelübersetzungen von Hieronymus.* Munich: Reidel.

CHAPTER 14

Augustine and the Close of the Ancient Period of Interpretation

Richard A. Norris, Jr.

BACKGROUND

Augustine (Aurelius Augustinus, 354-430 CE) was born in the town of Thagaste in the Roman province of Africa Proconsularis. His mother Monica, a pious Christian, enrolled him as a catechumen shortly after his birth, and such awareness as he had of the content of Christian faith and the style of Christian life he owed to her teaching and example. It did not include familiar acquaintance with any portion of the church's Scriptures or any "method" of interpreting them; and indeed his early education introduced him to quite another canon of literature, that of the grammar school, where he was immersed in the accepted classics of Latin literature, primarily Virgil and Cicero, as texts to be memorized, analyzed word by word, and studied for the rhetorical devices they employed to instruct, please, or move their readers. In the early stages of this exclusively literary and rhetorical education he apparently showed himself a gifted pupil. In any case, his mother and his father Patricius pressed him to pursue his education further, knowing that success in the business of words, in the calling of a rhetor, was the passport that could take their talented child out of the straitened life of a provincial town. Their financial sacrifices, and the patronage of a local grandee, Romanianus, enabled Augustine to pursue his studies first at Madaura and then at Carthage itself, where eventually his skill in the arts of rhetoric enabled him to set up as a teacher. In 383 — aged twenty-nine — he moved to Rome and then was appointed professor of rhetoric at Milan, an imperial capital, a year later. He had risen to the top of his profession and become a skilled and reflective artificer and interpreter of verbal constructions.

Principal Works of Augustine Illustrating or Bearing on His Exegesis

On Catechizing the Uninstructed (De catechizandis rudibus)
Against Faustus the Manichean (Contra Faustum Manichaeum)
The City of God (De civitate Dei)
Harmony of the Gospels (De consensu evangelistarum)
Confessions (Confessionum Libri XIII)
On Christian Doctrine, or *The Art of Christian Instruction (De doctrina christiana)*
Expositions of the Psalms (Enarrationes in Psalmos)
Letters (Epistulae)
On Genesis against the Manicheans (De Genesi adversus Manichaeos)
The Literal Meaning of Genesis (De Genesi ad litteram libri XII)
Incomplete Literal Commentary on Genesis (De Genesi ad litteram opus imperfectum)
Tractates on the Gospel according to John (In Johannis evangelium tractatus CXXIV)
On the Teacher (De magistro)
On the Morals of the Catholic Church and of the Manicheans (De moribus catholicae ecclesiae et de moribus Manichaeorum)
On the Lord's Sermon on the Mount (De sermone Domini in monte libri II)
Sermons (Sermones)
To Simplician on Various Questions (Ad Simplicianum de diversis quaestionibus)
On the Spirit and the Letter (De spiritu et littera)
On the Trinity (De trinitate)
On the Usefulness of Believing (De utilitate credendi)
On True Religion (De vera religione)

Initial Encounters with the Scriptures

It was in the course of this education, when still a student in Carthage, that Augustine took his first serious look at the church's Scriptures. At the age of nineteen he underwent a conversion to "philosophy," that is, to the search for human fulfillment *(beatitudo)* through wisdom, a search that was both intellectual and moral and was understood to involve a certain detachment from worldly values. This experience came to him in the act of reading a dialogue (now lost) of Cicero's, the *Hortensius,* an exhortation to love of wisdom. Given Augustine's upbringing, it was natural that he should turn, in pursuit of this ideal, to the Bible, which North African Christians understood to promulgate God's rules for the conduct of human life. That collection, however, once he examined it, disappointed and indeed repelled him. Scripture, he reports, "seemed to me unworthy to be compared with the nobility of Cicero" (*conf.* 3.5.9). He thought the language and diction of the old Latin versions that circulated in North Africa crude, as he did much of the content of the Old Testament, full as it was not merely of stories of doubtful accuracy but of polygamy, rapine, incest, and slaughter. He turned, therefore, to Manicheanism, a dualistic movement that claimed to embody true Christianity and certainly honored, as a source of wisdom, the Christ whom his mother confessed. For the young Augustine, the Manicheans represented an enlightened Christianity. Not only did they repudiate the Old Testament and its barbarities, moral as well as stylistic, and raise questions about the authenticity of the received text of the New Testament; not only did they deprecate the authoritarianism of the North African church and make their appeal not to faith, the servant of authority, but to reason; they also commended an ascetic way as essential to the search for fulfilling wisdom. Thus they satisfied at once Augustine's loyalty to the faith of his childhood, his mild contempt — normal in an upwardly mobile young intellectual — for "old ways," and his need for a strenuous ideal. He remained a practicing, if somewhat quizzical, Manichean until his arrival in Milan, by which time he had despaired of being entirely sure of anything and espoused the delicate skepticism of the Middle Academy as mediated through Cicero.

It was just at this point that Augustine once again encountered the Christian Scriptures — not as read by the Manicheans, at the foot of the letter and with intent to subvert, but as expounded by Ambrose, former governor of the province of Liguria and now the powerful and controversial bishop of Milan (374-97). Ambrose was the sort of person an Augustine could respect — not so much as an adept at the business of power, though he was that, but as a classically educated rhetor who, unlike the young African, was fluent in Greek as well as Latin and who in his preaching "every Lord's day" (*conf.* 6.3.4) brought to the interpretation of the Bible the techniques and insights of Greek exegetes in the tradition of Philo and Origen. Ambrose's preaching seemed, by its practice of an exegesis in the Alexandrian manner, to transpose the text of the Scriptures into a new and nobler key and to show how the "calumnies" of the Manicheans against the Law and the Prophets might be refuted. Ambrose commended to his congregation, as a "rule" for understanding the Scriptures, the Pauline statement that "The letter kills, but the spirit gives life" (2 Cor. 3:6) — a text that Augustine, as we shall see, was to muse upon for the rest of his life and employ variously in different connections.

The unexpected result of this encounter with Ambrose was that Augustine came, in his search for fulfillment in wisdom, to favor the way defined by catholic Christianity and even to recognize, not inconsistently with his new skepticism (cf. *util. cred.* 8.20), that the church was justified in its demand that people believe — that is, that they take on authority — truths that are difficult or impossible to demonstrate. "Since we were too feeble to discover the truth by pure reason and hence stood in need of the authority of holy writings," he was prepared to acknowledge the Scriptures as divinely supplied means of coming to "believe in God and to seek God." He had not lost his sense of the (superficial) absurdity and difficulty of many passages in the Bible, but Ambrose had taught him to perceive these phenomena as pointers to the "depth of the mysteries" *(sacramentorum)* taught there. The Bible, he understood, following long tradition, is "available to all for reading" and "would open itself to any and all by its understandable language and its unassuming style," but at the same time it rewarded the "close attention" of those who are not "light-minded" and are thus prepared to explore its profundities (*conf.* 6.5.8; cf. Sir. 19:4a).

Neoplatonist Lessons

At this point, when he was basically convinced "that in Christ . . . and by [the] Scriptures" God has "provided a way of human salvation, leading to the life that shall come to be after this death" (*conf.* 7.7.11), Augustine records how Neoplatonism, in the form of treatises by Plotinus and Porphyry, came to his aid as he wrestled with problems regarding the origin and nature of evil. In these writings, Augustine not only discovered an answer — new to him if not to Platonist or even Christian tradition — to the question of the nature of evil: it is not something that exists in its own right but is the corruption of something good. He also thought that he perceived in the Neoplatonist hierarchy of levels of reality, a scheme that was the substantive equivalent of the teaching of John 1:1-5. He equated the Johannine Word and Wisdom of God — that very divine Son of whom Paul had said that he was originally "in the form of God" (Phil. 2:6) — with the second hypostasis ("Mind" or "Intellect," *nous*) of the Plotinian scheme. Furthermore, in that "witness to the light" who "was not the light" (John 1:7-8) he saw imaged the human soul, which can find itself only by turning to this truth that illumines it from above. Augustine's discovery of Neoplatonism was thus intimately tied up with what were, for him, momentous insights into central New Testament passages. This occasioned an exegetical disclosure in which the philosopher's quest for wisdom and the believer's faith in God came together in a single motion of desire and intuition. "Wisdom," for him, now clearly meant "the light that lightens every human being" (John 1:9), the very mind of God expressed as the Word, the Son, of God.

Plotinus, however, had something further to teach Augustine: "I was admonished to return into myself" (*conf.* 7.10.16). In the Neoplatonist vision of things, the seeker's way to true wisdom, to the ultimate and fulfilling truth which is God, was an inward way. It moved not through things external to the self, but through its own interior awareness ("the eye of the soul"); and there the soul discovered, as Augustine describes his own experience of following this interior way, "an unchangeable light that lay above the very eye of the soul, above my mind" — that very same "light that enlightens every human being" (*conf.* 7.10.16; cf. John 1:9). Augustine could not sustain this vision, however, and thus in the very act of apprehending the light knew himself to be alienated from it. "I discovered that I was a long way from you," he writes, quoting Plotinus, "in 'the realm of unlikeness'" (*conf.* 7.10.16), that is to say, in the realm where things fall into isolation and mutual externality and subsist only in their not being something else.

This awareness of having somehow lost a hold on truth and goodness did not, however, alter Augustine's sense of the goal of his search for wisdom. It was now understood to be a knowledge, an intellectual "vision," of the truth that is God, but a knowledge in which God and the self — Paul's "interior self" (*ho esō anthrōpos*, Rom. 7:22) — communicate directly and so share an intimate presence to each other that is not externally mediated. In his account of the famous vision at Ostia (*conf.* 9.10.24), Augustine describes how he and Monica ascended "step by step" (*gradatim*) through "all corporeal things," including the heavens themselves, and then entered into their "minds" before touching upon "the realm of plenteousness unfailing," to participate in the life of the divine wisdom — but only momentarily. He proceeds then to lament the loss of this vision ("If only it might last!") even while explaining the mode of its occurrence (*conf.* 9.10.25): it occurs when all images are bypassed, when the soul itself is quiet and unselfconscious, and when "all language and every sign and whatever comes to be in passing is silenced." For then God

> himself alone would speak, not through them but through himself, so that we should hear his word not by means of the language of the flesh

nor the voice of an angel nor the sound of thunder nor a cryptic analogy, but we should hear himself, the one we love in all these things, and hear him apart from these. (*conf.* 9.10.25)

Such unmediated communication with God, occurring apart from signs (i.e., language of any sort), Augustine had already discerned in the "spring" that, according to Gen. 2:6, "came up from the earth and . . . watered the entire face of the earth." Seeing "earth" here as a symbol for the soul, he took the image of water welling up from within the earth as a similitude for God's direct, interior teaching of the soul; and he contrasted this mode of divine teaching with that symbolized by rain pouring down on the earth from dark clouds (Gen. 2:5) and so coming to the soul from outside "in the form of human words." This latter form of teaching is necessary to a fallen humanity that has forsaken God; but, writes Augustine,

it shall come to nothing. For now we see darkly *(in aenigmate),* like people searching for nourishment in the darkness of a rain cloud; but then "face to face" [1 Cor. 13:12], when the entire face of our earth shall be watered by the interior spring of flowing water. (*De Genesi adversus Manichaeos* 2.5).

This vision of the end (and presumably of Adam's unfallen state as well) intimates the shape of the salvation to which God "by the Scriptures" provides "the way." Yet the Scriptures themselves are an external medium in the form of human words and therefore, one must suppose, something of an *aenigma.* This obvious tension — between a goal in which mediation is to be overcome and the externally supplied "media" prescribed as the way to its attainment — gave Augustine material for much reflection and in the end, we shall see, affected his way of reading and using the biblical writings.

THE STUDENT OF THE SCRIPTURES

Augustine reports that after his encounter with "the Platonist books" he "greedily snatched up the awesome writing of [God's] Spirit, and most of all the Apostle Paul" (*conf.* 7.21.27). In fact, during the time of his conversion and baptism (386-87), he was just beginning to become acquainted with the Scriptures. He himself, after his (involuntary) ordination to the presbyterate at Hippo in 391, asked his bishop for time off to study the Scriptures in preparation for the duties of preaching, and in 392 he wrote to Jerome at Bethlehem to request Latin translations of Greek commentaries on biblical books (and especially those of Origen: *Epistle* 28.2). Needless to say, he read the scriptural commentaries of Jerome himself, and Jerome, even though the two never met, became Augustine's principal guide to understanding the Bible. This influence, together with that of Ambrose and no doubt Hilary of Poitiers, assured that Augustine would stand, broadly speaking, in the Alexandrian tradition of biblical interpretation. Unlike Jerome, however — for whose learning he maintained the greatest respect over the years, even when they (inevitably) quarreled — Augustine knew no Hebrew and even in his maturity read Greek only with difficulty. He was never a learned exegete, then: his interest in the Bible was that of a seeker, of a theologian whose mind never ceased to generate awkward questions, but above all of a preacher dedicated to showing people "the way" to God, which the Scriptures set out.

It is arguable that he developed, though not without the stimulus of a writer like the Donatist Tyconius, a fresh and unaccustomed reading of Paul — a reading whose echoes and adaptations have dominated much of medieval, reformation, and modern theology in the Latin churches of the west. The course of his developing understanding of Paul — usefully studied by Babcock (1979, 1982) and Burns (1980) — is reflected not only in his controversial writings against Pelagianism (and especially perhaps in the treatise *On the Spirit and the Letter*) and in brief commentaries on Romans and Galatians, but also in a crucial earlier work, *To Simplician on Diverse Questions*.

Augustine attempted four commentaries on the opening chapters of the Bible — two allegorical *(conf.* 11-13 and *On Genesis against the Manicheans)* and two literal *(Incomplete Literal Commentary on Genesis* and the twelve books of the final *Literal Commentary on Genesis)*. In the process he exhibited the restless intensity of his theological and exegetical probings. His exegesis is probably best studied, however, in his *Expositions on the Psalms,* the composition of which occupied almost thirty years; in a relatively early work, *The Lord's Sermon on the Mount;* in his homilies on the Gospel and First Epistle of John; and in his numerous sermons. Much of his exegesis, and not only in his early years as a Christian, was driven and given focus by Manichean attacks on the Scriptures of the Old Testament as catholics read and received them — attacks that he set out to answer systematically in *Against Faustus* and in his *Harmony of the Gospels.*

The Canon

Augustine is explicit about the list of books he reckons as Scripture: his canon, given in *The Art of Christian Instruction (doc. chr.)* 2.8.13, is the same as that acknowledged by the Council of Carthage of 397 (which he attended).

It differs very slightly, however, in its Old Testament list from that enjoined on the Egyptian churches by Athanasius in his thirty-ninth Festal Letter (367). Augustine's Old Testament was that of the Septuagint and thus included the books of the so-called "Apocrypha," to which Athanasius had assigned a secondary status, reckoning them suitable only for devotional reading. Indeed Augustine — perhaps unaware of Athanasius's views — attached great importance to the general agreement of the Latin- and Greek-speaking churches on the authority of this traditional Greek version of the Jewish Scriptures, whose contents were reproduced in the retranslations and revisions of the Latin Bible made by Jerome and eventually collected in the Vulgate. Augustine even objected to Jerome's project of translating Old Testament books directly from the Hebrew on the ground that the Septuagint enjoys "the weightiest authority" (*gravissima auctoritas, Epistle* 28.2) and had indeed been guided by God's Spirit (*City of God* 18.43; *doc. chr.* 2.15.22; 4.16.48).

Augustine's New Testament included, of course, "the Gospel in four books," the whole collection of writings traditionally assigned to Paul (including Hebrews, whose Pauline authorship Augustine, like Jerome, came to doubt), Acts, the Apocalypse of John, and seven "catholic" epistles. He was aware that not all churches agreed on his list, and he was prepared to acknowledge that a lesser degree of authority attached to writings that were not accepted by all catholic churches. His general principle in the matter of canonicity was to "follow the authority of the greatest number of catholic churches, among which are of course counted those that have merited possession of apostolic seats and reception of apostolic letters" (*doc. chr.* 2.8.12).

This appeal to authority is not casual. It illustrates Augustine's principle that one "must begin with faith" in order to "achieve understanding", later, if the moral quality of one's life permits (*util. cred.* 9.21-22.). It marks out, as suggested above, the foundation of Augustine's acceptance of the Scriptures. His desertion of the Manichean cause was at its core attributable to a conviction that the mind's and heart's search for wisdom and truth, since it is in the end a search for God, cannot be carried through apart from the guidance of some divine authority; and that authority he found, as we have seen, in "the way of the catholic discipline" (*util. cred.* 8.20; *conf.* 6.5.8), a discipline in which the Scriptures figured as the embodiment of a communication from God. What Augustine the rhetorician saw in the Scriptures, then, was the external, verbal communication of the divine Rhetorician. To understand his view of the Bible and his handling of it is to grasp what this way of perceiving the Scriptures entailed for him and how it fit in with his theological outlook.

Presuppositions

First of all, it entailed a conviction that the writings contained in the canon are inspired. Augustine is not perfectly clear about the nature of this inspiration. He asserts that God ministers "his Word to human beings through human beings" (*util. cred.* pr. 1.6). This occurred as the Holy Spirit guided the minds of the human authors by suggesting what they were to write (*con. ev.* 2.52); but such overruling guidance did not, at least in the case of the four evangelists, exclude differences of language, emphasis, detail, or point of view — any more than, in Augustine's view, the divergences of the Septuagint from the Hebrew texts represented a divergence from the intent of the divine Author of both. In practice, then, the inspiration of the Scriptures implied that the intent of the human authors, or of the text that they produced, is the same as that of the divine Spirit that inspires them; but it does not exclude significant diversity in the expression of that "mind" (*con. ev.* 2.128, 28). It does, however, exclude outright substantive inconsistencies, whether within the work of a single writer or among different writers giving accounts of the same subject matter. Acceptance of the authority of the church's Scriptures, then, requires that they be taken as truthful in what they intend to communicate.

The seriousness with which Augustine took this principle can be seen in his attack on Jerome's reading of Gal. 2:11ff. Jerome had interpreted the disagreement of Peter and Paul at Antioch as a bit of play-acting on their part, a pretense designed to force a decision about the issue of the inclusion of Gentiles in the church. Augustine argued that Jerome's position was intolerable, on the ground that it implied that a canonical writing contained a deliberate lie. The Scriptures, he maintained, could not contain any statement whose intent was to mislead readers (*Epistle* 82.3.24). His position was that if any passage or sentence made him suspect it of being untruthful, he would suppose either that the copyist had transcribed the text incorrectly or that the translator had made an error, or else that he himself had simply misunderstood it (*Epistle* 82.1.3). Needless to say, this position was important to Augustine not merely because the church's authority presented the Scriptures as trustworthy, but also because much of the substance of Manichean — and, in Porphyry's writing *Against the Christians,* Neoplatonist — criticism of Christianity was based on the allegation of inaccuracies and inconsistencies in the Scriptures.

Such concern for the reliability of the divine Rhetorician's teaching, together with Augustine's worries about the Manichean accusation that the texts of New Testament books had been interpolated and otherwise adulterated by the orthodox, provides a context for his real — though by no means consuming — interest in the task of establishing a sound Latin text of the biblical books. He strongly commends to serious students of the Scriptures what he himself never achieved, namely, thorough mastery of Hebrew and Greek, "in order that one may refer to the originals whenever the infinite variety of the Latin versions occasions some doubt" (*doc. chr.* 2.12.17). He preferred, among the Old Latin versions, the "Itala," traditionally employed in the churches of Rome and Milan, to the North African translations (*doc. chr.* 2.15.22); but he also appears gradually to have taken up with Jerome's revision of the Latin versions of the Gospels even while, as indicated above, he continued to prefer Latin translations of the Septuagint to any made from the Hebrew. Indeed what his textual work sought was a Latin that was transparent to the Greek of the Septuagint. He does not evince, however, the sort of interest in individual textual problems that one finds in a Jerome or an Origen. He often compares different versions of a single text, but does not in all cases feel obliged to decide which (if any) translation is best. He seems to think that differing versions express — or may express — the same meaning or intent *(sensus)* from differing viewpoints; and of course it is the intent informing the words that is essential. Thus, concerning Isa. 7:9, rendered as both "unless you believe, you will not understand" and "unless you believe, you will not persevere," Augustine thinks it unnecessary to choose since "to those who read wisely something weighty is conveyed by each of them" (*doc. chr.* 2.12.17). Similarly, in Ps. 87(88):10 the Septuagint has "physicians" instead of "giants," which Augustine understood to be the reading of the Hebrew. But he takes the Septuagint's version as an edifying, and of course inspired, paraphrase that indicates how "giants" ought to be understood (*en. Ps.* 87.10).

A second consequence of Augustine's understanding of the Scriptures as the divine Rhetorician's verbal communication — and a constant element in the tradition of early Christian exegesis that he inherited — is his perception of the canonical collection as a unity, not merely in the sense that it is, at base if not always on the surface, coherent and self-consistent, but also (a) that it has a single ultimate theme and (b) that any word, phrase, or image in it can be understood in the light of other occurrences of the same expression in other sections or books, regardless of their differing historical and literary contexts.

The first of these assumptions, to which we shall have occasion to return, is perhaps most obvious in Augustine's defense of the Old Testament against the Manicheans. Thus in writing against Faustus, Augustine takes the traditional line that the ceremonial commandments of the Law are prefigurations of the Christian dispensation and that the practices they enjoin are "types" (*typoi:* cf. 1 Cor. 10:6) or "shadows of things to come" (*skia:* Col. 2:17) intended for the edification of Christians (*c. Faust.* 6.2). That is the point of Augustine's famous saying that what lies hidden in the Old Testament lies open to view in the New (*civ. dei* 5.18; cf. *util. cred.* 5.9). Circumcision, for example, prefigures that "circumcision of the heart, in spirit and not in letter" of which Paul spoke (Rom. 2:29; *c. Faust.* 6.3; cf. *Sermon* 4.8-9); and as there was prefiguration in the Old Testament, so too there was direct prediction (*c. Faust.* 4.2). For that matter, as Augustine saw it, the present realities of Christian existence that the Old Testament foreshadows are themselves images that point beyond themselves to their perfection and fulfillment in the age to come. The present celebration of Easter points back to a past event but also signifies a "not yet" (*Sermon* 252.11). In truth, then, the theme of the Scriptures is one. The content is Christ, but Christ considered as the church's head and so as bound together with his "members." Otherwise stated, it is that one Word of God by which the world was created, which was spoken "in many and various ways" (Heb. 1:1) in the past, and which is not only enfleshed in Jesus the Christ, but also embodied and spelled out in these "many and various ways" in the Scriptures (cf. *en. Ps.* 61.17) as well as in the multiple realities of the created order.

This vision of the Scriptures means that for all his talk of prefiguration and prediction, and for all the seriousness with which he acknowledges, in other connections, the relativity of human habit and custom to time and place, he tends to treat the Bible and its language as *semel dictum,* that is, as a single "work" whose several parts are for all practical purposes simultaneous. It is this second, quieter assumption that shows itself in the ingenuity with which Augustine helps the Scriptures interpret themselves by assembling from various places phrases or statements that contain the same word or image as the phrase he is immediately concerned with and allowing them to determine its meaning. Addressing Ps. 45:3b in the Septuagint ("when the mountains are carried into the heart of the sea"), for example, he immediately looks for other places in the Scriptures where mountains are discovered in motion; and of course he finds what he wants at Matt. 17:20 (cf. 21:21). There Jesus assures his disciples that the very least endowment of faith will enable them to say "to this mountain 'Move hence and be cast into the sea,' and it will move." When the question arises what mountain "this mountain" is, Augustine answers it by reference to Isa. 2:2a ("In the last days the mountain . . . of the Lord shall be manifest"). This Isaianic mountain was, of course, understood, since at least the time of Origen, to refer to Christ (cf. *en. Ps.* 87.9); and hence when Isaiah says that this mountain is "on the top of the mountains" he alludes, Augustine says, to Christ's superiority to the Apostles, themselves mountains, who proclaim and so "carry" the Lord. The mountain, then, of Ps. 45:3b is Christ; and since "the sea" may be taken to refer to "this world," the reference to the mountain's being "carried" into the heart of the sea must be understood of the preaching of Christ to the Gentiles by the Apostles (*en Ps.* 45.6).

Finally, Augustine, like other ancient exegetes, presupposes — indeed assumes — that the Scriptures are full of passages or statements that are obscure or even, at first glance, difficult to make sense of or to credit. He would not have spoken, as Zwingli did later, about the perfect "clarity" of the Word of God, any more than would Irenaeus or Origen. Furthermore, like the exegetes of the Alexandrian school beginning with Philo, he perceived difficulties and obscurities in the plain sense of texts as deliberate divine contrivances, whose purpose was to stimulate further inquiry, to force the reader to go deeper, and so to "exercise" the mind in the understanding of mysteries. In other words, obscurities are indications of the presence of a "figural expression" (*figurata locutio*) in the proper and narrow sense, that is, one which creates "an allegory or a cryptic meaning" (*aenigma: doc. chr.* 3.11.17). The reference of these terms he explains in *De trinitate,* where, commenting on Gal. 4:24, he observes that "allegory" is a general term for "a trope in which one term is used to mean another" and thus stands in effect for any figural expression, while an *aenigma* is "an obscure allegory" (15.15), like Paul's reference to Hagar and Sarah as symbolizing the two Jerusalems.

This perception of the biblical text as full of cryptic passages had been conveyed to Augustine by the preaching of Ambrose (see above and *conf.* 6.5.8), and he reiterates it often. Following long tradition, he says that the Scriptures teach in part "openly," for anyone to understand, so that in the clear passages "are found all the things that convey the faith and the mode of life" (*doc. chr.* 2.9.14); but they also teach in part by "similitudes in word, deed, and mystery [*sacramentum*]," that is, by language that requires figural or alle-

gorical interpretation. Thus they are "adapted to the complete instruction
and exercise of the soul" (*ver. rel.* 17.33f.) and gradually raise it to a higher
level of understanding. The study of Scripture is therefore in part an ascetic
practice. It gradually cures the soul's blindness (e.g., *Jo. ev. tr.* 18.10-11; 35.6)
and trains it in the perception and understanding of divine mysteries; and the
act of clarifying its obscurities — overcoming the obstructions to understanding that the Spirit has provided — affords pleasure at the same time
(*mor.* 1.1.1), the sort of intellectual pleasure, perhaps, that only a trained
rhetor could delight in.

Literal and Spiritual

The elitism that Augustine betrays here, with his distinction between the ignorant and the learned, not to mention the obvious delight of the trained
professional in his own favorite business, should not be allowed to conceal
the seriousness with which he proposes that the text of the Bible has an odd
quality of depth. For all its plain speaking in certain passages, it can nevertheless be likened to rain descending out of a dark cloud (*Gn. adv. man.* 2.5) and
is full of puzzles and riddles. These of course serve a useful, and indeed a dual,
purpose. In God's providence, the Scriptures' obscurities both shield eyes unaccustomed to the light from levels of truth they cannot yet take in, and at the
same time tempt the proud (like Augustine!) to probe into the deep things of
God (*Gn. litt.* 5.8.6). They are, then, pointers to a "more" that is not so much
additional or supplemental truth as it is the same truth apprehended — gradually — in a different mode, at a higher level, and with more intense clarity
and delight. In this way, one can progress from faith to understanding
(*intellectus*), which is the product of faith, and ultimately to the fulfillment of
both in eternal life (*Jo. ev. tr.* 22.2; LXX Isa. 7:9).

This difference between the surface meaning of a scriptural text and its
deep — or heightened — sense Augustine normally characterizes by the contrast between "letter" and "spirit." He first encountered this distinction, as we
have seen, at the feet of Ambrose, but it carried the yet weightier authority of
Paul (cf. Rom. 2:29; 7:6; 2 Cor. 3:6), which is no doubt why it was fundamental
for Augustine's exegetical discourse. It is true that in the early treatise titled
The Usefulness of Believing he asserts that the Old Testament has a "fourfold
sense — historical, etiological, analogical, and allegorical" (*util. cred.* 3.5):
historical in that it relates events, etiological in that it conveys the "why" of
things said or done, analogical in that it coheres with the New Testament, and
allegorical when its statements are to be taken figuratively. Augustine never

employs or refers to this scheme again, however — nor indeed does it square with the famous four senses (literal, moral, allegorical, and anagogical) of the medieval schoolmen. Perhaps he came to think the apostolic distinction of letter and spirit both more correct and more economical. In any case, it would be easy to assimilate the first two of these senses to "the letter" and the second pair to "the spirit," since each of the latter, analogical and allegorical, involves going beyond the plain sense of what is said.

However that may be, what Augustine normally and most basically means by "letter" and "spirit" is "literal" on the one hand and "figurative" or "figural" on the other. This is apparent from his assertion that "the letter kills" means "that we are not to understand the figurative statements of Scripture in their literal sense . . . , but to look for their deeper significance" (*De spiritu et littera* 4.6). Further, what he means by "literal" and "figurative" can be gathered from the theory of signs as he develops it in his one hermeneutical treatise: a work whose title (*doc. chr.*), misleading to the modern reader, might possibly be rendered as *The Art of Christian Instruction.*

This crucial treatise Augustine composed in two stages. The first part (the Preface through 3.25.35) was likely completed around 397, just as he took up the writing of his *Confessions.* The work was then set aside, to be taken up and completed only thirty-odd years later (426-27). He describes the book as a set of "precepts for interpreting the Scriptures" (Preface 1), that is, for discovering what it means (Books 1-3) and conveying its sense in one's own words (Book 4). The work brings to scriptural interpretation the methods employed and taught by the classical *grammaticus* and the teacher of rhetoric — which is scarcely surprising in the case of a professional rhetorician like Augustine; but it also reflects his philosophical interests. It has been much studied in recent scholarship, and its genre and content have been considerably illuminated by the works of G. A. Press (1980, 1981, 1984), K. Pollmann (1996), and R. P. H. Green (1992) as well as by the useful collection of essays edited by Arnold and Bright (1995). As to the theory of signs itself, first taken up by Augustine in his early dialogue *On the Teacher,* the classic article of R. A. Markus (1957) and the later study of B. D. Jackson (1969) provide excellent analyses.

All words, Augustine avers, are signs: that is, they are sounds or written marks, things heard or things seen, which have the ability to make something other than what is heard or seen come to mind (*doc. chr.* 2.1.1). They are not "natural" signs (of which the classic example is smoke betraying the presence of fire), but what Augustine calls "given" signs: they are, that is, "signs . . . that living beings give one another in order to indicate as best they can what they feel [*motus animi*] or perceive or grasp conceptually." "Given" signs, then, are above all means of communication. They are employed "for the purpose of setting out and transmitting what the person who proffers the sign has in mind [*animo gerit*] to the mind of another person" (2.1.2; 2.2.3). Such signs are, at least in the present circumstances of the human race, essential to human society and fellowship; for "if human beings learned nothing from other human beings, love itself, that binds them one to another with the knot of unity, would gain no entrance for its work of making minds overflow and as it were mix in with one another" (Preface 6).

On the basis of these preliminary definitions, Augustine proceeds to explain that there are two ways in which words may signify: on the one hand, they may signify as "proper" *(propria)* signs when they are employed to refer to the things they were established to denote; on the other, they may signify as "transferred" *(translata)* signs "when the very things we denote by proper words are used to denote something else" (*doc. chr.* 2.10.15). The obvious course for the modern reader is to take Augustine's term *proprium* as equivalent to "literal" and *translatum* as equivalent to "figurative" or perhaps "allegorical"; and these translations will work most of the time. It is however important to be clear about what Augustine intends by such language. The literal sense of a word, for him, is simply the sense that it "owns" (hence *proprium*): what the word is normally employed to denote. A transferred sense of the same word occurs when the "thing" it normally denotes also functions as a sign and so points to something else (2.10.15; cf. *trin.* 15.15: "When the Apostle speaks of an allegory, he is applying the term not to a phrase but to a fact"). Thus when Paul quotes, "You shall not muzzle an ox . . ." (1 Cor. 9:9), the word "ox" means what it always means — an instance of a certain class of domestic animals. If the meaning is transferred, as Paul insists, that is not because the word "ox" is used in some odd way, but because the ox itself, to which the word "ox" refers, is being used and perceived as a sign: in this particular case, one that points to an apostolic preacher of the gospel. Hence Augustine can characterize a tendency to give literal readings of figural or metaphorical expressions as the "carnal" habit of mistaking sign for thing signified (e.g., ox for apostle: cf. *doc. chr.* 3.5.9–3.6.10; 3.8.12), a habit he associates with Jewish exegesis of Law and Prophets.

None of this, however, explains how figural language, and hence figural interpretation, works. Augustine's answer to this question is straightforward: it works by the intimation or (in the case of an exegete) the perception of a similarity. The movement from letter to spirit is a movement by way of analogy, then; and this proposition, it is worth noting, holds true both of what is called allegory and of what is called typology. To envisage the "mountain" of

Isa. 2:2a as Christ or to see the stretched-out firmament of Gen. 1:6 as signifying the Scriptures themselves (*conf.* 13.15.16) is to recognize an analogy. This entails, however, the conclusion that the same word or expression, as understood figurally, may mean different things in different places (*doc. chr.* 3.25.34-35), because the same "thing" can be similar to other "things" in many different ways. The word "leaven," for example, is used by Christ himself to mean both the outlook of the Pharisees (Matt. 16:6) and the hidden yet active presence of God's reign (Luke 13:21).

Of these two possible ways of taking scriptural language, Augustine plainly prefers a figural or allegorical reading. In the opening lines of his *Literal Commentary on Genesis,* he poses the question of how to interpret the creation narrative, but the very form in which he puts the question betrays his predilection. The issue for him is nothing so open and evenhanded as "literal or figurative," but "whether everything must be taken in accordance with the figurative sense only." He adds that "no Christian will dare say that the narrative must not be taken in a figurative sense" (1.1.1), in support of which thesis he adduces the evidence of Paul's practice (cf. 1 Cor. 10:11; Eph. 5:31-32). He nevertheless goes on to attempt a literal reading of the narratives of creation (and fall), partly at any rate because he wants to make it clear that there is no inconsistency between those narratives and the scientific cosmology of his day (cf. *Gn. litt.* 1.20.40-21.41). Augustine certainly does not deny, then, that the Scriptures have a literal meaning, even though, as we have seen, he is sure that where their literal meaning fails to make sense or offends his sense of right and wrong, one confronts a mystery (*sacramentum*), the plumbing of which requires the reader to go beyond the literal meaning. Furthermore, he is clear that the literal meaning, which conveys "deeds" or "happenings" (*res gestae),* is the necessary foundation of any deeper interpretation (*Sermon* 2.7). Nevertheless it is true to say that Augustine is always looking for the spirit in or behind the letter: he seems to regard the literal meaning of the Scriptures as an outward expression and evidence of the "mind" that governs them, much as an individual's words and gestures can be taken as indicators of the "personality" they embody. It is this perception of the Scriptures that appears to lie at the root of Augustine's proclivity for figurative exegesis.

How real this proclivity is can be gathered from Augustine's answer to when it is appropriate to resort to figurative or spiritual exegesis. From what has already been said here, it is evident that Augustine would accept the traditional answer to this question. Spiritual exegesis is, of course, required if the actual language of a text is figurative, but also if a text couched in literal language says something unworthy of God or inconsistent with Christian faith (*Gn. adv. man.* 2.2.3; cf. *conf.* 3.4.6). But *De doctrina christiana* seems to go beyond these canons. "Whatever there is in the divine utterance that cannot be referred to decent morals or to the truth of the faith" is to be taken as figurative discourse (3.10.14). Plainly this criterion has to do not with the way the words or signs in a text are used (that is, whether they are "proper" or "transferred") or, for that matter, with the content of any particular statement, but with what Augustine takes to be the ultimate subject matter *(res)* of all scriptural discourse. It legitimizes "spiritual" exegesis where a word or sentence is not directly addressing issues that concern "decent morals or . . . the truth of the faith."

To the reader of *De doctrina christiana,* this criterion, which permits the allegorization of almost everything, is nothing new. The first question Augustine takes up in that work is what the Scriptures are about, their *res* ("thing"), in Augustine's Latin. In Book 2, he suggests an answer to this question in a brisk formula to the effect that Christians read the Scriptures "in search of nothing other than the thoughts and will of their writers, and through them the will of God" (2.5.6). But he has already provided a lengthier and more detailed characterization of the *res* of the Scriptures in Book 1. Typically, he does this by asking what it is that human beings most properly and fruitfully desire or love — that is, what they can and should love for its own sake because their fulfillment or beatitude consists in possession of it. This he characterizes as the object of enjoyment or delight *(frui),* and he distinguishes it from "things" that are to be used *(uti)* — to be loved, that is, not for their own sake, but for the sake of the object of enjoyment and delight.

This object of enjoyment and delight Augustine of course identifies as the eternal and unchangeable "Trinity, a sort of single and supreme 'thing' that is common to all who enjoy it — if indeed it is a 'thing' and not the cause of all things; and if indeed it is a cause" *(doc. chr.* 1.5.5). By contrast, created things are not to be enjoyed but used with view to the enjoyment of God — that is, they are not to be loved for their own sake. The meaning of this distinction is carefully explored by O'Donovan (1982). For present purposes, it is enough to observe that human persons fall into the category of beings that are to be loved for the sake of God. Self and neighbor, that is, are to be loved for the sake of their common fulfillment in God, and the command to love neighbor as self means that the neighbor is to be loved as one who "is able to enjoy God together with us" (1.27.28).

As Augustine thus dilates upon the meaning of his habitual distinction between enjoyment *(frui)* and use *(uti)* and its implications for the shape of human love of God and neighbor, it is possible to see what is intended by his criterion for the use of "spiritual" or figurative exegesis: that of "decent morals" and "the truth of the faith." The seeking of God in love — and therefore

the interpretation of the Scriptures, which is a form of such seeking — has as
its goal the enjoyment of God, and this, as we have seen, constitutes human
well-being or, in his language, human beatitude. Such seeking and enjoying
of God is not, however, an affair of the lonely individual. To love neighbor
even as one loves self is, in the last resort, to seek the neighbor as one's companion in the love of God and, ultimately, in the enjoyment of God. Love of
God, in other words, is what constitutes true human community (the theme
of *City of God*), since it is God alone in whom all persons can share fully and
equally. Augustine's definition of the ultimate "thing" *(res)* to which the
Scriptures point is thus in the end his picture of that relation of self to God
and to other selves that used to be called "the chief end of man" — a relation
whose reality is grounded at once in the truths that faith grasps, that is, the
church's credal beliefs, and in the love they evoke. He believes that this is what
everything in the Scriptures is, in the last resort, from one point of view or
another, about. Hence, wherever this theme is not explicit, it is implicit, and
must be grasped by figurative as distinct from "literal" exegesis. This is the
point of Augustine's straightforward observation that "scripture prescribes
nothing save love *(caritas)* and condemns nothing save lust *(cupiditas)* . . .
[or] affirms anything save the catholic faith . . ." *(doc. chr.* 3.10.15). His addic-
tion to "spiritual" exegesis, whether in the form of allegory or typology, attests the seriousness with which he takes his underlying assumptions that the
theme of the Scriptures is single and it is set forth in varying ways in different
passages.

Plurality of Meanings

This theory of sign, and the account of the relation of "spirit" and "letter" in
the biblical text that it supports, represent an attempt — less formal and self-
conscious, perhaps, than an essay like the present one is bound to suggest —
to show how the Scriptures respond to the need of human persons to enter
and to share with one another the "mind" or "intent" of God. Communication between one mind and another is after all for Augustine the fundamental
purpose of language, as we have seen; and the words of the Scriptures are for
him means of access to God, even if they are also, as he intimates, authentically human words written down by particular individuals. "Spiritual" exegesis is in the end the sort of interpretation that is required when human words
are taken as divinely provided pointers to divine thoughts or purposes.

   This program, however, if program it is, creates problems of its own.
Augustine, as we have seen, never doubted that the Scriptures illustrated

Paul's observation in 1 Cor. 13:12 ("Now we see a reflection dimly [*per speculum in aenigmate*]"); or that this obscurity often rendered a meeting of minds between author and reader difficult to achieve. Nor were all these individual problems associated with particular texts. There were more general issues that Augustine had to wrestle with and reflect on more or less systematically.

One central problem, of course, was occasioned by the — potential and actual — multiplicity of different "readings" of a given text and the difficulty of choosing among them. He took this problem up explicitly in the *Confessions* (12.16.23-32.43, in connection with Gen. 1:1-2); and it was the topic to which he returned when in 426-27 he set out to complete *De doctrina christiana*, taking up the train of thought he had abruptly dropped almost three decades before (see *doc. chr.* 3.25.36-28.39). Despite the interval that separates them, the two discussions are mutually consistent, though each touches points omitted by the other. It was once not uncommon to assert that Augustine believed a text could have a plurality of literal meanings (e.g., Portalié 1960: 123); but it is not at all clear either that he ever raised that question or that his observations justify the view that he gave it a positive answer. Clearly, his discussion of the issue in *De doctrina christiana* is conducted under the general head of "ambiguities of figural expressions" (3.5.9: *verborum translatorum ambiguitates*).

In the *Confessions,* Augustine is clear that it is not always possible to ascertain the "intent" of an author, and certainly not that of Moses when he wrote the words, "In the beginning God created the heaven and the earth." For himself he is confident that those words mean that "by your [namely, God's] unchangeable Word you have made all things visible and invisible," but he is not certain whether it is this proposition or some other that Moses "had in mind" *(cogitaverat)* in using these words *(conf.* 12.25.33). If the intent of the human author, then, is taken to be the "literal" meaning, Augustine is saying that that *voluntas* ("intent") is not always available to a reader, even though it is an obligation of the interpreter to seek it *(doc. chr.* 3.27.38). God has brought it about that a great many of the pages of the Bible are "opaque and obscure" *(conf.* 11.2.3).

This does not mean, however, that the words of a text as they stand are open to any and every interpretation: Gen. 1:1 says certain things clearly, and excludes others *(conf.* 12.19.28). Nevertheless, by what it says it raises questions that a reader must and will answer, tacitly or explicitly, in order to make sense of its plain assertions and so to see what it says; and in supplying answers to these questions, different readers, as they mentally finish the text's meaning and so complement it, "see" different things. Augustine is prepared, in the *Confessions,* to apply the term "truths" to such differing interpretations (12.18.27), thus meaning not that there is no correct reading of a text, but that there is no *single* true account of its meaning. In *De doctrina christiana,* his phraseology is a bit more cautious, but it comes to the same point in the end. A reader, he says, may "elicit from the words" of a text a meaning not intended by the author, and it will count as true if it does not set itself against "right faith" *(recta fides),* and especially if it is based on other scriptural passages. Under those circumstances, being "supported by the truth," it is as acceptable as another reading of the same text (3.27.38).

Behind these worried lucubrations there lie two convictions. The first and most fundamental we have already encountered. It is that set forth in Augustine's criterion for legitimate use of figurative exegesis: namely, that what is said in any interpretation must conform to the twofold law of love and to the church's belief or creed *(fides).* Both of these convictions are scripturally derived, as he sees the matter, and not from obscure passages either. The second, however, is more difficult to state clearly. At base it has to do with Augustine's confidence that the truth into which the interpreter of a scriptural text enters is larger than any single "take" on it can appreciate and that God, Scripture's ultimate author, really does *intend* all the different "takes" human interpreters will produce, as long as they are consistent with the rules of love and of belief. He even allows himself to suppose that the human "author" of a text "perhaps saw, in the very words we seek to understand," the same meaning that we find there *(doc. chr.* 3.27.38); and thus he speculates — wistfully — that Moses might have "seen" and meant all the truths that readers have found in his text. What he is sure of is that "the one God adjusted the sacred text to the perceptions of many readers, perceptions that would envisage diverse truths" *(conf.* 12.31.42), or in other words that "the Spirit of God, who worked through [the author], foresaw with certitude" that a particular interpretation "would occur to some reader or hearer, or better, planned that it would occur . . ." *(doc. chr.* 3.27.38).

Tyconius's Rules

It was in the last decade of his life that Augustine resumed work on *De doctrina christiana* and composed the account given there of the ambiguity and plurality of meaning created in biblical texts by figural expressions. As we have noted, there was, by comparison with what he had said earlier on the same subject in the *Confessions,* little that was new in this account. What he added was a brief review of the various "manners of speech" *(modi locutionis)* or "tropes" the Scriptures employed — allegory, for example, or irony or catachresis — and then, in direct connection with this review, a summary of *The Book of Rules* of Tyconius (for the text see Burkitt 1894 and, for an English version, Babcock 1989).

This was a work whose interpretation had, by the problems it created for him and the insights it evoked, greatly stimulated Augustine's thinking about the Scriptures and their exposition. By incorporating an account of Tyconius's rules into *De doctrina,* Augustine both acknowledged a debt and struggled to fit Tyconius's ideas into the framework of his own hermeneutic.

A Donatist thinker, Tyconius had produced this work a few years before Augustine's baptism and had died less than a decade thereafter. The book was a proper, dense treatment of biblical interpretation which had at least two purposes: first, to formulate, in the shape of seven "mystic rules," a guide for understanding the Scriptures that would reflect the patterns according to which the thought of the Scriptures themselves moved; and second, to set out, in the very act of disengaging these rules, a theological understanding of the church as it exists in the present age — that is, in Tyconius's view, as a body in which good and evil are mixed until their final separation in the end time.

Augustine was introduced to this work early in his career at Hippo, and he pondered it, with great fascination, profit, and puzzlement, over a period of many years (*Epistle* 41.2). Both he and Tyconius, in their different ways, figured prominently in the struggle between catholic and Donatist that had rooted itself and ripened in North Africa in the course of the fourth century. Moreover, Augustine was indebted to Tyconius for many of his ideas on the issue that had, since the days of Tertullian, been the obsessive focus of North African theology — that of the character of the church in its relation to the "world." Augustine's most obvious borrowing is perhaps his picture of the church as "the whole Christ," which surely echoes the line taken by Tyconius in rule 1, "Concerning the Lord and His Body." Then there is Tyconius's statement — intended to illustrate and instantiate the principle that the Spirit hides "the general in the particular" (rule 4; cf. Burkitt 1894: 31.13) — to the effect that "Babylon, the city opposed to Jerusalem, is the entire world, which is represented through that part of itself found within this Jerusalem" (Burkitt 1894: 50.10-11; translation in Babcock 1989: 82). Here it is easy to discern an idea that Augustine, still musing in old age on his theme of two loves and two cities, would have found illuminating to say the least. On the other hand, he was genuinely puzzled and perhaps a bit angry that Tyconius had remained a Donatist even though, in *The Book of Rules,* he had denied the fundamental Donatist axioms that there is a "pure" church and that it existed only in North Africa in the form of the *pars Donati*. Despite his puzzlement, however, Augustine had no hesitation in exploiting Tyconius's ecclesiological views in his (fruitless) theological duel with the Donatists — and indeed in *The City of God*. For all that, his use of Tyconius in *De doctrina christiana* gives little sign of direct concern with the issues of the controversy between catholic and Donatist (for other views, see, e.g., the discussion in Kannengiesser and Bright 1989). In 426, indeed, when this material was added to Augustine's treatise, Donatism was no longer a principal object of his polemical energies. In this setting, what we have is Augustine's no doubt critical appreciation of Tyconius's rules as tools for exegesis.

The rules themselves deal, as one would expect, with recurring types of obscurity that occasion misunderstanding or confusion in readers who do not grasp certain principles that govern scriptural discourse (see the argument in Bright 1988). Thus a passage may speak of Christ and of his body the church — the body in which Christ himself unceasingly takes shape through the baptismal incorporation of believers into his identity; and the first rule, "Concerning the Lord and His Body," shows how it is possible to avoid confusion by learning to distinguish what is said of the whole (Christ in his body) and what is said of each of its parts. The second rule, "Concerning the Lord's Bipartite Body," shows how the Scriptures regularly speak of the church both positively and negatively, indicating thereby that it includes as members, and has included, not only honest believers but also members of the body of the devil. The third rule, "On the Promises and the Law," deals with the puzzle created by the Scriptures' habit of making human salvation conditional upon observance of the law while at the same time (and not least in the letters of Paul) insisting that it is conditional upon nothing but grace, that is, on the promise of God received by faith. This rule notes that the permanent members of Christ's body through the ages are those who live by the divine promise, while demands to keep the law are addressed to persons in whom faith and repentance must yet be wakened. (This rule, from whose treatment of Paul Augustine had learned a great deal, nevertheless disturbed him in the end because it appeared to compromise the principle of the priority of grace by attributing too wide a competence to human choice.) Rule 4, "Concerning the Particular and the General," indicates the Scriptures' habit of shifting between statements about individual persons and happenings and statements that, even if they refer to such "particulars," make sense only when applied to more "general" circumstances or states of affairs that characterize the existence of the church. Tyconius then, in rule 5, explores the puzzles created by the Scriptures' ways of talking about "extent of time" *(temporis quantitas)*. This rule explicitly appeals to the figure of synecdoche (part for whole and vice versa) to resolve certain questions about the accuracy of biblical statements about time, but then also to justify the view that the "thousand years" of Rev. 20:6 is to be applied to "the time of the church," that is, to the time of the conflicted growth of the body of Christ (cf. *civ. dei.* 20.7). The sixth rule, "On Recapitulation," takes a not dissimilar line. It points out that what the Scriptures say about a state of affairs that occurs at one time may be applied to an earlier or later state of affairs that "reiterates" the same — or rather a similar — state of affairs: a justification, this, of certain kinds of typology. Rule 7, "Concerning the Devil and His Body," seems to stand as a kind of counterpart to rule 1, since it shows how the Scriptures talk about Satan and his (human) train in the same ways that they talk about Christ and his body.

It is understandable that Augustine should read these "rules," which Tyconius had evidently understood to state norms that operate within scriptural discourse, as the equivalents of his "precepts," that is, as formulations of procedures for resolving obscurities. Augustine, in other words, read Tyconius in the light of his own assumptions and questions, and drew on him as an author who (among other things) had cast light on the question of how multiple meanings can be associated with the same "thing" referred to by transferred signs in the Scriptures. In particular, Augustine finds in Tyconius a recognition that the same "thing" can be a sign of opposite or contrary realities as well as of realities that are merely different (*doc. chr.* 3.25.36): the very point that he was making about the connotations of "leaven" — or of leaven — when he suspended work on his treatise in 397.

Augustine's general criticism of Tyconius (as distinct from his bluntly expressed distaste for Tyconius's views on freedom of choice and for his — to Augustine — incomprehensible Donatist loyalties) reveals this misunderstanding. He commends Tyconius's book to students on the ground that "it is a great help toward understanding the Scriptures" (*doc. chr.* 3.30.43), as indeed he has found it; but he thinks that the book promises too much when it suggests that its "rules" are all one needs to know how to understand "the entire law." "Not everything," he insists, "that is written in such wise as not easily to be understood can be searched out by means of these rules. On the contrary, there are many other tropes [*modi*] that are not contained in this set of seven" — tropes, Augustine avers, that Tyconius himself employs without naming them (*doc. chr.* 3.30.42). Augustine, then, sees Tyconius's rules not as attempts to articulate the underlying logic of scriptural discourse itself — a logic which, if followed, would unlock the depths of the Scriptures for a reader — but as a set of suggestions for handling certain types of scriptural obscurities (i.e., tropes: *doc. chr.* 3.37.56).

The reason for this, however, does not lie solely in his mistaken inclusion of Tyconius's *regulae* in a class with his own *praecepta*. It lies also in a significant theological difference, and specifically in a difference about the business or subject matter of Scripture, and, further still, about its function. When Augustine growls (*doc. chr.* 3.30.43) that Tyconius is presumptuous to claim that the principles enunciated in his seven rules "govern the hidden recesses of the entire law" (Burkitt 1894: 1.4), he is also, if tacitly, denying that the subject matter of the Scriptures is confined to questions raised by the Donatist controversy; for Tyconius's norms of scriptural discourse indicate that the character and destiny of the church is the dominant, if not the only, issue on the biblical agenda. By contrast, Augustine, as we have seen, thinks the Scriptures are intended in the last resort to establish communion of minds between God and God's human creatures; and his interest in the spirit as distinct from the letter, like his admission that a text may have more than one acceptable application or meaning, stems from his perception of the Scriptures as "sign" (not to say "mystery," *sacramentum*), that is, as the bodying forth of something that is larger and deeper than the sign, taken simply in and of itself, can convey.

Sign and Reality

In this way, Augustine's handling of Tyconius, as well as his meditations on plurality of meaning and ambiguity in the Scriptures, point to a further problem that underlies all his exegetical and hermeneutical reflections. This has to do not with the vagueness and ambiguity of "given" signs and their liability to variant interpretation but with their constitutional inefficiency in performance of the function of communicating knowledge. This issue came up in the relatively early dialogue *On the Teacher*, where Augustine insisted that words of themselves teach nothing: "On the contrary . . . we learn the force of the word . . . when we come to know the object signified by the word" (10.34). Words are either reminders of what we already know or stimuli to inquiry, and in cases where "what we already know" refers to the meanings of words and not the actual things signified (as, e.g., in most historical reports) they do not confer knowledge but merely evoke faith or belief. How then do the words of Scripture bring people to awareness of and communion with divine truths or realities?

He goes on to say:

> We do not pay attention to one who is making sounds . . . outside ourselves. We attend to the Truth which presides over our mind within us,

though of course words may admonish us to pay attention. . . . To this Wisdom every rational soul gives heed, but to each is given only as much as he is able to receive, in proportion to his own good or evil will (*mag.* 11.38).

This view — which we have already met and which Augustine reiterates in almost every period of his life — emerges again in *Confessions* 12. There he states that his knowledge of the truth conveyed by Moses' words derives not from the words themselves, but from the fact that he sees it to be "certain in your [i.e., God's] truth" (12.24.33), or, in other words, to be that which God, "the light of all truthful minds," shows "to be true" (12.18.27). Moses' words stimulate, then, recognition of a truth that is "seen" inwardly and not grasped indirectly through any external communication. Later still, Augustine notes that although the expression "the letter" normally means no more, as we have seen, than words taken in their ordinary sense, it can acquire a further and less neutral connotation when the opposition of spirit and letter coincides (as it often does in Augustine's mind: cf. *Sermon* 4.1) with that between flesh and Spirit — a contrast that is even more frequent in the Pauline letters than the former. In this developed sense of "letter," to take something literally is also to understand it carnally — that is, in the posture of the fallen Adam, for whom God, and so the truth, have become as it were foreigners that speak from "outside" because the self takes itself to be the spring of its own life (*spir. et litt.* 7.11, repeating a figure in *Gn. adv. man.* 2.5). In this case, "spiritual" understanding is not confined to the category of figurative statements, since even the moral commandments of the law, which are intended literally, can be truly and inwardly appropriated only when the Spirit sheds "the love of God" — that is, love for God, as Augustine understands this text — "abroad in our hearts" (Rom. 5:5; *spir. et litt.* 4.6).

Here, though perhaps not consciously, Augustine is reiterating, though in a modified form, the very position he had taken in *On the Teacher,* and here as there one can discern two aspects of how in his view "understanding" comes about. The first of these emerges in the implicit correlation of four polarities in Augustine's thinking: letter and spirit, flesh and Spirit, the external and the interior, and faith and understanding *(intellectus).* Augustine frequently interprets "spirit" as *intellectus,* and spiritual interpretation is characterized as understanding at the level of *intelligentia* (cf. *doc. chr.* 3.5.9). The rational faculty or "mind" is, therefore, the human spirit, and so the very heart of the human self. It is in fact the "interior self" of which Paul spoke, the ultimate seat of knowings and choosings. To understand something is thus not only to grasp and believe what a proposition "means" or affirms, but to make its truth inwardly one's own, to "see" and appropriate it intellectually. The transition, therefore, from faith or belief to understanding is a transition both from the external to the interior and from assent to truth as proposed by outward authority (sign) to truth inwardly appropriated as one's own through the ever-available illumination of the divine Wisdom; and all this simply is, from one point of view, the transition from letter to spirit.

There is however a second aspect of the position Augustine states in *On the Spirit and the Letter*. This second aspect is closely related to his insistence in the dialogue *On the Teacher* that the interior teaching of the divine Wisdom, or rather the mind's reception of it, is conditional upon "good will," a moral quality. If one asks further what this phrase "good will" means for Augustine, the answer is clear: it is that love of God and neighbor which, together with the faith that evokes it, is at once the essential content and the norm of scriptural teaching. It follows that one condition of understanding the Scriptures and appropriating their teaching inwardly is the possession of such love, at least in some degree: there is little gap here for Augustine between what the reader understands and the sort of person the reader is.

By the time he writes *On the Spirit and the Letter,* however, Augustine has openly surrendered the Plotinian faith that such "good will" is available in the here-and-now through a program of purification and intellectual *askēsis* — or for that matter that the interior teaching of the divine Wisdom is capable of being heard in its fullness by a fallen humanity to which God has become a stranger. The fellowship with God that the Scriptures aim to produce by stimulating interior understanding through the interpretation of externally given signs is, at least in its perfected form, something that belongs to the eschatological future; for the love upon which it ultimately depends is, in a fallen humanity, deflected to a focus on finite goods. It has to be taught, not only externally by the letter of the Scriptures, but internally by the Spirit's shedding love for God abroad in people's hearts — in a word, by the grace that gradually repairs human loving.

CONCLUSIONS

Augustine seems in the end to view the Bible on the analogy of God's self-communication in the incarnation. Each is a product of the humility of the eternal Word of God; for just as God's Word and Wisdom stoops for humanity's sake to take human flesh (*conf.* 7.9.13-14), so too it "descends to the discrete bits of sound that we make" (*ad particulas sonorum nostrorum*) so that "the single utterance of God is spread out over all the Scriptures," and "the one Word sounds through the many mouths of the saints" (*en. Ps.* 103, ser. 4.1). The essential exegetical precept, then, is that human beings must for their part imitate the humility of God: they must with docility and love apply themselves to treating the linguistic signs given by God as means of attuning themselves to the Wisdom that the signs intimate and embody. This process no doubt involves, in Augustine's mind, all the arts of the *grammaticus* and the rhetor — arts that he himself practiced with a fascinated devotion. The fruit of the process, however, is not merely knowledge but understanding *(intellectus)* — a having of something in common with God through the interpretive and self-transforming passage from letter to spirit. Hence Augustine can say, given his understanding of the "mind" expressed in the Scriptures, that "a person who is upheld by faith, hope, and love and steadfastly clings to them has no need of the Scriptures save for the purpose of teaching others" (*doc. chr.* 1.39.43); but one may be fairly sure that in the period of his anti-Pelagian writings he would have doubted whether any such person can exist before the eschatological consummation of all things.

Augustine the rhetor, however, loves the process as well as the end. This is evident not merely from his interest in languages, translations, and texts, or from the eagerness with which he commends to biblical interpreters the shared discourse — not itself strictly a biblical discourse — that is embodied in the traditional "liberal arts." It is further apparent in the delight he takes in noting how the various tropes, which rhetoricians studied in the compositions of classical authors and then imitated in their own oratory and writing, are used by the scriptural writers as well (*doc. chr.* 3.29.40; cf. 4.7.21), no doubt for the imitation of preachers. He also refers to Paul and other scriptural authors to illustrate the several styles that orators employed — simple, mixed, and grand; but he insists that in the biblical writers eloquence is the slave that follows along in the service of wisdom (*doc. chr.* 4.6.10) and in the service of readers or hearers.

Augustine's hermeneutic, especially as laid out in *De doctrina christiana*, was by no means without influence on later thinkers and writers. On the other hand, his exegetical writings themselves were probably not as influential in the Latin west as those of Jerome, Ambrose, or Ambrosiaster; and of course in the east they were unknown. In his exegetical practice there is little that is original: he is, in the end, an heir of the Alexandrian tradition, odd though that may seem in a North African interpreter. The distinctive characteristic of his hermeneutical thought is the way in which he ties together exegetical *(modus inveniendi)* and expository *(modus proferendi)* techniques, philosophical reflection on the theory of signs and theological understanding of the communion of human persons with one another and with God — all in a single vision of what is going on in biblical interpretation. This theory is, however, somewhat idiosyncratic in the sense that it grew out of Augustine's musings on problems that were the product of his own education and experience. He was not the founder, nor in any narrow sense the follower, of a "school."

BIBLIOGRAPHY

Arnold, D., and P. Bright (eds.)

1995   *"De Doctrina Christiana": A Classic of Western Culture.* Notre Dame: Notre Dame University Press.

Babcock, W. S.

1979   "Augustine's Interpretation of Romans (A.D. 394-396)." *Augustinian Studies* 10:55-74.

1982   "Augustine and Tyconius: A Study in the Latin Appropriation of Paul." *Studia Patristica* 17:1209-15.

1985   "Augustine and Paul: The Case of Romans IX." *Studia Patristica* 16.2:473-79.

Babcock, W. S. (trans.)

1989   *Tyconius: The Book of Rules.* Atlanta: Scholars.

Basevi, C.

1977   *San Agustin. La interpretación del Nuevo Testamento.* Pamplona: Ediciones Universidad de Navarra.

Bonnardière, A. M. (ed.)

1986   *Saint Augustin et la Bible.* Paris: Beauchesne. 2nd ed. ET by P. Bright: *Saint Augustine and the Bible.* Notre Dame: Notre Dame University Press, 1997.

Bright, P.

1988   *The Book of Rules of Tyconius.* Christianity and Judaism in Antiquity 2. Notre Dame: Notre Dame University Press.

Burkitt, F. C. (ed.)

1894   *The Book of Rules of Tyconius.* Cambridge Texts and Studies 3.1. Cambridge: Cambridge University Press.

Burns, J. P.

1980   *The Development of Augustine's Doctrine of Operative Grace.* Paris: Études Augustiniennes.

Green, R. P. H.

1992   "Augustine's *De Doctrina Christiana:* Some Clarifications." *Respublica Litterarum* 15:99-108.

Green, R. P. H. (ed. and trans.)
1995   *Augustine: De Doctrina Christiana.* Oxford: Clarendon.

Jackson, B. D.
1969   "The Theory of Signs in St. Augustine's *De Doctrina Christiana.*" *Revue des Études Augustiniennes* 15:9-49.

Kannengiesser, C., and P. Bright
1989   *A Conflict of Christian Hermeneutics in North Africa: Tyconius and Augustine.* Berkeley: Center for Hermeneutical Studies in Hellenistic and Modern Culture.

Markus, R. A.
1957   "St. Augustine on Signs." *Phronesis* 2:60-83.

O'Donovan, O.
1982   "*Usus* and *Fruitio* in Augustine *De Doctrina Christiana* I." *JTS* n.s. 33:361-97.

Pollmann, K. (ed.)
1996   *Doctrina Christiana. Untersuchungen zu den Anfängen der christlichen Hermeneutik unter besonderer Berücksichtigung von Augustins "De Doctrina Christiana."* Freiburg: Universitätsverlag.

Polman, A. D. R.
1961   *The Word of God According to St Augustine.* ET by A. J. Pomerans. London: Hodder and Stoughton.

Pontet, M.
1945   *L'exégèse de s. Augustin prédicateur.* Paris: Études Augustiniennes.

Portalié, A.
1960   *A Guide to the Thought of Saint Augustine.* Chicago: Regnery.

Press, G. A.
1980   "The Subject and Structure of Augustine's *De Doctrina Christiana.*" *Augustinian Studies* 11:99-124.
1981   "The Content and Argument of Augustine's *De Doctrina Christiana.*" *Augustiniana* 31:165-182.
1984   "*Doctrina* in Augustine's *De Doctrina Christiana.*" *Philosophy and Rhetoric* 17:92-120.

Ries, J.
1963   "La Bible chez S. Augustin et chez les Manichéens." *Revue des Études Augustiniennes* 9:201-15.

Williams, R. D.
1989   "Language, Reality, and Desire in Augustine's *De Doctrina.*" *Literature and Theology* 3:130-50.

CHAPTER 15

The Formation of the New Testament Canon and Its Significance for the History of Biblical Interpretation

Harry Gamble

The formation of the canon of the New Testament, together with the church's adoption of Jewish Scripture, determined what *is* the Bible for Christians. The formation of this canon is thus important for the history of biblical interpretation in that it defines the object of interpretation. Yet the formation of the canon cannot be understood as the historical point of departure for biblical interpretation, since the emergence of the New Testament canon was itself a result of interpretation of those documents that were ultimately included in it. Furthermore, the role of the canon has not been constant in the history of interpretation, but has varied with different periods and movements in the history of Christianity. This essay will briefly discuss, first, the early interpretation of those documents that would later constitute the canon, and second, the influences that have subsequently affected the hermeneutical force of the canon.

CANON FORMATION AS A DIMENSION OF SCRIPTURE INTERPRETATION

Recent Developments in the Study of New Testament Canon Formation

The history of the formation of the New Testament canon is long and complex, and, given the state of the evidence, not accessible in all details. Nevertheless, we can sketch its broad features. Study of the history of the canon has recently undergone a significant shift. It was once the prevailing view that the New Testament canon came into being at or near the end of the second century — some marginal issues remaining — and that its formation was mainly a reaction to second-century controversies with heterodox movements — Marcionism, Gnosticism, and Montanism (e.g., Harnack 1925; Zahn 1888; Leipoldt 1907; von Campenhausen 1972). Two developments in more recent scholarship have decidedly altered this conception of the history of the canon.

First, modern scholarship has clarified the problem by drawing a clear distinction between "Scripture" and "canon." The term "Scripture" refers to religiously authoritative writings, without regard to the scope of such literature; "canon," on the other hand, signifies a fixed and closed list or collection of such writings held to be exclusively authoritative (Sundberg 1968; Graham 1987a, 1987b). From the beginning, the church possessed as Scripture the Septuagint, the ancient Greek version of the Jewish Scriptures. Almost to the end of the second century, Christian references to Scripture have in view these Jewish writings, not Christian writings. Gradually, some Christian writings came to be read in Christian worship alongside Jewish Scripture and thus acquired a similarly scriptural status. Indeed, the Christian movement was actively interpreting Scriptures, both Jewish and Christian, well before it possessed a canon of either. This precanonical interpretation of Scripture was not only propaedeutic but prerequisite to the creation of the canon of the New Testament, and decisively influenced its content and shape.

Second, the older view depended heavily on the Muratorian fragment, a canon list traditionally dated to the late second or early third century and assigned a Roman provenance. Both this early dating and the Roman origin of the Muratorian canon list have been strongly challenged, however, and it is now widely regarded as a fourth-century list of eastern origin (Sundberg 1973; Hahneman 1992; but cf. Ferguson 1982; Metzger 1987). Thus, it appears that only in the fourth century did efforts begin in earnest to determine a canon, properly speaking, of Christian Scriptures. It is first with Athanasius of Alexandria, in his Easter letter of 367, that we discover a list of Christian Scriptures corresponding exactly to the New Testament we know. Athanasius was also the first to describe these writings as "canonical." It was even later, after broad accord was reached among ancient Christian communities of all regions, that the New Testament canon was fully established.

Hence, the present consensus holds that the formation of the New Testament canon, understood as a closed collection of exclusively authoritative Christian Scriptures, belonged to the fourth and fifth centuries, that it was the outcome of a long process, and that it was not mainly a response to controversies with heterodox movements. During the second and third centuries there were, to be sure, certain Christian writings — above all several Gospels, the letters of Paul, and a few other documents — which had come to enjoy an almost universal recognition and use as Scripture, but disagreements persisted about the status and value of other Christian writings, and there were corresponding differences in their use. The emergence and use of Christian Scripture, then, is a presupposition of the process of canon formation, but must be distinguished from the determination of a canon.

The older view has now been reasserted, however, by Trobisch (1996), who goes even farther and argues, chiefly on the basis of the contents and widely-shared conventions of ancient manuscripts, that there was already at the end of the second century not only a canon of Christian writings, but an actual edition of the New Testament as a whole and as we know it. He suggests that this edition, which bears the features of a uniform final redaction, had a clear and specific intention, namely to demonstrate the harmony and unanimity of the early Christian movement, and that it exercised decisive influence on the subsequent transmission of the documents. In this proposal, the process of canon formation is sharply foreshortened, given a specific editorial aim and method, and conceived as a literary as much as a theological event. The argument has, however, significant difficulties. Inferences backward from the great parchment codices of the fourth and fifth centuries (Sinaiticus, Vaticanus, and Alexandrinus) are not easily sustained by the fragmentary papyrus manuscripts of the second to fourth centuries. The diversity of opinions and usages attested for the third and fourth centuries would be hard to comprehend if a successfully unified canonical edition were already at hand by the end of the second century. The argument is nonetheless provocative, and valuably urges the potential importance of early manuscripts as evidence for the history of the canon. Without resolving all the historical questions, the present task is to consider the history of the canon from the point of view of the history of interpretation.

The Smaller Collections: Paul's Letters

The period between the first and fifth centuries, which compassed the production of Christian literature, its dissemination and use, and finally the formal canonization of some of it, was a fertile time for the interpretation of those writings. Indeed, in one of its most essential dimensions the history of the New Testament canon is nothing other than the history of the interpretation of those writings which were finally included in it. This is readily seen in the early history of many of these writings and in the shaping of those smaller collections (the four Gospels, the letters of Paul, and the Catholic Epistles) of which the New Testament canon is principally constructed.

To begin with the earliest extant Christian writings, little is known about the early circulation and collection of Paul's letters, and many theories have been proposed (see Lovering 1988). Paul's letters were important instruments of his missionary enterprise, pieces of correspondence addressed to individual local congregations and dealing with issues that had arisen in those churches. The particularity of address and concern that typifies Paul's letters inhibited their more general use by Christians at large, for it was not obvious that Paul's letters to individual churches were relevant to other communities (Dahl 1962). This problem was met by a catholicizing interpretation, which eventually was formulated in the idea that because Paul wrote to precisely seven communities, he intended to speak to the church at large (the number seven being taken as a symbol of wholeness or universality). Although this idea is not explicitly stated until later (Muratorian fragment, lines 48-50, 57-59; cf. Tertullian, *Adversus Marcionem* 5.17), it was embodied in what appears to have been the earliest edition of the corpus of Paul's letters, which emerged near the end of the first century and took the form of a collection of ten letters to seven churches (Dahl 1978; Clabeaux 1989; Gamble 1995).

Still earlier, before the letters were collected, the problem of their particularity was met by textual revision: some letters (Romans, 1 Corinthians; cf. Ephesians) were deprived of their original and specific addresses (and sometimes of other local matter) in favor of a more general address, undoubtedly to promote their wider circulation beyond their original recipients and thus to extend Paul's authority and influence (Dahl 1962; Gamble 1977). Equally remarkable was the composition after Paul's time of pseudonymously Pauline letters (Colossians, Ephesians, 1 and 2 Timothy, Titus, and possibly 2 Thessalonians), which were variously indebted to the epistolary and theological legacy of Paul and represent diverse efforts to interpret, elaborate, and apply Paul's authority and teaching to situations and problems of the late first and early second centuries. Some of these pseudonymous letters (Ephesians, Colossians, 2 Thessalonians) were incorporated into the earliest known edition of Paul's letters, which therefore already included an interpretive appropriation of Paul. Later, during the second century, this pseudonymous component of the ten-letter collection was enlarged by the inclusion of 1 and 2 Timothy and Titus. By means of these pseudonymous supplements to the authentic letters of Paul, the radical and controversial dimensions of the apostle's thought were to some extent domesticated and brought into the full service of the church. Thus the authority of Paul's teaching, originally local and specific, was broadened, contemporized, and applied through a continuing tradition of interpretation. The locus of this effort was the historic Pauline mission field. It was perhaps pursued under the auspices of a "Pauline school" (Conzelmann 1965, 1979; Schenke 1975) which was devoted to the heritage of Pauline Christianity and sought to cultivate and extend the apostle's influence.

Beyond the dissemination of his own letters and the production of Pauline pseudepigrapha, the interpretation of Paul was also informed by the development of biographical legends about Paul that became widely current and found deposit not only in the Acts of the Apostles but also in the *Acts of Paul* (Schenke 1975; MacDonald 1983). The epistle to the Hebrews, in spite of its appearance in the earliest surviving codex of the Pauline epistles, $\mathfrak{P}$46, probably had no original or early place among Paul's letters (cf. Trobisch 1989). Though well-known in the east in the second century, there were doubts about its authorship (Origen, in Eusebius, *EH* 6.25.11-14), and in the west it was either unknown or unacknowledged until the fourth century (*EH* 6.20.30; Jerome *Epistle* 129).

The collected letters of Paul became widely known during the second century (Dassmann 1979; Lindemann 1979; Rensberger 1981). Most Christian writers of the first half of the second century were acquainted with them but did not draw heavily on them, partly because the major issues that engaged Paul were then less pressing, and partly because, as the author of 2 Peter remarked (3:16), "there are some things in [Paul's letters] hard to understand, which the ignorant and unstable twist to their own destruction." The boldness and complexity of Paul's thought were a standing challenge to the interpretation of his letters. The most singular and radical interpretation of them was undertaken by Marcion of Sinope, who esteemed Paul as the only true apostle and teacher of the church and his letters (together with an edited version of the Gospel of Luke) as the exclusive repository of Christian revelation. By critical revisions of the letters aimed at eliminating interpolations and securing a true text (Clabeaux 1989; Grant 1993), Marcion sponsored an understanding of Pauline thought that was widely at variance with the church's and was soon repudiated as heretical. Yet Marcion's exclusive emphasis on Paul and his idiosyncratic interpretation of Pauline thought served as a stimulus to a more thoroughgoing interpretation and appropriation of Paul in the church at large. Christian Gnostic thinkers such as Basilides, Valentinus, Ptolemy, and Heracleon also made early interpretive use of Paul's letters (Pagels 1975; Rensberger 1981). Despite (rather than because of) these heterodox appeals to Paul, by the end of the second century Paul's letters were universally regarded as an authoritative and important source of Christian teaching.

They also became subjects of close reading and interpretation by such widely separated figures as Tertullian of Carthage, Irenaeus of Lyons, and Clement of Alexandria.

The Smaller Collections: The Gospels

The Gospel literature likewise was early subject to interpretation, and this interpretation led eventually to the formation of a fourfold Gospel. The very composition of the Gospels that later became canonical was a matter of the creative interpretation and appropriation of earlier oral and written traditions about Jesus. Mark's thematic redaction of oral traditions and early small written collections of Jesus-traditions gave rise to the narrative Gospel, and Matthew's and Luke's revisions of Mark in combination with other written materials, especially the sayings Gospel (Q), were critical interpretations that nevertheless preserved the narrative form (Koester 1990). Similarly, the Gospel of John offers an interpretation of largely distinctive source materials available to its author. In addition, many Gospels beyond these four had currency in the early church, some of which have come to light again through modern manuscript finds — the *Gospel of Peter,* the *Gospel of Thomas,* the "Unknown Gospel," among others (Koester 1980, 1990). At least some of these were independent redactions of oral tradition, which persisted alongside the written Gospels. It also appears that, just as each Gospel was intended to be complete and sufficient in itself, in the earliest period it was customary for each community to use but one Gospel, and thus individual Gospels became locally or regionally well-established in use and esteem. When the Gospels began to circulate and become more widely known in the early second century, however, problems of interpretation arose. Although in some instances it was a question how an individual document was to be understood, larger issues were posed by the sheer multiplicity of Gospels and the divergences among them.

A plurality of Gospels made suspect the adequacy of any one (Cullmann 1956; Merkel 1978). The term "gospel" originally had theological rather than literary force, designating the fundamental missionary proclamation of the church. In this sense the gospel was necessarily single and unitary (cf. Gal. 1:6-9). When, in the mid-second century, the word began to be used to designate documents recounting the activity and teachings of Jesus, there was a strong hesitancy to think in terms of numerous Gospels. Moreover, the considerable differences among the various Gospels was not lost on the early church, and constituted a problem for discussion from the second through the fifth centuries (e.g., Eusebius, *EH* 1.7.1-15; 3.24.5-13; the Muratorian list, lines 10-26; Augustine, *On the Agreement of the Gospels*). Though such differences might be rationalized, the use of more than one Gospel required an explanation and justification of their divergences (Merkel 1971).

We hear from Eusebius (*EH* 3.39.15-16) that already in the early second century Papias was defending Mark's Gospel, which had been criticized by comparison with another (Matthew, or possibly Luke), and characterizing Matthew as a collection of Jesus' *logia* (Kurtzinger 1983). Translation, or more likely intepretation, was at issue in relation to both. Papias himself composed a book on the interpretation of traditions about Jesus, some of which he clearly knew from Gospel documents, others from oral tradition. Papias can no longer be portrayed as one who rejected books in favor of oral tradition, for he valued both media (Alexander 1990). Marcion, near mid-century, championed the exclusive value of the Gospel of Luke because of its presumed association with Paul. Not much later the interpretation of the *Gospel of Peter* was in dispute in Syria, where some thought it docetic and unsuitable for use (Eusebius, *EH* 6.12.2). The Gospel of John was early in favor with Gnostic Christians and was, incidentally, the first Christian document to be the subject of a commentary, one by the Gnostic teacher Heracleon (Pagels 1973). It gained a broader foothold only slowly and with difficulty, not only because it was valued by the heterodox (the Montanists and Quartodecimans also appealed to it), but doubtless also because of its striking divergence from other Gospels in outline and content. It was under heavy dispute in Rome even at the end of the second century (Hillmer 1966). Broad recognition of the Gospel of John finally depended on the hermeneutical premise that it was to be understood as a "spiritual Gospel," less concerned with the outward facts than their inner meaning (Clement, according to Eusebius, *EH* 6.14.7). However, the other Gospels that were widely in use — Matthew, Mark, and Luke — also differed among themselves in problematic ways (Merkel 1971). Scribes consciously and unconsciously harmonized their readings, reducing the dissonance by textual alterations (Fee 1978; Baarda 1989; Ehrman 1993). The problem of such differences and the problem of the plurality of the Gospels were both addressed at a stroke by Tatian, who homogenized the texts of Matthew, Mark, Luke, and John (as well as some additional sources) into a single continuous narrative, the *Diatessaron*, which gained long-standing use in the Syrian church (Metzger 1977: 10-36; Baarda 1989; Petersen 1994).

Tatian's bold solution was outflanked by another, namely a collection of precisely four Gospels (Matthew, Mark, Luke, and John), or, more exactly, a fourfold Gospel, which came into being near the end of the second century (but cf. Hengel 1985). The earliest clear witness to the fourfold Gospel is

Irenaeus, who also devised a fanciful allegorical rationale for it (*Adversus Haereses* 3.11.8-9). The nature of this solution appears in the way the Gospels came to be titled: each is *the* (unitary) Gospel, but authorship is distributive ("according to"). Thus the Gospel remains one, but is witnessed by four. The establishment of this Gospel collection was a compromise between an indeterminate plurality of Gospels and the hegemony of any single Gospel. It was made possible also by the relatively wide early use made of these particular Gospels, which had enjoyed a broader currency than others and had gained a more authoritative position. At the level of interpretation, however, it meant that the Gospels were to be understood not merely in a biographical way, as if their truth lay in the literal text (Origen, *Commentary on John* 10.3.2), but also as testimonies of religious truth — the gospel (Cullmann 1956; Morgan 1981).

The Catholic Epistles, Acts, and Revelation

By the beginning of the third century, the collection of Paul's letters and the fourfold Gospel collection were in use almost everywhere as Christian Scripture. The third major collection that came to comprise the New Testament canon, the so-called Catholic Epistles, was much slower to develop. Of these letters, only 1 Peter and 1 John were much known or used in the second century. Apart from appropriations from the letter of Jude made in 2 Peter, there is no other early evidence for the use of this small letter. According to Eusebius (*EH* 6.14.1), Clement of Alexandria commented on these as well as on other "disputed" writings (2 John, Barnabas, etc.) in his *Hypotyposeis*. Beyond this, however, there is little evidence for the use of James, 3 John, or 2 Peter during the second century. The Catholic Epistles apparently came to be conceived and spoken of as a group of seven only in the fourth century, and first clearly by Eusebius (*EH* 2.23.25), although, with the exception of 1 Peter and 1 John, even he placed them in the category of "disputed books," not universally recognized as authoritative. Over against appeals to individual apostles (Marcion) or to esoteric apostolic traditions (the Gnostics), the Catholic Epistles, especially as a group, had the value of broadening the apostolic witness, thus counterbalancing the imposing collection of Paul's letters and giving a documentary basis to the notion of a consensus teaching derived from a group of primary apostolic authorities (Luhrmann 1981). It comports with this that, in early Greek manuscripts of the New Testament writings, the Acts of the Apostles is most closely associated not with Paul's letters but with the Catholic Epistles.

Beyond these three collections, the only two writings that eventually found their way into the New Testament canon were the Acts of the Apostles and the Revelation to John. Acts had a separate history from its original companion piece, the Gospel of Luke, and came into broad use only toward the end of the second century, perhaps as a result of the conflict with Marcion and Gnostic groups, for Irenaeus appeals to it as a proof of the unity of the apostles and their preaching. Indeed, its transmission in manuscripts mainly in connection with the Catholic Epistles sustains this hermeneutical function. As an ostensibly historical narrative, however, Acts offered sparse material for theological interpretation, and there is little commentary literature on Acts from the ancient church.

Very different is the case of Revelation. It was cited extensively among western Christian writers of the second century (Justin, Irenaeus, Tertullian) and had some early currency also in the east, where Melito of Sardis reportedly wrote a commentary on it (Eusebius, *EH* 4.26.2) and Theophilus of Antioch and Clement of Alexandria made use of it. Its authority was drawn into question in Rome because of appeals to it by the Montanists, but it retained esteem in the west generally. In the east, however, Revelation was early appropriated as a source and warrant of chiliastic eschatology. When in the third century a certain Nepos rejected allegorizing interpretation of Revelation in favor of a literal, chiliastic interpretation, he was attacked by Dionysius, bishop of Alexandria, who argued against the apostolic authorship of Revelation and insisted that the book could only be valued allegorically (Eusebius, *EH* 7.25). Dionysius's criticisms deeply eroded the standing of Revelation in the east and made allegorical interpretation the condition of its usefulness and authority.

The Third and Fourth Centuries

By the end of the second century, the Christian writings that had attained broad and uncontested scriptural standing were the fourfold Gospel, the thirteen letters of Paul, 1 Peter and 1 John, and Acts. Revelation was highly regarded in the west, Hebrews in the east. Many other documents were also in circulation and use, and bid fair for scriptural authority: various other Gospels (e.g., the *Gospel of Peter*, the *Gospel of the Hebrews*), Acts of various apostles, letters (James, Jude, 2-3 John, *1 Clement, Barnabas*), and some apocalypses (the *Shepherd of Hermas*, the *Apocalypse of Peter*). Although these enjoyed popularity for a period or in certain regions, only some secured any broadly authoritative standing. The availability of these other documents and the popularity of some of them are useful reminders that the canon which eventually emerged was the result not merely of collection, but also of selection.

The scope of Christian Scripture remained fluid through the third century and into the fourth. Generally, there is a perceptible correspondence between the scope of Scripture and the social context in which it was used: the extent of Scripture tended to be broader for teachers and their study circles (e.g., Clement and Origen), but narrower for bishops and their parish communities (e.g., Irenaeus and Athanasius; cf. Brakke 1994). How much remained in flux even in the early fourth century can be seen in Eusebius's evaluation of the status of Christian writings (*EH* 3.25.1-7; Robbins 1986). He puts into the category of "acknowledged books" the four Gospels, Acts, the letters of Paul, and 1 Peter and 1 John. Among the "disputed books" he places James, Jude, 2 Peter, and 2 and 3 John, as well as a variety of other books. This closely resembles the situation at the end of the second century and suggests that little had changed during the third century. Eusebius had an additional category, the "spurious books," those rejected as heretical or impious. This marks a change, since now some books are being decisively excluded, but it also shows that interpretation is a key factor.

Only later in the fourth century did efforts begin to draw up definitive lists making for a canon in the proper sense. Athanasius's list of 367 CE, noted earlier, was influential in Egypt, though not decisive (Ehrman 1983; Brakke 1994), and variations persisted in other regions. Syrian Christianity, for example, continued into the fifth century to admit only twenty-two books as authoritative (thus excluding 2-3 John, 2 Peter, Jude, and Revelation), while in Asia Minor the Council of Laodicea (363) endorsed the authority of twenty-six books (excluding Revelation), and in North Africa the Councils of Hippo (393) and Carthage (397) named the twenty-seven books of our New Testament. A full uniformity of usage, and thus a genuine canon of Christian Scripture, finally emerges only in the early fifth century.

This emergent canon was not, however, the product of particular formal decisions, whether episcopal or conciliar, for no such decisions were ever made that were effective for Christendom at large. Rather, it was one result among others of the developing consolidation of Christianity in liturgical, theological, and socio-institutional terms, and it must be understood in the context of that process. Most particularly, it was the outcome of Christian worship and preaching. The initial and fundamental sense of the term canon as applied to Christian writings was not "norm," but "list," specifically, the list of those writings that were acceptable for public reading in the service of worship. Writings read in that setting were interpreted and expounded to the gathered faithful in the homily immediately following the readings delivered by the one presiding over worship, ordinarily the bishop. Though this practice is first clearly documented in the middle of the second century (Justin,

Apol. I, 67), it must have reached well back into the first century since it follows a Jewish synagogal practice. It was due to their regular and repeated public reading that Christian writings became familiar to the largely illiterate body of Christians, were given close interpretation, gained authority, and thus became normative resources for Christian thought and life (Gamble 1995).

When in the early fourth century Eusebius canvassed the many writings that might be considered authoritative, he considered principally whether a document had been in public use in the churches from an early time (Hanson 1962) and thus rightly recognized the powerful authorizing force of traditional usage. Other criteria were sometimes employed to support or dispute the putative authority of particular documents, and these have been carefully studied (Ohlig 1972). Apostolicity was generally considered important, though this was not understood simply in terms of authorship, but signified an origin in the early period of the church, or conformity to what the church took to be apostolic teaching. Catholicity, or relevance to Christendom as a whole, was valued by way of eschewing obscure and esoteric resources. Orthodoxy, agreement with the church's faith, also was a key criterion, though used mainly to exclude rather than to sponsor a document. If the tradition of the church's faith served as a touchstone of scriptural authority, then it was understood to be somehow extrinsic to the writings that were judged by it, even though the faith of the Christian community had been nurtured and defined by many of the same writings that were judged canonical. Thus, just as Scripture, through public reading and expository interpretation, had molded the tradition of the faith, so also the tradition of the faith helped to shape the canon of Scripture. Such criteria were usually invoked *post facto:* they were less the reasons that documents gained canonical authority than modes of rationalizing or defending the authority that accrued to them through traditional use, or of discrediting the value of other documents. Such considerations must, however, have been tacitly and unsystematically at work throughout the church's use of its scriptural resources.

THE ROLE OF THE CANON
IN INTERPRETATION OF SCRIPTURE

The Fathers

We have seen that the interpretation of Scripture did not await the formation of the canon, but was fully pursued by the bishops and teachers of the church

from the second to fifth centuries. Beginning with Irenaeus, the fathers were
above all interpreters and expositors of Scripture, which was for them a richly
revelatory body of literature requiring the most careful study and reflection.
Although they employed many methods in their study — textual, philological, historical, typological, and allegorical — their approach to Scripture was
ultimately determined by its content. This content was adequately defined
even in the absence of fixed canonical limits: it included the traditional Scriptures of Judaism contained in the Septuagint and those Christian writings,
above all the Gospels and the Pauline letters, that were almost everywhere
read and esteemed in the church.

Most of all, it was the ideational substance of Scripture — its central
message as distinct from its exact textual scope — that determined the approach of patristic exegetes. This basic thrust of the Scriptures, the plot that
gave coherence and continuity to the whole, was called by Irenaeus the *hypothesis* ("governing sense," or "subject matter") of Scripture (*Against Heresies* 1.9-10 and passim; Hefner 1964; Norris 1994). Latin writers such as
Tertullian spoke of it as Scripture's *ratio* (*De praescriptione* 9), while
Athanasius called it Scripture's *skopos* (*Contra Arianos* 1.44, 53). The *hypothesis* or *skopos* of Scripture provided the interpretive framework and was in all
essentials identified with the rule of faith, that which was articulated in the
baptismal creeds and which stressed the creative activity of the one God and
the redemptive work of the incarnate Christ. This rule of faith, like the Scriptures themselves, was held to be received from the apostles, transmitted
through their disciples and successors, and preserved in the episcopate
(Irenaeus, *Against Heresies* 1.10.1; 3.3.3; Tertullian, *De praescriptione* 19-22).
This is not to say that the fathers merely found what they sought in Scripture;
rather, they believed the Scriptures and the tradition of faith were in ultimate
accord and that a proper interpretation of Scripture could be gained only
within the believing community under the leadership of apostolic successors.

Moreover, interpretation of Scripture was never pursued for its own
sake as a disinterested or merely scholastic enterprise. As diverse as their
methods or emphases were, the fathers' interpretation of Scripture was a
practical activity carried on for the sake of the Christian community, to instruct and to edify the faithful and to give expression to the central truths of
the faith. Hence it can be understood that patristic commentaries on scriptural books were largely, sometimes entirely, compilations of homilies on
scriptural texts that were read in *lectio continua* (sequentially, from beginning
to end) in worship and sequentially interpreted and expounded, usually
verse-by-verse, for the faithful.

The activity of scriptural interpretation, then, from the beginning through the great flowering of commentary in the fourth and fifth centuries, required no canon in the sense of a closed list of books, yet it presumed a shared recognition that at least some books were authoritative Scripture. Thus, it cannot be claimed that the canon as such constituted the basis of interpretation in the ancient church. Scripture was understood as both authoritative and coherent without a precise determination of its outer limits, because it had a broadly agreed core. At the same time, however, the interpretation of a particular passage, or even of a whole book, was undertaken with a view to its relations to those other passages and books which also had scriptural standing and thus had hermeneutical relevance. As diverse as those texts were, they were all approached as parts of a larger whole, the story of Scripture, within which were found consistency, direction, and sense.

Humanism and the Reformation

The interpretation of the Bible continued on patristic principles through the medieval period, and the canon, having become well-established, was simply taken for granted. With the Renaissance and Reformation, however, the significance of the canon for biblical interpretation came again to the fore. Humanism's recourse to classical sources, including the Bible, engendered a lively interest in Greek and Latin philology and an emphasis on the literal and historical meanings of ancient texts. Approaching scriptural texts with the methods and interests they brought to other ancient literature, humanist scholars moved toward a historical interpretation of the Bible, which then drew into question the relevance of the canon for historical understanding. Prominent humanists like Cajetan, Erasmus, and Colet freely doubted the traditional authorship, and hence the canonical authority, of Hebrews, James, and other catholic epistles, and of the Apocalypse (Metzger 1987).

These tendencies were bequeathed by humanism to the Reformation. The magisterial reformers used interpretive methods developed by humanist scholars, and the Reformation's emphasis on the classical sources of Christianity — the Scriptures and the fathers — mirrored the humanist interest in texts of Greek and Latin antiquity. The reformers took an interest in canonical issues, especially as they concerned the books that had been disputed in the ancient church. Their fresh and intensive reading of Scripture brought to light differences among canonical books and between the canonical writings and the teaching and practice of the church, thus sharpening the question of the nature and function of scriptural authority. Luther's principle of *sola scriptura* highlighted the Bible as the primary foundation and resource of

Christian teaching and emphasized its clarity and self-sufficiency *(scriptura sui ipsius interpretes)* for the conscientious reader. Even for Luther, however, Scripture was not free of difficulties, for different interpretations claimed to represent its literal sense. He adjudicated these claims by relying on Scripture's christological focus and gauged the authority of canonical documents by the critical principle *Was Christum treibet* ("What urges Christ"), that is, evangelical content. With this standard, Luther perceived significant differences within the Scriptures: superior in this respect were the Gospel of John, Romans, Galatians, and 1 Peter, while other canonical books were deemed deficient, especially James, Jude, Hebrews, and the Apocalypse (cf. Kümmel 1972). These latter Luther demoted by printing them at the end of his German New Testament, and he also generally overlooked them in preaching and theological argument. Thus, the canon was hermeneutically revised, though none of its traditional contents were actually eliminated. The Swiss reformers were less bold: Calvin raised questions about the authorship of some scriptural documents (Hebrews, 2 Peter) and among all the books of the New Testament neglected to write commentaries on 2 and 3 John and the Apocalypse. Zwingli explicitly repudiated the Apocalypse. Like Luther, however, they emphasized that the authority of Scripture rests not on the church's authority but on the self-evident, internal witness of the Holy Spirit. This conviction in principle deprived the canon of purely formal authority and permitted its contents to be questioned.

Historical-Critical Interpretation and Canonical Criticism

The historical-critical interpretation of Scripture had precedents in humanism and the Reformation, but took its rise principally from the Enlightenment, with profound consequences for the significance of the New Testament canon. The revolution in epistemology, scientific method, and human knowledge associated with the Enlightenment posed an enormous challenge to Christianity and to biblical authority and promoted a rationalistic approach to interpretation. Enlightenment thinking about history aided the revolutionary recognition that revelation and doctrine are historically conditioned. This meant that Scripture was not after all self-contained and self-explanatory but needed to be understood historically. Increasingly, the Bible was approached like any other ancient literature, that is, without dogmatic assumptions and with careful attention to the historical context of each constituent document.

The canon was regarded as a secondary and dogmatic phenomenon of little or no relevance for the interpretation of its contents. Rather, the historical understanding of a biblical document entailed a disregard for its place in the canon in favor of an emphasis on its original historical setting and aims. This has been the working principle of historical criticism in biblical studies up to the present. Thus, the historical criticism of the New Testament has thrown into relief disparities of chronology, circumstance, and thought within the canonical literature. It has also shown that the canon embraces a range of theological orientations which are not only diverse but to some extent incompatible, perhaps even mutually contradictory (Käsemann 1964; Dunn 1977). In these ways the historical interpretation of the New Testament has both discounted the relevance of the canon for interpretation and has rendered problematic a purely formal use of the canon as a theological norm. This has made it necessary to wrestle anew with the question of the nature and function of the New Testament canon as a norm for theological interpretation.

Two approaches to this problem stand out in modern discussion. The first, pursued mainly by Protestant scholars, has sought to locate the normative function of the canon not in terms of its scope and content but in a material principle *(Sachkriterium)* or center *(Sachmitte)* which is taken to be its essential and controlling feature, that is, a "canon (norm) within the canon (collection)." The aim is not to revise or reduce the contents of the canon but to identify a hermeneutical criterion by which to determine the fundamental meaning of Scripture and to employ that meaning as a theological norm (Lonning 1972). This view has failed, however, to produce any unanimity about what the authoritative element in the canon is (Schrage 1976; Kümmel 1968; Käsemann 1964, 1970). Catholic scholars have criticized the quest for a canon in the canon, objecting to its reductionism and arbitrary selectivity. They regard it as a symptom of the inadequacy of "Scripture alone" (Appel 1964; Küng 1963; Mussner 1964). Catholic scholars tend to affirm the unity and coherence of the canon as a whole, but since they too increasingly concede the theological diversity of the canon, it is unclear how equal authority can be accorded to all its parts. The essential difference between Protestant and Catholic approaches to this problem is that Protestant scholars seek an interpretive principle within the canon while Catholic scholars find it outside the canon in the authoritative teaching and confession of the church. Each view is, however, in its own way an acknowledgment that the formal canon does not by itself provide an effective theological norm for interpretation.

A second and more recent approach to the role of the canon in interpretation is known as "canonical criticism." While acknowledging the values of historical criticism, canonical critics claim that the canon should play a decisive role in the theological interpretation of Scripture. Here the canon, though a historically secondary context of its contents, is taken to be

hermeneutically primary. It is true that the canon is a hermeneutical construct not only by circumstance but to some extent also by design. As a literary phenomenon, the canon promotes the coherence of its own contents: the
meaning of individual documents is qualified and revised by the larger
whole, and the larger whole gives rise to new meanings through the textual
configurations created by the canon. Moreover, the sense that accrues to a text
within the canonical setting is not necessarily identical or even continuous
with its intrinsic, historical sense. Within this general approach which gives
hermeneutical primacy to the canon, however, there are decided differences
of emphasis and method. Childs has argued (1984) that theological interpretation of Scripture ought to proceed on the basis of the "final (canonical)
form" of a given text, irrespective of historical conclusions about its sources,
redactions, and variants, and with attention to its "full canonical context,"
that is, its intertextual relationships, conceptual and thematic, with other canonical documents. Thus, the literary setting of the canon, rather than the
original historical settings of the individual canonical documents, serves as
the touchstone of interpretation. Sanders (1976, 1984, 1987), on the other
hand, has argued that what is important about the canon is not the "final
form" or the "canonical context" of the documents, but the hermeneutical dy-
namics visible within the canon. He emphasizes the function of Scripture
within believing communities, arguing that, in the shaping of biblical literature, authoritative traditions were transmitted and stabilized, but also repeatedly adapted, revised, and reformulated as they were freshly reappropriated
by the community in response to changing situations. The hermeneutical
paradigms within the canon may then guide contemporary theological interpretation of Scripture.

    Canonical criticism, developed first in connection with the Old Testa-
ment canon, is in either of its main forms less helpful for the New Testament:
the history of New Testament literature is less protracted and complex, with
less distance and difference between early traditions and their textual
redactions, and between final textual redactions and the formation of the
canon. Yet it can yield real insights (Wall and Lemico 1992). The "canonical
sense" of a text, however, tends to be elusive and often hard to specify. In any
event, the putative canonical sense of a text is only one among others that
may be found in the canon and that may also have relevance for theological
exegesis (Dunn 1981; Brown 1981). So far as it is distinctive from others, the
canonical sense is not articulated by any biblical writer, but arises through the
canonical collocation of texts, and, accordingly, reflects above all the interpretive viewpoints of the church which shaped the canon.

    So far as the canon, by its scope and structure, promotes a construal of its contents that reveals the meanings they have come to have for the church, it is clearly relevant for theological interpretation. For the early church, however, it was not the canon as such but the *skopos* of the Scriptures that was decisive, and in the end it is perhaps the recovery of something like the *skopos* that both the search for a canon within the canon and canonical criticism aim to rediscover. While an adequate hermeneutic of the canon cannot be indifferent to historical criticism, it is equally clear that historical criticism cannot adequately explicate the meaning of the New Testament as a whole without attending to the hermeneutical force of the canon, or to the role that its contents have played in the life of the Christian community.

BIBLIOGRAPHY

Alexander, L.

1990 "The Living Voice: Skepticism toward the Written Word in Early Christian and in Graeco-Roman Texts." In D. J. A. Clines, ed., *The Bible in Three Dimensions*, 221-47. JSOTS 87. Sheffield: JSOT.

Appel, N.

1964 *Kanon und Kirche. Die Kanonkrise im heutigen Protestantismus als kontroverstheologisches Problem.* Paderborn: Bonifacius.

Baarda, T.

1989 "*Diaphonia — Symphonia:* Factors in the Harmonization of the Gospels, Especially in the Diatessaron of Tatian." In W. L. Petersen, ed., *Gospel Traditions in the Second Century: Origins, Recensions, Text, and Transmission*, 133-54. Notre Dame: Notre Dame University Press.

Brakke, D.

1994 "Canon Formation and Social Conflict in Fourth-Century Egypt: Athanasius of Alexandria's Thirty-Ninth Festal Letter." *HTR* 87:395-419.

Brown, R. E.

1981 *The Critical Meaning of the Bible.* New York: Paulist.

Campenhausen, H. von

1972 *The Formation of the Christian Bible.* ET by J. A. Baker. Philadelphia: Fortress.

Childs, B.

1984 *The New Testament as Canon: An Introduction.* Philadelphia: Fortress.

Clabeaux, J. J.

1989 *A Lost Edition of the Letters of Paul: A Reassessment of the Text of the Pauline Corpus Attested by Marcion.* CBQMS 21. Washington: Catholic Biblical Association of America.

Conzelmann, H.

1965   "Paulus und die Weisheit." *NTS* 12:321-44.

1979   "Die Schule des Paulus." In C. Andresen and G. Klein, ed., *Theologia Crucis —
        Signum Crucis: Festschrift E. Dinkler,* 85-96. Tübingen: Mohr.

Cullmann, O.

1956   "The Plurality of the Gospels as a Theological Problem in Antiquity." In Cullmann,
        The Early Church, ed. by A. J. B. Higgins, 39-54. Philadelphia: Westminster.

Dahl, N. A.

1962   "The Particularity of the Pauline Epistles as a Problem in the Ancient Church." In
        W. C. Van Unnik, ed., *Neotestamentica et Patristica: Freudensgabe O. Cullmann,*
        261-71. NovTS 6. Leiden: Brill.

1978   "The Origin of the Earliest Prologues to the Pauline Letters." In W. Beardslee, ed.,
        The Poetics of Faith: Essays Offered to A. N. Wilder, 233-77. *Semeia* 12. Missoula:
        Scholars.

Dassmann, E.

1979   *Der Stachel im Fleisch. Paulus in frühchristlichen Literatur bis Irenaeus.* Münster:
        Aschendorff.

Dunn, J. D. G.

1977   *Unity and Diversity in the New Testament.* Philadelphia: Westminster.

1981   "Levels of Canonical Authority." *HBT* 3:13-60.

Ehrman, B. D.

1983   "The New Testament Canon of Didymus the Blind." *Vigiliae Christianae* 37:1-21.

1993   *The Orthodox Corruption of Scripture: The Effect of Early Christological Contro-
        versies on the Text of the New Testament.* Oxford: Oxford University Press.

Fee, G. D.

1978   "Modern Text Criticism and the Synoptic Problem." In B. Orchard, ed., *J. J. Gries-
        bach: Synoptic and Text-Critical Studies 1776-1976,* 154-69. Cambridge: Cambridge
        University Press.

Ferguson, E.

1982   "Canon Muratori: Date and Provenance." *Studia Patristica* 18:677-83.

Gamble, H.

1977   *The Textual History of the Letter to the Romans.* SD 42. Grand Rapids: Eerdmans.

1985   *The New Testament Canon: Its Making and Meaning.* Minneapolis: Augsburg/Fortress.

1995   *Books and Readers in the Early Church: A History of Early Christian Texts.* New Ha-
        ven: Yale University Press.

Graham, W. A.

1987a   "Scripture." In M. Eliade, ed., *Encyclopedia of Religion,* 13:133-45. New York: Mac-
        millan.

1987b   *Beyond the Written Word: Oral Aspects of Scripture in the History of Religion.* New
        York: Cambridge.

Grant, R. M.

1993 *Heresy and Criticism: The Search for Authenticity in Early Christian Literature.* Louisville: Westminster/John Knox.

Hahneman, G. M.

1992 *The Muratorian Fragment and the Development of the Canon.* Oxford Theological Monographs. Oxford: Clarendon.

Hanson, R. P. C.

1962 *Tradition in the Early Church.* Philadelphia: Westminster.

Harnack, A. von

1925 *The Origin of the New Testament and the Most Important Consequences of the New Creation.* London: Williams and Norgate.

Hefner, P.

1964 "Theological Methodology and St. Irenaeus." *JR* 44:294-309.

Hengel, M.

1985 "The Titles of the Gospels and the Gospel of Mark." In Hengel, *Studies in the Gospel of Mark,* ET by J. Bowden, 64-84. London: SCM.

Hillmer, M. R.

1966 "The Gospel of John in the Second Century" (Ph.D. dissertation, Harvard University).

Käsemann, E.

1964 "The New Testament Canon and the Unity of the Church." In Käsemann, *Essays on New Testament Themes,* 95-107. London: SCM.

1970 *Das Neue Testament als Kanon: Dokumentation und kritische Analyse zur gegenwärtigen Diskussion.* Göttingen: Vandenhoeck und Ruprecht.

Koester, H.

1980 "Apocryphal and Canonical Gospels." *HTR* 73:105-30.

1990 *Ancient Christian Gospels: Their History and Development.* Philadelphia: Trinity Press International.

Kümmel, W. G.

1968 "Das Problem der 'Mitte' des Neuen Testaments." In *L'évangile hier et aujourd'hui. Mélanges F. J. Leenhardt,* 71-85. Geneva: Labor et Fides.

1972 *The New Testament: The History of the Investigation of Its Problems.* ET by S. M. Gilmour and H. C. Kee. Nashville: Abingdon.

Küng, H.

1963 "'Early Catholicism' in the New Testament as a Problem in Controversial Theology." In *The Council in Action,* 159-95. ET by C. Hastings. New York: Sheed and Ward.

Kurtzinger, J.

1983 *Papias von Hierapolis und die Evangelien des Neuen Testaments.* Regensburg: Pustet.

Leipoldt, J.
1907   *Geschichte des neutestamentlichen Kanons*. Leipzig: Henrichs.

Lindemann, A.
1979   *Paulus im ältesten Christentum: Das Bild des Apostels und die Rezeption der paulinischen Theologie in der frühchristlichen Literatur bis Markion*. BHT 58. Tübingen: Mohr.

Lonning, I.
1972   *Kanon im Kanon: Zum dogmatischen Grundlagen-Problem des neutestamentlichen Kanons*. Oslo: Universitetsforlaget.

Lovering, E. H.
1988   "The Collection, Redaction, and Early Circulation of the Corpus Paulinum" (Th.D. dissertation, Southern Methodist University).

Luhrmann, D.
1981   "Gal. 2.9 und die katholischen Briefe." *ZNW* 72:65-87.

MacDonald, D. R.
1983   *The Legend and the Apostle: The Battle for Paul in Story and Canon*. Philadelphia: Westminster.

McDonald, L. M.
1995   *The Formation of the Christian Biblical Canon*. Peabody: Hendrickson.

Merkel, H.
1971   *Die Widersprüche zwischen den Evangelien. Ihre polemische und apologetische Behandlung in der alten Kirche bis zu Augustin*. WUNT 13. Tübingen: Mohr.
1978   *Die Pluralität der Evangelien als theologisches und exegetisches Problem in der alten Kirche*. Bern: Lang.

Metzger, B. M.
1977   *The Early Versions of the New Testament: Their Origin, Transmission, and Limitations*. Oxford: Clarendon.
1987   *The Canon of the New Testament: Its Origin, Development, and Significance*. Oxford: Clarendon.

Morgan, R.
1981   "The Hermeneutical Significance of Four Gospels." *Interpretation* 35:376-88.

Mussner, F.
1964   "'Evangelium' und 'Mitte des Evangeliums.'" In B. Metz, ed., *Gott in Welt: Festgabe K. Rahner* I, 492-514. Freiburg: Herder.

Norris, R. A.
1994   "Theology and Language in Irenaeus of Lyon." *ATR* 76:285-95.

Ohlig, K.-H.
1972   *Die theologische Begrundung des neutestamentlichen Kanons in der alten Kirche*. Düsseldorf: Patmos.

Pagels, E.

1973   *The Johannine Gospel in Gnostic Exegesis.* Nashville: Abingdon.

1975   *The Gnostic Paul: Gnostic Exegesis of the Pauline Letters.* Philadelphia: Fortress.

Petersen, W. L.

1994   *Tatian's Diatessaron: Its Creation, Dissemination, Significance and History in Scholarship.* Leiden: Brill.

Rensberger, D.

1981   "As the Apostle Teaches: The Development of the Use of Paul's Letters in Second Century Christianity." Ph.D. dissertation, Yale University.

Robbins, G. A.

1986   "Peri tōn Endiathēkōn Graphōn: Eusebius and the Formation of the Christian Bible." Ph.D. dissertation, Duke University.

Sanders, J.

1976   "Adaptable for Life: The Nature and Function of the Canon." In F. M. Cross, W. E. Lemke, and P. Miller, eds., *Magnalia Dei, the Mighty Acts of God,* 531-60. Garden City: Doubleday.

1984   *Canon and Community.* Philadelphia: Fortress.

1987   *From Sacred Story to Sacred Text.* Philadelphia: Fortress.

Schenke, H.-M.

1975   "Das Weiterwirken des Paulus und die Pflege seines Erbes durch die Paulusschule." *NTS* 21:505-18.

Schrage, W.

1976   "Die Frage nach der Mitte und dem Kanon im Kanon des Neuen Testaments in der neueren Diskussion." In J. Friedrich, W. Pöhlmann, and P. Stuhlmacher, eds., *Rechtfertigung. Festschrift E. Käsemann,* 415-42. Tübingen: Mohr.

Sundberg, A. C.

1968   "Toward a Revised History of the New Testament Canon." *SE* 4:452-61.

1973   "Canon Muratori: A Fourth Century List." *HTR* 66:1-41.

Trobisch, D.

1989   *Die Entstehung des Paulusbriefsammlung.* NTOA 10. Göttingen: Vandenhoeck und Ruprecht.

1996   *Die Endredaktion des Neuen Testaments. Eine Untersuchung zur Entstehung der christlichen Bibel.* NTOA 31. Göttingen: Vandenhoeck und Ruprecht.

Wall, R., and E. E. Lemico

1992   *The New Testament as Canon: A Reader in Canonical Criticism.* JSNTS 76. Sheffield: JSOT.

Zahn, T.

1888-92 *Geschichte des neutestamentlichen Kanons.* Erlangen: Deichert.

CHAPTER 16

The Interpretation of Scripture
in the New Testament Apocrypha
and Gnostic Writings

Craig A. Evans

It is not possible to offer a comprehensive treatment of the interpretation of Scripture within this diverse and vast corpus of material. More than one hundred documents have been assigned to the "New Testament Apocrypha," and there are over forty documents in the Nag Hammadi library. The number grows if we include documents of the Old Testament Pseudepigrapha and Apocrypha (see chapter 9 above) that have been heavily edited and expanded by Christians. My intention is to give the reader a reasonably helpful sampling of the phenomena in certain defined areas and detailed study of several examples drawn from these areas. To give this survey more focus and to make it more manageable, I will limit discussion to a brief overview of the data found in the apocryphal Gospels and to a somewhat more extended analysis of several important biblical themes in Gnostic writings. Most of the study will focus on the use of the Old Testament in these later writings. The last section will, however, consider the use of the New Testament in the apocryphal and Gnostic writings.

THE USE OF SCRIPTURE IN THE APOCRYPHAL GOSPELS

The so-called apocryphal Gospels (or extracanonical Gospels, as some prefer) in large part follow the pattern of the canonical Gospels in their appropriation and interpretation of the Old Testament (see Evans 1993a; Stanton 1988; Hooker 1988; Barrett 1988; Carson 1988). Like their canonical counterparts, they explicitly quote Scripture (with or without introductory formulas), paraphrase Scripture (sometimes quite loosely and sometimes in conflations), and borrow words and phrases from Scripture. The purposes for this appropriation are apologetic, didactic, illustrative, corrective, and polemical.

The following selected list includes Old Testament quotations and allusions in the apocryphal Gospels that are not derived from the canonical Gospels but appear to be independent attempts to enrich the Gospel story by supplying explicit proof-texts, weaving scriptural language into the narrative, or adopting key words.

GNaz 2	Jesus says: "Unless what I have said is a sin of ignorance" (cf. Lev. 4:2; 5:18b).
GNaz 17	"Son of Joiada" (cf. 2 Chron. 24:20-22) instead of "son of Barachias" (as in Matt. 23:35; cf. Zech. 1:1).
GEbion 2	"John had a garment of camel's hair . . . and his food, as it says, was wild honey, the taste of which was that of manna, as a cake dipped in oil" (cf. Exod. 16:31; Num. 11:8).
GHeb 2	"It came to pass when the Lord was come up out of the water that the whole fount of the Holy Spirit descended on him and rested on him [cf. Isa. 11:2; 61:1] and said to him: 'My Son, in all the prophets I was waiting for you that you should come and I might rest in you [Sir. 24:7]. For you are my rest [cf. Ps. 132:14]; you are my firstborn Son [cf. Ps. 2:7; Exod. 4:22; Jer. 31:9] that reigns forever [cf. Ps. 89:29-30]."
GHeb 3	Jesus says: "Even so did my mother, the Holy Spirit, take me by one of my hairs and carry me away [cf. Ezek. 8:3; Bel 36] on to the great mountain Tabor."
GPet 2:5	Herod says: "For it stands written in the Law: 'The sun should not set on one that has been put to death' [Deut. 21:22-23; Josh. 8:29; 10:27]."
EpApost 3	Of Jesus the Apostles say: ". . . who by his word commanded the heaven and built the earth and all that is in it and bounded the sea that it should not go beyond its boundaries [cf. Job 38:10-11], and (caused) deeps and springs to bubble up and flow over the earth day and night; who established the sun, moon, and stars in heaven, and separated light from darkness [cf. Gen. 1:14]; who . . . has created man according to his image and likeness [cf. Gen. 1:26]. . . ."
EpApost 17	Jesus says: "I am wholly in the Father and the Father in me after his image and after his likeness [cf. Gen. 1:26-27]. . . ."

EpApost 19	Jesus quotes Ps. 3:1-8, which he introduces as "the prophecy of the prophet David concerning my death and resurrection" (see below for discussion).
EpApost 33	Predicting the persecution and later conversion of Saul of Tarsus, Jesus offers a very free rendition of Isa. 54:1 (with influence from Rev. 3:12; 21:2).
EpApost 35	Jesus again appeals to the "prophet David," quoting LXX Pss. 13:3; 49:18, 19b, 20, 21b to describe the "deceivers and enemies" of the church.
EpApost 36	The disciples question Jesus with an allusion to LXX Ps. 78:10.
EpApost 47	In describing the corrupt, who receive bribes, Jesus alludes to Isa. 5:23.
ProtJas 1:4	The righteous Joachim "fasted for forty days and forty nights and then said: 'I will not go down either for food or for drink until the Lord my God visits me'" (cf. Exod. 34:28; Deut. 9:9).
ProtJas 2:3	Anna's maid servant tells her that the Lord has shut up her womb (cf. 1 Sam. 1:3-8).
ProtJas 2:4–4:1	The story of Anna's prayer, lamentation, and angelic visitation is replete with scriptural allusions (Gen. 21:1-3; Ps. 1:3; Gen. 16:11; Judg. 13:2-7; 1 Sam. 1:9-11, 21-28).
ProtJas 6:2	Anna's song of praise, like the Magnificat (Luke 1:46-55), draws on 1 Sam. 2:1-10. Throughout this apocryphal account the language of Scripture is woven into the narrative.
AcPil 12:1	In a speech directed against Joseph of Arimathea for daring to request the body of Jesus for burial, we hear echoes of several passages of Scripture (1 Sam. 17:41-44; Lev. 19:18; Deut. 32:35).
AcPil 15:1	Jesus' ascension is compared to that of Elijah (2 Kgs. 2:1-18).
AcPil 16:5-7	When the witnesses of Jesus' ascension are questioned by Caiaphas, Annas, and the Sanhedrin, Scripture is appealed to for legal (Deut. 19:15; 34:5-6; Exod. 23:20-21; Deut. 21:22-23) and illustrative (Gen. 5:24; Jer. 10:11) purposes.

Every example in this list follows patterns that are discernible in the canonical Gospels. The tendency to find additional Scriptures for apologetic and doctrinal purposes parallels what we see in the patristic writings, especially those from the second and third centuries. Passages from the *Epistula Apostolorum* and the *Acts of Pilate* will serve as examples. In the first writing, Jesus assures his questioning disciples that they will receive incorruptibility. His assurance is based on Psalm 3:

Again we said to him, "In what form? In the manner of angels, or in the flesh?" He answered and said to us, "Look, I have put on (your) flesh, in which I was born and crucified and rose again through my Father who is (in heaven), that the prophecy of the prophet David might be fulfilled concerning what he foretold about me and my death and my resurrection, saying, 'O Lord, numerous have they become that strive with me, and many have risen against me. Many say to my soul, "There is no deliverance for you with God." But you, O Lord, are my protector; you are my glory and he who lifts up my heaven. With my voice I cried out to the Lord, and he heard me. I lay down and fell asleep; I rose up, for you, O Lord, are my protector. I will not be afraid of tens of thousands of people who set themselves against me round about. Rise up, O Lord; save me, my God. For you have cast down all who are my enemies without cause; the teeth of sinners you have broken. To the Lord is salvation and his delight in his people' [Ps. 3:1-8]. But if all the words that were spoken by the prophets are fulfilled in me — for I was in them — how much more will what I say to you truly happen, that he who sent me may be glorified by you and by those who believe in me." (*EpApost* 19, Schneemelcher 1991: 260-61)

Nowhere in the New Testament is Psalm 3 quoted, paraphrased, or even hinted at. Given what it says in v. 5, "I lie down and sleep; I wake again, for the Lord sustains me" (RSV; v. 6 in MT and LXX), this is surprising. The Psalm is, however, utilized by late-first-century and second-century Christian writers. Its appearance in the *Epistula Apostolorum* very probably reflects this usage and so is not independent. *First Clement* 26 quotes v. 5(6) as proof of the resurrection of Christians. Justin Martyr cites the Psalm, as uttered by the "spirit of prophecy," in discussing Jesus' resurrection (*Apol. I* 38); in *Dialogue with Trypho* 97, Justin appeals to Psalm 3 as David's prediction of Jesus' resurrection "on the third day." Irenaeus, in *Against Heresies* 4.31.2, appeals to the Psalm as evidence of the reality of the incarnation (that is, Jesus actually ate, drank, fell asleep, and woke up), but he later appeals to Ps. 3:5(6) as providing evidence of the resurrection. The *Epistula Apostolorum* thus reflects the type of *ad hoc* exegesis that flourished in early Christianity and third- and fourth-generation Christian understanding of Psalm 3 as predicting Jesus' death and resurrection.

The roots of this usage of Psalm 3 go back to pre-Christian traditions about David the prophet, who spoke through the Spirit and prophesied, which is already seen in 11QPs[a] 27:11 — according to which David "composed through prophecy given to him by the Most High" numerous psalms, including ones for use against demons — and in Mark 12:36 and Acts 1:16; 4:25. *Epistula Apostolorum* 35 has Jesus again appealing to the "prophet David," quoting LXX Pss. 13:3; 49:18, 19b, 20, 21b to describe the "deceivers and enemies" of the church.

The second example for our consideration is taken from *AcPil* 15:1, in which Jesus' ascension is explicitly compared to that of Elijah's (2 Kgs. 2:1-18):

> And Nicodemus stood up and stood before the council and said: "What you say is right. You know, people of the Lord, that the men who came from Galilee fear God and are men of substance, that they hate covetousness, and are men of peace. And they have declared an oath: We saw Jesus on the mountain Mamilch with his disciples. He taught them what you have heard from them. And we saw him (they said) taken up into heaven. And no one asked them in what manner he was taken up. Just as the holy scriptures tell us that Elijah also was taken up into heaven, and Elisha cried with a loud voice, and Elisha cast his cloak upon the Jordan, and crossed over and went to Jericho. And the sons of the prophets met him and said: Elisha, where is your master Elijah? And he said that he was taken up into heaven. But they said to Elisha: Has perhaps a spirit caught him up and cast him on one of the mountains? But let us take our servants with us and search for him. And they persuaded Elisha, and he went with them. And they searched for him for three days and did not find him, and they knew that he had been taken up. And now listen to me, and let us send to every mountain of Israel and see whether the Christ was taken up by a spirit and cast upon a mountain." And this proposal pleased them all. And they searched for Jesus and did not find him. But they found Joseph in Arimathaea and no one dared to seize him. (Schneemelcher 1991: 516)

Jesus' ascension from a mountain top (see Luke 24:51; Acts 1:9-11), as well as his Transfiguration on the mountain, in which Elijah makes an appearance (Mark 9:2-8), provides the inspiration for this imaginative narrative in the *Acts of Pilate*. But the substance of the narrative is a very loose paraphrase of 2 Kgs. 2:1-18, which narrates the ascension of Elijah. The author has Nicodemus recommend that a search for Jesus be conducted, just as one had been conducted for the mysteriously vanished Elijah. All the searchers find is Joseph of Arimathea, who earlier had provided the tomb. But of Jesus nothing was found.

The mystery of Elijah's translation was a subject of interest in late antiquity, as seen in the large number of pseudepigraphic writings attributed to the great prophet. It is also seen in Josephus: "Now about that time [the time of the death of the wicked Joram] Elijah disappeared [*ēphanisthē*] from among men, and to this day no one knows his end. He left behind a disciple Elisha. . . . However, concerning Elijah and Enoch, who lived before the flood, it is written in the sacred books that they became invisible [*aphaneis*], and no one knows of their death" (*Ant.* 9.2.2).

Comparison of Jesus with Elijah puts Jesus into a more impressive light. The parallel with the Old Testament figure enriches the story of Jesus' resurrection and ascension, and at the same time offers a measure of apologetic: Jesus must have been resurrected, for efforts to find his body proved fruitless.

These examples show how the writers of the New Testament Apocrypha interpreted Scripture using the same patterns, interpretive perspectives, themes, and exegetical methods as the New Testament writers did. Old Testament passages are appealed to as proof-texts, showing that the requirements of Scripture have been met (e.g., *GNaz* 2; *GPet* 2:5; *AcPil* 16:5-7) or that its prophecies have been fulfilled (e.g., *GHeb* 2; *EpApost* 19, 33, 35). Some of these Scripture citations include introductory formulas, some do not. Additional information concerning the events of Jesus' life or that of his mother is gleaned from the Old Testament (e.g., *GEbion*; *ProtJas* 1:4; 2:3; 6:2). These techniques are also found in the New Testament (see Evans 1989a). The infancy narratives exemplify this tendency. Prophetic passages cited as "fulfilled" punctuate the Matthean infancy narrative and provided the outline for the events that are narrated (e.g., the visit of the Magi and the flight to Egypt and settlement in Nazareth). The Lukan infancy narrative lacks prophetic proof-texts, but it offers various canticles which are replete with scriptural words and phrases (e.g., the Magnificat and the Nunc Dimittis [Luke 1:46-55; 2:29-32]). Thus, for Matthew, Scripture informs the events; for Luke, it informs the content of what the characters say.

INTERPRETATION OF THE OLD TESTAMENT IN THE GNOSTIC WRITINGS

M. Williams (1996) has brought to our attention the problematic nature of referring to "Gnosticism" in late antiquity. He has argued that, by lumping diverse materials together, scholars have created a synthetic construct that describes a religious phenomenon that probably never existed. The points that Williams has raised have merit. Although the present essay is not the place to explore them, the reader should bear in mind that references to "Gnostic" and "Gnosticism" in the discussion that follows are heuristic only. The documents that will be treated under this category are those that have been found in the Nag Hammadi Codices (NHC) and in the Berlin Gnostic Codex (BG). In what sense these writings reflect "Gnosticism" is left to those with expertise in this field.

Much Gnostic use of the books of the Old Testament appears to presuppose their authority and revelatory value, even if certain statements here or there are denied or corrected. It has often been observed that Deuteronomy, Isaiah, and the Psalms are the three most frequently cited books in early Judaism and Christianity. This is seen in the New Testament, the Dead Sea Scrolls, and rabbinic literature. Gnostic literature, however, prefers Genesis over Deuteronomy (see the index in Evans, Webb, and Wiebe 1993, pp. 467-545; for an extended discussion of Gnostic interest in the book of Genesis, see Tröger 1980). The reasons for this preference are not hard to find. Whereas Deuteronomy is chiefly concerned with the election and fate of Israel, Genesis is concerned with cosmic and human origins, themes of great interest to Gnostic writers, while the former are of little interest — certainly not sympathetic interest. Gnosticism, in most of its forms, was keenly interested in the origin of the world, the nature of God and the heavenly realm, and the plight and destiny of humanity (Rudolph, 1983), thus reflecting the fascination among writers and thinkers of late antiquity with the question of human and cosmic origins. The book of Genesis was widely appreciated, and not just by Jews and Christians. Pagan writers referred to it or were influenced by it (e.g., Ocellus Lucanus, *De Universi Natura* 45-46; Pseudo-Ecphantus, *Treatise on Kingship*; Porphyry, *Ad Gaurum* 11; Pseudo-Longinus, *De Sublimitate* 9.9). Moses himself was cited and discussed by many pagan writers (see Stern 1974; Gager 1972; e.g., Hecataeus of Abdera, *Aegyptiaca*; Apollonius Molon, *De Iudaeis*; Alexander Polyhistor, *De Iudaeis*; Strabo of Amaseia, *Geographica* 16.2.35; Pompeius Trogus; Ptolemy of Mendes; Nicarchus, *De Iudaeis*), a fact of which Josephus was much aware (in *Against Apion* he claims that Genesis and the other books of Moses influenced many Greek philosophers, even if the biblical books sometimes were misunderstood and misrepresented).

In the paragraphs that follow I will review Gnostic interpretive traditions concerning three elements of the early chapters of Genesis: creation (Genesis 1–2), the loss of paradise and Cain's murder of Abel (chs. 3–4), and the flood (chs. 6-9), along with the Gnostic identification of the creator as the demiurge, the inferior god. The closest analogies to these traditions are those writings that make up what is called the "rewritten Bible" (e.g., *1 Enoch, Jubilees, Books of Adam and Eve*, the *Genesis Apocryphon*, etc.). We will find that Gnostic writers not only cited and interpreted Genesis but, as has been observed by Pearson (esp. 1972, 1984, 1988), they also made use of Jewish interpretive traditions, many of which would eventually find their way into the Talmuds and the Midrashim (examples will be noted in the discussion below). The principal Gnostic texts we will examine are the *Apocryphon of John* (NHC II, 1; III, 1; IV, 1; BG 8502, 2), the *Tripartite Tractate* (NHC I, 5), the *Hypostasis of the Archons* (II, 4), and the *Origin of the World* (II, 5; XIII, 2). These texts offer what almost amounts to running commentary on the early chapters of Genesis. The authors of these texts vary in their assessments of the authority and revelatory value of Genesis. Much of the ancient book is accepted, some is rejected, and much of it is interpreted in new ways. Conventional understanding (or what we might think of as the norm in most Jewish and Christian circles) is often rejected.

The Creation Story

The Gnostic writings allegorize the Genesis story (or stories) of creation at many points. Gnostic cosmogony (ideas of the origin of the universe) and cosmology (ideas about the nature, purpose, and destiny of the universe) are drawn out of the story. The most noticeable feature of Gnostic exegesis of the creation story is its subversive dimension. It works as hard to turn the story on its head as it does to draw out of it ideas that can be exploited.

The principal points of contact between Genesis 1–2 and the Gnostic documents under consideration can be tabulated as follows (Evans, Webb, Wiebe, 1993: 74-81). It will be observed that all the principal elements of the creation story are taken up by the Gnostic writings under review.

Apocryphon of John (NHC II, 1)	Genesis 1–2
13.13-27	1:2b
14.13-24	1:26-27; 2:7
14.26-34	1:2b-4a, 7
15.1-12	1:26a, 27 (cf. 5:1b-2)
15.13–17.29	2:7a
19.22-33	2:7b
20.5-9	2:8
20.16-19	2:18, 22
20.33–21.7	1:26a; 2:7
21.13-16	2:21
21.16–22.5	2:8-9, 15-17 (+ 3:3)
22.6-8	2:25

22.20-25	2:21
22.28-30	2:21-22
22.32–23.5	2:21-23
23.9-16	2:23-24
23.28	2:9, 17

Tripartite Tractate (NHC I, 5)	Genesis 1–2
90.31-35	1:27, 31
96.17-24	1:1 (+ John 1:1-3)
96.26-31	1:1–2:25
100.36-39	1:31
101.3-5	1:2
101.6-8	1:3-31
104.26-30	1:1–2:25
104.31–105.35	2:7
105.2-3	1:26
106.1-2	1:26a, 27
106.18-25	2:7
106.25-31	2:8
106.34–107.8	2:16-17

Hypostasis of the Archons (NHC II, 4)	Genesis 1–2
87.11-20	1:2
87.20-23	1:3
87.24-33	1:26a, 27a; 2:7a
88.3-9	2:7b
88.7-9	1:2
88.13-17	2:7b
88.16	5:2b
88.19-24	2:19-20a
88.24-32	2:15-17
89.4-12	2:21-22
89.16-17	2:23

Origin of the World (NHC II, 5)	Genesis 1–2
97.30–98.3	1:2a
98.14-17	1:3
99.23-28	1:2

100.10-11	1:2b
100.31–101.2	1:2
101.3-9	1:6-10
101.9-11	1:26-27; 2:7 (cf. 5:1b-2)
101.12-13	2:7b
103.29-32	1:2b
104.3-5	1:3
104.13	1:2b
108.2-16	1:3-4
109.30-34	1:12
110.2-6	2:8a, 12
110.7-15	2:9b
110.18-20	2:9, 17
110.24-28	2:9b
111.21-23	1:12
111.24-28	1:20-21, 24-25
111.29–112.9	1:3-5, 14-18
112.33–113.1	1:26-27; 2:7
114.19-20	1:28
114.29–115.1	1:26a, 27; 2:7 (cf. 5:2b)
115.12-14	2:7b
115.25-27	2:2-3
115.27-29	2:8, 15
115.30–116.4	2:2-3, 7
116.4-8	2:21-23
116.21-24	2:21-22
116.28-29	2:9b, 17
117.28–118.5	1:3, 5b, 26-27, 31b; 2:2-3, 7
118.2-3	1:28a (cf. 6:1a)
118.19-23	2:16-17
120.19-24	2:19-20
123.34–124.4	1:28; 2:7

In the *Apocryphon of John* the creation story begins in 13.13-27, part of which reads: "Then the mother began to move to and fro. She became aware of the deficiency when the brightness of her light diminished" (13.13-15). The author thus alludes to Gen. 1:2b: "darkness was upon the face of the deep; and the Spirit of God was moving over the face of the waters." Moving "to and fro" is taken from "moving above" in Genesis. The disciple John, the alleged narrator of the *Apocryphon,* then asks the risen Jesus what the "moving to and fro" means. Jesus replies: "Do not think it is, as Moses said, 'above the waters.' No, but when she had seen the wickedness which had happened, and the theft which her son had committed, she repented. And she was overcome by forgetfulness in the darkness of ignorance and she began to be ashamed" (13.19-25). The author thus corrects Genesis and explains the pre-creation setting in terms of Gnostic mythology and dualism. The "theft which her son had committed" refers to the evil, "jealous" god (13.9) that had sprung from his archonmother and had begun creating the dark, physical world. This evil god earlier had been identified as Yaltabaoth (11.35), which is probably a corruption of Yahweh Sabaoth ("Lord of hosts"). (On his birth and naming, see 9.25–10.19.)

Two pages later in the Coptic text, we are told of the creation of the first human being:

> And he said to the authorities which attend him, "Come, let us create a man according to the image of God and according to our likeness, that his image may become a light for us." And they created by means of their respective powers in correspondence with the characteristics which were given. And each authority supplied a characteristic in the form of the image which he had seen in its natural (form). He created a being according to the likeness of the first, perfect Man. And they said, "Let us call him Adam, that his name may become a power of light for us." (15.1-13)

We have here an interesting combination of the creation of light (Gen. 1:3-4) and the creation of Adam (Gen. 1:26). This is necessary, for the evil god that created the physical universe could scarcely be expected to create light. He needs the power that light brings in order to sustain his world. Therefore, he creates Adam, in whom he may imprison the fallen sparks of light and who will "become a power of light for" the evil god and his demonic allies. The *Apocryphon*'s creation account goes on to describe in taxing detail the creation of every limb and organ of Adam — all with the assistance of the several demonic powers in league with Yaltabaoth (see 15.13–18.2).

With Adam's physical body assembled, it is time to give him life:

> And they said to Yaltabaoth, "Blow into his face something of your spirit and his body will arise." And he blew into his face the spirit which is the power of his mother; he did not know (this), for he exists in ignorance. And the power of the mother went out of Yaltabaoth into the natural body which they had fashioned after the image of the one who exists from the beginning. The body moved and gained strength, and it was luminous. (19.22-33)

It is obvious that this is an imaginative adaptation of Gen. 2:7: "Then the Lord God formed man of dust from the ground, and breathed into his nostrils the breath of life; and the man became a living being." The expectation that the newly created "body will arise" may owe something to 1 Corinthians 15, where Paul defends the resurrection by an appeal to the story of creation (vv. 45-49). The body's luminosity agrees with the earlier concern with the power of light, the very purpose for which the human was created.

The Genesis account goes on to narrate the creation of the woman: "The Lord God caused a deep sleep to fall upon the man, and while he slept he took one of his ribs and closed up its place with flesh; and the rib which the Lord God had taken from the man he made into a woman and brought her to the man" (Gen. 2:21-22). The *Apocryphon of John* gives the story an interesting twist: "This is . . . the first separation. But the Epinoia of the light which was in him, she is the one who was to awaken his thinking" (21.13-16). *Epinoia* means "thought" or "purpose." We are told that Epinoia hid herself in Adam. The allies of Yaltabaoth wished to extract her from Adam's rib. But they were unable to do it, so they made a woman, in the likeness of Epinoia, from Adam's rib, "not the way Moses said" (22.28–23.3). When Adam awoke from his sleep, he was able to recognize "his counter-image" as "bone from his bones and flesh from his flesh" (alluding to Gen. 2:23). The author goes on to tell of Sophia, "our sister" (that is, Jesus' sister), whose mission is to rectify the deficiency of the cosmos and awaken Epinoia hidden in Adam. This she does, and the female human and the male human recognize their fallen state and their ignorance (23.20-35).

Although different from this interpretation at many points, Philo's allegorical exegesis of the passage, in which he finds symbolism of mind and reason, is somewhat cognate (cf. *Leg. All.* 2.19-25, 35; *Heres* 257). Ultimately, the root of this tradition is found in personified Wisdom (the gender of both Hebrew *ḥokmah* and Greek *sophia*, "wisdom," is feminine), who says of herself: "The Lord created me at the beginning of his work. . . . When he established the heavens, I was there. . . . I was beside him, like a master workman" (Prov. 8:22-31). The association of Wisdom with creation is a commonplace in rabbinic interpretation (e.g., *Gen. Rab.* 1.1; *Targum Neofiti* Gen. 1:1) and probably contributed to the Gnostic myth of Sophia.

The Fall

Of equal importance to Gnostic interpreters was finding the cause of the human condition. The "tree of the knowledge of good and evil" (Gen. 2:9, 17; 3:3,

11-13) was of special interest. Adam, Eve, the snake, the garden of Eden, and the creator of earth (the demiurge) all demanded interpretation.

Apocryphon of John	Genesis 3–4
21.16–22.5	3:3
22.9-16	3:1-7
23.25-33	3:6-7
23.35-36	3:8
23.37–24.2	3:16b
24.6-8	3:21, 23-24
24.14-15	3:20
24.15-25	4:1-5, 8-9

Tripartite Tractate	Genesis 3–4
107.10-16	3:1-6, 13
107.17-20	3:23-24

Hypostasis of the Archons	Genesis 3–4
88.30-31	3:3b
89.13-15	3:20
89.31–90.2	3:1
90.2-5	3:2-3
90.6-12	3:4-5
90.13-19	3:6b-7
90.19-29	3:8-12
90.29-30	3:16
90.30–91.3	3:13-15
91.3-5	3:23-24a
91.5-7	3:16-19
91.7-11	3:17b-19a
91.11-20	4:1-5
91.20-30	4:8b-12, 15
91.30-33	4:25

Origin of the World	Genesis 3–4
110.7-15	3:22
110.24-28	3:22
110.31-33	3:5, 22

113.30-33	3:20
113.35–114.4	3:1
114.14-15	4:1b
116.4-8	3:20
116.24-25	3:16b
117.15	4:2a
118.24–119.6	3:1, 3-5
119.7-16	3:6-7a
119.23–120.10	3:8-19
120.26–121.13	3:22-24

According to the *Apocryphon of John,* it is Sophia who enters paradise and enlightens the female human and the male human. Because her mission is to set right the deficiency brought on by the loss of light from above and its imprisonment in the realm of darkness below, "she was called Life, which is the mother of the living" (23.20-24). Sophia enables the humans to taste perfect knowledge, while Jesus himself appears "in the form of an eagle on the tree of knowledge" (23.24-28). With thought (or Epinoia) awakened within them, the humans recognize their fallen state and their nakedness (23.30-35). They then withdraw from Yaltabaoth, evidently recognizing him for what he truly is. It is in this sense that they have received the knowledge of good and evil; that is, they are able to discern which gods are good and which are evil. Yaltabaoth retaliates by cursing his own earth and driving the humans out of Paradise. One of his allies then seduces the female human, who gives birth to the "bear-faced Eloim" (a corrupt form of *Elohim,* Hebrew for God) and the "cat-faced Yave" (Yahweh). The first offspring is unrighteous, the second righteous. They are given the names Cain and Abel. Yaltabaoth implants sexual urges in the woman so that she entices her husband to beget human after human. Ensnared by physical distractions, the man soon forgets what he learned from the tree of knowledge. In a state of stupor he can no longer remember his true identity, origin, or destiny. In short, he is in need of rescue and redemption (22.3–25.16).

The *Hypostasis of the Archons* (91.11-33) explains that the evil rulers of the physical world expelled the female human and the male human from the garden, throwing them into great distraction with lives of toil so that they might not be devoted to spiritual matters. They bore Cain and Abel, but Cain killed Abel. According to the *Valentinian Exposition* (NHC XI, 38.24-27), this happened because the evil god had breathed into them his spirit. Rabbinic tradition parallels this, claiming that Cain was not Adam's son (b. *Yevamot* 103b; b. ʿ*Avoda Zara* 22b; b. *Shabbat* 146a). In one Targum we are told that Cain was the son of Sammael the evil angel (*Pseudo-Jonathan* Gen. 4:1). Like

Gnostic exegesis, rabbinic tradition also speculates about the relationship of evil spirits to Adam and Eve (e.g., *Genesis Rabbah* 20.11 [on Gen 3:2]).

A more subversive interpretation of the Genesis account of the fall of humankind into sin can hardly be imagined than the Gnostic exegesis: eating from the forbidden tree was good, being punished for it was bad. The flood story continues the subversion within Gnostic exegesis.

The Flood

We have here yet another instance of the evil creator's clash with humanity, sometimes related to the "giants" of Genesis 6. These strange traditions offered ample opportunity for creative interpretation (cf. 4QAgesCreat 1.3-4; 1QapGen 2.1-26; *1 Enoch* 106:1-18; *3 Baruch* 4:10; *Origin of the World* [NHC II, 124] 21-25; *Pseudo-Jonathan* Gen. 6:2-4).

Apocryphon of John	Genesis 6–9
28.11-34	6:1-7
28.34–29.1	6:17
29.6-12	7:7
29.17–30.9	6:1-2, 4

Hypostasis of the Archons	Genesis 6–9
89.17-23	6:1-2
92.3-4	6:1a
92.4-8	6:7, 13, 17
92.9-14	6:14, 18b-20

Origin of the World	Genesis 6–9
124.21-25	6:1-4

According to the *Hypostasis of the Archons*, "humankind began to multiply and improve." This led some of the evil rulers to plot their destruction, though the "ruler of the forces" warned Noah, urging him to build the ark (92.3-18). The *Apocryphon of John* again corrects the Genesis account: "It is not as Moses said, 'They hid themselves in an ark'" (Gen. 7:7). No, not only Noah and his family escaped the flood, but "many other people from the immovable race . . . hid themselves in a luminous cloud" (29.6-12).

This subversive interpretation is consistent with the reinterpretations of the creation and the fall. Although varying in details, the Gnostic picture is relatively consistent: The evil god Yaltabaoth (sometimes spelled Yaldabaoth, or even Aldabaoth) was jealous of the humans and hoped to retain them in his dark, fallen world. Every effort on their part to escape, whether by acquiring knowledge from the tree or gradually improving after the expulsion from Paradise, was met with punitive action on the part of Yaldabaoth and his malevolent allies. This interpretation of the flood and the factors that led up to it is again in places analogous to early Jewish and rabbinic interpretive traditions. Yaltabaoth's jealousy parallels Jewish pseudepigraphic legends about demons who had intercourse with women (e.g., Targum *Pseudo-Jonathan* Gen. 6:4, which tells of two evil angels who fell to earth, so full of lust were they for women; cf. *1 Enoch* 6:1-8; Josephus, *Ant.* 1.3.1).

The "Jealous" God

One of the distinctive doctrines that tended more than anything else to drive a wedge between Gnostics, on the one hand, and Jews and Christians, on the other, was the Gnostic belief in two gods. Judaism and Christianity were monotheistic (although the former often accused the latter of compromising this cardinal doctrine through its exaltation of Jesus), but Gnosticism was plainly ditheistic. Many Gnostics held that Yahweh (or Yaldabaoth) came into existence through a prehistoric accident, that he created the earth as a prison in which to confine empowering particles of divine light that he captured shortly after his first appearance, and that he will continue to do all he can to prevent humans from acquiring knowledge of the truth and of their potential return to the true God of light. Many of these mythological elements have already been observed above in our review of Gnostic exegesis of Genesis 1–9.

Gnostic exegetes, therefore, searched the Scriptures for evidence of ditheism and for evidence that the creator was in fact an inferior god. The evidence for this plurality was somewhat similar to that adduced by Christians in arguing for the trinity, but the evidence for inferiority of the creator was adduced by passages in which God describes himself as "jealous."

Twice in the Coptic writings found at Nag Hammadi, Isa. 6:10 is cited as evidence of Yaldabaoth's malice and jealousy (*Apocryphon of John* II, 22.25-29; *Testimony of Truth* IX, 48.8-13). In both tractates the contexts are the same. Yaldabaoth, the "blind" and "ignorant" god, does not want Adam to eat of the tree of knowledge. Isaiah 6 is cited as proof of his malevolent nature. According to the *Apocryphon of John*, Yaldabaoth brought a "forgetfulness" over

Adam, which was not sleep in the literal sense (cf. Gen. 2:21), but a dullness of perception. The author cites Isaiah: "For he said through the prophet, 'I will make their hearts heavy that they may not pay attention and may not see.'" Isaiah 6 is similarly employed in the *Testimony of Truth*. Beginning on page 45, the Coptic text develops a polemic against Yaldabaoth (based on the same kind of interpretation of Genesis already observed). Furthermore, Yaldabaoth "envied" Adam for having eaten of the tree of knowledge (47.14-30). To support the claim that this kind of god is "malicious," the writer offers this paraphrase and comment (see Evans 1989b: 160-61, 225):

> I will make their heart thick,
> and I will cause their mind to become blind,
> that they may not know,
> nor comprehend the things that are said.   (Isa. 6:10)
>
> But these things he has said to those
> who believe in him and serve him!   (48.8-15)

To make the god of the Old Testament look all the more absurd, Gnostic authors sometimes appealed to his claims of uniqueness:

> And when he saw the creation which surrounds him and the multitude of the angels around him which had come forth from him, he said to them, "I am a jealous god [Exod. 20:5] and there is no other god beside me [Isa. 45:5]." But by announcing this he indicated to the angels who attended to him that there exists another god, for if there were no other one, of whom would he be jealous? (*Apoc. John* 13.5-13; cf. 11.20-21)

The author of the *Testimony of Truth* adds to this polemic (47.14–48.15). "What kind of god is this?" the author asks rhetorically. "First he envied Adam that he should eat from the Tree of Knowledge. And secondly he said, 'Adam, where are you?'" In asking this, the god of Genesis reveals his ignorance; he does not know where Adam is! After Adam eats of the tree, this god casts him out of the garden, thus revealing the extent of his maliciousness. He does not want Adam to possess knowledge and understanding, so he blinds the eyes and dulls the hearts of as many as he can (Isa. 6:10 is then cited). This god's inconsistencies may also be documented. He makes the devil a serpent in Genesis, makes the rod of Moses a serpent in Exodus, and has Moses fashion a serpent out of bronze in Numbers. Surely one should not trust a god who does such things. What may be inferred still further is that if such a god created the world in which humanity now finds itself, surely we should conclude that the world is intrinsically corrupt and beyond salvage.

THE USE OF NEW TESTAMENT WRITINGS
IN APOCRYPHAL AND GNOSTIC TEXTS

The question of the use of New Testament writings in Gnostic literature and the New Testament Apocrypha is often caught up in the debate surrounding the relative dating of these three groups of writings. Traditionally, the Gnostic writings and the New Testament Apocrypha were thought to have been written after the New Testament documents by at least fifty years and to be dependent on them. In recent years, however, some scholars, especially many who belong to the Jesus Seminar, have challenged this traditional view, claiming that some of the extracanonical Gospels are independent of the New Testament Gospels and that some of the Gnostic writings, if not as ancient as the Gospels, at least contain primitive, independent traditions (see Miller 1992). Assessment of usage of New Testament tradition in the apocryphal materials will vary greatly depending on how this question is answered. The most prudent approach is to avoid sweeping judgments: documents should be assessed on their own terms.

The *Gospel of Thomas* is probably the most frequently discussed extracanonical Gospel. Scholars today divide this document into a prologue and 114 sayings (or logia). *Thomas* survives in Coptic as the second tractate in Codex II of the Nag Hammadi library and partially in Greek in Oxyrhynchus Papyri 1, 654, and 655. POxy 654 contains *GThom* Prologue, 1-7, and a portion of 30. POxy 1 contains *GThom* 26-33. POxy 655 contains *GThom* 24, 36-39, and 77. Although the point has been disputed, most scholars contend that *Thomas* was originally composed in Greek and that the Oxyrhynchus Papyri stand closer to the original form of the tradition.

Many members of the Jesus Seminar believe that in its earliest form, the *Gospel of Thomas* was independent of the canonical Gospels and contained primitive and, in some cases, superior traditions. As such, they say, it should not be viewed as necessarily containing secondary, reinterpreted material derived from the canonical Gospels.

However, there are several factors that should give us pause before we accept the Jesus Seminar's high estimation of *Thomas* as an ancient and independent source. First, this writing alludes to more than half of the writings of the New Testament (all four Gospels, Acts, Romans, 1-2 Corinthians, Galatians, Ephesians, Colossians, 1 Thessalonians, 1 Timothy, Hebrews,

1 John, and Revelation; cf. Evans, Webb, and Wiebe 1993: 88-144), which suggests that it could very well be little more than a collage of New Testament and apocryphal materials interpreted, often allegorically, in such a way as to advance second- and third-century Gnostic ideas. Second, the traditions contained in *Thomas* hardly reflect a setting earlier than the writings of the New Testament, though members of the Jesus Seminar sometimes attempt to extract an early version of *Thomas* from the Coptic and Greek texts that are now extant (see Miller 1992). Third, *Thomas* contains a significant amount of material that is distinctive to Matthew ("M"), Luke ("L"), and John. If *Thomas* really does represent an early, independent collection of material, then how is one to explain the presence of so much M, L, and Johannine material? The presence of this material indicates that *Thomas*, at least in its extant Coptic form, has been influenced by the canonical Gospels. Fourth, features characteristic of Matthean and Lukan *redaction* are also found in *Thomas*, even in the Greek sayings preserved at Oxyrhynchus (compare Mark 4:22; Luke 8:17; POxy 655.5).

The evidence indicates that *Thomas* is secondary. Although it may in a few instances exhibit primitive, perhaps even independent tradition, on the whole, *Thomas* should be viewed as an interpretive assemblage of sayings of Jesus that in many instances has invested new meanings in the Gospel material. Several examples will make this clear.

Gnosticizing and elitist tendencies can be detected in *Thomas*. In the first logion, Jesus says: "Whoever finds the interpretation of these sayings will not taste death." We have here an unmistakable reworking of Johannine and Synoptic tradition: "Truly, truly I say to you, if any one keeps my word, he will never see death" (John 8:51; cf. Mark 9:1). In John the point is ethical, while in *Thomas* it is intellectual.

In *Thomas* 2 Jesus urges his followers to persist in the search for the meaning of his words, for when his follower "finds, he will become troubled. When he becomes troubled, he will be astonished, and he will rule over the All." "Ruling over the All" is a Gnostic doctrine; quest for such mastery becomes the goal of Jesus' exhortation to ask, seek, and knock (Matt. 7:7 = Luke 11:9). In the Synoptic tradition, Jesus does not specify precisely what his disciples are to seek. New understanding? New opportunities? Solutions to problems? Answers to prayer? *Thomas* takes advantage of the lack of specificity by pointing toward the acquisition of knowledge and self-mastery.

A similar tendency is seen in the fourth logion, where Jesus says, "For many who are first will become last, and they will become one and the same." The first part of the saying echoes the well-known saying that appears scattered about in the Synoptics (e.g., Mark 10:31). The last part of the saying is unique to *Thomas*. The hope of becoming single and unified is part of Gnostic eschatology and is expressed elsewhere in *Thomas* (11, 16, 23, 49, 75, 106, 114). The saying in logion 22 about making the male and female one and the same (cf. Gal. 3:28) is probably related to this idea.

Gnostic cosmology is apparent in logion 11, where Jesus says: "This heaven will pass away, and the one above it will pass away." The saying is found in Q (Matt. 5:18 = Luke 16:17) and Mark (13:31), but Jesus speaks of the passing of "heaven and earth." *Thomas*'s "one above [heaven]" refers to the Gnostic idea of a heaven above the heavens, where the god of light dwells. Part of Gnostic cosmology is that the end will be like the beginning. When the evil material universe implodes and is destroyed, that which is spiritual will return to the god of light. Jesus' reference to those who will find the kingdom (Matt. 25:34) becomes in logion 49: "Blessed are the solitary and elect, for you will find the kingdom. For you are from it, and to it you will return."

Gnostic soteriology features in the rewrite of Peter's confession at Caesarea Philippi (Mark 8:27-29). Peter's confession that Jesus is the Messiah is replaced with the apostle Thomas's confession: "Master, my mouth is wholly incapable of saying whom you are like" (logion 13). Here the Jewish messianic hope is replaced with esoteric soteriology. Jesus is understood to be the mysterious redeemer from heaven, with whom no one and nothing can be compared.

Elsewhere in *Thomas*, antipathy toward Jewish custom and piety is expressed. In logion 6, the disciples ask Jesus if they should fast, pray, or give alms. Jesus does not answer their question directly. But in logion 14, Jesus says: "If you fast, you will give rise to sin for yourselves; and if you pray, you will be condemned; and if you give alms, you will do harm to your spirits." This reply is clearly out of step with the canonical Jesus' stance toward the markers of Jewish piety. In Matt. 6:1-18, Jesus teaches what he regards to be proper fasting, prayer, and almsgiving. Although critical of "hypocrites," he does not denigrate these elements of piety. But in *Thomas*, these practices have no value. In logion 27, fasting and Sabbath observance are redefined in terms that are more suitable to a Gnostic perspective.

Much more material in *Thomas* could be adduced as evidence of a deliberate reworking of the Jesus tradition. In some instances, sayings of Jesus can be interpreted in gnosticizing ways without altering the wording appreciably. In other instances, slight alteration is required. In still other instances, wholly new material is added, either as a word or brief phrase, or in some cases a whole pericope.

The *Trimorphic Protennoia* (NHC XIII, 1) represents a completely different example of the use of New Testament tradition in a Gnostic document.

Here we do not have wholesale borrowing from writings of the New Testament, nor do we necessarily have a document that originated in Gnostic circles. It is probable that *Protennoia* emerged as a wisdom document, though whether from Jewish circles or pagan is impossible to say with certainty. There are numerous parallels with Old Testament and New Testament wisdom materials (see Evans, Webb, and Wiebe 1993: 401-14). But there are specific examples of secondary gnosticizing, where New Testament material, especially from the Gospel of John and Colossians, is adopted. The data do not support claims that *Protennoia* as a whole depends on John or Colossians or that either of these New Testament writings depends on *Protennoia*. The evidence suggests, however, that at a later stage in its development the *Protennoia* did come into contact with John and Colossians. A few examples will make this quite clear.

Protennoia (= "first thought") claims she dwells in the All and existed before all things (35.1-6). She goes on to describe herself as "the firstborn among those who came to be," the "invisible one" who exists in the "thought of the Invisible One" (35.4-9; cf. 35.24; 38.11-12). We probably have here an echo of the Christ hymn in Col. 1:15-18, which calls Jesus "the image of the invisible God, the firstborn of all creation," the one who is "before all things. . . . the beginning, the firstborn from the dead, that in everything he might be preeminent."

Evidence of direct dependence on Johannine tradition, especially John's prologue, is even more pronounced (Evans 1993b: 49-67). Protennoia's claim, "I descended to the midst of the underworld and I shone down upon the darkness" (36.4-5; cf. 46.30-32), echoes what the Johannine prologue says about the Logos: "The light shines in the darkness, and the darkness has not overcome it . . . the true light that enlightens every human was coming into the world" (John 1:5, 9). Protennoia later claims: "I am the Word who dwells in the ineffable Voice. I dwell in undefiled Light" (46.5-6). We have here an allusion to the opening words of the Prologue: "In the beginning was the Word, and the Word was with God . . . in him was life, and the life was the light of humans" (John 1:1, 4). Perhaps most telling of all is Protennoia's incarnational claim: "I revealed myself to them in their tents as Word and I revealed myself in the likeness of their shape. And I wore everyone's garment . . ." (47.14-17). This is an unmistakable allusion to John 1:14: "And the Word became flesh and dwelt among us, full of grace and truth; we have beheld his glory, glory as of the only Son from the Father." What makes the parallel especially close is the appearance in *Protennoia* of the Greek loanword *skēnē* ("tent"). The verbal cognate found in John's "and he dwelt [*eskēnōsen*] among us."

Gnostic fascination with the Johannine Prologue is evident elsewhere.

Thomas alludes to it: "Jesus said, 'I took my place in the midst of the world, and I appeared to them in flesh. I found all of them intoxicated; I found none of them thirsty" (logion 28; cf. John 1:14; 4:13-15; 6:35; 7:37). The *Gospel of Philip* (NHC II, 3) also alludes to the Johannine Prologue: "the Logos emanated from there [i.e., heaven]" (58.33; cf. John 1:1). *On the Origin of the World* (II, 5) says that the Logos was sent to proclaim the unknown (125.14-19; cf. John 1:1, 14), with Mark 4:22 partially quoted. In the *Second Treatise of the Great Seth* (VII, 2), the revealer (probably assumed to be Seth, as the title of the work implies; cf. 70.11-12) identifies himself as Christ (65.18), the Son of Man (65.19; 69.21-22), and as Jesus (69.21), who tells his disciples: "You do not know it because the fleshly cloud overshadows you. But I alone am the friend of Sophia. I have been in the bosom of the father from the beginning" (70.1-6; cf. John 1:1, 18). The *Teachings of Silvanus* (VII, 4) contains a cluster of predicates that in part derive from the Fourth Gospel: "For the Tree of Life is Christ. He is Wisdom. For he is Wisdom; he is also the Word. He is the Life, the Power, and the Door. He is the Light, the Angel, and the Good Shepherd" (106.21-28; 113.11-16; cf. John 1:1; 10:7, 9, 11, 14; 8:12; 9:5; 11:25; 14:6). The opening verses of the Prologue are echoed elsewhere in *Silvanus:* "the divine Word is God" (111.5; cf. John 1:1c); "the things which have come into being through the Word, who is the Son as the image of the Father" (115.17-19; cf. John 1:3). Similarly, the *Letter of Peter to Philip* (VIII, 2) has Jesus Christ (134.17) explain the "pleroma" (fullness) to his disciples: "I am the one who was sent down in the body because of the seed which had fallen away. And I came down in their mortal mold. . . . And I spoke with him who belongs to me, and he harkened to me. . . . And I gave him authority" (136.16-26; cf. John 1:11-12, 14). According to *Melchizedek* (IX, 1) Jesus Christ, the Son of God (cf. 1.3), "is unfleshly though he has come in the flesh" (5.6-7; cf. John 1:14). The *Testimony of Truth* (IX, 3) combines Synoptic and Johannine tradition: "The Holy Spirit came down upon him as a dove . . . accept for ourselves that he was born of a virgin and he took flesh" (39.26-31; cf. Mark 1:10; Matt. 1:18-25; John 1:14). The *Interpretation of Knowledge* (XI, 1), which alludes to and interprets New Testament passages throughout, probably echoes the Johannine prologue when it says: "It is the shape that exists in the presence of the Father, the Word and the height" (10.23-25; cf. John 1:1, 18). Later, we are told that the Son "appeared as flesh" (12.18; cf. John 1:14). Johannine language is probably echoed when the *Valentinian Exposition* (XI, 2) speaks of the revelation of the Father and the thought called the "Monogenes" (23.31–24.39; 28.22-25; 40.34-35; cf. John 1:18). The references to "Word" may also be Johannine (29.27, 30; 30.31).

CONCLUSION

We find in the apocryphal Gospels and the writings of the Gnostics an employment of Old Testament Scripture that is not significantly different from
its use by early Jewish and Christian groups. As with the latter, proof-texting,
spiritualization, and moralizing were common practices. The methods of
scriptural exegesis do not, therefore, in themselves demarcate boundaries between the bifurcating communities of faith, some moving toward what would
eventually be recognized as "orthodoxy" and others toward what would eventually be condemned as "heresy."

Gnosticism, however, did distinguish itself in that its exegesis broke
much more sharply with Israel's scriptural heritage than did those forms of
early Christianity that centered more closely (that is, more historically and
more literally) on the teachings of the Jewish Jesus. There was, to be sure, discontinuity between Christianity and significant components of Judaism, especially the emerging rabbinic form of Judaism. But this discontinuity, at
least in the first century, was not so great that Christianity could not remain
within the wider context of pluralistic Judaism. The radical discontinuity of
Gnosticism, with its ontological dualism, divided godhead, and denigration
of the God of Israel could not find a place in Judaism. Indeed, it eventually
could not find a place in most forms of Christianity, even those completely
Gentilized.

Gnostic usage and interpretation of New Testament literature is similar
in technique and perspective. Differences often occur in how Jesus is portrayed. The tendency is to portray Jesus as a visitor from heaven, which is
closer to the christologies of Paul and John, but more remote from the portraits of Jesus that we have in the Synoptic Gospels.

Study of the interpretation of Scripture in these diverse contexts is instructive. Among other things, it enables historians to gain a better understanding of issues that divided the communities of faith that emerged in the
first century. Although these communities appealed to a common sacred tradition, differing hermeneutics and worldviews led to radically divergent theologies and practices.

BIBLIOGRAPHY

Arab Republic of Egypt Department of Antiquities/UNESCO
1972-84   *The Facsimile Edition of the Nag Hammadi Codices.* 12 vols. Leiden: Brill.

Barrett, C. K.

1988   "Luke-Acts." In D. A. Carson and H. G. M. Williamson, eds., 1988: 231-44.

Beltz, W.

1976   "Gnosis und Altes Testament — Überlegungen zur Frage nach dem jüdischen Ursprung der Gnosis." *ZRGG* 28:353-57.

Bethge, H.-G.

1980   "Die Ambivalenz alttestamentlicher Geschichtstraditionen in der Gnosis." In K.-W. Tröger, ed., *Altes Testament-Frühjudentum-Gnosis: Neue Studien zu "Gnosis und Bibel,"* 89-109. Gütersloh: Mohn.

Carson, D. A.

1988   "John and the Johannic Epistles." In D. A. Carson and H. G. M. Williamson, eds., 1988: 245-64.

Carson, D. A., and H. G. M. Williamson (eds.)

1988   *It Is Written: Scripture Citing Scripture. Essays in Honour of Barnabas Lindars.* Cambridge: Cambridge University Press.

Charlesworth, J. H. (ed.)

1983-85   *Old Testament Pseudepigrapha.* 2 vols. Garden City: Doubleday.

1987   *The New Testament Apocrypha and Pseudepigrapha: A Guide to Publications, with Excurses on Apocalypses.* American Theological Library Association Bibliography Series 17. Metuchen: American Theological Library Association.

Charlesworth, J. H., and C. A. Evans

1994   "Jesus in the Agrapha and Apocryphal Gospels." In B. D. Chilton and C. A. Evans, eds., *Studying the Historical Jesus: Evaluations of the State of Current Research,* 479-533. NTTS 19. Leiden: Brill.

Evans, C. A.

1989a   "The Function of the Old Testament in the New." In S. McKnight, ed., *Introducing New Testament Interpretation,* 163-93. Guides to New Testament Exegesis 1. Grand Rapids: Eerdmans.

1989b   *To See and Not Perceive: Isaiah 6.9-10 in Early Jewish and Christian Interpretation.* JSOTS 64. Sheffield: JSOT.

1993a   "Luke and the Rewritten Bible: Aspects of Lukan Hagiography." In J. H. Charlesworth and C. A. Evans, eds., *The Pseudepigrapha and Early Biblical Interpretation,* 170-201. JSPS 14; SSEJC 2. Sheffield: JSOT.

1993b   *Word and Glory: On the Exegetical and Theological Background of John's Prologue.* JSNTS 89. Sheffield: JSOT.

Evans, C. A., R. L. Webb, and R. A. Wiebe (eds.)

1993   *Nag Hammadi Texts and the Bible: A Synopsis and Index.* NTTS 18. Leiden: Brill.

Fossum, J.

1985   "Gen. 1,26 and 2,7 in Judaism, Samaritanism, and Gnosticism." *JSJ* 16:202-39.

Gager, J. G.
1972   *Moses in Greco-Roman Paganism.* SBLMS 16. Nashville: Abingdon.

Grant, R. M.
1977   "Gnostics and the Inspiration of the Old Testament." In A. L. Merrill and T. W. Overholt, eds., *Scripture in History and Theology: Essays in Honor of J. Coert Rylaarsdam,* 269-77. PTMS 17. Pittsburgh: Pickwick.

Hooker, M. D.
1988   "Mark." In D. A. Carson and H. G. M. Williamson, eds., 1988: 220-30.

James, M. R.
1924   *The Apocryphal New Testament.* Oxford: Clarendon.

Kaestli, J.-D.
1981   "Une relecture polémique de Genèse 3 dans le gnosticisme chrétien. Le Témoignage de Vérité." *Foi et Vie* 80.6:48-62.
1982   "L'interprétation du serpent de *Genèse* 3 dans quelques textes gnostiques et la question de la gnose 'ophite.'" In J. Ries, Y. Janssens, and J.-M. Sevrin, eds., *Gnosticisme et monde hellénistique. Acts du Colloque de Louvain-la-Neuve (11-mars 1980),* 116-30. Publications de l'Institut Orientaliste de Louvain 27. Louvaine-la-Neuve: Institut Orientaliste.

Logan, A. H. B.
1979   "The Jealousy of God: Exod. 20:5 in Gnostic and Rabbinic Theology." In A. E. Livingstone, ed., *Studia Biblica 1978.* I: *Papers on Old Testament and Related Themes: Sixth International Congress on Biblical Studies, Oxford, 3-7 April 1978,* 197-203. JSOTS 11. Sheffield: JSOT.

MacRae, G. W.
1970   "The Jewish Background of the Gnostic Sophia Myth." *NovT* 12:86-101.

Magne, J.
1982   "L'exégèse du récit du Paradis dans les écrits juifs, gnostiques et chrétiens." *Augustinianum* 22:263-70.

Miller, R. J. (ed.)
1992   *The Complete Gospels.* Sonoma: Polebridge.

Pagels, E.
1986   "Exegesis and Exposition of the Genesis Creation Accounts in Selected Texts from Nag Hammadi." In C. W. Hedrick and R. Hodgson, eds., *Nag Hammadi, Gnosticism, and Early Christianity,* 257-85. Peabody: Hendrickson.

Pearson, B. A.
1972   "Jewish Haggadic Traditions in *The Testimony of Truth* from Nag Hammadi (CG IX 3)." In C. J. Bleeker, et al., eds., *Ex orbe religionum: Studia Geo Widengren . . . Pars Prior,* 457-70. NumenS 21. Leiden: Brill.
1975   "Biblical Exegesis in Gnostic Literature." In M. E. Stone, ed., *Armenian and Biblical Studies,* 70-80. Jerusalem: St. James.

1980 "Gnostic Interpretation of the Old Testament in the Testimony of Truth (NHC IX, 3)." *HTR* 73:311-19.

1984 "Jewish Sources in Gnostic Literature." In M. E. Stone (ed.), *Jewish Writings of the Second Temple Period: Apocrypha, Pseudepigrapha, Qumran Sectarian Writings, Philo, Josephus,* 443-81. CRINT II.2. Assen: Van Gorcum; Philadelphia: Fortress.

1988 "Use, Authority and Exegesis of Mikra in Gnostic Literature." In M. J. Mulder (ed.), *Mikra: Text, Translation, Reading and Interpretation of the Hebrew Bible in Ancient Judaism and Early Christianity,* 635-52. CRINT II.1. Assen: Van Gorcum; Philadelphia: Fortress.

Roberts, A., and J. Donaldson (eds.)

1989 *Ante-Nicene Fathers.* 10 vols. Reprint. Grand Rapids: Eerdmans.

Robinson, J. M., et al.

1988 *The Nag Hammadi Library in English.* Leiden: Brill/San Francisco: Harper & Row.

Rudolph, K.

1983 *Gnosis: The Nature and History of Gnosticism.* Edinburgh: Clark; San Francisco: Harper and Row.

Schneemelcher, W. (ed.)

1991 *New Testament Apocrypha* I: *Gospels and Related Writings.* Revised ET by R. McL. Wilson. Edinburgh: Clark/Louisville: Westminster.

1992 *New Testament Apocrypha* II: *Writings Relating to the Apostles; Apocalypses and Related Subjects.* Revised ET by R. McL. Wilson. Edinburgh: Clark/Louisville: Westminster.

Segal, A. F.

1977 *Two Powers in Heaven: Early Rabbinic Reports about Christianity and Gnosticism.* SJLA 25. Leiden: Brill.

1986 "Judaism, Christianity, and Gnosticism." In S. G. Wilson, ed., *Anti-Judaism in Early Christianity.* II: *Separation and Polemic,* 133-61. SCJ 2. Waterloo: Wilfrid Laurier University Press.

Stanton, G. N.

1988 "Matthew." In Carson and Williamson, eds., 1988: 205-19.

Stern, M.

1974 *Greek and Latin Authors on Jews and Judaism,* vol. 1. Jerusalem: Israel Academy of Sciences and Humanities.

1980 *Greek and Latin Authors on Jews and Judaism,* vol. 2. Jerusalem: Israel Academy of Sciences and Humanities.

1984 *Greek and Latin Authors on Jews and Judaism,* vol. 3. Jerusalem: Israel Academy of Sciences and Humanities.

Tröger, K.-W. (ed.)

1980 *Altes Testament-Frühjudentum-Gnosis: Neue Studien zu "Gnosis und Bibel."* Gütersloh: Mohn.

Weiss, H.-F.

1980   "Das Gesetz in der Gnosis." In Tröger, ed., 1980: 71-88.

Williams, J. A.

1984   "The Gospel of Truth: Witness to Second-Century Exegetical Traditions." *SBLSP* 23:1-10.

1988   *Biblical Interpretation in the Gnostic Gospel of Truth from Nag Hammadi.* SBLDS 79. Atlanta: Scholars.

Williams, M. A.

1996   *Rethinking "Gnosticism": An Argument for Dismantling a Dubious Category.* Princeton: Princeton University Press.

Wilson, R. McL.

1975   "Old Testament Exegesis in the Gnostic Exegesis on the Soul." In M. Krause, ed., *Essays on the Nag Hammadi Texts in Honour of Pahor Labib,* 217-24. NHS 6. Leiden: Brill.

1977   "The Gnostics and the Old Testament." In G. Widengren, ed., *Proceedings of the International Colloquium on Gnosticism: Stockholm, August 20-25, 1973,* 164-68. Stockholm: Almqvist & Wiksell.

1989   "New Testament Apocrypha." In E. J. Epp and G. W. MacRae, eds., *The New Testament and Its Modern Interpreters,* 429-55. The Bible and Its Modern Interpreters 3. Atlanta: Scholars.

Wintermute, O. S.

1972   "Study of Gnostic Exegesis of the Old Testament." In J. M. Efird, ed., *The Use of the Old Testament in the New and Other Essays: Studies in Honor of William Franklin Stinespring,* 241-70. Durham: Duke University Press.

Contributors

Peder Borgen, University of Trondheim

Dennis Brown, Manchester Grammar School, Manchester, U.K.

James H. Charlesworth, Princeton Theological Seminary

Philip R. Davies, University of Sheffield

Craig A. Evans, Trinity Western University

Harry Gamble, University of Virginia

Leonard Greenspoon, Creighton University

Alan J. Hauser, Appalachian State University

Donald H. Juel, Princeton Theological Seminary

Martin McNamara, Missionaries of the Sacred Heart, Blackrock, Co. Dublin

Esther Menn, University of Virginia

Richard A. Norris, Jr., Union Theological Seminary

Gary G. Porton, University of Illinois, Urbana-Champaign

James A. Sanders, Ancient Biblical Manuscript Center

Joseph Trigg, Christ Church, Port Tobacco Parish, LaPlata, Maryland

Duane F. Watson, Malone College

Frances Young, University of Birmingham

Index of Ancient and Modern Authors

Index of Subjects

Aaron
  and Golden Calf incident, 95
  and Moses, 259
  and Moses in the wilderness, 184-85,
    218-19
Aaron, with Moses
  in Christian exegesis, 296
Abel, as Cain's victim, 130, 134-35
  as type of Christ, 322
  in Gnostic texts, 436-37, 443
Abel, as Exemplar of Faith, 131-32
Abimelech, 218-19, 261
Abomination, 68
Abraham (Abram), 17, 36, 121, 152, 176,
    183, 261, 287, 327, 362
  and circumcision, 42-43, 188, 314
  and heavenly reward, 181
  and the well, 185
  as eponym, 238
  as inventor of the plow, 257
  as sire of Isaac, 187
  as type for land restoration, 76
  in parabiblical texts, 151-52, 257
  in paraphrastic listings, 131-32
  in Philo's commentaries, 135-36
  in Targums(im), 25
  life of, as creative history, 269-70

macrocosm to microcosm
  according to Philo, 122-24, 289-90
name etymology of, 123
promises toward, 39, 234-35, 258
  according to Paul of Tarsus, 292-94
testing of, 157
untruths told by, 175
within biblical history, 132
Adam, 25, 131, 273, 343, 349, 368, 385, 404
  and Cain, 443
  and free will, 264
  and Yaldabaoth
    in Gnostic texts, 445-46
  Apocalypse of, 254
  as genealogical patriarch, 246-47
  as last-created, 127
  banishment from Eden, 181
  creation of
    in Gnostic texts, 440
  Ezra's lament on, 270-71
  in Epistle of Barnabas, 314
  interaction with God
    anthropomorphism concerns on,
    326
  Testament of, 254
Adam and Eve, 188
  and evil spirits
    in Gnostic texts, 444

466

in Apocrypha, 270
on Jeremiah, 261
portrayals of women in, 99
transmission of Septuagint, 84
use of Psalms, 433
use of Septuagint, 15, 35, 105
Christian Translation
by Jerome, 356-62
Christianity, 4, 235-36
and Dead Sea Scrolls, 19, 243-45
and Greek philosophy, 42
and Manicheanism, 382-83, 386
and Neoplatonism, 383-85
as scriptured religion, 226-27
criticism of
from Manicheans, 389
development of canon in, 30-33, 103
heretical forms of, 138, 452
Gnosticism, 436-37, 445
in Augustine's background, 380-83
in North Africa, 382
precanonical references to Jewish
Scriptures, 410
separation from Judaism, 54
spread of, 10, 12, 240
use of Hebrew Bible, 436
use of Septuagint, 88, 98, 104-5, 107-8
Messiah concept in, 96
Chrysostom, John, 47, 366
and loaves and fishes, 344-45
moralizing of, 347-48
Church
and Augustine's writings, 380-97
and canonization of New Testament
texts, 22, 409-21
and Christ
grounding of gospel in, 40
Old Testament as prophecy of, 41-
42, 45
Song of Songs as prophecy of, 352
and continuation of prophetic age, 33
and early "fathers"
Jerome and Augustine, 48-50
and New Testament canon, 50-52
as body of Christ, 46, 328
"deceivers and enemies of"
in *Epistula Apostolorum,* 434

diversity of texts in, 231
figured as Jerusalem, 338
in apostolic succession, 330
"in" Christ
as Semitic concept, 240
orthodoxy vs. heterodoxy
not defined by canon, 53-54
not defined by interpretive method,
53-54
reactions to unity/diversity issues, 6-9
Church, Doctor of (Jerome), 355-68
Church, Early Christian
adoption of Septuagint (LXX) as
canon, 83-84, 284
influence of, on new texts, 104
and Clement, 308-9
and Justin Martyr, 316-18
and Polycarp, 311-12
and Second Clement, 309-10
and the *Shepherd of Hermas,* 312
as safe harbor
in Theophilus's text, 326
authoritative texts in, 339-40
"canon" in, 225-26
in Apostolic Age, 36-40
interpretive traditions of, 43
knowledge of Bible in, 299
observance of Passover in
Melito on, 322-24
oral readings in, 284
overarching message of, 248-49
use of Greek in, 245-46
Church, Early Christian Texts
use of Philo's writings in, 137-38
Church Fathers, 75
use of allegory and typology, 76
Church Order
Ignatius's writings within, 306-7
The *Didache* on, 311
Church Texts
use of question-and-answer format in,
128
Church Tradition
as basis for scriptural interpretation,
43
Cicero, 380
Augustine's study of, 382

Index of Subjects

477

Index of Primary Sources